AFTER SLAVERY

The Negro in South Carolina
During Reconstruction, 1861-1877

AFTER SLAVERY

The Negro in South Carolina
During Reconstruction, 1861-1877

Joel Williamson

Wesleyan University Press
Published by
UNIVERSITY PRESS OF NEW ENGLAND
Hanover and London

The University Press of New England
is a consortium of universities in New England dedicated to publishing scholarly and trade works
by authors from member campuses and elsewhere. The New England imprint signifies uniform
standards for publication excellence maintained without exception by the consortium members.
A joint imprint of University Press of New England and a sponsoring member acknowledges the
publishing mission of that university and its support for the dissemination of scholarship
throughout the world. Cited by the American Council of Learned Societies as a model to be followed, University Press of New England publishes books under its own imprint and the imprints
of Brandeis University / Brown University / Clark University / University of Connecticut /
Dartmouth College / Middlebury College / University of New Hampshire / University of Rhode
Island / Tufts University / University of Vermont / Wesleyan University

Printed in the United States of America

∞

Library of Congress Cataloging-in-Publication Data

Williamson, Joel.
    After slavery : the Negro in South Carolina during Reconstruction,
1861–1877 / by Joel Williamson.
        p.   cm.
    Reprint. Originally published: Chapel Hill : University of North
Carolina Press, c1965.
    Includes bibliographical references and index.
    ISBN 0-8195-6236-X
    1. Afro-Americans—South Carolina—History—19th century.
2. Reconstruction—South Carolina. 3. South Carolina—
History—1865-   I. Title.
E185.93.S7W73   1990
975.7'00496073—dc20   90-50317

5 4 3 2 1

To Marie

PREFACE

It is uniquely fitting that these pages come off the press precisely one hundred years after the great mass of Negro slaves in South Carolina spilled into freedom. *Century* is a word of deceptive roundness, but in the writing of modern history four generations of human existence offer a rather generous distance for evaluation. Scarcely a person now lives who was born into slavery, and scarcely a man can recall his father's relating how it felt to be white in a sea of black bondage. It is possible that we have now passed onto a new plateau, one where slavery and Reconstruction fall beneath the horizon of immediate memory and perspective rises a measure above personal passion. It is possible, also, that it is time to accept Francis Simkins' long standing invitation to "foster more moderate, saner, perhaps newer views" of Reconstruction.

In spite of its appropriateness, the centennial nature of this appearance is accidental. In the summer of 1959, when Professor Kenneth Stampp and I settled upon the Negro in South Carolina during Reconstruction as my dissertation topic, I hardly anticipated that the path to print would be so long and tortuous. In the beginning, I visualized a much less ponderous volume and a more narrow treatment, one which would parallel Vernon Lane Wharton's stimulating work on Mississippi, supplement George Tindall's pioneer labor in describing Carolina Negroes in the post-Reconstruction period, and update Alrutheus Ambush Taylor's 1924 study of the Negro in Reconstruction South Carolina. As my research and writing assumed book form, I found that the product of following revisionist advice was a broad-scale and time-consuming revision of a classic in revisionism: Simkins' and Woody's *South Carolina During Reconstruction*. In retrospect, I see this result as inevitable as the fact that historians in the last thirty years have traveled as the world has traveled. Racial attitudes that would have been called liberal in 1932 are rapidly becoming untenable. For example, it is no longer possible to assume that Negroes "naturally" possess any fixed cultural traits. Consequently, we approach our materials with new viewpoints out of necessity if not out of choice; we ask new questions of our sources and, just as important, we cease to ask all of the old. The world has traveled, we have traveled, and so, too, have our sources. We have added a vast number of printed pages to the store of information on Reconstruction, but, more important, we have raised our manuscript collections from an infancy in 1930 to a magnificent maturity in 1965. The responses of the manuscripts are twice novel: first, they reply to questions which could not have been asked a generation ago, and, second, they answer from an individualistic, deeply personal basis that gives a new and vital dimension to the study of history. Notwithstanding all of this, having passed along the road that Professors Simkins and Woody built, I am profoundly impressed with their scholarly craftsmanship and humanistic perception. Were I not of another generation and possessed of the infinitely broader research resources available, this book would not exist.

It is, of course, impossible to accord recognition to all to whom it is due. In seeking the sources of this book, my mind goes back in a sort of Joycean reverie to Julia, to Dempie, to Aunt Lulu, and to the other Negroes who did service in my father's house in less than decennial succession. There is, too, a montage of faces white and black and tan superimposed upon a background of the South Carolina town and countryside where I lived the first sixteen years of my life. And then I am in the University, attaining a sort of hothouse maturity. And then in the Navy, seeing a broad array of cultural alternatives, recognizing that racial attitudes are not immutable and that a valid cultural pattern can be aracial. And then at Berkeley, studying; and now I am home again attempting to define myself in describing others.

Narrowing my focus to individuals, I see a number of obligations. Above all, I am indebted to Professor Kenneth M. Stampp, who has somehow combined the roles of warm friend and faithful critic, never dictating but with marvelous restraint warning me against my trivial and intolerant self. I am grateful, too, to Professor Charles G. Sellers, also of Berkeley, who read the manuscript as a dissertation and encouraged me to translate it into book form. I owe thanks also to the anonymous reader who advised The University of North Carolina Press to print this book and, searching the manuscript with great skill and practiced perspicacity, offered suggestions for its improvement. I am deeply indebted to my friends and colleagues in the Department of History of The University of North Carolina at Chapel Hill who have nourished both this book and me with rare and gentle patience. Especially great is my obligation to Professors Frank W. Ryan, George Brown Tindall, and Frank W. Klingberg, and to Professor Carl N. Degler, of Vassar College, who helped me through difficult portions of the manuscript. Believing as I do that history is art and that every man is, ultimately, his own artist, I cannot blame whatever here is bad art upon my friends and advisors.

A glance at the manuscript bibliography only suggests the extent of my debt to the historian as archivist. Those who have borne my worst importunities are Dr. James Welch Patton, Dr. Carolyn A. Wallace, and Miss Anna Brooke Allan of the Southern Historical Collection of the Library of The University of North Carolina at Chapel Hill; Dr. Mattie Russell of Duke Manuscripts; Mr. E. L. Inabinett of the South Caroliniana Library; Mrs. Granville T. Prior of the South Carolina Historical Society; and Miss Judith Schiff of the Manuscripts Division of Yale University Library. My gratitude extends undiminished to the very able assistants of these archivists and historians. While I have not always used directly materials supplied by other institutions, I am no less grateful for the aid of their staffs, including that of Bennett College Library in Greensboro, North Carolina, the Manuscripts Division of the Library of Congress, and the Moorland Foundation at Howard University.

I also depended upon the very generous financial support afforded me by the Woodrow Wilson Foundation, the University of California Patent Fund, and the Southern Fellowship Fund. I wish to acknowledge my indebtedness to the Alumni Annual Giving funds and the University Research Council of The University of North Carolina at Chapel Hill for aid in publication of this book, and to the Ford Foundation for a grant under its program for assisting American university presses in the publication of works in the humanities and the social sciences. For typing assistance I am indebted to Gloria Byrd Brook; and for salvation from many grammatical errors of commission and omission to Nancy Mulberry Neustadt.

Chapel Hill
February, 1965

CONTENTS

AFTER SLAVERY

The Negro in South Carolina
During Reconstruction, 1861-1877

I...FROM SLAVERY
TO FREEDOM

To the great mass of Negroes in South Carolina, freedom came only gradually; but to the few—those ten out of every hundred who won their liberty during the war—freedom came with the traumatic and violent suddenness of human birth. These few were specially marked not only by the dramatic rapidity of their transition from bondage to freedom, but also by the facts that they chose liberty over slavery in the face of great hazards and that they fought and died to preserve their new status. Their story bears a particular significance in the history of the Negro in Reconstruction South Carolina.

The process of liberation began within seven months after the first Confederate shell burst over Fort Sumter. On November 7, 1861, a Union amphibious expedition occupied Hilton Head Island, at the mouth of Port Royal Sound. Before the end of the year, Union lines included St. Helena, Ladies, Port Royal, and a number of the smaller Sea Islands in the vicinity. The primary mission of the force was to establish an operating base for the South Atlantic blockading fleet. A more important and largely unforeseen result of the expansion of Union lines was the capture of some seven thousand slaves whose masters had fled to the mainland. That so large a number remained on the occupied islands was only partially caused by the rapid advance of the invaders. The Negroes themselves were largely responsible for their

capture, having resisted the strenuous efforts of their masters to carry
them inland. Those Negroes who remained testified that most masters
had attempted to persuade their slaves to flee with them, and, failing,
had tried to scare them into flight with warnings that the Yankees would
either shoot them or sell them "south" into the dreaded slave markets of
Cuba and other Caribbean islands. A few masters, it was rumored, had
shot some of their slaves in an attempt to force an evacuation. Although
one former plantation hand on St. Helena later stated that the "poor
whites" of Beaufort had made the Negroes "sensible" of the meaning of
the invasion, the large majority were apparently uncertain of their future
under the conquerors. Indeed, for months after the occupation, they
generally looked upon the Yankees with fear and suspicion. Insecure as
their prospects were, the Negroes were, nevertheless, quite certain that
the departure of their masters meant "no more driver, no more cotton,
no more lickin'," and for this they were obviously grateful.[1]

After the Port Royal invasion, the capture of large numbers of slaves
was made impossible by the thoroughness of both the Confederate
military and masters in removing bondsmen from areas of military
activity. Even under these circumstances, slaves persisted in their reluctance to leave the proximity of freedom. Louisa Gervais, the owner
of a James Island plantation, ordered her slaves driven from the island
by Confederate soldiers in the summer of 1863 in anticipation of a
Union assault, and in 1864 the mistress of a plantation on the mainland
in Beaufort District, desirous of moving her Negroes farther inland to
avoid Sherman's troopers, "feared the negroes might not go up, as
Willie [her husband] could not be there to make them."[2]

Although the Confederates succeeded in securing their slaves against
capture, they were never able to prevent a continuous sifting of Negro
fugitives through their lines to the islands. In the summer of 1862, more
than ten thousand Negroes were within the Union lines on the four
main islands in the Port Royal area, suggesting that three thousand
refugees had passed through the lines after the occupation.[3] By the end

1. *New South* (Port Royal), March 22, 1862; Elizabeth Ware Pearson (ed.),
Letters from Port Royal, 1862–1868 (Boston, 1906), pp. 181, 207; Elizabeth Hyde
Botume, *First Days Among the Contrabands* (Boston, 1893), p. 11; Ruppert S.
Holland (ed.), *Letters and Diary of Laura M. Towne, Written from the Sea
Islands of South Carolina, 1862–1884* (Cambridge, 1912), p. 27.
2. Louisa Gervais to J. Y. Simons, October 5, 1865, J. Y. Simons Papers;
Emma E. Holmes MS Diary, entry for January 1, 1865.
3. Edward L. Pierce, "The Freedmen of Port Royal," *Atlantic Monthly*, XII
(September, 1863), 299; *New South* (Port Royal), September 6, 1862; R. N. Scott

of the war, at least thirty thousand were within occupied territory which had expanded to include the islands south of Charleston, an outpost at Georgetown, and a coastal area roughly thirty miles wide from Charleston to the Savannah River.[4] The large majority of these were obviously refugees from the interior. Slaves escaping by their own resources maintained a constant flow of fugitives; but frequently the flow swelled to flood proportions as scores, hundreds, and, near the end of the war, thousands of slaves fled from their masters under the partial protection afforded by Union raiding expeditions into the interior.

The eagerness with which entire slave populations in affected areas seized upon the confusion occasioned by Union raids to flee evidenced their general willingness to undergo a reasonable risk to win freedom. Typical was their response to an expedition up the Combahee River in June, 1863. One rice planter, seeing the Union gunboats approaching, hastily ordered his slaves into the woods, only to observe them several minutes later running in the opposite direction, toward one of the boats. On a neighboring plantation, the overseer "ordered the negroes to the woods, but they refused to obey, and scattered." The overseer halted a portion of his charges only by shooting down a slave girl in their midst. On still another plantation, a number of slaves attempting to run the several miles to one of the gunboats were intercepted by mounted white men using "negro dogs." Despite the vigilance and vigor of the Southerners, the raiders returned to the islands with 725 refugees, "who are," as the Confederate commander in the area stated, "believed to have gone with great alacrity . . ."[5] The reaction of the slaves in the path of a Union raid up the South Edisto River in the following month indicated that not only were they eager to use this opportunity to escape their masters, but they knew of its coming well beforehand and had made their plans in advance. "The Negroes as soon as they heard the guns," wrote one rice planter several days after the raid, "rushed to my house and pillaged it of many things and principally wearing apparel." Left

et al., *The War of the Rebellion: A Compilation of the Official Records of the Union and Confederate Armies* (Washington, 1880–1902), Ser. 1, XIV, 191. Cited hereinafter as *Official Records*.

4. Whitelaw Reid, *After the War: A Southern Tour, May 1, 1865 to May 1, 1866* (Cincinnati, 1866), p. 80. In April, 1865, thirty thousand Negro refugees were under the direct supervision of military authorities in South Carolina. Probably as many as forty thousand were actually within the Union lines at this time.

5. *Official Records*, Ser. 1, XIV, 290–91, 301–8, 463; Botume, *First Days Among the Contrabands*, p. 51.

with only his house servants and after cataloguing the total or partial losses of his neighbors, the planter concluded that "everything tends to show the whole affair was pre-arranged," a view that was also expressed by a Confederate officer who witnessed the scene. The mistress of another plantation in the vicinity reported the same total desertion by her own slaves and by those of her father on an adjacent plantation. The Negroes, she declared, "showed the greatest delight" and "began to get ready as soon as they heard of the boat while it was some distance down the river." On her father's plantation "Dinah has gone, and Daphne and herself busied themselves in packing up and carrying off everything out of Papa's house."[6]

The grave dangers which individual fugitives endured to reach the Union lines indicated the high price that some slaves were willing to pay to win their freedom. The island press abounded in stories of such flights. For instance, in September, 1862, twenty-three Negroes, nineteen of them from a plantation on the South Carolina side of the Savannah River four miles east of the city of Savannah, eluded their masters, crossed undetected through an area thickly posted by Confederate troops, stole a dugout, and rowed across to the islands under the muzzles of Confederate pickets. In June the following year, after the Confederates had confiscated all the boats in the vicinity of the islands, eight Negroes from Savannah rowed and sailed a small dugout down the river and across the open sea to the islands. In March, 1864, a refugee named Sandy was recaptured on St. Helena by raiding Confederates, but he again escaped and returned to the island within a few days. Occasionally, fugitive slaves found safety by rowing out to the federal blockading fleet. In November, 1862, the Beaufort *New South* reported that five Negroes had escaped from Charleston by rowing past the Confederate forts and several miles beyond to a Union vessel. In March, 1864, the *Palmetto Herald* of Port Royal stated that four other slaves had followed the same channel to freedom.[7]

The most spectacular flight was that of a number of Negroes aboard the Confederate steamer *Planter*. These men were from the Port Royal area and had worked as sailors on the *Planter* for varying lengths of

6. J. B. Grimball to H. M. Manigault, July 14, 1863; Charlotte M. Manigault to her sister, July 12, 1863, John Berkeley Grimball Papers; *Official Records*, Ser. 1, XXVIII, Part I, 196, 198.

7. *New South* (Port Royal), September 8, 1862, June 21, 1863, November 22, 1862; *Free South* (Beaufort), April 2, 1864; *Palmetto Herald* (Port Royal), March 24, 1864.

time. When the ship was ordered to Charleston at the time of the invasion, the Negro members of the crew went with her, some bringing their families with them. In Charleston, the pilot of the ship, a mulatto then known as Robert Small (subsequently known as Robert Smalls), proposed to the Negro sailors that they escape, using the ship itself as a vehicle. Some declined, thinking the risk too great; most agreed. One night in May, 1862, while the captain was ashore, those who had families in Charleston rowed them out to the ship. In the early morning, they lifted the anchor and steamed out of the harbor. Passing under the guns of Fort Sumter at dawn, they gave the Confederate signal on the ship's whistle. To heighten the deception, Smalls broke into the captain's wardrobe, donned the officer's dress uniform, and paraded about the bridge, imitating the captain's distinctive gait. Taking the inland water route, they steamed for Beaufort, flying the Confederate flag. As they passed into St. Helena Sound and became visible to ships of the blockading fleet, they hauled down the Confederate ensign and ran up the Stars and Stripes. Shortly afterward, they landed safely in Beaufort. One of the sailors, while visiting his family on a St. Helena plantation several days later, told a Northern teacher that the crew had decided beforehand to blow up the steamer if threatened with capture because they knew the Confederates would show them no mercy.[8] Actually, the flight of the *Planter* was one episode in a continuing story. It was made more impressive than most in that the fugitives brought with them a sixty-thousand-dollar steamer. It was made more durable than most because the tale had unusual salability in the wartime Northern press, and because the hero, Robert Smalls "of *Planter* fame," later became the eminently popular leader among the Negro population of the Beaufort area.

A desire to be free only poorly describes the various and complex motives that spurred individual slaves to flight. Sometimes, the slave's desire for freedom from his master was reinforced by some more positive objective, such as a family reunion. Thus, York Polite, who had been working on the mainland at the time of the invasion, crossed the lines to rejoin his wife on St. Helena some five weeks afterward; and a Port Royal Negro woman who had been forcibly carried " 'way up in de country" by her master in 1861 returned early in 1865 following her "chillen" who had returned long since. Most fugitives, however, only vaguely understood what lay beyond the Confederate lines. They fled not so much to freedom as away from slavery. Freedom for these peo-

8. Pearson, *Letters from Port Royal*, pp. 46–47, 51.

ple simply meant an escape from the specific pains of slavery, both experienced and anticipated. One slave woman arrived with her two youngest children on St. Helena in April, 1862, having escaped from the mainland by hiding in "de ma'sh" all day and traveling by night. She was driven to flight by the action of her master who "had just 'licked' her eldest son almost to death because he was suspected of wanting to join the Yankees." Some fugitives were less specific in their reasons, simply judging the hazards of flight more tolerable than slavery. "I run away," declared one woman, "'cause master too bad; couldn't stay no longer." Not all refugees fled because they felt that their masters and slavery were all bad; some who claimed good masters, nevertheless, chose freedom. "Slavery is not so bad," said one man, speaking affectionately of his late master, "but liberty is so good." Another refugee, speaking in a church on St. Helena one Sunday in January, 1863, expressed his feelings with singular clarity. "I was brought up with the white folks," said he, "just like one of them; these hands never had any hard work to do. I had a kind master; but I didn't know but any time I might be sold away off, and when I found I could get my freedom, I was very glad; and I wouldn't go back again, because now I am for myself."[9]

When Union forces first occupied Port Royal, the United States government was willing to recognize the freedom only of those slaves whose labor had been used directly against the Union military. Yet it was unwilling to allow refugees to fall again under the control of rebel masters. Thus, the official status of refugees on the Sea Islands remained in limbo. However, it became increasingly evident that some practical, comprehensive program for organizing and employing the Negroes was imperative. Salmon P. Chase, then Secretary of the Treasury and an ardent abolitionist, seized the initiative. His agents had been active in the islands since the occupation, confiscating large quantities of cotton and, in a haphazard fashion, pressing the Negroes remaining on the plantations to commence operations for a new crop. To devise a more effective program, Chase enlisted the services of Edward L. Pierce, a Boston lawyer and abolitionist who had once been Chase's private secretary. Pierce was well suited to this task. Not only was he a friend to the Negro, but he was also a highly talented administrator

9. Holland, *Letters and Diary of Laura M. Towne*, p. 24; Botume, *First Days Among the Contrabands*, pp. 86, 139; Pearson, *Letters from Port Royal*, pp. 36–37; *Free South* (Beaufort), January 17, 1863.

who had left the ranks of his Massachusetts regiment during the previous summer to organize General Benjamin F. Butler's "contrabands"
on the Virginia peninsula. In December, 1861, Pierce hastened to Washington to confer with Chase, and in January and February he visited
the islands. Upon his return north, he proposed a two-part program.
Schools should be established to teach all, old as well as young, who were
willing to learn. Simultaneously, the Negroes on the plantations should
be organized to carry on the planting routine with two important innovations: they should work as individuals loosely supervised by white
superintendents, rather than in gangs as they had in slavery; and they
should be induced to work by the payment of wages rather than by the
use of the whip. "A system of culture and instruction," he explained,
"must be combined with one providing for their physical wants." He
thought the prospects of success excellent. "Never was there a nobler or
more fitting opportunity," he declared. However, official Washington
was not enthusiastic. The common retort of his opponents was that there
was no money for such a scheme.[10]

Forces already in motion were soon to provide Pierce with the
human and material resources needed to execute his program. On
February 6, 1862, while Pierce was in the islands, the commanding
general, Thomas W. Sherman, issued an order for the organization of
the Negro population precisely as Pierce subsequently proposed in his
report to Chase. Doubtful of his authority to use the means of the
government to activate the plan, the general appealed to the philanthropic
sentiments of the North for assistance. Abolitionist centers responded
immediately. In February and March, meetings in Boston, New York,
and Philadelphia established associations to recruit and pay the teachers
and the plantation superintendents required to implement the Pierce
plan. Before the end of the winter, the combined efforts of the Treasury
Department and the benevolent associations had placed a missionary
force in the islands, and organization on the plantations was under
Pierce's personal supervision.[11]

The Pierce program provided for the Negroes already on the plantations, yet the continuous influx of refugees, the employment of hundreds of Negroes by the government and by private parties, and the

10. Pierce, *Atlantic Monthly*, XII (1863), *passim;* Pearson, *Letters from Port
Royal*, p. v; Benjamin Quarles, *The Negro in the Civil War* (Boston, 1953),
pp. 94, 123–24.
11. *Official Records*, Ser. 1, VI, 222–23; Pierce, *Atlantic Monthly*, XII (September,
1863), *passim;* Pearson, *Letters from Port Royal*, pp. vi–ix, 1–14.

efficient prosecution of the war necessitated some more comprehensive organization. Consequently, in April, 1862, Secretary of War Edwin M. Stanton, by direct order, created a unique office in the Army—that of military governor. This officer was to function within the limits of the Department of the South, which at that time consisted of the islands in the Port Royal area and scattered, small outposts stretching southward to Key West, Florida. The military governor was directed to "take possession of all the plantations heretofore occupied by the rebels." Further, he was to "take charge of the inhabitants remaining thereon within the department, or which the fortunes of the war may hereafter bring into it with authority to take such measures, make such rules and regulations for the cultivation of the land and for protection, employment, and government of the inhabitants as circumstances may seem to require." Finally, the military governor was exclusively responsible to the Secretary of War in the performance of these specific duties.[12] Stanton's order indicated that he considered the Negro population on the Sea Islands a special and important case. His antislavery background and his subsequent behavior suggested that Stanton intended to test and to prove the capacity of the ex-slave to live in a free society. Thus, under peculiarly controlled conditions, the remaking of Southern society began in South Carolina less than a year after the commencement of the war.

On July 1, 1862, the military governor became the central authority concerned with the Negro population in the islands, and even the Pierce group passed under his control. The man chosen to fill the office was Rufus B. Saxton, a newly breveted brigadier general. During the next three and one-half years, Saxton was Washington's (and presumably Stanton's) chief spokesman to the civilian population of South Carolina, white and Negro, and his personality had a large influence in shaping the behavior of the Negro population during the Reconstruction period. A native of Deerfield, Maine, a graduate of West Point and a career officer in the army, Saxton came to Hilton Head with the assault force as a captain in the Quartermaster Corps. Like so many of his fellow officers, he was transformed by the war. On the eve of conflict, he was a plain-mannered, middle-aged, settled bachelor of unpronounced political views. By the end of the struggle, he had married one of the "pretty" Northern teachers on the islands; and Whitelaw Reid, in 1865, saw him as a handsome figure in dress uniform, with "black hair and luxurious English whiskers and mustache." His father

12. *Official Records,* Ser. 3, II, 152–53.

had been an enthusiastic abolitionist, yet Saxton undertook his new assignment with reluctance and out of loyalty to the government rather than out of sympathy for the Negro. "I was educated in its school and for its service," he explained, "and I thought it my business to do whatever it required." Events proved that Stanton had chosen his man well. Earnest and straightforward in manner, tireless in labor, Saxton made his administration felt at once. As his work progressed his antislavery potentialities became apparent. In the summer of 1862, Laura Towne, one of the Northern teachers on St. Helena, was pleased to find him "truly anti-slavery." When he left the state in 1866 to re-enter the regular service, the Negroes—particularly those in the islands—had come to recognize "Gen'l Saxby" as a devoted and ever-loyal friend.[13]

While Saxton was busily preparing himself to enter into his new duties, an intricate concatenation of events was in progress which would fix the official status of his charges before the end of the year. The Negroes on the Sea Islands were themselves a central element in the process, and the catalyst who made them so was Major General David M. Hunter, after March 31, 1862, commanding general of the Department of the South. Similar to Saxton in military background, the sixty-year-old commander was decidedly different in capacity and personality. After graduating from West Point in 1822, his prewar rise to the rank of major had been distinguished only by the fact that he had been Jefferson Davis's commanding officer in the First Dragoons. In 1860, he somehow gained the favor of President-elect Lincoln, and in the early months of the war his military star at last began to rise. In the fall of 1861, perhaps because he had a reputation for conservative politics and his "impulsive," "quick and decided," self-assertive demeanor suggested a capacity for action that Lincoln found rare among Union commanders, he was selected to relieve Fremont of his western command. Shortly thereafter, he assumed command of the Department of Kansas and, in March, 1862, was transferred to head the Department of the South. There it soon became apparent that the President had misread the general's politics.[14]

Within two weeks after assuming command of the Department,

13. Charles Howard Family, Domestic History, p. 169; Reid, *After the War,* pp. 80, 117; Pearson, *Letters from Port Royal,* p. 48; Holland, *Letters and Diary of Laura M. Towne,* p. 76.

14. James Grant Wilson and John Fiske (eds.), *Appletons' Cyclopaedia of American Biography* (New York, 1888), III, 321; Dudley Taylor Cornish, *The Sable Arm, Negro Troops in the Union Army, 1861–1865* (New York, 1956), pp. 15, 33; Holland, *Letters and Diary of Laura M. Towne,* p. 71.

Hunter issued a blanket declaration freeing the Negroes who had been captured in Fort Pulaski and on Cockspur Island, the spit of land in the mouth of the Savannah upon which the fort stood. Presumably, these people had been used by the Confederate military in the construction of the forts and their liberation was authorized by the provisions of the first Confiscation Act. On April 25, however, Hunter clearly exceeded his authority by placing the three states encompassed by his command under martial law, and on May 9, by announcing, with a logic that was at least novel, that since "Slavery and Martial Law, in a free country, are altogether incompatible; the persons in these three States, Georgia, Florida and South Carolina heretofore held as slaves are therefore declared forever free."[15] Possibly, Hunter thought that his actions would be upheld by his Washington sponsor. Most of the Northern missionaries in the islands, however, were dubious of its permanence, and E. S. Philbrick, one of the most practical among them, denounced the order as "premature and uncalled for."[16] In addition, the reaction among the Negroes on the islands was far from sensational. As Philbrick observed, they were virtually free already. Indeed, the teachers, superintendents, and ministers who went among them assumed that they were free, and the Negroes themselves seemed to accept such as being the case.[17] In the North reactions to the order were varied. Antislavery elements applauded loudly and held the island Negro population up for admiration. In Congress, however, border-state representatives raised such a furor that Lincoln moved quickly and decisively to crush his erstwhile protégé. On May 19, the President pointedly announced that "neither General Hunter nor any other commander or person" had authority to issue orders of emancipation.[18]

Four eventful months later, Lincoln promulgated his own plan of emancipation. In South Carolina, the proclamation was tantamount to a guarantee of liberation to every Negro within the Union lines. Yet, news of the Preliminary Proclamation, reaching the Sea Islands early in October, hardly caused any greater stir among either missionaries or former slaves than had Hunter's order. "Our first victory worth the name," commented Laura Towne, assessing the proclamation as a minor reward for much labor; meanwhile Philbrick reported from St. Helena: "Here the people don't take the slightest interest in it. They have been

15. *Official Records,* Ser. 1, XIV, 333, 341.

16. Pearson, *Letters from Port Royal,* pp. 50, 62.

17. Charles Howard Family, Domestic History, p. 105; Pearson, *Letters from Port Royal,* pp. 62–63.

18. Cornish, *The Sable Arm,* pp. 35–36; *Official Records,* Ser. 3, II, 42–43.

free already for nearly a year, as far as they could see. . . ."[19] Doubtless, the mass of the island population treasured the fact of freedom far more than they did the name.

Emancipation, after all, simply recognized a fact already established; but at the same time Hunter was pressing emancipation, he was also precipitating in his boot-first, blustering manner a question of immediate significance: Would and could freed Negroes fight in the ranks of the army to preserve their liberty? The question had been agitated in the North since the first days of the war. Within a week after his arrival in the islands, Hunter, acting on his own authority and in the face of what he considered to be military necessity, forced the issue by beginning the recruitment of a regiment of Negro soldiers.[20]

At a meeting called by Abram Murchison, a native Negro Baptist minister, 105 men were induced to enlist on April 7, 1862, and, within a week, Hunter was able to muster 150 Negroes into the service as the First South Carolina Regiment of Volunteers.[21] Thereafter, however, recruiting proceeded slowly. Most of the first volunteers probably were refugees from the mainland without employment. Those who had remained on the plantations and were engaged in planting their crops were far from enthusiastic. On St. Helena, it was reported that only one man volunteered, and the missionaries generally agreed that the Negroes were afraid of "being made to fight." Ironically, the missionaries, who supposedly knew the ex-slaves well, thought them incapable of facing white men in battle. "Five white men could put a regiment to flight," was the opinion of a superintendent; and a teacher was convinced "they are afraid, and they know it." On St. Helena, Laura Towne observed that the plantation hands generally regarded the maneuver as "a trap to get the able-bodied and send them to Cuba to sell," a remnant of the idea left by the fleeing masters some six months previously.[22]

19. Holland, *Letters and Diary of Laura M. Towne,* p. 92; Pearson, *Letters from Port Royal,* p. 91.

20. Joseph T. Wilson, an early historian of the Negro soldier, believed that Hunter's actions both in ordering emancipation and in beginning the Negro regiment were motivated primarily by military necessity. Joseph T. Wilson, *The Black Phalanx: A History of the Negro Soldiers of the United States in the Wars of 1775–1812, 1861–65* (Hartford, 1891), p. 146.

21. Quarles, *The Negro in the Civil War,* pp. 109–10.

22. Pearson, *Letters from Port Royal,* pp. 40–43; Holland, *Letters and Diary of Laura M. Towne,* p. 37.

Assuming that Negroes were reluctant to volunteer only because of their ignorance of the felicity of military life, on May 9, Hunter moved with characteristic decisiveness and lack of deliberation. Ordering all plantation superintendents to send their able-bodied laborers to Hilton Head, he dispatched squads of soldiers with fixed bayonets to execute the command. The suspicions of the Negroes were hardly lessened by the knowledge that Hilton Head was the traditional point of departure for slaves being sold in Cuba or by Hunter's neglect to tell the superintendents for what purpose he called these men. The Negroes were obviously apprehensive, but, as one missionary declared, "the whole thing was accomplished with much less *apparent* suffering than we had supposed possible." Laura Towne, observing the Negro men of her plantation gathering in the yard to leave with their military escort, noted that "some looked willing; others less so, but they all seemed to submit passively and patiently if not trustfully."[23] After having experienced a taste of camp life, Negro males responded much as Hunter had anticipated. Within a few days, some of the men returned to the plantations bringing reports of "comfortable quarters, good food and clothing." Miss Towne asserted that "nearly all are eager to go there again and serve in the forts," but they did not want to fight.[24]

The reluctance of Negro refugees to volunteer was manifest, but the greatest obstacle to Hunter's success in raising a Negro regiment was opposition from official sources. The President and elements in Congress were incensed by Hunter's presumption in enlisting Negroes. Brushing aside the general's attempt to justify his action by a strained interpretation of orders issued to his predecessor, Lincoln, on May 19, deprived Hunter's Negro troops of the appellation "soldiers" and revoked the freedom order that had accompanied the draft. Stubbornly, Hunter held the regiment together and continued to treat the men as an integral portion of his fighting force. The failure of officials to provide funds for paying his Negro troops, however, made some retrenchment inevitable. Early in August, Hunter released most of the regiment "for a time," supposedly to harvest the maturing crops. The one company that was retained was sent to garrison St. Simon's Island off the coast of Georgia.[25]

23. Pearson, *Letters from Port Royal*, pp. 38–41; Holland, *Letters and Diary of Laura M. Towne*, pp. 44–47.

24. Pearson, *Letters from Port Royal*, p. 42; Holland, *Letters and Diary of Laura M. Towne*, p. 54.

25. George Washington Williams, *A History of the Negro Troops in the War*

Even as Hunter dispersed his Negro troops, official policy shifted rapidly toward acceptance of the Negro as a soldier. As the summer waxed, the military fortunes of the Union forces waned. In Virginia, McClellan was hurled back from Richmond, and Lee began to march northward. In the West, early successes turned suddenly sour as Braxton Bragg began to move on Louisville. On the islands themselves, troops were withdrawn in such numbers for use in Virginia that Hunter felt constrained to abandon his northernmost outposts, reducing the area of his occupation by about a fifth.[26] Apparently moved by the crisis, Congress in July granted the President authority to enlist Negro soldiers. Even though Lincoln was still unwilling to act directly, he did allow Secretary Stanton, on August 25, to issue explicit orders to Saxton to arm five thousand Negro troops.[27] Shortly after receiving these orders, Saxton journeyed to Washington where he found that the administration had indeed decided to place in his hands the task of raising the first fully authorized Negro regiments. He returned to the islands in mid-October with a profound sense of the importance and urgency of his mission. The President and the North, he told one of the superintendents, looked to the organization of the first regiments "as a test experiment" to see if the Negroes would help defend themselves on the islands. If it were successful, then the Negroes could be enlisted on the mainland as they were liberated; thus, the proclamation of emancipation would become "a more terrible [and] effective weapon against the Southerners." Saxton immediately threw himself into the task of raising the five regiments authorized.[28]

This series of events suggests that official Washington was responsible for the formal induction of Negroes into the ranks of the Union military. Yet, the arming of the island Negroes was, at least in part, the result of the activities of the islanders themselves. During the summer the Negroes had reversed their attitude toward active combat against the Con-

of the Rebellion, 1861–1865 (New York, 1888), pp. 90–96; Quarles, The Negro in the Civil War, pp. 110–11; Thomas Wentworth Higginson, Army Life in a Black Regiment (Boston, 1890), pp. 274–75; Holland, Letters and Diary of Laura M. Towne, p. 83.

26. Official Records, Ser. 1, XIV, 363, 365.

27. Cornish, The Sable Arm, pp. 46–47, 50–55; Official Records, Ser. 1, XIV, 377–78.

28. Saxton's words were paraphrased by an assistant of the superintendent who interviewed Saxton. Pearson, Letters from Port Royal, pp. 86, 94, 97; Holland, Letters and Diary of Laura M. Towne, pp. 90, 91; New South (Port Royal), October 18, 1862.

federates. In August and September there were rumors that the islands
were to be evacuated entirely and the Negroes resettled in Haiti. Behind these rumors were the facts that Hunter had abandoned Edisto and
had announced his intention, should his forces be further reduced by
transfers, of evacuating all the islands except Hilton Head.[29] Further,
threatened disaster was given the substance of reality by sporadic Confederate raids on the islands and the capture of Southern spies on Port
Royal.[30] The imminent prospect of either leaving the islands or resub-
mitting to their masters apparently caused the Negroes to think more
favorably of military training. On many plantations superintendents
were able to organize and to drill the Negroes with arms provided by
the army. Some Negroes, acting on their own initiative, began to maintain watches along the beaches most exposed to enemy assaults, and,
on the night of October 23, the watch drove off two boats bearing Confederate soldiers attempting a raid on St. Helena.[31] Encouraged by this
change of sentiment, Saxton, on August 16, requested authority from
Stanton to enlist five thousand Negroes in the Quartermaster Department to be "uniformed, armed, and officered by men" detailed from the
Army. In effect, Saxton wanted to enlist Negro soldiers under the guise
of enrolling laborers for the Army. Stanton's order of August 25, explicitly authorizing Saxton to enlist five thousand Negro soldiers, was a
direct reply to Saxton's request. However, Stanton boldly ignored the
subterfuge of enlisting the Negroes as laborers and ordered their acceptance as soldiers on an equality with white recruits; and he added
the note that Saxton was authorized by a recent act of Congress (July
17, 1862) to certify the freedom of all who enlisted and of their wives,
mothers, and children.[32]

Entering the army, nevertheless, was quite different from defending
one's home, family, and self. Whereas many Negroes volunteered
"willingly" in the first few days of Saxton's recruiting campaign, some
offered themselves with "dismal forelornness," and others not at all.
When two officers appeared at a church on St. Helena on October 23
to seek recruits, all able-bodied males declined to attend.[33] On the
following Sunday, Sergeant Prince Rivers, a Negro veteran of the

29. Pearson, *Letters from Port Royal*, pp. 84–86; Holland, *Letters and Diary of
Laura M. Towne*, pp. 86, 90; Official Records, Ser. 1, XIV, 374.

30. Holland, *Letters and Diary of Laura M. Towne*, pp. 63, 69, 92.

31. Pearson, *Letters from Port Royal*, p. 89; Holland, *Letters and Diary of
Laura M. Towne*, pp. 86, 93; *Official Records*, Ser. 1, XIV, 189.

32. *Official Records*, Ser. 1, XIV, 374, 377–78.

33. Holland, *Letters and Diary of Laura M. Towne*, pp. 93–94.

Hunter Regiment, visiting the island on the same mission, suffered the same disappointment.

Confronted with the reluctance of the Negroes, Saxton intensified his recruiting efforts. Early in November, he organized the first company of Negro soldiers and paraded it ostentatiously in Beaufort. "Many of them were in the first regiment," wrote one observer, "and the regularity and steadiness of their marching was very creditable." New soldiers were given short leaves to visit their homes and seek additional volunteers.[34] In the first week in November, Saxton sent the company which had survived the demise of the Hunter regiment on a highly successful raid along the coasts of Florida and Georgia to bring away potential recruits, destroy Confederate salt works, break up picket posts, and—most important—"to prove the fighting qualities of the negroes (which some have doubted)." Equally successful was a raid up the Doboy River in Georgia some two weeks later by three companies of Saxton's men. On this occasion, a detachment of about thirty Negro soldiers coolly fought their way out of a Confederate ambush, proving, as one officer proudly noted, that they could fight as well in the open field as from behind barricades. The effect of these expeditions greatly improved the morale of the Negro troops, but the 550 men which Saxton mustered in mid-November and the more than one thousand Negroes employed as laborers by the Quartermaster and Engineering Corps in the islands virtually exhausted the "willing" manpower available in the Negro population.[35] The indefatigable Saxton then sought volunteers abroad. In December and January, he succeeded in raising more than four hundred recruits in the refugee-crowded outposts in Florida and at Georgetown, South Carolina. By January 31, 1863, the ranks of the regiment were filled. Under the command of Thomas Wentworth Higginson, Unitarian minister, writer, soldier, and long-time abolitionist, it was formally mustered into the service as the First South Carolina Regiment of Volunteers.[36]

When David Hunter returned to the islands on January 20, 1863, after a prolonged leave, he brought with him James Montgomery, the man who was to become the colonel of the Second South Carolina Regiment. Montgomery had gone to Kansas with John Brown and afterward became one of the most prominent leaders among the Jayhawkers. Failing to win command of the first Negro regiment raised in Kansas,

34. Pearson, *Letters from Port Royal*, pp. 104, 106–7.
35. *Official Records*, Ser. 1, XIV, 189–93.
36. *New South* (Port Royal), December 6, 1862; January 13, 31, 1863.

he went to Washington where he attached himself to Hunter whom he had probably known as the commander of the Department of Kansas a year previously. Middle-aged, vigorous, and aggressive, Montgomery was a striking figure, "a fiery westerner, full of fight and with sufficient confidence in himself," as one lady teacher in the islands observed. Bearded in the John Brown fashion, Montgomery brought the spirit of his mentor to South Carolina.[37] Like Brown, he sought to use slaves (refugee soldiers) to free slaves; and, again like Brown, his preferred tactic was the Kansas–style raid—swift, terrifying, and devastating, taking off all that could be carried and burning all that was left behind. Perfected in practice, the raid became the professional trademark of "Mon'gomery's boys" and, to some extent, that of the Negro soldier in South Carolina.

In command, Montgomery's first problem was to find enough recruits to fill his regiment. By early March, his ranks contained only 150 men, and 130 of these had been enlisted from among the refugees at Key West, Florida, an extremity to which even Saxton had not gone. For a Jayhawker, however, this was a sufficient beginning, and Montgomery knew where his recruits were. On March 10, he landed in Jacksonville along with Higginson's command and led a foray seventy-five miles inland, returning laden with booty and accompanied by a large number of potential soldiers—lately slaves.[38] In May and June, raids up the Ashepoo and Combahee rivers in South Carolina and an attack on the village of Darien, Georgia, supplied more recruits.[39]

Meanwhile, Hunter issued an order drafting all able-bodied Negro men remaining on the plantations. Confronted with the draft, many volunteered.[40] Others were seized in the night by squads of Negro soldiers. On one plantation on St. Helena, Betsy's husband was thus taken, leaving her with ten children and a "heart most broke." "Shan't live long, no way," she wailed, "oh my Jesus."[41] Those who attempted to evade the draft were roughly treated. Josh, who had fled to the

37. Cornish, *The Sable Arm*, pp. 103–4, 134; Holland, *Letters and Diary of Laura M. Towne*, p. 103.

38. Cornish, *The Sable Arm*, pp. 138–40.

39. Elizabeth Botume, a Northern teacher on Port Royal Island, found that most of the males belonging to families living in a refugee camp on "Montgomery Hill" were "wid Mon'gomery's boys in de regiment," suggesting that he drew heavily on the refugees for his recruits. Botume, *First Days Among the Contrabands*, pp. 50–62.

40. Holland, *Letters and Diary of Laura M. Towne*, p. 107.

41. Pearson, *Letters from Port Royal*, p. 185.

marshes, was tracked to his hiding place and when he again tried to elude his pursuers was shot down and captured.[42] Negro civilians suffered under the draft and resented the manner of its enforcement; yet, it was effective. "The draft is either taking or frightening off most of the men," lamented one of the superintendents at the end of March, 1863.[43]

Third, Fourth, and Fifth South Carolina Regiments were begun to accommodate the five-thousand-man force authorized; but neither raids on the mainland, where masters learned to be more careful in removing their human chattels from areas exposed to the raiders, nor an increasingly thorough draft sufficed to fill completely either these or Montgomery's regiment. By the end of the year, these three regiments last formed were consolidated and, as a part of the general re-organization of Negro troops, were redesignated the Twenty-first United States Colored Troops. Similarly, the First South Carolina became the Thirty-third United States Colored Troops, and the Second became the Thirty-fourth United States Colored Troops.[44] As Union lines rapidly advanced in the winter and spring of 1865, Negroes in the coastal areas supplied the manpower to complete the organization of the 102nd United States Colored Troops and to fill four more regiments—the 103rd, 104th, 105th, and the 128th United States Colored Troops.[45] Though all eight regiments served in the occupation, the last three were formed too late to participate in the fighting. Nevertheless, by the end of the war, 5,462 South Carolina Negroes had been recruited directly into the Army by Union authorities.[46] In addition, an unknown number joined the Fifty-fourth and Fifty-fifth Massachusetts Regiments (Negro), both of which remained in the Department of the South and actively recruited in the islands from the summer of 1863 until their discharge in 1866.[47]

42. *Ibid.*, p. 188.

43. *Ibid.*, pp. 184, 172–89, *passim.* See also: Holland, *Letters and Diary of Laura M. Towne*, pp. 107–8.

44. *Official Records*, Ser. 1, XXVIII, Part 2, 128; XXXV, Part 1, 34; *Free South* (Beaufort), April 2, 1864.

45. Wilson, *The Black Phalanx*, pp. 469, 476–77; Frank A. Rollin, *Life and Public Services of Martin R. Delany, Sub-Assistant Commissioner, Bureau Relief of Refugees, Freedmen, and of Abandoned Lands, and Late Major 104th U. S. Colored Troops* (2nd ed., Boston, 1883), pp. 200–2, 209–13.

46. Williams, *History of the Negro Troops*, p. 140, citing War Department Records.

47. Pearson, *Letters from Port Royal*, pp. 282–83.

In spite of the reluctance with which many Negroes volunteered and
the resistance that others offered to the draft, once in camp, the large
majority quickly adjusted to military life. For instance, January, a
draftee in the "First South" who had been pulled down from the in-
side of his chimney by a deserter-hunting squad only a few weeks before,
returned to his home on Coffin Point plantation in February, 1863,
fresh from a successful raid up the St. Mary's River. Proud and
boastful of the exploit, he was completely transformed in his martial
attitude and said he would not leave the army for a thousand dollars.[48]

Of course, there were a few men who never adjusted. During their
early history, the new regiments were plagued by desertions which were
freely excused on the ground of ignorance. Montgomery was personally unsympathetic with this plea, however, evincing the attitude
that the Negro soldiers ought to be treated in every respect as were the
white troops. One Sunday at dawn, Private William Span, having been
recaptured after his eighth or ninth defection, was brought before the
colonel in his tent. Montgomery asked Span if he wished to offer any
excuse. Span said no. "Then," declared the colonel, "you will be shot
at half past nine this morning." Precisely at 9:30 A.M., while the regiment watched, Span was marched out, the drums rolled, a squad of
Negro soldiers fired, and Span fell dead. By early July, 1863, desertion
was no longer a problem in Montgomery's regiment.[49]

Ultimately the capacity of the soldier is tested not in camp but in
the field, and in the field the Negro soon had ample opportunity to
prove himself. The first three regiments were literally born in the midst
of raiding expeditions on the mainland, and they early proved that
they could fight well in such encounters. During the assault on the
defenses of Charleston in the summer of 1863, they showed their white
brothers–in–arms that they could also perform creditably under the
severest conditions of orthodox warfare. The first laurels were won by
the Fifty-fourth Massachusetts, a Negro regiment which, on July 18,
1863, sustained heavy losses in a frontal assault that breeched the walls
of Fort Wagner, a key position in the defenses of Charleston. Even
though lack of support forced them to retire, there was no longer any
doubt either among the white troops or in the North at large that Negro
soldiers were equal to any.[50]

Even the Confederates implicitly conceded that these Negroes were,

48. *Ibid.*, p. 153.
49. *New South* (Port Royal), July 4, 1863.
50. Cornish, *The Sable Arm*, pp. 153–56.

indeed, soldiers. The Confederate brigadier who succeeded in getting scarcely a score of his thousand men engaged against the Combahee raiders on June 2, 1863, pronounced the raid a complete success. He could hardly have done otherwise since the raiders, between 2:00 A.M. and 2:00 P.M., steamed ten miles up-river, destroyed a military pontoon bridge, scattered pickets, burned six rice mills and the buildings on five plantations (pointedly leaving the Negro quarters unharmed), and escaped with 725 slaves and without casualties.[51] Considering armed Negroes as insurrectionaries, the announced intention of the Confederate government was to treat captured Negro soldiers as such. In South Carolina, this meant that they would be tried and, if convicted, hanged. Yet, after the assault on Fort Wagner, the Negro wounded who had been captured in the Confederate counterattack were returned along with the white wounded in a general exchange. Some of the Negro soldiers captured within the walls of Wagner by the Confederates were turned over to the state. Eighteen of these were tried under the insurrectionary laws of South Carolina. The state failed to win a conviction and, apparently, these and other Negro soldiers, afterward taken as prisoners of war, were regularly interned in Confederate military prisons.[52]

The assault on the defenses of Charleston brought the city itself under the guns of the Union forces and in September, 1863, Fort Wagner fell, giving the Union Army a reasonably defensible position within sight of the city. During the following year, the lines again became relatively stable, and the Negro troops reverted to their usual occupation—raiding operations along the coast.

In the fall of 1864, Sherman's approach from the interior drastically altered the military situation in South Carolina. In November, a Union force of some five thousand men, consisting largely of Negro troops, was ordered inland for the purpose of facilitating Sherman's advance. This first full-scale invasion of the mainland was designed to cut the Savannah and Charleston Railroad at Pocataligo. Incredibly bad generalship led the force astray and into the muzzles of an equal number of Confederates entrenched in a semicircle around them on a crest known as Honey Hill. Successive assaults by three Negro regiments

51. *Official Records,* Ser. 1, XIV, 290–308.
52. Cornish, *The Sable Arm,* pp. 157–58; James Amasa May and Joan Reynolds Faunt, *South Carolina Secedes* (Columbia, 1960), pp. 160–61. Interestingly, successful counsel for the defense was Edward McCrady, Yale '20, a prominent Charleston lawyer, and an ardent Unionist in the Nullification controversy.

over virtually impassable marshy terrain were repulsed after the assailants suffered heavy losses. Finally, the Union force withdrew, but
the beachhead on the mainland was held and gradually enlarged as the
Negro regiments hammered against Confederate positions before Pocataligo. Sherman's left wing, having come to the islands from Savannah
by sea, used the beachhead as its point of departure for the invasion of
South Carolina. As the Confederates withdrew before Sherman's army,
Negro troops occupied Pocataligo and moved rapidly northward along
the line of the railroad toward Charleston.

On the morning of February 18, while this force was still in motion,
the Confederates were hastily evacuating Charleston, leaving the city
in flames begun by burning military stores and exploding ammunition.
Union commanders on the islands southeast of the city, seeing the
billowing clouds of smoke and hearing the explosions, correctly concluded that the Confederates were abandoning Charleston. Even as
the last of the Confederate rear guard marched out of the city to the
northwest, troops of the Twenty-first United States Colored Troops
debarked on the deserted, grass–grown wharves at the lower end of the
peninsula. Minutes later, the entire Twenty-first and several companies
of the Fifty-fourth Massachusetts were in the city. The Twenty-first
marched up Meeting Street heralded by a Negro soldier who had somehow procured a mule upon which he rode and carried a banner bearing
the inscription "Liberty." Behind the Twenty-first came the Fifty-fourth
Massachusetts singing "John Brown's Body." The free Negro population
and those slaves who had managed to remain emerged from their
hiding places to greet the Negro troops enthusiastically. "An old woman,
who the night before had lain down a slave, and even on that morning
was uncertain of her master's movements," heard the shouts and ran
out. Unable to embrace the mounted herald, she hugged the mule,
exclaiming, "Thank God! Thank God!"[53]

The conflagration left by the Confederates was rapidly extinguished,
and the Union force made its occupation secure. The effect on the
Negro population was soon evident. The few masters remaining in
the city were deserted by their slaves. "The ex-slaves," a *Times* correspondent observed, "have become imbued with a spirit of freedom and
are determined to bear the yoke no longer." Most conspicuous was their

53. Luis F. Emilio, *History of the Fifty-Fourth Regiment of Massachusetts
Volunteer Infantry, 1863–1865* (Boston, 1894), pp. 254–86; Rollin, *Life and Public
Services of Martin R. Delany*, pp. 198–99; Quarles, *The Negro in the Civil War*,
pp. 326–28.

devotion to the Union cause, an affinity that was expressed by the hundreds of eager recruits who flocked to join the Negro regiments. In the first three weeks of the occupation, enlistments reached a peak of two hundred in one day, the young men yielding "to the persuasion of Negro soldiers by a show of bounty-money, allowances, rations, soldier-clothes, and chevrons." On March 29, after a particularly impressive celebration, three hundred men joined the ranks.[54]

Although Sherman's march from Savannah to Columbia and thence northeastward through Camden and Cheraw in January and February, 1865, had a large military significance, it offered freedom to comparatively few Negroes in the path of his advance. Indeed, scattered evidence indicates that Sherman's troops, unchecked by the organized consideration for the Negroes which Saxton administered along the coast, typically seized the possessions of Negroes as well as of whites, lured from their masters only the most productive slaves, and used these badly and for selfish ends. Emma Holmes, a spinsterish, twenty-six-year-old daughter of the "aristocracy," recorded in her diary that the Negro population of Camden was "terrified" by Sherman's coming. "The negroes all share the same fate as ourselves," she wrote after the army had passed, "everything ransacked and whatever was wanted stolen, though the Yankees told them they had come to free them and called them 'sis,' talking most familiarly." One elderly Negro, she remembered, saved his blankets from a group of bummers only by quick thinking and artful acting. Affecting "a tone of terror," he begged the blanket thieves not to mix those stolen from the house with his "as all the house girls had some catching disease. On hearing this, every one was hastily thrown, and off they went, making him a present of an old mule."[55] A letter allegedly written by one of Sherman's officers and found by one of the natives in the streets of Camden after the army's departure presumed to outline the Negro policy of the Sherman force. "The damned niggers," it asserted, "as a general rule, preferred to stay at home—particularly after they found out that we only wanted the able-bodied men (and to tell you the truth, the youngest and best looking women)." Occasionally, it added, an "influential secessionist" was repaid by having all of his Negroes removed. "But the useless part of these we manage to lose. Sometimes in crossing rivers, sometimes in other ways."[56] The authenticity of this letter is at least suspect; yet,

54. *New York Times,* March 9, p. 1; 18, p. 1; April 4, p. 9, 1865.
55. Emma E. Holmes MS Diary, entry for March 5, 1865.
56. Thomas J. Myers to his wife, February 26, 1865, Thomas J. Myers Papers.

available evidence suggests that it contained much truth. For instance, the owner of a plantation near Bamberg told a Northern traveler that Sherman had carried off about seven or eight of the best of his thirty-four slaves; and a large planter in Chesterfield District complained after Sherman's passage that his "cook and twenty-nine others of my negroes were carried off." That life with Sherman was not all that a Negro might desire was suggested by the Chesterfield planter's note, "3 have returned, have seen enough of it."[57]

As Sherman's troops passed through Camden, Negro troops moved inland from Charleston. By early March, they had established a new line anchored several miles inland from Summerville (a village on the South Carolina Railroad about twenty-five miles northwest of Charleston) and extending southward to include the line of the Charleston and Savannah Railroad. Thereafter, Union forces occupied an area which included the islands, a coastal strip some thirty miles wide from Charleston to Savannah, and an outpost at Georgetown. Opposing them were roving bands of Confederate cavalry scouts and a scattering of home guards. Again, the Negro soldiery reverted to raiding tactics.

By far the most impressive raid was led by General Edward E. Potter, who commanded twenty-seven hundred Negro troops, including the Fifty-fourth Massachusetts and the 103rd United States Colored Troops (South Carolina). On a sortie from the Georgetown outpost on April 5, Potter led his men eighty miles inland to Camden. The slaves, perhaps noting the prominent presence of Negroes among the soldiers, welcomed the invaders. In Camden, the Negro troops held a meeting, "of course attracting crowds and tremendous excitement prevailed, as they prayed their cause might prosper and their just freedom obtained." Unlike Sherman, Potter apparently took off only those who came willingly. When the Negro troops left Camden, Emma Holmes observed, "great numbers of servants went off from town, really crazy from excitement and the parade, as well as [the] idea of going to Charleston in carriages." Living in her mother's household in the village, she noted that two of their male servants had gone, "and, we believe, Mary and several others would have done so, save that they got there too late and were turned back by our men. Chloe and Judy do not deny it, but the former said 'if she had known in time that her son Thomas was

See also: Thomas J. Kirkland and Robert M. Kennedy, *Historic Camden* (Columbia, 1926), Part 2, pp. 169–70.

57. *The Nation*, II, No. 29 (January 18, 1866), 76; Allan MacFarland to R. H. Gourdin, May 22, 1865, Allan MacFarland Papers.

there, she would have gone. . . .' "[58] On the plantations, the effect of Potter's raid on the Negroes was much the same as in Camden. For example, of the 148 slaves residing on the Henry L. Pinckney planta- tion near Stateburg in Sumter District, forty-one followed Potter. In age, capacity, and family arrangements the fugitives represented a cross section of the slave population, suggesting that their only common distinction was a willingness to flee.[59] Potter returned to the coast with an estimated three thousand Negro civilians in his train, and it was be- lieved that the raiders had released as many more to make their own way to freedom.[60]

Potter's expedition was only one of many, and all elicited similar responses from the Negro population. On March 5, 1865, a group of sailors from the Union ships anchored near Georgetown raided through the area in the vicinity of Plantersville fifteen miles to the north "fol- lowed by many very excited colored persons who committed many excesses irrespective of all private property and in violation of all Chris- tian codes as to the claims and rights of man."[61] On April 10, A. S. Hartwell's Negro brigade, on a sortie from the lines around Summer- ville, marched northward through Monck's Corner to Pineville, returning April 12 with one thousand recent slaves in their van.[62]

April saw the end of the war in the east, but peace did not terminate the military careers of the Negro soldiery. By June, the Negro regiments were spread, as occupation forces, from Georgetown to Savannah and from the Sea Islands to the mountains; and their work of liberation was not yet done.

The Negro learned to soldier in the Union Army, and the military tradition so marked this generation that its vestiges were still apparent at the turn of the century. The Negro learned other things in the army, lessons equally durable and, perhaps more important, lessons that pre- pared him to face the perils of freedom as they had the hazards of war. Even the least intelligent, most ignorant Negro soldier shed his uniform with some understanding of subsisting in a money economy. Many left the army with considerable savings and virtually all left with bounty

58. Holmes MS Diary, entry for April 17, 1865.
59. Henry L. Pinckney MS Plantation Book, list of slaves and subsequent notations, January—April 24, 1865.
60. Emilio, *History of the Fifty-Fourth Regiment,* pp. 289–309.
61. MS Petition, The Citizens of Plantersville to the Military Commander at Georgetown, March 6, 1865, Sparkman Family Papers.
62. Emilio, *History of the Fifty-Fourth Regiment,* pp. 295–96.

money and adjustments in pay still due them. A large number used their funds to buy land, animals, and agricultural equipment; many invested their savings in a Freedman's Bank which was established in Beaufort specifically for the accommodation of soldiers and their families; and a few began businesses. In some degree, the horizons of the soldier were broadened by his military travels and by association with officers and comrades of diverse backgrounds. The more ambitious soldiers learned to read and write under the formal instruction of chaplains and the wives of officers. Finally, indoctrination and experience in military administration and martial justice had at least some applicability to civilian life.

Of transcendent importance were those less tangible acquirements—self-respect, leadership, and devotion to freedom and the Union. The very fact that they were fighting for their freedom rather than receiving it as a gift bred a spirit of pride among Negro soldiers. "Anoder ting is," Private Thomas Long said to his comrades in the camp of the First South one evening, "suppose you had kept your freedom without enlisting in dis army; your chillen might have grown up free and been well cultivated so as to be equal to any business, but it would have been always flung in dere faces—'Your fader never fought for he own freedom.' "[63] Moreover, in the First South—and apparently in most Negro regiments—care was taken to foster self–respect among the troops by treating them precisely as white soldiers were treated. Thus, the ex-slave in uniform soon learned to live in a social organization in which he had rights as well as obligations. The effectiveness of the instruction was illustrated by the refusal of large numbers of Negro soldiers to accept any remuneration at all when officials attempted to pay them—noncommissioned officers as well as privates—at the rate of $10.00 a month when white privates received $13.00. Despite the advice of their officers to take the amount offered and to trust the government to make amends later, the soldiers persisted in their refusal. "We'se gib our soggerin' to de Guv'ment, Cunnel," they explained to Higginson, "but we won't 'spise ourselves so much for take de seben dollar."[64] In time the government recognized their claim to equal pay for equal service, but the war was over before full recompense was made.

The Negro military also bred its own class of leaders. Since all the

63. Higginson, *Army Life in a Black Regiment*, p. 183.
64. *Ibid.*, p. 252; Cornish, *The Sable Arm*, pp. 184–95, *passim*. Three of the ten dollars paid to Negro troops were withheld for uniforms so that the actual monthly wage of the soldier was seven dollars, precisely the amount paid Negro laborers by the Quartermaster Department at Hilton Head.

non-commissioned officers in the Colored Troops were by military fiat Negroes, a ready-made opportunity to develop qualities of leadership among the men was provided. In the early days of their service, however, the privates apparently resented the authority seemingly arbitrarily given to some of their number. "I don't want him to play de white man ober me," was often heard in the camp of the First South. Yet, in time, they were taught to "take pride in having good material for non-commissioned officers among themselves, and in obeying them." Soon regimental drills were executed entirely by Negro subordinates.[65] Pre-eminent among the Negro leaders in the First South was Prince Rivers, a man who was later to become a prominent personality in Reconstruction politics in the state. As Higginson saw him during the war, he was an imposing figure, "being six feet high, perfectly proportioned, and of apparently inexhaustible strength and activity." Among the darkest of his race, the colonel thought his features "tolerable regular, and full of command." "He makes Toussaint perfectly intelligible," added the colonel, "and if there should ever be a black monarchy in South Carolina, he will be its king." Higginson's literary lavishness proved to be distressingly extravagant, yet Rivers was indeed possessed of high talents of military leadership. Even before the war, as a coachman in Beaufort, he had been recognized as an influential leader among the Negroes. He was one of the first to join Hunter's regiment and accompanied Hunter on a trip to New York in the spring of 1862, presumably to show the North what a Negro soldier could be. On Broadway, he was attacked by a mob infuriated at the sight of his chevrons, but he held his assailants at bay until the police arrived. Rivers was an active recruiter for the First South, and as its provost sergeant he was remarkably successful in the capture of deserters. Never regarded fondly by the men, he, nevertheless, received "implicit obedience." He could read and write well enough to verbalize his reports and Higginson thought him a better administrator than any of his white officers. Finally, he was devoted to the regiment, bitterly against the "Seceshky," and ardently for the Union. He was nearly the perfect soldier, with all the good and the bad which this meant. Perhaps, he revealed himself most fully when he described his reaction to a march to Beaufort and back to camp early in 1863. "And when dat band wheel in before us, and march on, ——my God!" he exclaimed, "I quit dis world altogeder."[66]

65. Higginson, *Army Life in a Black Regiment*, pp. 260–61.
66. *Ibid.*, pp. 56–57, 59, 62, 261; Pearson, *Letters from Port Royal*, pp. 104, 130–31; Williams, *History of the Negro Troops*, p. 95.

Only eight Negroes served as commissioned officers of the line in South Carolina. All were Northern bred, and none served in the first three Negro regiments raised in the state. Although sergeants in the First South, during the last months of the regiment's existence, performed all the functions of the discharged commissioned officers, Higginson failed (to his subsequent regret) to request commissions for these men, and his successor did so without success.[67] Two of the eight Negro officers, Martin R. Delany and O. S. B. Wall, were nominally assigned to the 104th United States Colored Troops but were actually detailed to special duty with Saxton. Delany, an editor, physician, African explorer, and amateur ethnologist—and withal, it should be said, an egomaniac and insufferable pedant—had a wide reputation as an abolitionist leader among the Negroes of the North and Canada. In February, 1865, he was commissioned a major by Stanton's explicit orders and sent to assist Saxton in the recruitment of Negro troops. In Charleston, during the spring, he was active in securing volunteers for the 103rd, 104th, and 105th United States Colored Troops. In the summer, he was transferred to the Bureau of Refugees, Freedmen, and Abandoned Lands (the Freedmen's Bureau) where he held his rank for three years, serving as the agent on Hilton Head Island.[68] O. S. B. Wall, a successful shoe and boot merchant in Oberlin, Ohio, was commissioned a captain at the express insistence of Stanton early in 1865. Wall, too, was sent to Saxton and passed into the Freedmen's Bureau, serving for some two years as a quartermaster in its Charleston headquarters.[69]

That the two Massachusetts regiments succeeded in supplying six of the eight Negro line officers was to be expected in view of the facts that their ranks mustered the most aggressive element in the Northern Negro population and that their bid for officer rank was pressed by John A. Andrew, the very able and energetic war governor of Massachusetts. In March, 1864, Andrew commissioned as a second lieutenant Stephen Atkins Swails, the first sergeant of Company F of the Fifty-fourth. Swails, born in Columbia, Pennsylvania, and at the time of his enlistment in April, 1863, a boatman living in Elmira, New York, had proved himself an aggressive front-line soldier. He had been cited for his part in the

67. Higginson, *Army Life in a Black Regiment*, p. 261.
68. Cornish, *The Sable Arm*, pp. 216–17; Williams, *History of the Negro Troops*, p. 142; Rollin, *Life and Public Services of Martin R. Delany*, pp. 176–80, *et seq.* Rollin's biography delineates the Delany character with unwitting fulsomeness.
69. Williams, *History of the Negro Troops*, pp. 142–43.

assault on Fort Wagner and was wounded during the charge of the 54th against Honey Hill in November, 1864. (He was to be again wounded during Potter's raid when he dashed across a railroad bridge and, with the assistance of some of his men, captured a Confederate locomotive.) Nevertheless, the War Department refused to verify his commission until January, 1865, when its attitude toward accepting Negro officers was suddenly reversed. Thereafter, Andrew moved quickly to commission ten other sergeants in the Fifty-fourth and Fifty-fifth. During the spring and summer, five of these were accepted by the Department.[70] Each of these six Negro officers served in the occupation forces and, at least one, Swails, remained to become a Bureau agent.[71]

The native Negro population was obviously proud of the capacity for military leadership displayed by soldiers drawn from their midst. Their response to the presence of Major Delany suggests that they were also pleased with the recognition that the commissioning of Negro officers implied.[72] There were more practical benefits, however. Those who had learned to lead in the army did not shed this ability with their uniforms. In politics, particularly, the transfer was evident. Three Negroes who had been sergeants in the First South sat in the Constitutional Convention of 1868.[73] One of these, Prince Rivers, served three terms in the state's house of representatives from Edgefield and Aiken counties. In the legislature, he commanded a following of some dozen other Negro legislators. After retiring from his seat in the house, Rivers became a trial justice residing in the village of Hamburg in Aiken County. Simultaneously, he was an important Republican leader in the counties in the vicinity of his home and also a captain and ultimately a major general of militia (hardly a ridiculous rank in view of his military experience and Higginson's estimate of his martial abilities). Another former sergeant of the First South who sat in the Constitutional Convention was Henry E. Hayne. Hayne settled in Marion County after the war and represented that district in the lower house of the legislature until his election to the office of secretary of state in 1872. Robert Smalls, who served throughout the war as the noncommissioned captain of the *Planter,* represented Beaufort in the

70. Emilio, *History of the Fifty-Fourth Regiment,* pp. 268, 296, 336; Cornish, *The Sable Arm,* p. 215.

71. Martha Schofield MS Diary, entry for January 3, 1866.

72. Rollin, *Life and Public Services of Martin R. Delany,* pp. 189, 223, 280.

73. Higginson, *Army Life in a Black Regiment,* p. 265.

Convention and later became a state senator, a representative in Congress, and a perpetually prominent figure in the politics of the state. W. J. Whipper, L. S. Langley, S. A. Swails, and M. R. Delany, and a number of other Northern Negroes came to the state as soldiers and stayed to do service in the Freedmen's Bureau and to take leading roles in Reconstruction politics. Swails became a representative, and later the senator, from Williamsburg County and the dominant Republican leader in that area. These were only the most successful political leaders arising from military origins; there were many more on the local level whose names were not so widely known.

South Carolina Negroes who fought in the army also learned to value their liberty and the Union. In the infancy of the First South, recruits tended to focus their loyalties upon individuals, particularly upon Saxton and Higginson, "de General" and "de Cunnel," as they called them. Within weeks, however, their allegiances shifted to rest upon ideals rather than men. One evening in December, 1862, Higginson overheard an informal speech by Corporal Prince Lambkin. The corporal began by reminding his audience of how, as slaves, they had longed for freedom, and he had predicted its coming. "Our mas'rs," he continued, "dey hab lib under the flag, dey got dere wealth under it, and ebryting beautiful for dere chilen. Under it dey hab grind us up, and put us in dere pocket for money. But de fus' minute dey tink dat old flag mean freedom for we colored people, dey pull it right down, and run up de rag ob dere own [loud applause]. But we'll neber desert de old flag, boys, neber; we hab lib under it for eighteen hundred sixty-two years, and we'll die for it now."[74] Corporal Lambkin's chronology was imperfect, but his message was clear: freedom and Union were inseparably bound, and these were the ideals—symbolized by the flag—for which they would fight to the death. At an emancipation celebration several days later the regiment endorsed this creed by singing "My Country 'Tis of Thee" with apparent spontaneity and obvious understanding and by enthusiastically receiving a stand of colors.[75] It was uniquely fitting, in South Carolina at least, that the Negro regiments ceased to be designated by the state of their origin and were called instead United States troops, for the title did indeed describe them well.

Loyalties generated among the troops spread through the Negro

74. *Ibid.*, p. 23.
75. *Free South* (Beaufort), January 10, 1863; Pearson, *Letters from Port Royal*, pp. 128–34.

population within the Union lines. Hardly a family failed to send a soldier to the army and all thought possessively of the Negro regiments. "Dey fought and fought and shot down de 'Secesh,'" exclaimed a delighted old Negro woman after one of the early engagements of the First South, "and ne'er a white man among 'em but two captains."[76] Pride turned to pain in the summer of 1863 as the Negro wounded poured down from the Charleston front. Many Negro civilians volunteered to serve in the hospitals, and cartloads of fruits and vegetables were sent unsolicited from the plantations to the hospitals.[77] Yet, the painful absence of fathers, brothers, and sons, the interminable lists of casualties which appeared week after week in the island press—"George E. Washington, dead of wounds; Abram Smith, wounded in the groin; Charles Polite, missing,"—seemed only to fix their loyalties more firmly.[78] The Emancipation Day celebration of 1863 had been organized and led by whites; those of the following years were organized exclusively by and largely patronized by Negroes. On January 1, 1864, more than four thousand Negroes paraded through Beaufort to a meeting ground where a dais had been raised bearing the names "Washington, Lincoln, Toussaint l'Ouverture." The Proclamation was read by the Reverend James Lynch, a Negro African Methodist missionary from Baltimore, and swords were presented to Saxton and Higginson by the Negro community. The ceremonies were followed by singing, a barbecue, and parading, a scene often to be repeated in South Carolina.[79]

In time, the love of freedom and devotion to the Union which marked the refugees of the war period evolved into a persistent, stubborn Republicanism that died only with him who had "fought for he own freedom."

76. Holland, *Letters and Diary of Laura M. Towne,* p. 94.
77. Pearson, *Letters from Port Royal,* p. 198.
78. *Free South* (Beaufort), July 25, 1863.
79. *Ibid.,* December 5, 12, 1863; January 9, 1864.

II...THE MEANING
OF FREEDOM

Freedom was a nominal legacy of the war, yet telling the slave that he was free did not make him so. Ultimately, the Negro had to establish his freedom by some deliberate, conscious act entirely his own, or he would remain a slave in fact, if not in name. Emancipation simply gave him that choice. With near unanimity, Negroes in South Carolina chose liberty.

In the spring of 1865, the news of emancipation and the close of the war filtered slowly into the hinterland of South Carolina. In mid-May, the commanding general of the Department of the South, Q. A. Gillmore, issued a proclamation declaring that governmental policy would soon be made known. "It is deemed sufficient, meanwhile," he said, "to announce that the people of the black race are free citizens of the United States, that it is the fixed intention of a wise and beneficent government to protect them in the enjoyment of their freedom and the fruits of their industry. . . ."[1] Upon hearing of the order, a few masters formally released their slaves. Francis W. Pickens, for instance, the secession governor of the state and an extensive planter on the Savannah River in Edgefield District, heard of the order on May 23, and on the same day he called his slaves together, acknowledged their emancipation, and con-

1. General Orders No. 63, Department of the South, reprinted in the *New York Times*, May 23, 1865, p. 1.

tracted to pay them for their labor during the remainder of the year.[2] Most slaveholders were not so forehanded, releasing their slaves only after occupation forces arrived from the coastal area late in May and subsequently. Even after the occupation was completed, a few masters, particularly among those living in the uplands in the extreme western portion of the state, stubbornly refused to recognize the new status of their Negro laborers. Under these circumstances, many Negroes became certain of their emancipation only by traveling to the lower districts with the men who still acted as their masters. A resident of Pendleton, visiting Columbia late in June with a neighbor and the neighbor's slave, noted with alarm that Toney, the slave, had "shown symptoms of demoralization since his arrival here." Apparently observing the presence of Union troops in the city and the formal recognition of emancipation generally accorded to the Negroes there, Toney "got somewhat excited and talked of making a 'bargin' when he returned to Pendleton." "No Negro is improved by a visit to Columbia," the Carolinian concluded, "& a visit to Charleston is his certain destruction."[3]

By whatever means the Negro learned of emancipation, the most obvious method of affirming his freedom was simply to desert the site of his slavery and the presence of his master. Patience Johnson, an ex-slave on a Laurens District plantation, must have expressed the sentiment of many freedmen when she answered a request by her mistress that she remain in her usual place and work for wages. "No, Miss," she declined, "I must go, if I stay here I'll never know I am free."[4]

Contrary to tradition, however, the typical slave upon hearing of emancipation did not shout with delight, throw his hat into the air, gather the few possessions he claimed, and run pellmell for Charleston. The great majority received the news quietly and began to make deliberate preparations to terminate their slavery definitely by some overt act. Representative of the reaction of the freedmen in the lower and middle districts was that of the Negroes on the Elmore plantation near Columbia. On May 24, as the secret channels of slave communication crackled with rumors of emancipation, an impatient field hand named Caleb ran away. On May 27, Union forces occupied Columbia. "We told the negroes they were free on the 30th"; noted young Grace Elmore, "they waited patiently and respectably." Nevertheless, the

2. MS Contract, May 23, 1865, Francis W. Pickens Papers.
3. J. K. Robinson to "Mrs. Smythe," June 28, 1865, A. T. Smythe Letters.
4. William Watts Ball, *The State That Forgot: South Carolina's Surrender to Democracy* (Indianapolis, 1932), p. 128.

freedmen initiated arrangements for separation. "Philis, Jane and Nelly volunteered to finish Albert's shirts before they left and to give good warning before they left," Grace reported, while Jack, the driver, "will stay till the crops are done." Not all of the freedmen were as explicit in stating their plans. "Old Mary, the nurse, took the news quietly on Sat evening; said that none could be happy without prayer, and Monday by day light she took herself off, leaving the poor baby without a nurse."[5]

In the upcountry, the same pattern prevailed. In Spartanburg District, David Golightly Harris first heard of Gillmore's emancipation order on June 5, but made no mention of the news to his slaves. On the same day, however, and apparently before Harris himself had heard of the order, York, one of his field hands, "disappeared." The remainder said "nothing on the subject" and continued to "work as usual." Desertion on neighboring plantations became increasingly frequent, and, in early July, another of Harris' slaves, Old Will, disappeared, "to try to enjoy the freedom the Yankey's have promised the negroes." By late July, it was rumored that some masters in the neighborhood were recognizing formally the freedom of their laborers. Finally, in mid-August, occupation forces stationed in Spartanburg ordered masters to explicitly inform the Negroes of their freedom. On August 15, most did so. When Harris made the announcement to his slaves, only one, Ann, left immediately, while "the others wisely concluded they would remain until New Years day."[6]

Desertion was a common means by which the ex-slave asserted his freedom; yet variations in the time and spirit of the desertion yield interesting insights into the Negro's attitudes toward his new status. Generally, freedmen who as slaves had labored as domestics, mechanics, and in the extractive industries departed at the first reasonably convenient opportunity. In doing so, they typically exhibited some degree of malice toward their recent owners. On the other hand, those who had labored in the fields generally finished the year in their accustomed places, and when they left seldom departed with expressions of ill will toward their late masters.

It is astonishing that among the servant or domestic class (where slave labor was reputedly least arduous and relations with the master most intimate and satisfactory), defection was almost complete. Corre-

5. Grace B. Elmore MS Diary, entries for May 24, 30, 1865.
6. David Golightly Harris MS Farm Journal, entries for June 5, 6, 14, July 6, 24, 25, August 14, 15, 16, 1865.

spondence and diaries of the period are replete with instances in which the master or mistress declared "all of our servants have departed."[7] The disintegration of the household staff of the Holmes residence in Camden was typical of the process in the larger houses. None of the dozen adult slaves on the staff departed with General Sherman, but two were lost to Potter's raiders in April. Early in May, two maids were discharged for insubordination, even though the mistress of the household persisted in her refusal to recognize the freedom of those who remained. Later in the same month, an occupation force arrived in the village, and the mistress told the servants of the emancipation order but refused to release them "because it was not at all certain that they would be freed." By mid-June, Isaac, Marcus, Mary (with her two children), and Catherine had, nevertheless, deserted the household without warning. The mistress became fearful that Chloe, eminently necessary to the house as cook and queen-pin of the serving staff, might go the same way. After a conversation in which the mistress presumed to explain President Johnson's position as implying that the slaves were not really free, she implored the cook "not to sneak away at night as the others had done, disgracing themselves by running away, as she had never done." Chloe agreed to stay, "but if she could she would like to go to Charleston in the autumn when the railroad was finished." Having won one battle, however, another was immediately lost. On the same day, Ann, the laundress, "poor deluded fool, informed mother she could not wash any longer, nor would she remain to finish the ironing . . . and off she went." By late August, even the "faithful" Chloe had left "after two days notice," and without waiting for the repair of the railroad. Thereafter, hired servants came and went at a rapid rate, and when they departed they usually did so in a cloud of irritation. "We have had a constant ebb and flow of servants," wrote Emma Holmes on October 1, "some staying only a few days, others a few hours, some thoroughly incompetent, others though satisfactory to us preferring plantation life." What was true in the Holmes household was true of their neighbors. "In every direction we hear of families being left without a single servant, or, those who stay doing almost nothing," reported Emma. "All have turned fool together."[8]

7. For instances, see: G. E. Manigault to his cousin, May 22, 1865, Heyward–Ferguson Papers; "R. R. E." (probably Ralph Elliott) to a friend, July 11, 1865, Habersham Elliott Papers; Meta Grimball MS Diary, entry for "February," 1865; Grace B. Elmore MS Diary, *passim*.

8. Emma E. Holmes MS Diary, entries for "End of May," July 15, 26, August 22, 25, October 1, 1865.

In the face of wholesale desertions the more pretentious white families were forced to resort to extremes. Many came to rely entirely upon the service of Negro children. "Our servants here behaved very badly & have all left us, with little exception," quipped one Camden resident in August. "Two of Patty's children are now waiting upon us, little William & Veny."[9] The vacuum in domestic labor, however, was most generally filled by the white ladies of the household. A gentleman refugee in the upcountry, noting the widespread desertion by domestics, was "struck by the cheerful & smiling manner" in which the ladies assured him that "It's a great relief to get rid of the horrid negroes."[10] In May, Emma Holmes had expressed the same spirit of independence. ". . . the servants find we are by no means entirely dependent on them," she wrote with a literary toss of her head. Yet, by mid-August, cheerful independence had soured into galling resentment. After a long day of arduous household labor, Emma complained, "but I dont like cooking or washing, even the doing up of muslins is great annoyance to me and I do miss the having all ready prepared to my hand." In late August, there was only fatigue. "I am very weary," she confessed, "standing up washing all the breakfast and dinner china, bowls, kettles, pans, silver, etc.—a most miscellaneous list of duties, leaving no time for reading or exercise."[11]

The frequency with which domestics deserted their masters discredits the myth of the "faithful old family servant" (the ex-slave) loyally cleaving to his master through the pinching years of Reconstruction. Most of the "faithful few" were literally old, or else very young, or infirm, or encumbered by family arrangements which made desertion impossible. James Hemphill, a wealthy lawyer and politician residing in Chester, indicated that faithfulness among this class of freedmen could be something less than a blessing—a feeling many of his contemporaries shared. "My crowd of darkies is rapidly decreasing," he reported to his brother in September, 1865. "Almost two weeks ago, my cook departed with her child. Last week, our house girl left, and this morning, another girl, lately employed in the culinary department, vacated. We still have six big and little—one old, three children, one man sick, so that you may perceive there are mouths and backs enough,

9. Martin S. Wilkins to J. Berkeley Grimball, August 5, 1865, J. B. Grimball Papers.

10. "R. R. E." (probably Ralph Elliott) to a friend, July 11, 1865, Habersham Elliott Papers.

11. Holmes Diary, entries for "End of May," August 14, 25, 1865.

but the labor is very deficient."[12] Three days previously, a former slave-holder in Abbeville District verbalized the same complaint. Of his fifteen slaves, only three remained, "one woman and her two children," who, he lamented, were "in place of a benefit . . . a heavy expense to me for their bread and clothing."[13]

Doubtless, some servants did remain with their late masters from motives of genuine loyalty and contentment. A Charlestonian wrote in September, 1866, that his "old" coachman and the coachman's wife held steadfast in their devotion to him all during the war and afterward.[14] Such instances were rare, however, and became increasingly so as Reconstruction progressed. An instance of real, but not unlimited, faithful-ness was provided by Patty, a Negro woman who had served the John Berkeley Grimball family for thirty-six years before emancipation, fleeing with them during the war from the coast to Greenville and remaining with them after emancipation. In the first disordered months of peace, she had taken out articles to sell and brought back food for the family, stubbornly refusing to take anything for herself. In January, 1866, when finally she did leave to join her son and husband in the lowcountry, she washed all the clothes, gave the young ladies of the house presents, and left two of her younger children to wait on the family.[15]

In spite of obvious and often painful realities, the myth of the "faith-ful old family servant" persisted both North and South and even grew in the years following Reconstruction. In 1881, John W. De Forest, a Connecticut Yankee who had been a Freedmen's Bureau officer in South Carolina and who certainly knew better, published a remarkably suc-cessful novel set in postwar Charleston. Among the host of noble stereotypes who crowded its pages were the "high bred," proud, but impoverished young "Miss Virginia Beaufort" of the Carolina aris-tocracy and her old crone of a servant, Maume Chloe, "the last faithful remnant of the feminine property of the Beauforts," who, of course, played her role to perfection and lived happily ever after.[16] Most Northerners were probably relieved to find that they had left their erstwhile charges in such good hands; but in the South the myth had a rather more tragic aspect. Living in a world they never made, life for

12. James Hemphill to W. R. Hemphill, September 11, 1865, Hemphill Papers.
13. William Hill to his brother, September 8, 1865, William Hill Papers.
14. Anonymous letter, September 2, 1866, Wilmot S. Holmes Collection.
15. Meta Grimball MS Diary, entry for February 20, 1866.
16. John W. De Forest, *The Bloody Chasm* (New York, 1881), p. 29, *et seq.*

Southerners was somehow eased by this small fiction which evoked a pleasurable image of the better world they had aspired to build. This was possibly what a lady of Charleston was saying in 1873 when she wrote to a friend upon the death of an elderly woman servant who had been her slave. "I feel a link has been broken, an occasion lamented," she sadly declared, "a really burial of what can never take place again."[17] And it could not, if, indeed, it ever had.

Mechanics and laborers outside of agriculture (in lumbering, mining, turpentine, and other industries) were as quick as domestics to leave their masters. Even where they did not desert their late owners, there was often a disposition to do so. In July, 1865, E. J. Parker, engaged in the turpentine business in the deep piney woods of Williamsburg District, despaired of inducing his former slaves to continue laboring for him even for wages. "I do not believe we shall hire our own negroes to work," he wrote to his partner; "it would be much better if we could hire other negroes. They would work much better." By late September, he had persuaded most of his late bondsmen to contract; but the conflict in their minds between economic necessity and their desire to be free of their recent master was evident. "They signed it with grate reluctance," Parker reported. "And Isaac Reid would not do it and had to take him to Kingstree. He cut up all sorts of Shines. Said he would suffer to be Shot down before he would sign it. That he did not intend to do anything for any man he had been under all his life."[18]

The liberty of freedmen engaged in agriculture to leave their former masters was restricted by the insistence of the occupation forces and the Freedmen's Bureau that plantation owners and laborers contract to harvest and divide the 1865 crop before parting. Many who did not contract found it convenient, nevertheless, to complete the agricultural season. But even as they worked they eagerly anticipated the New Year and the Christmas holidays that preceded it as a kind of second emancipation. Augustine Smythe, managing his mother-in-law's plantation, Lang Syne, near Fort Motte in Orangeburg District, described the expectancy among his laborers early in December. "The poor negro," he wrote to his mother, "besotted with ignorance, & so full of freedom, looking forward to January as to some day of Jubilee approaching, with all the difficulties & dangers of a free man's life to encounter, & none of

17. Eliza T. Holmes to Mary B. Chesnut, April 8, 1873, Williams–Chesnut–Manning Papers.
18. E. J. Parker to D. W. Jordan, July 24, September 29, 1865, D. W. Jordan Papers.

the experience or sense necessary to enable him successfully to battle with them, thinking only that freedom confers the privilege of going where & doing as they please, work when they wish, or stop if they feel disposed, & yet be fed, supported & cared for by his Master, lazy, trifling, impertinent! Mother, they are awful!"[19]

Christmas Day, 1865, saw many South Carolina plantations entirely deserted by their Negro populations. Smythe's plantation was thus abandoned, and, in Spartanburg District, David Golightly Harris recorded in his journal that all of his "negroes leave to day, to hunt themselves a new home, while we will be left to wait upon ourselves."[20] After visiting the plantation of a relative on February 9, 1866, the Reverend John Hamilton Cornish reported that, "Not one of their Negroes is with them, all have left."[21] Like many domestics, most of those field hands who remained on the plantations were very old, very young, ill, or encumbered. The mistress of the Ball plantation in Laurens District recalled at the turn of the century that at the end of 1865 "many of the negroes sought employment on other places, but the least desirable stayed with us, for they could not easily find new homes and we could not deny them shelter."[22]

This pattern was broken only on the very large plantations. Here, apparently, many freedmen deliberately chose to remain on the "home place."[23]

The inclination of domestics, mechanics, and laborers in the extractive industries and on relatively small plantations to leave their masters at the first reasonable opportunity while agriculturalists on the larger plantations remained suggests that desertion correlated very closely with the degree of proximity that had existed between the slave and his owner and, further, that the freedman was much more interested in leaving behind the personal remainders of slavery than he was the physical.

In South Carolina, the mass movement among the Negro population was not the "aimless," endless, far-flung wandering so often described.

19. To his mother, December 12, 1865, A. T. Smythe Letters.
20. Louisa Smythe to her aunt, December 21, 1865; A. T. Smythe to his mother, January 13, 1865; A. T. Smythe Letters; Harris Farm Journal, entry for December 25, 1865.
21. Cornish, Diary, entry for February 9, 1866.
22. Ball, *The State That Forgot*, p. 128.
23. Contracts for 1865 and 1866 on the Robert N. Hemphill plantation in Chester District, the MacFarland plantations in Kershaw, the H. L. Pinckney plantation in Sumter, and Mulberry on the lower Cooper River indicate that a high proportion of former slaves remained in their places.

Freedmen most often left their homes to separate themselves distinctly from slavery, but their destination was nearly always fixed by economic design or necessity. Most migrants resettled themselves within a matter of days or weeks and within a few miles of the place which, as slaves, they had called home. "In almost every yard," wrote Emma Holmes in June, 1865, "servants are leaving but going to wait on other people for food merely, sometimes with the promise of clothing."[24] Many former domestics went into the fields to labor, and, conversely, a few agricultural laborers entered household service. For instance, in February, 1866, the Grimballs hired Josey, one of their ex-field hands, and Amy, his wife, and their daughter, Delia, to replace the "faithful" Patty.[25] Also, Northerners on the Sea Islands, during and after the war, frequently drew their servants from among the plantation hands.

Large numbers of agricultural laborers left their native plantations during the Christmas season to camp in a neighboring village while they searched for an employer. Employment, however, was not always easily found. David Golightly Harris, visiting Spartanburg on New Year's Day, 1866, "saw many negroes *enjoying* their *freedom* by walking about the streets & looking much out of sorts. . . . Ask who you may 'What are you going to do,' & their universal answer is 'I dont know.' "[26] Augustine Smythe found much the same conditions prevailing in the vicinity of Fort Motte in Orangeburg District. "There is considerable trouble & moving among the negroes," he reported. "They are just like a swarm of bees all buzzing about & not knowing where to settle."[27]

Having proved their freedom by leaving their former masters, many Negroes, apparently, were soon willing to return to them. By late September, two out of the three servants who had deserted James Hemphill's Chester household had returned; and Cuffee, a domestic in the residence of John Richardson Cheves (a son of Langdon Cheves) in Abbeville, returned to his usual labors in October, 1865, after having savored both freedom and hunger downriver in Savannah.[28] A large number of agricultural laborers also returned to their native plantations after a short stay abroad. In mid-January, the wife of the manager of Lang Syne in Orangeburg District jested that "fifteen turkeys 'nebber come home,'" indirectly indicating that more than half

24. Diary, entry for June 15, 1865.
25. Meta Grimball MS Diary entry for February 20, 1866.
26. Farm Journal, entry for January 1, 1866.
27. To his mother, January 13, 1865, A. T. Smythe Letters.
28. James Hemphill to W. R. Hemphill, September 26, 1865, Hemphill Papers; Rebecca Cheves to J. R. Cheves, October 24, 1865, R. S. Cheves Papers.

of the laboring force had again settled in their places on the home plantation. Frequently, agricultural laborers returned to remain against the wishes of the owners. The manager of Lang Syne reported that one Negro woman had returned and asked to be hired. He refused but she declined to leave and secreted herself in one of the outbuildings. Several days later, she appealed over the manager's head to the owner of the plantation to order her acceptance and was again refused. Finally, the manager "walked her off," but later suspected that she was still hiding in one of the Negro houses.[29] A small planter in Union District cried out in anguish early in 1866 when some of his late slaves, being discharged, returned against his wishes and persisted in going into the fields and laboring alongside those he had agreed to employ.[30]

Apparently, many freedmen were driven to return to their old places by economic necessity. Isabella A. Soustan, a Negro woman who had somehow found freedom in a place called Liberty, North Carolina, in July, 1865, expressed her thoughts on the dilemma that many ex-slaves faced in their first year of emancipation. "I have the honor to appeal to you one more for assistance, Master," she petitioned her recent owner. "I am cramped hear nearly to death and no one ceares for me heare, and I want you if you pleas Sir, to send for me." Some few freedmen were willing to exchange liberty for security. "I don care if I am free," concluded Isabella, "I had rather live with you, I was as free while with you as I wanted to be."[31] Yet, even those who did return soon found that freedom bore no necessary relationship to geography.

While migrants were motivated by combinations of many desires, much of their behavior is explained by their love of the homeplace— the "old range" as they themselves rather warmly termed it. White contemporaries, perhaps obsessed with the idea that theirs was a white man's land, never fully appreciated the fact that Negroes, too, were strongly devoted to the soil upon which they had been born and labored. "The aged freedwomen, and many also of the aged freedmen," reported a Bureau officer, "had the bump of locality like old cats." Similarly, a local official of the state, frustrated in his attempts to resettle Negroes on public lands in Georgetown County, found this sentiment a serious deterrent. "Local attachment, you know, has always been a ruling

29. Louisa Smythe to her mother-in-law, January 15, 1866; A. T. Smythe to his brother, December 5, 1865, A. T. Smythe Papers.

30. Robert N. Gage to his sister, January 31, 1868, James M. Gage Papers.

31. To her late master (probably George C. Taylor), July 10, 1865, George Coffin Taylor Collection.

passion with the agricultural classes of our people," he explained to his superior.[32] Thus, ironically, the Negro frequently moved to get away from his late master, but he almost always moved to settle in the very locale where he had served in bondage.

The desire to return to the "old range" was particularly evident in the coastal areas in the year following the war. On the one hand, very nearly all the Negroes who had fled to the islands during the conflict returned to the mainland within the first two or three years of peace.[33] On the other hand, thousands of Negroes who had been taken inland by their masters during the war returned to the coast. In the months following emancipation, the stream of coastward migration was continuous, but as the upland farming season closed in October and November, 1865, the flow swelled into a flood. By December, it was estimated that Negroes were passing through Columbia at the rate of a thousand a month.[34] In January, the migration reached its crest and declined to a trickle by late February when the new planting season was underway.[35] Doubtless, it was the return of these freedmen to their coastal haunts that led Northern observers, virtually all of whom felt compelled to make the pilgrimage from Charleston to Columbia to see the ruins, to exaggerate the volume of Negro movement throughout the state and to conclude that the migrants were bound for Charleston simply because there "freedom was free-er." Later writers accepted and perpetuated these erroneous impressions.

Many of the coastward migrants moved with assurance of employment upon arriving at their destinations.[36] Many also returned without such guarantees, but with the aid of the Bureau and promises that work could be found in their native communities. Whatever their prospects, the road of the migrant freedman was never easy, and the obstacles they overcame to return home suggest the great strength of the

32. James H. Croushore and David Morris Potter (eds.), *John William De Forest, A Union Officer in the Reconstruction* (New Haven, 1948), p. 36; *Reports and Resolutions of the General Assembly of the State of South Carolina* (1871–1872), p. 369. Cited hereinafter as *Reports and Resolutions*.

33. For one example, the return of the freedmen to John Berkeley Grimball's Grove plantation, *see* John Berkeley Grimball MS Diary, entry for March 9, 1866, *et seq.*

34. *The Nation*, I, No. 26 (December 28, 1865), 813.

35. Croushore and Potter, *A Union Officer*, p. 36, fn.

36. *The Nation*, I, No. 26 (December 28, 1865), 812. Specific arrangements of this nature are also mentioned in F. H. Spawn to T. R. S. Elliott, December 12, 1865, T. R. S. Elliott Papers; John Colcock to James Gregorie, Gregorie–Elliott Papers; *The Nation*, II, No. 27 (January 4, 1866), 14.

pull of place upon them. From deep in the interior, many of them trudged along the ribbons of mud called roads to the fire-gutted city of Columbia. Riding with the driver in the "boot" of a westbound stagecoach one clear, cold December morning in 1865, one Northern traveler counted within a distance of eight miles thirty-nine Negroes walking toward Columbia. All were underclothed, miserable, and tired in appearance, carrying their possessions in bundles on their backs. One middle-aged Negro woman, he noted, was carrying a bundle on her head and a baby on her back. At the same time she was leading a little girl by the hand, while a small boy followed behind. As they passed, the driver shouted down to her, "Goin' down to Columby after you 'free, be ye? Well, go on."[37] From Columbia, they plodded some 100 miles along the line of the railroad to Charleston. There, while await-ing transportation to the homeplace by Bureau steamer, they took refuge in the deserted houses of their masters or in the burned-out buildings of the lower district.[38] In January, 1866, a Northern corre-spondent saw fifteen hundred of them camped on the waterfront, wretched and pitiable, some living in the open coal sheds along the wharves. As he walked among them, they cooked and ate their break-fasts around smoky fires, amidst "tubs, pails, pots and kettles, sacks, beds, barrels tied up in blankets, boxes, baskets, [and] bundles," while "hens were scratching, pigs squealing, cocks crowing, and starved puppies whining." An old woman belonging to a group bound for Colleton District catalogued their miseries. "De jew and de air hackles we more'n anyting," she declared. "De rain beats on we, and de sun shines we out. My chil'n so hungry dey can't hole up. De Guv'ment, he han't gib we nottin'. Said dey would put we on Board Saturday. Some libs and some dies. If dey libs dey libs, and if dey dies dey dies."[39] After such Odysseys, one can readily believe those early returnees who told a northern teacher on Edisto Island in June, 1865, that they were "glad to get back to their old homes."[40]

Some freedmen, cut loose from their moorings by war and emanci-pation, continued to drift wherever the winds and currents of chance

37. *Ibid.*
38. Martin S. Wilkins to J. B. Grimball, August 5, 1865, John Berkeley Grim-ball Papers; John Berkeley Grimball MS Diary, various entries, 1865 and 1866.
39. J[ohn] T[ownsend] Trowbridge, *The South, a tour of its Battle Fields and Ruined Cities, a journey through the desolated States, and talks with the people, etc.* (Hartford, 1866), pp. 537–38.
40. Mary Ames, *From a New England Woman's Diary in Dixie in 1865* (Spring-field, 1906), p. 63.

carried them; yet, by the spring of 1866, the great mass of Negroes in South Carolina had come again to settle upon the "old range."

In the first weeks of emancipation, many (perhaps most) freedmen interpreted their liberty as a temporary release from labor. "Already in the neighborhood they have refused to work & c," wrote Augustine Smythe in June, 1865, speaking of the vicinity of Fort Motte. The difficulty, he thought, lay in the presence of Northerners in the state. "Here we are having Yankee, Yankee, Yankee, White Yankee and nigger Yankee, till we are more disgusted with them than ever."[41] Early in July, an elderly planter living near Walterboro noted the prevalence of much the same sentiment. ". . . negroes generally very idle," he observed, "wandering about the country enjoying their freedom, tho to my mind wonderfully civil, under the circumstances."[42]

Yet, the mass of Negroes did not equate freedom with permanent idleness. In fact, they wanted to work, but only for themselves and at their own discretion. Almost universally, they showed an aversion to cultivating the great staple—cotton, and a willingness to grow food crops sufficient for themselves and their families. In March, 1865, for instance, the mistress of a Christ Church plantation, along with one of her neighbors, gave her slaves freedom to work or not as they pleased. "In every place they have gone to work planting for themselves on their usual places," she reported, meaning that the Negroes were cultivating the garden plots allowed them as slaves.[43] The average freedman expected to work for his own subsistence, but he wanted to choose the time and place of that labor. Late in May, 1865, Grace B. Elmore, living in her mother's house near Columbia, interviewed Philis, her maid, on the subject. Asked if she liked the idea of freedom, Philis answered "yes, tho she had always been treated with perfect kindness and could complain of nothing in her lot, but she had heard a woman who had bought her freedom from kind indulgent owners, say it was a very sweet thing to be able to do as she chose, to sit and do nothing, to work

41. To his aunts, June 11, 1865, A. T. Smythe Letters.

42. John W. Rutledge to Benjamin F. Perry, July 9, 1865, B. F. Perry Papers. As one might expect, the close of the agricultural season at the end of the year brought another period of general idleness. A Charlestonian wrote to his daughter early in January, 1866, that "in the plantations in general they refuse to work and some are insolent and obstinate . . ." N. R. Middleton to his daughter, January 10, 1866, N. R. Middleton Papers.

43. "Mother" to her son (probably Wilmot G. De Saussure), March 31, 1865, H. W. and W. G. De Saussure Papers.

if she desired, or to go out as she liked and ask nobody's permission, and that was just her feeling." Even so, Grace was assured, "Philis says she expects to work."[44]

When arrangements were satisfactory, the great mass of Negroes exhibited an eagerness to labor. Indeed, enforced idleness made the Negro agrarian uneasy. "We wants to git away to work on our own hook," explained a migrant waiting on a Charleston wharf for a steamer to return him to his home plantation. "It's not a good time at all here. We does nothing but suffer from smoke and ketch cold. We want to begin de planting business."[45] By the early spring of 1866, most Negro farmers had done precisely that.

Apparently, Negroes labored less arduously in freedom than they had in slavery. To many whites, the slowdown seemed a stoppage. During the hot, dry summer of 1865, when the woods were in danger of bursting into flames, a planter near Grahamville complained to the Bureau officer that "my negroes in the fairest weather refuse to go out to work at all, to save my place from danger of fire." A flagrant show of ingratitude, he thought, "as this was their old home, to which they said they were anxious to move, it seems now to avoid work altogether." However, he admitted, "they did do some work."[46] Similarly, the lessee of a lowcountry tract declared in early August that his plantation was "litterly taurn up" since "under the present labour system but little is done & what is done is badly done, it being impossible to get work done as it aught to be."[47] Planters above the fall line were also distressed. In Chester, James Hemphill lamented in September, "there is a general indisposition to labor, both among whites and blacks, and nothing is more needed than steady hard labor at present";[48] and an Abbeville resident declared, "the negro is so indolent and lazy that he is incapable of any exertion to better his circumstances."[49] A freedman's version was expressed on August 13, 1865, at Lewisfield, a small station on the North Eastern Railroad some forty miles from Charleston. There a Negro "asked the Yankee officer if they would be expected to do

44. Diary, entry for May 24, 1865.

45. Trowbridge, *The South,* p. 537.

46. Anonymous to B. F. Perry, n.d. (probably July, 1865), B. F. Perry Papers, quoting the author's letter to the local Bureau agent.

47. W. W. Bateman to J. L. Manning, August 2, 1865, Williams–Chesnut–Manning Papers.

48. To W. R. Hemphill, September 11, 1865, Hemphill Papers.

49. William Hill to his brother, September 8, 1865, William Hill Papers.

as *much* work as formerly. He replied certainly. Upon which the freedman said they did not intend to do any such thing."[50]

Of course, there were freedmen who lost the habit of labor during the transition from slavery to freedom. These tended to collect in the larger cities, on abandoned plantations, and, occasionally, on the farm of some larcenous poor white. Finding his former slaves encamped in his Charleston house late in the summer of 1865, one island planter "made arrangements to take his people back to Hilton Head and provision them, but only Anthony would then agree to go."[51] In time, however, the military and the Bureau were successful in clearing idlers from the population centers. More frightening to the whites than urban idlers were those in the country. Early in September, 1865, a planter near Georgetown complained to the absentee owner of a neighboring plantation that it was "being rapidly filled up by vagabond negroes from all parts of the country who go there when they please and are fast destroying what you left of a settlement. They are thus become a perfect nuisance to the neighbourhood and harbor for all the thieves and scamps who wont work."[52]

Idleness of this hardened sort soon dwindled to negligible proportions. Much of the continued malingering was apparently a manifestation of the Negro's dissatisfaction with his rewards under the new system, a sort of unorganized slowdown by which he fought his employer or prospective employer. Idleness, of course, had been a normal part of slavery, and it was no less evident among the whites than negroes. Sundays, Christmas, and New Year's Day were customarily holidays from labor for both races and remained so. Further, agrarian communities normally recognized the laying-by season in the early summer and the end of the harvest season in the fall and winter as periods of reduced labor, celebrations, and idleness. It is not surprising that the Negro in freedom continued to recognize them as such, and to relish them all the more.

Desertion, migration, and idleness were temporary as mass phenomena among the Negro population in postwar South Carolina. Much more lasting was the universal tendency among freedmen to identify their freedom with liberty to ignore the infinite minor regulations that

50. E. P. Millikey to R. H. Gourdin, August 14, 1865, R. H. Gourdin Papers.
51. Martin S. Wilkins to J. B. Grimball, August 5, 1865, J. B. Grimball Papers.
52. Charles Alston, Jr., to D. W. Jordan, September 1, 1865, D. W. Jordan Papers.

had been imposed upon them as slaves. They assumed new forms of dress, kept dogs and guns, hunted, and they traveled about without passes. Many refused to yield the sidewalks to the white gentry, omitted the slave-period obeisances, and rode horses or mules or in carriages in the presence of white pedestrians. They conversed in public and in secret with any number of other Negroes and entered into associations for a variety of purposes.

The master class, exasperated and outraged by the assertiveness of the freedmen, was particularly alert in noting and meticulously recording this metamorphosis of their erstwhile bondsmen. In Camden, early in April, 1865, Emma Holmes, attending services in the Methodist Church where the Negroes sat in the galleries, was incensed at the Negro women who wore "round hats, gloves and even lace veils, the men alone looking respectable."[53] A white resident returning to Charleston in June of the same year was appalled by "Negroes shoving white person[s] . . . [off] the walk. Negro women dressed in the most outré style, all with veils and parasols for which they have an especial fancy. Riding on horseback with negro soldiers and in carriages."[54] At the same time, a planter on the lower Cooper River complained that the Negroes would not stay out of Charleston, where they "claim they are free," and the women are frequently seen "with blue & pink veils, etc." The same planter was mortified while hunting in the swamps with a group of white gentlemen to encounter suddenly a number of Negro men engaged in the same entertainment, armed with shotguns and following the hounds like ebony images of their white superiors.[55]

To the freedman, his new liberty conveyed the right to assemble in public, to speak, and to celebrate—the cause most often and extravagantly celebrated being freedom itself. Celebrations occurred frequently, on plantations, in villages and towns, and pre-eminently in Charleston. The Negro community in Charleston was large, wealthy, well informed, and organized. Zion Church, having been established by the Presbyterians before the war primarily for the accommodation of their Negro members and having a seating capacity of two thousand, logically became the focal point of organized activity among the Negroes and their Northern friends.

Perhaps one of the most impressive parades ever seen in Charleston was staged by the Negro community on March 29, 1865, scarcely a

53. Diary, entry for April 2, 1865.
54. H. W. Ravenel to A. L. Taveau, June 27, 1865, A. L. Taveau Papers.
55. [—.—.] Deas to his daughter, July—, 1865, [—.—.] Deas Papers.

month after the occupation of the city. The marchers began assembling
at noon and a procession of about four thousand was soon formed. It
was led by two Negro marshals on horseback. Among the marchers
were fifty butchers carrying knives and preceded by a display of a large
porker. Then followed a band and the Twenty-first United States Colored Troops (the Third South Carolina Volunteers), a company of
school boys, and a car of Liberty carrying thirteen young girls representing the original thirteen states (which were cheered enthusiastically).
The main body of the parade consisted of eighteen hundred school
children with their teachers. The trades were represented by tailors
carrying shears, coopers with hoops, blacksmiths, painters, carpenters,
wheelwrights, barbers, and others. Eight companies of firemen wearing
red shirts paraded with their equipment. Also in the procession was a
cart bearing a mock auction block. While a boy rang a bell, an auction-
eer extolled the salability of two Negro women seated on the block
with their children standing around them. The cart carried a sign:
"A number of Negroes for sale." A long rope was tied to the cart and a
number of men were tied to the rope. Another cart bore a coffin displaying the signs: "Slavery is dead," "Who owns him, No one," and
"Sumter dug his grave on the 13th of April 1861." The cart was followed by mourners in black. Then came fifty sailors, a company of
wood sawyers, the newspaper carriers, and several clubs and associations.
The procession was three miles long and wound through the streets
below the Citadel. The Negroes, both participants and spectators, were
"wild with enthusiasm," reported one observer. "Good order and appreciation of freedom were evident."[56]

As the war drew to a close other mass meetings of Negroes followed
in rapid succession. On April 5, while Potter was making a sortie from
Georgetown, the Negroes of Charleston met in Zion Church and
passed resolutions thanking the army for their liberation.[57] Fort
Sumter, already reduced to rubble by artillery fire, might well have sunk
beneath the waters under the sheer weight of victorious abolitionists who
flocked from the North to stand upon its ruins. On April 14, Robert
Anderson himself returned to raise the flag over the ruins. Before the
ceremonies began, Robert Smalls brought the *Planter* alongside and
set ashore more than three thousand Negroes from the city. Remaining
aboard to watch the proceedings from the quarterdeck was the son of
Denmark Vesey, the man who forty-three years before had shocked

56. *New York Times,* April 4, 1865, p. 9.
57. *Ibid.,* April 11, 1865, p. 5.

the state—and, indeed, the South—with the threat of mass insurrection. "As the old silken bunting winged itself to its long-deserted staff, thousands of shouts, and prayers fervent and deep, accompanying, greeted its reappearance." And then the speeches began. "I have been a friend of the South," declared William Lloyd Garrison, and Henry Ward Beecher, Theodore Tilton, Henry Wilson, Joshua Leavitt, William D. Kelley, Joseph Holt, and George Thompson applauded.[58]

Other Negro communities were not long in following the example of Charleston. The editor of the *New York Times* praised the stand of the Negroes of Columbia in refusing to abandon plans to celebrate Independence Day in 1865 despite the protests of the whites. "They may not get the vote or court rights in this way," asserted the editor, "but there are a hundred petty regulations of the slave period which they can break to exert their influence. It is good that the white become accustomed to negro meetings."[59] In the village of Aiken on the Fourth, the Reverend Cornish observed that "the Negroes had a Pic Nic— somewhere, & a prayer meeting & a dance at the Hotel Headquarters."[60] Even in the remote hamlet of Spartanburg, scarcely a month after most of the slaves had been formally released by their masters, David Golightly Harris noted that "the negroes had a jubilee . . . at the village, the yankeys and the negroes going hand in hand."[61] Throughout Reconstruction, the Negroes made New Year's Day and Independence Day their special holidays and devoted them to the celebration of emancipation and union, concepts which were inseparably intertwined in their minds. On these days, even in the smallest villages, the Negro community usually staged some sort of jubilee.[62]

These celebrations were significant as assertions of freedom, but they were also important in other ways. They obviously gave the Negro population a feeling of unity and an awareness of the power that unity bestowed. Further, they pushed forth leaders from among their own numbers who, in time, would translate that power into political realities.

58. *Ibid.,* April 23, 1865, p. 2; Rollin, *Life and Public Services of Martin R. Delany,* pp. 193–95.

59. July 2, 1865, p. 4.

60. Cornish, Diary, entry for July 4, 1865.

61. Farm Journal, entry for September 23, 1865.

62. The *Intelligencer* (Anderson), July 7, 1870, reported celebrations of Independence Day occurring in seven upcountry villages and in Columbia in that year. The *Charleston Daily Republican,* July 7, 8, 13, 1870, recorded the same pattern in the lowcountry.

Freedmen often interpreted their liberty as a license to express
candidly, either by words or deeds, their true feelings toward the whites
in general and their late masters in particular.

Many Negroes continued to show the same respect and cordiality
toward individual whites which they had exhibited in slavery. "I have
been very agreeably disappointed in the behavior of the negroes," wrote
a young planter visiting Charleston in August, 1865. "They are as civil
& humble as ever. All I met greeted me enthusiastically as 'Mass
Gus.' "[63] In September, another visiting native white concurred. "The
negroes behave admirably," he reported to his wife, "when you consider
the ordeal of temptation & teaching they have passed through."[64] And
an elderly Charlestonian observed, "The negroes about town behave as
far as I see extremely well. I have met with nothing but respect and
good-will from them . . ."[65] On the plantations, returning masters
sometimes encountered the same response. "I met with universal polite-
ness from our former slaves," wrote a Beaufort District planter after a
visit to the family plantations in December, 1865. "They were glad
to see me & inquired after all the family."[66]

Yet, while many Negroes manifested cordial feelings toward the
whites, others exhibited insolence and insubordination. As the war
drew to a close, and before emancipation became a certainty, such displays often served as a device by which Negroes tested their freedom.
"There is quite a difference of manner among the Negroes," Grace
B. Elmore noted in Richland shortly after Sherman's passage, "but I
think it proceeds from an uncertainty as to what their condition will be.
They do not know if they are free or not and their manner is a sort of
feeler by which they will find out how far they can go." Grace's brother,
fresh from a visit to slave-rich lower Richland District, "found quite a
spirit of insubordination among the negroes who supposed they were
free, but they are gradually discovering a Yankee army passing through
the county and telling them they are free is not sufficient to make it
a fact."[67] As emancipation became assured many ex-slaves took obvious
pleasure in expressing heretofore concealed feelings of animosity toward their recent owners. In June, 1865, Edward, personal servant to
Henry W. Ravenel, accompanied his master from their refuge in

63. A. T. Smythe to his wife, August 19, 1865, A. T. Smythe Letters.
64. Ellison Capers to his wife, September 10, 1865, Ellison Capers Papers.
65. N. R. Middleton to his daughter, January 10, 1866, N. R. Middleton Papers.
66. "R. S. E." to his sister, December 19, 1865, Elliott–Gonzales Papers.
67. Diary, entry for March 4, 1865.

Greenville to Columbia. There Edward obtained permission from Ravenel to find his wife, and was given five of the master's last nine dollars to enable him to follow Ravenel to Charleston. Ravenel proceeded to Charleston where Edward subsequently appeared, but "was excessively insolent—told the Servant in the yard that he had no further use for me and that he had been left in Columbia to starve." The indignant Ravenal concluded: "So much for the fidelity of indulged servants."[68] Even more blatant was the insubordination of a "so-called" servant who, when ordered by her Charleston mistress to scour some pots and kettles, replied: "You betta do it yourself, Ain't you smarter an me? You think you is——Wy you no scour fo you-self."[69] Not all freedmen were so vociferous; many were content simply to ignore their late masters. "Rosetta, Lizze's maid, passed me today when I was coming from Church without speaking to me," wrote one aristocrat to his wife. "She was really elegantly dressed, in King Street style."[70]

A very few Negroes believed that freedom warranted the exercise of vengeance upon the whites—that theft, arson, and violence even to the extremity of homicide were justifiable retributions for their bondage. This sentiment was particularly apparent in areas subjected to Union raids and it persisted through the summer and fall of 1865. After Sherman had passed through Camden, a serious case of arson was narrowly averted, and "many other attempts at setting fire were discovered either just in time, or after some damage had been done—both in Camden and the surrounding country—keeping everyone in a constant state of anxiety and alarm."[71] In several communities, disturbances reached the proportions of insurrections. In March, in the vicinity of Christ Church on the lower Cooper River, an area which lay between the Union lines and Confederate pickets, the mistress of a plantation reported: "A band of armed negro men, principally from one of the neighboring plantations, until put to flight by Confederate Scouts, did without any authority for what they did, arming & marching about the country, stopping people on the highway with guns pointed at their heads, suddenly surrounding a man on his own plantation attending to his own affairs, going to peoples homes at night threatening them & in one instance I hear firing on the man who came out to see what the noise was about . . ." Another planter "was threatened with hav-

68. To A. L. Taveau, June 27, 1865, A. L. Taveau Papers.
69. Louisa McCord to A. T. Smythe, August 27, 1867, A. T. Smythe Letters.
70. Ellison Capers to his wife, September 10, 1865, Ellison Capers Papers.
71. Holmes, Diary, entry for March 27, 1865.

ing his house burned and himself shot if he tried to save a single piece of furniture."[72] The relief afforded by Confederate cavalry in this area was only temporary. In mid-July, a Cooper River planter complained that in Christ Church and St. Thomas Parishes and on the river, in general, the Negroes claimed everything and, in some cases, had driven away the owners. Five or six Negroes had come to three plantations—Richmond, Basis, and Kensington—and encouraged the freedmen to seize everything for themselves. "Insubordination & insolence," he concluded, were frequently observed.[73] Other lowcountry communities witnessed similar scenes. Near Plantersville in Georgetown District, a Union raid in March, 1865, released a large number of Negro slaves who were "indulging in the free use of wine & liquors obtained from the houses of former masters," and "preparing themselves for the commission of crime," "or worse, might break into open insurrection at any time."[74] "During the stay and after the departure of Genl Potters army," a group of Pineville planters complained in September, 1865, "the negroes evinced treachery and vindictiveness—illustrated by robbery, plundering, false accusation and insolence, in the three weeks after the departure of said army, by an open outbreak in arms—taking possession [sic] of and patroling this village night and day, threatening the lives of men and the chastity of women, & finally firing upon Confederate Scouts by whom they were dispersed."[75] During the same period on the mainland in the vicinity of Beaufort, a planter complained that robbery and theft were committed wholesale by the Negroes "& no redress given"; while "Mr. Chavis & others, as you are aware has been compelled with his Family to fly his home, from vagrant negroes, returned from the Islands, chiefly." Such was the case, he averred, "every where where officers of Colored troops have had jurisdiction any length of time."[76]

Notwithstanding the charges of the whites that Negro soldiers often instigated such disorders, the occupation rapidly established comparative peace. It is true, nevertheless, that the Negro population was most restless in those areas occupied by Negro troops—an area which included

72. "Mother" to her son (probably Wilmot G. De Saussure), March 31, 1865, H. W. and W. G. De Saussure Papers.

73. [—.—.] Deas to his daughter, July—and 15, 1865, [—.—.] Deas Papers.

74. MS Petition from the citizens of Plantersville to the Naval Commander in Georgetown, March 10, 1865, Sparkman Family Papers.

75. Petition of several planters of Pineville to the area commander, September 11, 1865, Trenholm Papers.

76. Anonymous to B. F. Perry, n.d. (probably July, 1865), B. F. Perry Papers.

the lowcountry from Georgetown to Savannah and, roughly, the southern half of the state from the sea to the mountains. The effect of the Negro military on the population of Aiken, as seen through the diary of the Reverend Cornish, presents a good case study. In June, 1865, the village was occupied by a detachment of the Thirty-third United States Colored Troops (the First South).[77] On Sunday, June 18, about twenty Negro soldiers entered the Baptist Church with the apparent intention of attending services. They were ordered by the white ushers to find places in the galleries. As some of the soldiers began to ascend the stairs, one of their number ordered them to halt, and the whole group attempted to take seats on the main floor. When some of the white men rose and blocked their way, the soldiers flourished their bayonets and began to curse. Finally, they were allowed to seat themselves below, but the church closed that evening. Monday morning, Cornish's serving woman, Phobe, used "intemperate" language in addressing the Reverend, and, upon being reproved, continued the abuse. When asked whose servant she was, Phobe answered, "My own servant." She was then told to recant or leave. She left. On the same morning, a Mr. Wood "was badly beaten by the 'Black and Blues,' " as the Negro soldiers were called. The beating brought the inspector general from Augusta, but on Saturday, August 5, there was another such "disturbance."[78]

It is difficult to distinguish fact from fiction in the disordered first weeks that followed the war; but the rumor circuit buzzed with tales of whites murdered by Negroes, usually their ex-slaves. Emma E. Holmes reported that William Prioleau returned to his lowcountry plantation after the Union forces had passed and spent the night, "but never woke again. His throat was cut from ear to ear." Another planter reported killed was William Allen, "who was chopped to pieces in his barn," as Emma graphically related.[79] A less impressionable recorder wrote from Walterboro early in July that "several citizens about Ashepoo & Combahee, eight or nine, have been murdered by negroes." Much of this lawlessness he blamed on the presence of Negro troops. "We have had them here and tho the officers & men behave as well as I had expected the soldiers (black) made great mischief among servants generally and plantation negroes particularly," he declared. "Things were bad before, but their influence made them infinitely worse."[80]

77. Higginson, *Army Life in a Black Regiment,* p. 265.
78. Cornish, Diary, entries for June 18 through August 5, 1865.
79. Diary, entries for "End of May," June 15, 1865.
80. J. W. Rutledge to "Colonel," July 9, 1865, B. F. Perry Papers.

The great mass of Negroes in South Carolina at the end of the Civil War hoped and expected that freedom meant that each would soon be settled upon his own plot of earth. Indeed, to the Negro agrarian freedom without land was incomprehensible. "Gib us our own land and we take care ourselves," a Union officer quoted as the sentiment of the mass of country Negroes in the spring of 1865, "but widout land, de ole massas can hire us or starve us, as dey please."[81] The desire for land touched all classes of former slaves. "She also said," wrote a young mistress late in May, paraphrasing the words of her maid, that "the commonest and most universal view was that each man would have his farm and stock and plenty to eat & drink and so pass through life."[82] The prevalence of this roseate view of the future among freedmen was confirmed by Mary Boykin Chesnut of Kershaw District, wife of a Confederate senator and general, and herself heiress to three generations of cotton culture, who reported that the Negroes "declare that they are to be given lands and mules by those blessed Yankees."[83] Similarly, a Northern correspondent, arriving in Orangeburg after a trip through the lowcountry, declared that the desire for land was active and widespread among the Negroes. "Some of the best regiments have white soldiers who tell the negroes they are the rightful owners of the land, that they should refuse to work or go to the islands to get lands."[84]

"Forty acres and a mule," that delightful bit of myopic mythology so often ascribed to the newly freed in the Reconstruction Period, at least in South Carolina during the spring and summer of 1865, represented far more than the chimerical rantings of ignorant darkies, irresponsible soldiers, and radical politicians. On the contrary, it symbolized rather precisely the policy to which the government had already given and was giving mass application in the Sea Islands. Hardly had the troops landed, in November, 1861, before liberal Northerners arrived to begin a series of ambitious experiments in the reconstruction of Southern society. One of these experiments included the redistribution of large landed estates to the Negroes. By the spring of 1865, this program was well underway, and after August any well-informed,

81. Reid, *After the War,* p. 59.
82. Elmore, Diary, entry for May 24, 1865.
83. Isabella D. Martin and Myrta Lockett Avary (eds.), *A Diary from Dixie, as written by Mary Boykin Chesnut* (New York, 1905), p. 396.
84. *The Nation,* I, No. 4 (July 27, 1865), 106.

intelligent observer in South Carolina would have concluded, as did the Negroes, that some considerable degree of permanent land division was highly probable.

The first step in this direction was taken in June, 1862, when Congress levied a direct tax on the states, apportioning a certain amount of the sum to South Carolina. The property of the occupied area in the islands thus became subject to its share of the tax. Since most of the owners were within the Confederate lines, 187 plantations passed into the control of the Treasury Department. During the first full year of its possession, 1862, the Department worked these lands through the agency of volunteer superintendents brought down from the North to supervise the labor of those Negroes who had refused to flee with their masters. The primary object of this experiment was to prove that the Negro could and would work profitably outside of the slave system. By the end of 1862, however, the government decided that these lands would be sold for the tax claims lodged against them. Before the sales occurred, three separate factions arose in the islands on the issue of just how the lands should be sold.

One party was led by Brigadier General Rufus B. Saxton, a West Pointer, career soldier, and late-blooming abolitionist, who after July, 1862, as military governor, was responsible for the Negroes on the plantations. Saxton pressed vigorously for the sale of lands exclusively to Negroes who would settle them on a pre-emption basis and subsequently be allowed to buy their homesteads from the government at nominal prices, payable in modest installments.[85] Strongly supporting Saxton was the Reverend Mansfield French, a New York Methodist missionary who had quasi-official charge of educating the island freedmen in mental and religious matters.[86] In the same camp were found most of the teachers, plantation superintendents, and physicians who had come to the islands to assist in the great experiment of reconstruction. Finally, among the most articulate of Saxton's supporters were the island journalists, particularly James G. Thompson of Beaufort, the editor of the *Free South*. Thompson proposed to punish the South for her apostasy and, at the same time, to reform her by the "division of land," among, as he said, "the children of the soil," by a "free press" which would do its "share toward electing an anti-slavery union governor in South Carolina," and by "free schools" where "White and

85. Holland, *Letters and Diary of Laura M. Towne*, p. 100.
86. *Free South* (Beaufort), December 12, 1863.

black, the 'poor white trash' and the 'nigger' will learn that 'knowledge is power' . . ."[87]

Diametrically opposed to the Saxton party was a faction led by the Treasury Department's tax commissioners for South Carolina, the men charged with the sale of the confiscated estates. Behind the commissioners, rather like the black-cloaked villain of melodrama, lurked a mysterious array of Northern speculators and army sutlers who conspired to control the land themselves and take advantage of the fabulously high price which Sea Island cotton then commanded.

A third faction was led by E. S. Philbrick, a very successful Boston businessman who had come to the islands early in 1862 as a plantation superintendent. He and his supporters in the North were certainly friends of the Negro, but they thought that he was unready for independent ownership and must first undergo a period of tutelage by carefully selected instructors—that is, by themselves. In addition, they feared (with good reason) that Negro purchasers might lose both their lands and their money either in the event the army evacuated the islands or in the uncertainty of tax titles in general.

In January, 1863, the tax commissioners announced their intention to sell a large number of plantations to the highest bidder at a public auction in February. The distressed Saxton promptly appealed to the antislavery commanding general of the department who suspended the sales on grounds of military necessity.[88] Thereafter, the tax commissioners somehow secured permission to sell forty-seven of the plantations. At the auction, six of these, consisting of some 2600 acres, were sold to Negroes at slightly less than a dollar an acre. Five of the six were bought by groups of Negroes who had pooled their savings (derived from the sale of services and goods to the whites) to outbid the speculators. Eleven plantations passed to the Philbrick company which resold them to their Negro laborers two years later; and the remainder, more than half the land sold, fell into the hands of the speculators.[89]

Of the approximately one hundred and fifty plantations still retained

87. *Ibid.*, November 21, 1863. Interestingly, Thompson sat in the Constitutional Convention of 1865 as the delegate from St. Helena Parish. Elected by the all-white vote of the missionaries on the islands, he was the only Republican among the 124 delegates attending the Convention.

88. *New South* (Port Royal), January 13, 31, 1863; *Official Records*, Ser. 1, XIV, 394–95; Pearson, *Letters from Port Royal*, pp. 147–52, *passim;* Holland, *Letters and Diary of Laura M. Towne*, p. 100.

89. Pearson, *Letters from Port Royal*, 152–71, 324, *passim;* Pierce, *Atlantic Monthly*, XII (September 1863), pp. 309–10.

by the government, a few were occupied by the military, some were leased to private parties to provide an income for experimental schools in the islands, but most were reserved by Saxton and operated by superintendents under his direction.[90] As the agricultural season of 1863 came to a close, Saxton again sought to divide the reserved area among the Negro laborers. Early in November, 1863, acting upon orders promulgated by President Lincoln, he issued a circular advising the Negroes to pre-empt farms for themselves on certain plantations. However, Lincoln's orders also authorized the sale of a score of plantations at public auction in plots not exceeding 320 acres. Since the tax commissioners were certain to use this authority and Negro purchasers would have to bid against speculators, this reservation made it unlikely that many Negroes would be able to buy their lands.[91] At Saxton's instigation, the Reverend French proceeded to Washington, where he apparently had important connections. Late in December, French won a new order from Chase and Lincoln that authorized a pre-emption program strikingly similar to that used in the West before the war. Single loyal persons over twenty-one years of age were allowed to choose and occupy twenty acres, and those with families, forty acres. Wives of absent soldiers and sailors were also allowed to claim forty acres. Interestingly, this was the first mention of forty-acre plots that was made in the islands. The price of the land was fixed at $1.25 per acre, two-fifths of which was due at the time the claim was filed and the remainder when the deed was issued. Under the new order, both whites and Negroes could purchase lots, but all buyers must have actually resided on government lands for six months during the time of the occupation. In effect, then, only teachers, superintendents, and Negroes were qualified as purchasers, and the troublesome speculator was excluded. "A statesman-like movement toward the reorganization of southern society," exulted editor Thompson through his *Free South* press. On the Sunday following French's return to the Islands from Washington, he, Saxton, and other officials met with the Negroes in the church in St. Helenaville where Saxton explained the new order and admonished the Negroes "not to sleep until they had staked out their claims."[92]

90. *Free South* (Beaufort), December 5, 12, 1863, March 26, 1864; Pearson, *Letters from Port Royal,* p. 327.
91. *Ibid.,* pp. 229–30.
92. *Ibid.,* pp. 243–44; Holland, *Letters and Diary of Laura M. Towne,* p. 129; *Free South* (Beaufort), January 16, 1864.

Events conspired to defeat Saxton's plans. Not all the Negroes wanted to buy land immediately, many preferring to work for wages until the permanency of their purchases would be certain.[93] Also, surveys were still incomplete, and those who did desire to stake out claims were unsure how to proceed. But most important, the tax commissioners and speculators now bestirred themselves and their friends in the government. A third order shortly arrived from Washington giving the commissioners blanket permission to sell the lands at auction. This they hastily proceeded to do, with the result that most were purchased by the speculators. The Negroes were much distressed by these maneuvers. Some refused to labor for the new proprietors; others agreed only with great reluctance.[94] Similar results followed sales in the winter and spring of 1865.

Saxton's more ambitious program for the division of the tax lands was defeated; yet, apparently, most Negroes on the islands who wanted farms had, by the end of the war, acquired small holdings. No figures on the number of Negro purchasers are available, but probably as many as five hundred bought lands either directly from the government or from private parties. In May, 1865, one of the superintendents reported that among the workers "about every family upon this place has got its five or ten acres" elsewhere on the island,[95] and Whitelaw Reid, visiting the islands in the following month, found that the market for land among Negroes was almost satiated.[96]

Farm animals and tools were also within the financial grasp of Negro farmers on the Islands, and they were even more successful in acquiring these than they were in the purchase of land. In March, 1864, for instance, on the Fripp Point Plantation on St. Helena, the Negro population outbid Northerners at a tax sale to acquire the entire stock of mules, oxen, cows, and agricultural implements.[97] In the same month, a lot of thirty-five condemned army horses sold at auction went entirely to Negroes at a cost of $3700.[98] Sherman's troops, passing through the islands in January, 1865, also brought numerous animals of Georgian heritage which they readily sacrificed to the Negroes for cash.[99]

93. Pearson, *Letters from Port Royal*, pp. 246–47.
94. *Ibid.*, pp. 244, 248, 254–55.
95. *Ibid.*, pp. 311–12.
96. Reid, *After the War*, p. 117.
97. Pearson, *Letters from Port Royal*, p. 255.
98. *Free South* (Beaufort), April 2, 1864.
99. Pearson, *Letters from Port Royal*, pp. 301–02.

The sale of plantations confiscated for taxes to Negro laborers was of minor importance when compared with the revolutionary potentialities of the War Department's policy of giving Negroes "possessory" titles to lands abandoned by their rebel owners. Promulgated on January 16, 1865, by Sherman's Special Field Orders Number 15, this program was ostensibly a practical solution to a large military problem—the disposition of vast numbers of Negroes who had followed Sherman to the coast and who had been, and were still, pouring through the lines in South Carolina. This it certainly was. Yet, the circumstances of its inception, the details of the design itself, and the manner of its execution suggest that the program was a continuation and a careful refinement of the very policies which Saxton and other friends of the Negro had matured during their three years of experience in the Sea Islands.

Sherman's orders were written upon the explicit instructions of Secretary Stanton during a visit to the islands and Savannah in January, 1865, and after a three-day conference with Sherman. Most interestingly, Stanton's host in the islands was Saxton, who thoughtfully arranged for the Secretary to observe closely the operation of the schools and plantations and to interview intimately Negroes as well as Northern schoolmistresses, superintendents, and missionaries–at–large. After returning to Washington, Stanton relieved Saxton's superior, J. G. Foster, as the commanding general of the Department of the South. Foster had been described as a "pro-slavery general"; he had been charged with collusion with the tax commissioners, the sutlers, and speculators; and he had, indeed, enforced the military draft upon the Island Negroes with excessive harshness. As his successor, Stanton named Oliver Otis Howard, the commander of Sherman's left wing, and a man who had shown a deep interest in the progress of the Negroes on the islands during his stay there in January. In addition, Saxton, who had earned only frowns from Foster, was promoted to the rank of major general in specific recognition of his services in the islands. Saxton's promotion pre-dated the settlement orders by only three days.

The actual draftsman of Sherman's Special Field Orders Number 15 is unknown, but even if Saxton himself had written the document it could not have been more in accord with his desires. The orders were poorly, and probably hastily, drafted, but the design of the program contemplated is, for the most part, evident. They set aside for settlement by the freedmen "The islands from Charleston south, the abandoned rice fields along the rivers for thirty miles back from the seas and the

country bordering the St. Johns River, Florida." Of course, at the time
the orders were issued, many of the islands south of Charleston were
not occupied by the Union forces and nowhere in South Carolina did
Union lines extend thirty miles inland. Moreover, Sherman's plans
obviously did not include the occupation of such an area by his troops.
Within six weeks of the issuance of the orders, however, the Union
lines in South Carolina did embrace almost precisely the area described,
and the new lines had been formed largely by the advance of Negro
troops attached to the Department of the South. The authors of the
orders apparently planned and executed an expansion to the mainland
of the policy of freeing the slaves and enrolling them to defend their
homes and free still more slaves—a policy which had been fixed in the
islands as early as the fall of 1862.

The details of the settlement program were significant. In essence,
each head of family (or the families of those in the government's service) who chose to do so could pre-empt "a plot of not more than forty
acres of tillable ground, . . . in the possession of which land the military
authorities will afford them protection until such time as they can
protect themselves, or until Congress shall regulate their title." In the
meantime, an inspector of settlements and plantations was to be detailed
whose duty it was "to visit the settlements, to regulate their police and
general management, and who will furnish personally to each head of
family, subject to the approval of the President of the United States, a
possessory title in writing giving as near as possible the description of
boundaries, and who shall adjust all claims of conflicts that may arise
under the same, subject to the like approval, treating such titles altogether as possessory." To facilitate the settlement of individual families, the whole bounty of any recruit, amounting to $300, might be paid
"to assist his family and settlement in procuring agricultural implements, seed, tools, boats, clothing and other articles necessary for their
livelihood." Finally, the orders provided that "on the islands and in the
settlements hereafter to be established, no white person whatever, unless military officers and soldiers detailed for duty, will be permitted to
reside; and the sole and exclusive management of affairs will be left
to the freed people themselves, subject only to the United States military
authority and the acts of Congress."[100] Thus, not only was Saxton's
land program for the islands finally to be realized, but also, at last, that
highly disruptive element—the speculator—was to be barred.

100. *Official Records,* Ser. 1, XLVII, Part 2, 60–62; *New York Times,* January
29, 1865, p. 1; Holland, *Letters and Diary of Laura M. Towne,* pp. 150–51;

The Sherman grants have often been interpreted as anticipatory of outright gifts of land to Negroes. Possibly this was true. Yet, neither Stanton, Saxton, French, Thompson, nor any of the leading liberal friends of the Negro in the Islands had ever proposed that land be given rather than sold to the Negroes. Indeed, even the Negro's most ardent and constant friends in the islands opposed giving the mass of freedmen anything. To the typical missionary, gratuities were reserved for hopeless cases and his very presence bespoke a faith in his hopefulness for the freedman's future. Probably those responsible for the orders hoped that Congress would legalize just such a program as Chase and Lincoln had sanctioned a year previously, that is, the sale of pre-empted lands to Negroes at nominal prices and on extended terms.

It is hardly surprising that the officer named to fill the position of executor of Sherman's Orders, under the title of inspector of settlements and plantations, was Rufus B. Saxton; and it was characteristic of Saxton that he immediately put the plan into effect. Within a week of the issuance of the order, he was in the process of resettling Negro refugees on Edisto Island (abandoned since the summer of 1862) under the protection of a Negro regiment.[101] By early May, there were some ten thousand Negroes settled on the island, many of them natives who had trod tortuous paths to come home again.[102] As the advance of Union forces rendered the islands to the north secure, these too were rapidly settled, particularly Wadmalaw, John's, and James islands.[103] Apparently no great numbers of Negroes were located on the mainland plantations, perhaps because they were less defensible against Confederate raiders.

By mid-April, Saxton was obviously pleased with his progress. Seated at the dinner table of his Beaufort home, "a fine, airy, large-windowed, many porched Southern residence" (which, incidentally, sat next to the home place of the fire-breathing secessionist Robert Barnwell Rhett), Saxton informed Whitelaw Reid that nearly thirty thousand Negroes had been located on the Islands and adjacent planta-

---

Pearson, *Letters from Port Royal*, p. 305; Botume, *First Days Among the Contrabands*, pp. 114–15; George R. Bentley, *A History of the Freedmen's Bureau* (Philadelphia, 1955), p. 45.

101. Pearson, *Letters from Port Royal*, pp. 306–7; Holland, *Letters and Diary of Laura M. Towne*, p. 154.

102. Ames, *From a New England Woman's Diary in 1865*, pp. 8, 16.

103. Martha Schofield, MS Diary, *passim;* Louisa Gervais to T. Y. Simons, October 5, December 18, 1865, Louisa Gervais Papers; Trowbridge, *The South*, pp. 541–42.

tions on the mainland. Twelve to thirteen thousand of these were recent comers, voluntarily settling "to the satisfaction of the negroes themselves," and living on rations loaned by the government.[104]

As Saxton indicated, during the first month, settlement was voluntary. However, early in May, Negroes drawing government rations in Charleston were given ten days to find homesteads on the plantations or suffer the loss of their allowances.[105] Thereafter, settlement under the Sherman program proceeded even more rapidly. Seemingly through Saxton's design, relatively few of the Georgia refugees were brought to South Carolina, and those who did come were assigned as wage laborers to plantations in the Port Royal area or were held in the refugee camps on Port Royal Island. Most of these seem to have returned to Georgia soon after the war.[106] Doubtless, Saxton was aware of the instinct that bound the Negro agrarian to his home, and the indications are that the Saxton party deliberately sought to utilize this affinity in building a new and permanent structure of land tenure in South Carolina.

Early in June, 1865, Saxton, as an assistant commissioner of the Freedmen's Bureau, became that agency's chief officer in South Carolina, Georgia, and Florida. This was, of course, precisely the area he had controlled as military governor for the Department of the South and as inspector under Sherman's orders. Moreover, the job itself was simply an evolution and expansion of his previous duties. O. O. Howard, lately Saxton's military superior in the Department, became the head of the Bureau, interestingly, upon the recommendation of Saxton himself, Stanton, and others.[107] Just as the authors of Sherman's order had hoped, Congress provided, on March 3, 1865, in the law creating the Freedmen's Bureau, that freedmen and loyal unionists could pre-empt forty acres of abandoned or confiscated lands, rent them at a nominal rate for three years, and buy them at any time within this period at a price fairly appraised.[108] In his first official order, issued on June 10, 1865, Saxton regularized the continuance of the Sherman program under the new law. On July 28, Howard sought to implement the system throughout his jurisdiction. Meanwhile, Saxton continued as before to seize abandoned lands wherever possible and to settle freed-

104. Reid, *After the War*, p. 117; *New York Times*, August 6, 1865.

105. *New York Times*, May 14, 1865, p. 2.

106. Pearson, *Letters from Port Royal*, pp. 306, 308–9; Botume, *First Days Among the Contrabands*, pp. 80–89.

107. Bentley, *Freedmen's Bureau*, pp. 51–52, 55.

108. *Ibid.*, p. 49.

men upon them. Before the end of August, he had claimed some 312,000 acres of plantation land in South Carolina. Professor Martin L. Abbott, a careful student of the subject, estimated that Saxton eventually settled about 40,000 Negroes under the program.[109]

With perhaps one out of every ten Negro families in South Carolina settled upon their own land by the late summer of 1865, and with the apparent intention of the government, through the Bureau, to guarantee the security of their tenure and to accommodate others, it is not surprising that the landless freedmen should have thought their chances of winning the same boon were excellent. Moreover, where Negroes settled, they revealed an inflexible determination to hold their ground. "We own this land now," the freedmen of one lowcountry plantation impressed upon their late master when he returned from the war; "put it out of your head that it will ever be yours again."[110] For a time, most owners believed that this was, indeed, a verity.

Thus, even in the early days of freedom, former slaves with amazing unanimity revealed—by mass desertion, migration, idleness, by the breaching of the infinite minor regulations of slavery, by a new candor in relationships with whites, and by their ambition to acquire land—a determination to put an end to their slavery. It is true that the Negro's freedom was still severely circumscribed a year after emancipation, and his experience during the whole term of Reconstruction could hardly be described as a success story. Yet, the Negro did not, upon emancipation, immediately jump a quick half-step forward and halt. In the favorable atmosphere generated by his political ascendency during Reconstruction, freedom for the Negro in South Carolina was a growing thing, flowering in areas political historians have often neglected. The growth was, in part, the result of cultivation by alien hands; but it was also the result of forces operating within the organism itself. The gains won during these early years enabled the Negro community to continue to move forward in vital areas of human endeavor in the post-Reconstruction period while, ironically, its political freedom was rapidly dwindling to virtual extinction. In this sense, far from being the disaster so often described, Reconstruction was for the Negroes of South Carolina a period of unequaled progress.

109. Martin L. Abbott, "The Freedmen's Bureau in South Carolina, 1865–1872" (unpublished Ph.D. Thesis, Emory University, 1954), *passim*.

110. Mary Boykin Chesnut, *A Diary from Dixie,* ed. Ben Ames Williams (Cambridge, 1949), p. 540.

III...TOWARD A
NEW ECONOMICS

Slavery was dead, and the vacuum in relations between labor, capital, and management created by its demise required filling. In nonagricultural pursuits, wage labor was rapidly and easily substituted. In agriculture, however, a highly complex and —for the South—novel pattern gradually evolved. Only in its broadest outlines was the new order prescribed by the victorious North. The infinite detail emerged in a largely free interaction between white employers and Negro employees. In this process, the Negro laborer revealed himself not only as capable of surviving in a competitive society, but also of improving his own material circumstances and of contributing to the total prosperity of his community.

As the war drew to a close, the victors clearly were determined that slavery would be replaced by a system of free labor. Just how the transition was to be effected, and precisely what the new system was to be, Washington had not yet decided. During the spring and summer of 1865, in the absence of specific instructions, economic policy in South Carolina was determined in the field by officials faced with the necessity of contriving means to meet the obvious exigencies of the civilian population around them.

At first, and to some extent throughout Reconstruction, military forces in the state were a source of official policy. By July, 1865, the Department of South Carolina had been created with headquarters at

Hilton Head and some seven to eight thousand troops blanketed the state. The commanding general was then Q. A. Gillmore, a graduate of West Point with high soldierly qualities and no apparent political ambitions.

During the summer and early fall of 1865, another agency of the national government became progressively more important in the state: the Bureau of Refugees, Freedmen and Abandoned Lands. Rufus B. Saxton, the assistant commissioner of the Bureau for South Carolina, recruited a staff of specialists and subassistant commissioners primarily from the ranks of the regiments assigned to occupation duty. In addition, a considerable number were enlisted from among the numerous educational and religious missionaries who had arrived before and after the capitulation. Until Saxton was relieved early in 1866, the Bureau in South Carolina was merely a continuation and elaboration in personnel, form, and policy of the organization which had dealt with problems involving the Negro population since 1862.

The problem facing military authorities in South Carolina in the summer of 1865 was the necessity of supplying the immediate needs of large numbers of freedmen for food, clothing, shelter, and medical care. The same problem on a smaller scale had been met by the joint efforts of the army and the benevolent societies in the Sea Islands during the war. The army regularly undertook to feed refugees recently arrived from the mainland until they could support themselves. Before March, 1863, the missionaries in the islands had distributed 91,834 garments, 5,895 yards of cloth, and $3,000 worth of agricultural implements to the freedmen.[1] Also, the missionary force included physicians, as well as teachers and superintendents. As the war drew to a close, the issue of army rations to freedmen and, indeed, to impoverished whites, increased to enormous proportions. The Bureau, empowered to issue food, clothing, and fuel to destitute freedmen and refugees, systematized and continued the practice. The dislocations caused by the war, the transition from slave to free labor, and the poor crops in 1865, 1866, and 1867 perpetuated the need for issues of rations well into 1868. The immensity of the problem is suggested by the facts that in the year following September 1, 1866, the Bureau issued 810,309 rations to freedmen in the state; and in July, 1867, over 15,000 Negroes were supported entirely by government issues.[2]

1. Benjamin Quarles, *The Negro in the Civil War* (Boston, 1953), p. 125.
2. *Report of the Secretary of War* (1867), 40 Cong., 2 Sess. House Ex. Doc. No. 1, Part 1 (Washington, 1868), p. 304.

Charity is hardly the term to describe the actions of Northerners in South Carolina. Both the benevolent societies and the government issued food, clothing, and fuel as gifts only to orphans, the aged, and infirm. All others received such assistance as loans, to be repaid in one form or another. For example, in the spring of 1865, a Northern teacher on Edisto Island quickly disabused the local Negroes of the idea that a barrel of used clothing recently arrived from the North was to be given away. She called in one of their leaders, Uncle Jack, to explain to the others "that they must pay for it with vegetables, eggs, chickens, or whatever they can bring in exchange."[3] Similarly, first as military governor and later as inspector of plantations, Saxton insisted that rations furnished to refugees and settlers be repaid.[4] Further, Bureau policy was to issue rations only in those cases where they were desperately needed and to cease issues as soon as possible. The meagerness of charity in the relief program was completely in harmony with the views of its sponsors. "Indeed, the most dangerous process through which the negro goes when he becomes a freedman is that of receiving the gratuities of benevolence in the shape of food and clothing," wrote a veteran missionary late in 1865. "If you wish to make them impudent, fault-finding and lazy, give them clothing and food freely."[5] Two years later, Laura Towne, who gave her life and much of her personal fortune to the education of the Negroes in the islands, concluded that it was better to "let the people suffer" than to demoralize them by general gifts of food.[6]

Even the Negroes themselves subscribed to the code of charity advanced by their benefactors. Many freedmen in real need refused to apply for rations. After his term as subassistant commissioner for the mountain districts, John W. De Forest asserted: "As far as I could compare the two races, able-bodied Negroes were much less apt to apply for rations than able-bodied 'low-downers' [poor whites]."[7] Those who did accept government aid usually understood that the issues were to be repaid and, by Saxton's testimony in April, 1865, some 17,000 of his

3. Mary Ames, *From a New England Woman's Diary in Dixie in 1865* (Springfield, 1906), pp. 69–70.

4. *New York Times,* August 6, 1865, p. 3.

5. *Ibid.,* February 11, 1866, p. 3.

6. Rupert S. Holland (ed.), *Letters and Diary of Laura M. Towne, 1862–1884, Written from the Sea Islands of South Carolina* (Cambridge, 1912), p. 187.

7. James H. Croushore and David Morris Potter (eds.), *John William De Forest, A Union Officer in the Reconstruction* (New Haven, 1948), p. 80.

first charges had already done so.[8] In the early postwar years, hard times made repayment difficult. In addition, during the political agitation of 1867 and 1868, the successful candidate for the congressional seat of the Charleston district, an ex-Confederate Army captain named Christopher Columbus Bowen, made considerable political capital for himself by advising the Negroes, as a lawyer, that they could not be legally bound to repay the rations advanced.[9] Nevertheless, the common reaction of the Negroes to government assistance was one of gratitude, and, politically speaking, it could not be said that the Negro bit the hand that fed him.

The key policy of military authorities in South Carolina in the late spring and summer of 1865 was, above all, to return the freedmen to their accustomed labors. Quite properly, officials viewed this as the real solution to the problem of relief. Under official pressure, most Negro agriculturists either located themselves on the Sherman grants, contracted with landowners to work for the remainder of the year for a share of the crop, or remained under such terms on the plantations where they were.

The occupation forces implemented this policy by various means. Positively, the military enjoyed the loyalty of the freedmen themselves, and the very presence of the blue uniforms and the promulgation of official desires through the soldiers usually won ready compliance from the Negroes. The occupation authorities and, in its turn, the Freedmen's Bureau, had the facilities to transport freedmen to places where labor was in demand and to provide them with rations until they became self-sustaining. Negatively, the government was able to wrest compliance from many of the most recalcitrant freedmen simply by ceasing to provide them with rations.[10]

8. Ames, *From a New England Woman's Diary in 1865,* p. 16; *New York Times,* August 6, 1865, p. 3.

9. C. C. Bowen to H. K. Scott, October 20, 1868, Freedmen File, Department of Archives, State of South Carolina. Cited hereinafter as Freedmen File.

10. The success of the government in the pursuit of this policy was particularly evident in Charleston where, early in May, 1865, the general commanding in the area ordered the Negroes coming in from the country to leave the city within ten days and settle upon the Sherman grants or to suffer the loss of their rations. By mid-June, the *Times* man noted that: "The throngs of colored people that were visible in our midst some time ago have scattered and settled down on the plantations. The short supply of rice in the government storehouses doubtless had much to do with their departure." *New York Times,* May 14, p. 2; June 14, p. 5, 1865.

Many freedmen settled upon Sherman grants and remained entirely under governmental control. However, a large majority of Negroes were forced to take employment on the lands of planters and, in many cases, under their late masters. Congress, in the law that created the Freedmen's Bureau, did not prescribe regulations to govern this situation. To instruct both planters and laborers in the ways of free labor and to protect the freedmen during the period of adjustment, local officials relied upon the method that Saxton had perfected in the islands during the war. This so-called "contract system" had emerged as the *direct result* of Saxton's failure to secure the sale of confiscated plantations exclusively to Negro laborers. As described in the previous chapter, most of these lands passed under the gavel into the hands of speculators. Suspicious of these entrepreneurs and stimulated by complaints of ill-treatment voiced by their Negro workers, Saxton, in April, 1864, invoked his military powers to require each employer to draft a contract covering the farming year. The contract detailed precisely the work to be required of the Negroes and the wages and goods in lieu of wages that the freedmen would receive in return. Saxton also ordered his agents to visit each plantation upon which private parties employed Negroes, to read the contract to the laborers, to adjust any differences then and there, and to note carefully on the contract itself the assent of each worker. Any laborer refusing to agree to each and all provisions was to leave the plantation immediately.[11]

During the late spring and summer of 1865, the officers of the occupation assiduously applied this method throughout the state.[12] The large number of manuscript contracts extant dated during the summer of 1865 suggests that the program was carried out with remarkable thoroughness. Typical of these contracts was one signed by the manager and marked by the 131 freedmen on one of the Alexander Hamilton Boykin plantations in Kershaw District on July 6, 1865, in the presence of Lt. S. J. Brooks of the Twenty-fifth Ohio Regiment of Volunteers. By its terms, the laborers were guaranteed not only their liberty by their

11. *Free South* (Beaufort), April 2, 1864.

12. For instances, see: *A History of Spartanburg County*, Compiled by the Spartanburg Unit of the Writer's Program of the Works Projects Administration in the State of South Carolina (n. p., 1940), p. 142; David Golightly Harris MS Farm Journal, entry for September 4, 1865; *New York Times*, June 4, 1865, p. 8; Whitelaw Reid, *After the War; A Southern Tour, May 1, 1865 to May 1, 1866* (London, 1866), p. 85.

late master, but also a third of the crop at the end of the year—certainly a savory first taste of freedom.[13]

Neither the relief, resettlement, nor the contract policies of the occupation were perfectly administered, and even had they been each contained intrinsic weaknesses. Nevertheless, in those critical months immediately following the war while Washington was still undecided as to how free the Negro was to be, these programs established a modus vivendi for the former slaves of South Carolina that sacrificed none of their hard-won freedom. At the same time, the victors were fashioning and improving the tools that they were to use to fix upon the South a relatively high standard of economic freedom for the Negro.

Before the war, the white population, North as well as South, had serious doubts whether or not the mass of slaves—if emancipated—could survive as free laborers. The Port Royal "experiment," which was in reality a bundle of experiments, had been designed in part as a test which would prove that a large mass of the least "civilized" slaves in the South could be re-educated to support themselves in a free economy. The results of the experiment in 1862 were inconclusive. In the following year, the Philbrick group set out to make the test under carefully controlled conditions. "Negro labor has got to be employed," explained Philbrick on the eve of launching his venture, "because it is profitable; and it has got to come into the market like everything else, subject to the supply and demand which may arise for all kinds of enterprises in which it chances to be employed." In brief: "We want first to prove that it is profitable, and then it will take care of itself."[14] Needless to say, it was profitable; a fact that Philbrick took great care to publicize throughout the North at the end of the year. By the close of the war, few informed Northerners had any doubts of the Negro's ability to survive in a free economy.

Southern opinion on the subject was by no means so unanimous. The Northern idea that necessity would compel the Negroes to labor only drew from the average Southerner the retort that "You can't do that way with niggers."[15] Some white Carolinians were convinced that

13. MS Contract, July 6, 1865, A. H. Boykin Papers.

14. Elizabeth W. Pearson (ed.), *Letters from Port Royal, 1862–1868* (Boston, 1906), pp. 220–21.

15. J[ohn] T[ownsend] Trowbridge, *The South, a tour of its Battle Fields and Ruined Cities, a journey through the desolated States, and talks with the people, etc.* (Hartford, 1866), p. 573.

nothing less stringent than slavery would keep the Negroes at labor; virtually all believed that some system of compulsion would be necessary. "We are in a transition to something better or worse," wrote one thoughtful Charlestonian early in the summer of 1865, "and I fear the latter very much, unless some system of labour is organized by which the negroes are compelled to work."[16]

In spite of their misgivings, most white Southerners frankly recognized the end of slavery, and many entered readily and in good faith into the "experiment" in free labor. "The institution of Slavery is I think with a few exceptions considered a thing past," wrote a low-country planter in August, 1865, "and the convention to meet in September next will pass an act to prohibit it for the future."[17] Some ex-slaveholders welcomed the end of the peculiar institution. A. L. Taveau, once a rice planter and a lesser light among the proslavery literati, before the war had believed "like a great many others" that slavery "was necessary to our welfare if not our existence," and that "these people were content, happy, and attached to their masters." The behavior of the Negroes during the war in deserting their masters "in the moment of his need," flocking "in herds to an Enemy whom they knew *not,*" and leaving "their, perhaps, really good Master whom they *did* know from infancy," led him, however, to conclude that "the Negro for forty years" had "been looking for the Man of Universal Freedom," and that he, Taveau, would not restore slavery if he could.[18] A few recent slaveholders regarded free Negro labor as an opportunity for unprecedented prosperity. "We will be better off, & be able to plant more successfully than we have ever yet," predicted a Cooper River grower in July, 1865, anticipating with unfeigned glee the prospect of himself being free of "old idle lazy negroes . . ." The same planter appeared to be not only willing, but eager to contract with some of his late bondsmen, signing an agreement for 1866 in September, 1865, and for 1867 in November, 1866.[19]

16. H. W. Ravenel to A. L. Taveau, June 27, 1865, A. L. Taveau Papers. See also: William Hill to his brother, September 8, 1865, William Hill Papers.

17. R. A. Pringle to W. R. Johnson, August 19, 1865, R. A. Pringle Papers. For evidence that such attitudes were common, see: *The Nation,* I, No. 4 (July 27, 1865), 106.

18. A. L. Taveau to William Aiken, April 24, 1865 (a draft), A. L. Taveau Papers. Taveau wrote several revisions of this letter, one of which appeared in the *New York Tribune,* June 10, 1865, under the title: "A Voice from South Carolina."

19. [—. —.] Deas to his daughter, July 15, 1865; MS Contracts, September 7, 1865, November 3, 1866, [—. —.] Deas Papers.

At the opposite extreme, however, there was a highly influential minority composed of former slaveholders who believed that the institution of slavery might, after all, be preserved and the Negro thus compelled to continue his labors. Warming under the increasing favor shown by the new President, Andrew Johnson, toward the "natural ruling element" in the South, these men were much encouraged in their proslavery stand. In April, even before the final capitulation of the Confederacy, lowcountry politicians journeyed to Washington and conversed with the President. They were pleased to learn that his manner was not at all hostile as the northern press had led them to expect. On the contrary, Johnson received them with gracious cordiality, and when they departed Southern gentlemen understood that their restoration to civil power would not long be delayed. While Johnson's provisional governor, Benjamin F. Perry, prepared South Carolina for readmission to the Union via a convention of the people scheduled for September, this postwar proslavery party gained strength. In July, an old resident of Colleton District estimated its power at the grass-roots level in his community. There was a conflict, he observed, between "the rich land owners formerly slave owners," many of whom still held "to the idea that slavery may yet be saved to them," and "the great jealousy of the poor" who "seem determined that it should not, even tho they butcher the whole race." "I ought not to say that such a spirit is general," he cautioned, "but it does exist, to what extent is not easily ascertained."[20] Even though their Presidential pardons committed them to recognize the abolition of slavery, some delegates-elect to the coming convention began to agitate for its preservation. Secession Governor Francis W. Pickens, one of the delegates who had accepted both his pardon and abolition in good faith, was alarmed by the resurgence of proslavery sentiment in his native district of Edgefield. "I found our people influenced by men taking the ground that slavery was not & could not be abolished, & swearing they would never submit to it &c," he warned Perry early in September.[21] Across the state in Chester, James Hemphill, a well-informed and highly astute political observer (as well as a delegate to the convention), saw disaster in the new proslavery movement. Recently returned from Washington where he had found "a strong party . . . pressing negro suffrage," Hemphill feared that the Negro party might "prove too powerful for President

20. John W. Rutledge to "Colonel," July 9, 1865, B. F. Perry Papers.
21. To B. F. Perry, September 7, 1865, B. F. Perry Papers.

Johnson and his friends, particularly if there is any disposition here to hold on to the peculiar institution, as some are inclined."[22]

Actually, the Convention of 1865 made quick work of the slavery issue. Perry pointed the way by declaring to the Convention that abolition was the price of readmission to the Union. A few delegates tried to eschew the question; a few others tried to word the provision to show elaborately that they acceded to emancipation only under duress. The large majority, however, voted for this simple statement: "The slaves in South Carolina having been emancipated by the action of the United States authorities, neither slavery nor involuntary servitude . . . shall ever be re-established in this State." Only eight delegates, led by A. P. Aldrich of Barnwell, stood against the provision.[23]

Having recognized the demise of slavery, the Convention turned to deal with the problem of regulating social, economic, and legal relations between Negroes and whites. It empowered the governor to appoint two commissioners to advise the next legislature on what changes in the laws were necessary to make them conform to the new constitution, and "especially to prepare and submit a Code for the regulation of labor, and the protection and government of the Colored Population of the State . . ."[24] Shortly thereafter, Perry appointed David L. Wardlaw and Armisted Burt, both of Abbeville, commissioners for this task. Apparently, Burt assumed responsibility for drafting the social and economic provisions of the Code, while Wardlaw dealt with the machinery of enforcement.

It was ironic that the so-called "Black Code" in South Carolina, one of those measures that the Radicals exhibited so conspicuously in displaying an unrepentent South still unwilling to do justice to the Negro, was actually designed as a system for the protection of the Negro To some extent, the Code was a concession to outside pressures, an initial payment on the price of readmission into the councils of the nation. "The President wishes to see that protection has been afforded or guaranteed to the freemen before the military authorities are removed," wrote Perry to Burt in mid-October, urging the latter to rush his draft of the Code to completion. "Congress will require it before our Representatives are allowed to take their seats in the Body," he added.[25] Yet, in every important way, the Code was purely a southern

22. To W. R. Hemphill, September 11, 1865, Hemphill Papers.

23. *Journal of the Convention of the People of South Carolina* (Columbia, 1865), pp. 11, 51–52.

24. *Ibid.*, p. 166.

25. B. F. Perry to A. L. Burt, October 15, 1865 (copy), B. F. Perry Papers.

document. "Protection for the Negro" in Washington, or Boston, or Topeka meant protection in his natural and, occasionally, in his civil and political rights. In Abbeville, Greenville, and, indeed, in South Carolina as a whole, protection for the Negro meant protection from himself, from his own inherent inadequacies. The Code, from the point of view of the "best" of the Carolina whites, was designed to provide, primarily, this latter form of protection. The problem was not simply one of semantics, but of fundamentally different racial philosophies. Whatever their racial likes or dislikes, most Northerners seemingly thought that the Negro was potentially a man like any other man except for the color of his skin. Perry stated one version of the southern view a year later: "If all the children in New York City were turned loose to provide for themselves, how many would live prosper and do well. The negroes are as improvident as children, and require the guardian protection of some one almost as much as they do."[26] Anyone who sought to enlarge the freedom of the Negro was liable to criticism as an enemy of the Negro, much as one who sought to place a child beyond the protection of its parents. Those who sought to treat the child more strictly might also be its enemies; but, as everyone knew, laxity, not severity, was the common error of the fond parent and more to be guarded against.

Paternalism, that best side of slavery, thus persisted in the Code and secured widespread endorsement. Armisted Burt personified the paternal tradition. "Tell all the Servants 'Howdy' for me, and write me about them," ran a typically thoughtful addendum to a letter to his wife in 1866.[27] In the minds of such men, there was no doubt that theirs was the wise, humane solution to the problem of race relations. Even after the Code had failed, Burt predicted that the Negroes "will soon find that the Southern people are their best friends."[28] Yet, paternalism did not mean that its adherents would yield one iota of their dominance. Burt, himself, in the state Democratic Convention in Columbia in August, 1868, voiced this sentiment when he urged his friends to fight for possession "of this country which was discovered by the white man, settled by the white man, made illustrious by the white man, and must continue to be the white man's Country. [Applause.]"[29]

Under such circumstances, it was hardly surprising that the Code

26. *New York Times,* October 7, 1866, p. 2.

27. A. L. Burt to his wife, February 14, 1866, A. L. Burt Papers. See also: A. L. Burt to his wife, February 22, April 1, 1866, A. L. Burt Papers.

28. *Ibid.,* July 2, 1866.

29. *Intelligencer* (Anderson), August 19, 1868.

presented to a special session of the legislature early in November prescribed in elaborate detail for the social, economic, and legal subordination of the Negro. In accordance with Perry's suggestions, Burt included provisions allowing employers to impose upon their employees "a deduction of wages" as a punishment for idleness and "neglect of duty &c"; requiring husbands "to work for the support of their families & not be allowed to leave them under any circumstances"; and ordering each family of Negroes "to support the old and helpless members."[30] In the economic sphere, Negro laborers of all classes were, in essence, forced to fix themselves to a "master." Desertion without good cause would result in the deserter's being ruled a vagrant and bound to serve a term with a master assigned by a jury of three freeholders. On the other hand, the conditions of labor were carefully stipulated, and laborers wrongfully discharged were entitled to collect wages for the entire contract period. As provided in the new Constitution (1865), district courts were established to function much as the public guardians of the Negroes.

The Code, in the form of four separate laws, was enacted late in November, 1865, during the regular session of the legislature. It was not passed easily and with little discussion as historians have previously maintained, however; the legislature seethed with dissension on this issue.

The sharpest criticism came from those who did not think the Code was severe enough. This element represented planters and leaders of the heavily Negro populated districts and the persisting proslavery party. Typical of the thinking of this group was that of one low-country planter who, in August, had envisioned the necessity of a Spartan-like system in which the whole white community would be mobilized to control the Negroes: "As for making the negroes work under the present state of affairs it seems to me a waste of time and energy. . . . No sheriff & Posse or Patrol, under civil rule will suit our wants. We must have mounted Infantry that the freedmen know distinctly that they succeed the Yankees to enforce whatever regulations we can make."[31] Edmund Rhett, once a "fire-eater" of the first rank and still an enthusiast for slavery, wrote to Burt in October while the Code was still unfinished, urging stringent regulations. Every citizen

30. B. F. Perry to A. L. Burt, October 15, 1865 (copy), B. F. Perry Papers (Duke); *Statutes of the State of South Carolina,* II, 269–85. Cited hereinafter as *Statutes at Large.*

31. E. P. Millikey to R. H. Gourdin, August 14, 1865, R. H. Gourdin Papers.

of the state, he lectured Burt, must have recognized that abolition "is unwise, injurious, and dangerous to our whole system, pecuniary and social." But, since it had been effected by force of arms, "it should to the utmost extent practicable be limited, controlled, and surrounded with such safe guards, as will make the change as slight as possible both to the white man and to the negro, the planter and the workman, the capitalist and the laborer." In other words, "the general interest both of the white man and of the negroes requires that he should be kept as near to the condition of slavery as possible, and as far from the condition of the white man as is practicable. . . . We must face the question," he concluded, "negroes must be made to work, or else cotton and rice must cease to be raised for export." To attain these ends, Rhett proposed a four-part program: Negroes and "their posterity" would be prohibited from acquiring *"Real Estate."* Each Negro would be required to have a fixed domicile, and those who deserted their places without the express approval of the authorities would be "taken up and put to hard labor upon public works in chain gangs." A laborer who violated his contract would be "held both as a vagrant and a criminal" and bound to his masters. Finally, "considering the prejudices prevalent against whipping," employers would be given the disciplinary powers normally possessed by garrison commanders over enlisted soldiers.[32] Such sentiments were well represented in the legislature. James Hemphill, sitting in the senate just before the Code was brought onto the floors of both houses, observed that "every individual member almost can find some ground of objection," and that "many think it too indulgent of the negro . . ."[33]

An attempt to mitigate the harshness of the Code before it passed the legislature came from those more perceptive politicians who were correctly reading the signals from the North. Even Rhett, who thought it entirely possible to enact the laws he recommended, suggested that "this is no time to do it," because "it will only strengthen the Black Republican Party, and render the admission of the State difficult." After the reunion, however, "I believe there will be little difficulty," he indicated, because "the administration will support us."[34] Rhett was something less than sincere in his public expressions; yet, in exchange for the return of political power to themselves, the mitigation party

32. Edmund Rhett to A. L. Burt, October 14, 1865, A. L. Burt Papers.

33. To W. R. Hemphill, November 7, 1865, Hemphill Papers. See also: *The Nation*, II, No. 29 (January 18, 1866), 75.

34. To A. L. Burt, October 14, 1865, A. L. Burt Papers.

candidly sought to satisfy the demands of the North on behalf of the
Negro. During September and October, when their confidence in
success was at a peak, this was the core of their strategy, and the approach was not without support among important elements of the white
population. "Unless you want to bring the north down on us," James
Chesnut had warned the state senator from Kershaw District as he
departed for Columbia, "repeal all laws enacted for negroes and leave
the emancipated negro and the white man on the same footing before
the law."[35]

The legislature had hardly assembled, however, before it became
apparent to the mitigationists that the great mass of white South Carolinians and most of their representatives would concede to the Negro
little more freedom than that contained in the version of the Code
presented by Burt, Wardlaw, and Perry. Noting the intransigence of
many of their constituents and the increasing insistence from the North
that its demands be met, the mitigationists became progressively less
sanguine. A week after the session began, James Hemphill, surveying
the political landscape from the vantage point of his seat in the senate,
dejectedly stated the case. "My impression is that our *Northern brethren,* who hold our fate in their hands, and who are par excellance the
negro's friends, will consider it too much a white man's law, and that
it does not sufficiently protect the freedmen against their former masters,"
he wrote in confidence to his brother. "It is a most difficult problem to
solve, and I do not believe that the great body of our people do yet
appreciate the great change that has taken place in the relations between the races."[36]

Even as the Code passed through the legislature, a cloud of futility
settled upon the effort.[37] By December, Hemphill was convinced that
the problem was, after all, beyond solution. The labors of the legislature,
he thought, "will prove fruitless," and "the U. S. Congress will take
the whole affair of the freedmen under their special charge, and make
laws which shall give them the protection which their Northern friends
may deem necessary." The Code, he explained, "will be regarded by
them as too much of a white man's law. Many of its provisions are
scarcely compatible with a state of freedom, and it will be hard to
persuade the freedom shriekers that the American citizens of African

35. "That was our first unalterable blunder—after the war—" concluded
Mrs. Chesnut. Mary Boykin Chesnut MS Diary, notes written in 1879.
36. James Hemphill to W. R. Hemphill, November 7, 1865, Hemphill Papers.
37. *The Nation,* I, No. 25 (December 21, 1865), 780.

descent are obtaining their rights." Readmission, in the idiom of the age, had also gone up the spout. "I think there is no probability that our members of Congress will be admitted to their seats," concluded the senator, "and that we will be out in the cold for some time."[38] Hemphill would have been distressed to know how perfectly prophetic he was.

The Code excited bitter animosity among the Negro population in South Carolina and in the North at large. In Charleston, the Negro community met in Zion Church to denounce the Code and to ask Congress for relief from such measures.[39] In the North, the Code became one of the stepping stones by which the Radicals ascended to overwhelming power in Congress.

Under the very able leadership of the newly elected governor, James L. Orr, the mitigation party recovered rapidly from its defeat on the issue of the Code. In mid-December, Orr vetoed an attempt by the legislature to rewrite the patrol laws so as to use that instrument of the slave period to enforce the provisions of the Code. In a stinging message accompanying his veto, Orr lectured the legislature on the obvious fact that since "the necessity [slavery] has ceased," the patrol laws "should be ignored."[40] In the following month, Orr arranged with the newly appointed commanding general of the department in which South Carolina was included to have the Code set aside by military fiat and "all laws" made "applicable alike to all inhabitants." This adjustment was facilitated by the close personal friendship between the new commander, Major General Daniel E. Sickles, and Orr, an intimacy dating from the high times of the National Democracy in the 1850's when both had been congressmen. Sickles, although unwilling to yield any of his authority, seemed disposed to allow white South Carolinians to adjust somewhat gradually to the demands of the new society.[41]

Under the highly astute guidance of Governor Orr, an interesting and significant movement developed among the white leadership to conciliate Northern sentiment and win readmission. Orr himself sought information from other Southern governors concerning methods their

38. James Hemphill to W. R. Hemphill, December 1, 1865, Hemphill Papers.

39. *Proceedings of the Colored People's Convention of the State of South Carolina, held in Zion Church, Charleston, November, 1865* (Charleston, 1865).

40. *New York Times*, February 25, 1866, p. 1.

41. D. E. Sickles to J. L. Orr, January 11, 1866 (telegram); J. L. Orr to D. E. Sickles, January 14, 1866 (telegram); W. H. Trescot to J. L. Orr, January 14, 1866 (telegram), D. E. Sickles Papers.

states had used to deal with their Negro populations. "It will be necessary to convene the legislature of this State at an early day to modify
our legislation of December last so as to conform to the 'civil rights Act,'
and the requirements of the Freedmens Bureau," he explained to the
governor of the Old North State, "and I am very anxious to lay before
the legislature when it assembles the legislation of our contiguous sister
States."[42] The replies probably raised the eyebrows of even the conciliationists. Georgia and North Carolina sent copies of their comparatively lenient Codes; the Republican governor of Virginia rather
acidly answered that "The freedmen in Virginia, I believe, enjoy all
the Civil Rights of white persons . . ."[43] Soon, several native white
journalists and many lawyers joined in denouncing South Carolina's
Code as cumbersome and unjust, urging greater flexibility in meeting
the demands of the North. The Charleston *Courier,* for instance, by
September, 1866, was damning the Code as "impractical."[44] In mid-
August, Orr was ready to call a special session of the legislature to
adjust the laws to treat Negroes and whites equally. Informing Sickles
of his intentions, Orr was told that when this was done the civil courts
would be allowed to resume jurisdiction over cases concerning Negroes,
a power which they had been denied since the occupation.[45]

Although the current of conciliation ran swiftly at the higher levels
of leadership, it did not, apparently, run deep. In January, 1866, an
elderly planter in Union District heavily discounted the optimism of the
conciliationists. "I can see none of that silver lining to the cloud which
cheers the eye of Senator Perry and Gov Orr & other political huck-
sters," he wrote to a friend. "The nigger wont work— he (the institution) will be a free nigger as free niggers always have been— they
will worry us until we will be forced to run them off to Yankee land
for sympathy, and then will come colonization and the white man's
Government."[46] Even the very rational Senator Hemphill objected to
the special session, arguing that Orr "might let the Code rock along
until the regular session of the Legislature, when the Members would

42. J. L. Orr to J. Worth, May 22, 1866 (copy), J. L. Orr Papers.
43. C. J. Junkins to J. L. Orr, May 28, 1866; J. J. Pierpont to J. L. Orr, May
30, 1866, Freedmen File.
44. *New York Times,* May 19, p. 8; June 2, p. 2, 1866; *Courier* (Charleston),
September 7, 1866.
45. J. L. Orr to D. E. Sickles, August 9, 1866 (copy); D. E. Sickles to J. L.
Orr, August 14, 1866, Freedmen File.
46. R. I. Gage to a friend, January 14, 1866, James M. Gage Papers.

have more leisure, and be in better plight for work."[47] In its special session in September, after a protracted debate in which expediency rather than a real change in sentiment seemed to be the ruling spirit, the legislature did go far toward granting economic and legal equality to Negroes. Nevertheless, it left a ragged residue of social restrictions concerning inter-racial marriages, domestic relations, and vagrancy unchanged.[48] Shortly afterward, with an admonition that all laws were to apply equally to all citizens, Sickles restored full judicial powers to the civil courts outside of the Sea Islands.[49]

The legislature acted with obvious reluctance; yet, even as it acted, the North was raising the price of reunion. Within a few weeks after it revised the Code, the legislature, in its regular session and with Orr's approval, flatly and nearly unanimously rejected the Fourteenth Amendment. With this action, the line was drawn; South Carolina would of its own volition and without a *quid pro quo* make no further concession to Negro equality. The initiative passed again to the North. If Johnson failed in his fight with the Radicals, then South Carolina would go down with him.

The policy of conciliation did not suffice to return normal power to the white leadership in South Carolina. Yet the alliance between Southerners and the national executive resulted directly in the reversal of the land redistribution program inaugurated under Sherman's orders and in changes in personnel in key offices which long worked to the disadvantage of the Negro population.

As described in the preceding chapter, during the late summer of 1865, Saxton was seizing abandoned plantations and settling Negroes upon them as rapidly as possible. Johnson was fully aware of this situation and of the damage it imposed upon his allies in South Carolina, but it was not until mid-August that he moved to oppose it openly, and not until mid-September that he pointedly ordered Howard to issue instructions which, if strictly enforced, would virtually have nullified the land program. By these orders all lands then held by the government were to be restored if they had not been abandoned "voluntarily" in support of the rebellion or if the rebel owner had been pardoned, a requirement the President himself could easily satisfy. Johnson also

47. To W. R. Hemphill, July 4, 1866, Hemphill Papers.
48. *Courier* (Charleston), September 22, 1866; *Statutes at Large*, XII, 366^{29}–366^{30}.
49. *New York Times*, October 7, 1866, p. 1.

decided with his attorney-general that all lands not actually sold, even
if condemned by the courts, would be returned to their former owners.[50]
In the meantime, on September 3, Saxton had been ordered by the
state's military commander to seize no more abandoned property.[51]
Without land, the redistribution program was obviously doomed.

Although it is striking that South Carolina landowners made no
move until after Johnson had acted in their favor, they then moved
rapidly to take advantage of this gap in the federal front. Owners of
plantations in the lowcountry took care to establish that the lands from
which they were absent were not abandoned. Many returned to their
county seats and others appointed friends, neighbors, or, in some cases,
former slaves, as agents in charge of their estates.[52] Owners of plantations already confiscated pressed vigorously for immediate restoration
by petitioning, retaining lawyers, or asking friends to represent their
interests to the authorities.[53] In Washington, William Henry Trescot,
ubiquitous as South Carolina's diplomat in the capital and the man who
had negotiated for the surrender of federal property to the state during
the secession crisis, was made the agent of the state for the purpose of
securing both pardons and restoration. By October 15, Trescott had
reported to his employers that all confiscated lands, less those condemned for taxes in the Port Royal area during the war, had been
ordered restored by the President.[54]

Yet, the game was not to be so easily won. Saxton and Howard
moved slowly and with great reluctance in executing the President's
wishes. His order of mid-September was not published in South Carolina until September 28, and even then it contained a proviso that land
cultivated by loyal refugees or freedmen would not be restored until
the crops were harvested or suitable compensation rendered, concessions
which the owners were unwilling to make.[55] In October, a highly

50. Reid, *After the War,* p. 307; George R. Bentley, *A History of the Freedmen's Bureau* (Philadelphia, 1955), pp. 95–96.

51. Martin L. Abbott, "The Freedmen's Bureau in South Carolina, 1865-1872,"
(Unpublished Ph.D. dissertation, Emory University, 1954), p. 86.

52. R. H. Colcock to James Gregorie, October 8, 1865, Gregorie–Elliott Papers;
Marta Lockett Avary, *Dixie after the War* (New York, 1906), p. 341.

53. MS Petition, September 23, 1865; Ralph Ely to O. O. Howard, September
22, 1865, Edward L. Stoeber Papers; Louisa Gervais to J. Y. Simons, October 5,
1865, Louisa Gervais Papers; R. E. Elliott to his sister, October 15, 1865, Elliott–
Gonzales Papers.

54. B. F. Perry to A. L. Burt, October 15, 1865, B. F. Perry Papers (Duke).

55. Printed Circular issued by the Assistant Commissioner of the Freedmen's

choleric Johnson personally, orally, and explicitly ordered Howard himself to go to South Carolina to effect a settlement "mutually satisfactory" to the freedmen and the owners. Doubtless as Johnson intended, Howard interpreted this to mean that complete restoration was mandatory. On October 19, Howard, assisted by Saxton, convened a large meeting of settlers on Edisto Island and with heavy heart informed the dismayed Negroes that their lands were to be returned to the planters. Nevertheless, in the machinery for restoration which he established on the same date, Howard created still another instrument for delay. A three-man board, consisting of an owner, a settler, and a Bureau agent, was named for each island. Before reclaiming his lands, the owner had to obligate himself to give the settlers all of the crops in progress, to permit them to retain their homes as long as they would contract with him, to renew leases indefinitely, and to allow the Bureau school to continue in operation. As agent in charge of this program, Howard appointed Captain Alexander P. Ketchum, an officer in the 128th United States Colored Troops assigned to Bureau duty and a man highly sympathetic with the settlers.[56]

After Howard's departure, Saxton and Ketchum made no concessions to the demands of the owners. In November, 1865, John Berkeley Grimball complained that his friend William Aiken had been "persistent at Gen Saxton's office with no result," and that many planters whose lands had been possessed by the settlers were beginning to expect the government to buy the land at its own price and give the Negroes permanent titles.[57] Another owner thought that "The Yankees have instilled into the negroes [sic] minds the belief that the Island country which they helped to conquer belongs to them, & they throw every obstacle in the way of the planters revisiting their plantations."[58] The last allegation was not entirely true. Nevertheless, early in February, 1866, Ketchum was still firm in his refusal to endorse any application for restoration.[59]

Highly effective opposition also came from the settlers themselves,

Bureau for South Carolina and Georgia, September 28, 1865, Heyward–Ferguson Papers.

56. O. O. Howard, *Autobiography of Oliver Otis Howard* (New York, 1908), II, 237–40; Printed Form, Commissioner's Special Field Order No. 1, Charleston, October 19, 1865, Edward L. Stoeber Papers.

57. J. B. Grimball to Meta Grimball, November 15, 1865, J. B. Grimball Papers (Duke).

58. John Bachman to E. Elliott, February 1, 1866, Elliott–Gonzales Papers.

59. Trowbridge, *The South,* p. 539; Abbot, "Freedmen's Bureau," p. 94.

who strenuously, bitterly, and even violently resisted dispossession. Many settlers were ex-soldiers who found it difficult to understand how the government could now ask them to give up their homes and take employment under the same men it had urged them to fight only a few months before. One committee of settlers expressed their feelings on this matter movingly, if ungrammatically: ". . . man that have stud upon the feal of battle & have shot there master & sons now Going to ask ether one for bread or for shelter or Confortable for his wife & children sunch a thin the u st should not aught Expect a man . . ."[60] All through the islands, settlers refused to concede any degree of recognition to the claims of the planters by contracting to work for them. A Northern teacher on Wadmalaw found the settlers determined not to "hire with a Rebel."[61] In many places, the Negroes organized militarily to hold their land and to prevent recent owners from even visiting the islands. "Mr. Seabrook, owner of Fenwick Isle," J. B. Grimball reported in mid-November, "told me yesterday that the Negroes on that Island were armed and have announced their purpose to allow no white man on it, and Edisto Isle is said to be much in the same state."[62] Two weeks later another planter delayed bringing his family into the lowcountry because "the Negroes are getting on their high horse & say they intend to fight for the land, particularly on Edisto."[63]

In several instances, the persistence of the owners drove the settlers to the very brink of violence. In one case, Bureau Superintendent Swails brought two recent Rebel owners to a plantation on Wadmalaw Island. There, he was challenged by one of the settlers as to his authority for doing so in the face of Sherman's order excluding from the area all whites not in the government's service. Swails drew his revolver and declared that to be his authority. Soon there was a musket shot and Negro men swarmed down from all directions. Swails then produced a paper from Saxton, but the Negroes advised the party to leave anyway. Followed by the Negroes, the party fled to the island's village, Rockville, where another superintendent assigned to the island talked them out of violence. One of the settlers who had surrounded the party subsequently told a Northern teacher that he had been wounded

60. Ames, *From a New England Woman's Diary in 1865,* p. 102.
61. Martha Schofield MS Diary, entry for December 6, 1865.
62. J. B. Grimball to his wife, November 15, 1865, J. B. Grimball Papers (Duke).
63. T. R. S. Elliott to his wife, November 28, 1865, T. R. S. Elliott Papers.

nine times while he was in the army and would be wounded nine times again before he would submit to a Rebel. "Oh, he says," quoted the teacher, "it was shaking the pistol in the mans face that has made us come here, such things kill us, if they had treated us as men we would not have harmed them—." "Ah," said another settler, "if dey com wid him [Swails], we'll not harm em, but if dey land here alone, we hab musket dat neber lie."[64]

In Washington, the owners were hardly more successful. In the first draft of a bill to extend the life of the Freedmen's Bureau, Howard secured the inclusion of a provision certifying the Sherman grants. Nevertheless, when passed in its final form on February 19, 1866, the bill validated the titles for three years only. In addition, the possibility of a general restoration was conceded by a stipulation declaring that any settlers dispossessed by restoration would be given an opportunity to buy or rent government lands elsewhere, presumably on the plantations confiscated for taxes.[65] Johnson's veto of the bill again left the issue unsettled. On the last day of February, 1866, Trescot complained to Governor Orr that Howard had previously promised to issue a comprehensive order for restoring the Sherman lands, but that he then claimed not to have the power to do so. Trescot was currently pressing the President for action and, sensing where the real difficulty lay, simultaneously winning friends in Congress. "I hired one or two of the radical members of the Committee," he reported, referring to the Committee of Ways and Means which was then considering the question of the tax lands, and had also secured from "general Garfield of Indiana, who is a radical," a promise to introduce a motion for the appointment of a subcommittee to study the restoration question.[66]

The impasse in Washington persisted through the winter and spring of 1866, but vital changes occurred in South Carolina that resulted in the practical dispossession of the Sherman settlers. Early in 1866, the relatively impartial commander of the occupation forces in South Carolina was relieved by the highly political Major General Daniel Sickles. Sickles would soon join the Radicals, but in the winter of 1866, he was still watching for a prevailing political wind and was not averse to promoting favor in both camps. Also, early in February, Rufus B. Saxton was relieved as the Bureau's assistant commissioner in South

64. Martha Schofield MS Diary, entry for January 3, 1866.
65. Bentley, *Freedmen's Bureau,* pp. 116, 118.
66. W. H. Trescot to J. L. Orr, February 28, 1866, Freedmen File. Actually, Garfield was from Ohio.

Carolina on the pretext that the army was being demobilized and
major generals of volunteers were no longer needed. Probably, Saxton
was dismissed at Johnson's insistence.[67] Saxton was replaced by Robert
K. Scott, also a major general of volunteers and a soldier of no fortune.
In his forties at the end of the war, he had led a varied and adventurous
life. As a young man, he had gone from Pennsylvania to the California gold fields. Afterward, he filibustered in Mexico and South
America, and, finally, returned to settle in Napoleon, Ohio. There, he
was moderately successful as a physician, merchant, and realtor. During
the war, he raised a regiment and ultimately commanded a brigade.
Before the end of the war, however, he was captured and brought to
Charleston as a prisoner. After his liberation, he was breveted a major
general. Politically, Scott was an undoubted Radical, but his radicalism
was less blatant than Saxton's, and he was markedly less sympathetic to
the Negroes. Within a month after Saxton's relief, Alexander Ketchum,
the man whom Howard had chosen to handle the restoration problem
on the Islands, was also discharged, allegedly because the Negro regiment upon which his commission rested was being disbanded.[68]

During the winter of 1866, Sickles simply used his administrative
power to do what Johnson and the owners had been unable to do by
judicial and legal means. First, he refused to recognize any claim for
which the settler did not have a warrant properly issued and signed by
Saxton himself precisely as Sherman had stipulated in his orders.
Since Saxton had urged the freedmen to settle first and leave the details until later, only about five thousand such warrants had been distributed. Further, many of these five thousand title holders had settled
on lands other than those described in their warrants. The refusal of
the military to recognize any papers which were in any degree erroneous
resulted, finally, in only 1,565 titles (representing some 63,000 acres),
being validated.[69] By the same order that disallowed the Negro Code,
Sickles also directed freedmen everywhere in the state to contract for
the coming year or to leave their places. In February, squads of soldiers
went through the plantations forcing those settlers without valid claims
either to contract with the owners or leave. Needless to say, the Negroes
concerned were greatly distressed by this display of steel by an army
in which many of them had fought. One northern teacher on John's
Island found that attendence in her school was diminishing because

67. Bentley, *Freedmen's Bureau,* p. 107.
68. Abbot, "Freedmen's Bureau," p. 95.
69. *Ibid.,* pp. 98–99.

"the people [were] so upset about contracting & having to leave—"[70] Scott protested this use of force but was quickly squelched by the imperious Sickles.[71] Bowing to the inevitable, Scott attempted to re-locate scattered settlers on the plantations where valid titles were most numerous; but, again, his efforts proved futile. He then concentrated on securing equitable contracts for the dispossessed and pressing the freedmen to labor faithfully. In this, he was largely successful and, by late spring, was enjoying the plaudits of the planters for his work.[72]

The Bureau bill which Congress passed over the President's veto on July 16, 1866, belatedly provided that holders of valid titles to Sherman lands were to be given leases on twenty-acre plots on tax lands in the Port Royal area with options to buy within six years.[73] Early in 1867, Scott relocated those settlers who chose to move.[74] The exchange was a poor bargain for the dispossessed, however, because virtually all the tax lands still held by the government had been sadly depleted by speculating lessees. By the end of the year, 1,980 Negro families, in-cluding those who had purchased tax lands during and immediately after the war, were settled on some 19,000 acres in the vicinity of Beau-fort.[75] The average plot was hardly large enough to furnish its owners a bare subsistence.

In November, 1868, the Bureau still held abandoned lands in South Carolina amounting to about seventy-five thousand acres. The owners of this land were not pressing the government for restoration; indeed, by 1868, restoration could be effected simply upon the application of the owner. Presumably, this acreage could have been divided into farms and allotted to freedmen. Yet, at the end of the year, the Bureau ordered this property either restored or summarily dropped, much as if its possession was an embarrassment to the government.[76] That Congress did not settle Negroes upon these lands suggests that, ulti-mately, even the Radical majority in Congress deliberately chose not to

70. Martha Schofield MS Diary, entry for February 21, 1866. See also: Ames, *From a New England Woman's Diary in 1865*, pp. 122–23.

71. Abbot, "Freedmen's Bureau," pp. 95–96; Bentley, *Freedmen's Bureau*, pp. 123–34.

72. *New York Times*, May 31, p. 5; June 11, p. 8, 1866; Abbot, "Freedmen's Bureau," p. 96.

73. *Ibid.*, p. 99.

74. Scott's Circular No. 2, dated January 9, 1867, was reprinted in the *New York Times*, January 27, 1867.

75. Abbot, "Freedmen's Bureau," p. 99.

76. *Ibid.*, pp. 100–1.

offer any further special assistance to Negroes aspiring to become land-owners. Perhaps, after all, both Congress and the North at large agreed with the editor of the *Nation* who stated in May, 1867, that land had to be earned rather than given as some Radical leaders desired.[77]

The tax lands were affected by the same currents that moved the history of the Sherman grants. Immediately after the war, the rebel owners of these plantations began to petition for the return of their estates. They found, however, that much of the land had already been sold. Moreover, a large part of the remainder was to be sold exclusively to freedmen on December 6, 1865. The previous owners then entered a prolonged struggle to regain their lands through legal and political action.[78] By the end of 1866, most of the land was sold, having been set aside in ten- and twenty-acre plots first for discharged Negro soldiers, and, subsequently, opened to all freedmen at $1.50 an acre. Badly used "school farms" found few buyers on the open market at $10.00 an acre.[79] Lands retained by the government were rented to freedmen at the nominal rate of $1.00 an acre per year. In 1871, Congress directed that all unsold lands be returned to their former owners upon payment of the taxes due and a ten-dollar penalty. No doubt, much of this was restored. In 1874, Myrtle Bank on Hilton Head was repossessed by its ante-bellum owner under this law. Thus, an estate worth perhaps $10,000 was regained for the payment of back taxes and penalties to the amount of $318.18. Those plantations which had already been sold were still subject to litigation, and many suits were instituted for their return. Eventually, however, the courts reinstated only those owners who had been minors during the war.[80]

In the winter of 1866, national authorities of all political complexions set out in earnest to re-educate Southerners of both races in the "natural laws" of economics as defined by the North. Officials viewed the problem as twofold. On one hand, employers had to be taught to treat their Negro employees humanely and to pay them a wage suffi-

77. *The Nation,* II, No. 46 (May 16, 1866), 394–95.
78. Richard De Treville to "Madam" (probably Emily Elliott, who had owned Myrtle Bank and Grove plantations on Hilton Head), January—, 1866, Elliott–Gonzales Papers.
79. *New York Times,* January 7, 1867, p. 1.
80. William Elliott to Emily Elliott, February 3, September 11, 1869; November 1, 1872; April 15, 1873; July 24, 1874; February 17, 1877, Elliott–Gonzales Papers.

cient for subsistence. On the other hand, Negroes had to be instructed in the necessity of constant and assiduous labor. Through their power to supervise the negotiation and execution of contracts between freedmen and their employers, the authorities sought to achieve these objectives.

Whites learned their lessons rather rapidly. At first, many employers contracted with Negroes without really being convinced that such was possible. One Cooper River planter admitted early in 1866 that Scott "seemed desirous of doing his duty both to employer and employees in the spirit of justice to both as far as he was competent." Yet, he lamented, "There lies the difficulty. The fairest minded of all these officials seems not to be able [to] comprehend the difference between the 'Nigger' freedman and the white northern laborer."[81] Authorities occasionally threatened to use force against employers. During the winter of 1866, the planters of Barnwell and Edgefield districts organized to keep wages of freedmen depressed to a level that threatened the very subsistence of their workers. Thereupon, Sickles announced his intention of removing the entire Negro population from these districts to areas where their labor was in demand and to maintain them by a special tax on the evacuated districts until they became self-supporting. Such a policy was beneficial to the freedmen, but exasperating to the whites. "Is not it shocking & inhuman," exclaimed Francis W. Pickens of Edgefield, who, incidentally, had just signed a very generous contract with his own 143 freedmen.[82] More often, officers of the occupation resorted to stern admonitions. Typical of these was a circular issued by Scott in January, 1868, in which he deplored the low wages which some planters were offering and advised the freedmen to contract only with planters of proved integrity. The planters, for their part, were advised to offer "liberal and fair contracts," and to pay money wages at the end of the season at a rate which they could afford and still profit, and upon which the laborer could support himself and his family.[83]

Some employers remained skeptical; most rapidly came to see large advantages for themselves in free labor. A few even grew enthusiastic after trying the system for several months. "The Freedmen are not sick these days," exulted a Chester District planter in August,

81. William Burney to T. B. Ferguson, February 1, 1866, Heyward–Ferguson Papers.
82. F. W. Pickens to J. L. Orr, February 16, 1866, Freedmen File.
83. Reprinted in the *New York Times,* January 6, 1868.

1866. "The Dr. has not been sent for this year, a remarkable thing for this Plantation that is A Happy change wrought by Emancipation. Another great relief to me is the absence of that old & familiar demand of, 'A piece of meat if you please.' "[84] That this idea had wide appeal among ex-masters was evident in the popularity of a parody on Poe which concluded: "But my victuals to the 'fly trap' of that nigger by my door, Shall be lifted, Nevermore!"[85]

Though they had previously regarded Northerners as interlopers and subsequently condemned military and Bureau officers as advanced agents of political oppression, soon after Sickles and Scott assumed offices in South Carolina many whites came to regard the soldiers and the Bureau rather favorably. In mid-January, Ralph Elliott, in Charleston maneuvering to resume planting operations, gleefully anticipated Saxton's removal. After the event occurred, he happily reported to his sister that Bureau rations were available for employees and, "as Sickles says the nigger must work," Northern capital was again to be had. Back on the land in Beaufort District in the second week in February, Elliott pronounced the military "now very helpful."[86] Armisted Burt, co-author of the Black Code, in Charleston on the date Saxton was relieved, observed that the Yankees intended to have the Negroes either contract or put to hard labor on public works. "I have no doubt the Yankees will manage them," gloated the man whose system for managing Negro labor had been nullified.[87]

The mass of Negroes learned their economic lessons more slowly than the whites, but it was not for lack of instruction. The message of the North to the freedmen of South Carolina was always the same, whether uttered by Chase, Garrison, Gillmore, or Sickles, by Saxton, Scott, Howard, or the lowliest of Bureau officers, or by Northern teachers, preachers, or businessmen. The theme constantly sounded was that only by unrelenting, hard labor could the Negro survive. Nevertheless, the coming of the new year, 1866, saw many freedmen unwilling to enter into labor contracts. "I have seen all the planters from Combahee, Ashepoo, Pon Pon et cet," a Beaufort area planter wrote to his mother from Charleston on January 13, 1866, "not one has yet been able to make the negroes contract . . ."[88]

84. R. N. Hemphill to W. R. Hemphill, August 11, 1866, Hemphill Papers.
85. Intelligencer (Anderson), November 30, 1865.
86. R. E. Elliott to his mother, January 13, 1866; R. E. Elliott to his sister, January 28, February 8, 1866; Elliott–Gonzales Papers.
87. A. L. Burt to his wife, January 29, 1866, A. L. Burt Papers.
88. R. E. Elliott to his mother, January 13, 1866, Elliott–Gonzales Papers.

A variety of reasons motivated this behavior. Many freedmen were, of course, displeased with the specific terms of contract offered by employers. Still, less explicit, more pervasive attitudes lay behind their refusal. One of these was suggested by a Chester District planter who found that "some & perhaps all of my people are determined to work under no white man & as I consider myself as belonging to that class I can't expect them to stay."[89] T. B. Ferguson, the manager of a Cooper River plantation, heard the same sentiments couched in stronger terms when he called his laboring force together early in January, 1866, and asked them (in the presence of a noncommissioned Union Army officer) if they would contract and get to work. They would not work, they replied, "for any rebel son-of-a-bitch." Some of their number then addressed the crowd and elicited general approval of the statement that "the Yankees had placed them there and there they would stay if they had to fight for it."[90]

The strongest and most enduring reason why Negroes refused to contract during the three-year period of military occupation was their hope for a land division and the common impression among them that any negotiations with their late masters might jeopardize their chances for success. This obstacle was most formidable during the fall of 1865 and the following winter. A Northern correspondent, after traveling through the lowcountry and the middle districts in October, November, and December, 1865, noted that freedmen everywhere were hoping for a division of the land and were not disposed to contract. On one plantation in Marion District, he observed that the Negroes would not contract even for a half of the crop, preferring to wait on the settlement of the land issue. "They tell what they'll do at Columby," said one, "and they tell another thing over to headquarters, and I goes for waitin' anyhow."[91] The white community quickly recognized a relationship between land division and a reluctance to contract and urged restoration of confiscated lands as the only solution. "The freedmen on the coast will not contract at all because they expect to get the lands and those in the interior contract only reluctantly," Governor Orr wrote to the President early in 1866, pointing out that experience had proved that "complete restoration will restore complete harmony."[92]

89. R. N. Hemphill to W. R. Hemphill, December 13, 1865, Hemphill Papers.

90. Captain H. S. Hawkins to the Assistant Adjutant General, January 5, 1866, Heyward–Ferguson Papers.

91. *The Nation,* I, No. 21 (November 23, 1865), 651; II, No. 27 (January 4, 1866), 48.

92. *New York Times,* February 5, 1866, p. 2.

During and after 1866, both the Bureau and the military worked
hard to convince the Negroes that there was to be no general division of
the land under the auspices of the government. Nevertheless, even in
areas which never experienced tax sales or Sherman grants, the hopes of
the freedmen died hard, and often violently. In Columbia in October,
1865, Grace B. Elmore noted in her diary that her brother had just arrived
from Fairfield District where a plot had been discovered among the
plantation Negroes "to rise and kill all the whites and take their land."[93]
Similarly, in January, 1866, a Charlestonian wrote to a friend that money
was scarce because of "the unsettled state of affairs here for the negroes
almost unanimously refuse to leave these plantations of which they
have possession." This was not only true of the Sherman grants, for,
as he noted, "Burr Pringle's negroes on Santee refused to contract
with him & being told they have to leave the plantations have burnt
down his house & have entrenched themselves on the place."[94]

As the 1867 agricultural season approached, another wave of unrest
swept through the Negro population. In December, 1866, about three
hundred armed Negroes met on a plantation about nine miles south of
Kingstree. By the report of white witnesses, they organized themselves
into six military companies and paraded back and forth. Speeches were
made and one Negro declared that "the D——d rebels have had their
way long enough, now they would have theirs." Any Negro who refused to join the conspiracy was to be killed, and one white resident
in the area reported, "It was rumored that they said they would have
land at all hazard."[95]

Again, early in 1868, while the all-Republican Constitutional Convention was sitting in Charleston, observers noted "a gradually growing
sentiment on the part of the freed people throughout the State" not to
contract until they saw that "something was decided in their favor by
the sitting of the Convention." Scott responded by requesting an official
pronouncement on the subject from the Convention itself.[96] That body
answered with a resolution stating unequivocally that it had no lands
at its disposal; "that no act of confiscation has been passed by the Congress of the United States, and it is the belief of this Convention that

93. MS Diary, entry for October 1, 1865.
94. John Colcock to James Gregorie, January——, 1866, Gregorie–Elliott Papers.
See also: Avary, *Dixie after the War,* pp. 341–45.
95. W. J. B. Cooper to a friend, December 11, 1866; S. W. Maurice and other
citizens to J. L. Orr, December 11, 1866, Freedmen File.
96. *New York Times,* January 29, 1868, p. 2.

there never will be, and the only manner by which any land can be obtained by the landless will be to purchase it."[97] Subsequent developments in the Convention suggested that the delegates were not entirely candid in this pronouncement, but apparently it did have the effect Scott desired.

It was inconceivable that the government would long allow the Negroes to remain unproductive. Even under Gillmore and Saxton authorities had always urged laborers to agree to reasonable contracts with employers. General Saxton himself attended a mass meeting of freedmen and employers in Sumter in December, 1865, to construct a model contract for agricultural laborers. In the following month, the garrison commander in Camden held a similar meeting in which the government's desires were explained.[98] Under Sickles and Scott, the same program was pressed even more vigorously.

The means employed by authorities to overcome the reluctance of freedmen to contract were various and not entirely coercive as Southern whites preferred to believe. The Bureau did much, positively, to induce Negroes to contract by providing transportation for freedmen to the plantations where they were to labor and by advancing them rations until their crops were harvested. In addition, the Bureau operated a mass employment office. A planter in the vicinity of Pocotaligo, after searching in vain for a laboring force, wrote to his wife early in February, 1866, that "Major Delaney (the negro) says he can furnish 200 hands or more & I will know the fact this evening as Willie will be here." On the next day, Willie returned and reported that Scott had indeed promised to send two hundred Negroes by a steamer and would advance the provisions necessary for making the crop.[99] Finally, as described earlier, the government was not unmindful of the obligation of the planters to pay their employees a fair wage.

When freedmen evinced a persistent reluctance to contract, persuasion was an obvious first resort of federal agents. In March, 1866, a Combahee planter spent a day and a half explaining to his former slaves the advantages of contracting but found they would not agree to work on Saturdays. In desperation, he obtained a letter from the

97. *Ibid.,* February 11, 1868, p. 5.

98. "D. G. M." to his mother, December 25, 1865, Williams–Chesnut–Manning Papers; Thomas J. Kirkland and Robert M. Kennedy, *Historic Camden* (Columbia, 1926), p. 198, quoting the *Camden Journal.*

99. T. R. S. Elliott to his wife, February 1, 1866, T. R. S. Elliott Papers. See also: Emma E. Holmes MS Diary, entry for February 15, 1866.

Bureau officer in the area advising the Negroes to contract to work the full six-day week, to which the freedmen then agreed.[100] The best persuasive efforts of the Bureau's agents did not always avail, however. In 1868, when a lowcountry planter leased a plantation, the Negroes told him they "dont want to see him on the place." He exhibited his proposed contract bearing Scott's personal endorsement. Still the Negroes refused, saying they would not work every day as prescribed by the contract, but only a day and a half or two days in the week.[101]

In the face of such intransigence, some agents simply by-passed the opposition of the freedmen. For instance, a planter in Chester District, "greatly harrassed with the Freedmen," had "endeavored to get them to sign a contract & have offered the 4th of the corn &c. the customary amt they are perfectly indignant, & will have their Rights or *nothing*." He expected, however, to take the proposed contract to the Bureau agent in the village "& he has promised to sign for them."[102] In cases of unyielding resistance, officials often resorted to varying degrees of coercion to force freedmen to contract. Ceasing to pass out Bureau rations to those not engaged to an employer was an obvious and highly effective device which Scott applied in some extreme cases soon after taking office.[103] In January, 1868, Scott applied this method throughout the state.[104]

When all else failed, authorities left no doubt in the minds of the freedmen that they would use force to eject them from plantations where they refused either to leave or to contract for the coming year. In 1866, for instance, a number of Negro laborers were marched off the premises of W. M. Burney's Cooper River plantation when they persisted in their refusal to contract.[105] In January, 1867, Scott, noting that many Negroes had not contracted (especially on the Sea Islands and along the Santee River) published his intention to remove all who refused to conclude agreements and to afford those removed none of the means of relief at his command.[106] Shortly afterward, a group of erstwhile

100. William Elliott to his mother, March 25, 1866, Elliott–Gonzales Papers.
101. "C. G. S." to "Mary" (probably Mary Elliott Johnston), March 2, 1868, Elliott–Gonzales Papers.
102. R. N. Hemphill to W. R. Hemphill, December 13, 1865, Hemphill Papers.
103. William Elliott to his mother, March 25, 1866, Elliott–Gonzales Papers.
104. *New York Times,* January 20, 1868, p. 2.
105. T. M. Montell to Lt. James Stann, November 21, 1865; H. S. Hawkins to Assistant Adjutant General, January 5, 1866; W. M. Burney to T. B. Ferguson, February 1, 1866, Heyward–Ferguson Papers.
106. *New York Times,* January 27, 1867, p. 6.

settlers on a plantation near Savannah declined to renew their contract with the planter, alleging him to be unfair. They also refused to move, apparently acting upon the advice of a Negro lawyer residing in the vicinity. The Bureau first showed its teeth when a Bureau agent appeared on the plantation with five soldiers. The Negroes remained adamant. The agent retired and returned with fifty soldiers. The Negroes then "crowded together in solid phalanx and swore more furiously than before that they would die where they stood before they would surrender their claims to the land." Insults led to leveled guns on both sides. One of the Negroes wearing a sword and belt shouted, "fall in guards," and a company of Negroes fell into ranks. The agent restrained his soldiers with difficulty and finally managed to withdraw his force.[107] The Negroes could not, however, stand against the army.

Having induced employers and employees to contract, the authorities of the occupation also assumed responsibility for seeing that the contracts were fulfilled, again influencing the freedmen with devices which they had used to win their assent to contracts. The great mass of freedmen honored their agreements more or less willingly. Where they did not do so, exhortation was a common resort of the Bureau man. For instance, in the summer of 1868, a Bureau officer in St. John's Parish, Berkeley District, wrote a sharp note to Moses, Peter, Neal, and Nancy on Shelbourne plantation. He had previously told them that their contract required them to work for the planter only two days in each week. He subsequently found that the planter loaned them four mules to work their own crops on their off days and that the freedmen had never labored more than two days for themselves anyway, "since you take Thursday of every week to fast, instead of working your crop, or laboring for rations, as you should have done." "Now you cannot prosper," he lectured, "unless you work, both white & Black, together without quarreling . . ."[108]

In serious cases, the authorities were quick to threaten the use of force to prevent the freedmen from falling into idleness. On St. John's Island, in May, 1866, an elderly Negro woman began to preach that she had had a revelation from heaven forbidding labor on Fridays and Saturdays. The idea gained wide acceptance as "God's truth," and on some plantations work stopped altogether on these days. Scott sent an emissary to tell the Negroes he would drive them all from the island

107. *Ibid.*

108. Bureau Agent, Oakley, to Moses, Peter, Neal, Nancy, "or other Freedmen who may be affected," June 4, 1868, J. B. Richardson Papers.

if they did not go back to work and the affair was quickly concluded.[109] Apparently, this disturbance was merely one manifestation of a wide-spread restlessness among the freedmen in the lowcountry. "Negroes working badly & half task," wrote one lowcountry planter in the late summer of 1866. In the crisis, Scott issued what Armisted Burt considered to be "pretty stringent orders" holding the Negroes to their contracts. Those who neglected their labor were to be arrested and "made to work on the public roads . . ."[110] Frequently, officers in the occupation forces authorized the use of physical punishment upon the freedmen whom they believed to be delinquent in honoring their contracts. In the upcountry district of Laurens, it was said that the garrison commander asked that shirkers be reported to him. One planter complained against two freedmen for malingering and the commander sent out two soldiers who tied the Negroes up by the thumbs. "The negroes begged to be flogged instead," a native white asserted.[111]

In many cases where some form of crop sharing was included in the freedman's wages, Bureau or military officers actually presided over the division. However, as the size of the occupation forces diminished during and after 1866, it became impossible for an officer to supervise the division on every plantation. Moreover, official attention was fully absorbed at the end of each season in settling those cases where a dispute had already arisen. Where an agent (or, as frequently happened, a referee appointed by him) did intervene, the typical solution was to "split the difference." This tendency and the availability of the agent as a mediator, however, apparently caused employers and employees to settle most disputes among themselves or through local magistrates.[112]

Thus, early in the Reconstruction Period, the North disallowed the attempt by white South Carolinians to replace slavery with a controlled system of labor. The North also denied the Negroes any special consideration in the form of rations and lands. Instead, the "contract system," derived from wartime experience in the Sea Islands, was used

109. *New York Times,* June 2, 1866, p. 2.
110. William Elliott to Ralph Elliott, June 16, 1866, Elliott–Gonzales Papers; A. L. Burt to his wife, July 2, 1866, A. L. Burt Papers; *New York Times,* July 4, 1866, p. 5.
111. William Watts Ball, *The State That Forgot: South Carolina's Surrender to Democracy* (Indianapolis, 1932), p. 127.
112. Croushore and Potter, *A Union Officer,* pp. 26–31, 73–74.

to re-educate South Carolinians of both races in the ways of liberal economics as they were then understood in the North. The success of the program is indicated by the fact that intervention by the federal authorities in relationships between individual employers and employees, intensive in 1865 and 1866, became progressively less important in 1867 and 1868, and ceased entirely by 1869 when such affairs were surrendered entirely to the officers of the state.

IV...BLACK AND WHITE:
CONFLICT AND ADJUSTMENT

The broad framework of a new economics for the South was prescribed by the North, but the infinite detail evolved in a species of economic warfare between white employers and Negro employees. In South Carolina, the Negro laboring population was seriously disturbed by many aspects of its early postwar situation and reacted against the employers in seeking a remedy. In turn, Negro laborers were adversely affected by the retaliatory tactics of employers. Ultimately, however, each group was forced to adjust its demands to meet the needs of the other, and economic relations between Negroes and whites crystallized into new patterns which began to disintegrate only in the middle of the twentieth century.

The greatest cause of dissatisfaction among Negro workers was a lasting reluctance on the part of the whites to recognize completely the freedom of their Negro employees. Typical was the attitude of a Laurens gentleman who "has said he wishes negroes to leave their freedom over the fence when they come in his yard. . . . he meant they had to still act as slaves." Also typical was the re-action of the Negroes who replied that they had had their freedom "too short a time to let go so soon."[1] Often this attitude came to the sur-

1. "Wife" (probably Mrs. Robert Pelot) to her husband, March 11, 1866, Lalla Pelot Papers. For other expressions of the same sentiment, see: B. S. Holmes to

face in labor contracts. In proposing an agreement for 1866, one planter inserted a provision requiring the freedmen to call him "master," and it was more than a slip of the pen which led a Berkeley District planter, as late as 1868, to draft a contract that bound his Negro workers "to be strictly as my slaves in obeying his [the overseer's] orders & instructions & in performing all work necessary to the well organization of the plantation."[2]

A continuation of the violence of the slave period was a logical concomitant of this attitude. "I have made up my mind to treat the darkies as I have always done so far as respect is concerned toward myself," a planter on the lower Savannah River confided to a friend in the summer of 1866. "On one or two occasions I have floored them, and I believe it has not a very bad effect."[3] The freedman might grieve that he was still subjected to the punishments of slavery, but he could also complain that freedom exposed him to certain hazards from which he had been relatively immune while his life and health had a pecuniary value. For example, John B. Glymph, a planter, admitted shooting an ex-slave who had insisted on having a federal officer see his contract.[4] Sometimes, Negroes who refused to contract with their late masters were "carried off" by vindictive whites, and hired assassinations became a major business. Texas Brown, Confederate cavalryman, deserter, bandit, and all-round bad man, plied his trade in the Piedmont for a year after the war, offering to kill anyone, white or black, for the very reasonable fee of five dollars.[5] Simultaneously, Dick Colburn, a former Confederate Army officer, led a hundred "Regulators" or "Reformers" in Edgefield District in hiring their services to planters "to interfere with the blacks to compel them to remain in the employ of their old masters," and, as one Union officer testified, "they have murdered as many as eight or ten for refusing to do so."[6] Under Saxton, Bureau officials in South Carolina sedulously collected reports of "outrages"

Nickels J. Holmes, December 11, 1867, N. J. Holmes Papers; "H. R. G." (probably Harriett Gonzales) to "Emmie," January 8, 1868, Elliott–Gonzales Papers.

2. *The Journal of the Joint Committee on Reconstruction at the First Session of the Thirty-Ninth Congress* (Washington, 1866), II, 240. Cited hereinafter as *Joint Committee Journal.* MS Contract, 1868, J. B. Richardson Papers.

3. S. C. Bee to B. S. Williams, ——, 1866, B. S. Williams Papers. See also: J. C. Lumpanger to D. W. Jordan, June 29, 1865, D. W. Jordan Papers.

4. *Intelligencer* (Anderson), July 27, 1865.

5. James H. Croushore and David M. Potter (eds.), *John William De Forest, A Union Officer in the Reconstruction* (New Haven, 1948), pp. 15–21.

6. *New York Times,* April 9, 1866, p. 5.

upon freedmen, and these were widely publicized in the North. Southern politicians and their friends claimed that the prevalence of such
outrages was exaggerated by the opposition; yet, it was common
knowledge among the whites that such occurrences were frequent, and
most seemed to accept them as the natural result of the peculiar circumstances of postwar life.

Many Negro laborers were also disturbed by the refusal of some
whites to contract with them under any conditions. Indeed, planters
were not laggard in availing themselves of the opportunity "free labor"
offered to discharge their less productive ex-slaves. "I want to get rid
of all my negroes with the exception of two or three," wrote an Orangeburg planter at the end of the agricultural season in 1865.[7] Intentions
were not always translated into action; nevertheless, discharges were
often numerous and employees were not overly sensitive to the human
suffering which such dismissals entailed. In Chester District in December, 1865, a planter reported that some employers were summarily
dismissing their late bondsmen. "Some persons are hauling them out
below here & putting them down in the Road—bad weather for outdoor
living."[8] Hard times brought mass discharges beyond the desires of
employers. A small planter near Bishopville in January, 1868, described
at length the disastrous results of the previous farming season and
added: "Negroes are out of employment by thousands without any
means of support, stealing, house-burning &c are of daily occurrence
all over our State. They roam the Country armed & have destroyed
nearly the seed [those necessary for reproduction] of Hogs & Cattle."[9]
On many plantations dismissals, combined with other causes, resulted
in the progressive diminution of the Negro population. In July, 1865,
for example, cotton planter A. H. Boykin of Kershaw District contracted with 131 freedmen and ten years later with only twelve.[10]
Similarly, in January, 1865, Henry L. Pinckney listed the names of
148 slaves in the journal of his Sumter District plantation. By 1868, his
laboring force had been reduced to sixteen hands.[11]

Many Negroes were discharged by their employers for political
reasons. In the fall of 1868, an Edgefield sawmill operator warned his
five Negro laborers that if they voted Republican, "they can no longer

7. A. T. Smythe to his brother, December 5, 1865, A. T. Smythe Letters.
8. R. N. Hemphill to W. R. Hemphill, December 13, 1865, Hemphill Papers.
9. J. M. Dennis to J. Y. Harris, January 14, 1868, J. Y. Harris Papers.
10. MS Contracts, July 6, 1865, February 1, 1875, A. H. Boykin Papers.
11. H. L. Pinckney MS Plantation Journal, entries for January 5, 1865, and
January—, 1868.

work for me." When three proved unwilling to commit themselves, he reported, "I thereupon told them I would dispense with their services."[12] In the same election, the Democrats of Anderson County broadcast a warning to Negroes to follow those "who own the Land upon which you labor, and who furnish the Money by which you are paid for your labor . . ."[13] In some places, the names of ardently Republican Negro laborers were circulated among planters and exchanged between agricultural associations. After the election of 1870, for instance, the secretary of the Martintown Agricultural Club wrote the president of the Rocky Pond Agricultural Club: "We have recd your list of pro-scribed negroes, which was read before our meeting to-day, and members furnished with a copy. We herewith send you a list of those proscribed by this Club . . ."[14] Discharges for political reasons were not always so well organized and public. A small farmer residing in Spartanburg County in 1869 reported that he had employed "old Daniel Allen" for two years and "we never had a word but because I would not take his Radical son in law with him he left me so no more."[15]

Still another source of dissatisfaction among Negro agrarians was the disinclination of some owners to rent lands to them, an irritation which was aggravated by the fervent desire of many Negroes to work inde-pendently of direct white supervision. One lowcountry aristocrat de-plored "a disposition with many persons to rent their lands to negroes. . . . It will be hard ever to recover the privileges that have been yielded to the negroes."[16]

Occasionally, landowners and employers entered into "gentlemen's agreements" to refuse to rent land to Negroes and to minimize other concessions generally. On December 23, 1865, only two days after Saxton had met the freedmen and planters from three districts in the village of Sumter to discuss contract arrangements for the coming year, the planters held a private meeting in the same place and agreed "not to hire their neighbor's negroes, or rent any land to them."[17]

12. G. R. Ghiselin to R. H. McKie, October 27, November 2, 1868, R. H. McKie Papers.

13. *Intelligencer* (Anderson), October 7, 1868.

14. R. H. McKie to the President of the Rocky Pond Agricultural Club (copy), December 24, 1870, R. H. McKie Papers.

15. Edward Lipscomb to Smith Lipscomb, June 30, 1869, Edward Lipscomb Papers.

16. William Heyward to James Gregorie, June 4, 1868, Gregorie–Elliott Papers.

17. "D. G. M." to his mother, December 25, 1865, Williams–Manning–Chesnut Papers.

More often, agreement was achieved informally within the tightly knit employer class. A Cooper River planter considered paying his workers half the rice crop of 1866 for their labor; however, when he learned that all the other planters on the river were allowing them only a third, he lined out "one half" in his proposed contract and wrote in "one third" as the freedmen's share.[18]

Negroes also complained of the wages, or share in lieu of wages, offered by the planters. In Chester District in 1866, an extensive planter found his laborers "perfectly indignant" at his offer of a fourth of the crop for their work.[19] Even when the terms of labor were fairly and carefully determined by a conscientious employer, Negro workers remained suspicious of the white man. In Spartanburg District, David Golightly Harris found that he could afford to rent land and supply animals and implements to his former slaves for no less than two-thirds of the crop. When one of his renters grumbled at the bargain, Harris agreed to "modify the terms by giving him more time to work for himself." Even so, the landlord noted, "they are no judges, and fear to trade for fear they will [be] cheated & have no confidence in themselves or in the white man."[20]

Sometimes, wage payments for extra labor beyond the terms of the share contract gave the Negroes cause for complaint. In the summer of 1867, for instance, an Orangeburg planter was elated over the prospect of a good cotton crop and his arrangements with the Negroes for harvesting it. "All the extra women, Diana, Katey, Penny, old Maum Lucy, are preparing to pick the cotton." Yet, the "price of picking" had not been settled. By late September, the planter was in high dudgeon. "One more day past & I am still alive & kicking, tho' not a little chafed & worried to-night by the negroes who came to me about cotton picking," he informed his wife. "I got real mad and gave them a piece of my mind which they did not relish much but which they had to swallow. They are the biggest fools I ever knew."[21] The rub, of course, was that the Negroes were demanding higher wages.

Free labor under the contract system occasioned other, lesser complaints from Negro workers. In the lowcountry, where many planters

18. W. M. Burney to T. B. Ferguson, February 1, 1866; MS Contract, 1866, Heyward–Ferguson Papers.

19. R. N. Hemphill to W. R. Hemphill, December 13, 1865, Hemphill Papers. See also: Robert I. Gage to his sister, January 31, 1868, J. M. Gage Papers.

20. MS Farm Journal, entries for January 4, 11, 1866.

21. A. T. Smythe to his wife, August 16, September 24, 1867, A. T. Smythe Letters.

followed the practice of hiring laborers to work two or three days out of each week, there was frequent disagreement on the specific days to be worked and the total laboring time required.[22] Indicative of another class of grievances expressed by the Negroes was the refusal of the Negro population of a Union District plantation to accept a contract provision which required them to have written permission from the owner whenever they left the premises. ". . . dont think a nigger's free if he cant roam at liberty," observed the employer in disgust.[23] Freedmen were also frequently offended by being pressed to perform labor not included in their contracts. The Bureau officer in Georgetown reported in the fall of 1865 that army officers were assisting planters in compelling freedmen "to do work not called for under their contracts."[24] A Cooper River rice planter met only obstinacy and impudence in the spring of 1866 when he attempted to persuade his workers to perform extra labor on the crop in which they had a half interest. Drafting a contract for future consideration at about the same time, the employer included a provision requiring the laborers to be "civil."[25]

In the early years of freedom, many Negro laborers were disgruntled by the actual rewards that they reaped from their work. Of course, very often meager returns originated in poor farming practices and unpropitious weather. Yet, the average Negro worker "could not understand how the advances which had been made to him during the summer should swallow up his half or third of the 'crap.'"[26] It was natural that in his frustration the freedman should turn against the apparent author of his ills—his employer. "Of the complaints against the whites," reported a Bureau officer, "the majority were because of the retention of wages or of an alleged unfairness in the division of the crops."[27] Sometimes, however, employers did deal unfairly with their employees. "A large number of Farmers finding they are making nothing, put off to Chester with some fictitious complaint to the Provost Court & have their hands discharged," reported one planter during the summer of 1866. The result, he noted, was that the vicinity was "in-

22. "C. G. S." to "Mary" (probably Mary Elliott Johnston), March 2, 1868, Elliott–Gonzales, Papers; Bureau Agent, Oakley, to Moses, Peter, Neal, Nancy, "or other Freedmen who may be affected," June 4, 1868, J. B. Richardson Papers.
23. Robert I. Gage to a friend, January 14, 1866, J. M. Gage Papers.
24. *Joint Committee Journal*, II, 225. See also: E. J. Parker to D. W. Jordan, November 1, 1865, D. W. Jordan Papers.
25. [—. —.] Deas to his daughter, April 18, 1866, [—. —.] Deas Papers.
26. Croushore and Potter, *A Union Officer*, p. 73.
27. *Ibid.*, pp. 29–30.

undated with Idle darkies wandering about without homes or employment." The fault, he believed, lay with the Yankee Colonel, "an old army officer" who "loves Liquor & Cares very little for Sambo."[28]

Whether the grievances of Negro laborers were real or imaginary, they soon developed an impressive array of weapons by which they sought to promote their interests within the evolving economic order. Many Negro laborers resisted unfavorable contract terms by refusing to conclude agreements, hoping that delay in beginning the planting operation would force the employer to yield the desired concessions. Typical was the experience of William Elliott. In the spring of 1866, he was attempting to muster a laboring force to cultivate long-staple cotton on Cheeha plantation on the Combahee. At first, he was unable to persuade the Negro residents on the plantation to contract with him. They were "civil," but they had already planted their "patches" and were working for their food on the plantations of neighbors who were "capable of feeding them, and sadly in want of hands." Elliott attempted to break the solid front presented by the laborers by contracting with Jacob, a "faithful" retainer from the slave period. Failing, the planter complained that "even he is indifferent, wanting only to squat and have all he grows." Specifically, Jacob refused to plant five or six acres of cotton for a half share. "He prefers planting two & having all the provisions he may make for himself—this in consideration of his past important service to the family," Elliott explained. "I told him I thought the obligation lay the other way. He is eaten up with self-esteem & selfishness." Elliott then tried unsuccessfully to contract with Negroes on neighboring plantations where he had heard that the hands "are awaiting a better offer." Early in April, Elliott finally converted Jacob, and together they again attempted to persuade other former slaves of the Elliott family on Cheeha, the Bluff, and Oak Lawn plantations to contract. After a great amount of negotiating, a contract was written to which all agreed.[29]

Negro laborers soon developed other coercive techniques for forcing their claims upon prospective employers. Many simply refused to leave the plantation at the end of the agricultural season. Such tactics often caused great distress among employers. In 1868, a Union District planter fired all his Negro workers when they persisted in their

28. R. N. Hemphill to W. R. Hemphill, July 6, 1866, Hemphill Papers.

29. William Elliott to his mother, March 14, 25; April 2, 26, 1866, Elliott–Gonzales Papers.

demand for one-half the crop to be produced during the coming year. Finally, seven recanted and accepted his terms. The remainder either departed voluntarily or were driven away. Then Carolina, one of those who had left, returned with her four children, only one of whom was old enough to work. Also "back came Frank & Ret. I have refused to give them rations, told them I dont want them but they are working with the other negroes. What am I to do?" cried the anguished planter. "I cannot afford to feed them & I know that they will not earn their bread." The success of this maneuver ultimately depended upon the sympathy of the employer for his employees, and even the kindest employers often had mixed feelings. As this gentleman admitted, "I have no scruples about running off the young ones but it is a painful duty with the old ones. What will become of the poor creatures—the country is full of just such cases."[30] In the face of a hostile master, the sit-down strike was liable to fail, as an elderly freedman in Sumter District found in 1867. "Old Gage got so bad that Frank put him off," his late mistress reported, "but had to threaten to burn his house before he wd go."[31]

Freedmen very early learned the power of united action in presenting their demands to prospective employers. A Northern correspondent noted in November, 1866, that the freedmen were exhibiting a tendency to meet together to redress grievances. "There is a large general movement in the interior districts to change the conditions of labor, especially to increase the compensation for labor," he reported. The movement "is entirely spontaneous on the part of the freedmen," and while they bore the "symptoms of something very like a Northern 'strike,' are yet totally free, as far as I can judge, from any tendency toward disorder or violence."[32] Mass meetings did occur, but practical negotiations were usually carried on by the Negroes on each plantation acting in concert.

Occasionally, combinations of Negro laborers generated strikes of a "wildcat" variety, arising spontaneously and threatening or actually doing violence. To the native white, this was not a "strike"; it was a "rising," an insurrection.[33] During the late summer of 1876, such a movement reached very large proportions among the Negro laborers on the

30. Robert I. Gage to his sister, January 31, 1868, J. M. Gage Papers. See also: "Wife" to her husband, March 11, 1866, Lalla Pelot Papers.

31. "Mother" to her children, March 4, 1867, J. B. Richardson Papers.

32. *New York Times,* November 30, 1866, p. 2.

33. For an instance of the use of the term in this relation, see: "Mother" to B. S. Williams and his wife, June 30, 1871, B. S. Williams Papers.

rice plantations of the lower Combahee river. The primary object of the strike, as some of its leaders told Negro trial justices attempting to halt the disturbances, was to force the planters to pay cash wages instead of advancing provisions and promising them a share of the profits. "Thear Striking was for the wanting the money," one trial justice reported to the governor, D. H. Chamberlain.[34] In addition, apparently, the strikers wanted an increase in wages. The Combahee strike, or riot, as it is called, resulted in violence against both Negroes and whites. R. B. Elliott, a prominent Negro politician who visited the scene of the strike, reported that the strikers were forcing the whole Negro community to join in the movement so that "all classes of workmen are compelled to demand higher wages, and women and children are now beaten as well as men." Shortly before, he had seen Lieutenant Governor R. H. Gleaves, a Negro who resided in the vicinity, use "actual bodily interposition" to halt an armed assault of strikers on a group of whites.[35] Working through local officials, Governor Chamberlain gradually restored order. ". . . say to them," he directed the local sheriff, "that they have a right to refuse to work for low wages but they have no right to make others join them against their will, that if they molest those who are willing to work they violate the law, and will be arrested and punished." He added, however, that he sympathized with wage reform and asked the sheriff to "advise [the] planters for me to be liberal."[36]

Negro laborers, frustrated in their relations with employers, sometimes indulged in vengeance upon the persons or property of the whites. An Edgefield sawmill operator, previously mentioned, who had fired three of his laborers for refusing to forego "their votive privilege," wrote three days later that during the night "about 15ft in length was cut from my saw belt & carried off. I suppose it was done in consequence of my discharging the hands."[37] Arson, because the act was easily and cheaply committed and its authors not easily discovered, was a favored weapon of disgruntled Negro laborers. After several Negroes had been discharged from a plantation in Kershaw District, one of the barns was burned. "Toney and his sett are the party," wrote the manager im-

34. William Middleton and other trial justices to Governor D. H. Chamberlain, September 13, 1876, Freedmen File.

35. R. B. Elliott to Governor D. H. Chamberlain, September 12, 1876, Freedmen File.

36. Sheriff Terry to Governor D. H. Chamberlain, September 26, 1876 (telegrapher's copy); Governor D. H. Chamberlain to Sheriff Terry, September 26, 1876 (telegrapher's copy), Elliott–Gonzales Papers.

37. G. R. Ghiselin to R. H. McKie, November 5, 1868, R. H. McKie Papers.

mediately afterward, accusing his former employees. It was presently found that, indeed, Toney and a friend had induced Tom, a feeble-minded Negro still working on the plantation, to arrange the conflagration.[38] During times of tension, particularly after the end of the farming season and before the commencement of another, the local press teemed with reports of farm buildings burned by unknown hands. That the whites were responsive to these threats was indicated by the advice of the owner of a lowcountry plantation to his manager. "In dealing with the negroes please use forbearance and management to accomplish your ends," he counseled, "a recourse to other means may cause the buildings to be laid in ashes, as was the case in my late brother's place near Mobile Alabama. Deal Kindly with the poor creatures and you will accomplish as much or more than by harsh measures."[39]

Arson was sometimes committed with a murderous design. Emma E. Holmes reported from Camden early in 1866 that "Mr. Bull lately turned off his negroes because they would not work and, shortly after, the overseer's house, where he and the boys were living, was set on fire at night and they escaped only with their lives and a little clothing." Mr. Bull then settled his family in the gardner's house "and another night, while preparing for bed, stooped to pick up something just in time to escape a whistling bullet."[40]

Failing to agree with his employer upon terms for the coming year, an obvious resort of the Negro worker was to seek arrangements in other places. Thus, the end of each agricultural season saw movements of Negroes away from the sites of their past labors.

Some plantations were entirely abandoned by their Negro populations. "On the Wateree," wrote an heiress of the cotton aristocracy, "all of the negroes where Frank and Wm are have left—"[41] In the first year of freedom, of course, such movements were primarily an exercise by the Negroes of their new liberty. Soon, however, desertion became a potent and lasting weapon in the hands of the laborer.

In some instances, the removal of the Negroes was permanent. The Reverend John Cornish saw three cotton plantations belonging to his

38. A. H. Boykin to L. D. De Saussure, February 4, March 24, April 12, 1868, A. H. Boykin Papers.

39. W. M. Burney to T. B. Ferguson, October 23, 1865, Heyward–Ferguson Papers.

40. Diary, entry for January 15, 1866.

41. "Mary" (Johnstone) to her mother, January 24, 1866, Elliott–Gonzales Papers.

wife's family which were totally abandoned by the Negroes in 1866 and 1867. Moreover, these estates were never restored to full productivity during the Reconstruction Period, and such planting as was done upon them was done by strangers to the land.[42] In the rice areas, abandonment was the rule rather than the exception. Of the fifty-two rice plantations lying on the Cooper River immediately north of Charleston, forty-three were not cultivated at all in 1866, forty-five lay barren in 1867, and each year the remainder were operated with laboring forces much reduced.[43] Even though attempts were made to revive the cultivation of rice in South Carolina, they were never successful. One agricultural authority declared in 1883 that "much" lowcountry rice land was withdrawn from use after the war because of "uncertain labor" and a decrease in the price of the product. He estimated that in Colleton District between one-fourth and one-half the rice acreage was abandoned.[44]

Nevertheless, tradition has exaggerated the size and misinterpreted the nature of these migrations. At least through the Reconstruction Period, a considerable number of Negroes remained on the very plantations where they had served as slaves. In 1874, Thomas Taylor, a very able planter in Richland County, told a Northern reporter that most of his ex-bondsmen were still working for him.[45]

The vast majority of those who did leave the "homeplace" in 1865 and 1866 did so only to take up employment elsewhere in the same community. After one or more seasons, many moved again to still another plantation in the same neighborhood, or, in some cases, returned to the homeplace.[46] Apparently, interplantation migrations diminished greatly after 1866. On Montrose plantation in Chesterfield District, in 1867, twenty of the twenty-five Negro workers who had

42. J. H. Cornish MS Diary, entries for February—November 23, 24, 1866, et seq.

43. James B. Heyward MS Plantation Book, a list of fifty-two plantations lying on the Cooper River with data for 1846, 1866, and 1867. Heyward–Ferguson Papers.

44. James C. Hemphill, *Climate, Soil, and Agricultural Capabilities of South Carolina and Georgia: Department of Agriculture. Special Report No. 47* (Washington, 1882), pp. 17–21.

45. *New York Times*, July 4, 1874, p. 5. *See also:* J. H. Cornish MS Diary, entries for December 8, 9, 1866.

46. For instances among the ex-slaves of B. S. Holmes of Laurens, see: "Mother" to N. J. Holmes, July 25, 1866; B. S. Holmes to N. J. Holmes, August 20, 1867, N. J. Holmes Papers.

labored there during the previous year contracted to remain.[47] Early in Reconstruction, most Negro workers seem to have established more or less permanent relations with a single employer. Of the twenty-seven Spartanburg Negroes who testified on this point before the Ku Klux Investigating Committee in 1871, one-third had lived and worked on the same plantation since emancipation. Only two of the twenty-seven had changed employers at the end of the 1870 planting season. Five workers were in their second year with their current employers (or lessors), four were in their third year (one of these having returned to the place where he was born a slave), and four were in their fourth year.[48] Negro workers in the lowcountry behaved in much the same manner. For instance, on Mulberry, one of the few rice plantations on the Cooper River that operated continuously throughout the period, the slave population remained through the 1865 harvest and stayed either on the plantation itself or in the vicinity year after year until they died.[49]

Not all the Negroes who left their employers at the end of the season were able to find new homes. At least a portion of these lapsed into idleness—in itself a means of combating the employer class. The lowcountry planter who had "floored" one or two of his laborers in 1866 found a number of Negroes in his community still unemployed in May, 1867. They preferred to be "very idle" rather than contract with employers who needed their labor, and, the pugilistic planter lamented, "the garrison nearby gives no help."[50] Voluntary idleness among Negroes was not a widespread phenomenon, but it was an enduring one. In Spartanburg County in the summer of 1874, one farmer complained that "the description" which his brother had given him of the Negroes in Alabama "in regard to avoiding work and trying to make their living by the slight of hand or stealing is in conformity with what we observe among our own people."[51]

The rapid increase in the urban Negro population was, of course,

47. MS Contracts, ——, 1866, January 1, 1867, Allan MacFarland Papers.
48. *The Ku-Klux Conspiracy. Testimony taken by the Joint Select Committee to inquire into the condition of affairs in the late insurrectionary States* (Washington, 1872), III, IV, and V, *passim*. Cited hereinafter as Ku-Klux Conspiracy.
49. James B. Heyward MS Plantation Book. Slaves belonging to Mulberry were listed in February, 1865, and entries were made subsequently as they died. The last entry was made in 1902.
50. S. C. Bee to B. S. Williams, May ——, 1867, B. S. Williams Papers.
51. Edward Lipscomb to Smith Lipscomb, June 19, 1874, Edward Lipscomb Papers.

closely related to rural unemployment. The villages and towns and the
city of Charleston were natural collecting places for unemployed agriculturalists. "There is a good deal of idling among the negroes," reported a Northerner recently arrived in the piedmont town of Greenville in the late summer of 1866. "We see daily, in the streets of this
country town, groups of three or four to a dozen idling, or playing
marbles, or some game requiring little physical exertion."[52] In the
decade following 1860, the Negro population of Charleston increased
by more than three thousand, so that by 1870 Negroes outnumbered
whites in the city by more than four thousand.[53] The Negro populations
of Columbia and Greenville increased with astonishing rapidity and,
in some cases, entirely new villages were created with a large proportion of Negro citizens.

Possibly 10 per cent of South Carolina's Negroes left the state during
Reconstruction. Most of these, suggesting a continuation of the prewar
flow of labor, moved to Florida, Arkansas, Mississippi, Louisiana, and
Texas. The movement was underway at the end of the 1865 farming
season and recurred to some extent at the end of each successive season.[54]
The largest emigration took place during the late fall and winter of
1866–1867, and one can imagine that among the emigrants there were
many Negroes who had left their homeplaces at the end of 1865, spent
an unhappy year on another plantation, and were then inclined to
resort to extremes. The number who emigrated can only be approximated, but all indications point to a vast movement. A correspondent
in Columbia averred, on "good authority," that by late March, 1867,
twenty-five thousand Negroes had departed from the Carolinas and
Georgia, while a Charleston writer put the number of Negro emigrants
from South Carolina alone at fifty thousand.[55] In Anderson District,
in January, 1867, "crowds" of Negro laborers were observed leaving
for the West, and De Forest estimated that a thousand left the predominately white districts of Greenville and Pickens in the fall of 1866.[56]

52. *New York Times,* September 17, 1866, p. 1. See also: *Intelligencer* (Anderson), November 25, 1868.

53. Robert Somers, *The Southern States since the War* (New York, 1871),
p. 53.

54. Mary Johnstone to her sister, February 9, 1866, Elliott–Gonzales Papers;
Daily Republican (Charleston), February 19, 1870.

55. *New York Times,* April 2, p. 5; February 28, p. 2, 1867.

56. *Appeal* (Anderson), January 16, 1867; Croushore and Potter, *A Union
Officer,* p. 130. See also: *New York Times,* January 16, 1867, p. 2.

Economic self-improvement was the primary motive for such removals. Indeed, professional agents representing planters in other states supervised most movements. To the prospective emigrant, they offered free transportation and promised considerably better wages than were paid in South Carolina, where a fortunate worker received about $15.00 a month. Agents of Florida planters offered $12.00 to $20.00 a month in addition to subsistence, while those from Louisiana and Arkansas promised $15.00 and subsistence.[57]

Many Negroes did, in fact, improve their circumstances by emigration. Jake, once a slave in Laurens District, wrote to his former master from his farm in Ouachita County, Arkansas, in February, 1867, that he was doing well with the help of his two large boys. "I once thought I wanted to come back to that old country," he admitted, "but I believe I have given up that notion."[58] Similarly, Jesse McElroy, who had probably been a free Negro in Kershaw District during slavery, reported himself contented with his farm near Galveston, Texas, in April, 1868.[59] Many of the Florida settlers expected to acquire eighty acres of government land under a law passed by Congress soon after the war. By 1910, one out of every two Negro farmers in Florida owned his own farm, a degree of independence which was exceeded only in Virginia and Kentucky.[60]

Various other motives re-enforced economic self-interest to prompt Negro emigration from South Carolina. Some Negroes left to join relatives. Often, Carolinians who owned plantations elsewhere transported laborers from the state. Wade Hampton, living on his Mississippi estates in January, 1866, wrote to his sister in Richland District requesting her to ask a neighbor "to tell the negroes that their families here want them to come out and that I will pay the passage of all who will come." Further, if the neighbor "can hire 100 negroes—hands—for me, I wish that he would do so."[61] In July, 1873, a group of more than fifty Negroes calling themselves the "Zion Travelers" followed

57. *New York Times*, January 16, p. 2; February 28, p. 2, 1867; Croushore and Potter, *A Union Officer*, pp. 130-31.

58. "Jake" to W. D. Simpson, February 5, 1867, W. D. Simpson Papers.

59. Jesse McElroy to a friend, April 22 [1868], Bonds Conway Correspondence.

60. *New York Times*, January 7, p. 1; 16, p. 2, 1867; Bureau of the Census, *Negro Population in the United States, 1790-1915* (Washington, 1918), p. 478. Cited hereinafter as *Negro Population*.

61. Letter to Mary Fisher Hampton, January 1, 1866, contained in Charles E. Cauthen (ed.), *Family Letters of the Three Wade Hamptons, 1782-1901* (Columbia, 1953), p. 117.

their minister-leader out of Spartanburg County. Their destination was a "promised Land" which their Moses declared lay precisely 160 miles northwest of the village.[62] Others, less religiously inclined, were freed from jails on the promise that they contract to work in another state.[63] Finally, many Negro laborers, especially the younger, doubtless moved from place to place within and without the state simply from a thirst for adventure. Changing scenes certainly made difficult labor more bearable, and a sizeable number probably chose to "go walk" or "to hunt vittel," as they said, when there was no compelling reason for them to do so.[64]

In 1871, the Reverend Elias Hill, a Negro leader in the American Colonization Society, gave still another reason why some two thousand South Carolina Negroes took advantage of the Society's offer of free transportation to Liberia. ". . . we do not believe," he declared, "it possible, from the past history and from the present aspect of affairs, for our people to live in this country peaceably, and educate and elevate their children to that degree which they desire."[65] Visiting the organization's ship, the *Golconda,* in Charleston in November, 1866, a it made ready to sail, a Northern correspondent found that its 600 berths had been easily filled by young Negroes with high hopes.[66] By March of 1867, the Society had received applications from an additional 642 Carolina Negroes for transportation to Liberia.[67]

Even though the number of emigrants was offset by births among those who remained, the movement did create temporary and local shortages of labor in South Carolina. In May, 1866, one Laurens District planter mentioned a "scarcity of labor," and another complained in February, 1869, that "We have not got many freemen yet and I

62. *A History of Spartanburg County.* Compiled by the Spartanburg Unit of the Writer's Program of the Works Projects Administration in the State of South Carolina (n.p., 1940), p. 173.

63. Croushore and Potter, *A Union Officer,* p. 103.

64. *New York Times,* December 30, 1868, p. 2.

65. *Ku-Klux Conspiracy,* V, 1410; *News* (Charleston), November 18, 1867.

66. *New York Times,* November 20, 1866, p. 5.

67. *Daily Courier* (Charleston), March 6, 1867. Of course, the *Golconda's* passengers included Negroes from many states. For instance, the 312 people who embarked for Liberia in November, 1867, included families from Columbus and Macon, Georgia, Dover Court House, Tennessee, and Philadelphia. The only Carolina family on board, Alfred and Nancy Holley and their eleven children, came from Mars Bluff. MS List of Emigrants for Liberia, embarked on Ship *Golconda* off Charleston, S. C. (American Colonization Society), November 17, 1867, South Carolina Historical Society, Charleston.

dont expect that we will get any now, it is so late now that they have all got homes now, what few there is in [the] country." The latter explained: "There is about one half of the negroes that was in our state disappeared and know body knows where nor whence they have gone and it is a very hard matter for the farmers to [get] hands enough to work the lands and there fore there will be hardly half crop made in South Car."[68] Employers were slow to respond to the dearth of Negro labor, whenever and wherever it occurred. A native white journalist noted in January, 1867, that the whites did nothing to encourage or to hamper emigration, but he believed that the departure of the best rather than the worst workers sorrowed them.[69] In Charleston, a month later, a Northern correspondent rather optimistically thought that the planters, alarmed by the labor exodus, were offering better wages and considering giving Negroes increased political privileges to induce them to remain.[70]

Negro emigration from the state greatly decreased during the 1870's. Although the wages of Negro laborers in South Carolina usually lagged behind those of other states, they did tend to increase gradually; and the demand for labor in other Southern and Southwestern states diminished. During the decade preceding 1880, the number of Carolina-born Negroes living in other states decreased by about four per cent.[71]

Even after having contracted, Negro laborers sometimes became disgruntled with their work. They evinced their dissatisfaction by various devices, many of which had been perfected during the slave period. Thus, white employers complained bitterly of the Negro's proclivity to do poor work, or little work, or no work at all, and of his malingering and insolence. One Sumter District planter experienced most of these and recorded his irritation in his plantation book: May 5, 1866, "all the hoe hands slothful in work, except Capt. Margaret"; June 8, "Milley dismissed from the field for bad work & insolent language. Miley asked pardon & restored"; and under no date, "Amy

68. J. S. Holmes to N. J. Holmes, February 25, 1869; S. L. West to N. J. Holmes, [May —, 1866], N. J. Holmes Papers.

69. *New York Times,* January 16, 1867, p. 2.

70. *Ibid.,* February 28, 1867, p. 2.

71. *Compendium of the Tenth Census of the United States* (Washington, 1883), I, 480. Decennial census reports will be cited hereinafter by *Census* and reference to the year in which the census was taken.

stopped work on the 15th & refuses to go in the field."[72] In the early years of freedom, such occurrences were frequently observed.[73]

Although the worker forfeited his share of the crop or wages due, an impromptu departure was an obvious way out of an unsatisfactory contract. Moreover, desertion often produced the desired effect of irritating the late employer. On one of the Richardson estates in Clarendon District in 1866, Phocian Boston was labeled a "bad negro" for having abandoned his duties at the plantation mill precisely when his services were most in demand. Like many deserters, however, his departure was not permanent; he returned to the same plantation in 1875 as a renter.[74] The sudden defection of household servants was most irritating to the whites, and led them to recall fondly the advantages of the peculiar institution. "We are out of a cook again," lamented James Hemphill in Chester in December, 1867, "one came last week, stayed a week, and left without notice. . . . The antipathy to constant labor is inherent in the African, . . . certainly slavery had many objectionable features, but it also had its points for all parties."[75]

After the passage of the first Reconstruction Act in March, 1867, a final resort of the Negro laborer in his struggle with employers was political action—a weapon which was, indeed, most efficacious. Negroes in the Reconstruction Period clearly understood the possibilities of using political means to gain economic ends. Even during the first year of political activity by Negroes, laborers looked eagerly at political prospects. "The hands are working well just now, tho' they were very much afflicted with freedom & voting when I first came up," reported the manager of an Orangeburg District plantation in August, 1867. "They evidently felt large!"[76] The meeting of the exclusively Republican Constitutional Convention in the winter and spring of 1868 was expectantly scrutinized by the Negro population. "Can you not stir up the Freedmen or are they waiting on the Convention?" asked an

72. H. L. Pinckney MS Plantation Book, entries as indicated.

73. R. S. Cheeves to L. Cheeves, October 24, 1865, R. S. Cheeves Papers; E. J. Parker to D. W. Jordan, December 24, 1865, D. W. Jordan Papers; B. S. Holmes to N. J. Holmes, August 20, 1867, N. J. Holmes Papers; Edward Lipscomb to Smith Lipscomb, July 5, 1868, Edward Lipscomb Papers; Keating S. Ball MS Plantation Journal, entry under the year 1870.

74. J. B. Richardson to a friend, August 6, 1866; MS Contract, 1875, J. B. Richardson Papers.

75. To W. R. Hemphill, December 11, 1867, Hemphill Papers.

76. A. T. Smythe to Louise Smythe, August 16, 1867, A. T. Smythe Letters.

anxious Kershaw planter of his manager, while the mistress of a low-country plantation observed that "the freed people are *universally dissatisfied*."[77]

Republican politicians were quick to capitalize on the interest of the Negroes. The members of the Convention, through stay law measures, homestead provisions, bankruptcy regulations, land policy, and war debt repudiation, showed themselves to be friendly to the lower economic classes. Typical of the many motions of this nature offered in the Convention was that of James M. Allen, a native white delegate from Greenville. Allen proposed an ordinance to prohibit landlords from charging rents of more than a third of the grain crops or a fourth of the cotton or tobacco crops when they supplied only the land and to limit their rental income to one-half of all crops when they supplied land, stock, and feed.[78]

Once in power, Republican legislators created a pattern of laws favoring the laboring class, a pattern which was successfully defended by them throughout Reconstruction.[79] In its special session in the summer of 1868, the first Republican legislature considered a rash of bills to protect the agricultural laborer.[80] During its regular session in December, 1868, it established a Bureau of Agricultural Statistics ostensibly to promote diversification in agriculture, scientific methods, and the importation of Northern capital.[81] In actuality, the Bureau, through its most active agent, Martin R. Delany, operated much as a state-level Freedmen's Bureau in seeing that justice was done to Negro laborers. Other key elements in the legislative program were laws regulating crop liens. These laws generally represented an attempt to transfer advantage under the credit system from employers or lessors to employees or lessees.[82]

Probably, more important than their official acts was the unofficial agitation sparked by the Republican leadership. A planter on the lower

77. L. D. De Saussure to A. H. Boykin, January 21, 1868, A. H. Boykin Papers; "C. G. S." to Mary [Johnstone], March 2, 1868, Elliott–Gonzales Papers.

78. *Proceedings of the Constitutional Convention of South Carolina* (Charleston, 1868), p. 184. Cited hereinafter as *Convention Proceedings, 1868.*

79. For a defense of the lien law by Republican legislators late in 1875, see: *Intelligencer* (Anderson), December 9, 1875.

80. For instances, see: *Journal of the Senate of the State of South Carolina* (Special Session, 1868), p. 26. Cited hereinafter as *Senate Journal. House Journal* (Special Session, 1868), p. 314.

81. *New York Times,* December 28, 1868, p. 1.

82. See below, pp. 171–72.

Ashepoo in August, 1868, complained to Governor Scott that a speaker claiming to represent him had been instructing the Negroes in the area not to work for less than $1.50 per day.[83] Occasionally, such agitation became formidable. In November, 1869, Robert Brown Elliott, a Negro legislator from Edgefield County, led a state labor convention which pressed for one-half of the crop for the laborer under share arrangements, or a straight daily wage of from seven cents to a dollar.[84] Republican politicians carried this idea into the fields. "Senator Wimbush [a native Negro Republican leader] & some new Scalawag Converts are going about making speeches, & advising the freedmen to demand the Half &c," complained a Chester County planter in November, 1869. "The Consequence is that every thing is in Confusion, & will remain so until the New Year."[85]

The fact that the judicial and executive systems of the state were almost wholly in the hands of Republicans after 1868 redounded greatly to the economic benefit of the Negro, upon whose suffrage the party depended. While white Republican officers of the state were often flagrantly biased in favor of Negro workers, literally hundreds of Negroes—lately of the laboring class—were appointed to the lowest judicial office, that of trial justice or magistrate. Since these courts had jurisdiction in cases involving $100.00 or less, the great majority of disputes between employers and employees came before them. When the scales of justice were thus tilted, the bias probably favored the employee. In Spartanburg County, in 1869, David Golightly Harris submitted to arbitration proceedings in a dispute with a Negro renter; he subsequently lamented his action. "To day Warren & I had an arbitration at the mill concerning the rent & fencing he was to pay & to do. The arbitrators (as usual) divided the claim & gave me about ½ that I should have had." He concluded: "This is the consequence of dealing with negroes, one can not get justice of a negro."[86] Even in the higher courts, exact justice for white employers was liable to suffer through the bias of Negro jurors. Clearly, such was the expectation of an association of Beaufort County planters who used immigrants to settle on their land and work for them, but required imported laborers to agree

83. A. R. Heyward to Governor R. K. Scott, August 11, 1868, Freedmen File.
84. *Daily Republican* (Charleston), November 30, 1869.
85. R. N. Hemphill to W. R. Hemphill, November 15, 1869, Hemphill Papers. See also: T. P. Bailey to R. H. McKie, February 20, 1871, R. H. McKie Papers.
86. MS Farm Journal, entry for October 28, 1869. See also: Trial Justice File, Department of Archives, South Carolina.

beforehand not to resort to a jury settlement of any dispute with their employers as long as Negroes participated on juries.[87]

Republican officials of both races were prone in administrative procedures to favor Negroes loyal to the party over white Democrats. "I handed your letter to W. A. Giles and he read the contents and replied to me that he knew as much as your letter contained and he will not act upon the 2 notes," an Abbeville planter complained to his lawyer after an official had refused to pursue two Negro renters indebted to him. "I believe that W. A. Giles is a Radical at hart for he Will do all that lays in his power for a Radical Negro," the planter asserted. "Peter Hunter and Peter Martin is boath Radical Negroes, Major Burt," he explained. The planter was afraid to press the matter aggressively lest another group of Radicals in the sheriff's office execute their threat to retaliate by arresting his sons.[88]

During Reconstruction, white employers were quick to devise means to counteract the effects of inadequate or intractable Negro labor. Many of these were implied in the discussion above; but there were other, less direct devices which, nevertheless, made deep impressions upon the economic history of the Negro. Thus, white employers occasionally abandoned their operations altogether or reduced them to adjust to the supply of pliable Negro labor. Frequently, the employer either supplanted or supplemented Negro labor with that of himself, his family, other native whites, Northern whites, or immigrants from abroad. Like the Negro laborer, he, too, had a final resort in political action.

In many cases the abandonment of entire plantations resulted, not from the unwillingness of the Negroes to work as mentioned above, but from the landowner's refusal to attempt to employ Negroes as free laborers. "The Negro can never be made to work as when a slave, and the wear and tear on those who have to follow them will in time kill many of our young men or drive them to other pursuits, it is telling fearfully on many men," opined one lowcountry planter who had retired from active operations.[89] Many of his contemporaries concurred.[90]

Still, few planters could afford to abandon the use of their lands entirely. Most found a much more satisfactory solution in simply de-

87. *The Nation,* X, No. 236 (January 6, 1870), 2.

88. J. A. Martin to A. L. Burt, December 6, 1869, A. L. Burt Papers.

89. William Heyward to James Gregorie, January 12, 1868, Gregorie–Elliott Papers.

90. S. L. West to N. J. Holmes, May —, 1866, N. J. Holmes Papers.

creasing their laboring force to include only their most efficient and
co-operative laborers. The case was admirably presented in the correspondence of Robert W. Hemphill, a substantial Chester County planter.
"I may kick off some of a poorer sort, & carry on to a limited extent,"
he declared at the end of his first season as an employer of free labor.
During the following summer, he anticipated still further reductions:
"My own share [of the crop] will not allow me to carry on so largely
the coming year. I will have to reduce my force Considerably & every
one else will do the same. Now what is to become of those thrown
out of employment is beyond me to see." In the spring of 1871, curtailment continued as he wrote, "have reduced my force this year
three plows. am becoming more disgusted with the business every
year . . ." In January, 1873, he noted that such sentiments were common and that "most every one in our County is turning Merchant to
get clear of the vexations & annoyance of the negro labour."[91] This
pattern was most apparent among middle and lowcountry planters
with large land holdings, but it also occurred in the upcountry. David
Golightly Harris, in Spartanburg County, reported the same attitude
in his community in 1868. "The farmers are talking of working less
land," he observed, "& almost entirely discarding the Radical negro
race."[92] Reportedly, some farmers also reduced their need for labor
by turning from cotton to cereal production, crops which required
considerably less human effort to cultivate.[93]

"If the reality ever comes on me that I must labor," wrote the aristocratic William Heyward in June, 1868, "I am sure I cannot do it, I
must then lie down and die."[94] While Heyward may have been a representative spokesman of his class, it was, after all, a very small class, one
generally confined to Charleston and the lowcountry, and his was not
typical of the thinking of the great mass of white Carolinians. On the
contrary, most whites—men, women, and children—appear to have labored in Reconstruction both with their hands and their heads as they had
never worked before, earnestly, diligently, almost desperately. Particularly was this true in the upcountry where land holdings had always been
comparatively small, where many farms had been worked by the families

91. R. N. Hemphill to W. R. Hemphill, December 13, 1865; August 11, 1866;
January 6, 1873; R. N. Hemphill to Robert Hemphill, April 30, 1871, Hemphill
Papers.
92. MS Farm Journal, entry for June 20, 1868.
93. *Intelligencer* (Anderson), January 6, 1876.
94. To James Gregorie, June 4, 1868, Gregorie–Elliott Papers.

who owned them (occasionally assisted by hired white laborers), and where masters had often worked in the fields beside their half-dozen or dozen slaves.[95] As the time grew near when his ex-slaves were to leave him, David Golightly Harris noted in his journal that his young sons, Willie and James, were learning to plow. "I fancie that they will have some of it to do now the negroes are to be freed," he concluded.[96]

Many planters had great difficulty in securing white labor outside their own families. Plantation manager A. T. Smythe, in Orangeburg District in December, 1865, found it impossible to get white laborers.[97] In Spartanburg District, David Golightly Harris had no success in his attempts to employ whites to do domestic work. "I tried to hire some white women to live with & assist my family with their work," he explained. "They do not like the idea of becoming 'Help.' but time & privation is telling hard on some, & they are learning to work for a living." A year later, he tried in vain to hire a "Miss story," a "poor white" girl, who had, nevertheless, ambition enough to walk twenty-eight miles in an unsuccessful attempt to obtain an issue of government corn.[98] Even when they could be hired, landowners often discovered that native whites were unsatisfactory substitutes for Negro laborers. David Harris' experience is again revealing. After renting his land to three of his former slaves in 1866, he turned in disgust and leased only to whites in 1867. Still, at the end of the season, he saw only failure and further frustration. "My own renters (white men) have sadly disappointed me," he complained. "Paying me nothing while I am to pay my debts as best as I can." During the following year, he agreed to rent to two Negroes and two white tenants, apparently deciding to strike a balance.[99]

In spite of obstacles, white tenancy did become common in the upcountry during Reconstruction. Although it was not, apparently, as prevalent in the lowcountry, it did exist there. The mistress of Social Hall, a plantation in St. Paul's Parish near Adams Run, reported in January, 1868, that two white men had contracted to farm a part of the

95. B. W. Holmes to N. J. Holmes, December 11, 1867, N. J. Holmes Papers; *New York Times*, January 15, 1869, p. 2; *A History of Spartanburg County*, pp. 183–84.

96. MS Farm Journal, entry for November 10, 1865, *et seq.*

97. A. T. Smythe to his brother, December 5, 1865, A. T. Smythe Letters.

98. MS Farm Journal, entries for March 8, 1866; June 9, 1867.

99. *Ibid.*, entries for December 25, 1867; April 17, 1868. See also: J. A. Mitchell to his sister, January 13, 1867, J. A. Mitchell Papers.

land for half the crop. "They are well recommended," she added, "and good men."[100]

There was some sentiment among Carolina planters for bringing agricultural laborers down from the North; however, the idea was never popular. A Northern farmer who had settled in Aiken for purposes of health urged others of his class to come South; at the same time, he warned young men without capital to stay away, since "there is no demand for labor."[101] Southern whites, too, rejected the idea, perhaps following the cue of a legislative committee which offered the opinion in November, 1866, that Northern laborers would not adopt the mores of the South.[102]

Under the circumstances, it is hardly surprising that among native whites in the early years of Reconstruction the importation of foreign labor was the most popular solution to the problems presented by the free Negro worker. To some extent, the idea was promoted by politicians and journalists who saw in the immigrants a mass of white voters, and by ex-slaveholders out of simple malice against their late bondsmen for no longer being their slaves. However, the movement was chiefly an indication of the pessimism with which the white community regarded the Negro as a free laborer. One pro-immigration element candidly expected the Negro, deprived of the protection and guidance of the whites, to vanish as a race. In this context, the immigrant was to supply the competition which would keep the Negro toiling until his demise and then, conveniently, flow easily into the labor vacuum.[103] Other proponents of immigration expected the Negro to survive, but they looked to an influx of willing white labor to supplement the available supply and stimulate both Negroes and native whites to greater effectiveness. "Let your old niggs know that you [can] do without them," a Batesburg physician counseled his landowning father in advising him "to try some foreigners" as their neighbors were doing.[104]

100. "H. R. G." to "Emmie," January 8, 1868, Elliott–Gonzales Papers.

101. *New York Times*, August 3, 1865, p. 5; September 27, 1868, p. 3.

102. *Ibid.*, December 3, 1866, p. 2.

103. For this trend of thought, see: M. S. Wilkins to J. B. Grimball, August 5, 1865, J. B. Grimball Papers; Ralph Elliott to his mother, January 13, 1866, Elliott–Gonzales Papers; *The Nation*, I, No. 21 (November 23, 1865), 651; *New York Times*, December 3, 1866, p. 2; May 7, p. 5; July 5, p. 5, 1868; February 16, p. 2; July 19, p. 5, 1869.

104. T. S. Fox to John Fox, February 25, 1875, John Fox Papers. See also: "Mother" (probably Mrs. William Elliott) to "Hattie," June 29, 1869, Elliott–Gonzales Papers; *New York Times*, December 3, 1866, p. 2.

In this atmosphere, a host of immigration projects emerged. Occasionally, individual planters made their own arrangements. Thus, B. F. Crayton of Anderson, in December, 1875, had four German families at work on his plantation. In that month, he brought in twelve additional families consisting of fifty-two people, and, soon afterward, he announced his intention of re-settling still others.[105] Potentially, by far the most effective organization for promoting immigration was the Bureau of Immigration, an agency of the state government created by the legislature in 1866 after a year of careful consideration. A partial answer to the disallowance of the Black Code, the Bureau pushed its work vigorously forward. However, only 248 immigrants were induced to enter the state before the Republican legislature abolished the Bureau in 1868. Ironically, it was replaced by the Bureau of Agricultural Statistics, whose real purpose was to promote the interests of Negro labor.[106] The demise of the Bureau by no means killed the immigration movement. Private organizations—such as the Immigration Society of Newberry—persisted, while the press and various agricultural and political associations displayed an abiding interest in the subject.[107]

The results of all the immigration projects were hardly impressive either in numbers, or in satisfaction to employers and employees. Altogether, probably less than a thousand immigrants were induced to settle permanently in the state, and few of these stayed in the fields. In 1880, only about 6 per cent of the total foreign born population worked in agriculture. The immigrants then constituted barely 1 per cent of the population and this was only three-fourths of what the proportion of foreign-born had been in 1860.[108] Moreover, employers found that immigrant labor could be fully as unreliable as Negro labor. "Many families here entirely discarded the blacks & get industrious Irish women who like 'new brooms' give great satisfaction for a time, but too often prove to be Drunkards &c &c," reported one lady of Charleston.[109]

105. *Intelligencer* (Anderson), December 2, 16, 1875; January 13, 1876.

106. *Reports and Resolutions* (1865), p. 191; *New York Times,* March 13, p. 4; November 29, p. 2, 1866; March 2, p. 2; April 21, p. 1, 1867; June 1, p. 5; December 28, p. 1, 1868.

107. For instance, the Patrons of Husbandry, after its organization in the state in 1871, repeatedly expressed its interest in immigration. See: Harry Aubrey Chapman, "The Historical Development of the Grange in South Carolina" (Unpublished Master's Thesis, Furman University, 1952), *passim.*

108. Harry Hammond, *South Carolina Resources and Population, Institutions and Industries* (Charleston, 1883), p. 391.

109. Louise Porcher to A. Burt, December 11, 1866, O. T. Porcher Papers.

Apparently, alcohol, as well as other afflictions, also pursued Irishmen into the fields. "Our people are much in the spirit of getting foreigners," reported a Laurens County woman in the summer of 1868, "but some have tried Irishmen and they are worse than the negro, they drink and gamble worse and some of them are very trifling."[110] Also, employers soon learned that the immigrant might present all the problems of the Negro laborer, and add a few uniquely his own. One planter near Columbia obtained a German family of five, including three very young children. He soon found that the wife would not work, the children could not because of their youth, and that he was unable to communicate with any member of the family, he making "no progress in their language & they none in English." A neighboring planter, having some special talents as a linguist, hired the family, and soon found that the wife was demoralizing her husband and children because she wanted only to go "back to Germany."[111] Even after it reached the field, immigrant labor was expensive to maintain. The wages and rations that the Newberry Society prescribed for its charges were nearly twice those of Negro workers, and the fringe benefits—quarters, garden plots, and fuel privileges—were much more generous than those allowed Negroes.[112] Under these circumstances, it is hardly surprising that well before the end of Reconstruction, the majority of white employers had come to recognize that immigration was no solution to their labor problem.

Whites were well aware that politics afforded a means of controlling the labor of the Negro. During the summer and fall of 1865, when they felt that at least local political power was theirs, the Black Code and lesser legislation were submitted as partial solutions to the labor problem. After federal authorities moved decisively to reclaim that power in January, 1866, and subsequently passed it rather deliberately into the hands of the Republican party in the state in June, 1868, the white community was strongly motivated to regain political potency by a consciousness of its economic value. In November, 1869, Robert Hemphill said what many of his friends were thinking: "the labour of this Country is gone up, & unless we Can redeem the state at the Election next fall we are doomed."[113] Needless to say, Hemphill was dis-

110. "Mother" to N. J. Holmes, July 7, 1868, N. J. Holmes Papers.
111. E. B. Turnipseed to T. S. Boinest, January 24, 1869, T. S. Boinest Papers.
112. Circular, a Charleston agent, November 1, 1867, revised March 1, 1868; Circular, Newberry Immigration Society, September 6, 1869, T. S. Boinest Papers.
113. R. H. Hemphill to W. R. Hemphill, November 15, 1869, Hemphill Papers.

appointed in that year and in the elections of 1872 and 1874. In their frustration, some employers resorted to physical force. In a minor degree, the Ku Klux disturbances were a reflection of this trend. Yet, the real push came in 1876 and 1877, and it should excite no surprise that white employers of Negro labor—particularly planters—supplied a large part of the leadership and swelled the ranks of the Redeemers.[114]

The crucial fact in the economic history of South Carolina during Reconstruction is that, ultimately, both whites and Negroes adjusted their demands to the requirements imposed by the North and to the needs of each other. In view of their traditional relations, this was accomplished with a rapidity that was amazing. In retrospect, it is easy to see that some adjustment was virtually inevitable. The white man needed the labor of the Negro to make his capital productive; the Negro needed the white man's capital to earn a subsistence. Yet, the prejudices, the bitterness and suspicion that filled the minds of both white and Negro complicated an already difficult problem. In this context, possibly the political dictation of the North was actually salutary in that it forced each group to cut through the fantastical problems of race so that all might deal with the real and pressing problem of economic necessity. Under these circumstances, the economically dominant whites were forced to concede much to the Negro worker which would have come—if at all—only later and with more difficulty. Further, the Negro received benefits and (as will be described subsequently) rewards which facilitated his adjustment to the new economics. From the Northern point of view, probably in no area was Reconstruction more completely successful. At least in the legal sense, the Negro was transformed from a slave into a "free" economic agent. If that freedom was sometimes limited—as it obviously was—the Negro had the same alternatives possessed by his Northern white contemporary; he could submit, starve,

114. Harry Aubrey Chapman, the historian of the Grange in South Carolina, asserted his belief that politics—contrary to the rules of the organization—were discussed during and after Grange meetings. It was, he thought, not "without significance that Wade Hampton, a member of the Grange himself, addressed the group at its annual meeting in February, 1875, and was elected governor of the state in 1876; and that D. Wyatt Aiken was one of the two Congressmen elected that same year." "Up to this time," Professor Chapman concluded, "Granges were unable to accomplish anything with the Reconstruction government in power, but after the whites regained control of the state government in 1877, with the removal of federal troops, they were given full consideration." Chapman, "The Grange in South Carolina," p. 42.

or move. Even among Negroes themselves, few would have asked for more.

Within the economic realm, the white community was perhaps quicker to adjust to the changing order than were the Negroes. Even those whites who were least sympathetic with Negroes nevertheless recognized a temporary or partial dependence upon them. In December, 1865, the Columbia correspondent of the *New York Times* reported that some planters in the area were considering immigration. "But," he added, "it is evident that for some years to come these lands must depend upon the present population of freedmen for culture."[115] An important number of whites were inclined to make a virtue out of the necessity imposed by the North. In a Christmas Day proclamation in 1865, Governor Orr urged "kindness, humanity and justice" upon the whites in their relations with the freedmen. "Under such a policy," he predicted, "the majority of them will labor patiently and faithfully, and the eye will be greeted everywhere with blooming fields, fruitful harvests and well-filled granaries."[116] Several weeks later, in a letter to Francis W. Pickens, he gave a practical suggestion for the application of his advice when he recommended that planters, themselves, should voluntarily divide their lands into forty- and fifty-acre plots upon which individual Negro families would live and work. Pickens, a planter with large land holdings, approved, but added the more generous thought that one-hundred-acre plots might be necessary to provide each with the water, wood, and other resources required to operate a farm efficiently.[117] At the end of the 1866 farming season, both Orr and the legislative committee appointed to study immigration were pleased with the "amount of voluntary labor" which the Negro had performed.[118]

A glimmer of prosperity in 1867 and a fair return on a less-than-perfect crop in 1868 coincided with a rising sentiment among white employers that Negro labor was not only necessary, but desirable and, indeed, preferable to any other. Strangely enough, his very prejudices suggested to the white employer good reasons for adjusting to the new status of the Negro in order to retain his services as a laborer. For instance, it was generally believed that the Negro, physically, was

115. *New York Times,* January 4, 1866, p. 1. See also: *The Nation,* I, No. 21 (November 23, 1865), 651.

116. *New York Times,* January 4, 1866, p. 1.

117. F. W. Pickens to J. L. Orr, February 16, 1866, Freedmen File.

118. *New York Times,* November 28, p. 5; 29, p. 2, 1866.

uniquely adapted to the culture of rice or cotton, that he was immune from the illnesses of the lowland rice and long-staple cotton plantations, and that he could labor all day under a blazing sun that would prostrate a white man. There were also social reasons why Negro labor was preferable to white. D. Wyatt Aiken, who subsequently became the leading Granger in the state, in 1870 told a meeting of Carolina planters that the importation of culturally inferior white laborers might lead to social leveling. ". . . let us have no social equality with our laborers," he cried. However offensive this declaration may have sounded to Charleston ears still attuned to German and Gaelic, it doubtless touched the hearts of many of Aiken's colleagues.[119] The advantage of having economic inferiors whose subordination was reinforced by supposedly perpetual biological and social inferiority was obvious.

The advent of a predominantly Negro legislature in June, 1868, served to heighten the white employer's appreciation of the Negro as a laborer under the previous regime. Native whites now fondly thought that South Carolina would be a veritable Eden were it not for the Radicals. J. W. W. Marshall of Abbeville, a close friend of Orr and a land speculator with large holdings in the South and Mid-west, verbalized this feeling in writing to his wife from Council Bluffs, Iowa, in the summer of 1868. "As slow as the negro is in our country," he declared, "If it was not for the political & financial situation in the South I would prefer to remain there, but I am affraid it will be allmost intolerable for a decent person to remain there & raise a family as long as the negro has control of our country."[120] A year later, in Chester County, even the perennially pessimistic planter Robert Hemphill saw some hope. "My Freedmen are Industrious & respectful," he wrote, "& I am convinced (by kind treatment & fair & Just dealing) would do well were it not for the abominable Carpet Baggers."[121]

During the early 1870's, the adjustment of the whites was virtually completed. A traveler in South Carolina in November, 1870, found "little or no disparagement of the negro as a labourer among respectable countrymen, who need his services and employ him." "On the contrary," he asserted, "there is much appreciation of his good qualities, and much greater satisfaction with what he has done, and may yet be trained to do, as a free labourer, than one might be prepared to find."[122] By

119. *Daily Republican* (Charleston), May 6, 1870.
120. To his wife, August 28, 1868, J. W. W. Marshall Papers.
121. To W. R. Hemphill, June 9, 1869, Hemphill Papers.
122. Somers, *The Southern States since the War,* p. 60.

the close of the 1875 farming season, even Robert Hemphill, who repeatedly threatened to desert the planting profession, was apparently
reconciled. "I suppose I will get A few Hands," he announced, "&
continue the business in some shape Next Year."[123] The only fly remaining in the economic ointment was, of course, the "abominable
Carpet Baggers."

By their actions, rather than their words, Negroes revealed a ready
willingness to adjust to the evolving economic order. One indication of
their adaptability was the increasing facility with which the great mass
of Negroes entered into contractual relations with employers. Even
while the first flush of freedom was driving many Negroes away from
their ex-masters, a few were earnestly seeking employment in their
old places. "Dick found me out soon after my arrival, is humble &
anxious to contract with the family for the next year," wrote a lowcountry planter in January, 1866, upon returning to his estate for the
first time after the war.[124] In many areas, contracting had been a
painful, tedious process in 1865 and 1866; but, by 1867, it was easy for
those planters who had gained reputations for dealing fairly with
their laborers. "I have 45 hands & can get as many as I require," reported one employer in February, 1867, after having collected a laboring
force in the previous year only with great difficulty.[125] Two years later,
David Golightly Harris found the Negroes of Spartanburg County
eager to contract for 1869. "At this time there is lively times in the
country, renting land," he observed. "The white people are a little
careless, while the negroes are getting more anxious to find homes."[126]
Once employed, the same progress was seen in the performance of
Negro labor. Particularly as prosperity returned complaints gave way
to expressions of satisfaction and even pleasure. "I am hard at work
here," wrote a Beaufort planter in the spring of 1867, "have hands
enough & am agreeably surprised at the ease with which they are
managed. We intend planting 150 acres short cotton & 20 acres of corn,
have 7 mules & 13 contracted hands—outside labour can be obtained

123. To W. R. Hemphill, December 4, 1875, Hemphill Papers.
124. Ralph Elliott to his mother, January 13, 1866, Elliott–Gonzales Papers.
For similar expressions, see: M. S. Wilkins to J. B. Grimball, August 5, 1865,
J. B. Grimball Papers; and F. H. Spawner to T. R. S. Elliott, December 12, 1865,
T. R. S. Elliott Papers.
125. T. R. S. Elliott to his mother, February —, 1867, Elliott–Gonzales Papers.
126. MS Farm Journal, entry for December 5, 1868.

to a sufficient extent."[127] A year later, in Lancaster, a militantly Democratic planter conceded that "We are getting on very well with our Freedmen [who] continue still to work very well."[128] Similarly, the Reverend John Cornish, visiting his plantation near Adams Run, recorded that the work being done by his Negro farmers "was like plantation work in olden time when good crops of fine cotton were made."[129] By 1874, Thomas Taylor, a very extensive planter in Richland County, was able to state that if his Negro laborers were "well watched," they worked better than before they were freed.[130]

"Your brother Joe had less advantages than either of you three," the mistress of a plantation admonished one of her sons in 1871, "and he works as hard or harder than any negro."[131] In this backhanded way have Southerners—in spite of the myth that idleness is inherent in the Negro—recognized the capacity of the black man for labor. The phrase "works like a Negro" and its variants contained the kernel of the Southern white's attitude toward the Negro as an economic entity. He is the laborer par excellence. As such and in his proper place he is not only desirable, he is indispensable to the Southern economy. "The white planter," stated a native white agricultural expert in 1882, "cannot get on without the skillful and competent help of the colored farm laborer."[132]

For his part, even in the heyday of his political ascendency, the Negro laborer was forced, eventually, to moderate his terms to meet the needs of his employer. "The nig," wrote a Georgetown druggist in the spring of 1873, "ever desirous of change, gives trouble & altho labor politically 'mirabile dictu' contracts capital, he is obliged eventually to seek the landholder to keep from starving."[133]

Thus, by mutual consent occurred the marriage between the labor of the Negro and the capital of the white; a union of convenience certainly and possibly one of necessity, but no less a marriage for all of that.

127. R. E. Elliott to T. R. S. Elliott, March 13, 1867, T. R. S. Elliott Papers.
128. E. B. Mobley to E. W. Bonney, April 10, 1868, E. W. Bonney Papers.
129. MS Diary, entry for May 19, 1868.
130. *New York Times*, July 4, 1874, p. 5.
131. Mrs. R. E. Bonney to her son, February 16, 1871, E. W. Bonney Papers.
132. Hemphill, *Climate, Soil, and Agricultural Capabilities of South Carolina and Georgia*, p. 38.
133. T. P. Bailey to R. H. McKie, March 26, 1873, R. H. McKie Papers.

V...NEW PATTERNS IN ECONOMICS

Before the end of Reconstruction, the Negro in South Carolina found that the pattern of his employment was already well defined. In agriculture, he belonged to one or more of four distinct groups. Either he rented the land upon which he worked, labored for wages, sold his supervisory skills as a foreman or a manager, or owned his own land.

In the first days of freedom, the Negro agrarian usually found himself in one of the first two categories. His desire to rent land was strong and persistent. He was also averse to working for wages and, especially, to working in gangs under direct supervision. David Golightly Harris, visiting Spartanburg village on January 4, 1866, observed: "The negroes all seem disposed to rent land, & but few are willing to hire by the day, month or year."[1] Occasionally, the desire to rent became a mania. "I am about renting some land on the aint (Aunt) Juriy Hemphill place to Bek, Smith Sam & Peggy," wrote a Chester County planter in November, 1869. "They have hardly corn for Bread & will make nothing but are rent Crazy & must be gratified."[2]

1. David Golightly Harris MS Farm Journal, entry for January 4, 1866.
2. R. N. Hemphill to W. R. Hemphill, November 15–16, 1869, Hemphill Papers. See also: T. R. S. Elliott to William Elliott, February 1, 1875, T. R. S. Elliott Papers.

In the first years after manumission, renting was poor economics for most freedmen. Few had the managerial experience, and fewer still had the capital necessary to succeed as independent renters. Moreover, the late 1860's was a period of agricultural depression. Landowners were aware of these problems and, in addition to their aversion to renting land to Negroes for social and political reasons, they opposed the practice as economically unsound. "Negroes will not do to rely upon as croppers," journalized David Harris in the spring of 1869. "They will not [look] far enough ahead to do any good."[3] As buildings, fences, ditches, and lands deteriorated under the neglect of successive tenants, resistance to renting to either blacks or whites became stronger among landowners. In the spring of 1868, Harris recorded a complaint frequently heard: "I have no little trouble to get my renters to do such work [maintenance], & have almost determined never to rent again. I sometimes think that if I can [not] hire hands to work my land as I want it done, it shall not be worked at all."[4]

Possibly, the Negro renter made his choice against the clear dictates of agrarian economy because he wanted to free himself from the pattern of life he had known as a slave. As a wage laborer, he would have continued to live in the plantation village and to work in gangs under the eye of the white man. As a renter, he labored independently and lived with his family upon his own farm, having either moved a cabin from the plantation village or, as frequently happened, having built a new one upon his plot of earth.

Statistically, the "rent crazy" Negroes often had their way. A generation after emancipation, 37 per cent of the Negro farmers in the state were renters, a large majority occupying plots of less than fifty acres.[5] Indeed, renting became the usual form of land tenure in the upcountry. For instance, of thirty-four Negro farmers who testified on the subject before a Congressional committee in the spring of 1871, twenty-one were renters, eight were wage laborers, and five owned their own land.[6] Further, renting existed in considerable degree in every part of the state. "The negroes who cultivated cotton, as a general rule, rented land from their former masters," reported one native several decades later.[7]

3. MS Farm Journal, entry for March 27, 1869.
4. *Ibid.*, entry for March 22, 1868. See also: Robert Somers, *The Southern States since the War, 1870–1871* (New York, 1871), p. 60.
5. *Negro Population*, pp. 528, 624.
6. *Ku-Klux Conspiracy*, III, IV, and V, *passim.*
7. William Willis Boddie, *History of Williamsburg County, South Carolina, 1705 until 1923* (Columbia, 1923), p. 449.

Negro renters paid their landlords in a variety of ways, but, generally, the method of payment belonged to one of two broad categories. In South Carolina in 1880, about one-quarter of the farm operators of both races compensated landlords with a share of the crop.[8] Renting land for a share of the proceeds tended particularly to pervade those areas where cotton was grown; and, even after the return of prosperity, many planters (or landowners) continued to adhere to the system, deeming it more profitable than slavery.[9] This was especially true in the upcountry. "In the upper counties the negroes work better and the masters treat them fairly, so that in some cases farms are still worked on shares with a profit to both parties," reported a Northern correspondent in 1874.[10]

The proportion of the crop paid for the use of land normally varied from one-half to three-quarters, depending largely on the goods and animals that the landlord supplied in addition to the land.[11] The share arrangement was thus capable of endless variety and complexity. For instance, in Edgefield District in 1866, Alfred rented a certain acreage from his late master for one-third the expected crop. However, for the cultivation of another plot, Alfred was to get a tenth of the gross yield in payment for his services as stockminder, then the owner was to have a third of the remainder as rent, and the last two-thirds was to go to Alfred as wages.[12]

In 1880, slightly less than a quarter of the farm operators in South Carolina were renters who paid their landlords a fixed-cash rental.[13] Like share-renting, the term fixed-cash renting covered a wide variety of

8. James Calvin Hemphill, *Climate, Soil, and Agricultural Capabilities of South Carolina and Georgia* (Washington, 1882), p. 33. "Share-cropping" is a poor term to describe this practice. Negro wage laborers who worked as a gang and were paid by a share of the crop were also share-croppers. Thus, a very different practice was contemporaneously referred to by the same name. "Share-renting" perhaps, describes this first class more accurately.

9. *Ibid.,* pp. 31–32.

10. *New York Times,* July 4, 1874, p. 5.

11. Hemphill, *Climate, Soil, and Agricultural Capabilities of South Carolina and Georgia,* p. 32. A thorough study of Spartanburg County indicated that the proportion there varied from one-half to two-thirds. *A History of Spartanburg County* (Compiled by the Spartanburg Unit of the Writer's Program of the Works Project Administration in the State of South Carolina) (n.p., 1940), p. 184. Cited hereinafter as *A History of Spartanburg County.*

12. MS Contract, January 1, 1866, Pickens-Dugas Papers. See also: J. H. Cornish MS Diary, entry for May 19, 1868.

13. Hemphill, *Climate, Soil, and Agricultural Capabilities of South Carolina and Georgia,* p. 33.

methods of payment. A common device was the payment of the rent by a specific quantity of a given crop. Thus, in St. Paul's Parish, Colleton District, in December, 1865, "Miles (a Freedman of Colour) and Alfred E. Stokes of the same place" agreed to rent sixteen acres of land from Charles H. Rice for the coming season. The rental was to be paid in November, 1866, and consisted of sixty-four bushels of corn and a third of the "peace and fodder that may be made."[14] Frequently, Negro renters paid a money rental for their land. For instance, a planter near Adams Run filled his plantation with renters at five dollars per acre, whereas another planter in St. Andrews Parish, in 1872, had difficulty finding renters at three dollars an acre.[15] Occasionally, labor was given in total or partial payment of rent. In Spartanburg County, David G. Harris recorded the terms of a contract with a Negro renter for 1869: "Prince morris has built a house[,] garden[,] cut a ditch & cleared an small field. He gives me Sim's [his son's] labour this year for this land."[16]

To meet the needs of the renter, the landlord, the crop, and of the land itself, rental arrangements often assumed a bewildering complexity as various methods of sharing and paying produce, cash, and labor were combined to provide a satisfactory rental. In 1871 in Colleton County, seven renters (two of whom may have been white) agreed to six different arrangements with the same landowner. Benjamin Kelley agreed to pay the owner a fourth share which was to be used by Kelley himself to improve the house on his rented plot. A pair of renters agreed to work a mule for the owner on a given field and to pay the owner a half of the yield from this field in addition to the fourth due from their main plot. Didemus Allen agreed to farm four acres and to pay the owner two bushels of corn per acre and a fourth of all else he grew. Jerry Smith, a Negro, agreed to pay on Christmas Day, 1871, $12.00 plus a fourth of the produce from a twenty-acre plot that he was allowed to use.[17] In the following year, Jerry contracted with the owner to set up ten thousand turpentine boxes on his land and to divide the profits of the enterprise evenly.[18]

14. MS Contract, December 25, 1865, J. D. Bivens Papers.

15. J. H. Cornish MS Diary, entry for May 20, 1868; "G. I. C." to W. P. Miles, April 4, 1872, W. P. Miles Papers.

16. MS Farm Journal, entry for June 5, 1869. *See also:* MS Contract, January 1, 1866, Pickens-Dugas Papers.

17. MS Contracts, January —, February —, 1871, J. D. Bivens Papers.

18. MS Contract, February —, 1872, J. D. Bivens Papers. For examples of similar complexity on upcountry estates, see: David Golightly Harris MS Farm

Contrary to the general impression, the plantations of South Carolina did not at the end of the war immediately crumble into many small parts. Indeed, probably most plantations continued to be worked, on a reduced scale, as integral units using wage labor. In the rice districts, fragmentation was impossible since the production of that crop required dikes, ditches, and flood gates which could only be constructed and maintained by a number of laborers organized under a well-financed management. Although few rice plantations were restored to full productivity during Reconstruction, many of these were operated as units.[19] On the other hand, many cotton plantations were indeed divided into small farms and operated under the rental system. Even in the cotton areas, however, some plantations continued to be operated as units for some time after the war,[20] and many planters who rented portions of their lands to others frequently retained large "home places" which they managed themselves.[21]

Employers placed restrictions upon Negro wage laborers that were much more onerous than those imposed upon renters by landlords. The amount, the time, and, frequently, the quality of the wage hand's labor were closely prescribed in his contract, and any delinquency in his performance was severely penalized by fines. In the early years of Reconstruction, the task—the unit of labor used in the slave period—was widely utilized. Ideally, a task was an amount of work which an adult Negro of average abilities could do well in a day's time. The contract signed by thirty-six wage laborers on the Peter B. Bacot plantation in Darlington District in 1867 was typical: "The said servants

---

Journal, entry for June 5, 1869; R. N. Hemphill to W. R. Hemphill, December 4, 1875, Hemphill Papers.

19. T. R. S. Elliott to his son, June 2, 1874, T. R. S. Elliott Papers; K. S. Ball MS Plantation Journal, entry for March 14, 1874, et seq.; Gabriel Manigault to Louis Manigault, November 29, 1876, Louis Manigault Papers; MS Contract, January 21, 1867, Sparkman Family Papers; The Nation, XIV, No. 365 (June 27, 1872), 418–19; XV, No. 367 (July 11, 1872), 22.

20. MS captioned "Division of Laborers share of Dec. 1865 crop," H. W. and W. G. De Saussure Papers; MS Contract, ———, 1867, P. B. Bacot Collection, MS Contract, February 20, 1866, J. J. McIver Papers; numerous manuscripts and correspondence between A. H. Boykin and L. D. De Saussure, June 22, 1865, et seq., A. H. Boykin Papers; MS Contract, April 14, 1867, D. T. Crosby Papers; MS Contract, ———, 1866, George Wise Papers.

21. For instances, see: MS Farm Journal, entries for June 18, 1866; August 23, December 25, 1867; July 27, 28, September 21, October 6, 1868; June 5, 1869; R. N. Hemphill to W. R. Hemphill, December 4, 1875, Hemphill Papers; MS Contract, ———, 1866, F. W. Pickens Papers.

agreed to perform the daily tasks hitherto usually allotted on said plantation, to wit: 125 to 150 rails; cutting grain 3 to 6 acres; ditching & banking 300 to 600 feet; hoeing cotton 70 to 300 rows an acre long; corn 4000 to 6000 hills. In all cases where tasks cannot be assessed, they agree to labor diligently ten hours a day."[22] While the task system of measuring labor tended to persist in the rice areas, elsewhere there was a general trend toward substituting a given number of hours of labor per day. Ten hours daily was the usual requirement, beginning at or shortly after sunrise and ending at sunset, with greater and lesser periods of freedom allowed for the noon meal as the days lengthened and shortened. Often, attempts were made to control the quality of labor by including in contracts provisions binding Negroes to work "as heretofore," or to "the faithful discharge of his duties as an industrious farm labourer doing whatever he is directed to do . . ." The fine for "absence, refusal or neglect" was everywhere fifty cents for each day lost, and illness gave no exemption from the penalty. Absence from the plantation without leave was subject to fine at the rate of two dollars a day. Persistent absence or misbehavior was punishable by expulsion from the plantation and forfeiture of any claim to wages at the end of the year.

Contracts also included a host of minor regulations designed to enhance the efficiency of the laborer. Typically, the laborer was "not to leave the premises during work hours without the consent of the Proprietor or his Agent," and "not to bring visitors without permission." On some plantations, laborers were committed to observe silence in their cabins after nine o'clock in the evening, "to bring no ardent spirits at any time upon the plantation," and not to have private livestock or pets or to converse with one another in the fields. Often, the laborers as a group were required to supply from their numbers a foreman, a nurse when sickness occurred, a stockminder, and a watchman for the harvested crop. Employers also sought to use the contract to enforce a proper demeanor upon their Negro employees. Thus, laborers were often bound to "perfect obedience," promptness, diligence and respectful conduct," or "to conduct themselves faithfully, honestly & civilly," or to be "peaceable, orderly and pleasant," or "reliable and respectful and to mind all directions," or "to be kind and respectful to Employer and Agent," or to "treat the Employer with due respect." Disrespectful behavior, evidenced by "impudence, swearing; or indecent and unseemly language," was often punishable by fines. Finally, the

22. MS Contract, ——, 1867, P. B. Bacot Collection.

laborer was invariably bound to pay for the loss or injury of tools and animals either through neglect or by his willful act.[23]

In return for his toil, the agricultural laborer was paid by combinations of goods, services, and cash. In the early postwar years, most received at the end of the season a share of the crop, commonly a third of the gross yield. As with share-renting, the proportion taken by the employer depended largely on the degree to which he maintained his employees. In 1869, an upcountry editor averred that contracts usually granted the laborer a third of the crop in lieu of wages. However, he added, if the employer fed the laborer a weekly ration of four pounds of meat and one peck of meal with small allowances of coffee, salt, sugar, and lesser items, the share granted was a fourth.[24] Share-wage arrangements were often very complicated. For example, on the Mac-Farland plantation in Chesterfield District, in 1866, twenty-five Negro workers agreed to share evenly with the landowner the net profit of the year after a fourth of the cotton crop or seven bales, whichever was less, was deducted for rent and the overseer's wages and other expenses had been paid.[25]

Neither the share nor the specific amount of money the laborers received for their share was the ultimate measure of the individual's wages. On virtually every plantation, wage laborers contracted as a group, and the share which they earned collectively was divided among them in proportion to the working capacity of each as agreed upon in the contract itself. Thus, a full hand was paid a certain amount, while three-quarter, half, and quarter hands received proportionately less. In addition, employers promised "to furnish each family with quarters on his plantation & a garden plot and the privilege of getting firewood from some portion of the premises indicated by the Employer . . ." Also, laborers were sometimes allowed an "outside crop." A. H. Boykin, in Kershaw County, in 1875, permitted his dozen workers to cultivate as much land as "each thinks he can work every other saturday . . ."

23. MS Contract, January 1, 1866, ———, 1868, Pickens–Dugas Papers; MS Contract, ———, 1866, Heyward–Ferguson Papers; MS Contract, ———, 1866, George Wise Papers; MS and Printed Contract, February 20, 1866, J. J. McIver Papers; MS Contract, April 14, 1867, D. T. Crosby Papers; MS Contracts, June 22, July 6, 1865, January 23, 1868, A. H. Boykin Papers; MS Contract, ———, 1868, J. B. Richardson Papers; MS Contract, January 21, 1867, Sparkman Family Papers; MS Contract, ———, 1867, R. B. Bacot Collection; MS Contract, February 4, 1868, G. W. Spencer Papers.

24. *Intelligencer* (Anderson), January 28, 1869.

25. MS Contract, January 1, 1866, Allan MacFarland Papers.

Further, he promised to let each employee keep "one cow & one hog," not unusual concessions ten years after emancipation. Occasionally, special allowances were made for family chores. On Dean Hall plantation on the lower Cooper River, in 1866, the contract provided that "only half a day's work on Saturdays will be required of female employees who are heads of families." Employers usually agreed to advance goods and services to their employees, the costs of which were deducted from their share at the end of the season. Whether a part of the contract or not, most employers were forced to supply rations to their employees to enable them to finish the season. In addition, they often advanced other items: tobacco, salt, molasses, blankets, overcoats, shoes, taxes, medical care, and even, with striking frequency, preachers' salaries, coffins, and grave sites. Sometimes, too, the laboring force was required to pay a fraction of the cost of fertilizer, insurance, bagging, and rope—all of which were advanced in the same manner by the employer.[26]

Although it was true that many impoverished planters had no other resort in the early postwar years when cash was scarce, there are indications that many planters and laborers deliberately elected, at first, to use the share system. "I found very few [planters]—not more than one or two, who were offering monthly wages," wrote the owner of extensive lands on the Cooper River in February, 1866. "All on the Cooper River as far as I could learn were offering a share in the crops whether from a want of ability to pay wages &c or because they believed an interest in the crop would secure a more steady course of labor and prevent stealage, I know not, perhaps both."[27] Many Negro workers, themselves, preferred shares to cash wages. "The negroes will not contract for wages," reported a lowcountry planter in the winter of 1866.[28] In the fall of the same year, the majority of a large meeting of Negro laborers gathered in Sumter rejected a suggestion to change to cash wages, clinging "to their preference for a moiety of the crops."[29] One planter

26. MS Contracts, June 22, 1865; January 23, 1868; February 1, 1875; L. D. De Saussure to A. H. Boykin, December 27, 1869, A. H. Boykin Papers; MS Contract, ——, 1866, Heyward–Ferguson Papers; H. L. Pinckney MS Plantation Book, entry for April —, 1866, et seq.; MS Contract, January 1, 1866, Allan MacFarland Papers; MS Contracts, September 7, 1865; March 3, 1866, [—.—.] Deas Papers.

27. W. M. Burney to T. B. Ferguson, February 1, 1866, Heyward–Ferguson Papers.

28. T. R. S. Elliott to his wife, February 1, 1866, T. R. S. Elliott Papers.

29. New York Times, November 30, 1866, p. 2.

thought the Negroes preferred goods to money because they feared: "Maybe it git lak Confeddick money."[30]

Nevertheless, the great majority of planters shifted to money wages within the first few years after the war. Even in 1867, the number of planters paying cash wages, either entirely or partly, greatly increased. A cotton planter on Cooper River who ran "ten steady plows & more as the necesity [*sic*] calls for them and 30 hoe hands" wrote to a friend in the spring of 1867 that "We pay money for our labour half cash at the End of Each month."[31] A Northern correspondent reported in that year that the few Sea Island planters who could afford it had shifted to monthly wages; and another, writing in 1874, asserted that the share system had been "entirely abandoned" in the lowcountry a year or two after the war and that most planters "now pay their hands monthly wages."[32]

A preference for cash wages also spread among Negro laborers. In June, 1874, a planter on the Combahee River reported that "The negroes now work for money & I have to send out & pick them up where I can get them, & am obliged to take what I can get in order to get along." Such was still the case in the following winter: "Uncle Hawk is here with some hands that know how to work & will work here all the week, they work for money, exclusively, & don't draw from the Commissary."[33] As described earlier, the Combahee Riots in 1876 were partly caused by the desire of Negro laborers for payment of their wages in cash.

Definitions of the amount of labor demanded of an employee who worked for cash and the manner in which his wages were paid varied widely. On the whole, however, both were much less complicated than share agreements, and the parties concerned often dispensed entirely with formal, written contracts. A Combahee planter described one of his arrangements in 1875: "I have hired John Barnwell to Plow & attend to the mules at $5.00 per month, & give him 2 lbs meat & a package of flour per week . . ."[34] In the early postwar years, planters, suspicious of the constancy of Negro labor, were prone to withhold a portion

30. Myrta Lockett Avary, *Dixie after the War* (New York, 1906), p. 345.

31. P. O. Craddock to T. R. S. Elliott, April 27, 1867, T. R. S. Elliott Papers.

32. *New York Times,* June 19, 1867, p. 2; July 4, 1874, p. 5.

33. T. R. S. Elliott to William Elliott, June 2, 1874, February 1, 1875, T. R. S. Elliott Papers.

34. *Ibid.,* February 1, 1875. For other examples, see: John Berkeley Grimball MS Diary, entry for October 12, 1872; W. B. Burney to T. B. Ferguson, December 8, 1865, Heyward–Ferguson Papers.

of their employees' wages until the crop was harvested. In Newberry District, in 1866, for instance, an employer contracted to retain half the wages due his employees until "after summer work begins," and the other half until the end of the year to insure "faithful performance."[35] By the end of Reconstruction, however, most wage laborers were paid daily, weekly, or monthly, had contracted with their employers individually rather than collectively, and had taken a giant step away from the organizational forms of slavery.

Cash wages were also paid for part-time labor. Employees working on shares were paid cash for extra work. For instance, in 1867, the owner of Dirleton plantation on the Pee Dee contracted to pay fifty cents per day in wages to those share-laborers who would do "plantation work," particularly "carpenter work," beyond the terms of their contract.[36] Extra labor, on and off the plantation, was hired "to get the crop out of the grass," or to assist in its harvesting. Gathering in the cotton crop was a usual occasion for hiring additional laborers, and the standard rate of fifty cents per hundred pounds of cotton picked soon became the fixed wage.[37] In the lowcountry, many Negroes owning or renting small plots worked as day laborers whenever they could. In 1868, the Reverend John Cornish was breakfasting with John Jenkins at Gardenia Hall near Adams Run when "quite a gang of negroes came up the avenue with their hoes in hand, looking for work—John sent them into his cotton field—gives them 20cts a task—if very hard 25cts. In this way John is cultivating 30 odd acres of cotton this year—has but one hand constantly employed, & that is his plough man—"[38]

In the Sea Islands generally, and on some rice plantations on the Cooper River, the payment of wages by a combination of land allotments and cash called the "two-day system" came to be widely practiced. As applied to cotton on the Sea Islands, the system involved the laborer's giving two days of work a week (usually Monday and Tuesday) during the ten-month working season in return for quarters, fuel, and five to seven acres of land to work as he wished. Additional labor performed for the planter was paid for in cash at the rate of fifty cents a day or task. "Laborers prefer this system," asserted an agri-

35. MS Contract, ——, 1866, George Wise Papers. See also: MS Contract, ——, 1868, Pickens–Dugas Papers.

36. MS Contract, January 21, 1867, Sparkman Family Papers.

37. Somers, *The Southern States since the War,* pp. 60–61; *New York Times,* June 19, 1867, p. 2; W. A. Law to his wife, August 29, 1874, W. A. Law Papers.

38. J. H. Cornish MS Diary, entries for May 19, 21, 1868.

cultural expert in 1882.[39] The system was also applied to rice culture. Gabriel Manigault, having just completed the 1876 season on Rice Hope on the Cooper River, urged his brother Louis, who had had an unsuccessful year in rice on a Georgia Sea Island, to exchange land for two days' labor a week and to hire workers for two more, thereby cutting his cash expenses from $5,000 to $3,000 a year and avoiding "the paying of wages at every step."[40] The "two-day system," too, was capable of infinite variation. In 1868, for instance, rice planters near Adams Run were said to give two and a half acres of rice land, two pounds of bacon, and four quarts of corn in exchange for three days of labor each week.[41] Here again, possibly, the preference of the Negro worker for the "two-day system" marked his desire for greater independence in economic pursuits.

A third class of Negro agricultural worker emerged under the title of "foreman," or, less frequently, "agent" or "manager." Functionally, the foreman was the all too familiar "driver" of the slave period trading under a new label. Francis Pickens inadvertently recognized this fact when he drafted his first contract to employ his ex-slaves as free laborers. In that document he, at first, bound his workers "to obey faithfully the Overseer or Driver." Having second thoughts, he crossed out the word "Driver" and substituted "Agent."[42] The primary function of the foreman (as that of the driver had been) was the day-to-day assignment of tasks to individual laborers and seeing that they were properly done. Unlike the driver, however, the foreman did not carry a whip as his badge of office, and his demeanor was often in sharp contrast with that of the driver. In 1868, the mistress of El Dorado, a lowcountry plantation, noted this development with disgust. "The work here consists in going out at 9 & hoeing in a very leisurely manner till 12—when they disappear for the day," she reported. "The 'foreman' escorts the women with an air of gallantry—& Mary P. one day heard him saying in the most courteous manner—'Hide your grass, ladies, hide your grass.'"[43] Further, the foreman frequently assumed the obligations of a full

39. Hemphill, *Climate, Soil, and Agricultural Capabilities of South Carolina and Georgia*, p. 13; *New York Times*, July 24, 1869.

40. Gabriel Manigault to Louis Manigault, November 29, 1876, Louis Manigault Papers.

41. John Berkeley Grimball MS Diary, entry for August 29, 1868.

42. MS Contract, May 23, 1865, F. W. Pickens Papers.

43. "C. G. S." to "Mary" (probably Mary Elliott Johnstone), March 2, 1868, Elliott–Gonzales Papers.

field hand, laboring alongside his charges and, thus, becoming more of a leader among equals than a superior. Contracts typically bound all hands to obey the foreman equally with the owner, and occasionally, foremen possessed the power to discharge "disrespectful and idle or unfaithful" employees.[44] Foremen were doubtless numerous because plantations which continued to be farmed as a unit invariably relied upon the services of at least one member of this class.

The foreman sometimes earned only as much as a full hand, sometimes more. In 1866, H. L. Pinckney made James, an ex-slave who had not been a driver, foreman over some thirty-three field hands on his Sumter District plantation. For his trouble, James seems to have received only a full hand's share of the crop. Two years later, Pinckney broke his force into three groups of which James, Mitchell (another Negro), and the owner himself were the leaders. James and Mitchell, apparently, received only the shares due full hands.[45] Francis Pickens, in contrast, was very liberal in compensating his foremen. In 1866, he agreed to pay Jacob, who had been one of his drivers in the slave period, $100 at the end of the year and to keep him and his five dependents "in the old fashion." Comparatively, two years later, Pickens employed a "field labourer" for the year at $60 and maintenance.[46]

Largely out of the ranks of the foremen, there arose a higher level of agricultural supervisors who might be described collectively as the "managerial class." Managers differed from foremen in that their primary concern was with yearly, rather than daily, operations, though they usually performed both functions. In essence, the manager substituted for the absentee owner. He planned the crops, scheduled the various phases of cultivation and harvesting, executed the schedules, kept the records, attended to the health, welfare, and efficiency of the laboring force, and prepared, shipped, and frequently marketed the finished product. The manager might also do field work, but he was clearly more than a field hand. He was the fully authorized agent of the owner, filling an office which before the war was dominated by whites. Frequently, the manager received a special share of the profits from the owner. Occasionally, he became the lessee of the plantation and operated it for his own profit and, thus, passed into the entrepreneurial class where he competed directly with white men.

44. For instance, see: MS and Printed Contract, February 20, 1866, J. J. McIver Papers.

45. H. L. Pinckney MS Plantation Book, entries headed "1866" and "1868."

46. MS Contract, ——, 1866, F. W. Pickens Papers; MS Contract, ——, 1868, Pickens–Dugas Papers.

The Negro manager in action was personified by Adam R. Deas. He had been born a slave, the son of Robert, a driver on The Grove, a rice plantation near Adams Run belonging to John Berkeley Grimball. In July, 1863, during an inland raid conducted by Union gunboats and a portion of the First South Carolina Volunteers, he fled to the Union lines along with the entire Negro population of The Grove, including his father, his mother Amy, and his grandmother Sally. Like so many refugee families, they pre-empted a plot on Edisto Island in the spring of 1865 and remained there through 1866. In the spring of 1866, however, Robert contracted with Grimball to serve as caretaker of The Grove and an adjacent rice plantation, Pinebury, which was also owned by Grimball. In return, Robert was allowed to farm whatever portion of land he chose with a mule provided by Grimball. Adam's mother and grandmother, however, elected to remain on Edisto, partly because they had already begun a crop.

Through 1868, Grimball attempted unsuccessfully to resume profitable operations on his two rice plantations. In 1865 and 1866, he and his son, Arthur, were unable to induce their ex-slaves to return from their Edisto homes. In 1867, Robert persuaded a few Negroes to plant rice on The Grove, paying a third of the produce as a rental. Since Grimball did not provide seed rice and advances, some of these laborers had to earn expenses by working on neighboring plantations and the yield was both late and scanty. In 1868, Pinebury, the buildings of which had been razed and the fields neglected since 1863, was taken up by a Negro manager named Henry Jenkins with the same unsatisfactory results.

In November, 1868, Grimball sent for Adam Deas. Deas, in a letter written in his clear, squarish script, promised to come to Grimball in Charleston within a week. "I was at the Grove on Thursday afternoon," he wrote, catching a scene. "The people are all busy thrashing & I met my father cleaning out the house, expecting you up. I hope the family are all well." In Charleston, early in December, he called on Grimball and agreed to act as the owner's agent in restoring Pinebury to productivity. What happened to Pinebury during the next eleven years was adequate testimony to Deas's worth as a manager. On December 5, Adam returned to the country and on December 9 he wrote: "The time being so Short I was out from 6 oclock this morning up [to] 10½ oclock to night, the Place being in Such bad order & no Building. It is ahard Task for me to gat any one, but up to this date the 9th, I have the Promise of 15 hands who Expect to move Right on the Plantation." On December 21, while laborers were searching for places for the coming year, he again reported to Grimball: "Everybody & my Self are Standing quite Still at present Waiting for Jan . . . So you must allow me a little Chance, I cant go to Work With a Rush, because I have no money." In concluding, he advised Grimball to take any offer for the lease of The Grove which he might receive.

In January, 1869, Deas mustered a score of rice hands on Pinebury and by early February was hard at work. Apparently, however, he had located his family on the Gibbes' plantation, near Willtown, perhaps because there were no buildings remaining on Pinebury. ". . . I was down to the Plantation Purty Much all this Week, and We are trying to do the Best We Can," he informed Grimball. "Just now the men are Buisy Building & preparing Some Where to Put their Provision & Seed Rice." He rejected Grimball's idea of transferring some Pinebury acreage to the Grove. "I don't think Sir that you aught to take a way any of the Pinebury land to Put with the Grove because If We Should not be able to Plant all of It this Season We will Want It to put in order this Summer for the next Season and I am trying to get the Place full up." Several days later, Deas wrote that nothing had been done on the Grove for the coming season. On April 1, while some planters were still seeking laborers, he reported: "We are trying to Push things through in the Best Way We Can We have one Square under water & in a day or 2 We Will have 2 more." By the end of June, the crop was planted. "We have Planted 74 acres of Rice & 50 acres of Corn. We are Now trying to Keep the Grass out of What is Planted." During 1869, Deas acted as Grimball's "agent and nominal leasee" for Pinebury. The payment for his services was a fifth of Berkeley's rental fee of five bushels of rice for each acre of rice land planted and one bushel of rice for each acre of high ground cultivated. On October 26, Deas's commission produced $142.92 in cash.

In 1870, Deas worked on Pinebury under the same terms, but a better yield on increased acreage raised his income to $233.74. In 1871, he received $243.84 for his portion of the crop. In July, 1871, Deas journeyed to Charleston where he signed a three-year contract with Grimball to "cash" rent Pinebury himself for 1000 bushels of rice a year. Hardly had Deas returned to Pinebury when the area was lashed by a hurricane. Nevertheless, by September 3, he reported that the laboring force was hard at work and would soon repair the damage to flood gates, dikes, ditches, and the crop. In 1872, Deas actually leased Pinebury for himself, generously agreeing to pay Grimball the rental which the owner would have received under the previous system only if the plantation were under maximum cultivation. Deas, apparently, intended to profit by using the two-day system to pay his laborers, a system which Grimball had steadfastly refused to utilize. Deas's income from Pinebury in 1872 was about $800, roughly half the salary of a South Carolina circuit judge. By some means Grimball broke the three-year lease, and, in 1873, Deas agreed to manage Pinebury for two-thirds of the yield of 105 acres of rice to be planted. Grimball's share of the crop sold for $946 and Deas's for twice that amount. Deducting $600 in expenses, Deas's income for the year was approximately $1300. Thus, Deas, for the first time, derived a higher income from managing Pinebury than its owner received as a rental.

Grimball was unhappy with the contract for 1873. Even in April, 1873, he had pressed Deas to plant more than the 105 acres stipulated in the agreement. However, a scarcity of laborers prevented further expansion. On June 30, Grimball met Deas in the Charleston office of their marketing agent, Ingraham, and told him he would only agree to share equally both expenses and profits in 1874. In August, Grimball thought that Deas was unwilling to agree to these terms, "says he has made nothing by planting," and complained that even the present terms were too high. Deas was to write his decision. Ultimately, Deas offered Grimball a cash rental of $1200, due on December 1, 1874, and Grimball accepted. The rent was no longer fixed by the acreage planted, and Deas expanded to the fullest the area under cultivation. Perhaps with the benefit of information from the marketing agent, Grimball estimated that Deas's sales grossed $4975 in the year 1874. If this were true, after deducting the expense of planting the increased acreage, Deas's income for the year was about $3,000, a handsome figure in view of the fact that the governor of South Carolina earned only $3,500 during the same period. Grimball agreed to a cash rental in 1875 also, and Deas's profits were probably similar to those of 1874.

Again unhappy with the terms of the contract, Grimball offered, in the summer of 1875, to rent Pinebury to Deas in 1876 for either $1625 in cash or one-third of the net profits. Finally, they agreed to plant at least 150 acres in rice, and the owner was to get a third of the net profits. However, a poor crop and poorer prices produced only about $900 for Grimball and twice as much for Deas. In 1877, they agreed to share both expenses and profits equally. At the end of the year, Grimball resolved to offer Deas a straight 10 per cent commission on profits to act as his manager. It is not clear whether Deas accepted or not, but he did remain in control of Pinebury in 1878 and 1879.

Finally, on December 20, 1879, in a letter addressed to John Berkeley Grimball at 19 Lynch Street, Charleston, Deas severed his connection with Pinebury and gave the owner some parting advice: "It is true I dont expect to plant pinebury next year but things there are moving too slowly. Other planters are moving and you should too, otherwise you allow the hands to Scatter off And it is so much trouble to Get them together again. I know that you dont like to Commence your work until January, but you throw things to far back why Sir you ought [to] be Ploughing now, Giving the Lands to the Rain and Frost." Unfortunately for Pinebury, Grimball did not take Deas's advice. At the end of the year, he gave management of the plantation to his son Lewis, a physician and druggist who had been singularly and repeatedly unsuccessful in his profession. Grimball, himself, remained in Charleston, visiting old friends and being visited, presiding over sessions of the Charleston Library Society, ordering books for the Library, and writing over and over again ever-diminishing lists of the ill-paying stocks and bonds of his and his wife's estates.[47]

A similar story could be told of Bacchus Bryan, a Negro who managed five other hands in planting rice, cotton, and provision crops on a plantation in the vicinity of Adams Run. From 1866 through 1876, Bacchus agreed with the owner, Reverend John Cornish, each year to pay half the yield in return for the use of the land and the advance of supplies. Bacchus's profits were much less spectacular than those of Adam Deas but were probably nearer those of the average manager. For instance, in 1869, Bacchus's share of the cotton crop sold for about $160, and this probably constituted nearly the whole of his cash income for the year.[48]

The Negro manager was a persistent figure in post-Reconstruction South Carolina. In 1888, a Northerner returning to the Sea Islands twenty-five years after he had first come there as a teacher, found that Cuffee, who had been a foreman on one of the plantations, was managing a stock farm for a Northern firm.[49] In 1900, however, there were

47. A composite from: John Berkeley Grimball MS Diary; J. B. Grimball Papers (Southern Historical Collection, University of North Carolina); J. B. Grimball Papers (Manuscript Division, Duke University Library); and J. B. Grimball Papers (South Caroliniana Library, University of South Carolina); *passim.*

48. J. H. Cornish MS Diary, *passim.*

49. Charles Howard Family, Domestic History.

only 180 farm managers among the 85,000 Negro farm operators in South Carolina, and probably most of these were less like the entrepreneurs Adam Deas and Bacchus Bryan than the salaried Cuffee.[50]

"We all know that the colored people want land," cried the carpetbag delegate from Barnwell District to the members of the Constitutional Convention which assembled in Charleston in January, 1868. "Night and day they think and dream of it. It is their all in all."[51] The speaker hardly exaggerated; yet, at that time, relatively few Negroes had entered the class of agricultural landholders. Some free Negroes had owned land (and, indeed, slaves) before the war, a negligible number had been given lands by their late masters after emancipation,[52] and some two thousand had secured titles to lands on the Sea Islands. But, in view of the desires of Negro agrarians, these were, after all, mere tokens. Under the circumstances, it is hardly surprising that Negro agriculturalists simply shifted the focus of their expectations from the federal to the state government, and that local Republican leaders, mindful of where their strength lay, were anxious to accommodate them.

Doubtless, many Negro voters would have favored confiscation. "I know how hard it was to beat down that idea," declared a Massachusetts man on the floor of the Constitutional Convention. "It has been in their minds that government would some day present them with their old homes and old farms. There is no gentleman on this floor from the country who does not know how much he has had to contend with when he has had to oppose that desire which has been uppermost in the hearts of the people."[53] A few of the most radical of Republican leaders endorsed confiscation. A scalawag delegate to the organizing convention of the Republican party, held in May, 1867, was "perfectly disgusted with the negroes, that they advocate confiscation of lands..."; and as late as the campaign of 1870, the scalawag boss of Laurens County was vigorously preaching confiscation with the result, one resident observed, that "none of the men want to work, all looking forward to

50. *Negro Population,* p. 607.

51. *Convention Proceedings,* 1868, p. 385.

52. For instance, in October, 1868, Washington, a Negro servant residing in Sumter District, was awarded the highly suggestive bequest of forty acres and a mule by his dying master. *Intelligencer* (Anderson), November 11, 1868, copying the Sumter *Watchman.*

53. *Convention Proceedings,* 1868, p. 402.

next month when they expect to get land & houses."[54] White anxiety concerning confiscation was partially justified, but much of the furor was generated by an overly timorous white community. In Spartanburg, in November, 1867, a prospective purchaser of a plot of land was too cautious when he reneged because he was "afraid of confiscation."[55] Furthermore, there were Conservative politicians who were not above promoting and playing upon the anxieties of their friends. "Knowing that the Radicals had scared the Southern people with *Confiscation* by Congress, from the path of honor and patriotism, I thought I would scare them back again with *Confiscation* by the negroes," B. F. Perry wrote to one of his supporters in the spring of 1867. "You have lived long enough in the world . . . to know that most persons are influenced more by their *fears* than by their honor," concluded that gentleman of highly vaunted democratic reputation.[56]

Confiscation met with the early, persistent, and successful opposition of the main body of Republican leadership. In the convention of the party in July, 1867, the idea was not even formally introduced;[57] in the field, campaigners subsequently adopted the same attitude;[58] and the Constitutional Convention of 1868 with the full assent of its Negro delegates pointedly asserted that "The only manner by which any land can be obtained by the landless will be to purchase it."[59] Two years later, in a political meeting at Christ Church, native Negro A. J. Ransier was still answering the charge that Republicans had offered Negroes forty acres and a mule. "We had never," he declared, "promised any such thing, but on the contrary advised the people to buy lands by saving their money, and not to expect confiscation or the possession of lands that were not theirs, nor ours to give them . . ."[60]

To some extent, Republicans rejected confiscation as inexpedient— that is, that titles conferred might be impermanent, that Congress might disallow such a measure, or that whites might be driven to violence.

54. Lizzie Perry to A. L. Burt, May 11, 1867, B. F. Perry Papers; Mrs. J. W. Motte to her son, September 3, 1870, Lalla Pelot Papers.

55. Harris MS Farm Journal, entry for November 21, 1867.

56. To F. M. Nye, May 25, 1867, B. F. Perry Papers.

57. *New York Times,* August 9, 1867, p. 2. Nash had opposed confiscation publicly as early as April, 1867; see *ibid.,* April 15, 1867, p. 5.

58. *Intelligencer* (Anderson), September 4, 1867; *New York Times,* October 11, 1867, p. 1.

59. *Convention Proceedings,* 1868, pp. 213, 293. See also: *New York Times,* February 11, 1868, p. 5.

60. *Daily Republican* (Charleston), May 16, 1870.

Primarily, however, they refused confiscation because they felt it was contrary to the natural laws of economic morality; it would be useless, they argued, even pernicious, to legislate against the fiats of classical economics. "The sooner the public mind is disabused of that impression, the sooner every man knows that to acquire land he must earn it," declared W. J. Whipper, a Northern-born Negro delegate, to the convention, "the sooner he feels the Government has no lands to dispose of or to give him the better. Do what is necessary to protect the laborer in his labor and you will effect the greatest possible good."[61]

Republican leaders were strong in their rejection of confiscation, but by no means did they abandon the use of political power to achieve the popular goal of a division of large landed estates among their supporters. Ultimately, they settled upon two complementary but separate programs. One of these involved the purchase of lands by the state for division and resale to actual settlers. By the spring of 1869, acting upon an ordinance of the Constitutional Convention, the Republican legislature had created a Land Commission which was to purchase, by the issue of bonds guaranteed by the state, lands at public sales and "otherwise." Under a land commissioner these acquisitions were to be surveyed, divided into smaller tracts, and sold to settlers at the purchase price. The settler would pay taxes on the land and 7 per cent interest yearly on the principal of the loan. One half the plot was to be under cultivation within three years, at which time payments on the purchase price would begin and would extend over such period as the legislature directed.[62]

Almost from its inception the land program was hamstrung by political involvement. At least some Radical politicians thought that the partisan purposes of the relocation scheme were as important as the economic goals. In October, 1869, for instance, a leading Republican concurred in a statement by the land commissioner that party interest dictated "That in the upper counties it is necessary to purchase large tracts, so that colonies may be planted of sufficient strength to help, & protect each other, and to be the nucleas [sic] of education &c &c &c. . . . We must draw the union people to points where they will be a power & mutual supporters."[63] In addition, the office of land commissioner, itself, soon became a political pawn. The first incumbent was Charles

61. *Convention Proceedings*, 1868, p. 402.
62. *Ibid.*, 1868, pp. 179–80, 196–97, 309, 380, 400–03, 439, 507–09, 651, 788. See also: *New York Times*, February 19, p. 2; 22, p. 2, 1868.
63. R. J. Donaldson to C. P. Leslie, October 15, 1869, Samuel Dibble Papers.

P. Leslie, an aging, erratic, unscrupulous New Yorker who was given the office, it was said, to compensate him for losing the United States marshalship which he really wanted.[64] Whatever talents Leslie may have possessed were turned immediately to filling his own pockets, an occupation at which he was very adept. Using $200,000 in bonds authorized by the legislature, Leslie began to buy land at a rapid rate.

A very few purchases were well made at sheriff's sales, from the executors of estates, and by conscientious agents with an eye for a bargain. For instance, Henry E. Hayne, an ex-sergeant of the First South Carolina, acting as Leslie's agent in Marion County, arranged to buy 1734 acres of land for $1,500. The tract contained, by Hayne's report, 200 acres of "good swamp land, a splendid range for cattle &c and good corn and grain land. The balance is good upland, a large portion of woodland. There is good water on the place, several good buildings." The tract was then rented for $100 yearly, suggesting that the offered price was reasonable. But more to the point: "A number of citizens are prepared to purchase small tracts of this property from the State."[65]

Unfortunately, most purchases were made by men less reliable than Hayne. In Darlington County, Leslie's agent bought lands at a sheriff's sale supposedly for the land agency. He later changed the titles to indicate that he had bought them on his own account and then re-sold the land to the state at twice the price he had paid.[66] Throughout the life of the commission, a suspiciously large number of purchases were made from men directly involved in Republican politics—including Governor Scott, himself.

The secretary of state, Francis L. Cardozo, a Negro, had never approved of the choice of Leslie as land commissioner and soon refused to participate as a member of the advisory board. As rumors of fraud and mismanagement in the Land Commission began to circulate, Cardozo and other Negro leaders—including Rainey, Whipper, Elliott, Ransier, and Nash—moved to force Leslie out of his post. Dominant in the legislature in the winter of 1870, these men refused to pass a proposed bill authorizing the issuance of an additional $500,000 in bonds for the use of the commission. Leslie and others were very anxious to win the new issue because they had already overspent the amount

64. *Intelligencer* (Anderson), March 18, April 22, 1869.

65. To C. P. Leslie, October 11, 1869, Samuel Dibble Papers. By the end of 1871, this tract was fully settled, doubtless by "citizens" of color. *Reports and Resolutions (1871–1872),* p. 396.

66. R. W. Boyd to J. R. Cockran, October 23, 1877, Samuel Dibble Papers.

initially authorized. It was arranged, finally, that Leslie would resign and the legislature would sanction the new issue. According to the subsequent testimony of N. G. Parker, treasurer of the state until 1872, Leslie demanded and got $25,000 in return for his resignation and the surrender of his one-twelfth share in the Greenville and Columbia Railroad. To raise this money, Parker arranged the fraudulent purchase by the commission of some 27,000 acres (one portion of which was appropriately known as "Hell Hole Swamp") for about $119,000 nominally, but actually for much less.[67] D. H. Chamberlain, then attorney-general, discovered that the title to one of these tracts was faulty and that Parker and his associates were aware of the fault. However, he did not expose his findings.[68]

One of the demands of the Negro legislators was the appointment of a Negro as land commissioner. The stipulation was met, but the choice was unfortunate, falling upon R. C. De Large, a native Charlestonian, still young in 1870 and very ambitious politically. Parker later asserted that De Large was Scott's choice and that the latter arranged his appointment so that De Large could steal enough money to unseat scalawag Congressman C. C. Bowen of Charleston, Scott's most bitter personal and political enemy.[69] True or not, De Large was in fact immediately caught up in a year-long, vitriolic campaign against Bowen from which he emerged victorious. During De Large's absence, the scalawag comptroller-general, apparently, took the lead in administering the land program. Again, most purchases were made at exorbitant prices through the agency of or directly from officers of the state, and by 1871 the funds of the commission were exhausted.[70] They were never renewed, but the quality of lands purchased during De Large's tenure did improve somewhat. The improvement may have resulted from the closer scrutiny to which Cardozo and Chamberlain subjected prospective transactions. Since Cardozo, as secretary of state, had to record purchases and Chamberlain, as attorney-general, was responsible for the legitimacy of titles, each man was in a position to block suspicious transactions. During the De Large period, interested parties were,

67. MS Affadavit, January 23, 1878, signed by N. G. Parker, Samuel Dibble Papers.

68. D. M. Porter to N. G. Parker, June 6, 9, 1870; D. M. Porter to D. H. Chamberlain, June 6, 1870 (copy by Porter), Samuel Dibble Papers.

69. Daily Republican (Charleston), March 2, 1870; MS Affadavit, January 23, 1878, signed by N. G. Parker, Samuel Dibble Papers.

70. Reports and Resolutions (1871–1872), pp. 340–78, 1003–27.

apparently, willing to solicit their approval for purchases and the degree of control which they exercised was considerable.[71]

Criticism within the Republican party during the spring and summer of 1870 forced many officials to defend their connections with purchases made by the commission.[72] Chafing under charges that professional politicians were obstructing the efficient administration of the land program, an aroused legislature ordered the land commissioner to report immediately, formed a joint committee to investigate the program, and passed legislation clarifying the conditions of settlement on state lands.[73] Ultimately, the legislature assigned the duties of the land commissioner to the secretary of state, and, thus, Cardozo, himself, assumed responsibility for the program. A very able administrator, Cardozo quickly systematized the haphazardly kept records of the office, ascertained the location of the one hundred thousand acres in twenty-three counties which belonged to the state, investigated the degree to which these lands were settled, and arranged to receive regular payments from the settlers.[74] In April, 1872, the advisory board permitted the commissioner to base the price of lots (those already sold, as well as those remaining unsold) upon their actual value rather than the price which the state had paid for them. Immediately, a wave of additional settlers moved onto state lands. On one state-owned plantation on St. John's Island, for instance, fifteen lots which had lain barren for two years were promptly settled by Negro families.[75]

Henry E. Hayne, who succeeded Cardozo as secretary of state in 1872, continued the good work. He improved the administration of the program still more by appointing a single agent, J. E. Green, to replace the many county agents. Green familiarized himself with each tract, encouraged settlement, and made collections. In 1874, Hayne reported that the administration of the program under the new system cost only 8 per cent of collections, whereas before expenses had often exceeded revenues.[76] On one occasion, when settlers were about to be

71. For evidence, see: MS Payment Order from J. L. Neagle to N. G. Parker, March 12, 1870, endorsement by R. C. De Large, March 15, 1870, Samuel Dibble Papers; J. H. Rainey to R. Dozier, January 24, May 26, 27, June 3, 1870; R. Dozier to J. R. Cockran (copy), October 6, 1877, Richard Dozier Papers.

72. *Daily Republican* (Charleston), May 3, July 15, August 17, 1870.

73. *Ibid.*, January 7, 26, 30, March 3, 1871; *Reports and Resolutions (1870–1871)*, pp. 1256, 1266, 1405–8, 1703.

74. *Reports and Resolutions (1871–1872)*, pp. 340–78, 1003–27.

75. *Reports and Resolutions (1872–1873)*, pp. 49, 165.

76. *Reports and Resolutions (1874–1875)*, p. 069.

evicted from their Darlington County plots because of a fault in the title purchased by the state, Hayne used the resources of the commission to correct the deficiency.[77] The humane policy of the state was further revealed in February, 1874, when the legislature, following a poor farming season in some areas and a money scarcity which generally prevailed after the panic of 1873, authorized the commissioner to postpone payments in cases where subsistence was endangered.[78]

Strangely enough, although they did not buy new lands to perpetuate the program, the Redeemers continued and improved still further the administration of the Land Commission. Through litigation they added about 1300 acres to the program, the only addition made after 1870. Further, they refunded taxes paid by settlers before titles were granted, it being customary for titleholders to pay tax claims against real estate, in this case the state itself. In November, 1877, about 47,000 acres or one-half of the state's lands remained unsettled. The Redeemers reduced prices on unsold plots, surveyed tracts more suitably, allowed occupants to reduce the size of their farms to adjust to their ability to pay, and passed on the lands of those unable to pay to other settlers.

The end result was that by the late 1880's nearly all the state's lands had been disposed of to actual settlers; and by the early 1890's approximately 2,000 families had obtained titles to farms through the agency of the Land Commission.

Perhaps the most effective scheme of land redistribution implemented by Republicans in South Carolina was also the most subtle. In its earliest form, it was conceived as a heavy tax on unused land. This tax was expected to force owners of such lands either to bear the burden of the tax from their other resources, to put the land under cultivation and thus employ laborers or renters, or to allow the land to be sold either to the state for resale or directly to private parties. As it matured, the basic concept expanded. Not only would unused lands be heavily taxed, but all property, real and personal, used and unused, would be so burdened. Thus, all capital would be forced into full productivity, or, in essence, would be confiscated and sold. One anticipated result of the program was that a large quantity of land would be offered for sale at prices that the landless could afford to pay. Also, heavy taxation would support a prospective expansion of public services rendered by the state: internal improvements; care for the

77. R. W. Boyd to J. R. Cockran, October 23, 1877, Samuel Dibble Papers.
78. Reports and Resolutions (1874–1875), p. 069.

insane, orphans, and indigents; a modern penitentiary; a streamlined and efficient judiciary; and, most important, a system of public education from primary to university levels. Heavy taxation, then, was the core of the Republican program in Reconstruction South Carolina. It was a program designed to give its supporters land, educational opportunity, and other benefits that would imbue them with a spirit of loyalty to the party and insure its continuance in power.

From its birth, the Republican party in South Carolina consciously and deliberately advocated land division through taxation. "We must drive them to the wall by taxation," cried one carpetbagger to a Republican convention in the summer of 1867.[79] While the convention was more circumspect in its choice of words, its resolution on the subject was commonly interpreted as an endorsement of a tax program which, as one Negro delegate observed, "would force owners of large tracts of waste lands to sell and give us a chance."[80] As the campaign for the Constitutional Convention of 1868 proceeded, the tax program supplanted confiscation in popularity. Such a program, one observer noted, would be as effective as confiscation, "and yet avoid the strenuous opposition that any scheme of general land pillaging would infallibly meet with in the North."[81] Perhaps, with this criticism in mind, the Convention itself decided to tax all real and personal property at a single, uniform rate based upon actual values. This amendment did not mean that the party had deserted the tax program. The carpetbag delegate who was soon to become the treasurer of South Carolina put the case succinctly:

> Taxes are always (at least in hard times) a burden, will be assessed yearly upon all lands, and they must be paid. The expenses of the State (constantly increasing, will be a continual drag upon those who attempt to carry on large landed estates with a small amount of money,) will alone force sufficient lands upon the market at all times to meet the wants of all the landless. This Convention will cost the State quite a large sum of money. A legislature will soon assemble, and that will cost money. Education, once limited, is to be general, and that will be expensive; and, to keep up with the age, it is fair to presume that the State tax will be greater next year than this, and increase yearly; this will be felt, and will be the

79. *New York Times*, July 31, 1867, p. 1.
80. *Ibid.*, p. 2.
81. *Ibid.*, October 11, 1867, p. 1; *Intelligencer* (Anderson), September 4, 1867.

stimulus to many for owning less land, and cause them to
see the necessity for disposing of their surplus.[82]

The Convention adopted other measures which were to supplement
the tax program. It requested and obtained from the military authorities a stay law—or rather order—designed to delay forced sales of lands
to allow the landless an opportunity to accumulate capital and the
tax program time to depress land prices.[83] Once the agriculturalist
had acquired a small holding, the Convention sought to protect him
against the direct effects of forced sales in civil actions by a constitutional provision that exempted from such sales a homestead worth
$1000 and personal property worth $500.[84] A suggested corollary to
the tax program would have required state officers to subdivide all
tracts sold for taxes into plots of 160 acres or less. This proposal met
with the sympathy of the Convention, but the majority ultimately
decided that no satisfactory defense could be made against monied
men buying as many plots as they chose.[85]

Once in power on the state level, Republicans hastened to carry
out the tax program. The burden of taxation was shifted from mercan-
tile interests to landed property, and the total tax bill increased rapidly
to astounding heights. During Reconstruction, the amount of taxes
levied and collected every year was well over a million dollars; before
1860 it had always been considerably less, and, during the Orr regime,
had been only about $600,000—less than one dollar each for every man,
woman, and child in the state.

Some Republican politicians contended that the state tax rate in
South Carolina was no more than in some Northern states. Such,
indeed, was the case, but the whole story of taxation in South Carolina
was not told by the *state tax rate*. Actually, the rate was kept deliberately low, but other variables in the tax equation were manipulated
to raise the tax bill ever higher. In addition to the state levy, each county taxed its property owners for the administration of regular county
affairs and for special purposes such as new buildings and roads.

82. *Convention Proceedings,* 1868, p. 457. The speaker, N. G. Parker, might
have added that public thievery, in which profession he was soon to become a
dean, would also be expensive. For discussions on the effect of school and poll
taxes, see: *ibid.,* pp. 646, 873.

83. *Ibid.,* pp. 113–48, *passim.* See also: *New York Times,* February 11, 1868,
p. 5.

84. *Convention Proceedings,* 1868, pp. 105–8, 308–24, 452–75, 488–506, 846.

85. *Ibid.,* pp. 160–63.

Furthermore, the school tax was often quoted separately. Thus, E. Gelzer, in Abbeville County in 1871, paid a state tax of only $59.64; but, at the same time, he paid a $25.56 county tax and an $8.52 school tax.[86] Property owners residing in towns and cities paid municipal taxes as well. Census returns indicate that Carolinians paid $2,800,000 in state and local taxes in 1870, an enormous sum by prewar standards. Of this amount, $1,600,000, including the school tax, went to Columbia, while almost half was consumed locally.[87]

A second variable in the tax equation was the value placed on property for tax purposes. Before the advent of the Republican regime, the tendency was to undervalue property in assessing it for tax purposes; after, the tendency was drastically reversed. This weapon for increasing taxes was sharpened by the authority given to the governor to appoint and remove assessors within each county and by the creation of a State Board of Equalization with power to decrease or increase (two- or threefold if it wished) the assessment of a given county. There was abundant evidence that this power was abused during the first six years of Republican rule. A meeting of Conservative white leaders in Columbia in 1871 admitted that the state tax rate (about 1 per cent at that time) was not excessive but complained that assessments were unduly high.[88] Wide fluctuations in the total of assessments between 1869 and 1873 show clearly that this power was freely used. For instance, in 1870, the figure was placed at $184,000,000. In the hard election year of 1872, it was reduced to $146,000,000, only to be raised again after the election.[89] Even some Republicans deprecated such blatant unfairness. Martin R. Delany, the former major, stated in 1871 that lands were often sold at one-half to one-fourth of the assessed value. "Land in South Carolina is greatly depreciated," he declared, "while taxes have become proportionately higher."[90] "Taxes are enormous," exclaimed a Northern businessman residing in Charleston, voicing a fact all too well known among his landowning Carolina contemporaries.[91]

Astonishing as the tax bill was in the aggregate, it was even more astounding to the individual taxpayer. In May, 1871, a Chester County

86. MS and Printed Tax Bill and Receipt, December 29, 1871, A. L. Burt Papers.
87. *Census* (1870), III, 8–11. *See also: House Journal* (1871–1872), pp. 7–8.
88. *Daily Republican* (Charleston), March 24, 1871.
89. Walter Allen, *Governor Chamberlain's Administration in South Carolina: A Chapter of Reconstruction in the Southern States* (New York, 1888), p. 296.
90. *Daily Republican* (Charleston), March 24, 1871.
91. W. H. Taylor to J. Wilbur, March 22, 1871, J. Wilbur Papers.

planter lamented: "I have paid $400.00 Dollars of Tax this year & expect to pay about $300.00 in the fall making $700 in all. before the war my Tax was from 30 to 50 Dollars. Where does the money go?" By January 6, 1873, he had paid $365 in taxes for that year and would have to pay another large tax bill before the year ended. "I can go to some other place (say Augusta) & live comfortably on my Tax," he asserted.[92]

Republican reform Governor Daniel H. Chamberlain, who held office from November, 1874, until he was ousted by Hampton in April, 1877, made a determined and partly successful attempt to reduce the tax burden. In this he was ably assisted by Secretary of the Treasury Francis L. Cardozo. In 1874, Chamberlain recommended to the legislature an across-the-board reduction in expenditures and, soon thereafter, executed a re-assessment of taxable property throughout the state which very nearly equalized assessed and market values. When the legislature passed a tax bill in the spring that exceeded his recommendations, Chamberlain courageously vetoed it, and in the legislative session of 1875–1876 he succeeded in reducing the rate of taxation from 13 to 11 mils.[93]

Chamberlain won much praise and considerable support from the native white community for his efforts, but other circumstances were operating in the fall of 1875 to turn the tide of taxpayer sentiment against him. In the counties and cities where corruptionists remained entrenched, local tax rates were largely beyond the control of the governor. In spite of Chamberlain's reforms, these drove the total tax bill for their areas to great heights. In heavily agricultural Kershaw County, yearly taxes (county and education, as well as state) amounted to about 2 per cent of the total value of taxable property. Taxpayers, under such circumstances, were hardly impressed with the fact that Chamberlain had saved them from a 2.2 per cent levy. One upcountry editor queried, "Does this mean reform or confiscation?"[94] Even in counties under native white control, where local levies had been kept at a consistent minimum, Chamberlain's moderate gains were more than offset by the decline in cotton profits and the increase in food costs which began in the fall of 1875. "Our crops are poorer, the prices range much lower than for years past, while flour and bacon are higher,"

92. R. N. Hemphill to W. R. Hemphill, May 9, 1871, January 6, 1873, Hemphill Papers.
93. *News and Courier* (Charleston), July 15, 1876.
94. *Intelligencer* (Anderson), December 9, 1875.

complained an Anderson County editor early in December. When he learned that the tax rate for his county was to be about 1.5 per cent he cried, "Thus our worst fears are realized."[95]

The results of the Republican tax program were everything that its authors anticipated—and more. Vast quantities of land were forfeited to the state every year, and others passed under the hammer to satisfy judgments rendered in civil suits. When the Republicans took office, the state held only about 23,000 acres of land forfeited for taxes.[96] This figure dwindled into insignificance as tax foreclosures by the Radical government proceeded. In the early 1870's, the local press, particularly in the middle and lower counties, abounded in advertisements of tax sales.[97] During the state fiscal year which ended October 31, 1873, officials reported 270,000 acres of land as forfeited for about $21,000 in taxes; and in the following year the figure rose to more than 500,000 acres. Interestingly, the twelve counties in which the most land was forfeited were precisely those dozen counties in which the proportion of Negro to white voters was highest.[98]

White landowners in the lower counties were convinced that Republican tax collectors were, indeed, conspiring to "drive them to the wall." One Georgetown plantation owner complained in the spring of 1869 that the county tax collector had told him he did not know how much his tax would be or when it would be determined. "The scallawags and capt Baggers would no doubt like right well to see my place advertised and sold for taxes," he surmised. "I trust they will not be gratified."[99] John Berkeley Grimball could have added that confiscation by hook was fully as possible as by crook. In the spring of 1873, he was surprised to see that Pinebury, which Adam Deas was operating, was up for sale within two weeks for delinquent taxes. Hasty inquiry revealed that his tax payment had gone astray and much ado at the county seat eventually brought rectification. In January of the following year, when the tax collector visited Charleston for the convenience of residents owning land in Colleton County, Grimball proceeded to the appointed place prepared to pay his dues, only to find that the collector had fled to avoid meeting a rival claimant to his office. For

95. *Ibid.,* December 9, 30, 1875.

96. *House Journal* (1868, Special Session), pp. 203–4.

97. Francis Butler Simkins and Robert Hilliard Woody, *South Carolina During Reconstruction* (Chapel Hill, 1932), pp. 180–81.

98. *Reports and Resolutions (1874–1875); (1875–1876);* Table H in the Report of the Comptroller General for each year.

99. A. W. Dozier to Richard Dozier, May 8, 1869, Richard Dozier Papers.

some days, he tried to locate the elusive collector, always arriving just after the tax agent had departed, pursued by his rival. Finally, he succeeded in passing the duty to the post office by resorting to the use of registered mail.[100]

In the fall of 1875, as agricultural profits declined and the price of foods increased, economic distress began to spread into the white counties. In 1873, no land had been forfeited for taxes in Anderson County, and, in 1874, only two acres were lost to the state. In December, 1875, however, the editor of the local newspaper noted that "a very large amount of property was sold" at the monthly sheriff's sales for the execution of tax and civil judgments against property.[101]

The losses of property owners were not entirely reckoned in the number of acres forfeited. Obviously, all labored under the burden of paying unusually high taxes on lands which had never yielded so little income. J. B. Grimball paid state and local taxes on Pinebury amounting to $119.36 in 1873 and $136.08 in 1874. During the same period, he received about $1200 yearly by leasing the plantation to Adam Deas. Thus, the tax on the property amounted to about 10 and 11 per cent of the gross income in 1873 and 1874 respectively, and, in terms of productivity, these were banner years for Pinebury.[102] Taxpayers were also distressed by the extremes to which they were forced to save their lands from the sheriff. The widow of the most prominent Know-Nothing leader in ante-bellum South Carolina complained to a friend in 1874: "Having six pieces of property not yielding me one dollar, and those demons after taking my Plantation from me, have this year levied 50 per cent Taxes which I have had to sell Silver to pay."[103] Similarly, in 1872, a Charlestonian, noting that the ownership of a plantation "will *cost* me a good deal" during the year, complained: "I don't think you cd get any attempt at resistance in any part of the Old State to an immediate Confiscation of all the property of the whites if the so called Legislature ordered it."[104]

The price of land in South Carolina was depressed after the war and continued to decline until 1868.[105] Even after prosperity returned, prices

100. MS Diary, entry for January —, 1873, *et seq.*; A. Schaffer to J. B. Grimball, April 16, 1873, J. B. Grimball Papers.

101. *Intelligencer* (Anderson), December 9, 1875.

102. MS Diary, entry for January —, 1873, *et seq.*

103. Ann Pamela Cunningham to a friend, March 27, 1874, Ann Pamela Cunningham Papers.

104. "G. I. C." to W. P. Miles, April 4, 1872, W. P. Miles Papers.

105. *Senate Journal* (1868, Special Session), p. 18.

remained relatively low. In some measure, this v as a result of the uncertain political situation; but, more particularl), it was the fruit of the Republican tax program. In 1870, one upcountry farmer painted the picture rather deftly:

> Our country is in a bad condition. Negroes have every thing in their own hands, and do as they please. The Legislature is radical out and out. All or nearly all of our County officers are negroes. The consequence is that lands and every other kind of property is taxed so high that they have decline twenty five percent in value since last fall. Every little negro in the county is now going to school and the public pays for it. There is a negro school near Billy Turners, with over fifty schollars and lands principally are taxed to pay for them. This is a hell of a fix but we cant help it, and the best policy is to conform as far as possible to circumstance . . .[106]

It is evident that many Negroes took advantage of these conditions to acquire lands by purchase. Unfortunately, no census of Negro farm owners was taken in South Carolina before 1890, but in that year 13,075 Negro farmers owned farms of some size.[107] Since only about 4,000 Negroes obtained lands through government agencies, roughly 9,000 Negro farmers must have bought farms through their own efforts during the generation that followed emancipation. A large portion of these realized their desire for land during the eight years of Republican rule. In 1870, Reuben Tomlinson, a Northern missionary who came to the Sea Islands during the war and remained to become a Bureau educator and a state legislator, declared on the floor of the House of Representatives that "If we could get together the statistics of the laboring men who have during the past year become land owners through their own exertions and industry, we would be perfectly astounded."[108] Random evidence seems to bear out this assumption,

106. A. W. Moore to E. H. Dabbs, April 30, 1870, A. L. Burt Papers.

107. *Negro Population,* p. 470. Significantly the proportion of Negro farmers who owned at least some land to the total number of Negro farm operators remained substantially unchanged from 1890 to 1910. In 1890, the proportion was 20.3 per cent; in 1900, it was 20.0 per cent; and in 1910, 21.0 per cent. This suggests that the most ambitious Negro agriculturalists acquired property early and retained it, a presumption further warranted by the low incidence of mortgaged indebtedness on farms owned by Negroes. *Ibid.,* pp. 470, 588, 607, 610.

108. *Daily Republican* (Charleston), April 9, 1870.

for one cannot travel far into contemporary writings without encountering numerous incidental references to the sale of land to Negroes.[109]

It is improbable that many Negroes acquired land through co-operative purchases, but on at least two occasions, Negroes formed associations for the purchase of lands. In January, 1868, in the low-country, F. L. Cardozo described one such operation to his colleagues in the Constitutional Convention: "About one hundred poor colored men of Charleston met together and formed themselves into a Charleston Land Company. They subscribed for a number of shares at $10 per share, one dollar payable monthly. They have been meeting for a year. Yesterday they purchased 600 acres of land for $6,600 that would have sold for $25,000 or $50,000 in better times. They would not have been able to buy it had not the owner through necessity been compelled to sell."[110] In 1872, a similar group acquired a 750-acre estate on Edisto Island.[111]

The Negro generally paid his poll tax and his one– or two–dollar levy on personal property cheerfully,[112] but once he had acquired lands, he was subject to the same adverse effects of the Republican tax program as his white neighbors. Contrary to the design of the politicians, small holders suffered equally with large. In 1874, a Northern traveler visited the home of a Negro farmer who had bought his land two years previously with two hundred hard-saved dollars. "Now the cabin has fallen into decay, the rain and wind come through great cracks in the walls of the one cheerless room, the man and his wife are in rags, and the children run wild about the parched and stony fields, clothed very much as they were when they first saw the light. Negro voters are not exempt from the visits of the tax gatherer, and it is almost certain that the poor fellow's place will, with many others, be forfeited to the State at the next sale for delinquent taxes."[113] It is hardly surprising that Negro property owners were observed in one lowcountry community in January, 1877, paying taxes for the support of the Hampton government while a Republican still sat in the governor's office.[114]

109. For instances, see: B. D. McCreery to A. L. Burt, January 1, 1871, A. L. Burt Papers; MS Note, n.d., Samuel Dibble Papers.

110. *Convention Proceedings,* 1868, p. 117. See also: *New York Tribune,* June 30, 1869.

111. Hemphill, *Climate, Soil and Agricultural Capabilities of South Carolina and Georgia,* p. 14.

112. *Daily Republican* (Charleston), October 23, 1869.

113. *New York Times,* July 4, 1874, p. 5.

114. J. H. Cornish MS Diary, entry for January 26, 1877.

Native white resistance to the aggressive tax program of the Republicans was at first tentative and cautious. There was, after all, no assurance that Republican rule through Negro voters would ever end and an imprudent resistance might close doors which could never be re-opened. Nevertheless, almost as soon as the first Republican tax bills reached the taxpayers a quiet desperation crept into Conservative politics. "Negro laws will ruin any people," an upcountry farmer advised his brother during the summer of 1869, "those that was not broke by the old debts will be by tax my tax was 57 dollars & 30 cents. I have paid but how long I can do so I dont no but we still hope for better times we think in the year 1870 we will be able to change the law making power . . ."[115] In 1870, native whites looked anxiously to the polls and placed their trust in a "Reform" Republican candidate for governor. "If the Radicals gain the day what is to become of us, I don't see how we can stay in the country," a Laurens resident wrote to her son on the eve of the elections "for our taxes will be increased, and we will be under the very heels of the Radicals."[116] The election was lost and taxes rose as expected. Among John Berkeley Grimball's papers there is an artifact, a clipping from a March, 1871, issue of a Charleston paper. What Grimball saved was an article which concluded with the sentence: "This is a TAXATION which is tantamount to CONFISCATION."[117] Several weeks later, an upcountry woman wrote to her cousin: "I have nothing of a political nature to communicate that would interest you,—nothing much talked of these days except Taxation & the Ku Klux."[118]

It was characteristic of the native white community that their anxiety should lead to meetings and that meetings should soon assume some state-wide organization. The state-wide conference took place in May, 1871, under the name of the Taxpayers' Convention. Even though the convention included Negroes, carpetbaggers, and scalawags, as well as rising young professional politicians within the ranks of the Conservatives, it was dominated by the prewar aristocracy—men such as Chesnut, Kershaw, Aldrich, Trenholm, Porter, Trescot, Bonham, and Hagood. Indeed, it was generally conceded that no comparably distinguished body of men had met in the state since the Secession Convention.

115. Edward Lipscomb to Smith Lipscomb, June 30, 1869, Edward Lipscomb Papers.
116. Mrs. J. W. Motte to her son, September 3, 1870, Lalla Pelot Papers.
117. *Daily News* (Charleston), March 24, 1871, J. B. Grimball Papers.
118. "M. E. B." to her cousin, May 4, 1871, W. W. Renwick Papers.

Nevertheless, the leadership remained cautious. The debates were temperate, no Republican officeholder was personally impugned, and the resolutions were innocuous: it was in essence a whitewash of the Republican regime.[119]

The Moses administration (1872–1874) brought still higher taxes and consequent agitation among the whites. ". . . our tax this year is full one third higher than last year and it looks to me like that it will finally result in confiscation of the land by Taxation," wrote a Laurens planter in February, 1873.[120] The whites called another Taxpayers' Convention for February, 1874. "Things are blue enough here & the taxation is practically confiscation," wrote a resident of Georgetown in January, "I trust there may be some good in the Taxpayer's [sic] Convention this time."[121] The desperation of the whites rapidly became less quiet, particularly as they began to read signs outside the state which suggested that Negro rule might not be perpetual. The tone of the convention of 1874 was radically different from that of 1871. An impressive delegation of gentlemen from the convention journeyed to Washington where they formally presented to both Grant and the House of Representatives a vigorous indictment of the Republican regime in South Carolina. "It has been openly avowed by prominent members of the Legislature," the memorial of the convention declared, "that taxes should be increased to a point which will compel the sale of the great body of the land, and take it away from the former owners." Perhaps the most important result of the convention was the legacy of organization which it left to the white community. Largely under the leadership of the "Bourbons," local Tax Unions were formed which were to function as the watchdogs of persons in office. These organizations were very active in the 1874 campaign and in supporting the reform programs of the Chamberlain administration.[122] In the fall of 1875, however, the Tax Union rapidly lost ground to more radical elements among the native whites and, by 1876, had virtually ceased to exist.

During 1876, native whites stymied the Republican tax program by extra-legal means. In the fall of 1876, they refused to pay taxes to the

119. *Proceedings of the Tax-Payers' Convention of South Carolina, Held at Columbia, beginning May 9th, and ending May 12th, 1871* (Charleston, 1871), *passim*. See also: Simkins and Woody, *Reconstruction in South Carolina*, pp. 156-59.

120. H. P. Sharpe to his nephew, February 3, 1873, J. McK. Sharpe Papers.

121. T. P. Bailey to R. H. McKie, January 16, 1874, R. H. McKie Papers.

122. A. P. Aldrich to James Chesnut, [November] 5, 1874; October 30, 1875, Williams–Chesnut–Manning Papers.

Chamberlain government which claimed victory in the November elections while they voluntarily paid 10 per cent of the previous year's levy to the Hampton government. By general concert, native whites also refused to buy lands being sold for taxes. In December, 1876, in Charleston County numerous parcels of land had been forfeited for some $200,000 in taxes and costs, but not one single purchaser could be found for any of these. Once firmly in power, the Redeemers hastened to restore forfeited lands to the tax books and allow delinquents generous limits within which to repair their deficiencies.[123]

Although the great mass of Negroes in Reconstruction South Carolina earned their living through agricultural pursuits, others worked as domestics, as skilled or unskilled laborers, and as business and professional men.

With the exception of agriculture, the domestic class was by far the most numerous economic group. These found employment in various capacities in the homes of the whites. Negro men became butlers, valets, coachmen, gardeners, and handy men. Negro women became housemaids, personal maids, cooks, laundresses, nurses, and serving girls. As described earlier, a general reduction in household staffs occurred immediately after the war. As Reconstruction progressed, further reductions ensued. Typical was the H. L. Pinckney plantation near Statesburg, in Sumter District, in June, 1866, where a unique arrangement prevailed in which ten domestics—two cooks, two houseboys, a house servant, a gardener, a nurse, a housemaid, a washer, and "Louisia—(little)"—were included with thirty-nine agricultural workers in a contract by which all would receive a third of the crop. By 1868, the total work force had been reduced to sixteen, only three of whom were domestics.[124]

In relations with his employer, the Negro domestic experienced grievances similar to those felt by his agrarian contemporaries. His responses, too, were much the same. In a sense, however, he was freer to express his dissatisfaction since desertion—the ultimate reply to unsatisfactory conditions—could follow the daily or weekly payday and he need not forfeit or await the division of a crop. Occasionally, individual domestics revealed a persistent reluctance to remain with any single employer very long. In 1872, in Charleston a Negro cook

123. *Reports and Resolutions (1877-1878)*, p. vi.
124. H. L. Pinckney MS Plantation Book, entries for "June," 1866, and "January," 1868. See also: MS Contract, ——, 1867; Peter B. Bacot MS Diary, entry for "1870," Peter B. Bacot Collection.

told her employer that she was leaving the household, not because she was dissatisfied with her position but "because, ma'am, it look like old time to stay too long in one place."[125] However, like their brothers in agriculture, most Negro servants adjusted to the new order during the first years of Reconstruction and established rather permanent relations with a single employer. For instance, in 1870, a lady residing in a large household in the village of Chicora wrote: "We have only made one change in our domestic arrangements since you left [a year previously] & that is in the outdoor department, the indoor servants are all with us still & we go on so smoothly & comfortably that I hope it will be long before we have to make any change."[126]

A glimpse into the life of a servant girl working in one of the Campbell households in Charleston in 1868 is preserved in a letter from her to her aunt in Camden. The girl, Celia Johnson, was a member of a "free" Negro family living in Camden and had come to Charleston as a servant. To her aunt's invitation to visit Camden, she replied that she would like to, but it was too "hard to get away from Mrs. Campbell, and hard to get money." Not all of Celia's life was drudgery. "I spent last Sunday night with sister Mary Stewart, and went to a meetin to the African church. We heard a blind man preacher and had good times." But, there was work to be done. "Excuse this short letter as I am very busy ironing," she concluded. "All the way I will get to go home is to promise to come back in October. If I don't I will make hard feelings . . . I have been sleeping upstairs so long that you will have [to] get me an upstairs room when I get there. I don't know how to sleep down stairs."[127]

In slavery, large numbers of Negroes had performed relatively unskilled labor in the lumbering and turpentine industries and in construction, particularly railroad construction. In freedom, many laborers continued the occupations which they had learned as slaves and these were joined by freedmen who had never before had an opportunity to leave the fields. Frequently, the choice was made even more attractive by the prospect of higher and certain wages in industry. In 1873, a resident of the once rice-rich county of Georgetown noted the growing profitability of the production of naval stores and commented: "The turpentine interest being very lucrative, controls a great deal of

125. *The Nation*, XV, No. 372 (1872), 105.
126. Susie Hanckel to Robert Gourdin, November 6, 1870, R. H. Gourdin Papers.
127. To Epsey Johnson, July 3, 1868, Bonds Conway Correspondence.

labor & the Rice fields suffer thereby."[128] The war, itself, promoted the growth of the laboring population outside of agriculture. During and after the war, hundreds of Negro laborers found employment in the Quartermaster and Engineering departments of the army and in the Freedmen's Bureau. The dislocations of the war and of the months immediately following left large numbers of Negroes in Charleston and in the towns and villages of the interior. These often earned a subsistence by working as stevedores, street cleaners, yardkeepers, porters, draymen, messengers, and at other unskilled jobs. The repair of war–worn and torn rail lines and a boom in the construction of new lines gave at least temporary employment to several thousand Negro laborers. Many others found jobs in a new and fantastically profitable industry—the mining of phosphates for processing into fertilizers. Some of the rock was dug from tidewater river beds by giant dredges, but large deposits lay on or near the surface of the land. These "land deposits" were mined with pick and shovel, wielded by Negroes under the supervision of white foremen. "A common laborer will raise a ton a day, for which he is paid $1.76," wrote an agricultural expert in 1882. "The product of the land rock is about 100,000 tons a year."[129] Negroes struggling to retain their small farms in the Sea Islands during the hard years following emancipation must have viewed the rise of the phosphate industry as providential.

Many of the free Negroes of Charleston had long earned their living as artisans. A month after their liberation, the Negro tradesmen of the city participated in a parade, described earlier, which indicated the diversity of their occupations and the solidity of their organization. Free Negroes in other centers of population followed much the same pattern on minor scales. Further, emancipation freed numerous slaves who had been trained in the trades, particularly in those connected with plantation maintenance. Thus, literally thousands of more or less proficient blacksmiths, carpenters, wheelrights, masons, plasterers millers, mechanics, and engineers (who had operated steam engines supplying power to rice threshers, cotton gins, sawmills, and flour mills) became "free" economic agents.

Many of these, of course, were only partially trained for their occupations, and many combined the practice of their trade with other pursuits (e.g., farming) in order to support themselves. Still, a few

128. T. P. Bailey to R. H. McKie, March 26, 1873, R. H. McKie Papers.

129. Hemphill, *Climate, Soil, and Agricultural Capabilities of South Carolina and Georgia,* p. 50.

Negro tradesmen attained eminence as artists in their work. The Noisette family in Charleston, for instance, was nationally praised for the products of their nursery and the elder Noisette gained a creditable reputation as botanist.[130] Ben Williams, a Negro shoemaker in Columbia, was awarded a premium in November, 1869, "for the second best lot of shoes" exhibited at the annual fair of the State Agricultural and Mechanical Society.[131]

In Reconstruction South Carolina, Negroes tended to withdraw or abstain from entering certain trades, leaving them entirely to whites. "The well wishers of the negro race see with regret that they seem to have little inclination to take to mechanical pursuits," reported a Northern journalist from Charleston in 1870. ". . . it is a rare thing to find a negro adopting the trade of blacksmith, or carpenter, or any other requiring skilled labor."[132] This particular gentleman was apparently suffering from myopia induced by the fact that he did not, in truth, wish very well for the Negro race, but he did glimpse a part of a large trend among tradesmen. The results of this retirement of the Negro tradesman is evident in the business directory of the state published in 1880. In the entire state, it listed no Negroes among the cigarmakers, coopers, or coppersmiths, and only one Negro dyer and cleaner was polled. Furthermore, outside of Charleston there were no Negroes listed as tailors, dressmakers, tinners, upholsterers, wheelwrights, or builders and repairmen; in Charleston about half of the tradesmen engaged in each specialty were Negroes.[133] Although the evidence is by no means conclusive, for obviously many Negro tradesmen continued to serve white customers, there was also a trend toward Negro tradesmen serving Negro customers exclusively. In Spartanburg District, in the winter of 1867, David Golightly Harris probably touched a deep reason for this tendency. Vexed at the inefficiency of the white man he had chosen to run his flour mill, he had reached the point of exasperation. "I have an idea of puting Paschal to the mill," he wrote. "But some say a negro will drive all the customers away. . . . Everything is a botheration."[134] Charleston, again, was perhaps exceptional in this respect.

Probably most Negro tradesmen worked independently and a few

130. Noisette Family Papers.

131. *New York Times,* November 19, 1869, p. 3.

132. N. S. Shaler, "An Ex-Southerner in South Carolina," *The Atlantic Monthly,* XXVI, No. 153 (July, 1870), 58.

133. *South Carolina State Gazetteer and Business Directory* (Charleston, 1880), *passim.*

134. David Golightly Harris MS Diary, entry for December 23, 1867.

worked for established white employers, but many were also businessmen in that they kept shops in which their goods or services were sold.
In addition to those in the trades, a large number of Negroes engaged
in small enterprises, such as the flourishing trade in supplying firewood
to Charleston from the neighboring islands.[135] More typical of small
Negro-owned businesses, perhaps, were those of Beverly Nash who
operated a produce stand in Columbia in 1867 and later opened a coal
and wood yard, and of Samuel Nuckles, a political refugee from Union
County, who, in 1871, operated a drayage wagon in the same city.[136]
Occasionally, Negroes embarked upon large-scale undertakings in
business. For instance, in the spring of 1866, "The Star Spangled Banner Association" led by Tom Long, a veteran of the First South, raised
$20,000 by $15 to $100 subscriptions with which they opened a store
at Beaufort and acquired a steamer to operate along the coast under
the captaincy of Robert Smalls.[137] During the Republican ascendency,
Negro politicians participated in ventures darkened in greater or lesser
degree by partisan shadows. Thus, F. L. Cardozo and J. H. Rainey
were two of the twelve stockholders in the Greenville and Columbia
Railroad Company and, with several other Negro leaders, charter
members of the Columbia Street-Railway Company. However, the
most striking successes in business were made by individuals in private
life who gradually accumulated capital and expanded the scope of their
operations. John Thorne, who had apparently led in a co-operative
land purchase on Edisto Island in 1872, ten years later owned 250 acres
of land on the island, "an extensive store and storehouse," and a
comfortable residence. "He also runs a gin-house with six gins, and
last year ginned out upwards of 400 bags of cotton of 300 pounds each,
for which work he received four cents per pound. He advanced largely
to several colored planters, and is worth from $15,000 to $20,000."[138]

Although not numerous, the Negro professional class was very influential during and after Reconstruction. Ministers, politicians, and
lawyers led the professions, while teachers and medical doctors formed
a rather weak second rank, both in popular influence and economic
importance. Each of these groups will be discussed subsequently in
contexts which are appropriate to their work.

135. J. T. Trowbridge, *The South, a tour of its Battle Fields and Ruined Cities,
a journey through the desolated States, and talks with the people, etc.* (Hartford,
1866), p. 538.

136. *New York Times*, August 9, 1867, p. 2; *Ku-Klux Conspiracy*, IV, 1158–65.

137. *New York Times*, April 2, 1866, p. 1. See also: ibid., June 11, 1866, p. 8.

138. Hemphill, *Climate, Soil, and Agricultural Capabilities of South Carolina
and Georgia*, p. 14.

VI...THE FRUITS
OF FREEDOM

O ne final question remains. What rewards did the
Negro reap from his labor as a free man?

For the Negro in agriculture, the answer was largely determined
in two steps; first, by his productivity, and second, by the degree in
which his product was taxed to satisfy the costs of production. The
remainder fixed his standard of living.

The productivity of the Negro farmer depended primarily upon his
willingness to work, the hazards of nature, and his managerial abilities.
As described earlier, in the first few years following emancipation there
was considerable controversy as to whether the Negro would work
as hard voluntarily as he had under the compulsions of slavery. However, as various groups adjusted to the new economic order, there was
general agreement that Negroes worked as well in freedom as they
had in bondage. This opinion was strengthened by the fact that agricultural production in South Carolina, which ultimately depended
upon the effectiveness of Negro labor in the fields, rose steadily during
Reconstruction. The rise was particularly evident in cotton yields
which increased from 30,000 bales in 1865 to 310,000 bales in 1876.[1]

1. Harry Hammond, *South Carolina Resources and Population, Institutions and
Industries,* State Board of Agriculture (Charleston, 1883), p. 359. In the year
preceding September 1, 1866, 112,000 bales of cotton came into the market from
South Carolina. In the following year, 162,000 bales were sold. The crop of

Improvement was also evident in the production of other crops. Over the decade of the 1870's, corn output increased by 50 per cent, wheat by 20 per cent, and oats by 400 per cent.[2] By 1870, even rice production, in spite of its many encumbrances, had reached about 25 per cent of its 1860 level, and soon stabilized at about one-third of the yield of 1860.[3]

However, the rewards of the most assiduous and skillful laborers were often swallowed in one giant gulp by the adverse effects of nature. In 1866, the entire state was struck by a drought which dwarfed agricultural production generally.[4] During the first half of the following year, planters became increasingly sanguine of a banner crop only to have their hopes dashed by a very dry May and June followed by torrential rains in July and August. The damage was particularly severe in the lowcountry and especially in the Sea Islands. There, many planters had not driven the rain-fed grass from the fields before a novel enemy, the caterpillar, made his awful appearance.[5] Localized disasters (floods, rice birds, caterpillars, cotton worms, and hurricanes) continued to occur throughout Reconstruction. After 1867, however, there followed a seven-year period in which nature was relatively kind to the farmer, and it was under these auspicious circumstances that the Negro farmer improved his material situation and gained a large measure of economic independence.

By good management, the farmer might minimize the hazards of nature. Diking and ditching might control the flow of rain water, the use of Paris Green might limit the ravages of the ever voracious caterpillar, and an alert watch might keep the rice birds out of the

---

1868 reputedly yielded 180,000 bales; that of 1869, 251,000 bales; and in 1870, 224,000 bales were produced. The crop of 1871 supplied 271,000 bales and that of 1872 sent 374,000 bales into the market. See: Printed sheet: "Cotton Crop of the United States, for the year ending September 1, 1867," Office of the *Commercial and Financial Chronicle*, New York, A. H. Boykin Papers; *New York Times*, October 19, 1868, p. 5; February 5, 1869, p. 2; Edwin De Leon, "The New South," *Harper's Monthly Magazine*, XLVIII (January, 1874), 276.

2. James Calvin Hemphill, *Climate, Soil, and Agricultural Capabilities of South Carolina and Georgia* (Washington, 1882), p. 3.

3. De Leon, *Harper's*, XLVIII (1874), p. 276; *News and Courier* (Charleston), September 1, 1873, September 1, 1876.

4. *New York Times*, August 24, 1866, p. 5; James H. Croushore and David M. Potter (eds.), *John William De Forest, A Union Officer in the Reconstruction* (New Haven, 1948), p. 73.

5. *New York Times*, June 19, p. 2; September 4, p. 2, 1867; January 6, p. 2, 1868; J. M. Dennis to J. Y. Harris, January 14, 1868, J. Y. Harris Papers.

fields. A prospective renter might choose a farm of the size and quality best suited to his resources, and both the renter and the land-owner might place the right crops in the right fields. The yield might also be enhanced by the careful selection and preservation of seed, close cultivation, judicious use of fertilizer, and utilization of the proper tools from among the increasing variety of improved implements avail-able. Of course, the ability to manage well depended in part upon the financial resources of the farmer, but good management might reflect, too, a knowledge of agricultural lore and a willingness to per-form hard labor.

In their first year of independence, Negro farmers, as a class, were probably less expert managers than their white contemporaries. After all, the school of slavery had not been designed to teach the Negro a course in farm management. Most individual Negro farmers who prospered immediately after emancipation seem to have sprung from the driver class, a class which had often slipped into managerial func-tions during the slave period. The dissatisfaction of many landowners with renters of both races was described above. However, landowners frequently ascribed incompetence as managers specifically to Negro renters. "They will do as day labourers," wrote David Golightly Harris in 1867, "but not as managing farmers." In 1868, he elaborated: "Ne-groes will not do to rely upon as croppers. They will not [look] far enough ahead to do any good." In 1869, he tried in vain to have his renters keep the banks and ditches in his bottom land in repair to prevent a flooding which occurred in May. "Much damage would have been prevented, if my hired [renting] negroes had fulfilled their contracts and had cleared out & cleaned off the banks of the creek," judged Harris, himself a skillful manager. "I am getting tired of negro farmers," he concluded wearily, "they are only calculated to worry the owner & injure his land."[6]

In time, Negro farmers either became more or less able managers, or they lost their lands to those who were more capable. Nevertheless, even the best farmers among the Negroes were susceptible to the same difficulties and foibles experienced by white farmers. The general lack of capital in the 1860's and the scarcity of good seed in 1866 and 1867 hampered the Negro farmer's efficiency just as it did that of the white. The Negro farmer was also no less the victim of the cotton and fertilizer manias. In 1869, a freedman was said to have planted cotton on a rented plot within the city limits of Columbia where a garden

6. MS Farm Journal, entries for March 27, 1867; June 20, 1868; May 18, 1869.

would have yielded twice the income.[7] Negro farmers also joined in
heaping "an enormous, almost fabulous quantity of Guano and other
Fertilizers" upon the soil of South Carolina.[8] In one important respect,
that of close cultivation, Negro farms were probably better managed
than those of the whites. To some extent, this was the result of necessity; the size of farms operated by Negroes ranged far below that of
the whites. In 1900 about five out of every eight Negro farms consisted of from ten to forty-nine acres; and, in 1910, the average number
of acres of improved land on Negro farms was 26.8. In other words,
65.9 per cent of the total acreage of the typical Negro farm was under
cultivation. At the same time, 43.9 acres, or 36.6 per cent, of the average
white farm was actively worked.[9]

Even if the Negro farmer were willing to work, even if he perfected
his managerial skills and overcame the hazards of nature, he was not
assured of success. For then he still had to face the perils of the market
place where wide fluctuations in the prices of his produce, steadily
increasing costs of production, processing, and marketing, and the invariably high cost of credit posed serious threats to his success. These
obstructions, real in themselves, seemed even more ominous to the
farmer because they appeared to move by the direction of some unseen,
mysterious hand steadfastly inimical to his interests.

Cotton was important to the Negro agrarian because it was his
main—frequently his only—source of cash income. If the Negro farmer
bought goods which increased his standard of living, he usually did
so with money derived from his cotton crop. However, during the
first two years in which the freedman planted cotton he reaped only
frustration. For several months after the war, middle-grade cotton sold
in Charleston for premium prices ranging around fifty cents a pound.[10]
Inevitably, prices would have declined, but as the first cotton crop to
be raised entirely by free labor came into the market in the fall of 1866,
it continued to command a good price, ranging from forty to thirty
cents a pound.[11] For the typical farmer, however, good prices in 1866

7. *New York Times,* May 24, 1869, p. 2.
8. J. M. Dennis to J. Y. Harris, June 25, 1870, J. Y. Harris Papers.
9. *Negro Population,* pp. 604, 610.
10. For instance, in December, 1865, L. D. De Saussure sold 122 bales of
middling cotton in Charleston for fifty-three and one-half cents a pound. L. D. De
Saussure to A. H. Boykin, December 4, 1865, A. H. Boykin Papers.
11. Printed Circular, "Cotton Crop of the United States, for the year ending
September 1, 1867," Office of the *Commercial and Financial Chronicle,* New York,
A. H. Boykin Papers.

were offset by poor yields. Nevertheless, during the spring of 1867, cotton farmers—by nature, perennially hopeful—went earnestly to work and planted a large acreage. With good weather, and, presumably, good management, they expected an excellent harvest to sell at last year's prices. On September 30, 1867, as the cotton fields of South Carolina were turning from dusty green to a dazzling white, middling cotton was selling in Charleston at thirty cents a pound. By late November when farmers were picking the cotton plant bare of its last fruit, the price had fallen to a disheartening fifteen and one-half cents. Prospects were further dimmed as natural causes reduced the harvest far below expectations. "Half crops and hardly half price will use up the very best managing people," lamented a Marion merchant who was soon to turn scalawag.[12] In some areas, planters had borrowed heavily from their factors, offering their cotton crops and other possessions as security. "The entire cotton crop failed to meet the liens & in many instances of my own acquaintance the Factors have stripped the Planters of everything not leaving them enough to subsist upon," wrote one irate Bishopville farmer. Negro agriculturalists of all classes shared in the disaster. "Negroes are out of employment by thousands without any means of support," he observed.[13]

During the six-year period from 1868 through 1873, fair prices and good weather combined to bring relative prosperity to cotton farmers in South Carolina. A somewhat diminished yield in 1868 commanded prices ranging through the lower twenties. Good yields in 1869, 1870, and 1871 sold at prices that were declining only gradually. A very large crop in 1872 sold at eighteen and nineteen cents a pound, and an excellent crop in 1873 sold at about fifteen cents a pound.

Then came the reaction. In 1874 and 1875, declining prices were accompanied by declining yields (which perhaps reflected the withdrawal from the field of the least efficient producers). By September 1, 1876, middling cotton was selling at the depression price of ten cents a pound, probably less than it cost the average farmer to produce it.[14] ". . . cotton is low and will continue so untill after it gets out of the hands of the planter," complained a Darlington County farmer to his wife in the summer of 1874, reflecting the rising spirit of rebellion among farmers of both races.[15]

12. C. Graham to W. A. Law, December 1, 1867, W. A. Law Papers.
13. J. M. Dennis to J. Y. Harris, January 14, 1868, J. Y. Harris Papers.
14. L. D. De Saussure to A. H. Boykin, December 4, 1865, et seq., A. H. Boykin Papers.
15. W. A. Law to his wife, August 25, 1874, W. A. Law Papers.

While Negro farmers were fighting declining cotton prices with increased production, the costs of producing their crops were steadily rising. To some extent, increasing costs reflected a general trend upward in prices during the period. However, the Negro farmer doubtless found small comfort in this fact when he paid his rent and taxes, bought seed and rations, and paid the high fees charged for ginning, threshing, bundling, and shipping his products to markets. Even the cost of selling his crop was high because factors customarily charged 3 per cent of the gross sale price for disposing of farm products.

Fertilizer, the most important item in increasing production, was also the key element in increasing operating costs. Beginning in 1868 and 1869, tens of thousands of tons of fertilizers were lavished every year upon the cotton plant. In 1873, for instance, 56,000 tons were poured into the ground to produce a yield never before equaled in the state.[16] In the early 1880's, Sea Island planters were yearly spreading half a ton of phosphates upon every acre of cotton land.[17] Fertilizer was fantastically expensive, selling at prices ranging from forty to seventy dollars, and its cost fell not only upon the landowner and renter, but upon the share-laborer as well. Typical was the experience of Negro laborers on the A. H. Boykin plantations in Kershaw County who paid a third of the cost ($3,000) of thirty-nine and a half tons of "Soluble Pacific Guano" and seven tons of dissolved bones used in 1870, and a third of the cost (about $3,250) of fifty tons of acid phosphate used on two of the plantations in 1871.[18]

Another costly item in the budget of the Negro agriculturalist was credit. In the first full year of freedom, credit took the form of advances of rations, seed, and tools by landowners. At the end of that year, these advances were repaid from the laborer's share of the crop. After 1866, this system of advancing persisted in arrangements where laborers worked for a portion of the crops. According to the usual contract, advances were interest free, to be "charged at Market prices," and an accurate accounting was to be kept by the employer.[19] However, such was not always the practice. A resident of the lowcountry

16. *New York Times,* September 8, 1873, p. 4.

17. Hemphill, *Climate, Soil, and Agricultural Capabilities of South Carolina and Georgia,* pp. 7–9.

18. L. D. De Saussure to A. H. Boykin, April 2, 1868; December 20, 1869; February 21, March 10, 29, 1870; January 25, March 24, 1871; April 19, 1872; March 4, 1874, A. H. Boykin Papers.

19. MS Contract, January 23, 1868, A. H. Boykin Papers.

informed a friend in 1866 that planters commonly advanced rations
to their laborers, "but the percentage charged the negroes on which is
enormous."[20]

Even the most honest and generous planters held their laborers
strictly to account for advances. At the end of the year, some workers
did emerge from the settlement with cash in their hands, but most were
forced to surrender all or nearly all of their wages to cancel their debts.
The end result was that the typical laborer earned only enough to pay
for what he had consumed during the year—though, of course, his rate
of consumption was increasing. The division that occurred on the
A. H. Boykin plantations in Kershaw County in December, 1869, suggests the nature of a usual settlement. There, a hundred laborers received, on paper, $6,537.48 for their third of the cotton crop. After
deducting a third of the fertilizer and the insurance costs and advances
of bacon, salt, molasses, straw, blankets, and overcoats, the balance due
the workers was estimated at less that $4,200, or about forty-two dollars
for each hand. On one of these plantations in 1874, only $500 was re-
quired to settle accounts with a dozen laborers.[21]

Share-laborers in the rice fields experienced much the same results.
On Dirleton plantation in Georgetown County in 1868, thirty-six laborers earned $2,365.01 (or an average of $65.69 each) after deductions
had been made for lost time, seed rice, and the use of five yoke of
oxen belonging to the employers. One fractional hand earned only
$12.18 beyond expenses, another $2.50, and another $2.40. The largest
amount earned by a full hand was $132.34, and the foreman was paid
$156 for his services.[22]

As wage laboring supplanted share laboring, the practice of advancing fell into disuse. Employees subsequently received the usual
ration of about three pounds of bacon and a quarter bushel of cereal
weekly as a part of their wages, or were paid its cash equivalent. In
1882, one expert estimated that agricultural wages in South Carolina
ranged from five to ten dollars monthly, in addition to rations, but
were never more than fifteen dollars. Authorities differ on the monthly
wages paid agricultural laborers in the state during Reconstruction.
Certainly, wages varied widely in different places and times. However,

20. William Elliott to his mother, March 25, 1866, Elliott–Gonzales Papers.
21. L. D. De Saussure to A. H. Boykin, December 20, 27, 1869; December 20,
1874, A. H. Boykin Papers.
22. MS list of "Expenses," ——, 1868; MS Contract with notes, January 21,
1867, Sparkman Family Papers.

estimates ranged from about ten to thirteen dollars a month, excluding room and board worth about five dollars a month.[23]

What and how much the laborer could buy with his wages can only be approximated. A very general comparison is suggested by the fact that in Barnwell, in 1866, rice sold for twelve and one-half cents a pound, bacon for sixteen cents, and coffee for twenty-five cents. At the same time, in Charleston, a pair of cottonade pants cost two dollars, and a cotton sack coat was valued at five dollars.[24]

Agricultural laborers received credit through advances; renters and landowners obtained credit by giving the lender a mortgage on their prospective crops. Essentially, this so-called "lien" (or mortgage) system was simply the advance system adapted to meet the peculiar circumstances of these two classes of agriculturalists. While even the most extensive white planters were drawn into the vortex of the lien whirlpool in the 1880's, during Reconstruction the large majority of liens were given by the farmers of smaller plots, "usually renters, for advances made by the landlord, or more frequently by the storekeeper."[25] Even though the value of the average lien was steadily rising, that amount did not seem excessive before the close of Reconstruction. In 1879, the average value of 50,358 liens in eighteen counties was $86.83. In the following year, the average value of 67,518 liens in the same counties was $109.[26] Furthermore, one lien might well cover credit for rent, seed, fertilizer, and provisions. In short, it might finance the crop beyond the means of the farmer.

In the fall of 1866, the legislature began to regularize the lien system with the passage of a law which allowed the lender a first lien on the crop when the agreement was properly registered in the office of the county clerk of court.[27] Early in their ascendency, Republicans reversed the emphasis of the law by an amendment which allowed the

23. Hemphill, *Climate, Soil, and Agricultural Capabilities of South Carolina*, p. 32; *New York Times*, September 17, 1866, p. 1; *A History of Spartanburg County*, p. 184; "Report on Cotton Production in South Carolina," House Misc. Doc. No. 42, 47th Cong., 2nd Sess., Pt. 6, p. 521; Edward Young, "Labor in Europe and America," House Ex. Doc., 44th Cong., 1st Sess., No. 21, pp. 74-77.

24. *Sentinel* (Barnwell), June 30, 1866; *Daily Courier* (Charleston), October 13, 1866.

25. *A History of Spartanburg County*, p. 185.

26. Hemphill, *Climate, Soil, and Agricultural Capabilities of South Carolina and Georgia*, p. 41.

27. *Statutes at Large*, XIII, 366^{12}–366^{13}.

"laborer," whether a renter or a laborer, the *first* claim on any crops he produced.[28]

As the payment of fixed rentals in cash or produce came into use, landlords normally required tenants to give them liens on the entire crop to guarantee its payment. For example, in 1869, six of the eight renters on David Harris' Spartanburg lands paid a fixed rental, and all six gave him "a mortgage on the entire crop for the pay."[29] In 1874, the legislature regularized this practice by defining the use of rented land as an advance for agricultural purposes and, as such, subject to the lien law. If the landlord duly recorded the arrangement, it became a first lien. However, the renter was still protected by a provision which limited the amount that a landlord could claim under a lien to one-third of the gross harvest.[30]

Liens were also used for special purposes directly related to the production of the crop. Thus, liens were sometimes executed for the purchase of seed, agricultural tools, draft animals, and other costly items. Probably the most important of this class was the fertilizer lien, a document which became increasingly common in the 1870's. In every community there were a number of agents representing fertilizer companies. Of necessity, these agents granted credit to farmers and protected themselves by taking a mortgage on the crop.[31] Conceivably, one crop might have three principal liens resting upon it: one for the use of the land, another for general provisions, and still another for fertilizer.

Liens frequently covered not only the prospective crop, but the debtor's personal and real property as well. In Clarendon County, in February, 1874, Doc Harrington and five other Negro renters made their marks on a lien which bound them to pay James B. Richardson 1900 pounds of cotton on October 1 of that year for advances received. To guarantee the loan, they mortgaged not only their crops, but "all our Horses, Mules and Stock which at the date of these presents we have, hold, own or possess." Unable to pay the debt in cotton, Doc Harrington, subsequently, executed a bill of sale by which he assigned ownership of a yoke of oxen to Richardson.[32] The requirement that

28. *Revised Statutes of the State of South Carolina* (Columbia, 1873), pp. 557–58.

29. MS Farm Journal, entry for June 5, 1869.

30. *Statutes at Large*, XV, 788–789, 844.

31. For an example, see: L. D. De Saussure to A. H. Boykin, March 7, 1872, A. H. Boykin Papers.

32. MS Contract, February 13, 1874, J. B. Richardson Papers.

the advance be repaid in cotton, a readily saleable commodity, was typical and lent authority to the oft-repeated charge that the lien system tended to perpetuate and promote a one-crop economy.

In the early postwar years, the landlord typically provided all the credit available to the tenant. However, there soon appeared a novel source of rural credit, the country store, which largely deprived the landlord or planter of this function. The origins of the country stores were varied. A significant number were begun by planters themselves as convenient instruments by which to issue advances to their laborers or renters. Frequently, the very building which had been used in the slave period to issue rations to the Negroes, the commissary, also housed the store.[33] Some country merchants, such as M. C. Clement in Adams Run, had operated stores before the war and, afterwards, had entered into the business of advancing seed and rations to renters and laborers upon the authority of the landlord, and, thus, passed on to the pursuit of the lien system.[34] However, a large number of these businesses were established as entirely new enterprises, and many of these were begun by persons more or less alien to the community in which they were located. Northern-born merchants were particularly active in this way in the Sea Islands after the war. Typical of this group was Reuben G. Holmes who had been a washing machine salesman in Boston and, after the war, came South to open a store near Beaufort. During the early postwar years, he advanced provisions to the Negro islanders for cotton, and, as late as 1879, was still a merchant in the area.[35]

As the Negro farmer or agricultural laborer found credit available through the storekeeper, he became increasingly independent of the landowning class. Wage laborers no longer needed to marry their fortunes yearly to one planter or another in order to secure a bare subsistence. Now, they could demand cash wages on a weekly or

33. For example, in 1868, the mistress of Social Hall, a lowcountry cotton plantation, operated a store through which all except one of the laborers on the plantation were paid; and, in 1876, John Berkeley Grimball established the same kind of store on his rice plantation, The Grove, near Adams Run. "Mrs. A. J. G." to her mother, May 3, 1868, Elliott–Gonzales Papers; J. B. Grimball to Arthur Grimball, January 23, 1876, J. B. Grimball Papers (Duke).

34. Various letters from M. C. Clement to J. B. Grimball, J. B. Grimball Papers (Duke).

35. Interestingly, Holmes was the delegate to the Constitutional Convention of 1868 who presented the ordinance which embodied the concept of the Land Commission. R. G. Holmes Papers, *passim.*

monthly basis, working wherever wages were highest, and living on provisions purchased with cash or on credit at the store. The more thrifty and ambitious among them could use the storekeeper's credit to establish themselves independently as small landowners or renters. Negroes who were renters found they were no longer bound to deal exclusively with their landlords (their former masters), and tended to ally themselves with storekeepers who were often more liberal in racial and political attitudes. Indeed, with surprising frequency, store-keepers became Republicans.[36] A pronounced hostility grew between white landowners as opposed to white storekeepers and their Negro allies. This antagonism was heightened by planter suspicion that storekeepers universally bought "seed cotton," that is, unginned cotton presumably stolen from the fields either by outsiders or by the land-lord's own tenants or laborers. "Three stores and three Duggens [possibly saloons?] at Black stock & more building besides numbers in the County & almost all buying Cotton in the seed from thievish Niggers," observed Robert Hemphill in 1873, voicing a complaint common among his class.[37] Frequently, landowners concluded that storekeepers not only bought stolen cotton from the Negroes, but that they actually encouraged the Negroes to steal cotton to settle their debts, a belief which occasionally led to open violence. Thus, in 1871, a Confederate veteran from Georgia who ran a store in Williamsburg County had his entire stock burned and narrowly averted being whipped by a band of alleged Ku Kluxers who accused him of buying seed cotton.[38]

While Negroes were politically allied with some merchants, their incomes were nevertheless heavily taxed by the merchant as well as by the planter. To some extent, the high cost of credit was merely a reflection of the high rates of interest which prevailed in the state throughout Reconstruction. Creditors and planters who made advances to Negroes themselves borrowed money in Charleston and New York at "extortionate" rates ranging from about 12 to 36 per cent per year, and occasionally agreed to pay even higher rates.[39] Even in the relatively

36. *Daily Republican* (Charleston), July 13, 1870.

37. To W. R. Hemphill, January 6, 1873, Hemphill Papers.

38. *Ku Klux Conspiracy*, III, 35-85. For similar charges made by a Northern plantation manager in the Sea Islands, see: *New York Times,* August 1, 1866, p. 1.

39. J. B. Heyward to W. H. Heyward, March 16, 1866, Heyward–Ferguson Papers; R. E. Elliott to T. R. S. Elliott, March 13, 1867, T. R. S. Elliott Papers; H. Gourdin to Robert Gourdin, August 19, September 12, 1874, R. H. Gourdin Papers.

promising year of 1872, a Marion merchant found that the interest rate was then about 1.5 per cent each month.[40] The local operator passed these charges along to his own debtors, Negro and white, and frequently added some of his own manufacture.

To evade the legal maximum yearly interest rate of 7 per cent, those who advanced provisions usually charged "time prices," that is, a credit price which was much higher than the cash price on the same item. In March, 1872, A. H. Boykin bought nine tons of fertilizer for $990 (or $110 a ton) on eight months' credit, while the best quality of that commodity could have been purchased for $70 a ton in cash.[41] Even the cash prices of goods in country stores were artificially inflated, and fantastically high mark-ups were normal in the plantation stores where labor was exchanged for goods through account books kept by the planter-merchant. The mistress of Social Hall, heiress to a name pre-eminent in ante-bellum Carolina society, in 1868 explained to her mother the manner in which she operated the store on the plantation of her husband, General Ambrusio Gonzales: ". . . I determine the prices of the last [cloth]——the Gen. thinks I am too exorbitant but I tell him I am sure the nigs do not do 'full work'—A piece of nice blue check which costs 88 cts by the piece, your Jewess' of a daughter gets 60 cts for—& the freedmen get 12 yds at a time. I have now a box of assorted candy to tempt them—but as these articles are paid for in work of course my satisfaction at getting high prices is greatly diminished."[42] The rationalization that such practices were justified by the poor quality of labor performed by the Negro was common among whites. Probably many agreed with the historian of Williamsburg County who blamed the situation on the North which had taught the Negroes to work as little as possible and live off the whites. Thus, "honest landowners" turned to taking all they could from their Negro tenants. There was more than a grain of truth in the folksy rhyme which the first generation of freedmen came to chant at "settling-up time":

> Naught's a naught, and five's a figger,
> All for the white man and none for the nigger.[43]

40. C. Graham to W. A. Law, May 16, 1872, W. A. Law Papers.
41. L. D. De Saussure to A. H. Boykin, March 7, 1872, A. H. Boykin Papers.
42. "Mrs. A. J. G." to her mother, May 3, 1868, Elliott–Gonzales Papers.
43. William Willis Boddie, *History of Williamsburg County, South Carolina 1705 until 1923* (Columbia, 1923), p. 453.

The central fact of the Negro's experience in the economic sphere is that he realized—in spite of the general and particular hazards which obstructed his progress—an appreciable improvement in his standard of living. To many Northerners, the emergence of the Negro as an independent consumer was a major contribution to national economic progress. E. L. Pierce, the leading spirit in the Port Royal "Experiment," envisioned the results of allowing Negroes "the opportunity of labor and earning wages." Viewing the materialistic panorama, he exclaimed, "What a market the South would open under the new system!"[44]

Even compared with the most affluent element in the white community, some Negroes achieved high material and cultural incomes under the new regime. "In Charleston and other large cities at the South there are colored people, tailors, butchers, and tradesmen, who maintain their families in very good style," reported a Northern traveler from Charleston in 1874. "Your correspondent recently spent an evening at the home of a colored man whose house was furnished with every modern improvement, whose table was supplied with choice meats and rare wines, and whose daughters had admirably solved the sweet mysteries of Schubert's and Bach's most difficult music."[45] Without doubt, Charleston, presenting many free Negro families which had been prosperous in the ante-bellum period, could have offered a number of similar cases. Even outside Charleston, some Negroes achieved a standard of living well above that of the average white. Negro governmental officials in Columbia, Beaufort, and Georgetown rivaled Charleston tradesmen in the elegance of their material and cultural surroundings. In Columbia, three of the Rollin sisters, the social arbiters of Negro and Radical society in the city, lived near the Capitol in a comfortable, white frame house with a garden and a fountain in the rear. By all reports, the house was well furnished. "Thick carpets covered floors; handsome cabinets held costly bric-a-brac; a $1,000 piano stood in a corner; legislative documents bound in morocco reposed with big albums on expensive tables," reported one indignant lady.[46] A fourth sister became the wife of Negro politician Robert Brown Elliott

44. Edward L. Pierce, "The Freedmen of Port Royal," *The Atlantic Monthly*, XII (September, 1863), 311. See also: Whitelaw Reid, *After the War; A Southern Tour, May 1, 1865, to May 1, 1866* (London, 1866), p. 116; *New York Times*, August 6, 1865, p. 3.

45. *Ibid.*, July 4, 1874, p. 5.

46. Myrta Lockett Avary, *Dixie after the War* (New York, 1906), p. 356; *New York Herald*, June 13, 1871.

who owned a house of comparable elegance. Because of the affluence of their husbands, the wives of Beverly Nash and C. M. Wilder were given the leisure and means to take leading roles in charitable activities, particularly those concerned with the orphanage and insane asylums maintained by the state. In this manner they acted much as club women of more recent times have done.

There were, of course, many Negroes who fared worse, materially, in freedom than they had in slavery. The same traveler who saw Charleston Negro society at its best in 1874 also thought that the "great majority of the colored population lived in the most abject, the most deplorable, wretchedness and poverty."[47] Poor crops and declining prices for Sea Island cotton in the early postwar years did indeed leave many lowcountry Negroes in the direst circumstances. A Northern teacher living in the Sea Islands reported that many of the "refugees" who had returned from the Islands to their mainland homes after the war "lived on roots and acorns." Others who acquired small holdings on the islands lived in rude shacks and "mud huts," suffering and sometimes dying from starvation and exposure.[48]

Nevertheless, the great mass of freedmen registered a progressive improvement in their material situations. By 1870, when prosperity was again widespread, the change had become obvious. In the spring of that year, a Republican partisan in the upcountry village of Ninety-Six reported that "the proprietors of farms have made money since the war," but the laborers (Negroes) had not progressed quite so rapidly. However, the laborers' "wages, or part of the crop, has been increased some this year, and if there is a good crop made this season they will get their just and full half share next year." Meanwhile, he observed, some Negroes "have acquired stock and are going on their own hook; and generally they enjoy a great many more of the pleasures and comforts of every day life."[49] Soon afterward, an English observer judged that such progress was prevalent: "That the Negroes are improving, and many of them rising under freedom into a very comfortable and civilized condition, is not only admitted in all the upper circles of society, but would strike even a transient wayfarer like myself in the great number of decent coloured men of the laboring class and of

47. *New York Times,* July 4, 1874, p. 5.

48. Elizabeth Hyde Botume, *First Days among the Contrabands* (Boston, 1893), pp. 225-77, *passim; New York Times,* June 14, p. 5, 1869; July 4, p. 5, 1874.

49. *Daily Republican* (Charleston), April 18, 1870.

happy coloured families one meets."[50] By 1882, a native white author
could write that even on the Sea Islands, where the Negro population
had suffered so severely in the late 1860's, the more thrifty had acquired
"comfortable little fortunes to which they are gradually adding from
year to year"; and "there is hardly a colored man who does not own
a horse or mule, a cart, and a cow as well as household goods and agricultural implements."[51]

The material progress of the Negro was not measured entirely by
his acquisition of farms and stock, homes and furnishing, food and
clothing. Negro communities were also building their own churches
and schools, and paying the salaries of teachers and ministers long
before its members had won material security.[52] In freedom, Negroes
were also able to avail themselves of the professional services of physicians and lawyers, to use transportation facilities, attend entertainments,
dine in restaurants and patronize bars and saloons. Further, they were
able to support numerous social and economic co-operative organizations among themselves: reading clubs, fire companies, military companies, burial and insurance associations, and fraternal organizations.

The material progress of the Negro community was also indicated
by the money which it did not spend. Institutional saving began in
Beaufort in August, 1864, when a group of liberal Northerners founded
the Freedmen's Savings Bank of South Carolina primarily to induce
Negro soldiers to save their pay and bounties. In October, 1865, this
organization merged with a savings institution in Charleston to become the National Freedmen's Savings and Trust Company. While
Negroes were still serving in the ranks of the army, the company's
assets amounted to about $200,000; however, in the lean years of 1866,
1867, and 1868, deposits steadily declined. In March, 1869, the bank
credited some $91,000 to 1224 depositors reflecting a general return of
prosperity. In March, 1870, it held $132,000 for 2154 depositors; in
October of the same year assets reached $165,000; and, in 1873, some
5500 depositors had invested about $350,000 in the bank. A few of the
depositors were white, but most were Negroes, as one observer noted
in 1870: "Go in any forenoon, and the office is found full of negroes

50. Robert Somers, *The Southern States since the War, 1870–1871* (New York,
1871), p. 54.
51. Hemphill, *Climate, Soil, and Agricultural Capabilities of South Carolina
and Georgia*, pp. 14–15.
52. For instance, Martha Schofield's school in Aiken was largely supported by
the Negroes themselves. Martha Schofield MS Diary, entries for March 20, 1869,
through March 24, 1871, *passim*.

depositing little sums of money, drawing little sums, or remitting to distant parts of the country where they have relatives to support or debts to discharge." In 1874, however, poor management caused the bank to fail. In spite of this disastrous experience, Negroes subsequently deposited substantial sums in other banks. For instance, in Charleston, in 1876, Negro investors had placed some $125,000 in institutions under white management.[53]

By the end of Reconstruction, improvement in the material circumstances of the Negro population was evident, and its effects upon the Negro's actions and attitudes were becoming manifest. In 1882, a native white agricultural expert caught glimpses of the pattern:

> A canvass of the counties in this State shows that the negro is building up his own fortunes and that he is gradually acquiring a property interest in the government. Many notable instances of thrift among colored farmers and mechanics could be given. No accurate account of the number of the colored property holders in the State has ever been taken, but it is a significant fact that on the sea islands alone the negroes own lands that are worth fully $500,000, acquired by hard industry and economical living. Of late years there has been an encouraging decrease in crime.[54]

It is a patent truth that Negroes in South Carolina during this period did not win material security in any way comparable to that of the whites. Yet, measured by the admittedly minimal standards of his existence in slavery, Reconstruction was, for the Negro, a tremendous success, a success which possibly might never have been achieved had not his temporary political ascendency—rightfully or wrongfully—turned doubtful economic issues in his favor. The momentum gained was no doubt slowed by the reversal of the political tide in 1876 and 1877, but, during the dark and difficult decades which followed, political repression never quite became economic regression.

53. *The Nation*, I, No. 25 (December 21, 1865), 779; *New York Times*, August 6, p. 3, 1865; June 11, p. 8, 1866; May 12, p. 1, 1865; *Daily Republican* (Charleston), June 11, 1870; Somers, *The Southern States since the War*, pp. 54–55; *News and Courier* (Charleston), August 1, 1873; December 30, 1874; O. O. Howard to Governor R. K. Scott, January 31, 1870, Freedmen File; George Brown Tindall, *South Carolina Negroes, 1877–1900* (Columbia, 1952), p. 142.
54. Hemphill, *Climate, Soil, and Agricultural Capabilities of South Carolina and Georgia*, p. 37.

VII... RELIGION: WITHDRAWAL AND REFORMATION

The withdrawal of Negroes from churches dominated by native whites was the most striking development in religion in South Carolina during Reconstruction. Secession began with emancipation, and, in terms of numbers, was largely accomplished within months after the close of the war. In June, 1865, an informant in Charleston wrote: "In fact the colours are separated now as to churches. The Blacks now have Calhoun & Zion, Old Bethel, also I believe another Methodist church, Morris St. Baptist and perhaps some other old churches to themselves."[1] By the end of Reconstruction, separation was practically universal.

After the secession process was completed, approximately half the Negro church-going population belonged to churches that had been formed by Northern missionaries during and immediately after the war. In the early postwar months, the activities of Northern missionaries were not directed solely toward re-orienting the Negro's religious inclinations in a Northerly direction. Indeed, the initial aim was to effect a complete reconstruction of the entire religious and moral fabric of southern society. As late as 1871, after a decade of labor in the state, the South Carolina Conference of the Methodist Episcopal Church (Northern) declared that the "religious institutions of the South are

1. J. K. Robertson to Mrs. Smythe, June 28, 1865, A. T. Smythe Letters.

corrupted, and her garments are moth eaten," presumably by the "barbarism of slavery and the demoralization of war." The reverend body concluded, "We firmly believe that God's great means of righteous reconstruction in this country are *religious,* rather than *political.*"[2]

It is hardly surprising that South Carolinians were unwilling to offer their religious institutions for reform along Northern lines. The refusal of Southern whites to submit to a religious conquest angered many Northern missionaries in the state. " 'Jeshurun is waxing fat,' and gives fair warning that unless gratified, he intends 'to kick,' " observed one Northern churchman in Charleston; and another feared that "the war is ending too *soon* and too *abruptly* for the good of the South or the peace of the County."[3] Unable to work with their Southern brothers, Northern missionaries were led to work against them. Logically, their evangelistic efforts concentrated upon the conversion of the Negro, and thus, they contributed directly to the work of separation. In South Carolina, six Northern churches were active in this movement: the Methodist Episcopal Church (Northern), the African Methodist Episcopal Church, the African Methodist Episcopal Church Zion, the Presbyterian Church (United), the Baptist Church (Northern), and the Reformed Episcopal Church.

In terms of zeal, organization, growth, and permanent influence, the Northern Methodists were by far the most impressive missionaries in South Carolina. One of their first representatives was Mansfield French, a New York minister who arrived with the invasion in 1861 and became one of the prominent Port Royal "Experimenters."[4] French's activities ranged far beyond the religious sphere, but in January, 1864, Timothy Willard Lewis came to Beaufort from a Methodist pulpit in Worcester, Massachusetts, for the explicit purpose of carrying on missionary labors.[5] From his arrival until his death in the early 1870's, Lewis devoted his time and his considerable talents to this single task. Informally allied with the many Methodist ministers and local preachers then serving in the army, he carried his evangelism wherever the sol-

2. Adopted Report of the Religious Condition and Wants of the Country, South Carolina Conference, *Minutes of the Annual Conferences of the M. E. Church for the Year 1872* (New York, 1872), p. 11. Cited hereinafter as *Northern Methodist Minutes.*

3. Hunter Dickinson Farish, *The Circuit Rider Dismounts; a Social History of Southern Methodism, 1865–1900* (Richmond, 1938), pp. 36, 37.

4. *New South* (Port Royal), March 15, 1862.

5. *Free South* (Beaufort), January 9, 1864.

diers went. One of his most effective collaborators was Benjamin Franklin Whittemore, a Massachusetts Methodist minister who had come South as the chaplain of a Maine regiment and who before the end of the summer of 1865 had become well known to the Negroes of Darlington and Camden. Another was Benjamin Franklin Randolph, a Northern-born Negro and also a Methodist minister, who arrived in Hilton Head in 1864 as chaplain of the Twenty-sixth United States Colored Troops.[6] In February, 1865, Lewis "entered the city of Charleston with the conquering Union army only to find in it empty churches, deserted school-houses, and scattered and abandoned flocks." A decade later, a colleague described the importance of Lewis's work: "For weeks, if not for months, neither white nor black could have had a pastor's prayer, a minister's blessing, a sacrament, or even a Christian burial, if he had not been there to supply them all." The result was the early entrance of several thousand Carolina freedmen into the Northern Methodist Church. "To these very men, rather than to the ministers born on their own soil, the colored people turned, recognizing in them their natural protectors and friends."[7]

Before 1876, the hierarchy of the Northern Methodist Church equivocated on the question of absolute racial equality within its Southern branches. Their ambivalence reflected, of course, their desire to recruit both Negroes and Southern whites into their fold. While the hope of a reunion with the Southern Methodist still lived, the church allowed the missionary ministry within each conference to prescribe its own racial policy. In South Carolina, where virtually no native whites and thousands of Negroes chose to join the Northern Church, the policy was active, aggressive opposition to discrimination. Weeks after the occupation of Charleston, Lewis used this appeal to win Negro members away from Charleston's Trinity Church, to which both Negroes and whites belonged. The native white ministry pleaded with the Negro membership "to stay with us in your old places in the galleries." But Lewis assured them that "there will be no galleries in heaven," and invited them "to go with a church which makes no distinctions." The entire Negro membership supported Lewis and, subsequently, formed the nucleus of Centenary Church, which has ever

6. John M. Gould, *History of the 1st–10th–29th Maine Regiment* (Portland, 1871), p. 597; *House Journal* (1868–1869), p. 15.
7. Henry J. Fox, "Our Work in the South," *Methodist Review*, January, 1874, pp. 31–32.

since been one of the strongest Northern churches in the South.[8] Although there were temporary reversals in Lewis's aracial policy, under his influence and that of his strong-minded co-workers, Northern Methodists in the state remained firmly committed to this ideal throughout Reconstruction. For instance, in 1871, the South Carolina Conference adopted a report which accurately echoed Lewis's convictions. "We re-affirm," it declared, "our solemn conviction that the true basis of organization in State or Church is without distinction of *race* or *color*; and to pander to the prejudices of the white or black race in this regard, will displease our common Father, and bring only evil and disaster in the end."[9] Probably the South Carolina Conference came closer than any other Northern Methodist group in practicing the impartial racial program which it preached. So thoroughly was the program executed that it is difficult to determine the color of members or ministers within the Conference because the records are uniquely mute on the point.

The visitation of Bishop Gilbert Haven in the fall of 1873 lent a new measure of authority to the racial liberalism of the Conference. Even though he was often denounced by members of his own church for his radicalism, this red-haired, fiery-eyed, strong-voiced, portly proponent of miscegenation had been elevated to high office in the church partially because of his very militancy in the abolitionist cause. Even his presence in South Carolina was an insult to the native whites, and he hastened to add the anticipated injury. "If you want to see the coming race in all its virile perfection," he wrote from Charleston in a public letter on his favorite theme, "come to this city. Here is amalgamation made perfect." On the alleged mixtures of Negro with Pinckney, Rhett, Barnwell, and Calhoun blood, he grew perfectly rhapsodical. "What exquisite tints of delicate brown; what handsome features; what beautiful eyes, what graceful forms," he sang. "No boorish Hanoverian blood here, but the best Plantagenet. . . . It is an improved breed— the best the country has today. It will be so reckoned in the boudoirs of Newport and the court of Washington ere many years. . . . Let the white man make the less white lady his wife, and let her not de-

8. William H. Lawrence, *The Centenary Souvenir, Containing a History of the Centenary Church, Charleston, and an Account of the Life and Labors of Reverend R. V. Lawrence, Father of the Pastor of the Centenary Church* (Charleston, 1885), *passim*.

9. *Northern Methodist Minutes*, 1872, p. 11.

grade herself by any voluntary association of sin."[10] The blasphemy was officially continued when Haven, within weeks, presided over the annual session of the South Carolina Methodist Conference in Columbia.[11]

The unqualified acceptance of Negroes into the membership, ministry, and councils of the Northern Methodist Church in South Carolina alienated Southern Methodists and precluded the possibility of converting any significant number of native whites. But the policy was eminently successful in promoting the growth of the church among Negroes. Even at the time of its first formal conference, in April, 1866, Northern Methodism was already firmly established, having 2,750 members and 288 applicants on probation in nine churches and in numerous "preaching places." Charleston claimed more than half of the membership, and the islands to the south supported a sprinkling of small congregations. Already, however, the church was reaching well into the interior. Inland stations were led by Camden where a young Canadian missionary, William J. Cole, began a church in November, 1865. "The colored people hailed him with joy as a messenger God-sent," another missionary wrote. "A circuit was immediately organized, and he lived to see [in 1867] ten preaching places established and an ample church erected and nearly paid for, and over six hundred members gathered into the fold." Beginnings had also been made in Orangeburg, Darlington, Summerville, and Sumter. This large establishment was served by only three full ministers—Lewis, Cole, and Alonzo Webster, a New Englander who came to Charleston to join Lewis soon after the occupation. The three were assisted by Mansfield French (who was still in the army), one defecting Southern Methodist minister, and four Negro ministers who were accepted on trial.[12]

Thereafter, Northern Methodism expanded with astonishing rapidity. By 1874, the South Carolina Conference, with 26,000 members, was the second largest in the South, and the roll of 5,000 probationers indicated that it was still growing at a prodigious rate.[13] Its churches blanketed the state from Charleston to Spartanburg and southward to

10. Farish, *The Circuit Rider Dismounts*, pp. 213–14; Ralph Ernest Morrow, *Northern Methodism and Reconstruction* (East Lansing, 1956), p. 184.

11. *Northern Methodist Minutes*, 1874, p. 7.

12. *Ibid.*, 1866, pp. 61–62; 1867, p. 11; Morrow, *Northern Methodism and Reconstruction*, p. 45.

13. Fox, *Methodist Review*, January, 1874, p. 35.

the Savannah, invading the citadels of Southern Methodism.[14] For two years after 1866 it boasted a press edited by Webster and, after 1869, a university, both heavily subsidized by the Claflin family of Boston.[15] But, most of all, it came to be led by a zealous, able ministry of several score. A few of these had transferred from Northern pulpits, and the native white ministry had furnished a very few. The majority, however, were native Negroes.[16] The recruiting and the training of these last were the most effective means of promoting the spread and permanency of the Methodist Church in South Carolina.

In the early days of freedom, probably many recruits for the ministry sprang from the religious leaders of the slave period. A pioneer in the Southern work asserted that "Veteran preachers among the late slaves were prompt to offer their welcome services."[17] In South Carolina, Francis A. Smith was perhaps typical of this class. Born in Charleston in 1812, as a boy he joined the Methodist Church. For over forty years he was a class leader, an exhorter, a local preacher, and, finally, for thirty-five years a member of the South Carolina Conference. Carried out of the church of "his choice" (as his official eulogy read) by the secession of the Southern Methodists in 1844, he eagerly returned to the "old church" after the occupation. His son, known as Francis Smith, was one of the first four Negroes admitted to ministry in the Conference. The elder Smith became a deacon in 1868, and a minister in 1871. Thereafter, "he resided in Charleston, laboring with his hands for a livelihood, and supplied feeble churches in the vicinity until his death."[18]

Many other Northern Methodist Negro ministers had been religious leaders among slaves. Henry D. Owens was among the first Negroes admitted to the ministry in the Conference, as were the younger Francis Smith, J. A. Sasportas, and Thomas Phillips. Owens was also active in the Sea Islands even before the church was formally established in the state. Martha Schofield, teaching on Wadmalaw in 1865 and 1866,

14. *Northern Methodist Minutes,* 1874, pp. 7–9.

15. Morrow, *Northern Methodism and Reconstruction,* p. 55.

16. L. C. Matlack, a leader in the Methodist movement in the lower South during Reconstruction, noted in 1872 a similar distribution among his denomination's ministry in the South at large. Of 630 traveling ministers in 1871, 260 were white, and 370 were Negro. Of the 260 whites, only about 50 were Northerners. L. C. Matlack, "The Methodist Episcopal Church in the Southern States," *Methodist Review,* January, 1872, p. 108.

17. *Ibid.*

18. *Northern Methodist Minutes,* 1881, p. 70.

noted in her diary in February, 1866: "Henry Owens, colored preacher, dined here——." And again in March: ". . . we slept on sofas last night & let H. Owens have our bed! ! !"[19] J. A. Sasportas ministered to the Summerville church throughout Reconstruction and became the first Negro in the Conference to be made a presiding elder. Thomas Phillips, filling the Orangeburg pulpit, brought the membership of his congregation to 1059 in 1869, the fourth largest in the Conference.[20] Abram Middleton, admitted to the ministry on trial in 1867, had been a leader in the Negro community in the Beaufort area during the war. He remained at his Barnwell station for ten years; thereafter, returning to Beaufort as the presiding elder of the Port Royal District.[21]

Perhaps half a dozen Northern Methodist ministers were won from dissident elements among the African and Zion Methodist churches. Some of these, apparently, brought their congregations with them. For instance, soon after emancipation, Thomas Evans became a preacher in the African Church in the vicinity of Monck's Corner. "But when he found an opportunity to connect himself with the MEC he gladly came within its fold, feeling that in it all of the rights of his manhood would be duly respected, and all the blessings of Christian fellowship and labor would be freely extended without invidious distinction on account of race or previous condition." He enjoyed "great success" in his labors among the rice workers along the lower Cooper River, but in 1874 both he and his wife died of malaria.[22]

The lasting strength of Northern Methodists in South Carolina grew from the young dedicated churchmen who emerged from the native membership to join the ministry. The large majority of ministers admitted on trial by the Conference belonged to this class, and the figures in the early years are indeed impressive. Thus, eighteen ministers were admitted in 1867; sixteen in the following year; eight in 1869; thirteen in 1870; and thirty-two in 1871.[23] As a group, the younger

19. Martha Schofield MS Diary, entries for February 25, March 1, 1866; *Northern Methodist Minutes,* 1866, p. 62. One evening in June, 1866, Martha Schofield dined in company with Owens, Lewis (whom she described as a "massachusetts Methodist preacher"), and Capt. Chamberlain, who ten years later was the governor of South Carolina. Martha Schofield MS Diary, entry for June 2, 1866.

20. *Northern Methodist Minutes,* 1866, pp. 61–62; 1867, pp. 13–14; 1868, pp. 10–11; 1869, pp. 10–12; 1870, p. 10; 1876, pp. 9–10.

21. *Ibid.,* 1867, pp. 13–14; 1877, pp. 7–8.

22. *Ibid.,* 1875, p. 7.

23. *Ibid.,* 1867, *et seq.*

ministry was eminently better trained for its mission than their elders. Many attended Baker Institute in Charleston, which had been founded by Lewis in 1865, and, at first, staffed by Webster and himself. After Baker Institute became the theological department of Claflin University, future ministers enjoyed the broader educational opportunities offered by the cluster of institutions and their faculties in Orangeburg. Christopher W. Lucas was of this new generation. Born a slave on the Round O in Colleton County in 1849, Lucas was converted to Methodism soon after the war. He first became a local preacher, and, in 1870, was admitted on trial as a minister. Stationed at Walterboro, the county seat of Colleton, he soon gathered a flock, built a church, and organized a country circuit on the upper Ashepoo. In 1871, he was ordained a deacon, and, in 1875, an elder. In 1879, at the age of thirty, he died of "exposure and over-work."[24]

Even though the South Carolina Conference held firmly to its commitment to racial equality throughout Reconstruction, the leadership in the Methodist Church in the North moved steadily toward official recognition of racial distinctions. The favored plan was the organization of a separate conference for each race in each area. In the nationwide General Conference in 1872, a movement to allow voluntary separation in this manner was barely defeated by a coalition of New Englanders and those Southern conferences which were largely Negro in membership. Meanwhile, however, separation became a reality without official sanction as each conference in the South came to be dominated entirely by one race or the other. In the General Conference of 1876, voluntary separation won approval, and the division of the races within the church was largely accomplished by 1881.[25] A staunch proponent of racial equality within the church lamented the desertion of the ideal as a surrender to the Southern charge that their church was the "Nigger Church." In 1892, he recorded the sequel. "As a result our white and colored members became, most unfortunately, estranged from each other, until to-day, in many places, the fraternal relations of our white to our colored work is less cordial than that between the Southern Church and our colored work."[26] In South Carolina, in 1881, where only 69 whites stood among 36,000 Northern Methodists, the effect of the prevailing trend was not, of course, to

24. *Ibid.*, 1879, p. 63.
25. Morrow, *Northern Methodism and Reconstruction*, pp. 191–97.
26. A. E. P. Albert, "The Church in the South," *Methodist Review*, March, 1892, p. 238.

separate these few whites from the Negroes. However, in 1877 the
white ministry began returning to the North. Though many remained
during the next few years (Webster, for instance, became the presiding elder of the Port Royal District in the 1880's), and others came
to teach at Claflin University, by 1894 only one white minister remained
in the Conference.[27]

In spite of the defection of their white allies, Northern Methodism
in South Carolina continued to be a healthy, growing institution under
the leadership of the native Negro ministry. In 1890, it mustered a
membership of 43,000, which, by 1906, had increased to 54,097. In size,
it was the third largest denomination among Carolina Negroes; in
wealth, unity, strength, and the educational level of its ministry, it
was first.[28]

The African Methodist Episcopal Church—an exclusively Negro
body established by Richard Allen in Philadelphia in 1786 and formally
sanctioned by Bishop Asbury—had been active in Charleston before
the war. However, the pressures exerted by the white community after
the Denmark Vesey insurrectionary scare of 1822 caused it to withdraw
from the state. In 1863, the African Church re-entered South Carolina
in the person of the Reverend James Lynch, a missionary from Baltimore who soon became a prominent Negro leader in Beaufort.[29]
Doubtless, Lynch developed a following in the Sea Islands, but he did
not organize a formal congregation until a year later, after he had
moved to Savannah.[30]

Following the capture of Charleston, Daniel Alexander Payne was
ordained a bishop and given the task of carrying the banner of African
Methodism into the Southeast. Payne had been born free in Charleston
in 1811. He attended the Minor Moralist Society's School and worked
as a shoemaker, tailor, and carpenter. In 1829, he opened a school
for free Negro children but discontinued teaching after the passage
in 1834 of restrictive legislation by the insurrection-fearing whites. He
then went to Gettysburg, Pennsylvania, to attend the Lutheran Theological Seminary, and enlisted in the ministry of the African Church.

27. *Northern Methodist Minutes, 1877, et seq.*; George Brown Tindall, *South
Carolina Negroes, 1877–1900* (Columbia, 1952), p. 192.
28. United States Bureau of the Census, *Religious Bodies,* I (Washington,
1906), 558–59.
29. *Free South* (Beaufort), December 5, 1863; January 9, 1864.
30. Farish, *The Circuit Rider Dismounts,* p. 27. It was perhaps this James
Lynch who later became secretary of state in Reconstruction Mississippi.

He subsequently took a leading role in the establishment of Wilberforce University in Greene County, Ohio—an area heavily populated
by Negroes and a stronghold of the African Church.[31] In Charleston,
in May, 1865, Payne assembled a Conference of four Northern and
twelve Southern African Methodist ministers, and launched a well-
planned missionary effort.

A church exclusively Negro had its obvious appeal, one that was
consciously and effectively emphasized by the African Methodist leadership in South Carolina. Under Payne's influence, the first Conference
resolved that a separate religious organization was necessary for the
Negro. Racial prejudice among whites both North and South, Payne
argued, precluded worship at the same altar. "Colored men who had
admitted to a distinction in the House of God had lost half their manhood," he declared.[32]

Paradoxically, the success of the African Church in the South was
greatly facilitated by the friendly attitude of Southern Methodists.
Though Southern Methodists were reluctant to lose their Negro members, when the loss was recognized as inevitable they preferred to
surrender them to the African Methodists rather than to their old rivals,
the Northern Methodists.[33] In Charleston, in 1865 and 1866, Southern
Methodists gave this spirit material form when they allowed the African
Methodists to use Trinity Church while the African Church was under
construction. In the same vein, in Camden, a Methodist Church building was sold to the African Methodist Episcopal Church; and white
Carolina Methodists, in 1866, approved the acceptance of fraternal
delegates from the African Church in the next General Conference of
Southern Methodists.[34]

In the first year of its evangelism in the Southeast, African Methodism grew prodigiously. The second annual conference, in 1866, announced a membership of over 22,000, most of whom were South

31. "Daniel Alexander Payne," *Dictionary of American Biography*, IV, 324;
Historical Records Survey Program, Division of Professional and Service Projects,
Works Projects Administration, *Inventory of the Church Archives of Michigan,
AMEC, Michigan Conference*; Detroit, MHR Survey Project, September, 1940,
pp. 1-4.
32. Quoted in: Francis B. Simkins and Robert Hilliard Woody, *South Carolina
During Reconstruction* (Chapel Hill, 1932), pp. 385-86.
33. Matlack, "The Methodist Episcopal Church in the Southern States," p. 110.
34. Simkins and Woody, *Reconstruction in South Carolina*, p. 387; Thomas
J. Kirkland and Robert M. Kennedy, *Historic Camden* (Columbia, 1926), pp.
288-89.

Carolinians. For the first few years, the primary problem of the Church was not membership but ministry. In 1867, for instance, there were only thirteen ministers attempting to serve, with lay assistance, a flock which must have numbered about 30,000.[35] The work of these few was, of necessity, indeed impressive.

Pre-eminent among the African ministry was Richard Harvey Cain. Cain, a mulatto, had been born free in Greenbriar County, Virginia, and as a child, was carried by his father to Gallipolis, Ohio. He entered the ministry while still a young man; but feeling the need of a formal education, he enrolled in Wilberforce University in 1860. Subsequently, he became a leader in the church, and, in 1865, occupied an important Brooklyn pulpit. Cain was one of the first four African Methodist ministers to enter South Carolina as the war drew to a close. Then forty years old his was a striking appearance, distinguished by squarish features and a bristle mustache. Self-assertive, a poised and experienced speaker, he soon acquired a commanding influence among Negroes in the Charleston area. An indication of his power was suggested by the fact that in the immediate postwar period, when few new buildings were being erected in Charleston, he organized the construction of Emmanuel Church, a huge edifice containing two thousand seats and costing $10,000.[36] In addition to his ministerial labors, Cain was editor of the *Missionary Record,* the highly successful journal of the Conference. Although his political activities were extensive and not free from charges of corruption, Cain, rising to bishop in 1880, retained his position of religious leadership until his death in 1887.[37]

In the decade following 1866, these few pioneer ministers of the African Church in South Carolina were supplemented by hundreds of native Negro recruits to the ministry. Though endowed with natural talents of religious leadership, many of these novices were poorly educated and of doubtful denominational loyalty. Educational deficiencies were ameliorated by the establishing of Payne Institute in Cokesbury in

35. Simkins and Woody, *Reconstruction in South Carolina,* p. 386.

36. A native white minister wrote to a friend in October, 1865: "Houses are being repaired but I see no new ones building—except the African Methodist Church in Calhoun St, opposite Zion [Presbyterian] Ch." C. P. Gadsden to a friend, October 27, 1865, A. T. Smythe Letters.

37. *Biographical Directory of the American Congress, 1774–1949* (Washington, 1950), p. 954 (Cited hereinafter as *Congressional Biography* [1950]); Daniel Alexander Payne, *Recollections of Seventy Years* (Nashville, 1888), p. 332; George Washington Williams, *History of the Negro Race in America from 1619 to 1880* (New York, 1883), pp. 580–81; Simkins and Woody, *Reconstruction in South Carolina,* pp. 131–32, 386–87, 546–47; *A. M. E. Church Review,* III, 337–50.

1871, and its expansion into Allen University in Columbia in 1881 raised the educational level. However, the problem of loyalty was not so easily solved, and internal dissensions, often centered in rather shallow personality conflicts, long plagued the church. In 1873, Cain, himself, became the center of such a storm. Denounced by another African minister, Christopher Wesley, as "no child of Heaven, and not fit to be a brother of the Church" because of his political and financial involvements, Cain secured Wesley's dismissal from the Conference. Wesley then entered the Northern Methodist Conference and vigorously continued the verbal battle.[38]

In spite of internal difficulties, the Conference continued to grow. By the end of Reconstruction, the African Methodists, with 44,000 members and 1,000 ministers, was the second largest Negro denomination in the state.[39]

The history of the African Methodist Episcopal Zion Church, often called the "Zion Church," in Reconstruction South Carolina has passed largely unrecorded. Only four years younger than the African Methodist Church, the Zion Church was a close national rival in appeal and in numbers. Perhaps because it moved unobtrusively into the state from western North Carolina and because its leadership was never active politically, the Zion Church escaped the notice of the press of the larger cities. The church remained heavily localized in the northwestern counties, particularly those contiguous to North Carolina. Nevertheless, the Zion Church did organize a South Carolina Conference in Chester in 1867. In 1890, its 130 churches and 45,880 members outnumbered those of the Northern Methodists, and were only slightly fewer than those of the African Methodists.[40]

Northern Presbyterian missionaries were also active in the northern middle counties, particularly after the reunion of the various branches of the church in the Northern states in 1869. While never impressive in numbers, Presbyterians did mold a stable, well-led organization which offered its members a planned system of parochial schools, along with a stern Knoxian theology. James Hemphill, a resident of Chester and an influential layman in the Associated Reformed Presbyterian

38. *New York Times*, June 15, 1874, p. 2; *Northern Methodist Minutes*, 1874, p. 7.

39. Simkins and Woody, *Reconstruction in South Carolina*, p. 387, citing *Minutes of the A. M. E. Church*, 1876, pp. 31–33.

40. James Walker Hood, *One Hundred Years of the African Methodist Episcopal Zion Church* (New York, 1895), pp. 359–60; *Census* (1890), IX, 563.

Church, writing to his clergyman brother, provides a glimpse of the
Northern missionary in the field in 1871:

> . . . the Northern Presbyterian Church have now a colored
> church near the depot, making three Presbyterian Churches in
> the village, where there should be only one. By the way, as
> there were no services in any of the white churches last Sab-
> bath, I went to the said colored church, and heard Mr. Loomis
> their minister. I was very much pleased. Indeed I have not
> heard a more appropriate discourse in a long time. After I
> went, several gentlemen expressed regret that they had not
> known as they would like to go. Mr. Loomis appears to be a
> gentleman, and as far as I have heard he has conducted him-
> self as a Christian Minister. Yet he has received no kindly
> courtesy or recognition from either Minister or layman. The
> Episcopal minister Mr. Stewart, a young man, told me that he
> called on him, and thought he should have the right hand of
> fellowship. I have not heard of any attention from any Presby-
> terian A. R. minister. A good many persons are afraid of
> their shadows, and fear to move, lest they may make a wrong
> step.[41]

Robert Hemphill, James's brother and a planter in lower Chester
County, observed the Northern Presbyterians gathering for a convention
in Chester several months later: "I was at the Dep.[ot] the other day
when the African Presbytery assembled at that place, among the distinguished arrivals was your old scool [sic] mate Dick Reed [a Negro
who had been a tenant on Robert's plantation and, presumably, a
family slave], A delegate from Mt. Olivet. Dick had on such a Huge
pair of spectacles that I told him he was liable to be arrested under the
Shalabarger Bill as a disguised K. K."[42] At the end of Reconstruction,
Northern Presbyterians in South Carolina numbered several thousand,
and, by 1916, had grown only slowly to 8,320 members.[43]

Northern Baptists were informally active in the Sea Islands early
in the war. For several years after 1865 agents of the Baptist Home
Missionary Society spoke in much the same spirit as did their Northern
Methodist contemporaries, of reorganizing Southern religion. A few

41. James Hemphill to W. R. Hemphill, January 25, 1871, Hemphill Papers.
42. R. N. Hemphill to W. R. Hemphill, May 9, 1871, Hemphill Papers.
43. United States Bureau of the Census, *Religious Bodies*, I (Washington, 1916), 574.

Baptist missionaries were active religious organizers. Benjamin Franklin Jackson, for instance, established a very strong church in Columbia. The dozen missionaries in the state concentrated their efforts primarily, however, upon the promotion of the educational interests of the church.

The Protestant Episcopal Church survived the secession crisis without a formal split, and when the war was over the members easily effected a reunion. The missionary efforts of the Northern elements within the church differed from those in the other denominations in that they were channeled through the native white Southern branches.

In 1873, however, the so-called "Cummings Schism" emerged in Kentucky as a separate body which gave Negro members and ministers full control within their own churches. In 1875, P. F. Stevens, a white Southerner, came to South Carolina as the missionary of the "Reformed Episcopal Church." The Reverend John Cornish met him on the cars of the Charleston and Savannah Railroad in August of that year; ". . . met Rev. P. F. Stevens, who having renounced the ministry of the Episcopal Church, & been deposed, is now acting in the Cummings Schism, & on his way to Edisto Island to deforme the Negroes."[44] Stevens's efforts were only moderately successful; by 1888, he was bishop of the new church which, by 1906, had a meager membership in South Carolina of 2,252.[45]

At the end of Reconstruction, about one hundred thousand Negroes in South Carolina belonged to churches inaugurated by out-of-state missionaries. Probably slightly more than this number belonged to churches which had been established by the self-inspired secession of Negro members from churches dominated by Southern whites.

The great mass of those Negroes who withdrew, without direct external impetus, from the native churches were Baptists. In 1858, about twenty-two thousand Negroes were formally enrolled members of Baptist churches in South Carolina. In addition, several times this number received religious instruction from Baptist ministers or from Negroes especially designated for the task and supervised by the clergy and laymen of the church. In neither case did the Negro have any voice in the government of his religious organization. In fact, as the classic historians of Reconstruction in South Carolina have asserted, the primary objective of the whites was to reconcile the Negro to his condition.[46]

44. MS Diary, entry for August 26, 1875.
45. Tindall, *South Carolina Negroes*, p. 200; *Religious Bodies*, 1906, I, 558.
46. Simkins and Woody, *Reconstruction in South Carolina*, pp. 382–83.

Once freedom was achieved, exclusively Negro Baptist churches appeared everywhere, growing either out of the "praise meetings" on the plantations or out of the secession of Negro members from churches dominated by whites. Less that a year after the occupation of the Sea Islands, the first independent Baptist Church with an exclusively Negro membership was organized. Its leader and minister was an ex-slave and slave exhorter, Abraham [Abram] Murchison, and its membership consisted of seventy Negroes who had been converted while slaves and fifty others who were recruited following the invasion.[47] After the war, secession movements by Negroes within white-dominated churches were opposed by Southern whites of all denominations. The Baptists shared this general desire to keep Negroes in their "accustomed place in the galleries." However, when the virtually universal wish of the Negro membership for separation became apparent, the Baptists, consistent with their traditional commitment to religious freedom, were the first to sanction and even encourage such separation. Moreover, the congregational organization of the Baptists facilitated multiplication by division, because secessionists merely required letters of dismissal certifying their good standing. The secessionists could then enter a covenant to form a spiritual church, select a minister, and secure his ordination by other ministers. By 1874, the secession process was practically complete; only 1,614 Negroes remained within the old establishments.[48]

It was in the nature of Baptist faith and organization that numbers grew rapidly while centralization proceeded slowly. The early pattern of growth was one in which strong local leaders established numerous churches in one locale, and gradually brought other churches, founded separately, into association with them. Monroe Boykin, an ex-slave and long a member of the Baptist Church in Camden, was such a leader. In 1866, he led the secession of sixty-six Negro members from the First Baptist Church in Camden and established the Mount Moriah Baptist Church. Ordained by two Northern missionaries, he became Mount Moriah's first minister, a post which he filled until his death in 1904. During this ministry Boykin also "established most of the old Baptist churches for negroes now existing in the counties of Kershaw, Lancaster, Sumter and Clarenden."[49] Another such leader was Alex-

47. *New South* (Port Royal), August 17, 1862.
48. Simkins and Woody, *Reconstruction in South Carolina*, p. 385.
49. Kirkland and Kennedy, *Camden,* p. 279; Albert Weitherspoon Pegues, *Our Baptist Ministers and Schools* (Springfield, 1892), pp. 75–78.

ander Bettis, a highly talented man who as a slave had managed his mistress's Edgefield plantation and had been admitted to the Baptist Church in Edgefield and commissioned an exhorter. Immediately after the war seventeen Negro members of his church in a secession movement called him to become their minister. Against the opposition of the Edgefield Association, he secured ordination and proceeded not only to establish this church but to found more than two score others.[50] In Columbia, in the summer of 1867, the Reverend William Johnson, a Negro, succeeded in building Cavalry Baptist Church, the pulpit of which was filled in 1870 by the energetic and politically minded Northern missionary, Benjamin Franklin Jackson.[51]

Intercongregational organization among the Negro Baptists emerged only gradually. In 1867, the Morris Street Baptist Church in Charleston, with the most eminent congregation in the state, led in the formation of the Charleston Association, which eventually spread to include the Boykin churches in the Camden area. Simultaneously, Bettis formed his churches into two associations. There were other similar arrangements, but withdrawals, reformations, and consolidations rendered organizational structures above the congregational level impermanent and ineffective.[52]

A new height of unity was achieved in 1876 when most of the state's Negro Baptist churches were represented in a convention held in Sumter for the purpose of promoting their educational, missionary, and Sunday school work. Prime leaders in the movement were E. M. Brawley and Jacob Legare, the pastor of the Morris Street Church. Brawley's labors were particularly important in promoting unified action by Negro Baptists. Born free in Charleston in 1851, he attended school there until 1861 when he went North to enter a Philadelphia school. After the war, he returned to Charleston and apprenticed as a shoemaker, but again, in 1870, returned North to attend Howard and Lewisburg Colleges. At Lewisburg, he joined the Baptist Church, was licensed a minister, and, after graduating in 1875, returned to South Carolina as a missionary of the American Baptist Publication Society. He immediately became very active in the co-operative en-

50. Alfred W. Nicholson, *Brief Sketch of the Life and Labors of Rev. Alexander Bettis* (Trenton, South Carolina, 1913), *passim*.

51. *New York Times,* July 1, 1867, p. 1; *Daily Republican* (Charleston), February 12, 1870.

52. Pegues, *Our Baptist Ministers and Schools,* p. 149; Nicholson, *Alexander Bettis*, pp. 33–34; Kirkland and Kennedy, *Camden,* p. 279.

deavors of the local Baptists. In 1876, he became the permanent executive agent of the Colored Baptist Educational, Missionary, and Sunday School Convention which consisted of some 100,000 members and 350 ministers. After 1880, through the Convention, South Carolina's Negro Baptists were represented in the National Baptist Convention.[53] Bettis's was the only major Baptist organization that remained outside the union.[54]

Southern Methodists were only slightly less opposed to the withdrawal of their Negro membership than were the Baptists. Indeed, the earliest efforts of the Methodists in the postwar period were directed toward keeping the Negro membership "within the fold." The first Methodist mission to the slaves begun in the United States had been initiated by the South Carolina Conference. As the bonds of slavery tightened in the thirty years preceding the Civil War, the concern of the church for its Negro members seems to have grown. By 1860, over 44,000 Negro members, more than those of all other state denominations together, were formally within the church. This interest in the religious welfare of Negroes continued after emancipation. In 1865, the first postwar conference of Methodist ministers in South Carolina advised quarterly conferences to license Negroes to preach and exhort whenever possible. It further asked the laity to "continue as heretofore your arrangements for their accommodation in all the churches, that, frequenting the schools of catechetical instruction, and occupying their accustomed places in the house of God; they may receive from the lips of a pure and spiritual ministry the messages of the Gospel, and rejoice with you in participation of the benefits of common salvation."[55] The same approach was taken by the General Conference of Southern Methodists which met in New Orleans in the following spring.[56]

It soon became obvious that most Negroes would not remain in a church that did not afford them complete equality, and Southern Methodists soon allowed Negroes to depart freely and encouraged their entrance into the African Church. Under these circumstances, the desertion of the Negro membership was rapid. In 1867, there were only 8,000 Negroes in the South Carolina Conference, and, by December, 1870, the number had dwindled to 1500.[57] In the latter year,

53. Pegues, *Our Baptist Ministers and Schools*, pp. 78–82, 149–50.
54. Tindall, *South Carolina Negroes*, pp. 189–90.
55. Farish, *The Circuit Rider Dismounts*, p. 165.
56. *New York Times*, April 22, 1866, p. 3.
57. Simkins and Woody, *Reconstruction in South Carolina*, p. 385; *Minutes*

the General Conference of the church authorized the establishment of a separate church for those members who desired to join an exclusively Negro organization. Thus, the Colored Methodist Episcopal Church of America (often called the Colored Methodist Church) was begun under the auspicies of the white clergy and soon passed into complete independence. Perhaps because of this tardy beginning, Colored Methodists were never numerous. In 1890, the South Carolina membership was only 3,468, and by 1916, had grown only modestly to 4,850.[58] Meanwhile, the number of Negroes in the parent church steadily diminished. In December, 1871, about 1300 Negroes remained in the Southern Church; in 1873, there were 653; and in 1876, only 421.[59] In 1885, the Bishop of the South Carolina Conference reported a white membership of 54,858, and a Negro membership of 76, "mostly sextons." "Think of our Church in South Carolina as solidly white," he concluded with more than a touch of accuracy.[60]

Unlike Baptists and Methodists, the Presbyterians of South Carolina never willingly released their Negro members. In the ante-bellum period, the state's Presbyterians were no less zealous than the Methodists in ministering to the spiritual needs of the slave population. A pioneer in this work was Dr. J. L. Girardeau who, in 1850, organized Zion Church in Charleston with special provisions made for a Negro membership. By 1860, about 5,000 of the 13,000 Presbyterians in the state were Negroes. After the war, both the clergy and the white laity labored arduously to retain their Negro members, apparently spurred primarily by their apprehension that the Negro's inherent incapacity would cause him to fall away from the faith and jeopardize his soul. "Let us remember their infirmities and not be too hasty," the saints of Harmony Presbytery warned their churches in October, 1865. In the fall of the same year, the Presbytery resolved "to continue to instruct them by preaching, catechetical teaching, and all other means

of the Eighty-Third Session of the South Carolina Annual Conference of the Methodist Episcopal Church, South (Charleston, 1871), p. 10.

58. Census (1890), IX, 609; Religious Bodies, 1906, I, 558–59.

59. Minutes of the Eighty-Fourth Session of the South Carolina Annual Conference of the Methodist Episcopal Church, South (Charleston, 1872), not paginated; Appletons' Annual Cyclopaedia, 1873, p. 485; 1876, I, 530.

60. Quoted in A. B. Hyde, The Story of Methodism (Greenfield, Massachusetts, 1867), p. 339.

of improving their spiritual condition."[61] The same attitude was reflected in the actions of the other South Carolina presbyteries.

The manner in which the work was carried on varied. In many
cases, Negro members continued to worship with white congregations
as before. Increasingly, however, Negroes tended to meet separately
while being served and controlled by the white ministry. Thus, Zion
Church in Charleston was reorganized with some seven to eight hundred Negro members, but it was governed by a white eldership and
pastored by Dr. Girardeau, its founder. Ladson Chapel, a missionary
activity in Columbia, operated in the same fashion, as did a number of
rural stations.[62] Many Negro Presbyterians found this arrangement
satisfactory, at least temporarily. In Chester District, in August, 1866,
Robert Hemphill noted the results of such a plan: "The Rev. Brice
is preaching one third of his time to the Cold. people at Maj. Ray's
School House. He has large crowds to hear him, & they seem to be
pleased with the idea of having preaching to themselves. I am afraid
it is all owing to the novelty of the thing."[63] In October, 1870, Harmony
Presbytery went so far as to employ a colored minister, the Reverend
J. H. Ghee, to work as a special missionary among the Negroes.[64]

The best efforts of white Presbyterians delayed only briefly the
desertion of their Negro membership. In many cases, Negroes simply
departed without leave. In the fall of 1866, Bethel Presbytery, in the
northwestern quarter of South Carolina, reported that most of its
Negro members had withdrawn. In other instances, Negroes asked
their Presbyteries for permission to withdraw and establish separate
congregations within the same structure. In the spring of 1867, the
Negroes of Rock Presbyterian Church in Abbeville District petitioned
the South Carolina Presbytery for separation. The Presbytery, in reply,
recognized "that our colored people are entitled to all the rights and
privileges which justly belong to any other class of Christians, among
these is the right to vote for their ecclesiastical rulers and to fill any
ecclesiastical office for which they may be personally qualified . . ."
Yet, the petition was denied because, as the Presbytery rather illogically
contended, "We are all one in Christ Jesus . . ." Quite clearly, Presbyterians were still unwilling to commit to Negroes the keeping of

61. Quoted in Frank Dudley Jones and W. H. Mills (eds.), *History of the
Presbyterian Church in South Carolina Since 1850* (Columbia, 1926), p. 120.
62. *Ibid.,* pp. 117-18, 121.
63. To W. R. Hemphill, August 13, 1866, Hemphill Papers.
64. Jones and Mills, *Presbyterian Church in South Carolina,* p. 125.

their own souls. Nevertheless, within three years, Negroes had largely withdrawn from the churches of this Presbytery.[65] Harmony Presbytery, in the middle districts, had the same experience, seeing "its former negro members slowly but inevitably drifting away from its control." In Charleston Presbytery, where the Northern friends of Negroes charged the Southern Presbyterians with attempting to keep the Negro membership in submission, the fight was long and bitter. Nevertheless, by the fall of 1873, the Presbytery was ready to recognize defeat. With great misgivings as to the intellectual and moral qualifications of the Negroes for independence, it moved slowly to follow a recommendation of the General Assembly of the Southern Presbyterian Churches that separate Negro presbyteries be established.[66]

At the end of Reconstruction, only a few Negroes remained within the Presbyterian churches of South Carolina, and most of these worshipped apart from their fellow churchmen of lighter hue. Many belonged to independent presbyteries, exclusively Negro, but still more or less related to the churches and presbyteries from which they had sprung. In time, a number of these passed through independence and into the fold of the Northern Presbyterians.[67]

The 3,000 Negroes who belonged to the Episcopal Church at the end of the war reflected the prevailing separatist tendency. Some joined other denominations, while a few remained in their usual places. The Reverend John Cornish indicated in his diary that Negroes attended Episcopal churches in every part of the state throughout this period. However, the number present at any one service rarely exceeded a dozen; they sat in places set aside for them, and, of course, they did not participate actively in church affairs.[68] In 1876, in all of South Carolina, only 262 Negroes were members of white churches.[69]

Apparently, most Negro Episcopalians withdrew from their previous affiliations and established churches of their own with the blessings of the whites and without losing their diocesan connection.[70] Thus, an Episcopal clergyman wrote to a colleague from Charleston in October, 1865: "I find the coloured people friendly to me personally, but the majority of those that belonged to my church have organized a congre-

65. *Ibid.*, pp. 130–37.
66. *Ibid.*, pp. 116–28.
67. Tindall, *South Carolina Negroes,* pp. 201–2.
68. MS Diary, *passim.*
69. Simkins and Woody, *Reconstruction in South Carolina,* p. 385.
70. *Ibid.*, p. 392.

gation of their own."[71] This new congregation, St. Mark's, had been established before the end of May. It met in the chapel of the Orphan House, and called to its pulpit a venerable white minister, J. B. Seabrook, who continued to serve them throughout Reconstruction.[72] In 1866, St. Mark's moved for admission to the Diocesan Convention. If admitted, Negro laymen would have gained a voice and a vote in the government of the church. St. Mark's was advised to wait until it was firmly established. In 1876, when most other Negro Episcopal congregations were passing into the rebel Reformed Church, St. Mark's presented a formal application for admission to the Convention. The application was referred to a commission which, in 1876, submitted a report opposing approval of the petition. On the floor of the Convention in that year, a majority of the lay delegates voted against admission. Since both orders had to approve, the petition was denied even though most of the clergy and a majority of the whole body favored the cause of St. Mark's.[73]

The inclination of the Episcopal laity to exclude Negroes from the church was not confined to denying them representation in the Diocesan Convention. There was also a clear tendency to exclude them entirely from worship in churches with whites, a movement which the clergy steadfastly opposed. These conflicting attitudes produced a crisis in the church in Plantersville a year after the close of Reconstruction. There Rector Benjamin Allston faced a vestry determined to bar Negroes from the church entirely. In advising the besieged Rector, Bishop Howe pointed out that in Summerville the galleries had been removed, but that half a dozen Negro members "were provided for by the vestry who assigned them seats in the room for the whites." The Bishop could not conceive of any member desiring to "exclude the colored people" from the Plantersville church, and did "not recall a single church in the Diocese wh. ever thot' of saying to a colored person you are excluded from our public worship, & have no part in it, & sld not come here to offer prayer & receive instruction in divine things." The objection, the Bishop thought, must be "merely to the indiscriminate mixing of black & white in the seats of the church," and not a desire "to exclude from public worship with the whites the few colored per-

71. C. P. Gadsden to a fellow clergyman, October 27, 1865, A. T. Smythe Letters.

72. Emma E. Holmes MS Diary, entry for "End of May," 1865; Tindall, *South Carolina Negroes*, p. 195.

73. An excellent discussion of the Negro in the Episcopal Church in the postwar period is contained in Tindall's *South Carolina Negroes*, pp. 194–200.

sons who may wish to attend." If necessary, he concluded, separate services or another building might be provided for the Negroes, "but I have no thot or expectation that the colored people will thus throng you & press you; it will only be the few, & those household servants, who will attend the services of the church."[74] Nevertheless, two weeks later, after the Rector had preached a sharply pointed sermon on the subject, the vestry passed a resolution which, in the Bishop's words, "affirmed the principle that no place cld be provided for colored persons to receive the instruction of the Church or its sacraments, & that they are not to be admitted to the building."[75]

The Catholic Church in Charleston succeeded during Reconstruction in retaining its prewar Negro membership of several score, a unique event in that time and place.[76] By 1906, the number of communicants had risen to 170, thus remaining, as always, a very minor proportion of the Negro population of the city.[77]

Church affairs among Negroes during Reconstruction differed in no essential respect from that of their white contemporaries. Indeed, the organization, ritual, and theology of the Negro churches were direct and conscious imitations of corresponding denominations in the white community. The most distinctive trait of the black man's religion was probably its emulation of the white ideal. Yet, there were differences which imparted to the Negro churches a flavor not generally shared by their white neighbors.

White observers were often disturbed by what they considered excessive emotionalism in the religious exercises of Negroes. "The Freedmen has had a protracted religious meeting here for the last ten days," reported a Presbyterian layman from Chester in July, 1866, "Colored preachers from different parts of the Country have been here. They carried on most extravagantly, day and night."[78] Eight years later, a farmer living on Goncher Creek in Spartanburg County made the same point. "Yet the Freedmen is getting on badly in our State in every respect," he wrote. "They do not advance in the least, in any

74. W. B. W. Howe to Benjamin Allston, September 16, 1878, Benjamin Allston Papers.

75. *Ibid.,* October 1, 1878.

76. Estimated from the number of children enrolled in the Catholic school for Negroes in 1870. *Daily Republican* (Charleston), April 27, 1870.

77. *Religious Bodies,* 1906, I, 558–59.

78. J. C. Hemphill to W. R. Hemphill, July 4, 1866, Hemphill Papers.

thing they have cut loose from us, and our Churches, and gone to themselves and they are making there [*sic*] mark in regard to Visions and Trances, they See and hear a great many Wonderful things."[79]

Dancing, a practice which would have seemed scandalous in a white church, was a quasi ritual in some Negro churches. A Northern teacher on Edisto in the summer of 1865 attended such a meeting. The session began with a hymn and a prayer by the "elder." "They sang again, then the sisters walked round in a circle with short, quick steps, swinging their arms and singing, 'Oh! Lord, don't be offended. Oh! Lord, don't judge me hard,' and much more of the same strain. They kept this up a long time, the meeting lasted till long after mid-night."[80] Two years later, a Columbian noted the emergence of a group of "Dancing Baptists" among the Negroes of his city. This group met every other Saturday night in the church, and, after prayers and exhortation, proceeded to spend the night in dancing. "They dance to the singing of hymns, keeping time in regular cadence; and change from one figure to another in a great variety of ways, sometimes passing around and across by twos, and sometimes with hands linked, forming a general circle in the 'hands-round' style." The observer was careful to note that such meetings were a "kind of aside-scene to the church proper," and the regular services continued on Sunday in the usual manner.[81]

Compared with his white contemporaries, the Negro came to church often and stayed late. On February 13, 1870, for instance, the African Methodist Church at Sumter and Camden Streets in Columbia advertised a program which included prayer meeting at 6 A.M., Sunday school at 9:00 A.M., and preaching at 10:30 A.M., 3:30 P.M., and 7:00 P.M.[82] Almost every holiday, religious and secular, occasioned late hours in the churches. A Northerner in Charleston on Christmas Eve, 1866, reported: "Last night the negro churches, of which there are several in the city, were densely thronged by freed people of both sexes, who spent the entire night in singing, praying and mutual exhortations, with an enthusiasm that would have put to the blush the religious zeal of many a white devotee."[83] On New Year's Day, 1871, the Reverend Cornish,

79. Edward Lipscomb to Smith Lipscomb, June 19, 1874, Edward Lipscomb Papers.

80. Mary Ames, *From a New England Woman's Diary in Dixie in 1865* (Springfield, 1906), pp. 80–82.

81. *New York Times,* February 24, 1867, p. 3.

82. *Daily Republican* (Charleston), February 12, 1870.

83. *New York Times,* December 31, 1866, p. 1.

walking past the African Methodist Church in Aiken at about 5:00 A.M., heard "shouting and singing."[84]

Many whites would have agreed with the Spartanburg farmer who thought the Negro too prone to see visions and to indulge in trances and similar performances. Indeed, there was a tendency in the Negro church to emphasize the mystical, nonintellectual qualities of Christianity. Higginson noted something of this proclivity among his troops in the Sea Islands during the war when phrases such as a "religious army," or "Gospel army," crept into the vocabulary of his regiment.[85]

There was also a distinct puritanical strain in the Negro church. Negro followers of Northern Methodism were directed to eschew "dram drinking, tobacco and loose women," and avoid the temptations offered by "the dance, the theater, the horse race, the card table, and the opera."[!][86]

Finally, Negroes seemed to draw from their churches a special sense of fatalism, a resignation to the tragedies of life. "We have to go as God commands us," wrote a Camden Negro from the far side of Texas, "be that what it may. If our way is hard we must bear it, and we should be resigned." That such should have become a part of the faith of the freedman is hardly surprising in view of the function of the church in the slave system.[87]

The religious ardor of Negroes during Reconstruction has probably been overemphasized. Each of the tendencies mentioned above occurred in some degree and in some form in the churches of the whites. If they stood out in the Negro community, it was possibly because the socio-economic circumstances from which they sprang were more prevalent among Negroes than whites. The organization of Negro churches and the format of worship which they followed duplicated those of the whites. "Christ and Him Crucified" was the root and branch of their theology, precisely as it was that of the whites. It was, indeed, all that they knew; it was all that they had been taught.[88]

84. J. H. Cornish MS Diary, entry for January 1, 1871.

85. Thomas Wentworth Higginson, *Army Life in a Black Regiment* (Boston, 1890), pp. 53–54.

86. Quoted in Morrow, *Northern Methodism and Reconstruction*, p. 145.

87. Jesse McElroy to a friend, April 22, 1868, Bonds Conway Correspondence.

88. After hearing a sermon by a Southern Presbyterian minister who had spent twenty years of his life tending to the spiritual needs of Negroes, a New York Presbyterian residing in Charleston in 1871 declared, "I do not know that even in my youth, I ever heard such tremendous Calvinism." M. C. M. Taylor to Jeremiah Wilbur, January 23, 1871, Jeremiah Wilbur Papers.

If Negro ministers preached the message in its elemental form during
the early days of Reconstruction, movements were also inaugurated to
train a ministry capable of delivering a more sophisticated interpretation.
In sum, at the end of Reconstruction, Negro churches differed in no
important respect from those of the whites.

Like its white contemporary, the Negro church often performed
most unchurchly functions. For instance, it was obviously a source
of entertainment for some—a point of relief in lives which might
otherwise have been interminably dull. It was this aspect of Negro
religious practice which most often offended sensitive whites. Martha
Schofield, visiting the African Methodist Church in Aiken in 1869,
observed that "so many went up to the communion table, and kneeled
while the Minister said 'eat this bread as the body, drink this wine
as the blood of Christ'——" But, she scolded, "I saw two young girls
laugh & do it with less reverence than I would look upon any dead——"[89]
Negro churches also engaged directly in a variety of educational
activities and, perhaps as important, they supplied close support to the
educational efforts of other institutions. In the difficult early years of
her labors in South Carolina, Martha Schofield was sustained and com-
forted by the evident gratitude of the membership of local Negro
churches. Attending a meeting on Wadmalaw in October, 1865, she
heard a Negro preacher tell his flock: "Ye must tank de Lord he hab
put in de harts of dese people to cum down h'ar & teach ye to read
his word. dey has cum across rivers and over de great ocean on purpose to teach ye, and now if ye dont want to slight de Lord, dont
slight dem, for he sent em—" In the summer of 1869, having begun
her Normal and Industrial School in Aiken, she was visited by the
local African Methodist minister, J. E. Hayne, who announced a
meeting in honor of her and her assistant. The gathering was held
in the church in the afternoon. J. N. Hayne, the Negro senator from
the county, presided, and the Reverend Hayne spoke. "All thanked
us and urged the necessity of education," Miss Schofield reported, and
a resolution of appreciation was passed and sent to the press. Gratitude
was often manifested in forms more substantial than words. When
Schofield School was in danger of bankruptcy in the spring of 1871,
an exhibition was held in the African church which raised forty-two
dollars for the school and prevented its closure.[90]

89. MS Diary, entry for June 12, 1869.
90. *Ibid.*, entries for October 29, 1865; June 23, 1869; March 24, 1871.

Negro churches manifested an interest in the physical as well as the spiritual welfare of their members. In the late summer of 1865, a Northern traveler found that the Negro members of the Presbyterian Church in Columbia were supporting two very old Negroes who were unable to provide for themselves.[91] Relief on a broad scale was sought for his flock by Methodist minister Abram Middleton of Barnwell, when a prolonged drought in the spring and summer of 1876 diminished the vegetable crop and crushed credit. It was feared, he averred, "that many of the inhabitants will be compelled to sustain life by eating green corn." Using the *New York Times* as his vehicle, the Reverend Middleton appealed "to the rich and charitable people of the North for assistance for these distressed and afflicted people."[92]

It would be surprising if Negro churches, so much a part of the Negro community in every other way, were not also politically active. Negro churches tended to support Republican measures, just as their leaders and members, as individuals, universally became Republicans. There was no more possibility of bipartisan politics in the church than there was of a bipartisan membership. Yet, there was a question of activism—of the active use of the church proper in political affairs— and the degree of political activity varied widely between denominations and between individuals within denominations.

Northern Methodists were well to the fore in political leadership. Mansfield French came to the Sea Islands with the occupation in 1861 and fought harder and longer than any other man in the state for land grants for Negroes. In the first session of the Republican legislature, he received strong support for a seat in the United States Senate.[93] In early March, 1867, the nine thousand members of the church in South Carolina and Florida, then conveniently represented by their ministers in conference in Charleston, hailed "with joy" the inauguration of Congressional Reconstruction.[94] Benjamin Franklin Randolph and Benjamin Franklin Whittemore, both Methodist ministers, were two of the first rank leaders in the organization of the Republican party in South Carolina. Randolph, "a tall, stalwart mulatto," was born in Kentucky in the early 1820's. He moved to Ohio as a child, received a common school education, and was graduated from Oberlin.

91. *The Nation*, I, No. 11 (September 14, 1865), 332.
92. *New York Times*, July 22, 1876, p. 2.
93. *House Journal* (Special Session, 1868), p. 81.
94. *Northern Methodist Minutes*, 1867, pp. 13–14; Morrow, *Northern Methodism and Reconstruction*, p. 223.

As a young minister, he became the chaplain of a Negro regiment in South Carolina. Afterward, he edited a paper in Charleston and served in the educational division of the Bureau. Along with Whittemore, he was active in the Constitutional Convention of 1868. The Conference of 1868 assigned him to the ministerial station in Columbia, but he was soon dispatched to the state senate by Orangeburg County. In October of that year, his rather flamboyant political career was cut short by assassination.[95] Whittemore, who had filled a Methodist pulpit in Mauldin, Massachusetts, before becoming an army chaplain, served churches in Sumter and Darlington in the early postwar years. In 1868, he was elected to Congress but resigned in the spring of 1870 under threat of expulsion for having admittedly sold a cadet's appointment to West Point. He subsequently became Darlington's state senator and held that office until he was forced to flee from the state in 1877. Under Henry J. Fox, Northern Methodists also moved into the University of South Carolina, using it as a base for activities clearly political.[96] As an editor in Charleston and Orangeburg and as president of Claflin University, Alonzo Webster was active in advancing the interests of Methodism, Republicanism, and the Negro.[97] In addition to Randolph and Whittemore, at least three, and perhaps four other Methodist ministers, were members of the Convention of 1868.[98] Occasionally, these and other Methodist ministers took seats in the legislature.

Political activity among African Methodist leaders was less concerted than among Northern Methodists. Where political activity was high, it was found to be sparked by the energy of a dynamic, but local, leader. In Sumter, for instance, the Reverend William E. Johnston [or Johnson] became the dominant Republican of his race, serving as a delegate to the Convention of 1868, and, subsequently, as a state senator. The most spectacular personality politically, as well as religiously, among the African divines was R. H. Cain. One Negro contemporary thought that his huge Emmanuel Church in Charleston was "one of the strongest political organizations in the State." Utilizing

95. *New York Times,* October 28, 1868, p. 5.

96. Fox, *Methodist Review,* January, 1874, pp. 29–45, *passim.* See also: *Weekly Republican* (Charleston), October 25, 1876.

97. Morrow, *Northern Methodism and Reconstruction,* p. 222.

98. *Convention Proceedings,* 1868, pp. 6–7; *Northern Methodist Minutes,* 1868, pp. 10–12. These were Abram Middleton of Barnwell, R. J. Donaldson (white) of Oro, William Barrington (white) of Kingstree, and possibly Joseph White of Lynchburg.

his very able editorial talents in the *Missionary Record* and his remarkable gift of leadership, Cain built up a political following in Charleston that never deserted him. In the Convention of 1868, he took a prominent part in the debates and passed immediately into the state senate. After one term, he retired from the senate and became a very successful lobbyist in Columbia during the 1870–1871 session of the legislature. Cain had been involved in land speculation soon after his arrival in the state, but, in 1871, he ambitiously contracted to buy two thousand acres of land near Charleston, payments to begin six months afterward. He subdivided the area, named it Lincolnville, and sold twenty-five lots before the previous owners foreclosed for his failure to make any of the promised payments. In spite of complaints, he was not then indicted and, indeed, was elected to Congress in November, 1872. Eventually indicted for fraud, he delayed the prosecution until a settlement was agreed upon; but again he failed to satisfy his obligations under the new agreement. Indicted for libel by another African Methodist minister whom he had driven from the church, he refused to come from Washington to face trial. He helped win Charleston for bolting "reformers" in 1874, but lost his Congressional seat. In 1876, he was again returned to Congress and served that term. Until his death in 1887, he remained highly effective as a religious, political, and social leader among the Negro population of the Charleston area.[99]

Without doubt, there were individual leaders in each denomination who turned their churches into political vehicles. A certain Reverend Jackson, a Negro minister heading a church in Charleston, was reported to have dramatically turned out of his flock all who voted the bolters' ticket in 1874.[100]

However, Negro Baptists, Zion Methodists, Methodists, Presbyterians, and Episcopalians generally maintained a distinct separation between religion and politics. When there was involvement, it was of a mild sort, such as Martha Schofield's visit to the Baptist Church in Aiken on March 14, 1869, to attend a celebration of Grant's inauguration. Her assistant read Grant's oath, and Miss Schofield "told them Grant with all his power, could not do as much for them as they could do for themselves, that now in this state 'all men were equal before the law,' it depended upon their own efforts to raise them into power—

99. Congressional Biography (1950), p. 434; *New York Times*, June 15, July 3, 1874; Simkins and Woody, *Reconstruction in South Carolina*, p. 472; Tindall, *South Carolina Negroes*, p. 154; *Convention Proceedings*, 1868, *passim*.

100. *New York Times*, December 1, 1874, p. 1.

that they must be masters of their passions, & vices and habits, must be guided by the spirit of truth written in their own hearts &c—— Then the minister arose & said 'Friends I have heard many words since freedom, but none purer and better than those just spoken by our worthy friend &c'——"[101]

Even in the Northern Methodist and African churches, there were powerful elements which resisted political involvement. Bishop Payne, the leader of African Methodism in the state during Reconstruction, was never politically prominent. T. W. Lewis, the pioneer organizer of the Northern Methodists, strove valiantly to keep the spiritual ideals of the church above all others and clearly before the eyes of its leadership. In the Conference of 1871, he drafted and the assembly approved a resolution which declared: "We pledge ourselves to hold no entangling alliances with any party organizations, or accept of any political or secular office which may injure our influence and prevent our rebuking sin on account of party ties or obligations."[102] Lewis died shortly afterward, while the sins to which he probably referred were still in the form of vague rumors. Had other Northern missionaries, particularly Northern Methodist missionaries, preserved the moral objectivity Lewis visualized, the nature of political reconstruction in South Carolina might have been significantly altered.

101. Martha Schofield MS Diary, entry for March 14, 1869.

102. *Northern Methodist Minutes,* 1871, pp. 11–12. Before 1867, Randolph and Whittemore, the two men most responsible for marrying the name of Northern Methodism to Reconstruction politics in South Carolina, were employees of the Bureau rather than professional missionaries. In 1867, they were admitted to the Conference on trial and did not receive ministerial assignments until 1868. Randolph's assassination terminated his period of trial; and Whittemore withdrew voluntarily before his trial period ended and after his expulsion from Congress. Thus, neither was admitted to full ministry by the Conference. *Northern Methodist Minutes,* 1867, p. 13; 1868, pp. 10–12; 1871, pp. 7–8.

VIII...EDUCATION: PROGRESS
AND POVERTY

E ven before the coming of the Yankee missionaries to South Carolina, Negroes had evinced a
widespread interest in education for themselves and their children.
Before 1834, when the legislature prohibited the teaching of reading
and writing to slaves, a few Negro children had attended schools along
with their white masters. In 1874, a prominent Chester lawyer recalled
this fact when he wrote to his brother about a mutual acquaintance, a
Negro, ". . . old Dick Reed who went to school with us in juvenile
days, before it was discovered that a nigger should not be allowed to
read."[1] In Charleston, many nonslave Negro children had attended
schools maintained by the free Negro population of the city and by
sympathetic whites. Even after "free persons of color" were required
by the restrictive law of 1834 to have a white person present at each
class meeting, schools maintained by free Negroes continued to operate.[2]
Many other Negro children were taught at home, illegally beyond the
scrutiny of whites. Finally, before and after 1834, a few free Negro
children were sent to schools in the North and abroad to complete

1. J. C. Hemphill to W. R. Hemphill, November 13, 1874, Hemphill Papers.
2. *The Nation*, I, No. 25 (December 21, 1865), 779; J[ohn] T[ownshend]
Trowbridge, *The South, a tour of its Battle Fields and Ruined Cities, a journey
through the desolated States, and talks with the people, etc.* (Hartford, 1866),
p. 570.

their education. What was true of the free Negro community of Charleston was also true in some degree of free Negro communities in smaller towns. Correspondence between members of the Conway, Boykin, McElroy, and Johnson families of Camden, for instance, indicates that they possessed literary abilities at least equal to that of their average white contemporary.[3]

It is evident that at the time of their emancipation a large number of Negroes (perhaps 5 per cent) had already acquired some knowledge of reading and writing. Among the great mass of freedmen, of course, the level of achievement was very low. Some had laboriously taught themselves, others learned from barely literate companions, and still others had been taught sporadically and casually by their masters. Yet, Negroes, like whites, exhibited a wide diversity of achievements in literacy. Elias Hill of York County, who was born a slave, crippled at seven, and bought into freedom by his father, was almost entirely self-educated. Rudimentary as his learning was, by 1871 he had become a teacher and Baptist minister. On the other hand, Francis Louis Cardozo was exceptionally well educated. Cardozo's mother was reputedly half-Indian and half-Negro, and his father was J. N. Cardozo, an economist and editor of an ardently anti-nullification newspaper in Charleston in the 1830's. As a young man, Cardozo was sent to the University of Glasgow. He afterwards studied theology in Edinburgh and London and was ordained a minister in the Presbyterian church. He served the Temple Street Congregational Church in New Haven, Connecticut, during the war and within weeks of the occupation of Charleston by Union forces returned to that city.[4]

Northern missionaries who came to the Sea Islands in the winter of 1862 placed free schools on a par with free labor as primary requisites in the reconstruction of Southern society. About half of those who came had been engaged as teachers by various Northern benevolent associations and were assigned to conduct schools on the occupied plantations. As the occupation progressed, other teachers followed. Early in 1863, there were some two score Northern educators on the Sea Islands working in more than thirty schools and teaching between two and three thousand scholars. Origins of individual teachers spread from

3. Bonds Conway Correspondence, *passim.*

4. Francis B. Simkins and Robert Hilliard Woody, *South Carolina During Reconstruction* (Chapel Hill, 1932), pp. 116–17; *The Nation,* I, No. 25 (December 21, 1865), 779; *Southern Patriot* (Charleston), July 10, 11, 1832; *Ku-Klux Conspiracy,* IV, 1179; Bertram Wallace Korn, *Jews and Negro Slavery in the Old South, 1789–1865* (Elkins Park, Pennsylvania; 1961), p. 51.

Massachusetts to Ohio, and academic preparations ranged from the best of Harvard and Yale to that of normal school graduates who had been teachers of the poor. Regardless of background, most of these educational evangelists subscribed to the purpose of Charlotte Forten, a young mulatto from Philadelphia and a graduate of the grammar and state normal schools in Salem, Massachusetts, who had come "for the good I can do my oppressed and suffering fellow creatures."[5] On the Islands, the Northern teachers were often assisted by ex-slaves who had somehow acquired a smattering of education. John Milton and another Negro were already teaching a school in Beaufort when the Northern teachers arrived. Ned Lloyd White—"who had picked up clandestinely a knowledge of reading while still a slave"—and Uncle Cyrus assisted in the school in St. Helena village; Anthony kept four schools on Hilton Head Island; and Hettie, an Edisto slave, continued to teach her refugee pupils at St. Helena village after Edisto had been abandoned in the summer of 1862.[6]

Immediately after the occupation of Charleston, the military seized the buildings that had housed the city's free school system, and, under the superintendence of James Redpath, popular biographer of John Brown and a long-time abolitionist, a Bureau of Education was established. Two weeks after the first Negro troops had marched through the streets of Charleston, Redpath opened the Morris Street School to some 1200 children, 200 of whom were white. By the end of the month, 3,114 children were attending seven schools, staffed by 83 teachers of whom 74 were "loyal Charlestonians of both races." F. L. Cardozo became the principal of one of the larger schools.[7]

Early in the fall of 1865, Reuben Tomlinson, a Pennsylvania Quaker who had been general superintendent of St. Helena Island since 1862 under Saxton, became the superintendent of education in South Carolina under the Freedmen's Bureau, an office which he continued to hold for nearly three years.[8] There can be no doubt of Tomlinson's devotion to the cause of educational reform in South Carolina or of his exceptional abilities. Yet, as the Bureau's chief educator in the state

5. Edward L. Pierce, "The Freedmen of Port Royal," *Atlantic Monthly*, XII (September, 1863), 303; Benjamin F. Quarles, *The Negro in the Civil War* (Boston, 1953), p. 176.

6. Pierce, *Atlantic Monthly*, XII (September, 1863), 298–307, *passim*.

7. T. P. O'Neale to R. H. Gourdin, June 3, 1865, R. H. Gourdin Papers; *New York Times*, April 16, 1865, p. 3; *The Nation*, I, No. 25 (December 21, 1865), 779; Quarles, *The Negro in the Civil War*, p. 328.

8. Printed order signed by Saxton, October 6, 1865, E. L. Stoeber Papers.

his powers were severely limited. His primary duty was merely to supply the physical surroundings in which learning was to take place— the buildings, the furniture, the books—but in every case the teachers were appointed and paid exclusively by private organizations, principally by the Northern societies. To some extent, Tomlinson's friendly, often warm, personal relationships with the officers of the associations minimized the hazards of such a dyarchy.[9] Nevertheless, the number of scholars who could be accommodated in Bureau schools was ultimately limited by the resources that Northern philanthropy could muster. This upper limit was reached within months after the end of the war and remained fairly stable into the spring of 1868.

In view of the prescribed restrictions, the record of the Bureau in education in South Carolina is impressive. By mid-October, 1865, about 6,000 pupils were enrolled in 48 schools taught by 108 teachers, 80 of whom were Northerners. These were concentrated in the islands and in Charleston, but schools had also been established in Columbia, Greenville, Orangeburg, Summerville, and Georgetown. Other schools were being formed in Camden, Florence, Darlington, Sumter, and Cheraw.[10] The nature of Tomlinson's work is suggested by the fact that during the first half of 1867 he spent $22,551.12 on the construction and rental of school buildings, transportation of teachers, and other school purposes.[11] A part of these expenditures was devoted to the construction of Howard School in Columbia. With a capacity for about 700 pupils, this school soon earned a reputation for quality comparable to that of the best white schools in the state. During its first years, the school functioned with about 450 regular scholars under a faculty of ten or eleven teachers, most of whom were paid initially by the New York Branch of the Freedmen's Union Commission, later by the Presbyterian Freedman's Society of New York, and ultimately by the state of South Carolina as staff members of the public school system. By 1870, of a faculty of eleven ladies, eight were Northerners and three, all in the primary department, were native Negroes.[12] In the spring of 1868, the

9. For instances of Tomlinson's intimate relationships with the societies, see: Robert P. Carson to Reuben Tomlinson, October 6, 1866; Anna P. Steavesen to Reuben Tomlinson, May 8, 1867, Freedmen File.

10. *The Nation,* I, No. 25 (December 21, 1865), 779.

11. *Report of the Secretary of War* (1867), House Ex. Doc. No. 1, Part 1, 40th Cong., 2nd Sess. (Washington, 1868), p. 653.

12. *New York Times,* July 29, 1867, p. 1; February 25, p. 2; July 5, p. 5; December 25, 1868, p. 2; July 4, p. 3, 1869; *Daily Republican* (Charleston), July 5, 1870.

Bureau had participated in the establishment of 56 Negro schools, employing 101 white and 37 Negro teachers to instruct an actual average attendence of 5,854. Moreover, these schools conducted Sunday classes for an additional 2,271 scholars. It was estimated that other schools which had no direct connection with the Bureau mustered about the same number of scholars.[13] Bureau Commissioner Howard estimated that 20,000 pupils were enrolled in Bureau and private schools in South Carolina in mid-October, 1867.[14]

Attitudes toward Negro education generated by the white community during Reconstruction were to have far reaching effects upon the progress of the movement in South Carolina. The initial response of the whites, as one might expect, was almost entirely negative. Tomlinson, having toured the state immediately after taking office in the fall of 1865, reputedly said that the whites "were not only indifferent but entirely opposed to the educating of the negroes . . ."[15]

This antagonism persisted at the grass roots level throughout Reconstruction. A native white member of the Constitutional Convention of 1868 recognized that there were "strong objections" in many localities to Negro schools, arising, as he said, from the "prejudice and ignorance" of the lower classes.[16] Occasionally, whites actively exhibited their opposition. In Lexington, in 1866, a group of white men attempted to interrupt a night class in a Negro school and threatened violence upon the son of the teacher, herself the widow of an Episcopal minister.[17] In Newberry, a contractor building a Negro school was threatened by a band of armed men, and a young lady teacher, sent by the Vermont Methodists, "was subjected to the meanest sort of insults and persecutions."[18] More frequently, the whites, secure in their belief in the inherent superiority of their race, exhibited their disfavor in the form of humorous ridicule. A Laurens woman wrote in 1876:

> I was very much amused on Saturday witnessing a procession of little & big negroes, the scholars of Mr. Wade Hix, at present, quite a great man among the colored folks. An ex-

13. *New York Times,* March 23, 1868, p. 5.
14. Oliver Otis Howard, *Autobiography of Oliver Otis Howard* (New York, 1908), II, 339.
15. *The Nation,* I, No. 25 (December 21, 1865), 779.
16. B. O. Duncan of Newberry, *Convention Proceedings,* 1868, pp. 889–90.
17. *New York Times,* May 25, p. 5; July 1, p. 3, 1866.
18. Howard, *Autobiography,* II, 383.

amination was held that day by four gentlemen. His scholars, they say, did him great credit. After the examination, several speeches were made by *colored gentlemen,* and four appointed as officers of the day. They then formed a procession and walked through the streets, waving a flag, made by Mr. Seibert, the Motto was "knowledge is power." The little darkies had on white dresses, low neck & short sleeves, and blue sashes, some with sun shades.[19]

A year later a young Erskine College student commented in the same vein on a similar occasion. "Several of the boys and myself," he wrote to his father, "went on last Saturday to the Celebration of a Negro S. School about 6 miles distance where 'Night Blooming Cereus' in the *shape* of Negro stench abounded freely. I think *they* did very well to be *'Beasts.'* Their exercise consisted of speaking extracts & reciting pieces of Poetry."[20]

As Reconstruction progressed, elements within the native white leadership came to grant a qualified support to Negro education. Governor James L. Orr, heading a democratic movement within Conservative ranks, led his followers to support popular education for Negroes as well as for whites. "I think such things are the first movings of the waters," wrote F. L. Cardozo from Charleston to his Northern friends, "in the formation of public opinion, in favor of educating the colored people, and giving them their rights."[21]

The churches, the traditional conservators of erudition in the state, led those favoring the education of Negroes. In 1867, South Carolina Baptists urged the establishment of Sunday schools by the various churches for the instruction of Negroes in academic subjects.[22] The poverty of most of the churches prevented effective action, but Episcopalians, aided by their fellow religionists in the North, made impressive beginnings in the establishment of Negro schools. In 1866, largely under the leadership of the Reverend A. Toomer Porter of Charleston, contributions were obtained from Northern Episcopalians. Porter used these funds to employ Southern Episcopalians to teach Negroes in the Franklin Street School in Charleston. Subsequently, Porter visited O. O. Howard in Washington,

19. Mary Motte to "Julia," July 10, 1867, Lalla Pelot Papers.
20. J. C. Hemphill to W. R. Hemphill, July 27, 1868, Hemphill Papers.
21. *New York Times,* March 21, 1866, p. 8. See also: February 20, p. 4; 25, p. 1; November 15, p. 4, 1866; *Intelligencer* (Anderson), August 2, 1866; *House Journal* (1866), p. 88.
22. *Convention Proceedings,* 1868, p. 890.

and together they obtained the use of the United States Marine Hospital to house another school for Negroes. This school was supported by the Freedman's Commission of the Protestant Episcopal Church. "The teachers all but one are Charleston ladies," wrote a visitor in 1874. "The rooms are capacious, well arranged & fitly furnished. The teachers are evidently patient, & pains taking, the evidence of which is in the good order, & highly creditable progress of their pupils."[23] In 1870, the Catholic church in Charleston also entered the field of Negro education by opening a school for the children of Negro members on the grounds of St. Peter's.[24]

As Negro education proceeded under both Bureau and private auspices, the upper strata of native white society evinced a general shift in their attitudes. In 1867, Tomlinson, after another tour of the state, declared that not "half a dozen men of intelligence" were opposed to the Bureau's school program.[25] In the following year, a native white member of the Constitutional Convention expressed the same opinion. He admitted that "opposition to the education of the colored people was strong at the close of the war." However, he declared, citing the actions of the churches in general and of the Baptists in particular, "it is rapidly dying out among sensible men; indeed among educated Christians it is already entirely dead."[26]

Neither of these observers fully stated the case. The white leadership had, in fact, passed from opposition to support of Negro education; but even the most liberal of the native whites qualified their support in two vital respects: education for the average Negro should be confined to the rudimentary level; and there should be no "mixing" of the races in the schools. Probably the legislature, and certainly Orr, expected the state to finance Negro education only to the extent of appropriating for this purpose a portion of the taxes paid by the Negroes themselves.[27] Further, the churches sought only to teach the Negro masses their special versions of Christian morality and to educate a chosen few for the pulpit. Even this small concession was made, in part, as a device to free their former

23. J. H. Cornish MS Diary, entry for June 5, 1874.

24. *Daily Republican* (Charleston), April 13, 27, 1870.

25. Laura Josephine Webster, *The Operation of the Freedmen's Bureau in South Carolina* (Northampton, Massachusetts, 1916), p. 133.

26. *Convention Proceedings,* 1868, pp. 889–90.

27. *Daily News* (Charleston), February 15, 1867; *New York Times,* February 23, 1867.

slaves from "the perverting instruction of persons claiming to be the special friends of the Negro."[28]

Behind these attitudes was the virtually unanimous acceptance by the native white community of the basic assumption of the proslavery argument: that the Negro was inherently inferior to the white, at worst a "beast" of a high order and at best a human of a low order. The Negro's "inferior brain" might well absorb reading and writing and simple arithmetic, but subjects requiring "the logical faculties united with the memory," such as algebra and grammar, were beyond his grasp.[29] It was futile, therefore, to offer the mass of Negroes more than an elementary education. A native white correspondent of the *New York Times* accurately summarized the attitude of his class when he reported, in December, 1868, that "all parties desire to see the negro get some education—as much as he can take."[30]

Native whites were virtually unanimous in their opposition to "mixing" the races in the schools.[31] Of course, during the slave period, some Negro children had attended schools operated by whites for white children. In the first few months after the occupation of Charleston, both Negro and white children attended Redpath's schools, though separate class rooms were provided for each race. Two hundred of the 1200 students enrolled in the Morris Street School in March, 1865, were white. These children attended classes on the second floor, while the Negro pupils occupied the first and third floors. During recess, however, children of both races played together in the schoolyard.[32] Observing this practice, a scandalized native white teacher wrote caustically: "The place is now an African Heaven, Redpath a John Brown desiple [*sic*] has all the Schools open and the negro and whites Pell Mell altogether. his zeal in behalf of this race is remarkable a low ill bread [*sic*] person both in manners and appearance."[33]

As the opposition of the white community crystallized, mixing, even in this limited form, disappeared. The schools operated by both the

---

28. *South Carolina Baptist Convention Minutes*, 1866, pp. 226, 238–51.

29. *New York Times*, July 4, 1869, p. 3.

30. *Ibid.*, December 25, 1868, p. 2.

31. Unanimity among the whites even reached into Radical Republican ranks. In the Constitutional Convention of 1868, only four members voted against the opening of the public schools to both races and all four were native whites. *Convention Proceedings*, 1868, p. 902.

32. Quarles, *The Negro in the Civil War*, p. 328.

33. T. P. O'Neale to R. H. Gourdin, June 3, 1865, R. H. Gourdin Papers.

Bureau and the benevolent societies, although supposedly open to both races, actually were attended by an insignificant number of whites, and perhaps even these were the children of Northerners. A correspondent of the *Nation,* visiting the Bureau's schools in Charleston in November, 1865, found no white children in attendance.[34] This pattern was reflected throughout the state. In 1867, it was reported that there were only fifteen white children in the Bureau's schools, and, in the following year, a member of the Constitutional Convention stated that not a single white child was then a pupil in "the freedmen's schools."[35] The social pressure that produced such uniformity was suggested by the experience of a white mother who sent her two young daughters to an exclusively Negro missionary school in a remote portion of Port Royal Island. Having withdrawn her daughters from the school in spite of the absence of other, all-white educational facilities, the mother, in the fall of 1867, explained her reasons to the teacher: "I would not care myself, but the young men laugh at my husband. They tell him he must be pretty far gone and low down when he sends his children to a 'nigger school.' That makes him mad, and he is vexed with me."[36]

The white community, determined to keep its children out of schools open to or attended by Negroes, was no less determined to exclude Negroes from schools that it controlled. When the native white school board of Charleston recovered the use of its buildings in 1867, Cardozo's Morris Street School was set aside for Negro children, and three others were opened for the exclusive use of the whites.[37] Probably many semi-public schools in villages throughout the state managed to retain their all-white character through provisions in their charters that allowed their all-white boards of trustees to fill vacancies in their ranks themselves. Such was certainly the case with the common school in Aiken.[38] Separation was also the distinct rule in the schools sponsored by various native white religious institutions. O. O. Howard, visiting Episcopal schools in Charleston, found that one was exclusively white and another, in the Marine Hospital building, was "filled with pupils called 'colored,' but

34. *The Nation,* I, No. 25 (December 21, 1865), 779.

35. *Daily News* (Charleston), April 18, 1868; *Convention Proceedings,* 1868, p. 890.

36. Elizabeth Hyde Botume, *First Days Among the Contrabands* (Boston, 1893), pp. 257–58.

37. *House Journal* (Special Session, 1868), p. 258; George Brown Tindall, *South Carolina Negroes, 1877–1900* (Columbia, 1952), p. 218.

38. J. H. Cornish MS Diary, entry for August 26, 1870, *et seq.*

actually presenting the spectacle of all shades as to the hair, the eyes, and the skin."[39]

Early in 1868, a particularly astute *Times* correspondent accurately summarized the status of native white sentiment on the coeducation of the races: "From what I have learned conversationally during my stay here, intelligent citizens are perfectly willing to be taxed for the support of free colored schools and the education of the colored race, but most emphatically do they object to the affiliation of their children with negroes under the same roof and teachers."[40]

So verbal on other matters, the mass of Southern whites were not articulate as to why they opposed "mixing." Perhaps it seemed unnecessary to them to offer explanations of why they spurned association with their inferiors. In rare cases when native whites were forced to advance reasons for their opposition to projects involving biracial education, the arguments offered were highly specious. One common theme was that such a policy would aggravate and extend the "war of races" to the children. James L. Orr appealed to the first Republican legislature to establish separate schools: "In the new relation between the two races there already exist causes enough for bickering and controversy, and the prudence of grown people is taxed to its tension to prevent disagreeable antagonisms. No greater cruelty could be inflicted by legislation upon parents of children of the two races than that which is contemplated by this objectionable feature of the constitution."[41] Several weeks before, a native white delegate to the Constitutional Convention had advanced in graphic detail precisely the same argument.[42]

The Negro community, through its leaders expressed dissatisfaction with separation in the schools. Apparently, their opposition did not spring primarily from their sensitiveness to the racial distinction which separation implied, but from the denial of equal opportunities in education. Negroes saw an obvious injustice in being forced to pay taxes to support institutions from which they and their children were barred, and they sought to use their position as taxpayers to pry concessions from governmental units dominated by native whites. In June, 1867, the Union League Association in Columbia, represented by an all-Negro committee, petitioned the city council for relief from taxation for the support of certain public services unless these services were made avail-

39. Howard, *Autobiography*, II, 340.
40. *New York Times,* February 11, 1868, p. 5.
41. *House Journal* (Special Session, 1868), pp. 44–45.
42. The delegate was B. O. Duncan of Newberry. *Convention Proceedings,* p. 891.

able to them. "We are willing and desire to be a law-abiding people," they declared, "but we don't think that we should be compelled to pay a tax to support the city alms and orphan houses and free schools, when we are not represented, but we are willing to pay all other taxes that may be justly imposed upon us. We are willing and would gladly pay the objectionable taxes complained of, when provisions are made for all citizens alike." A few weeks previously, D. Motte, a Negro resident of Charleston who had paid a tax of $3.15 for the support of schools that excluded his children, raised the same question—confined in this instance to public schools only—with the local Bureau officer who referred it to headquarters. The Columbia City Council evaded the issue by replying that it was the state and not the city which levied the tax in question. In Charleston, the school board met the problem by providing separate facilities for the races when the public schools were opened in the fall of 1867.[43]

The political leaders of the Negroes early committed themselves to the ideal of universal public education without racial distinctions. The first state convention of the Republican party which met in Charleston in March, 1867, declared its support of "a uniform system of common schools, which shall be open to all without distinction of race, color or previous condition—such system to be supported by a general tax upon all kinds of property."[44] A second state convention which met in Columbia in July, 1867, reflected this sentiment.[45] The Negro delegates to the Constitutional Convention of 1868 were unanimous in their support of a section in the new constitution that declared: "All the public schools, colleges, and universities of the State, supported wholly or in part by the public funds, shall be free and open to all the children and youths of this State, without regard to race, color or previous condition."[46] Closely related was a provision that after the schools were "thoroughly organized" all children between six and sixteen years of age should attend school for at least twenty-four months. Thus, the public schools were to be open to all children, and all children were to be required to enroll in some school, either public or private. Presumably, poor white children would be forced to attend public schools with Negroes.

43. *New York Times,* July 1, 1867, p. 2; Major G. A. Williams to Lt. Col. H. W. Smith, May 4, 1867, and Enclosure, Tax Receipt of D. Motte, 1867, Freedmen File.
44. *New York Times,* March 27, 1867, p. 8.
45. *Ibid.,* July 31, 1867, p. 1.
46. *Convention Proceedings,* 1868, p. 889.

Although Negro leaders agreed on the ideal of universal biracial education, they disagreed on how and when the goal was to be realized in the face of concerted and determined opposition from the white community. A minority of Negro delegates led by Northern-born B. F. Randolph and L. S. Langley believed that they were creating a system in which parents who were unable to enroll their children in private schools would be immediately compelled to send them to public schools attended by Negroes. Randolph, a graduate of Oberlin, a Bureau teacher, recently an assistant Bureau superintendent, and a Methodist minister, stated the case for his group succinctly: "We are laying the foundation of a new structure here, and the time has come when we shall have to meet things squarely, and we must meet them now or never. The day is coming when we must decide whether the two races shall live together or not ..." Langley, who had taught in the military's Negro schools near Beaufort, agreed. "If we are Republicans," he told the convention, "let us have a Republican Government, and stand by our principles."[47] A Northern correspondent accurately interpreted this as "an attempt ... by a strong faction to force colored children into schools and colleges among the whites."[48]

A large majority of the delegates of both races, however, believed that their votes had established a system in which separation was denied in theory but in practice would be abandoned immediately only in sparsely populated districts where separate facilities were not economically feasible. As mass education proceeded, "prejudice must eventually die out" and result in the peaceful abolition of separation. F. L. Cardozo, chairman of the committee on education, expressed this view in the convention. "We have not said there shall be no separate schools," he argued in discussing the public school system. "On the contrary, there may be separate schools, and I have no doubt there will be such in most districts." Separate public schools, he thought, conformed not only to the wishes of the whites. "I have no doubt, in most localities, colored people would prefer separate schools, particularly until some of the present prejudice against their race is removed," Cardozo asserted. "In Charleston, I am sure such will be the case. The colored pupils in my school would not like to go to a white school." In less populous districts, however, the expense of separate facilities would be prohibitive, and, in these cases, "we simply give those colored children who desire to go to white schools, the privilege to do so." Whites might send their

47. *Ibid.*, pp. 690, 747–48.
48. *New York Times*, March 4, 1868, p. 8.

children to private schools, but "for ten or fifteen white children to demand such a separation, would be absurd; and I hope the Convention will give its assent to no such proposition."[49] Charlestonians R. C. De Large and A. J. Ransier, along with A. C. Richmond of Berkeley and John A. Chesnut of Kershaw, supported Cardozo's argument.[50] Even though some white parents would thus be allowed to keep their children out of schools that admitted Negroes, these delegates by no means abandoned their pursuit of racial equality in the schools. Indeed, De Large asserted that "if there is a place in the State where no distinction should be made, or in this country, it should be in the school house, or in the Church." But they believed their age to be one of general progress in which prejudice and discrimination would gradually dissolve, and their concessions to expediency rendered meaningless. J. J. Wright, a Pennsylvania-born Negro then residing in Beaufort, concurred and added that at that moment he did "not believe the colored children will want to go to the white schools, or vice versa."[51]

Modest as they were, the most conservative aspirations of the Negro leadership were doomed to disappointment. Governor H. K. Scott, previously head of the Freedmen's Bureau in South Carolina, followed Orr's lead in urging the legislature to establish separate schools for Negroes and whites. "I deem this separation of the two races in the public schools a matter of the greatest importance to all classes of our people," he declared. Failure to do so would repel "the whites from the educational training that they so much need," whereas the adoption of such a policy would allow the government to "rely upon time and the elevating influence of popular education, to dispel any unjust prejudice that may exist among the two races of our fellow-citizens."[52] The idea that the whites could be educated out of their prejudices in a separated school system which could then be organized without regard to race dominated official Republican thought on the subject throughout Reconstruction.

Still, sentiment for mixed schools did not die entirely with the adjournment of the convention. Justus K. Jillson, a well-informed Massachusetts educator who had come to the state as a Bureau teacher and remained to serve the state as superintendent of education throughout the period of effective Republican control, was conscientiously opposed

49. *Convention Proceedings,* 1868, pp. 691, 706, 901.
50. *Ibid.,* pp. 688–92, 748–49, 899–900.
51. *Ibid.,* pp. 692–93.
52. *House Journal* (Special Session, 1868), pp. 44–45.

to separation. In the summer of 1874, he told a Northern reporter "that, should the question arise, he would feel it his duty to decide that negro children were entitled to the benefit of every free school in the State."[53] Yet Jillson's direct authority was greatly circumscribed by the school law. In one area in which he was clearly empowered to act, he ambitiously ordered the faculty of the state's School for the Deaf and Blind, at Cedar Springs in Spartanburg County, to receive Negro students precisely as they did white children. The native white faculty resigned in protest, and Jillson, rather than yield, closed the school. The faculty continued to work with some of its students privately, and, in 1876, Jillson capitulated, re-opening the school under an arrangement which separated the children according to race. Thus, paradoxically, color was distinguished where no color was seen; but the rigid rule of separation had been partly breeched in a conspicuous incident.[54]

It is possible—as Cardozo anticipated—that Negro and white children in some of the more remote districts attended the same school and were taught by the same teacher. In Kershaw County, in 1870, for instance, there existed a school in which some two score children of both races were divided into first, second, and third grades. Even here, apparently, some racial distinction was made, the "colored" children being listed separately on the school roster.[55]

In this manner, the rule of separation in education was practiced throughout Reconstruction. In 1874, a *Times* correspondent found that separation was universal in South Carolina's public schools, and that in remote areas only white schools existed. In Charleston, he found Cardozo's pride, the Morris Street School, now in the public system, staffed completely by native whites and attended exclusively by Negro children.[56]

The actions of Negroes under these circumstances suggest that they were more interested in obtaining educational opportunities for their people than in "mixing" colors in the public schools. While demanding education for all children, Negroes in the legislature said little about "mixed" schools at the elementary level. A Northern visitor in 1874 observed that the mass of Negroes "with that moderation and good sense for which they have been noted, as a class, since the war, have never made any effort to force their children into the white schools, and it is

53. *New York Times,* July 3, 1874, p. 1.
54. *A History of Spartanburg County,* p. 179.
55. MS list of students, D. W. Jordan Papers.
56. *New York Times,* July 3, 1874, p. 1.

believed they will be wise enough never to take advantage of the doubtful privilege given them by the Constitution."[57] Negroes did, indeed, resent separation in the public schools because of the social attitudes which it reflected. But so long as educational opportunities for the two races were not blatantly unequal, Negroes did not attempt to press the moral issue at this level. After the Redemption, as Negro parents saw their children deprived of educational benefits which white children enjoyed, their resentment grew into bitterness and, all too often, into hatred. Politically, the Redeemers had no choice but to maintain racially separated public schools. For a time, however, they did provide Negroes with educational opportunities roughly equivalent to those of the whites. Within a few years, it became obvious that the majority of voters opposed even this, and the quality of education offered to whites rapidly advanced beyond that provided for Negroes.

The story of education in South Carolina under the Republicans has often been told in detail, and most accounts are in close agreement.[58] On the common school level—the primary target of Republican educational efforts—a broad, generally enlightened scheme of universal, compulsory education was inaugurated. It was partly crippled, however, by placing excessive power in the hands of local authorities who were usually ill-informed and often venal. In advanced schools—as those between the common school and the college or university levels were usually called—the state made little progress. In this area, agents of Northern societies realized considerable success in working with Negro students. In higher education, the white community actually regressed, largely because of its withdrawal from the University of South Carolina when it was opened to Negroes. On the other hand, by entering the University and other institutions established specifically for their benefit, Negroes enjoyed significant advances in higher education.

Experts agree that the Republicans planned an intelligent, progressive common school system in South Carolina. Among those who designed the new system were men who brought to their task substantial experi-

57. *Ibid.*
58. Amory Dwight Mayo, "The Final Establishment of the Common School System in North Carolina, South Carolina, and Georgia, 1863–1900," *Reports of the Commissioner of Education* (1904), I, 1026 *et seq.*; Edgar Wallace Knight, *The Influence of Reconstruction on Education in the South,* Teachers College, Columbia University (New York, 1913), pp. 63–89; Simkins and Woody, *South Carolina During Reconstruction,* pp. 434–43; Tindall, *South Carolina Negroes,* pp. 209–10.

ence as teachers and educational administrators both in South Carolina and the North. Cardozo, Jillson, and Langley led the convention's committee on education in outlining a program which—in spite of the lengthy and often acrimonious debates on the poll tax, compulsory attendance, and separation of the races—was accepted by a large majority of the delegates with only minor changes. Reuben Tomlinson, for three years the head of the Bureau's educational organization in the state, became the first chairman of the education committee of the House of Representatives. Jillson held the same position in the Senate until he became the nominal head of the state system as the superintendent of education, an office which he held by popular suffrage until the fall of 1876. After inexplicable delays, the legislature, in February, 1870, finally put the plan into effect.[59]

The program provided for the compulsory education of all children for a minimum of two years. Primary responsibility for its execution lay with popularly elected commissioners of education in each county. Counties were divided into school districts, each under the supervision of three elected trustees who were responsible for the operation of their school or schools. The trustees depended heavily on the county school commissioner, who controlled educational funds and, with two other persons appointed by himself, licensed teachers. The commissioner was charged with keeping the schools open as long as his funds allowed, annually visiting each school and advising the teachers, making statistical reports to the superintendent, and seeing that the curriculum included "the common branches of an English education," and United States history. The relation of the state superintendent of public instruction to the system was almost entirely advisory. He could license teachers, but his primary duties consisted of the purely mechanical tasks of keeping records and making reports, collecting and disseminating information, and allotting school funds through the various county commissioners.[60] Financial support for the schools was to be derived from a state property tax and a special poll tax.

The real fault in the system lay not in its design but in its execution. It is true, as was frequently charged, that the scheme was ambitious; but it was hardly too ambitious, and none of the leaders was so naive as to

59. *Southern Enterprise* (Greenville), March 3, 1869.

60. The General Assembly passed basic legislation establishing the school system in February, 1870. However, a temporary measure was passed in September, 1868, and the Act of 1870 was re-cast in better form in March, 1871. *Statutes at Large*, XIV, 23–25, 339–48, 574–84.

believe that it could be made fully effective immediately. "We are not to legislate for a day or a week," a Negro delegate declared to the convention during the discussion on the school system, "but to lay a foundation that will be for the general welfare of the people in all future time . . ."[61] It is also true that the plan was expensive, but the draftsmen of the system anticipated a period of prosperity—soon to be realized— when the state could afford the expense. Further, in view of the high tax program envisioned, Republicans considered the cost of the system an argument in its favor. Nevertheless, the full burden of school support was not placed upon property holders. Persons without property, declared J. J. Wright, "have children to be educated, and we claim that they should pay a tax for the support of the schools." An annual tax of $1.00 (a poll tax) was levied on every male over twenty-one years of age, a tax which bore directly and heavily on the Negro population. In reply to the argument that Negroes had no money, Wright replied, "Let him smoke less segars, or chew less tobacco."[62] Finally, it has frequently been alleged that the primary defect in the system was the placing of excessive power in the hands of the county commissioners. Yet, if all of the commissioners had been as effective as was R. H. Reid of Spartanburg County (a conservative native white in a Democratic county), giving control to the superintendent in Columbia would not have seemed an obvious reform. Actually, blame for the shortcomings of the system must be shared by the legislature, the county commissioners, and the voters who allowed abuses to persist.

In view of the number of experienced educators in their midst, the Republican legislature was astoundingly inept in dealing with school matters. It was in its third session before it passed the school law in completed form, even though Tomlinson reported within weeks after the beginning of the first session that his education committee in the House would present a "fully matured" plan in the second session and did so.[63] The delay was critical. In a period in which the Negro school-age population numbered 200,000 and was increasing at the rate of 10,000 annually, the imperfect, temporary provisions of the legislature prevented even the best-intentioned administrators from doing more than bringing already existing schools into the system. In August, 1870, George F. McIntyre, the school commissioner for populous Colleton County, de-

61. *Convention Proceedings,* 1868, p. 724.
62. *Ibid.*
63. *House Journal* (Special Session, 1868), pp. 258–59; Knight, *Influence of Reconstruction on Education in the South,* p. 73.

clared that since February of that year, when the school law in full
form was finally passed, he had established twenty-five schools and
would have done so before had the legislature acted earlier.[64] A bad
situation was made worse in the fall of 1868 when the Northern benevolent societies curtailed their operations. The combined efforts of the
societies and the Bureau, which ended its educational efforts in the state
in 1870, had never provided instruction for more than 20,000 Negro
children. Their withdrawal from the field before the state system was
well underway was disastrous.

In 1871, perhaps spurred by charges that the selfish machinations of
"professional politicians" caused this delay, the legislature moved briskly
forward. It recast the school law and increased the appropriation from
the $50,000 of the preceding two years to $190,000. This, together with
the haphazardly collected poll tax, was expected to yield $261,000 for the
schools. The legislature had acquired speed, but it had hardly acquired
wisdom in educational matters. In the same year, it considered a bill
to require the trustees of each district to build at least one school for
200 pupils before November, a ridiculous gesture in view of the fact that
many districts had school populations far below that figure. The legislature unwittingly omitted from a revised version of the appropriations
bill the customary authorization for a special property tax in the
Charleston district for the support of its schools, an oversight which, had
it passed unnoticed, would have crippled Charleston's public school system.[65] During the next five years, legislative appropriations and special
taxes levied for the schools amounted to nearly $300,000 annually. This
sum, combined with the poll tax, should have produced revenues of
about $400,000 a year, which was sufficient to send every school-age child
in the state to school four months a year.[66] Yet, at least a quarter of this
money was lost through political corruption.

No doubt, large amounts were diverted to personal and political
purposes after being passed to the county school commissioners. But
corruption was not the only disease prevalent among the commissioners.
After an interview with Jillson in the summer of 1874, a northern
reporter was impressed with "the ignorance, incompetency, and neglect
of duty on the part of school officers." On the first count, he elaborated:
"In many cases rice-field hands, and other negroes who can neither read

64. *Daily Republican* (Charleston), August 29, 1870.
65. *Ibid.*, January 17, March 2, 1871.
66. Knight, *Influence of Reconstruction on Education in the South*, pp. 78–80;
Simkins and Woody, *South Carolina During Reconstruction*, p. 436.

nor write, are elected to the office of Commissioner; they in turn appoint Trustees and Examiners who do not know one letter from another, and the result is that teachers are selected who should themselves be the pupils in some primary school."[67] By way of illustration, he might have included the following sample, written by the school commissioner of Richland County: "The foller ring name person are Rickermended to the Boarde for the Hower [Howard?] Schoole . . . . haveing Given fool sat ed fact Shon in thi tow Last Years."[68]

By 1874, a broad movement to reform the administration of the school program was under way. In the gubernatorial campaign of that year, both D. H. Chamberlain, the regular Republican nominee, and the "reform" candidate favored a reorganization. Once in the governor's chair, Chamberlain attacked the "absolute" powers of the county school commissioners.[69] In a celebrated case in Chester County, a Negro senator, Dublin Walker, who had previously been the school commissioner, was prosecuted by a Republican solicitor, convicted by a predominately Republican jury, and sentenced with a vengeance by Thomas Jefferson Mackey, a Republican judge, for improperly using school funds. Yet, the problem was not so simply solved. Some Negroes tended to regard the results of reform as persecution of their race. As a native white lawyer observed of Walker's departure for the penitentiary: "There was much weeping the day he left among the brethren. They look upon him as a martyr."[70] When the Redeemer superintendent of education took office in 1877, he found only twelve school commissioners who had both zeal and capacity (most of these in the white counties), a number of others who had zeal and might improve in capacity, but the rest had neither.[71]

Republican reformers were more successful in winning the promise of progressive improvement in the quality of teacher training. In 1873, under the enthusiastic and able direction of Mortimer A. Warren, a Northern-born educator, a State Normal School was begun in Columbia. Various Northern sponsors established other normal schools in Aiken, Orangeburg, and Charleston. A large proportion of the more than 400

67. *New York Times,* July 3, 1874, p. 1.
68. John S. Reynolds, *Reconstruction in South Carolina, 1865–1877* (Columbia, 1905), p. 122.
69. Walter Allen, *Governor Chamberlain's Administration in South Carolina: A Chapter of Reconstruction in the Southern States* (New York, 1888), pp. 27, 55, 172.
70. J. H. Hemphill to W. R. Hemphill, October 2, 1875, Hemphill Papers.
71. *Reports and Resolutions* (1877), p. 382.

teachers who were added to public school faculties during Chamberlain's administration were graduated from these schools.[72]

The Chamberlain administration also sought to nourish sentiment among both races in favor of public education. That popular support did exist, in spite of the inroads of corruptionists, was evident in the financial assistance which local communities afforded their schools outside of official channels. For example, even though the state paid only $128,000 for schools in "the year of good stealing," 1872, local contributions raised the pay of teachers, alone, to $268,000, and there were similar contributions during the next three years.[73] Seeking support from all elements, the reformers addressed themselves to the whites, many of whom agreed with the native white educator who declared "that Christians should welcome the opportunity to educate the Negro."[74]

Although Republican reformers actually realized only minor gains during Chamberlain's administration, Democratic campaigners in 1876 adopted virtually intact the Republican program for reorganizing the public school system. Once in office, the Redeemers passed an amendment to the constitution which established a special and permanent tax for the support of schools and, by law, centralized public school administration precisely as Chamberlain had sought to do. With these improvements, the Redeemers were able, for a time, to honor Hampton's pledge of better schools for the Negroes. In the decade and a half after 1880, however, the state's per capita expenditure for Negro pupils declined by more than half, while that for the whites increased slightly.[75]

Hampered by apathy, incompetence, disorganization, desertion, and betrayal, the pell-mell assault on public ignorance launched by the Reconstruction regime nevertheless won impressive gains. Near the end of 1869, before the new system had received any substantial financial aid from the state, slightly less than 10 per cent of the school-age population attended 381 schools staffed by 528 teachers who were supported by a variety of means, including gifts, tuition, local levies, and promises. By June, 1870, after the enactment of the first comprehensive school law, and after expenditures by the state had nearly trebled, 15 per cent of the school-age population attended twice as many schools staffed by 734

72. Allen, *Governor Chamberlain's Administration,* p. 173; see also: Warren's reports in *Reports and Resolutions* (1873–1874), *et seq.*

73. Knight, *Influence of Reconstruction on Education in the South,* p. 79, fn. 85.

74. *A History of Spartanburg County,* pp. 180–81. See also: M. R. Warren to W. R. Hemphill, February 22, 1876, Hemphill Papers.

75. Tindall, *South Carolina Negroes,* pp. 210–17.

teachers. Four-fifths of these schools were supported partly or entirely by state funds. In 1871, when state expenditures for schools were again substantially increased, 32 per cent of the school-age population were enrolled in 1,639 schools employing 1,898 teachers. At the end of the first year of the Chamberlain administration, 46 per cent of South Carolina's school-age children were attending 2,580 schools staffed by nearly 3,000 teachers. During the following year, in spite of strong pressures for economy in all branches of state expenditures, attendance in the public schools reached a peak of 123,000 pupils, representing roughly one-half of the school-age children in the state. During the revolutionary months of 1876 and 1877, attendance by both races declined, but by 1880 enrollment was higher than ever.

The Negro community shared in this general progress in public education. The number of Negro children enrolled in public schools rose from some 8,200 in 1869 to 70,800 in 1876, representing an increase from 9 to 44 per cent of the Negro population of school age. At the same time, Negro teachers assumed an ever-growing share of the educational burden. In 1873, a quarter of the teachers in the public schools were Negroes. By 1876, more than one-third of the teachers were Negroes; and of the 1,087 Negro teachers employed only 44 were Northern born.[76]

During Reconstruction, advanced schools for Negroes did not exist in the state system outside of Charleston and Columbia. Without success, Chamberlain repeatedly suggested to the legislature that provision be made for the establishment of "one or more" such schools in each county.[77] The few advanced schools for Negroes that were established were created by Northern benevolent societies or religious bodies.

As public schools began to form at the primary level, private educational groups naturally shifted their efforts to fill the void beyond the common schools. Thus, in 1869, the South Carolina Conference of the Methodist Church (Northern), which had operated nine schools in South Carolina, noted that the inauguration of the public system would "relieve the church of this portion of her responsibilities," and turned its educational efforts to higher institutions.[78] Similarly, Martha Schofield

76. Relatively complete statistics on education are available in the yearly reports of the superintendent which were published in *Reports and Resolutions* beginning with the 1869–1870 edition. See also: Knight, *Influence of Reconstruction on Education in the South*, pp. 75, 76, 79, 85–86; *New York Times*, November 27, 1875, p. 4.

77. Allen, *Governor Chamberlain's Administration*, pp. 55, 173.

78. Thomas H. Pearne, "The Freedmen," *Methodist Review*, July, 1877, pp.

abandoned elementary education for the establishment, in 1868, of Schofield Normal and Industrial Institute in Aiken. Mather Industrial School was begun near Beaufort; and the famous Penn School on St. Helena, which was started in 1862, became the Penn Normal and Industrial School. In 1872, the American Missionary Association, which under Cardozo's leadership had pioneered in the training of Negro teachers by the establishment of Avery Normal Institute in Charleston in 1865, founded the Brewer Normal, Industrial, and Agricultural Institute in the upcountry village of Greenwood.[79]

Among the churches, the Northern Presbyterian Committee of Missions for Freedmen was early in the field of advanced education. Many congregations in the state had their own lower schools and, by the end of Reconstruction, three higher schools were prospering under Northern Presbyterian auspices: Wallingford Academy in Charleston, Fairfield Normal School in Winnsboro, and Brainerd Institute in Chester. By 1877, these three schools boasted an enrollment of 676 students.[80] Two advanced schools of the Reconstruction Period later became Negro colleges. Benedict Institute, begun by Northern Baptists in 1871, mustered 118 students under one professor in 1877, but over the next three decades grew rapidly and was renamed Benedict College.[81] Payne Institute, established in Cokesbury in 1871 by the African Methodists, was later moved to Columbia where, in 1880, it became the core around which Allen University was organized.

The curricula of the advanced schools presented a wide variety of vocational and academic subjects. Many of them offered terminal education for teachers and ministers, and supplied practical training in the domestic arts, agriculture, and the trades. A primary object, however, was to prepare students for college level instruction, and in this the advanced schools did yeoman work.

472, 473; Ralph Ernest Morrow, *Northern Methodism and Reconstruction* (East Lansing, 1956), p. 162.

79. Martha Schofield MS Diary, various entries; Rupert S. Holland (ed.), *Letters and Diary of Laura M. Towne, 1862–1884, Written from the Sea Islands of South Carolina* (Cambridge, 1912), *passim*; Tindall, *South Carolina Negroes*, pp. 223–24, 225.

80. Pearne, *Methodist Review*, July, 1877, pp. 469–70; Luther P. Jackson, "The Educational Efforts of the Freedmen's Bureau and the Freedmen's Aid Societies in South Carolina, 1862–1872," *Journal of Negro History*, VIII (January, 1923), 8.

81. Pearne, *Methodist Review*, July, 1877, p. 474; Tindall, *South Carolina Negroes*, pp. 231–32.

At the end of Reconstruction, Negroes who were qualified could attend any one of three institutions of higher learning in South Carolina: Claflin University, the South Carolina Agricultural College and Mechanics Institute (both in Orangeburg), or the University of South Carolina in Columbia.

The Northern Methodists chartered Claflin in 1869. The nucleus of the institution was Baker Theological Institute which was transferred from Charleston to Orangeburg for the purpose. The Claflin family of Boston provided most of the financial support for the new university and gave it its name. Alonzo Webster, the Massachusetts minister who had led in the founding of both the Institute and the university, became its president. Throughout Reconstruction, some seven to ten Northern Methodist ministers, their wives, and daughters staffed Claflin. In addition to the theological department, the university offered a preparatory department "which will take a few bright and promising children of both sexes," a normal department open to students "who can read and write well," and a four year college course. Obviously, the level of instruction at Claflin during Reconstruction hardly deserved the appellation "higher education." However, college courses were begun in 1878. As instruction improved, the number of scholars gradually increased, until, by 1876, there were more than a hundred enrolled in the university.[82]

In 1872, the legislature created South Carolina Agricultural College and Mechanics Institute which was, in effect, made an industrial department within Claflin University. Supposedly, the industrial department was also the state's agricultural and mechanical college under the Morrill Land Grant Act of 1862. The state maintained some control over the department by measuring out yearly appropriations. These it derived from the fund created by the investment of the state's land scrip. The state's authority was also manifested through a peculiar arrangement in which a board of trustees appointed by the legislature joined with the board of Claflin University in governing the industrial department.

Actually, much of Claflin's early prosperity sprang from its association with the generously financed industrial department. By the end of Reconstruction, that department had a 250-acre experimental farm in operation, shops for the training of carpenters and blacksmiths, and

82. *Minutes of the Sixth Session of the South Carolina Annual Conference of the Methodist Episcopal Church, held at Claflin University, Orangeburg, South Carolina, December 22, 1870* (Charleston, 1871), advertisement. See also advertisements in subsequent local issues of the minutes of the Conference.

a budding faculty of its own. In the clearly separated system which the Redeemers established in 1878, the department, ambitiously redesignated Claflin College, became the state's institution of higher learning for Negroes, while the University of South Carolina was altered to serve the same purpose for the whites. However, the close connection between privately owned Claflin University and publicly financed Claflin College continued. Edward Cooke, a New England Methodist minister who relieved Webster as president of Claflin University in 1875, was also the chief officer of the college.[83]

In January, 1866, the state reopened venerable South Carolina College and, with the nominal addition of several professional schools, changed its name to the University of South Carolina. However, hard times, as well as hard feelings, militated against its prosperity. In 1868, the year in which the Republican party came into power, its total enrollment was only 113. By the following spring, the number of scholars had dropped to sixty-five.[84] Many members of the faculty joined the departing students. For a time, the whites hoped their University might be spared and even offered to barter the Citadel buildings in Charleston to house a university for Negroes in exchange for the promise of an all-white institution in Columbia.[85] The Radicals scorned the offer, however, and their intentions became increasingly clear. In March, 1869, the legislature prohibited racial discrimination in the University, and shortly afterward named two Negroes to the Board of Regents.[86] The father of two of the sixty-five students remaining read the signs accurately: "I suppose that the S. C. University will go up the spout, under the new regime of the Carpet bagger and Scallawags and negroes. I am somewhat puzzled as to what I shall do with Charles. John will be through. The Rads have strangled the N. C. and Alabama Universities and ours will follow suit I suppose."[87]

In the early 1870's, Northern Methodists spearheaded a movement to fill university chairs with professors with pronounced Republican convictions. One of these, Henry J. Fox (who had had extensive experience as an educator and administrator in Methodist schools in the

83. *Reports and Resolutions* (1871–1872), pp. 172–75; *Reports and Resolutions* (1877–1878), pp. 829, 831; *Reports and Resolutions* (1879), p. 364; *Northern Methodist Minutes,* 1876, p. 9; Ralph Ernest Morrow, *Northern Methodism and Reconstruction* (East Lansing, 1956), p. 168.
84. *New York Times,* October 28, 1868, p. 5.
85. *Ibid.,* December 25, 1868, p. 2.
86. *Statutes at Large,* XIV, 203–4.
87. J. H. Hemphill to W. R. Hemphill, May 18, 1869, Hemphill Papers.

North), assumed the presidency; and another, A. W. Cummings, a
defecting Southern Methodist who had been the financial agent of
Claflin University, became the chairman of the faculty.[88] The transition was completed suddenly in October, 1873, when the first Negro
student, Henry E. Hayne, former sergeant in the Union Army and
South Carolina's secretary of state, was admitted to the law school.
After the ensuing exodus, Thomas G. Clemson, the son-in-law of
John C. Calhoun, lamented, "I see L'abord has taken his departure
& is rid of the humiliation of this sphere & with the fall of the University of S. C. as bad as was the curriculum of that school it was the
last hope."[89] Shortly thereafter, Negroes formed a majority on the
Board of Regents, and, in 1874, Richard T. Greener, a Negro who had
"stood in flattering proximity to his highest compeers when graduating
at Harvard," took the chair of mental science.[90]

Scores of other Negro scholars followed Hayne into the University.
Through comparatively liberal appropriations and a system of state-
financed scholarships the University enjoyed a rather striking prosperity under the aegis of the Republicans. During the year preceding
October, 1875, it claimed an enrollment of 233 students, 91 of whom
were on state subsidies. Interestingly, of the 233, 102 were in the preparatory department, 107 in "Academical Schools," 20 were studying law,
and two were in medicine.[91] The races were mixed in the University,
but even in its best years under the Chamberlain administration, conservative whites did not send their sons there. Only a tenth of the
students were whites, and most of these bore names that suggested
that their fathers were prominent professionals in the Republican party
or were Northern missionaries.

The eagerness of freedmen of both sexes and all ages to acquire
at least a rudimentary education was a truism. As soon as schools were
established in the Sea Islands, Negroes thronged to them and a year
later, according to the leader of the experiment, their avidity for learning had not abated.[92] As the educational missionaries followed the

88. *Northern Methodist Minutes,* 1873, p. 6; 1874, p. 8; 1876, p. 10; 1877,
p. 7; Hunter Dickinson Farish, *The Circuit Rider Dismounts; a Social History
of Southern Methodism, 1865–1900* (Richmond, 1938), p. 142.

89. T. G. Clemson to A. L. Burt, November 16, 1873, T. G. Clemson Papers.

90. Henry J. Fox, "The Negro," *Methodist Review,* January, 1875; Carter G.
Woodson, *A Century of Negro Migration* (Washington, 1918), p. 124.

91. Allen, *Governor Chamberlain's Administration,* p. 173.

92. Pierce, *Atlantic Monthly,* p. 303.

armies inland, the masses of Negroes who flocked to newly established schools showed the same desire for knowledge. "All manifest a degree of earnestness in their studies which is not excelled by white children," a journalist wrote of the Negro students in a Bureau school in the upcountry village of Anderson in 1866. "Out of the school-house, one sees them on door steps or by the roadside, conning their lessons, with an appearance of wisdom which is often ludicrous."[93] In the early period, adults seemed hardly less thirsty for knowledge than children. Higginson thought that the "love of the spelling-book" among his men was "perfectly inexhaustible."[94] Although the number of adults attending schools tended to decrease after the first year of freedom, the desire of adults to have their children educated seemed to grow stronger as Reconstruction progressed. "The people are hungry and thirsty after knowledge," declared a Negro delegate from Beaufort to the Constitutional Convention. "They seem to be inspired with a spirit from on high that tells them that knowledge is the only source by which they can rise from the low and degraded state in which they have been kept."[95]

In spite of the frequent and pointed declaration by Northern teachers along the Carolina coast during the war that there was no difference in learning ability between whites and Negroes, virtually all native whites and a large number of Northerners believed at the time of emancipation that Negroes were capable of absorbing only a limited education. "I am convinced," wrote the Bureau officer in Greenville, who was by no means unsympathetic with the freedmen, "that the Negro as he is, no matter how educated, is not the mental equal of the European."[96] Frequent assertions by teachers that Negro students learned as readily as the white and denials by educators that he was capable only of elementary education indicate that such doubts died slowly, if at all. After touring the state in 1874, a Northern reporter found it necessary to declare: "The statement that after a certain point colored children did not advance so rapidly in their studies as white ones is very emphatically denied by some of the most experienced teachers in the State." A visit to the Morris Street School in Charleston and an interview with the principal, a native white, provided a

93. *Intelligencer* (Anderson), May 24, August 2, 1866.

94. Thomas Wentworth Higginson, *Army Life in a Black Regiment* (Boston, 1890), p. 25.

95. *Convention Proceedings,* 1868, p. 726.

96. James H. Croushore and David M. Potter (eds.), *John William De Forest, A Union Officer in the Reconstruction* (New Haven, 1948), p. 117.

case in point. "Mr. Doty, who has been principal of the school for a number of years, states that, in his opinion, negro children learn quite as readily as white ones. Their desire for information, or 'thirst for knowledge,' as he expressed it, is much greater."[97] By the end of Reconstruction, the presumption that the Negro was incapable of absorbing higher education began to crack under an accumulating mass of evidence. The more astute among the native whites then shifted from a disbelief in the ability of Negroes to learn to a fear that the Negroes might surpass the whites in this respect. Edward McCrady, who advocated white supremacy of a paternal variety, voiced this fear in a speech at Erskine College. "But I do tremble," he declared, "at the idea that the time should come when the negroes of the South, forced by outside pressure and sustained by outside aid, should at least for the while, be better educated than the masses of the whites."[98]

The availability of schools and the eagerness (and the ability) of Negroes for learning combined to produce an impressive record of actual academic performance. In 1863, after the schools on the Sea Islands had been open sporadically for several months, E. L. Pierce reported on the progress of the scholars. "The advanced classes," he wrote, "were reading simple stories and didactic passages in the ordinary school-books, as Hillard's Second Primary Reader, Willson's Second Reader, and others of similar grade. Those who had enjoyed a briefer period of instruction were reading short sentences or learning the alphabet. In several of the schools a class was engaged in an elementary lesson in arithmetic, geography, or writing."

Unfortunately, the instruction was not without a political bias. When Pierce visited one school in Beaufort, he found the teacher and her pupils reciting their geo-historical catechism:

> Teacher: What country do you live in?
> Class, *in unison and loudly:* United States.
>
> What state?
> South Carolina.
>
> What Island?
> Port Royal.
>
> What town?
> Beaufort.

97. *New York Times,* July 3, 1874, pp. 1–2. See also: *New York Times,* August 6, 1865, p. 3; *The Nation,* 1, No. 24 (December 14, 1965), 746.
98. Tindall, *South Carolina Negroes,* pp. 212–13.

Who is the Governor?
General Saxton.

Who is your President?
Abraham Lincoln.

What has he done for you?
He's freed us.[99]

The performance of Negro scholars in advanced schools became more impressive. In 1874, a Northern correspondent reported that in Charleston and Columbia "there are classes of black children who are exceedingly proficient in natural philosophy, advanced history, and higher mathematics, and it is stated that they are more willing and anxious to learn than most white children of the same age." The same writer found that students in the Morris Street School in Charleston did algebra, twelve- to fourteen-year-olds answered questions in ancient and modern history, and both sexes read well and with understanding.[100] Even in 1869, in the village of Beaufort, young Negro scholars were boasting to their country cousins that they were studying "algeeber" and "passin" (parsing), much to the discomfiture of the latter whose small school had not then reached such academic heights.[101]

In the University, where the Negro scholar could obtain the highest level of education available to him in South Carolina, a broad range of academic performance was registered. A Republican journalist, attending the spring exercises in 1874, frankly noted that some of the students, Negro and white, spoke only "poorly," some spoke "well," and the speeches of William M. Dart and T. McCants Stewart (both Negroes) were "excellent."[102]

Impressive as they were, both major and minor educational achievements among Negroes in South Carolina before 1877 were confined to the few. Bare literacy, the *sine qua non* of education, made only slight gains during the period. The prodigious efforts of the early postwar years reduced illiteracy among Negroes from perhaps 95 per cent in 1865 to an estimated 85 per cent in 1868, and, if the census figures can be believed, to 81 per cent in 1870. Yet, the curtailment of the educational efforts of the benevolent societies, the termination of the Bureau's educational activities in 1870, the delay in the organization

99. Pierce, *Atlantic Monthly,* pp. 303, 306.
100. *New York Times,* July 3, 1874, pp. 1–2.
101. Botume, *First Days Among the Contrabands,* p. 275.
102. *Daily Union* (Columbia). March 13, 1874.

of the public system, its inefficiency once established, and the disruption of the schools during the confusion of the Redemption combined to handicap education severely and to increase the actual number of illiterates in the growing population. In sum, in 1870, there were 290,000 illiterates in the state over ten years of age, and a decade later the figure had risen to a staggering 370,000.[103] During the same period, the proportion of illiterates in the Negro population dropped only 2.5 per cent from 81 per cent to 78.5 per cent. Thus, in 1870, only two out of every ten Negroes could read and write with any proficiency, and, in 1880, the proportion remained substantially unchanged.[104]

Glimpses behind the raw figures of the census attest not only to their general accuracy, but suggest that learning was achieved by the urban few rather than the rural many. In the early 1870's, an agent of the Peabody Board, which was especially interested in the establishment of advanced schools in the more populous areas, found that 679 of the 800 Negro children of Columbia were in school.[105] On the other hand, in the hundreds of surviving manuscript contracts agreed to by Negro agricultural laborers, almost none were able to sign their names.[106]

Obviously, educational accomplishments during Reconstruction fell far short of needs. Nevertheless, such as they were these achievements became highly significant factors in the subsequent progress of the Negro.

Many Negro leaders of the best quality did rise without the benefit of a formal education; but, the eminent men of the post-Reconstruction period were frequently intimately associated with the formative years of Negro education in South Carolina. Two of the three most prominent Negro politicians, Thomas E. Miller and George Washington Murray, illustrate this point. Miller, born as a "free person of color," attended schools in Charleston and after the war matriculated in Lincoln University in Pennsylvania. In 1874, he became the school commissioner of Beaufort County, and, in 1876, he entered politics professionally. He served several terms in the General Assembly and two terms in Congress before 1896, when he became the president of the state's college for Negroes, a position which he held for fifteen years.

103. Simkins and Woody, *South Carolina During Reconstruction*, p. 439.
104. *Census* (1870), I, 5, 427; (1880), I, 920, 924.
105. Knight, *Influence of Reconstruction on Education in the South*, p. 76.
106. For one exception, see: MS Contract, February 13, 1874, J. B. Richardson Papers.

Murray, a native of Sumter County, was orphaned by the war but
secured sufficient learning to become a teacher and attend the University
of South Carolina from 1874 to 1876. In the 1890's, he was the last
Negro to represent South Carolina in Congress.[107]

The educated elite was also the vital element which sparked the
increasingly successful assault against ignorance in the Negro community after Reconstruction. From their own ranks, they supplied the
teachers and administrators who bore the brunt of the battle, but, more
important, they led in organizing a broad base of popular support.
Their success is measured, in part, by the remarkable performance of
Negro teachers who reduced illiteracy among their people from 78.5
per cent in 1880 to 64 per cent in 1890, and still further to 52.8 per cent
in 1900.[108] This feat is all the more impressive because it was accomplished during a time when an increasingly hostile legislature scaled
the yearly expenditure on Negro pupils in the public schools down-
ward from $2.51 per capita in 1880 to $1.05 in 1895.[109]

The direct relationship between the educational efforts of the Reconstruction period and the progress subsequently achieved in the
schools is ideally illustrated in the personal history of William A.
Sinclair. Sinclair, born a slave in Georgetown, was sold away but returned after emancipation to live with his father. He attended the local
schools, studied at Claflin and then entered the University of South
Carolina. When the University closed, he continued his education at
Howard University in Washington, where he earned bachelor's, master's, and theological degrees. After a brief association with Andover,
he took a position in Nashville with the American Missionary Association, and there he earned a medical degree from Meharry Medical
College. Ultimately, he returned to Georgetown to become the principal of the public school and, thus, to contribute to the advancement
of a new generation of leaders for the Negro community.[110]

Less learned than Sinclair and Dart were the thousand Negro
teachers who not only continued their labors after the Redemption but
recruited for their profession the most promising of their students.
Between 1876 and 1900, the number of Negro teachers trebled; and
however inadequate their means, they performed a truly Herculean

107. Tindall, *South Carolina Negroes*, pp. 54–58, 59–61, 144, 148–49, 150–51,
204–05.
108. *Negro Population*, pp. 415, 419.
109. Tindall, *South Carolina Negroes*, p. 216.
110. William A. Sinclair, *The Aftermath of Slavery* (Boston, 1905), p. ix.

task. The students of the Reconstruction Period taught the teachers to the next generation; and the efforts of both, combined with the mass support of the Negro community, enabled the Negro to move forward in education during an age in which all external and internal circumstances seemed to conspire against his progress.

IX...RACE RELATIONS: ATTITUDES, IRRITATION, AND VIOLENCE

The white community largely determined the nature of relationships between the races in post-bellum South Carolina. The basic assumption underlying the attitudes of the whites was that the Negro race was inherently and immutably inferior to their own. The argument supporting this assumption and, hence, the white man's attitudes toward the Negro, had been developed well before emancipation. In essence, it was conceived as a rationalization of slavery, but both the argument and the attitudes which it generated lived long after slavery had died.

Like the society which gave it birth, the proslavery position was capable of both mercurial evolution and rigid staticism. Generally the argument passed through two grand phases. During the colonial period and far into the Jeffersonian years, Southerners argued that slavery was justified, primarily, as a means of civilizing the Negro. Taking their cue from their European cousins, early Southerners looked upon Negroes as their cultural inferiors. Rising with the ground swell of scientificism and rationalism, seeing an unfolding physical and moral universe which they were rapidly mastering, it was not strange that Southern whites saw cultural difference as cultural inferiority and discriminated against Negroes and Indians, both slave and free, upon these grounds. Incipient masters as they were, the discrimination was not at first well defined, but by the end of the first century of colonization the color line was clearly and unmistakably drawn.

Yet the very system which damned the Negro in this way also held out to him the promise of eventual redemption. The assumption was that association with the white man would civilize the Negro, and there was nothing in the system which ruled that Negroes could not attain a cultural parity with their white neighbors. In this view, slavery was but a school for the Negro, an institution which would die of atrophy when the period of tutelage had passed. The belief that total liberation lay somewhere in the future was given the semblance of reality by the partial acculturation of the great mass of slaves, by the freeing of a few, and by the emergence of a host of emancipation societies in the Southern states.

In the third and fourth decades of the nineteenth century, a profound change occurred in the Southern interpretation of slavery. This shift in thought coincided with a rising conviction among Southerners that they could not, or would not, exist in a society without this form of human bondage. With rather frightening precipitancy Southerners turned away from arguing that slavery was merely a temporary aberration, a short but necessary interval on the path from Africa to the West. Now it became a touchstone peculiarly their own, a talisman which would guide them in the construction of a society of transcendent excellence. As their thinking about slavery altered, so too did their attitudes toward the Negro. Southerners now argued that Negro inferiority was not merely cultural but natural, a permanent, inbred, incurable affliction which uniquely fitted that race to perpetual slavery.

Virtually every field of creative intellectual activity in the South turned its energies to buttressing the new faith. Ministers were in the vanguard. Assiduously they searched their Bibles anew for words to sanctify the eternal enslavement of the Negro. They found them in abundance. Natural scientists, eminent scholars such as Henry W. Ravenel, argued that the races had been separately created, that the Negro and the white were not the fruit of a common genealogical tree. The Negro, they asserted, was biologically unique, an intermediate species suspended somewhere between the animal and human worlds. Economists contended that slavery was not only necessary to Southern prosperity, but essential to the Negro's very existence, that without the guidance of the whites the childlike, improvident Negro would perish. Early-day sociologists maintained that perpetual Negro slavery was a social "mudsill," a foundation upon which the South would erect a superior civilization. Medical men concluded that Negroes possessed strange immunities and weird physical adaptations which fitted them to labor in the fields as white men never could. William Gilmore Simms, Henry Timrod, Sidney Lanier, and other Southern writers turned their whole creative efforts to works which established a convenient color code, damning black as forever inferior (and, indeed, evil) and praising white as good and true. Simultaneously, Southerners at large argued that the Negro was happy in slavery; it was the one social estate congenial to his nature; it was, in short, a positive good.

Having passed through three decades of repetition and refinement, the new proslavery persuasion evolved an elaborate and rigid ritual well before the Civil War began. It had developed a unique vocabulary, an intellectual shorthand of ideas and assumptions, and a facile jargon, all of which were intelligible only to the initiated. In the mind of the South, the educated South, the new argument approached a complicated and well-integrated synthesis of all knowledge justifying perpetual slavery.

Inevitably the question arises: Against whom were the Southerners contending? Unburdened by the immediate moral problem of slave ownership in their midst, many and perhaps most Northerners accepted Negro inferiority as a postulate. Slavery might seem wrong to some Northerners, but it did not necessarily follow that even those devotees of antislavery regarded the Negro as the equal of the white. Most Northerners who cared hardly understood the language of proslavery apologists, and the few who did seldom bothered to answer. Furthermore, most Northern intellectuals were much too busy constructing arguments to convince themselves that slavery was wrong to heed seriously the polemics of the opposition. Nor was the proslavery plea addressed to articulate critics within the South, for these did not exist. Ultimately, the argument was the South's answer to itself, each man's reply to his own conscience, to his unspoken criticism of the peculiar institution.

Spawned to justify slavery, the argument asserting the Negro's inherent inferiority did not die with emancipation. After a generation of self-indoctrination, for such it was, Southerners could hardly be expected to concede that emancipation by the sword invalidated their argument or altered the basic nature of the Negro. Reconstruction correspondence is replete with restatements of the argument. Occasionally, its tenets were adapted to shifts in scientific theory. "The work goes far to strengthen my own views as to the difference in the origin of the two races," wrote former Governor Francis Pickens to former Governor A. G. Magrath in 1867 concerning a borrowed book. "I see Agassiz has come out on the same side lately, & says he would have come out before, but he feared people might suppose he was for slavery." Agassiz, Pickens explained, had recently conducted an experiment which indicated that "the clean footed [bird] was higher in progressive procreation" than the web-footed. "So too of the negro, no full blooded negro can open his fingers as clean as a white man, between his fingers there is a ligament of skin at the root which looks partly like webb. So in like manner there is a skin or webb between the toes of an old full blooded negro. And the inference is that he is lower in progressive procreation than the white man."[1] Most often, however, the argument was repeated in a language essentially unchanged. "The African has been, in all ages, a savage or a slave," declared B. F. Perry in 1866. "God created him inferior to the white man in form, color and intellect, and no legislation or culture can make him his equal . . . His color is black; his head covered with wool instead of hair, his form and features will not compete with the caucasian race, and it is in vain to think of elevating him to the dignity of the white man. God created differences between the two races, and nothing can make him equal."[2] After 1867, many comprehensive reproductions of the argument in book form circulated in the state. Interestingly, one of these was written by Hinton Rowan Helper, the North Carolinian whose denunciation of slavery had caused such a furor in the late 1850's. Dedicating his work to the ideal of bringing the nation "under the Exclusive Occupancy and Control of the Heaven-descended and Incomparably Superior White Races of Mankind," Helper hoped that after the Fourth of July, 1876, "No Slave nor Would be Slave, No Negro nor Mulatto, No Chinaman nor unnative Indians, No Black nor Bi-colored Individual of whatever Name or Nationality, shall ever again find Domicile anywhere Within the Boundaries of the United States of America . . ."[3]

Precisely as before the war, Northerners could scarcely translate the jargon of the proslavery profession. A Bureau officer in Greenville

1. F. W. Pickens to A. G. Magrath, February 19, 1867, F. W. Pickens Papers.
2. *New York Times*, October 7, 1866, p. 2.
3. Hinton Rowan Helper, *Nojoque; a Question for a Continent* (New York, 1867). See also: Hinton Rowan Helper, *The Negroes in Negroland; the Negroes in America; and Negroes Generally* (New York, 1868).

was astounded by the effectiveness of Perry's use of the old arguments
to fight Negro suffrage; but he was also amused at "the Confusion of
certain Radical pundits, who did not know what the governor is (or
was) talking about."[4] Scarcely a Southerner raised a critical voice
against either slavery or the persisting assumption of innate Negro
inferiority. Those few who did so seem usually to have had strong
affiliations abroad. For instance, A. L. Taveau, who in 1865 concluded
that the ideal of the happy slave was a "delusion," had been educated
primarily in France by his *émigré* father.[5] Joseph E. Holmes, a Laurens
county native who lived in London in the early postwar years, put
both Negroes and whites into the framework of a neatly preserved
Jeffersonian universe. "I know well how hard it is for men to give up
preconceived notions or opinions or make allowances for the effects of
education & circumstances on others," he lectured his young nephew
from the South, then a student at Edinburgh. "You I suppose think the
negro by nature an inferior race & that he should be made to keep that
lower position. I believe his origin as good as my own & I claim nothing
of natural rights for myself that I am not ready to concede to him." A
year later, he continued in the same rare vein:

> The government must educate the negro & treat him in all
> respects as it does other men & white people must recognize
> the same civil rights for him as they claim for themselves, or
> else it will ever be a war of races & life & property in the south
> will be precarious enough, and the sooner the whites kill off
> the whole race of darkies hip & thigh the better, unless they
> conclude to leave the country & live apart from the negro or
> conclude that a perfect acknowledgment of the equality of rights
> & duties is the true policy . . . For your own good. For the bless-
> ing of your home & neighborhood I hope you will go home to
> pacify & conciliate the discordant elements. If however you
> like war better than peace, strife & hatred better than love &
> good will, it is easy to be pleased on that score. We can any
> of us get up a row at any time by impudence & insolence, by
> hard words & frowning looks, by saying to any of our fellow
> creatures stand aside for I am your superior.[6]

4. James H. Croushore and David M. Potter (eds.), *John William De Forest,
A Union Officer in the Reconstruction* (New Haven, 1948), p. 192.

5. A. L. Taveau to William Aiken, April 24, 1865, A. L. Taveau Papers.

6. Joseph E. Holmes to Nickels J. Holmes, August 29, 1866; November 24,
1867, N. J. Holmes Papers.

Few Southern whites could be so objective, and even fewer were openly so. Nevertheless, native whites continued as before the war to rehearse to one another the same hackneyed phrases arguing the Negro's incorrigible inferiority, suggesting that it was still themselves against whom they were contending.

Applied to the hard realities of Reconstruction times, the persisting assumptions of the proslavery argument generated in the white community a clear, complex, and, within its own context, logical pattern of attitudes toward the freedman.

A central theme of native white thought was that Negroes should be subordinated to whites whenever and wherever contact between the races occurred. Emancipation hardly altered this attitude. The subordination of the freedmen had obvious economic advantages for whites of all stations, but in the minds of the dominant group it also had higher purposes. Most important, it was God's way. Dr. John Bachman, a New York Lutheran clergyman transplanted to South Carolina soil during the ante-bellum period and closely identified with the low-country aristocracy, wrote to a friend in September, 1865, that he hoped for the most stringent regulations for the freedman, that "the negro be placed in the situation for which God intended him—the inferior of the white man."[7] Negro subordination was also natural law. "The resistance to social equality is a law of race—a law of nature," argued a Columbian in December, 1868, "and has existed in all ages and in all places. It exists to-day in New York and in New England, as well as here, and always will."[8] Without conceding that Negroes could be made the equals of whites, many whites continued to believe that slavery had been God's plan for civilizing the Negro. "What is to happen to the negro and white?" asked a young Columbian in her diary in March, 1865, as the prospect of freeing the slaves loomed before her. "Has God taken this means of making the negroes suffer bodily as did the Israelites, placing them in bondage to a superior people, in order to force intelligence and civilization upon them?"[9] Many of her contemporaries would have answered in the affirmative, and some would have added that emancipation was another step forward in a divinely inspired process. To rice planter Robert A. Pringle it seemed "as if Providence has forced upon us the civilization of the negro & now

7. John Bachman to E. Elliott, September 11, 1865, Habersham Elliott Papers.
8. *New York Times,* December 25, 1868, p. 2.
9. Grace B. Elmore MS Diary, entry for March 4, 1865.

that that has been accomplished we are forced to submit to having them freed in our midst and the work of making him an intelligent free laborer capable of providing for himself given us to do."[10] In freedom, as in slavery, subordination was thus necessary to the cultural elevation of the Negro, just as the student is below the master. Finally, subordination was essential to the Negro's very existence. "The negro is the most inferior of the human race, far benenath the Indian or Hindu, and how can it be expected that they will be the white Man's equal," asked Grace Elmore. "It will be with them as with the Indian whereever [sic] the white has found foot hold, the negro will disappear except where he is kept in subjection, and consequently where it will be in the interest of the master to promote the welfare of the body and soul."[11]

For most native whites, verbalization and elaborate rationalizations were unnecessary. Slavery itself had offered sufficient prima facie evidence of the inferiority of the Negro, his subordination was in the natural order of things, and the practical income from the system was obvious and desirable. The determination of the masses to keep the freedman in subjection was expressed by their actions rather than their words.

Native whites also commonly believed that the co-existence of the two races was impossible, that nature had made them incompatible. Grace Elmore, observing the state of relations between Negroes and whites in June, 1865, caught the flavor of this feeling. "Both parties are very indifferent and the most that is felt is polite and gentle interest in the affairs of each other," she noted. "In most instances there is I think a bitter feeling & a sharp antagonism between the two races. I almost believe they are natural enemies and that only their relative positions [in slavery] bound them in affection as well as law together."[12] The failure of the Black Code and the continuing "misbehavior" of the Negro in an unstable political and social order confirmed native whites in their belief that the two races could not live together in peace. Complaining of larceny by Negroes during the summer of 1866, a Laurens woman wrote: "I believe they will have to leave the country or the white people will leave them for they will kill and destroy so much that we cannot flourish together."[13] After the inauguration of Con-

10. R. A. Pringle to W. R. Johnson, August 19, 1865, R. A. Pringle Papers.
11. Grace B. Elmore MS Diary, entry for March 4, 1865.
12. Ibid., entry for June 25, 1865.
13. "Mother" to Nickels J. Holmes, July 25, 1866, N. J. Holmes Papers.

gressional Reconstruction, many native whites believed that the issue had been irrevocably drawn. "The negro & the white (Southern) man cannot fraternize," concluded a Laurens native in 1868. "They are compelled to be distinct and I may also say hostile classes. One or the other will rule."[14]

Directly reflecting the general belief in inherent Negro inferiority was the expectation that the race was soon to disappear entirely from the Southern scene, by a common analogy, just as the Indian had gone. He would die primarily because the Yankee had deprived him of the protection previously afforded by his master and could offer no viable substitute. Thus bereft, the Negro himself would be incapable of wresting a subsistence from the forces of nature. Seeing the beginning of the end as Sherman entered the state in January, 1865, Henry Ravenel confided to a friend that he refused to grieve over the death of Tom, "a faithful servant," because, as he explained, "deep & dark as is the ruin approaching for all of us, the woe impending over this hapless race seems infinitely greater. What is to become of these luckless wretches when crushed upon the nether millstone of Yankee pity?"[15] In June, 1865, Mary Chesnut saw in the destruction of the economic aristocracy of the South the destruction also of the Negro. "Better teach the Negroes to stand alone," she admonished Andrew Johnson and the North, "before they break up all they leaned on."[16] Several months later, in Abbeville District, a late slaveholder concurred: "They will perish by hunger and disease and melt away as snow before the rising sun."[17]

Many native whites believed that competition with the superior white race would hasten the demise of the Negro. A Northern reporter in Orangeburg in July, 1865, thought that the Southern people were "nearly unanimous" in this opinion.[18] Three years later, a native white correspondent of the *Times* was "solemnly impressed with the conviction that the colored race in the South is destined to die out under the operation of natural causes," and that, like the Indian, "the darker and inferior race must go to the wall," driven to this end by "being in contact and competition with a superior race."[19]

14. J. D. Young to his sister, May 1, 1868, W. D. Simpson Papers.
15. H. W. Ravenel to R. H. Gourdin, January 21, 1865, R. H. Gourdin Papers.
16. Mary Boykin Chesnut, *A Diary from Dixie,* ed. Ben Ames Williams (Cambridge, 1949), p. 539.
17. William Hill to his brother, September 8, 1865, William Hill Papers.
18. *The Nation,* I, No. 4 (July 27, 1865), 107.
19. *New York Times,* June 1, 1868, p. 5; see also January 15, 1869, p. 2.

During the early years of freedom, a high rate of mortality among Negroes and the emigration of many from the state lent an appearance of validity to the theory that the black race was destined to vanish. However, federal and state censuses soon showed the Negro population as actually increasing. Under such evidence "the vanish theory" rapidly ceased to be a part of the Southerner's thinking. It was supplanted in part by the expectation that the rate of increase among whites would outstrip that of the Negroes and eventually reduce the latter to an insignificant proportion of the total population.

Many whites, perhaps most of those in the middle and lower districts, believed that the incompatibility of the two races would lead to an open "war of the races" in which the Negro would meet his sudden demise.

This attitude, too, was a logical concomitant of a continuing current of ante-bellum Southern thought. Whatever else it might have been, slavery was also a system for keeping Negroes in subjection. Force was more than a convenient element for control; the very real danger of insurrection made it necessary. In South Carolina itself, within the memory of many whites still living during Reconstruction, two widespread conspiracies had been discovered. On July 4, 1816, a score of Negroes in Camden had plotted to seize the state arsenal in that town and thus give arms to a mass of insurrectionists. Five years later, in Charleston, the Denmark Vesey conspiracy was discovered and proved to be even more formidable as a threat to the sense of security of the white community. In addition, Carolinians had constantly before them the horrible examples of actual slave insurrections in other places. They were particularly frightened by a successful revolt of the Negroes of Santo Domingo in the 1790's and by the sanguinary Nat Turner rising in Virginia in 1831. During the 1830's, even as they lavished their intellectual energies upon the elaboration of the proslavery argument, South Carolinians turned their organizational energies toward perfecting a system of slave control unprecedented in severity. The slave code was revamped, repressive legislation for the better regulation of both the free Negro and slave populations enacted, and the traditional method of enforcing the system, the patrol, revitalized.

Ultimately, slavery rested upon force, an overriding, all-pervasive force employed not solely by the relatively few Southerners who owned slaves, but by the white community as a whole. (In a sense, the patrol institutionalized the white community's interest in slavery, in the control of the Negro.) In South Carolina, the patrol was formally begun in the early eighteenth century and, though nominally separate, existed in close conjunction with the militia. Every able, adult white male was constrained to join both groups. For service in the patrol no compensation was given, indicating the spirit of public necessity which lay behind it. Significantly, each district (county) in the state was divided into regiments and each regiment into "beats." The same men who made up the militia company in a beat were organized into several patrols which took turns in maintaining a moving, and, usually, mounted watch on the activities of the Negroes. This group was authorized by law to exercise an immediate discipline over Negroes, both slave and free, which was in many ways more harsh than that which the slaveholder himself was legally granted. Moreover, the slaveholder could not interfere with the patrol as it performed its duties upon his slaves. So central was the patrol to the political and social fabric of South Carolina that its area of responsibility, the beat, became the local area of governmental organization, and the term remained in use until it was changed to "township" by the Republicans in 1868. In its first century of existence, the patrol occasionally lost its alertness. After 1816, however, it was active almost continually, realerted again and again by insurrections, by the discovery of insurrectionary plots, and by rumors of both. Throughout the three decades preceding the war, while the proslavery argument was developing to a crescendo of intensity, and particularly after John Brown's raid, the patrol maintained a feverish activity which abated only slightly after the military situation had attained some stability early in the war. After a century and a half of such surveillance, it is small wonder that Negro folklore produced a song which advised the sable brother, "Run, nigger, run, or the patrol'll get you."[20]

Having lived all their lives under such tension, most whites, particularly those in the heavily Negro districts of the lowcountry, believed that the inevitable result of emancipation and the removal of the restraints previously exercised on the Negro would be racial violence. Significantly, they most often spoke of the expected war of races as if it were a mass insurrection of slaves, as they termed it, a "rising." The mistress of a plantation near Columbia subsequently recalled those first anxious days: "Opposite, in a settlement of our houses left on the lot, the negroes were packed and sang as only they could sing in these times, the nights through, keeping our spirits alive and awake to expectation of a horde pouring into our houses to cut our throats and dance like

20. Thomas J. Kirkland and Robert M. Kennedy, *Historic Camden*, Part 2 (Columbia, 1926), p. 193.

fiends over our remains."[21] Having passed through the lower and middle districts in the summer of 1865, a Northern traveler found this fear "almost universal."[22]

As the summer passed without any widespread insurrection occurring, native whites began to look forward to the Christmas season as the time of rebellion. The Fourth of July (Independence Day!) and Christmas or New Year's Day had marked a large number of insurrections and planned insurrections. Ironically, in South Carolina during the antebellum period, it became almost traditional for whites to anticipate these occasions with anxiety rather than pleasure. After emancipation, far from abating, these apprehensions were greatly increased by the deliberate agitation of some Union officials, army officers, and troops (particularly Negro troops), by the failure of others to present a stern face to the Negro, and by the rising dissatisfaction of Negro laborers with the results of their economic arrangements during the first year of freedom. Hearing in October of a thwarted conspiracy among the Negroes to rebel near Winnsboro, a young Columbia woman fearfully predicted: "They will be tried by a military court in Winnsboro and will not be hung, so that the whole countryside will be unsafe. Dr. Sims stated that the Yankee troops had encouraged their belief that land would be given them and when the higher officers denied this, the negroes became desperate. The negroes are organizing and drilling and will certainly rise."[23] As Christmas approached tension increased. In Abbeville District, a young woman whose husband would be absent during the holidays was invited by Judge Wardlaw, one of the authors of the Black Code, to stay with his family "as there is fear that the negros [sic] on the plantations will rise in rebellion about that time."[24] Early in December, near Fort Motte in Orangeburg District, a young planter was warned by his stockman that his Negro laborers would attack the barns near the end of the month when "hungary came." The thoughts which passed through that young man's mind during the next few weeks were perhaps shared by many white Carolinians. "Adger you have seen nothing over your way of the freedman as [he] really is," he cautioned his brother. "If they are already planning for an attack on barns &c. what are we to look for? I confess I am very anxious. I am

21. Sally Elmore Taylor MS Memoir.
22. *The Nation,* I, No. 4 (July 27, 1865), 107; I, No. 11 (September 14, 1865), 331.
23. Grace B. Elmore MS Diary, entry for October 1, 1865.
24. Rebecca S. Cheves to J. R. Cheves, November 19, 1865, R. S. Cheves Papers.

trying to do my best here, am out early & late, but meet with sour looks, & uncivil words." A week later, the planter, a battle-tested veteran of the Confederate Army, was even more timorous. Denouncing the improvidence of the Negro in a letter to his mother, he added:

> ... And then when to their animal nature, ready for anything like riot or robbery is applied the teachings & drillings, which those negro troops that have infest our country have been so eager to inculcate, when from the ignorant he rises into the bloodthirsty & revengeful brute, eager to possess all he sees, unable to look beyond the present but merely acting under the direction of blind & maddened impulse, of animal desires & passions. Mother I shuddered yesterday, when I was having some hogs killed, to see the fiendish eagerness in some of them to stab & kill, the delight in the suffering of others![25]

Native whites moved to meet the imagined menace with the same spirit, language, and action with which threats of insurrection had been met during the slave period. Governor Perry, in October, 1865, asked the legislature to restore the militia to full strength to guard against "insurrection and domestic violence."[26] The legislature responded with alacrity. The patrol laws were rewritten much as if the Negro were still a slave and candidly looked to the suppression of Negro revolts. By joint resolution the governor was "authorized to employ, as far as may be necessary, the militia and volunteer police forces of this State for the purpose of enforcing the Patrol Laws of the State, so far as they are applicable to the changed condition of society under the new Constitution, and of preserving law and order in the State."[27] The volunteer police force was, of course, the patrol. The new governor, James L. Orr, vetoed the modified patrol law on the ground that any patrol was incompatible with the Negro's freedom. Thereafter, organization of the "volunteer police" as a sort of posse proceeded only slowly despite the circulation of a rumor that a widespread plot had been discovered among the free but oppressed Negroes of Jamaica to rebel on Christmas Eve, burn Kingston, and massacre its citizens.[28] However, early in 1866, the militia was re-established in its traditional form. For instance, General

25. A. T. Smythe to John Smythe, December 5, 1865; A. T. Smythe to his mother, December 12, 1865, A. T. Smythe Letters. For indications of the prevalence of such thinking, see: *The Nation*, I, No. 21 (November 23, 1865), 651.

26. *Intelligencer* (Anderson), November 2, 1865.

27. *Reports and Resolutions* (1865), pp. 195–96.

28. *Intelligencer* (Anderson), November 30, December 7, 14, 1865.

Order Number One for the Ninth Brigade prescribed the same "beat" boundaries which had existed before the war.[29]

The failure of the Negroes to rise in mass rebellion during the winter of 1865–1866 relieved the anxieties of the whites only temporarily. Again, in the following winter, white citizens were gravely concerned over "threats of insurrection" among the Negroes.[30] During the months in which Negro voters were rising to political power, many whites still feared a war of races. A Charleston physician, writing to his brother in February, 1868, anticipated a rebellion in the North against the Radicals, "and we will have to guard ourselves against the negroes while they are fighting it out there."[31] The spectre of Negro insurrection and inter-racial war would mark the mind of the South for many years to come.

At least some whites looked eagerly forward to the vanishing of the Negro race, either by violence or otherwise. Contemporaries believed that such an attitude was particularly prevalent among the less affluent elements of the white community. A Northern traveler in the sand hills southwest of Columbia in December, 1865, lodged a night in the home of a "low white" widow. She had lost a son at Petersburg, but she "niver knowed" why the rich folks brought on the war. "They's lost all their niggers, and she was mighty glad of it. She wished them and the niggers had been at the bottom o' the sea."[32] Such anti-Negro attitudes were hardly less prevalent among late slaveholders. "I am utterly disgusted with the race," wrote one aristocrat, "and trust that I may some day be in a land that is purged of them."[33]

The attitudes evinced by freedmen toward native whites were largely responses to attitudes manifested by whites themselves. In freedom the Negro obviously resented having been held in slavery. But resentment seldom passed into hatred, either against their late masters or against the whites generally, and the desire for revenge was certainly an alien emotion. Even among the fevered agitations of war, Thomas Wentworth Higginson was struck by "the absence of affection and the absence of

29. MS General Order No. 1, 9th Brigade, January 5, 1866, South Carolina Militia Papers.

30. W. J. B. Cooper to a friend, December 11, 1866; S. W. Maurice and others to James L. Orr, December 11, 1866, Freedmen File; J. A. Mitchell to his sister, December 5, 1866, J. A. Mitchell Papers.

31. J. B. Elliott to Habersham Elliott, February 2, 1866, Habersham Elliott Papers.

32. *The Nation*, II, No. 28 (January 11, 1866), 47.

33. H. W. Ravenel to A. L. Taveau, June 27, 1865, A. L. Taveau Papers.

revenge" in the feelings of his Negro troops toward their former owners. "It was not the individual, but the ownership, of which they complained," he interpreted.[34]

Negroes were nonplused by white anxiety. "What for we rise?" scoffed a Charleston Negro in the summer of 1865, "we have our freedom now."[35] The inevitable "war of races" was also discounted by the Negro leadership. "Have you any fear of a war of races here, in this State?" asked a Northerner of Beverly Nash in 1867. "Oh, no!" Nash answered. "I hope not. I don't see why we should not all live peaceably together."[36]

Even though Negroes were not liable to engage in any general armed rebellion against the whites, they nevertheless resented the assumptions of the proslavery argument and the subordinate status in society which these assumptions assigned to them. In slavery they had resisted subjection by rebellion, flight, sabotage, incendiarism, insolence, and a thousand and one minor defiances. In freedom the Negro resented attempts at his subordination as he had resented slavery, and he expressed his resentment by the same means. As he gained political power, he added new forms of resistance, and the feelings of the race found voice in an articulate, burgeoning leadership. He asserted the equality of his race with others; or, rather, he declared the cultural meaninglessness of race. "All bloods are one," cried the Reverend Henry Turner, a Carolina-born Negro who had recruited colored troops in Washington during the war, to a mass meeting of Negroes in Columbia in April, 1867. "The difference of race is nothing," he continued, arguing that it was simply the result of climatic variations. What he wanted was "universally equal rights—white, negro, Indian—all, without reference to the flatness of his nose or the length of his heel."[37] The Negro also argued that his intelligence, his integrity, and his capacity fitted him for participation in the ordinary affairs of society. Once in power, he moved to achieve this goal, and he saw no halfway house in freedom.

Negroes, collectively, were suspicious of the intentions of the white community as a group. They frequently assumed that the whites were plotting to damage them in their posture as free men; and the plot, they believed, often included violence. A case in point occurred in the village

34. Thomas Wentworth Higginson, *Army Life in a Black Regiment* (Boston, 1890), pp. 249–50.
35. *The Nation,* I, No. 11 (September 14, 1865), 331–32.
36. *New York Times,* August 9, 1867, p. 2.
37. *Ibid.,* May 5, 1867, p. 1.

of Anderson in July, 1868. Mary, a Negro girl of "notorious" reputation, suddenly disappeared from the village. The Negroes, convinced that she had been killed by the whites and her body thrown into a near-by river, "drug" the stream in search of the corpse. After much agitation within the Negro community, a white man reported having seen Mary in Walhalla, a village some forty miles distant by rail. The Negroes distrusted the testimony of the white man, saying that it was a trick conceived by the whites to halt their investigation. The Negro community then sent an agent to Walhalla, where he found and interviewed Mary. He returned to Anderson and reported his conversation with the girl in detail. Still, most of the Negroes refused to believe the girl had not been murdered by the whites, saying that the whites had bribed their emissary to tell this story.[38]

The attitudes thus assumed by each race toward the other made friction between them inevitable. Frequently, the conflict ended with a feeling of irritation; often it flared into open violence, and occasionally the violence assumed a horrendous magnitude.

Irritation between the races was a continuing occurrence, correlated in large measure with the assertiveness of Negroes. In the early postwar months, many whites were offended by the mere freedom of their slaves. Many directed their irritation not at the liberators but toward the freedmen themselves. In July, 1865, for instance, a Cooper River rice planter complained that the freedmen were disgustingly presumptuous and revealingly confessed that many Negroes he had liked best as slaves he now disliked most.[39] Difficulties in adjusting to a new economic order often gave positive substance to irritation, but as Negroes gained political power occasions for racial friction multiplied. That the Negro had become a voter was a thorn in the side of many native whites. In the presidential election of 1868, one ancient aristocrat regretted that he could not support Chase because "he goes for Negro suffrage, which is so horrible to us."[40] Several months later, the best advice which a dying man could give to his body servant was: "Miles, serve your God, and let politics alone."[41] The presumption of the Negro in seeking public office still further exasperated the whites. Noting that a mulatto had been nominated for secretary of state by the Republicans in 1868, a

38. *Intelligencer* (Anderson), July 29, 1868.
39. [—.—.] Deas to his daughter, July 1, 1865, [—.—.] Deas Papers.
40. William Heyward to James Gregorie, June 15, 1868, Gregorie–Elliott Papers.
41. Anonymous to Mrs. Cicero Adams, February 11, 1869, N. A. Nicholson Papers.

Charleston physician pronounced South Carolina "a miserable land to live in."[42] Seeing Negroes actually in office heightened the outrage. As the big guns noisily saluted the inauguration of South Carolina's first Republican governor in July, 1868, the widow of an old planter sat in her house near the campus of the University writing to her daughter in Charleston, struggling to find words sufficiently vitriolic to describe the "crow-congress," the "monkey-show," the "menagerie" which was the legislature and the "Yankee-nigger government programe" which was the constitution.[43]

Native whites were not always able to abstain from contact with Negro officials, and they seldom came away from such encounters without a feeling of having been degraded. "We are being made, however, day by day, to realize the equalities of all things," complained a Charleston lady, "and brings to my mind the scenes I have read of during the Revolution in France of the hundred days, when the Nobility were so terribly treated. Surely our humiliation has been great when a Black Postmaster is established here at Headquarters and our *Gentlemen's Sons* to work under his biddings."[44] Neither was the native white lawyer in a commanding position when pleading before a Negro judge or Negro jurors. A lawyer who had left the state chided one who had remained, suggesting a typical reaction: "Well, Dick, you have a charming Supreme Court in S. C. now—a contemptible scallawag occupying the seat once adorned by O'Neal and Dunkin, and two carpet baggers (& one of them a *negro*) in the seats once graced by Wardlaw & Withers. How do you feel before such a Bench? When you address such creatures as 'your Honors,' dont the blood boil or grow chill in your veins? and how can you say 'Gentlemen of the Jury' to a panel of loathsome, leather-headed negroes?"[45] After appearing before this Supreme Court, another lawyer pronounced it "a damnable farce!"[46] Occasionally, however, whites found themselves totally under the thumb of Negro authorities. A native white inmate of the insane asylum wrote to a friend in the ministry asking his help in securing his discharge. The minister advised him to read his Bible. The patient replied with more than paranoic emotion that "if the stupid Negroes who act as Regents of

42. J. B. Elliott to Habersham Elliott, February 2, 1868, Habersham Elliott Papers.

43. Louisa S. McCord to her daughter, July 9, 1868, A. T. Smythe Letters.

44. Eliza T. Holmes to Mary Boykin Chesnut, April 8, 1873, Williams–Chesnut–Manning Papers.

45. A. W. Dozier to Richard Dozier, March 21, 1870, R. W. Dozier Papers.

46. B. W. Rutledge to G. W. Spencer, February 6, 1870, G. W. Spencer Papers.

this Institution had read the Bible as much or as long as either my Wife or I have done, they would not need when sitting as a board on Such Cases as mine, to ask the Stupid and insulting questions that some of them now do when exercising their brief authority While I appear before them."[47]

Irritations might have remained merely irritations had there not been individuals on both sides who were prone, almost eager, to do violence to members of the other race.

To an extent, a readiness for violence was a part of the social order of the white community and was not pointed directly at Negroes. On occasion, the "code of honor" might demand that the most refined white citizen commit mayhem upon his fellows. One Bureau officer thought that poor whites sometimes murdered "black 'uns" not because of their color, "but simply kill them in the exercise of their ordinary pugnacity."[48] Nevertheless, even in slavery the Negro had been a special object of violence by the militant element in the white community, a violence from which a slave's pecuniary value did not always exempt him. Physical force and the threat of bodily harm was, traditionally, the ultimate means of controlling the Negro. Such was the case in slavery, and it did not cease to be so afterward.

The Negro was well aware, and doubtless the whites intended that he should be, that aggressiveness on his part would draw down upon him sudden, overwhelming, and awful violence. Particularly in periods of political turmoil, the threat became general and darkly menacing. In the heat of the campaign of 1876, an Abbeville farmer wrote to his cousin in North Carolina: "The Negroes here are more uneasy than they have ever before been, and not without very good reasons either, for there is a great many whites will hurt them with just the least provocation."[49]

Readiness for violence was not the exclusive monopoly of the white man. Yet, as with the whites, not all of the violent propensities of Negroes were directed against whites for racial reasons. Negroes subscribed in full to the "code" idolized by the whites, and, while the Negro's rationales may not have been as elaborately matured, the results were equally bloody. As Negroes organized politically, their potential for violence was more often turned against the whites as a race. It was,

47. J. H. Cathcart to W. H. Hemphill, January 4, 1875, Hemphill Papers.
48. Croushore and Potter, *A Union Officer*, p. 153.
49. J. L. Harris to J. W. Holland, July 11, 1876, J. W. Holland Papers.

after all, but a short step from fighting to gain one's freedom to fighting to preserve it. During the campaign of 1876, R. H. Cain was reported to have written in the *Missionary Record* and repeated to a large gathering of Negroes in Charleston: "There are 80,000 black men in the State who can use Winchesters and 200,000 black women who can light a torch and use a knife." During the same period, Negro women were reported to be "carrying axes or hatchets in their hands hanging down at their sides, their aprons or dresses half-concealing the weapons."[50]

There were numerous incidents, of course, in which individual whites assaulted Negroes for reasons in some degree attributable to racial differences. In the summer of 1865, William Lemons, a hotel clerk in Newberry, attacked and beat Burrel Mayes, a mulatto, for asking Lemons to hold his carpetbag. Interestingly, Mayes was nearly white and had served as a Confederate soldier, enlisting in Columbia, it was said, under the name of John Brown.[51] Contrary to tradition, Negroes also instigated and won violent encounters with whites. In the spring of 1870, an Abbeville planter wrote to a friend in Virginia that, "One negro has with the assistance of others whipped and beat three white men at Abbeville Court-House one of them was John Turner from Buck Level. This negro I expect will be the next Sheriff. He speaks of running for the office. If he runs he will be sure to be elected and we will be in a worse fix than now."[52] Similarly, in 1876, a medical student in Charleston related the experience of a young friend who "was walking with the young ladies and a negro run against them, when they were near home, after Turner got them home he went back and went for the 'nig' and was giving him 'fits' when two other negroes came up and doubled on him, and one of them struck him in the head with a brick bat, which laid him out for a while. Then they ran off."[53]

More indicative of racial antagonisms were recurrent conflicts involving more or less organized groups of whites and Negroes. In such encounters individuals frequently were not personally acquainted with their opponents and recognized the enemy solely by the color of his skin. Here, obviously, the color line was distinctly drawn. During Reconstruction, violence of this nature fell into four rather distinct, non-successive phases. The first phase followed immediately after the war and continued for approximately a year. It was characterized by riots

50. Myrta Lockett Avary, *Dixie after the War* (New York, 1906), p. 362.
51. *Intelligencer* (Anderson), July 27, 1865.
52. A. W. Moore to E. H. Dabbs, April 30, 1870, A. L. Burt Papers.
53. J. E. Renwick to his brother, January 5, 1876, W. W. Renwick Papers.

almost devoid of political content. The second phase, beginning with the
political elevation of the Negro and terminating with the end of the
elections of 1868, produced violence which arose from altered political
conditions. In the third period, from October, 1870, through the summer
of 1871, the so-called Ku Klux Klan disturbances reached their height.
Violence in the final and most fevered period coincided with the
campaign of 1876.

Between July, 1865, and November, 1866, there were three major race
riots in South Carolina. Two of these were between white Union
soldiers and Negroes. After a shooting skirmish in the Market Place
in Charleston on Saturday, July 8, organized groups of a New York
Zouave regiment kept up a running fight with Negro soldiers of the
Twenty-first United States Colored Troops (formerly the Third South
Carolina) well into the following week. The riot was stopped only by
exiling the Zouaves to Morris Island.[54] In Marion, in the spring of 1866,
a gang of soldiers went on a spree which ended with the burning of the
house of "courtesan" Kate Lewis (color unknown) and the building
used as a school for the freed people, "several of whom were beaten
quite severely."[55] More accurately suggestive of things to come was
a riot which occurred between native whites and Negro Charlestonians
in June, 1866. A scene typical of this and later riots was staged on
Sunday, June 24, at 8:00 in the evening. At that time, a mob of about
twenty-five Negroes turned into Tradd Street from King and halted in
the front yard of a house where a young man, George F. Ahrens, stood
on the portico watching them. Presently, a white man, Richard M.
Brantford, happened to turn into Tradd from Orange Street at the opposite end of the block. Perceiving the militant disposition of the
Negroes, he tried to run away. With cries of "Charge" and "Fire" by
several of the Negroes, they hurled a shower of bricks on the fleeing

54. *New York Times,* July 16, p. 3; 24, p. 2, 1865.
55. *Intelligencer* (Anderson), April 19, 1866, quoting the Marion *Star.* Antagonism between Northern white troops and Southern Negroes was, of course,
not unusual. Higginson had seen it in the islands during the war. Higginson,
Black Regiment, pp. 16, 251. Native whites were alert to record a continuation
of this attitude among the occupation forces. A young student in Columbia in
October, 1868, wrote that the men of the garrison "are itching to get a shot at
the negroes and the officers too if they try to take the nigger side, for they are
radical mostly." Edward R. Crosland to his mother, October 31, 1868, Edward
Crosland Papers. For the existence of the same spirit during the Ku Klux riots,
see J. M. Dennis to J. Y. Harris, July 6, 1871, J. Y. Harris Papers.

Brantford. The first missile thrown hit the fugitive in the back. Then one of many struck his head and he fell to the pavement. Scipio Fraser, one of the rioters, shouted "Kill the rebel son of a bitch." "Then the crowd gathered around him, as he lay on the ground," Ahrens testified, "kicked him and struck him with brick bats. They then left him and I saw two colored men come up Tradd Street, picked up Brantford and carried him home.... The same evening ... Scipio Fraser came into my yard and was talking about the riot. He said: 'I, and no one else, killed the rebel son of a bitch, and he is not the first, nor he will not be the last I will kill.' "[56] A week later, Charleston was still racked by sporadic fighting.[57]

In the interior during this period, violence of the mass sort was characterized by the assaults of roving bands of outlaws upon hapless Negroes who came their way. In addition, more or less respectable groups of white citizens organized as "home police," or vigilantes, or militia attempted to keep the Negro population under control. In Orangeburg District, in November, 1866, the first clear case of lynching occurred when a mob of whites summarily dispatched two Negro men who had, allegedly, "way-laid" on the road and "killed with axes" a widow and her eight-year-old daughter.[58]

A second wave of violence coincided with the rise of the Negro to political power. During this period, Negroes were as often the aggressors as were the whites. In the fall of 1867, the Union League Club of Hunnicutt's Crossing in Pickens District, after killing a young man in a fight with the white membership of a local debating club, assumed control of the neighborhood. For several days, they marched about in a military fashion, bearing arms, arresting and imprisoning whites whom they accused of participating in the riot.[59] Several months later, in Orangeburg District, "a military company of negroes" surrounded the house of a Mr. Hane who, supposedly, had shot a Negro. They held the white man as a prisoner "with the avowed intention of hanging him in case the wounded negro should die." Hane was later delivered to a magistrate, but the whites learned that the lynch rope in Orangeburg was racially impartial.[60] As the Republicans progressed to political

56. *House Journal* (Special Session, 1868), pp. 169–73.

57. *New York Times,* July 10, 1866, p. 5.

58. David Gavin MS Diary, II, 404; *New York Times,* November 20, 1867, p. 5.

59. *Report of the Secretary of War* (1867), I, 370–467.

60. *New York Times,* January 10, 1868, p. 8.

dominance, Negroes became increasingly restless. In several areas incendiarism was rampant, and in Williamsburg District and on John's
Island large groups of Negroes were said to be organizing militarily, in
the latter case "to patrol the island and keep down the white people."[61]

Anxious elements within the white community retaliated in kind,
particularly in the upcountry counties where the Negro population was
not in an overwhelming majority. In its most violent form, white retaliation was an irregular campaign of terrorism against Radical leaders.
Interestingly, the whites reacted violently only after the state elections of
1868 had been lost, and there was no hint at the time (though this certainly came later) that any such organization as the Ku Klux Klan lay
behind it. On June 1, 1868, Solomon George Washington Dill, senator-
elect from Kershaw District, was assassinated in his home.[62] When the
legislature convened several weeks later, members were mysteriously
warned that if they dared return to their homes after the session they
would be killed. As a Northern-born Negro member later declared, on
the eve of adjournment each member asked himself, "Will it be I?"[63]
Shortly after the close of the session, James Martin, an Irish immigrant
who had become a Radical member from Abbeville, was "pursued by a
gang of ruffians" from Abbeville Courthouse and killed.[64] In mid-
October, B. F. Randolph, a Northern-born Negro Methodist clergyman,
was shot dead by unknown parties at Donaldsville, while on a speaking
tour.[65] Several days after Randolph's demise, the president of the Union
League Club in Newberry, a Negro named Lee Nance, was assassinated
in his front yard by a band of mounted whites.[66]

The organization of the Negro militia was the specific Radical
answer to these offerings of violence by the whites. When the legislature reconvened during the winter of 1869, it hastened to pass the law
necessary to organize the militia fully. It also authorized the governor to

61. MS petition of several citizens of Kingstree to Governor James L. Orr,
July 26, 1868, Freedmen File; New York Times, September 28, 1868, p. 5.

62. Kirkland and Kennedy, Historic Camden, p. 201.

63. New York Times, October 22, 1868, p. 5; House Journal (1868–1869), p. 46.

64. House Journal (1868–1869), p. 27.

65. Intelligencer (Anderson), October 21, 1868; New York Times, October 19,
p. 1; 28, p. 5, 1868. Interestingly, the assailants in each of these cases were never
satisfactorily identified. A white man of doubtful sanity confessed to killing
Randolph for money, but before he identified his employer or employers the
supposed assassin was, himself, killed by persons unknown. Journal (Bennettsville),
December 24, 1868; Southern Enterprise (Greenville), December 8, 1869.

66. Intelligencer (Anderson), October 28, 1868, quoting the Newberry Herald,
October 21, 1868.

buy 2,000 stand of arms "of the most approved pattern."[67] However, even as the legislature acted, violent outbursts became less frequent and by late spring had virtually ceased. Politicians promptly pre-empted the higher ranks in the militia and the paper organization was completed, but only a few local units were actually established.

During the spring of 1870, the situation changed drastically when incumbent Governor Scott deliberately revitalized the militia and transformed it into a giant political machine for use in combatting his enemies within and outside of the Republican party. Legally, white men could have joined the militia as enlisted men; indeed, technically, they were required to join. In reality, however, whites simply refused to serve in militia companies in which Negroes were their equals or, occasionally, their superiors, and the governor refused to accept all-white companies. Therefore, whites were effectively excluded. But there was no dearth of Negro volunteers. Few young men could resist the attractions of militia service: dashing, varicolored uniforms, shining arms and clattering accoutrements, the roll of the drum, the intricate and endless ritual of the drill, and the incomparable comaraderie of fellows under arms. On the eve of the election of 1870, the militia rolls had swelled to include more than ninety thousand men. The highest ranks were of course, held by Scott's friends; but the key officers were actually the captains of local companies. Almost invariably, they were strong characters in the Negro community, sometimes noted for their prudence, often for their bellicosity. Demanding and, frequently, enjoying the complete loyalty of their men, they often failed to accord the same measure of loyalty to their nominal commanders. Some of them used their men badly, deliberately maneuvering them in ways menacing to the whites or calling out their companies to settle personal grudges.

Ultimately, the so-called Ku Klux riots of 1870–1871 occurred not because Negroes were organized in militia companies, but because the Negro militia was, in certain areas, heavily and effectively armed. From the Southern white's point of view, a well-armed Negro militia was precisely what John Brown had sought to achieve at Harper's Ferry in 1859. It was, in short, an insurrection with a high potential for disaster. The Ku Klux riots, it is true, did have a political flavor; but the flavor was of frustration, not hope. It is highly significant that the first outbreak on October 19, 1870, occurred only after the election was over. Having lost the state elections, native whites were bitter, but no white leader seemed to think that any amount of violence would recall the

67. House Journal (1868–1869), p. 131; New York Times, April 21, 1869, p. 2.

results of the election or improve the political prospectus for 1872. Quite clearly, the Ku Klux riots were also influenced by any number of local and personal enmities, but these were merely ancillary to the main body. Whites were also irritated and alarmed by the very existence of the Negro militia, but irritation and fear led to action only when and where the militia was armed.

This conclusion is supported by the fact that the counties which suffered most from violence were also the counties in which the Negro militia was most heavily and effectively armed. Since Scott had arms enough for barely a tenth of his force, he chose to issue the bulk of those in counties where the normal Republican majority was jeopardized by white intimidation. To the Laurens militia, he sent 620 breech-loading, rifled muskets, 50 Winchester rifles, and 18,000 rounds of ammunition, that is, roughly 10 per cent of the total distributed. It was in Laurens that the first and bloodiest of the riots took place. Comparably large quantities of arms and ammunition were dispatched to the militia in Spartanburg, Newberry, Union, Chester, York, Fairfield, Kershaw, and Edgefield counties. Each of these was also a center for large-scale violence. On the other hand, no arms were issued in the heavily white counties of Oconee, Pickens, and Greenville, and only 96 muskets were sent to Anderson and Abbeville counties together. In each of these areas, there were no significant outbreaks. The same pattern generally prevailed in the lowcountry where the Negro population was heavy. In the Fifth Regiment, centering in Marion and Georgetown, only ninety muskets were given the militia and no riots occurred. The only exceptions were Charleston and Beaufort countries where the militia was both well organized and well armed. Here, however, the primary purpose was probably exhibitory rather than militant.[68]

The signal importance of arming the militia in precipitating the Ku Klux disturbances was also revealed in the unerring, almost instinctive accuracy with which even the least organized white mobs focused as if by careful concensus upon the seizure of the arsenals of the militia as their goal. This was dramatically evident in the Laurens riot. Since early September, 1870, whites had been aware that a large quantity of arms and ammunition had been received by the local militia and stored by them in their armory on main street and in the fortresslike barn behind the house of their colonel. Beginning with a fist-fight between a native white and a carpetbagger on the town square, within a few minutes and apparently spontaneously the struggle grew into a shooting

68. *Reports and Resolutions* (1870–1871), pp. 521–611.

attack on the militia's armory. During the next few hours, the "volunteer police" managed, quite legally, to seize all of the guns in both the armory and the barn and deposit them in the courthouse. Within a day after the militia was disarmed, violence ceased.[69] In Newberry, York, Chester, and Union counties confrontations and running battles between the Negro militia and white "citizen's committees" produced the same result.[70] In Spartanburg, the same pattern developed over a period of several months. On September 23, 1870, in Columbia, 192 breech-loading, rifled muskets were drawn for the Spartanburg militia.[71] On the following day, whites in Spartanburg were greatly agitated by a rumor that twenty-four boxes of Winchesters and seven boxes of ammunition had arrived for the militia and were stored in the county jail. On November 17, some twenty to fifty men, "fantasticly attired," unsuccessfully assaulted the jail. Thereafter, the arms were secreted by the authorities. During the ensuing four months a rash of Ku Klux visitations broke the peace of the county. A number of those visited were militiamen, whose houses were searched for arms. On March 22, 1871, the last large-scale raid was made on the house of a man whose son was the local militia brigadier. It was suspected that the arms had been hidden there. In Spartanburg, as elsewhere, peace was restored only after the arms were withdrawn.[72]

To label these riots the result of a Ku Klux "conspiracy" is inaccurate and misleading. These affrays were largely spontaneous. There was no conspiracy above the very local level, and often none existed there. There were local organizations of Klansmen in South Carolina in 1870 and 1871, but it is highly doubtful that any of these were organized before this time and it is a virtual certainty that no statewide or even widespread organization of the order ever existed. In the Laurens riot, the most murderous of the sequence, white participants made no attempt to disguise themselves in the fashion of the Klan and were not members of that society. Yet, the racial and social objects of the Klan were in perfect harmony with the objects of the white community, and it was hardly necessary for white males to swear solemn oaths, perform rituals,

69. The complete story of the Laurens riot is provided by an eye-witness, Mary Motte, in a series of letters to her son in Missouri. Mary Motte to Robert Motte, September 3, 1866, and following, J. R. and Mary Motte Papers.

70. *New York Times*, March 13, p. 3; April 28, p. 1, 1871; *Ku Klux Conspiracy*, Vols. III, IV, V.

71. *Reports and Resolutions* (1870–1871), p. 593.

72. *A History of Spartanburg County*, pp. 150, 153–54, 156; *Ku Klux Conspiracy*, Vols. III, IV, V.

and wear costumes to pursue the same ends. There was a unity of feeling and action in the white community which rendered forms unimportant. Actually, all those more or less impromptu organizations which the Radicals chose to call Klans were only up-dated versions of the patrol, revitalized to meet still another "rising" by the Negroes. This was probably what the editor of the *Nation* meant when he very astutely observed that "the South before the war was one vast Ku-Klux Klan."[73]

The published record suggests that all responsible leaders of the white community deprecated the lawlessness of the rioters. However, private correspondence indicates that the great mass of white Carolinians were pleased by the results of a terrorist program. "It may seem very disloyal & Ku Kluxish in me, but I am exceedingly delighted at the Union & York 'outrages (?),' " wrote a Georgetown druggist in February, 1871, concluding that such events "will teach the misguided African to stand in the subordinate position nature intended."[74] In Chester County, planter Robert Hemphill noted that one of his Negro neighbors was visited by the Klan for "having guns in store, & . . . acting the Big man & fool generally," and another was threatened by the Klan for having, in his capacity as overseer of a public road, "ordered out his hands, & among them some white men which gave offence." Declared Hemphill, "The K. K.s are an excellent institution if kept in proper bounds. They have been of immense benefit in our county."[75] In Spartanburg, a small farmer hoped that the Klan would so frighten Negro legislators that they would resign and prevent his being "sold out for taxes in a year or to more." He explained: "There is a new sort of beings got up called KKs that has made a powerful show. These kks whip and kill as they pleas."[76] One group of Klansmen fleeing across Edgefield county in November, 1871, en route to political asylum in Georgia probably never discovered that the band of mounted men pursuing them were not irate federals but local citizens fervently attempting to congratulate them upon their work.[77] When alleged Klansmen were arrested, virtually the entire white community leaped to their

73. *The Nation*, VII, No. 167 (September 10, 1868), 204.

74. T. P. Bailey to R. H. McKie, February 20, 1871, R. H. McKie Papers.

75. R. N. Hemphill to W. R. Hemphill, April 20, May 9, 1871, Hemphill Papers.

76. Edward Lipscomb to Smith Lipscomb, April 11, 1871, Edward Lipscomb Papers.

77. Anonymous to Dr. James Renwick, November 14, 1871, W. W. Renwick Papers.

defense.[78] After several were convicted, the white community negotiated for their freedom much as if they were soldiers taken as prisoners of war. Quite obviously, the mass of native whites felt that a little Klanning was a good thing.

As an instrument for disarming the Negro militia, violence was a success. As a political tool promising ultimate victory, however, terrorism was a failure. Negroes were indeed frightened, but they were neither scared into the Democracy nor away from Republicanism. Moreover, violence simply provided more excellent grist for the Radical mill, allowing Northern Republicans to profit electorally at home by waving the freshly bloodied shirt and Southern Republicans to invoke the aid of the federal military. Finally, Negroes themselves might be driven to meet violence with violence, and in the lowcountry this could only mean disaster for the whites. Rather deliberately, the white leadership weighed the consequences of further violence and, during the winter and spring of 1871, moved to halt it. On March 13, a native white delegation waited on Governor Scott and secured his promise to recall the arms of the militia, since, as Scott asserted, "their arms provoked asaults and violence that otherwise would not have arisen."[79] In the following month, Scott kept his promise. Responding, the white leadership took to the stump and by mid-summer, 1871, had squelched the riotous elements as decisively as if the mobs had been under their military command. Ironically, in Spartanburg, where a series of public meetings were held for this purpose, one of the speakers was a legislator who had been a local Klan leader.[80]

The fear of some white leaders that Klan violence might lead to retaliation by Negroes was well grounded in fact. In the middle and lower portions of the state, indignation within the Negro community was marked. Late in March, 1871, a resident of Georgetown reported that the "negroes here of late have become quite outrageous in the town . . ."[81] On July 1, 1871, in Barnwell County a group of twenty-five armed Negroes attacked the house of a white man who had reputedly wronged one of their number. They wounded the owner, his wife, and his mother and killed a white man who happened to be visit-

78. Wade Hampton was a leading organizer in a statewide movement to raise money and engage lawyers to defend supposed Klansmen. Wade Hampton to A. L. Burt, October 22, November 25, 1871, A. L. Burt Papers.
79. *New York Times*, March 22, 1871, p. 2.
80. *A History of Spartanburg County*, pp. 153–54.
81. T. P. Bailey to R. H. McKie, March 27, 1871, R. H. McKie Papers.

ing the owner at the time of the raid.[82] In Camden, three days later
(on the fifty-fifth anniversary of a major insurrectionary threat), the
Negro militia attempted to rescue one of their number from the town
marshal by whom he had been arrested. A riot was narrowly averted
only by the intervention of cooler heads which prevented "the street
from flowing with blood."[83]

During the summer, the white community itself put a stop to further
Ku Klux outbreaks; nevertheless, in October, Scott persuaded Grant to
suspend the operation of the writ of *habeas corpus* in nine counties, some
of which had been the scene of only minor disturbances. The military
moved in and hundreds of arrests were made. The proceedings were
long drawn out. In hearings before federal commissioners, presentments
of grand juries, and finally on trial before federal district courts in
Columbia and Charleston, stories of Ku Klux atrocities were repeated
in all their brutal and gory detail again and again. Even some conservative native whites were revolted by the awful exhibition.[84] However, the
great mass of native whites learned only one lesson: that a show of force
in areas where they were numerically strong brought about similar displays in areas where Negroes were safely in the majority, and that the
continued use of violence ultimately produced a crushing imposition of
federal power. Under the circumstances, force was seen to be an instrument of restricted usefulness. For some five years after the summer of
1871, with only sporadic and scattered interruptions, the white community sought to gain its ends through persuasion rather than force.

By 1876, political prospects had changed. Only three Southern states
remained under Radical control. The last to free itself had been Mississippi which, in 1875, had combined the careful, controlled use of force
with the threat of unlimited violence to overwhelm its Negro majority.
During the Redemption struggle in Mississippi, the Grant administration
had shown itself unwilling to intervene as it had, say, in South Carolina
in 1871. South Carolina consciously and deliberately took its cue from
Mississippi.

The instrument which a major element of the Redeemer leadership
forged to do violence upon and to threaten the Negro voter was the
"Rifle" and "Sabre" Clubs. The forging began in Edgefield, Barnwell,
and Aiken counties during the campaign of 1874 when the Negro

82. *New York Times,* July 4, 1871, p. 1.
83. Kirkland and Kennedy, *Historic Camden,* pp. 208–09.
84. A. M. Seibels to John Fox, December 24, 1871, John Fox Papers.

militia of Edgefield was again supplied with state arms. The whites reacted by organizing themselves into rifle and sabre clubs, many of which had existed in previous times as social clubs more or less devoted to the cultivation of the military arts. In this instance, conflict was averted by the timely arrival of United States troops. Presumably peace was restored by Governor Chamberlain's withdrawal of the arms of the militia and ordering the dissolution of all military organizations, both Negro and white, within the county.[85] However, far from dissolving, the white clubs remained active and, indeed, proliferated throughout the state. By the summer of 1875, the captain of a club in Abbeville had the temerity to ask the governor to supply his men with arms.[86] As the more violent element in the Redeemer leadership became increasingly strong after the fall of 1875, these military clubs emerged as a primary political tool.

The first and highly successful use of force was made by the whites of Edgefield, Barnwell, and Aiken counties, a stronghold of the militant "straightout" Democracy. Early in the spring of 1876, the Negro population in this area grew restive. Doubtless they heard the false rumor that several Negroes had been lynched in Edgefield for the murder of a white couple. Meanwhile, a displaced Negro politician from Georgia named Doc Adams was allowed to re-organize and re-arm a Negro militia company in Hamburg. A village of some five hundred people, Hamburg was unique. Lying directly across the Savannah River from Augusta, it had been a major depot on the route connecting Charleston with the upcountry. After a railroad bridge was built between Hamburg and Augusta, the village declined rapidly. By 1876, it had become partly a ghost city, inhabited almost exclusively by Negroes and governed completely by Negro officers. Its most important citizen was Prince Rivers, recently the first sergeant of the First South Carolina Regiment of Volunteers and, for several years, a leading member in the legislature. In the summer of 1876, Rivers was both the trial justice for the Hamburg area and a major general of militia. He had originally organized Hamburg's militia company in 1870 as a part of the Scott campaign. Since that time the unit hardly existed other than on paper. Under Adams, however, the company included about eighty men who drilled frequently in the streets of Hamburg and were armed with the best Winchester rifles. The sequel is worthy of close scrutiny because it

85. *New York Times,* September 1, p. 5; 27, p. 1; 28, p. 1; October 6, p. 1; 7, p. 1; December 1, p. 1, 1874; January 22, p. 6; 27, p. 6; 30, p. 4, 1875.

86. R. R. Hemphill to D. H. Chamberlain, August 25, 1875, Hemphill Papers.

indicates the manner and spirit in which white Democrats used force in the campaign of 1876.

On July 4, 1876, Adams was drilling his company on a deserted street in Hamburg when two young white men approached in a buggy. Finding the militia obstructing their advance, the whites demanded the right of way. After a hostile exchange, both parties retired. Later, the father of one of the young men retained Matthew C. Butler to press charges against Adams and other officers of the company for obstructing the highways. Butler, recently a major-general of Confederate cavalry and a prominent Reform politician, was a leading lawyer of Edgefield, and most importantly, a leader if not the commander of the Edgefield County rifle and sabre clubs.

On Saturday morning, July 8, General Butler called on Rivers and demanded that he investigate, in his capacity as trial justice, Adams's conduct in the incident. In the negotiations which ensued, Adams declined to accede to Butler's demands, first, that his militia surrender their arms and, second, that the captain apologize personally to the young men. Finally, the militia refused the advice of Rivers that they give up their rifles and withdrew to their armory, a large brick structure standing alone near the bank of the Savannah.

The primary object of the whites in pressing the issue, apparently, was the disarming of the Hamburg militia. One of the militiamen had been told by a white friend on the day before the riot that their arms were to be taken by force if necessary. Also, a white citizen of Hamburg subsequently testified that he had overheard General Butler tell another man Saturday afternoon before the riot that "they wanted those guns and were bound to have them." Yet the circumstances suggest that the whites preferred taking the arms by force rather than having them surrendered. In adding his demand for a personal apology to terms which were already unacceptable to the Negroes, Butler probably hoped to push the issue to a forceful settlement. Furthermore, the whites were obviously prepared for a fight. Immediately after the militia retired to its armory, several rifle and saber clubs from remote parts of the county appeared on the scene and must have been in the saddle well before this impasse was reached. Militant Redeemers were set to provide the Negro voter with a horrible example of the awful force which lay behind the white man's threats.

The whites quickly surrounded the armory. At 7:30, filling the still summer air with rebel yells, they opened fire. The militia answered in kind. Thirty minutes later, the Negroes drew first blood. McKie Meriwether, aged nineteen, was killed instantly when struck in the head by a Minie ball. The whites then wheeled in a cannon from Augusta and fired two rounds of grape and two of scrap into the armory, driving the defenders into the cellar. About ten o'clock, the Negro marshal of Hamburg was cut down by rifle fire as he attempted to escape across a fence at the rear of the armory. The first lieutenant of the militia company was captured as he fled and was shot down in the midst of his captors while General Butler was questioning him. At eleven o'clock, the armory was stormed and by midnight the town had been thoroughly sacked and twenty-nine Negroes captured, not all of whom belonged to the militia. Doc Adams was one of those who escaped.

At one o'clock Sunday morning, Butler departed, ordering a detail of twenty-five men to escort the prisoners to the county jail in Aiken. Enroute the guard separated four of the most prominent Negro leaders from the rest, took them aside and ordered them to run. As they ran, three of the guards shot them down. Several other Negro leaders were saved from the same fate by a party of Georgians in the guard who, after much pleading, were allowed to take them to Augusta. The main body of prisoners were then ordered to run and the guards fired into them with undetermined effect.[87]

The reaction of the native whites to the Hamburg riot was much the same as the response evoked by the Ku Klux raids. The Conservative press generally deplored such outrages, but, as Chamberlain observed, these disturbances were seen to have practical advantages for the whites which induced them "to overlook the naked brutality of the occurrence, and seek to find some excuse or explanation of conduct which ought to receive only unqualified abhorrence and condemnation . . ."[88] The response of the Reverend Cornish substantiated Chamberlain's analysis. Even after attending the hearing in which Butler and some seventy or eighty other rioters were arraigned, Cornish refused to

87. There are numerous contemporary accounts of the Hamburg Riot, each having a pronounced political bias. The most informative reports are contained in: *South Carolina in 1876. Testimony as to the Denial of the Elective Franchise in South Carolina at the Election of 1875 and 1876*, Sen. Misc. Doc. No. 48 (3 vols.), 44th Cong., 2nd Sess. (Cited hereinafter as *South Carolina in 1876); Recent Election in South Carolina, Testimony Taken by the Select Committee on the Recent Election in South Carolina*, House Misc. Doc. No. 31 (3 parts), 44th Cong., 2nd Sess. (Cited hereinafter as *Recent Election in South Carolina*). Not entirely accurate but relatively impartial accounts appeared in the *New York Times*, July 10, p. 1; 12, p. 5; 14, p. 1; 18, p. 2; 19, p. 5; August 3, p. 1, 1876.

88. D. H. Chamberlain to U. S. Grant, July 22, 1876, quoted in the *New York Times*, August 7, p. 5, 1876.

believe that the affair was anything but a Radical ruse. "Taking the negro testimony only on both sides," he concluded "it would appear that the Hamburg riot was gotten up designedly by the Radicals for political purposes." Further, he felt that the state's case against the white rioters was "gotten up" for the purpose of political persecution.[89]

Politically, the Hamburg riot abruptly ended Chamberlain's alliance with Conservatives of the fusionist persuasion. It also brought about a temporary reversal in Grant's policy of not interfering militarily in the internal policies of the Southern states. Responding to pleas from Chamberlain and Senator T. J. Robertson, the President ordered the army into the state to maintain order. Garrisons all along the Atlantic seaboard were soon stripped of troops for the purpose. By election day, there were more federal soldiers in South Carolina than at any time since the close of the war.[90] The result was a curtailment in the actual use of force by the militant Democracy. Nevertheless, in mid-September, rifle and sabre clubs in the Edgefield, Aiken, and Barnwell area again precipitated a riot in which two whites and an estimated fifteen Negroes were killed. Even greater disaster was prevented, however, when a small detachment of United States infantry arrived in time to halt an attack by some eight hundred white men on an entrenched force of one hundred Negroes near Silverton.[91] A month later, a skirmish in which a white man was killed and a white person and two Negroes were wounded occasioned a similar confrontation. But, again, a small contingent of federal troops arrived to force the whites to desist.[92]

89. J. H. Cornish MS Diary, entry for August 10, 1876.

90. Nevertheless, there were never enough federal troops to afford Negroes adequate protection. This was partly because of Custer's defeat at the Little Big Horn on June 25, 1876, after which the army depleted its eastern posts and recruited vigorously to fight the Sioux War. When the political and racial situation in the South became critical, the army had to strain its resources to the maximum by channeling men recruited for the Sioux War into the South and by reducing eastern garrisons to the care taker level to create an inadequate force of some 2,500 soldiers for Southern duty. These few had to move either by foot or rail and major elements were shifted between Columbia, Tallahassee, and New Orleans so that their effectiveness was severely limited. There is reason to doubt that the administration could have smothered violence under a military blanket even had it chosen to make the attempt. *Use of the Army in Certain of the Southern States,* House Ex. Doc. No. 30, 44th Cong., 2nd Sess., pp. 13 ff.

91. *New York Times,* October 16, p. 1; 24, p. 1, 1876; J. H. Cornish MS Diary, entries for September 5, 19, 20, 1876; *South Carolina in 1876.*

92. Alvin Hart to D. A. Tompkins, October 24, 1876, D. A. Tompkins Papers; *New York Times,* October 20, 1876, p. 1.

In other places and, after mid-October, in those three most agitated districts, the militant wing of the Democracy was constrained to rely more on the threat of violence than its actual implementation in attempting to frighten Negroes away from the polls.

Among Negroes indignation rose to the danger point. In Columbia, on July 20, R. B. Elliott called a convention of leading Negroes to protest the Hamburg murders and consider a course of action. Particularly in Charleston did tempers flare. On July 10, a mass meeting of Negroes declared that, "The late unwarrantable slaughter of our brethren at Hamburg, by the order of Gen. M. C. Butler, of Edgefield County, was an unmitigated and foul murder, premeditated and predetermined, and a sought-for opportunity by a band of lawless men in the county known as Regulators, who are the enemies of the colored race in that county, composed of ex-Confederate soldiers, banded together for the purpose of intimidating the colored laborers and voters at elections, and keeping the 'negroes in their place,' as they say."[93] A week later, another such meeting indicated that the Negroes would fight if another such outrage occurred. The assembly resolved to ask Chamberlain to bring Butler and his followers to justice. One speaker declared that he "hoped the Republican party would show them that a colored man's life was as good as a white man's," and a voice in the crowd cried, "Put Chamberlain out if he don't stand by us." Meanwhile, a large crowd of Negroes, unable to press into the meeting hall, filled the sidewalks and the streets near the entrance. They refused to move to allow the street car to pass and when a policeman arrested one of the immovables the crowd freed him by force.[94]

Thereafter, the situation became increasingly explosive. In the lowcountry, where the Negro population outnumbered the white by more than three to one, roles were reversed. Here, Negroes were menacing and whites were fearful. Early in September, the Combahee rice workers threatened mass violence, and even though this disturbance was almost entirely economic in its origin the whites interpreted it as another Negro "rising." During the evening of September 6, rioting broke out in Charleston when a Negro mob assaulted a group of Democrats. In the fight which followed one of the whites was killed and several wounded. "The rioters held King Street, the main thorough-

93. The Address of the meeting, reprinted in the *New York Times*, July 24, 1876, p. 6.

94. *Ibid.*, July 21, 1876, p. 2, quoting the Charleston *News and Courier*, July 18, 1876. See also: *New York Times*, July 24, 1876, p. 6.

fare, from midnight until sunrise," a *Times* correspondent reported, "breaking windows, robbing stores, and attacking and beating indiscriminately every white man who showed his face."[95] Elderly Charlestonians later recalled hearing cries in the night of "Kill them! Kill them all! Dis town is ours!" On the following day, Negro rioters retired to the back streets where they continued their attacks for several days, defiant of whites and authorities alike. Terrified, whites stuck to their houses, shutters closed and shades drawn.[96] Hamburg was strikingly reversed as whites were terrorized by roving bands of rioting, looting Negroes. "When the riot took place in Charleston," wrote a Carolinian a decade afterward, "Wade Hampton *told* me he shed tears when he heard of the cowardice of his fellow townsmen."[97] Six weeks later, a political meeting at Cainhoy, a village ten miles up-river from Charleston, ended in a shooting riot in which one Negro and four whites were killed.[98] Again in Charleston, on the day following the election, a street brawl over election returns produced a general melee between the races in which one white and one Negro were killed.[99] For the whites of the lowcountry, violence was obviously no solution to the political problem.

Long after the election was over, an atmosphere of fear hung over both Negroes and whites in South Carolina. A totally unfounded rumor that the rifle and sabre clubs were ravaging the Negro population of Abbeville County and that several captured Negroes had been horribly poisoned in the Anderson jail gained wide currency during December, 1876. In February, 1877, in Charleston, an old resident found the Negroes "far from quiet or civil," and "much disposed to unprovoked annoyance." Many of the young white men, he added, had "resumed their pistols lest they be again caught unprepared."[100]

Once in office, the Redeemers hastened to reduce the military potential of the Negro community to a point where it posed no serious threat to white domination. Rifle and sabre clubs quickly gained legal status by being mustered into the militia under the Hampton govern-

95. *Ibid.,* September 8, p. 5; 11, p. 8, 1876.

96. Avary, *Dixie after the War,* p. 362.

97. C. W. Moise to F. W. Dawson, September 15, 1885, F. W. Dawson Papers.

98. *New York Times,* October 17, p. 4; 18, p. 4; 21, p. 3; 31, p. 2, 1876; Avary, *Dixie after the War,* p. 362.

99. *New York Times,* November 9, p. 1; 16, p. 1, 1876.

100. *Ibid.,* December 11, p. 1, 1876; Anonymous to "Belle," February 23, 1877, W. H. and W. G. De Saussure Papers.

ment. The transition was only thinly veiled. In reply to a request by the captain of the Brunson Mounted Rifles that his unit be commissioned, Hampton's secretary relayed the governor's approval. "Of course it must not be a *Rifle Club*," he cautioned.[101] Strangely, some elements of the Negro militia were retained and continued active into the twentieth century. However, the Negro militia was distinctly separated from the white, its numbers comparatively small, and its displays were always ornamental and never militant.[102] On July 6, 1877, the state's adjutant and inspector general ordered local units to collect arms and ammunition "now in the hands of members of disbanded companies or of private persons . . ."[103] With the execution of this order the balance of military power shifted definitely in favor of the white community. Thereafter, no white person in South Carolina need fear more than an isolated and temporary threat of injury at the hands of Negroes. On the other side, any Negro could expect a show of aggressiveness on his part to be met by galloping, crushing, merciless violence from the white community.

101. B. A. Williams to Wade Hampton, February 19, 1877; Wade Hampton to B. A. Williams, February 23, 1877, B. A. Williams Papers.

102. George Brown Tindall, *South Carolina Negroes, 1877–1900* (Columbia, 1952), pp. 286–88.

103. E. W. Moise to B. A. Williams, July 6, 1877, B. A. Williams Papers.

X...THE SEPARATION
OF THE RACES

The physical separation of the races was the most revolutionary change in relations between whites and Negroes in South Carolina during Reconstruction.

Separation had, of course, marked the Negro in slavery; yet the very nature of slavery necessitated a constant, physical intimacy between the races. In the peculiar institution, the white man had constantly and closely to oversee the labor of the Negro, preserve order in domestic arrangements within the slave quarters, and minister to the physical, medical, and moral needs of his laborers. In brief, slavery enforced its own special brand of interracial associations; in a sense, it married the interests of white to black at birth and the union followed both to the grave. Slavery watched the great mass of Negroes in South Carolina, but those Negroes who lived outside of the slave system were not exempt from the scrutiny of the whites. Even in Charleston, the free Negro community was never large enough to establish its economic and racial independence. In the mid-nineteenth century, as the bonds of slavery tightened, the whites were forced to bring free Negroes under ever more stringent controls and to subject their lives to the closest surveillance.

During the spring and summer of 1865, as the centripetal force of slavery melted rapidly away, each race clearly tended to disassociate itself from the other. The trend was evident in every phase of human endeavor: agriculture, business, occupations, schools and churches, in every aspect of social intercourse and politics. As early as July of 1865, a Bostonian in Charleston reported that "the worst sign here . . . is the growth of a bitter and hostile spirit between blacks and whites—a gap opening between the races which, it would seem may at some time result seriously."[1] Well before the end of Reconstruction, separation had crystallized into a comprehensive pattern which, in its essence, remained unaltered until the middle of the twentieth century.

There is no clear, concise answer to the question of why separation occurred. Certainly, it was not simply a response of Negroes to the prejudiced fiat of dominant whites; nor was it a totally rationalized reaction on the part of either race. Actually, articulate whites and Negroes seldom attempted to explain their behavior. Yet, the philosophies and attitudes each race adopted toward the other lend a certain rationality to separation, and, if we are always mindful that this analysis presumes a unity which they never expressed, can be applied to promote an understanding of the phenomenon.

For the native white community, separation was a means of avoiding or minimizing problems which, they felt, would inevitably arise from the inherent inferiority of the Negro, problems which the North, in eradicating slavery and disallowing the Black Code, would not allow them to control by overt political means. In this limited sense, segregation was a substitute for slavery.

Thus, first, total separation was essential to racial purity, and racial purity was necessary to the preservation of a superior civilization which the whites had labored so arduously to construct, and suffered a long and bloody war to defend. After the war, that civilization was embattled, but not necessarily lost. Unguarded association with an inferior caste would obviously endanger white culture. In this view, children were peculiarly susceptible to damage. "Don't imagine that I allow my children to be with negroes out of my presence," wrote the mistress of a lowcountry plantation in 1868, "on one occasion only have they been so with my knowledge."[2] Even the Negro wet nurse, that quintessence of maternalism upon which the slave period paternalist so often turned his case, emerged as the incubus of Southern infancy. "We gave our infants to the black wenches to suckle," lamented an elderly white, "and thus poisoned the blood of our children, and made

1. *New York Times,* July 11, 1865, p. 4.
2. Mrs. A. J. Gonzales to her mother, May 3, 1868, Elliott–Gonzales Papers.

them *cowards* . . . the Character of the people of the state was ruined by slavery and it will take 500 years, if not longer, by the infusion of new blood to eradicate the hereditary vices imbibed with the blood (milk is blood) of black wet nurses."[3] Adults, of course, were not immune to racial contamination. Casual associations across the color line might lead to serious ones and to the total pollution of the superior race. Particularly might this be so of the poor, the ignorant, and the feeble-minded, but even the aristocracy had to be watched. Shortly after Redemption, an anonymous Carolinian was incensed at a rumor that Wade Hampton had dined at a table with Negroes in the home of the president of Claflin, the leading Negro university in the state. "Who shall say where it will stop?" he warned. "Will not dining lead to dancing, to social equality, to miscegenation, to mexicanization and to general damnation."[4]

Separation also facilitated the subordination of the inferior race by constantly reminding the Negro that he lived in a world in which the white man was dominant, and in which the non-white was steadfastly denied access to the higher caste. Further, the impression of Negro inferiority would be constantly re-enforced by relegating the baser element, whenever possible, to the use of inferior facilities. The sheer totality of the display alone might well serve to convince members of the lower caste that such, indeed, was in the natural order of things.

Many whites had envisioned the early elimination of the freedman from the Southern scene, and many had eagerly anticipated this event. In time, however, it became evident to all that the Negro would be neither dissolved nor transported to Africa. In a sense, separation was a means of securing the quasi elimination of Negroes at home. It was, perhaps, a more satisfactory solution than their demise or emigration, since it might produce many of the benefits of their disappearance without losing an advantageous, indeed, a necessary supply of labor.

Finally, separation was a logical solution to the problem posed by the widespread conviction that the races were inherently incompatible outside of the master-slave relationship. If the white man could not exist in contentment in the proximity of Negroes, then partial satisfaction might be achieved by withdrawal from associations with mem-

3. C. W. Moise to F. W. Dawson, September 15, 1885, F. W. Dawson Papers. See also: A. L. Taveau to William Aiken, April 24, 1865, A. L. Taveau Papers.
4. Anonymous MS, n.d., South Carolina Reconstruction Papers. This document was probably found among the papers of Martin Witherspoon Gary. The text indicates that it was written shortly after Redemption.

bers of the inferior caste. This spirit was evident among some of the wealthier whites who voluntarily dispensed entirely with the services of Negro domestics. Elderly William Heyward, in 1868 still second to none in the ranks of the rice aristocracy, stopped taking his meals at the Charleston Hotel because, as he said, he found "the negro waiters so defiant and so familiar in their attentions." "A part of the satisfaction is," he explained to a friend, "that I am perfectly independent of having negroes about me; if I cannot have them as they used to be, I have no desire to see them except in the field."[5] Planters were often manifesting precisely the same sentiment when they deserted their land and turned to grain culture, or to the use of immigrant labor. Separation was also a way of avoiding interracial violence. B. O. Duncan and James L. Orr, both native white Republicans, argued against mixing in the public schools because they were convinced that minor irritations between children would generate major altercations between parents of different races. Conceived as a means of avoiding violence, separation, ironically, was subsequently enforced by the use of violence.

The Southern white did not always have a clear reason why racial "mixing" (as they called it) in a given situation was wrong, why the color bar should be leveled in one place and not in another. Nevertheless, he had no difficulty in recognizing a breach of the proprieties when he saw it. A young Carolinian visiting New York in the summer of 1867 was outraged by the degree of mixing he observed there: "I can now say that I have seen the city of cities, and after I have seen it it is nothing but vanity and vexation of spirit. Here you can see the negro all on equal footing with white man. White man walking the street with negroe wenches. White man and negroe riding to gether. White man and negroes sit in the same seat in church or in a word the negro enjoys the same privileges as the white man. They address each other as Mr and Miss but notwithstanding all this we (the southern boys) say what we please and when we please. . . ."[6]

Contrary to common belief, the separation of the races was not entirely the work of the whites. Suspicious, resentful, and sometimes hateful toward the whites, chafed by white attitudes of superiority, and irritated by individual contacts with supercilious whites, Negroes, too, sought relief in withdrawal from association with the other race. In many instances, the disassociation was complete—that is, many Negroes

5. William Heyward to James Gregorie, June 4, 1868, Gregorie–Elliott Papers.
6. J. H. Young to J. W. White, August 5, 1867, J. W. White Papers.

left the state. During the war, Corporal Simon Crum of the First South Carolina declared his intention of leaving South Carolina after the capitulation because, as he phrased it, "dese yer Secesh will neber be cibilized in my time."[7] For those who could not or would not leave, alternative forms of withdrawal were possible. A major facet in the new pattern of agriculture was the removal of Negro labor from the immediate supervision of white men. As the Negro agriculturalist moved his labor away from the eye of the white man, so also did he move his family and his home. Plantation villages became increasingly rare as Negro landowners and renters either built new houses on their plots or, in a rather graphic symbolic display, laboriously dragged their cabins away from the "Negro street." Negroes in the trades and in domestic service followed similar trends. Furthermore, Negroes chose to withdraw from white-dominated churches, though they were often urged to stay, and they attended racially separated schools in spite of the legal fact that all schools were open to all races. Negroes also tended to withdraw from political association with members of the white community.

Finally, on those few occasions when Negroes entered into polite social situations with whites, Northern as well as Southern, they were often ill at ease. For instance, while driving along a road near Columbia, a planter and his wife met William, "a fine looking light mulatto" who had been their stableboy as a slave. William was driving a buggy and seated beside him was a young white woman, elegantly attired. The woman was a "Yankee school marm," probably one of the new teachers in Columbia's Negro school. As he passed his late master and mistress, the Negro averted his gaze and did not speak. The following day, he approached the planter and apologized for having been escort to a "white woman." He had met the teacher at a celebration, he explained, and she had insisted on his taking her to see the countryside.[8]

During Reconstruction, the Negro's withdrawal was never a categorical rejection of the white man and his society. In the early days of freedom, it was primarily a reaction against slavery, an attempt to escape the unpleasant associations of his previous condition and the derogatory implications of human bondage. However, as the memory of slavery faded, a more persistent reason for withdrawal emerged. Essentially, it was the Negro's answer to discrimination. Almost in-

7. Thomas Wentworth Higginson, *Army Life in a Black Regiment* (Boston, 1890), p. 266.
8. Sally Elmore Tayler MS Memoir.

variably, attempts by individual Negroes to establish satisfactory relations across the race line were unsuccessful, and, all too often, the pain of the experience was greater than the reward for having stood for principle. During Reconstruction and afterward, only a few were willing to undergo such pain without the certainty of success. It was much easier, after all, simply to withdraw.

Withdrawal as a solution to the race problem was by no means satisfactory to the Negro leadership. Implicit in the behavior of Negro leaders during Reconstruction was a yearning for complete and unreserved acceptance for members of their race by the white community. However, overtly, and rather politically, they carefully distinguished between "social equality" and what might be appropriately termed "public equality." For themselves, they claimed only the latter. "Our race do not demand social equality," declared W. J. Whipper, a member from Beaufort, on the floor of the house of representatives in Columbia. "No law can compel me to put myself on an equality with some white men I know," he continued, and, turning cynically on a native white Republican who had vigorously defended separation, concluded, "but talk about equality and the member imagines he must take you into his arms as he probably would your sister, if she was good looking."[9] Two years later, Martin Delany, a man who expressed pride in his blackness, said much the same thing to a large Charleston audience. "I don't believe in social equality; there is no such thing," he shouted. "If we want to associate with a man, we'll do it, and without laws."[10]

What the Negro leadership did insist upon was public equality, that is, absolute civil and political parity with whites and full and free access to most public facilities. These latter included restaurants, bars, saloons, railway and street cars, shipboard accommodations, the theater, and other such places of public amusement. Once they gained political power, Negro leaders hastened to embody this attitude in legislation. Within a week after the first sitting of the Constitutional Convention of 1868, a Negro delegate introduced a resolution which was eventually included in the state's bill of rights: "Distinction on account of race or color, in any case whatever, shall be prohibited, and all classes of citizens shall enjoy equally all common, public, legal and political privileges."[11] Similarly, one of the first bills passed by the Republican

9. *New York Times,* August 20, 1868, p. 2.
10. *Daily Republican* (Charleston), June 24, 1870.
11. *Convention Proceedings, 1868,* pp. 72, 353–56, 789–92.

legislature prohibited licensed businesses from discriminating "between persons, on account of race, color, or previous condition, who shall make lawful application for the benefit of such business, calling or pursuit." Convicted violators were liable to a fine of not less than $1,000 or imprisonment for not less than a year.[12] During the debate on the measure in the house, not a single Negro member spoke against the bill, and only five of the twenty-four votes registered against it were cast by Negroes, while fifty-three of the sixty-one votes which secured its passage were those of Negro legislators.[13]

Negro Congressmen were no less ardent in championing the same cause in Washington, particularly in 1874, when a federal civil rights bill was up for consideration. ". . . is it pretended anywhere," asked Congressman R. B. Elliott, who had only recently been denied service in the restaurant of a railway station in North Carolina on his journey to the capital, "that the evils of which we complain, our exclusion from the public inn, from the saloon and table of the steamboat, from the sleeping-coach on the railway, from the right of sepulture in the public burial-ground, are an exercise of the police power of the State? . . . . Are the colored people to be assimilated to an unwholesome trade or to combustible materials, to be interdicted, to be shut up within prescribed limits?" Several days later, in the same place, Congressman R. H. Cain declared, "We do not want any discrimination to be made. I do not ask any legislation for the colored people of this country that is not applied to the white people of this country. All that we seek is equal laws, equal legislation, and equal rights throughout the length and breadth of this land."[14]

It was upon this emotional, uneven ground that an essentially new color line was drawn. It was established in a kind of racial warfare, of assaults and withdrawals, of attacks and counterattacks. Nevertheless, well before the end of Reconstruction, both forces had been fully engaged and the line was unmistakably formed.

Even before the Radicals came into power in South Carolina in 1868, native whites had already defined a color line in government-supported institutions, on common carriers, in places of public accommodation and amusement, and, of course, in private social organizations.

12. *Statutes at Large,* XIV, 179; see also pp. 337–38, 386–88.
13. *House Journal* (Special Session, 1868), pp. 218-23; *New York Times,* August 20, 1868, p. 2.
14. *Congressional Record,* II, Part 1, 43rd Cong., 1st Sess., 408, 566.

The degree of separation in each of these areas varied. In many instances, obviously, some compromise between expense and the desire for complete separation had to be made. Usually, the compromise involved the division of available facilities in some manner. If this was thought to be inconvenient, Negroes were totally excluded.

Typical was the treatment of Negro and white prisoners in the state penitentiary under the James L. Orr regime. Criminals of both races were confined in the same institution but were quartered in separate cells. Ironically, the racial concepts of white prison officials sometimes redounded to the benefit of Negro inmates. Minor violations of prison rules were punished every Sunday by the offenders being tied closely together, blindfolded, and forced to work their way over a series of obstacles in the prison yard. The chief guard explained that the white offenders were placed in the most difficult middle positions of the "blind gang" because "they have more intelligence than the colored ones and are better able to understand the rules of the institution."[15]

It is paradoxical that the Negro leadership, once in office, pressed vigorously for an end to separation in privately owned facilities open to the public but they allowed a very distinct separation to prevail in every major governmental facility. The most obvious instance was the schools, but the distinction also stretched into the furthermost reaches of gubernatorial activity. For example, a visitor to the state insane asylum in Columbia in 1874 found that "The Negro female inmates occupy a separate part of the same building" in which the white women were housed.[16]

On the other side, within a month after they had gained the vote, Negroes in South Carolina opened a frontal attack against racial discrimination on common carriers. Typical was their assault on the Charleston Street Car Company. At the time of its inauguration, the facilities of the company consisted of double tracks running the length of the peninsula with a spur branching off near the mid-point. Horse-drawn cars, each manned by a driver and a conductor, ran along the tracks at regular intervals. The cars contained seats in a compartment, and front and rear platforms. Before the cars began to run in December, 1866, the question of the accommodation of Negro passengers was thoroughly canvassed. "Proper arrangements will in due time be made

15. *House Journal* (Special Session, 1868), Appendix A, p. 110.
16. J. E. Bomar to his children, November 26, 1874, E. E. Bomar Papers. See also: Sally Elmore Taylor MS Memoir.

to allow persons of color to avail themselves of the benefits of the railway," the management assured the Negro community, but it had not then decided between providing "special cars" for the Negroes as was done in New Orleans, or "assigning to them a portion of the ordinary cars as is more usual in other cities."[17] Negro leaders rejected both alternatives. As a Northerner wrote from Charleston in January, 1867, "Every scheme that could be devised that did not contemplate the promiscuous use of the cars by whites and negroes alike, was scouted by the Negro paper here; and the result is that negroes are now debarred the use of the cars altogether, unless they choose to ride upon the platform."[18]

But here the matter did not rest, as the following press account from the *New York Times* will show:

> On Tuesday afternoon, March 27, after the adjournment of the Freedmen's mass meeting in Charleston, S. C., an attempt was made by some of them to test their right to ride in the street car, which is denied them by the rules of the Company. One of them entered a car, and declined to leave it when requested to do so by the conductor, who at the same time informed him of the Company's rules. The conductor, however, insisted that he should at least leave the inside of the car, and finally his friends, who found he was liable to be forcibly ejected if resistance were offered, persuaded him to yield. On its return trip the car was filled at the same place by a crowd of negroes, who rushed into it, to the great discomfort of the white passengers, and although remonstrated with and appealed to by the conductor, declined to go out. The driver then attempted, by direction of the conductor, to throw his car from the track; and failing in this, unhitched his horses and left the car. The negroes attempted to push the car forward, and threatened personal violence to the conductor, but the arrival of the police and detachments of soldiers caused the negroes to disperse. Other cars were in the meantime entered in the same way, and the negroes, finding the conductors would not permit them to ride, endeavored to interrupt the travel of the cars by placing stones on the track . . .[19]

17. *Daily Courier* (Charleston), October 15, December 17, 1866.
18. *New York Times,* January 7, 1867, p. 1.
19. *Ibid.,* April 2, 1867, p. 1.

The military soon restored order, but the Negro community prepared to bring the case before the courts.[20] By early May, Negroes were actually riding in the cars, and, by early June, the military commander, Sickles, had issued an order prohibiting racial discrimination on railroads, horse-cars, and steamboats.[21] Sickles's successor, Canby, continued to enforce the rule.[22]

After the Negro gained political power, the battle against discrimination became more intense and assumed a wider front. The so-called antidiscrimination bill, passed in the summer of 1868, on paper was a most formidable weapon. In essence, it imposed severe penalties upon the owners of public accommodations who were convicted of discrimination. Burden of proof of innocence lay on the accused, and state solicitors (public prosecutors) who failed to prosecute suspected violators were themselves threatened with heavy punishments.

The effect of the new legislation on common carriers was immediate. A Northern teacher returning to Beaufort in the fall of 1868, after a few months' absence in the North, observed a portion of the results:

> We took a small steamer from Charleston for Beaufort. Here we found a decided change since we went North. Then no colored person was allowed on the upper deck, now there were no restrictions,—there could be none, for a law had been passed in favor of the negroes. They were everywhere, choosing the best staterooms and best seats at the table. Two prominent colored members of the State Legislature were on board with their families. There were also several well-known Southerners, still uncompromising rebels. It was a curious scene and full of significance. An interesting study to watch the exultant faces of the negroes, and the scowling faces of the rebels . . .[23]

The same legislation applied to railway facilities; and, apparently, it was applied without a great amount of dissent. Adjustment was made easier, perhaps, by the acquisition of some of the railroad companies by Radical politicians within the state, or by Northern capitalists, and by the close understanding which usually prevailed between Republican officeholders and those Conservatives who managed to retain

20. *Ibid.*, April 20, 1867, p. 1.
21. W. E. Martin to B. F. Perry, May 7, 1867 (copy), A. L. Burt Papers.
22. *New York Times*, August 20, 1868, p. 1.
23. Elizabeth Hyde Botume, *First Days among the Contrabands* (Boston, 1893), pp. 267–69.

control of their railroads. While formal discrimination was not practiced by railway operators, unofficial racial separation did occur on a
large scale. On all of the major lines first- and second-class cars were
available. Most Negroes apparently deliberately chose to ride in the
more economical second-class accommodations, and virtually all of the
whites—particularly white women—took passage on the first-class cars.
The separation thus achieved was so nearly complete that the first-class
car was often referred to as the "ladies' car."[24] It is highly relevant that
the first Jim Crow legislation affecting railroads in South Carolina
provided for the separation of the races only in the first-class cars,[25]
because, of course, this was the only place on the railroads where there
was any possibility of a significant degree of mixing.

During and after Reconstruction, some Negro passengers on the
railroads could afford to and did share first-class accommodations with
whites, but even this limited mixing was not welcomed by the mass of
whites. For instance, a Northern white woman had an interesting and
revealing experience while traveling from Columbia to Charleston via
the South Carolina Railroad early in 1871:

> I must tell you of a scene I saw in the cars coming from
> Columbia. . . . After we were all seated a black man entered
> suitably dressed with black pants, black coat, *no* jewelry, trailing
> a cane. As he came on a man (white in complexion) rose up
> quickly and grasped the ebony hand with great impressment,
> and offered him the seat at his side. The colored representa-
> tive, for such he was, took the seat close to the other, & they
> commenced a rapid conversation. My ear was arrested at once
> by the most painful profanity. It came from the *negro*. This
> [was] an exercise of his freedom, as a slave he would never
> have dared to utter a word of the kind.

When the Negro representative was reproved by a fellow passenger
who happened to be a well known Presbyterian minister, he "took it
quietly, and then went out of the car, into the one, (second class I
think they called [it]) in front of us." After the minister debarked, the
Negro "came back, took a seat by himself, and behaved as well as any

24. *New York Times,* October 19, 1868, p. 1; *Intelligencer* (Anderson), October
21, 1868.

25. George Brown Tindall, *South Carolina Negroes, 1877–1900* (Columbia,
1952), p. 301.

person could."[26] A year later, a lady of the lowcountry complained of her trials on a trip by rail from Charleston to Unionville. "Grabbed snatches of sleep on the train on the way in spite of our colored neighbors," she reported to her husband.[27] Thus, until 1898, it is possible to find instances in which individual Negroes rode the rails seated in the same cars with the most aristocratic of whites; but economic and social lines re-enforced the color line, and the mixture was never generally and freely made.[28]

In the winter of 1869–1870 and through the summer which followed, a concerted attempt was made by the Negro leadership to win the full acceptance of Negroes into all places of public amusement, eating, drinking, and sleeping. Special provisions for the accommodation of Negroes at public entertainments had been made in ante-bellum times, but physical separation of the races was invariably the rule. In December, 1868, Charles Minort, a mulatto restaurateur and lesser political figure, nearly provoked a riot in a Columbia theater by presuming to seat his wife and himself in the front row, a section traditionally reserved for tardy white ladies. Presumably, he should have chosen seats among the other Negroes present who "had taken their seats, as has always been the custom, in the rear."[29] Minort yielded to the clamor of the whites in the audience, but, a year later, the Negroes of Charleston instituted judicial proceedings against the manager of the Academy of Music for refusing to mix the races in the boxes of the theater. The management barely succeeded in winning a postponement but was able to complete the season before the case came to trial.[30]

In the spring of 1870, Negro leaders in Charleston launched an attack against discrimination in restaurants, bars, and saloons. On March 25, for instance, Louis Kenake, accused of violating the anti-discrimination act, was brought before Magistrate T. J. Mackey and put on a bond of one thousand dollars while awaiting trial. Other white restaurant keepers of Charleston united to oppose and test the

26. M. C. M. Taylor to Jeremiah Wilbur, March 13, 1871, Jeremiah Wilbur Papers.

27. Margaret Grimball to John B. Grimball, July 3, 1872, J. B. Grimball Papers.

28. Negro leaders in this period experienced more difficulty in winning admission to first-class cars in other states. For instance, in December, 1869, three Carolina Negroes sued the Richmond and Danville Railroad for ejecting them from the first class cars of that Virginia line. *Horry News* (Conway), December 24, 1869.

29. *New York Times*, December 25, 1868, p. 2.

30. *Ibid.*, January 25, 1870, p. 2.

validity of the act, but, in the week which followed, at least six additional charges were lodged against operators of such businesses.[31] The assault was not confined to Charleston and demonstrations by Radical politicians were frequent during the campaign of 1870. In April, a Laurens woman wrote to her son in Missouri that "On Monday the yankees & some negroes went to Hayne Williams' and asked for drink, which 'Ward' refused them, that is, to drink at the gentlemans bar. They quietly marched him off to jail, & locked the doors, putting the keys in their pockets. The family are all at Spartanburg, we look for H. Williams to night, and I am afraid of a fuss, for he is a great bully."[32] In the same month, during a Radical meeting in Lancaster, a Negro was refused service in a local bar with the comment that no "nigger" could buy a drink there. Lucius Wimbush, a Negro senator, hearing of the incident, went to the bar, ordered a drink, and was refused. He immediately had the barkeeper arrested and placed under bail.[33] Strangely, not all such suits were against whites. "1st case under Civil Rights Bill today," a Greenville merchant noted in his diary in August, "negro indicts Henry Gantt [a Negro and well-known local barber] for not shaving him where he shaves white persons—— What is to come from it no one knows."[34]

Negroes were also ambitious to open sleeping accommodations to their race. In the summer of 1868, as the first Negro legislators gathered in Columbia, native whites had been extremely apprehensive that they would attempt to occupy rooms in the city's hotels. Even *The Nation,* which had applauded the opening of common carriers to both races, declared that hotels were another and "delicate" matter, where separation was everywhere observed.[35] The white community was vastly relieved to find that no such invasion was attempted, one upcountry newspaper having sent a special correspondent to Columbia to ascertain the fact.[36] Nevertheless, when Negro legislators debated the antidiscrimination bill early in the session, they made it very clear that hotels were included. William E. Johnson, the African Methodist Minister then representing Sumter County in the statehouse, noting that the management of Nickerson's Hotel was concerned lest Negroes apply

31. *Daily Republican* (Charleston), March 26, 28, 29; April 2, 1870.
32. Mrs. J. W. Motte to Robert Motte, April 27, 1870, Lalla Pelot Papers.
33. *Daily Republican* (Charleston), April 13, 1870.
34. William L. Mauldin MS Diary, entry for August 22, 1870.
35. *The Nation,* VII, No. 164 (August 20, 1868), 142.
36. *Intelligencer* (Anderson), August 26, 1868; *New York Times,* July 12, 1868, p. 5.

for rooms, declared that if he found private accommodations filled he would want to know that this resort was open to him. George Lee, a Negro member from Berkeley, observed that a group of junketing legislators had recently failed to find lodging in Greenville and that this law was desired to prevent that sort of occurrence. "Equal and exact justice to all," he demanded, ". . . it is what we must have."[37] Negroes were subsequently allowed to attend meetings in Columbia hotels, but it is apparent that none were ever given lodging.

Negroes also decried the fact that places of permanent rest occupied by whites, as well as those of a more temporary variety, were denied to their race. For instance, S. G. W. Dill, the native white Radical who was assassinated in Kershaw in the summer of 1868, and Nestor Peavy, his Negro guard who was killed in the same assault, were buried in racially separated cemeteries.[38]

Thus, from 1868 until 1889, when the antidiscrimination law was repealed, Negroes in South Carolina could legally use all public facilities which were open to whites. However, in actual practice, they seldom chose to do so. "The naturally docile negro makes no effort at unnecessary self-assertion," a Northern visitor in Charleston explained in 1870, "unless under the immediate instigation of some dangerous *friends* belonging to the other race, who undertake to manage his destiny."[39] This particular reporter was certainly prejudiced against the race; but four years later another Northern observer congratulated the Negroes of South Carolina on the "moderation and good sense" which they exhibited in their "intercourse with the whites." He concluded, "They seldom intrude themselves into places frequented by the whites, and considering that in South Carolina they have a voting majority of some thirty thousand and control the entire State Government, it is somewhat remarkable that they conduct themselves with so much propriety."[40] Indeed, after 1870, even the Negro leadership hardly seemed inclined to press further their political and legal advantage to end separation. Of the numerous charges lodged under the antidiscrimination law, not a single conviction was ever recorded.[41]

37. *New York Times,* August 20, 1868, p. 1.

38. Thomas J. Kirkland and Robert M. Kennedy, *Historic Camden,* Part Two (Columbia, 1926), p. 202.

39. N. S. Shaler, "An Ex-Southerner in South Carolina," *The Atlantic Monthly,* XXVI, No. 153 (July, 1870), 58.

40. *New York Times,* July 4, 1874, p. 5. The pattern of separation was also impervious to any effects from the Civil Rights Act of 1875.

41. Tindall, *South Carolina Negroes,* pp. 292–93, citing the Charleston *News and Courier,* November 5, 1883.

Even when Negroes pressed themselves in upon the prejudice of whites, the latter adjusted by total or partial withdrawal, so that a high degree of separation was always and everywhere maintained.

Some whites responded to the pressure by total withdrawal, that is, by leaving the state entirely. Of course, many of those who left South Carolina did so primarily for economic reasons, but many also departed from purely racial motives. A Winnsboro lawyer and pre-war fire-eater revealed the thinking of many emigrants when he asked William Porcher Miles, in April, 1867, how he could live in a land where "Every 'mulatto' is your Equal & every 'Nigger' is your Superior." Pronouncing the Negro majority "revolting," he advised Miles to go to England. ". . . I have no doubt you could succeed & at any rate wd not have as many Negro Clients & negro witnesses to offend yr nostrils as in these USA. I can't conceive of any ones remaining here who can possibly get away—Suppose, it were certain, wh. it is not, that no U S Congress will ever pass a Law requiring that your Daughter & mine shall either marry Negroes or die unmarried. Still the Negro is already superior to them politically & to their Fathers also, & must ever be so henceforth."[42]

As the prospect of the elevation of Negroes to political power grew increasingly imminent, restlessness among white Carolinians rose. Joseph Le Conte, nationally famous scientist and a professor at the University of South Carolina, bespoke the minds of many of his colleagues in the fall of 1867. "The prostration of every interest in the Southern States first by the war, & then by the prospect of Negro supremacy, is so great that every one is at least making inquiries in anticipation of being compelled to leave for more favored regions," he wrote to a fellow academician at Yale. "If the present program is carried out it is quite certain that living in these states is simply impossible."[43] Once the Negro was in power, the flood of white emigration swelled. "Better make terms with the Wild Comanches," wrote one exiled Carolinian from the tangles of western Arkansas in 1872, "than hourds of Radicals . . ."[44]

Of course, not every white Carolinian was able to leave the state, but even among those who remained there was a strong current of

42. G. I. C. to W. P. Miles, April 13, 1867, W. P. Miles Papers.
43. Joseph Le Conte to W. D. Whitney, November 28, 1867, W. D. Whitney Papers.
44. Victor W. Johns to F. W. McMaster, January 9, 1872, F. W. McMaster Papers.

sentiment for emigration. "I shd. be better satisfied to live and raise my children in a 'white man's country;' and will do so if I can," declared one Baptist clergyman on the eve of the ratification of the Constitution of 1868.[45]

For those who did remain there were lesser degrees of withdrawal. In the one area in which the Negro gained a definite ascendency, politics, a large number of whites simply refused to recognize his dominance beyond a necessary, minimal level. In 1870, and in the two state-wide elections which followed, more than ten thousand white voters actually abstained from voting because both regular and "reform" tickets recognized the political existence of the Negro. "They don't like to give up the dead issues of the past," explained a Bishopville farmer to a Virginian, "and are apprehensive that their acknowledgement of the Negroe's Civil and political equality will lead to social leveling."[46] One of those who refused to vote gave as his reason the statement that: "I wish no affiliation with niggers & a platform acknowledging the right of the negro to vote & hold office simply discourages the efforts of the Northern Democracy. The privilege may be *allowed the negro at this time to vote & c* but it is certainly not a right."[47] Many of those who voted the reform ticket did so only with grave reservations. While honoring "Hampton, Butler, Kershaw & gentlemen of that character" for their "courage and endurance" in attempting to fashion a program in 1870, a Charleston aristocrat asserted that: "Some of us have been unable to bring ourselves to admit the right to give the negro these rights of citizenship & are therefore unable to join in the canvas, but even we who are, possibly of this mistaken conscientious opinion, will vote the Reform Union (as it is called) candidates & rejoice at their success."[48] Even those who actively campaigned as Reformers, while embracing the Negro politically, kept him at arm's length socially. Attending a Reform speaking and barbecue in 1870, the Reverend Cornish noted that the participants dined at two tables, "the negroes at one & the whites at another."[49]

After Negroes were firmly entrenched in official positions in government, native whites evinced a distinct tendency to refrain from associa-

45. Basil Manly, Jr., to Charles Manly, April 15, 1868, Basil Manly, Jr., Letters and Letterbook.

46. J. M. Dennis to J. Y. Harris, May 21, 1870, J. Y. Harris Papers.

47. T. P. Bailey to R. H. McKie, May 12, 1870, R. H. McKie Papers.

48. W. G. De Saussure to W. P. Miles, September 21, 1870, W. P. Miles Papers. The writer was mistaken in including Hampton in this group.

49. J. H. Cornish MS Diary, entry for September 3, 1870.

tions which recognized the authority of Negro officers over white citizens. For instance, in the heavily Negro county of Abbeville, in 1870, a distresssed guardian asked one of the magistrates, who happened to be a Democrat, to dispatch a constable to return an orphan girl stolen away from his house. "When you send for Laura," he begged, "please send a white man, as she is a white girl under my charge, and I would not like to subject her to the mortification of being brought back by a colored man. Besides that I would be censured by the community as they would know nothing of the circumstances of the case."[50] Very often, avoiding communication with Negro officeholders was an easy matter for the whites. In the predominantly white counties, Conservatives were always able to retain some offices. In the counties where the Negroes were heavily in the majority, there were usually white Republicans in office through whom the local whites might and did conduct their business with the government. Contrary to tradition, when carpetbaggers and scalawags were actually in office, and there was every prospect that they would remain so throughout the foreseeable future, the white community did not think them all nearly so odious personally as subsequent reports suggested. Even in the middle counties, where the native Negro leadership predominated and scalawags did tend to be political opportunists, native whites still found means of avoiding contacts with Republican officers which, to them, would have been humiliating. A typical resort was that of the white citizens of Camden who arranged for the introduction of a bill in the legislature by a conservative representative from the white county of Lancaster because, as a Camdenite indicated, "our Representatives were coloured, and scalawags."[51]

Withdrawal was also the means by which native whites combatted attempts by Republican officials to end separation in institutions supported by the government. The withdrawal of native whites from the University and the State School for the Deaf and Blind at the prospect of Negro admissions are illustrations of white determination either to maintain separation or to dispense with the services afforded by related state institutions. If the Radicals had attempted to end separation in the common schools, it is virtually certain that the whites would have removed their children from these schools too. As one post-Redemption proponent of universal education argued, separation was essential to academic progress. Only by this means, he explained to Governor Hampton, could it be achieved "without any danger of social equality—*and this is*

50. E. F. Powers to R. R. Hemphill, May 21, 1870, Hemphill Papers.
51. R. A. Bonney to Dock Bonney, August 2, 1868, E. W. Bonney Papers.

the great bug bear."[52] Doubtless, it was the threat of withdrawal by the whites which dissuaded the Radical leadership from further attempts to end separation in institutions over which they had, by political means, absolute control.

Whites also refused to engage in normal civic activities in which the color line was not distinctly drawn. Thus, native whites chose not to join militia companies in which Negroes participated and were reported to be extremely apprehensive of being forced to undergo the "humiliation" of joining a mixed company.[53] Too, whites were reluctant to sit with Negroes in the jury box. An elderly Spartanburg farmer verbalized his feelings on this point in the summer of 1869: "When I go to court & see negroes on the jury & on the stand for witnesses it makes me glad that I am so near the end of my race to sit on a jury with them I dont intend to do it we have a law that exempt a man at 65 & I take the advantage of it."[54] This kind of withdrawal often reached odd extremes. In the spring of 1870, at the peak of the Negro leadership's drive for admission to privately owned public accommodations, the white Democrats of the Charleston Fire Department refused to decorate their engines and join in the annual parade because Negro fire companies were being allowed to march in the procession.[55]

This general withdrawal of whites from participation in civil affairs resulted in a tendency within the white community to govern itself outside of the official system. As Reconstruction progressed, this peculiar form of dyarchy approached its logical culmination. In its last days, the Tax Union came very close to the establishment of a separate government within the state when it considered collecting a ten-mil tax from its members and supervising its expenditure, thus depriving the incumbent Radicals of the staff of political life.[56] A year later, during the period of the dual government, a similar plan was actually implemented while the Hampton regime governed the whites and the Chamberlain government served, virtually, a Negro constituency.

Native whites also tended to withdraw from public places where the color line could not be firmly fixed and the Negro could easily assert his equality. "The whites have, to a great extent—greater than ever before—

52. Anonymous to Wade Hampton, November 13, 1877, Freedmen File.

53. *New York Times,* May 24, 1867, p. 2.

54. Edward Lipscomb to Smith Lipscomb, June 30, 1869, Edward Lipscomb Papers.

55. *Daily Republican* (Charleston), April 30, 1870.

56. *Intelligencer* (Anderson), December 2, 1875.

yielded the streets to the negroes," wrote a Columbian on Christmas Day, 1868.[57] Similarly, in Charleston, in the late spring of 1866, a young aristocrat noted that the battery with its music and strollers had been yielded to the ladies and gentlemen of non-noble lineage on Saturdays, and by all whites to the Negroes on Sundays. On Saturdays, he declared, "the battery is quite full of gentlemen and ladies but it is not much patronized by the elite. . . . On Sunday afternoon the ethiops spread themselves on the Battery."[58]

The same reaction was manifested by the whites wherever the Negro leadership succeeded by legal means in ending separation. For instance, when Negroes won admission to the street cars of Charleston, the whites simply withdrew. "On Sunday I counted five Cars successively near the Battery crowded [with] negroes, with but one white man, the Conductor," wrote a native white in May, 1867. "The ladies are practically excluded."[59] When the Academy of Music was threatened with a discrimination suit in 1870, the white community replied with a counter-threat to withdraw its patronage and thus close the theater.[60] Adjustment which fell short of complete separation remained unsatisfactory to whites. "Even the Theatre is an uncertain pleasure," complained a Charleston lady in 1873, "no matter how attractive the program, for you know that you may have a negro next to you."[61] Probably many of her contemporaries found the exposure too damaging and stayed home.

The social lives of native whites were, of course, absolutely closed to Negroes. Access to the homes of the whites was gained by Negroes only when they clearly acquiesced in the superior-inferior relationship dictated by the owners, and even then entrance was often denied. "I told him I would never allow negroes to go in it while I owned it," wrote a Laurenville woman, incensed that a man who had bought her former home had rented it to Negroes. In spite of the fact that some Negro domestics lived in quarters behind the houses of their employers, whites were already rejecting Negroes as neighbors. A real estate agent in Aiken in 1871 responded to this sentiment when he refused offers from Negroes for city lots at triple prices because, as he explained to the owner, "purchasers among the whites will not settle among the Negroes, and I am

57. New York Times, January 2, 1869, p. 2.
58. Berkeley Grimball to Elizabeth Grimball, June 10, 1866, J. B. Grimball Papers (Duke).
59. W. E. Martin to B. F. Perry, May 7, 1867 (copy), A. L. Burt Papers.
60. New York Times, January 25, 1870, p. 2.
61. Eliza M. Smith to W. P. Miles, January 16, 1873, W. P. Miles Papers.

afraid to sell to only a few of the latter."[62] Negroes were also not permitted to join any of the numerous social organizations in which native
whites participated. The Patrons of Husbandry (the Grange), waxing
strong in the state in the early 1870's, was not only exclusively white in
membership, but was accused of widening the racial gap by its attitudes
and actions toward Negroes.[63] Of course, such separation had been
practiced before, but the exclusion of the Negro in freedom from the
social organizations of the whites was not so much tradition as it was
deliberate decision. For instance, witness the outrage of an officer of the
Donaldsville Lodge of Good Templars at a careless assertion by the
Abbeville *Medium* that the Lodge had admitted Negroes to membership. "I want to inform you," he lectured the editors, "that we have no
negroes in our Lodge of Good Templers as you stated in your Last
paper that we had formed a Lodge of Good Templers Numbering 45
including children & negroes. we don't take negroes in our Lodge.
If you Do dont send me any nother number."[64]

The average Northern white residing in South Carolina during Reconstruction was only slightly less inclined than his native white
contemporary to enforce racial separation. During the war, of course,
Negro troops were organized in separate regiments, bivouacked in
separate camps, and, when wounded, housed in separate hospitals.[65]
After the war, although still sympathetic to most of the interests of the
Negro, many Northern residents continued to draw a very distinct race
line. In March, 1867, presumably under the influence of a man who had
commanded a Negro brigade, many of the whites on St. Helena moved
to establish a separate church from which Negroes would be excluded.
Further, two months later when the Negroes of the island met to form
a Republican organization, most of the Northern white residents boy-
cotted the meeting, saying they were "going to have a *white* party."[66]
Apparently, at least some of this sentiment carried over into the Constitutional Convention of 1868, because, as a Northern correspondent observed, white delegates occupied the front rows while Negroes filled the

62. Mrs. Robert Pelot to her husband, March 11, 1866, Lalla Pelot Papers;
F. A. Ford to James Conner, November 27, 1871, James Conner Papers.

63. William A. Law to his wife, August 29, 1874, William A. Law Papers; *A
History of Spartanburg County*, p. 168.

64. O. P. Gordon to R. R. Hemphill, June 21, 1874, Hemphill Papers.

65. Emma E. Holmes MS Diary, entry for April 7, 1865; Rupert S. Holland,
*Letters and Diary of Laura M. Towne, 1862–1884, Written from the Sea Islands
of South Carolina* (Cambridge, 1912), p. 116.

66. Holland, *Letters and Diary of Laura M. Towne*, pp. 177–78, 182.

seats at the rear of the hall.[67] By 1870, separation also marked the formal social life of the official community in Columbia. Governor Scott, himself, set the precedent. In January, 1869, it was noted that no Negroes attended the traditional annual ball of the governor. The omission caused a great out-cry—the loudest of which, incidentally, came from Franklin J. Moses, Jr., the native white speaker of the house who became the next governor of the state on the suffrage of a Negro electorate. Governor Scott responded to the criticism by holding open house every Thursday evening to which all comers were welcomed. It was soon observed, however, that only Negro politicians called at that time.[68]

Informally, there was considerable social intercourse between Negroes and some Northern missionaries and white Radical politicians, Southern as well as Northern in birth. For instance, as revealed through her diary, the Quaker schoolmistress Martha Schofield never thought or acted in any way discriminatory against Negroes as a race.[69] Frank Moses, politically the most successful of the scalawags, after 1868, publicly, repeatedly, and consistently supported unreserved equality for Negroes. Similarly, in Charleston, in 1870, a scandalized aristocrat declared that Mrs. Bowen, the wife of scalawag Congressman Christopher Columbus Bowen and the daughter of a unionist leader in the nullification controversy in the 1830's, "is reported to receive negro visitors. . . . thank Heaven," he added gratefully, "that Mr. Petigru cannot see her degradation . . ."[70] Perhaps in time the quantity of interchange increased slightly. A Northern observer, visiting the state in 1874, noted that the "shoddy" Northerners living in South Carolina "hob nob" with the blacks in the bars and have them at home and that "at least two politicians of Charleston have married colored wives . . ."[71] Taken at large, however, most white Republicans apparently accepted "public equality" for Negroes; but only a few broadened their toleration to accept Negroes into their social activities.

Separation is, of course, a relative term. It was obviously not possible for Negroes and whites to withdraw entirely from association with each other. If intimate contact led to irritation and violence, it also led to warm personal friendships—often with the superior-inferior, paternal

67. New York Times, January 27, 1868, p. 2.
68. Ibid., February 6, 1869, p. 2; January 25, 1870, p. 2; Charleston Daily Republican, February 19, 1870.
69. Martha Schofield MS Diary, passim.
70. W. G. De Saussure to W. P. Miles, September 21, 1870, W. P. Miles Papers.
71. New York Times, July 9, 1874, p. 1.

bias, but no less real for all of that. Cordiality could and did breach the barrier of race. Yet the fact remained that it was difficult to establish a human bond across the color chasm and, once established, the tie had to be assiduously maintained against the constant erosion induced by a thousand and one external forces of social pressure.

That there was sometimes tenderness between individuals of different races is abundantly evident. On the Elmore plantation near Columbia, in the fall of 1865, the young white master was nightly importuned by the Negro children to get out his fiddle and play. Frequently he did so, the dozen or so Negro boys and girls dancing around the fire, begging for more after the fiddler had exhausted himself in a two-hour concert.[72] The concern of many late masters for their ex-slaves was matched by the interest of individual Negroes in the welfare of their recent owners. A freedman seeking relief for a white family from a Bureau officer explained his motivation: "I used to belong to one branch of that family, and so I takes an interest in 'em."[73] Occasionally, ex-slaveowners retained the friendship and assistance of their erstwhile bondsmen when all others had deserted them. Thus, in the summer of 1873, in an area of Chester county where alleged Klansmen had been active two years previously, planter Robert Hemphill noted the death of a neighbor, John McCluken. "I called one morning & found him dead & the dogs in bed with him," he reported. "Strange to say there was no white person ever called to see him. The negroes were the only persons who gave him any attention at all."[74]

Sometimes, intimacy became miscegenation. The census reports are uncertain witnesses and contemporaries are typically mute on the point; but scattered references suggest that racial interbreeding was markedly less common after emancipation than before. "Miscegenation between white men and negro women diminished under the new order of things," a Bureau officer later wrote. "Emancipation broke up the close family contact in which slavery held the two races, and, moreover young gentlemen did not want mulatto children sworn to them at a cost of three hundred dollars apiece. In short, the new relations of the two stocks tended to separation rather than to fusion."[75] A Northern traveler visiting the state in 1870 concurred: "From all I could see and learn,

72. Grace B. Elmore MS Diary, entry for October 1, 1865.
73. James H. Croushore and David M. Potter (eds.), *John William De Forest, A Union Officer in the Reconstruction* (New Haven, 1948), p. 65.
74. R. N. Hemphill to W. R. Hemphill [Summer, 1873, Hemphill Papers.
75. Croushore and Potter, *A Union Officer,* p. 132.

there are far fewer half-breed children born now than before the
Rebellion. There seems, indeed, a chance that the production of original
half-breeds may be almost done away with. . . ."[76]

Legal, moral, and social pressures exercised by the white community
upon its members, as well as the physical separation of the races suggest
that these were valid observations. The Black Code pointedly declared
that "Marriage between a white person and a person of color shall be
illegal and void," and when the code was revised in 1866 this portion
emphatically remained in force.[77] Children born of Negro mothers and
white fathers, so recently especially prized for their pecuniary value,
became simply illegitimate issue and a liability to the community. In
addition, the laws of bastardy came to be applied against the fathers of
mulatto children. Perhaps most important was the fact that, in the
minds of the native whites, children of mixed blood personified the
adulteration of the superior race and embodied in living form the failure
of Southern civilization. Many whites, turned to soul-searching by their
defeat, fixed upon miscegenation as their great sin. "It does seem strange
that so lovely a climate, and country, with a people in every way superior
to the Yankees, should be overrun and destroyed by them," wrote a rice
aristocrat in 1868. "But I believe that God has ordered it all, and I am
firmly of opinion with Ariel that it is the judgement of the Almighty
because the human and brute blood have mingled to the degree it has
in the slave states. Was it not so in the French and British Islands and
see what has become of them."[78]

Just as complete separation of the races was physically impossible,
there was little possibility that miscegenation might entirely cease. One
does not have to travel far into contemporary sources to discover
instances in which white men had children by Negro women. In 1867,
a lowcountry planter, accused of fathering the mulatto child of his
Negro house servant, wrote plaintively to his mother: "This child was
begotten during my absence in Charlotte & Charleston, from the middle
of December until nearly the middle of January, & the Father of it was
seen night after night in Emma's house, this I heard on my return, but
as it was no concern of mine I did not give it a thought. She was *free*,
the Mother of 5 Children & could have a dozen lovers if she liked. I
had no control over her virtue."[79] In 1874, a planter on the Cooper River

76. Shaler, *Atlantic Monthly*, XXVI, p. 57.

77. *Statutes at Large*, XII, 270, 366[29]–366[30].

78. William Heyward to James Gregorie, January 12, 1868, Gregorie–Elliott
Papers.

79. T. R. S. Elliott to his mother, October 20, 1867, T. R. S. Elliott Papers.

in St. John's noted the existence of circumstances on his plantation which might have led to similar results. "Found a white man staying with one of the colored people on the place," ran the laconic note in his journal. "He being engaged in rebuilding Mayrents Bridge."[80] Some of these liaisons were of prolonged duration. In 1870, Maria Middleton, a Negro woman, brought suit against a Pincville physician for failure to support her three children which he had allegedly fathered. Strangely, the defendant's lawyer did not deny the paternity, but sought dismissal on the plea that the plaintiff had no legal grounds for suit.[81]

Once in power, the Radicals hastened to repeal the prohibition against interracial marriage. Thereafter, informal arrangements were sometimes legalized. In the spring of 1869, a reporter stated that three such marriages had occurred within the state—a Massachusetts man had married a Beaufort mulatto woman, and two white women had married Negro men.[82] In 1872, the legislature explicitly recognized interracial unions by declaring that the "children of white fathers and negro mothers may inherit from the father if he did not marry another woman but continued to live with their mother."[83]

There were a surprisingly large number of cases in which white women gave birth to children by Negro fathers. During his stay in Greenville, Bureau officer John De Forest heard of two such births and noted other instances in which white women were supported by Negro men. Such situations, he believed, were largely the result of the loss of husbands and fathers in the war and the destitution of the country generally.[84] In 1866, in neighboring Pickens District, a case came into the courts in which Sally Calhoun, "a white woman of low birth," and a Negro man were brought to trial for the murder of their child. Ironically, the Negro was freed, though obviously implicated, and the woman was convicted and imprisoned.[85] Apparently, some of these liaisons were far from casual as a Spartanburg farmer rather painfully suggested to his brother in Alabama: "My dear Brother as you have made several Enquiries of me and desiring me to answer them I will attempt and endeavor to do So to the best information that I have on the Various Subjects alluded to by you the first Interrogatory is Relative to

80. Keating S. Ball MS Plantation Journal, entry for February 5, 1874.
81. *Daily Republican* (Charleston), June 7, 1870.
82. *New York Times*, May 24, 1869, p. 2.
83. *Statutes at Large*, XIII, 62–63.
84. Croushore and Potter, *A Union Officer*, p. 138.
85. *House Journal* (Special Session, 1868), Appendix A, pp. 134-35. See also: *New York Times*, November 9, 1866, p. 1.

John H. Lipscomb's daughter haveing Negro Children, I am forced to answer in the affirmative no doubt but she has had two; and no hopes of her Stopping. . . ."[86]

By the end of Reconstruction, Negroes had won the legal right to enjoy, along with whites, accommodations in all public places. In reality, however, they seldom did so. On the opposite side of the racial frontier, the pattern of separation was fixed in the minds of the whites almost simultaneously with the emancipation of the Negro. By 1868, the physical color line had, for the most part, already crystallized. During the Republican regime, it was breached only in minor ways. Once the whites regained political power, there was little need to establish legally a separation which already existed in fact. Moreover, to have done so would have been contrary to federal civil rights legislation and would have given needless offense to influential elements in the North. Finally, retention of the act had a certain propaganda value for use against liberals in the North and against Republican politicians at home. Again and again, the dead letter of the law was held up as exhibit "A" in South Carolina's case that she was being fair to the Negro in the Hampton tradition. After the federal statute was vitiated in the courts, after racial liberalism had become all but extinct in the North, and as the Negro was totally disfranchised in South Carolina, the white community was ready and able to close the few gaps which did exist in the color line, and to codify a social order which custom had already decreed.

Ultimately, the physical separation of the races is the least important portion of the story. The real separation was not that duo-chromatic order that prevailed on streetcars and trains, or in restaurants, saloons, and cemeteries. The real color line lived in the minds of individuals of each race, and it had achieved full growth even before freedom for the Negro was born. Physical separation merely symbolized and reinforced mental separation. It is true that vigorous assaults by one side or the other forced the enemy to yield his forward trenches and to alter slightly the precise line of the color front. It is also true that material changes in post-Reconstruction Southern society pushed the trenches into areas which had not existed before. This often gave the illusion of basic change, of a breakthrough by the dominate whites in the war of races, whereas, actually, it merely represented the extension of the old attitudinal conflict onto new ground, only to bring with it the stalemate

86. Edward Lipscomb to Smith Lipscomb, June 19, 1874, Lipscomb Family Papers.

that marked the struggle elsewhere. Viewed in relation to the total
geography of race relations, the frontier hardly changed; and the rigidity
of the physical situation, set as it was like a mosaic in black and white,
itself suggested the intransigence of spirit which lay behind it. Well
before the end of Reconstruction, this mental pattern was fixed; the
heartland of racial exclusiveness remained inviolate; and South Carolina
had become, in reality, two communities—one white and the other
Negro.

XI...THE NEGRO COMMUNITY

In South Carolina during Reconstruction there existed a strange paradox in the attitude of the Negro toward the society of the white man. On one side, there was an instinctive tendency to withdraw from an association which had been painful in the past and was certain to be painful again. On the other side, white society provided the cultural ideal which the Negro strove to achieve. Consciously, deliberately, he rejected the heritage of Africa. Intuitively, he rejected the legacies of slavery. Thus he denied the past. He had been born, as Negro orators were fond of saying, on the day of emancipation and in his infancy he had assisted in the deliverance of the Union. His identity was inseparably bound with that of the nation. In this sense, he was the most American of Americans. Yet, his Americanism was more than patriotism. It was the complete acceptance of the American way, unqualified by St. Patrick's Day, schutzenfest, or synagogue. Rejecting the past, the Negro was uniquely free to—and did—become acculturated in a degree which none of his neighbors of lighter hue could ever approach. His labor, his church, his God, his clothes, manners, speech, education, thoughts, his values, and even his name were a microcosm of contemporary Southern civilization. Withdrawn from white society, Negroes built a community exclusively their own, quite apart, quite distinct from that of the whites, but withal as nearly perfect in its reflection as a mirrored image. There were flaws, of course. Negroes never accepted the white man's interpretation of Negro character.

Further, the Negro community never approximated the economic wealth of the whites, and, occasionally, it was unable to offer satisfactory replicas of institutions embodied in white society. For instance, Negroes were never able to produce a theater which was exclusively Negro, nor were they able during Reconstruction to create a university comparable in quality to the ideal established by the whites. During Reconstruction, in South Carolina, Negroes generally searched for perfection within their half of a dyarchical civilization. But because the replica must always be, in some degree, an imperfect representation of the original, the pursuit never held the promise of ultimate satisfaction. And thus the Negro faced his dilemma: should he strive to construct a surrogate white culture for himself, or should he move to take a full share in the white community and suffer the pain which the attempt, whether or not successful, would inevitably involve? Again and again, drawn by the bright, white light he moved close, and even as he drew near was seared by the heat of the very thing he would embrace. Again and again, burned, chastened, perhaps resolving never to so punish himself again, he withdrew, but even as he moved away felt drawn again. Attraction and repulsion, this was the Negro's special paradox, the yin and the yang of his existence in this familiar yet alien land. At the end of Reconstruction, the dilemma remained. The Negro had not yet made his decision.

At the time of emancipation there were minor traces of their African heritage among the Negroes of South Carolina. A very few had actually been born in Africa. Such was perhaps the case with Nero, once a slave on Limerick plantation on the lower Cooper River, whose meat ration always consisted of beef rather than the usual pork because, it was said, he was a Mohammedan.[1] In Greenville, an elderly Negro named Uncle Peter was also known as Kangaboonga because he had been "born in Africa, Sar."[2] On the Sea Islands, a Northern teacher found several Negroes who bore tattoo markings on their faces. One of the oldest, Monday, remembered the sea voyage to Charleston, and another, "Maum Katie," recalled worshipping in Africa.[3] Northern residents on the Sea Islands generally agreed that among American Negroes, the islanders had advanced least in acculturation, and many thought that they saw the vestiges of Africa in the language, superstitions, and dances of the

1. W. J. Ball MS Plantation Books, Vol. 3.

2. James H. Croushore and David M. Potter (eds.), *John William De Forest, A Union Officer in the Reconstruction* (New Haven, 1948), p. 55.

3. Rupert S. Holland (ed.), *Letters and Diary of Laura M. Towne, 1862–1884, Written from the Sea Islands of South Carolina*, pp. 22, 144, 176–177.

freedmen. Attending a "shout" on St. Helena in 1862, a Northern
teacher pronounced the wild, shuffling, circular dance to be "certainly
the remains of some old idol worship."[4]

With the exception of these vestigial remains, whatever else slavery
may have done to the Negro, it de-Africanized him. The master did not
share his profits with his slave, but he did share—indeed he forced upon
his bondsmen—his way of life. Even on the Sea Islands, the slave became a part of a world-wide economic system, was Christianized, and
was taught the social morality of the whites. In other areas, cultural
assimilation was virtually complete. In 1866, a Northern correspondent
wrote that "in the upper country, especially in the mountain districts,
they rise in intelligence and in social condition, and approach more
nearly to the whites with whom they are thrown into contact."[5] Another Northern writer reported that in Charleston some Negroes were
"unusually intelligent," and had "assumed the dress, manners and speech
of the whites to perfection."[6]

Excluded from the cultural society of the whites, unable to achieve
full satisfaction by emulating that society from without, some few
Negroes were led to attempt to avoid the dilemma by reviving and
exalting their African heritage. This current of sentiment hardly de-
serves the significance the term movement implies. It did not, for
instance, have the depth and perception which might have led it to the
obvious expedient of appropriating—for the use of all Afro-Americans—
the Islamic culture which some Negro Africans possessed. Nevertheless,
as Reconstruction progressed, some more thoughtful Negroes in South
Carolina evinced an interest in filling the void in the preslavery history
of the American Negro with evidences of ancient and excellent civiliza-
tions in Africa. While the predominantly Negro convention sat in
Charleston in 1868 to draft a new constitution for the state, Martin
Delany, who had traveled extensively in the Niger River Valley in the
1850's negotiating treaties for the settlement of emancipated slaves,
queried a Yale professor: "Weren't [the] first 16 Gk letters invented by
Egyptians or Africans?"[7] During Reconstruction, several hundred

4. *Ibid.*, p. 20; E. L. Pierce, "The Freedmen of Port Royal," *Atlantic Monthly,*
XII (September, 1863), 303; *New York Times,* May 20, 1866, p. 1.

5. *Ibid.*, November 9, 1866, p. 1.

6. *Ibid.*, May 20, 1866, p. 1.

7. Carter G. Woodson, *A Century of Negro Migration* (Washington, 1918),
p. 80; Martin R. Delany to W. D. Whitney, February 29, 1868, W. D. Whitney
Papers.

freedmen returned to Africa via Charleston, and, after the Redemption, there was widespread interest in a general emigration.[8] Furthermore, Negro churches consistently indicated their willingness to support missionary labors in Africa. Perhaps Negroes were attempting in this way to create an alternative culture truly their own, one that would allow them to reject that of the whites if they so chose. More probably, they were only attempting to give the Negro a cultural background somehow comparable to that of the whites and thus, by becoming in some degree different, become still more like their fellow Americans of Irish, German, or Jewish ancestry. It is worthy of note that when emancipated slaves did return to settle in Liberia, the society which they created was as nearly American, and Southern, as circumstances permitted.[9]

Slavery Americanized the Negro, but it also impressed upon him its peculiar marks. In adjusting to the conditions imposed by their bondage, Negroes cultivated certain traits that persisted in the early years of freedom. Northerners working on the plantations behind the lines found the Negroes timid, evasive, suspicious, mendacious, malingering, and inclined to commit petty thievery.[10] Well into Reconstruction, observers commented on sexual promiscuity among Negroes. In 1867, an amazingly well-informed Northerner residing on a plantation near Beaufort reported that hardly a girl on two plantations near by had reached the age of fifteen or sixteen without giving birth to a bastard and that eight women were then pregnant by men other than their husbands.[11] Yet, if slavery had imposed vices, it also imposed virtues. The colonel of the First South found his men obedient, submissive, and easily organized— certainly admirable qualities in soldiers. "I have heard of no man intoxicated, and there has been but one small quarrel," he testified after a year of command. "I suppose that scarcely a white regiment in the army shows so little swearing."[12] Similarly, a British visitor in 1870 noted that the Negro "continues, save on election nights or other periods

8. George Brown Tindall, *South Carolina Negroes, 1877–1900* (Columbia, 1952); MS List of Emigrants for Liberia, embarked on Ship *Golconda* off Charleston, S. C. (American Colonization Society), November 17, 1867.

9. R. Earle Anderson, *Liberia, America's African Friend* (Chapel Hill, 1952), p. 5, *et seq.*

10. Elizabeth W. Pearson (ed.), *Letters from Port Royal* (Boston, 1906), pp. 89, 227.

11. *New York Times*, April 20, 1867, p. 1.

12. Thomas Wentworth Higginson, *Army Life in a Black Regiment* (Boston, 1890), p. 18.

of great excitement, to turn into bed at the early hour in the evenings prescribed to him by a sort of curfew law in the days of slavery."[13]

Slavery had in large measure destroyed the African, but in freedom the Negro himself hastened to destroy the slave. He rejected many of the traits nurtured in slavery as incompatible with his new status. "I ain't got colored-man principles," Corporal Landon Simmons of the First South declared to his colonel, "I'se got white gemman principles."[14] As used by Negroes themselves, the term "nigger" scornfully denoted the way of the Negro in slavery. Thus, a Negro girl was overheard in the streets of Charleston, in the summer of 1874, labeling the rendition of a tune by her male friend as "nigger like"; and an elderly Negro urging his mules along, sagaciously asserted that "Niggers and mules is hard to drive."[15] Some Negroes employed their freedom to adopt virtues which they could not afford in slavery; others used it to cultivate vices which (at least ostensibly) had been denied to them. Intoxication, profanity, and fighting were soon all too common among freedmen. The Reverend Cornish spent one Saturday evening in 1875 in a room over a "grog shop" operated by one of his vestrymen in Barnwell. "In the street in front of the grogshop are heard the voices of Negroes, boisterous laughter, wrangling, & awful profanity," he exclaimed in clerical indignation.[16]

Rejecting Africa, rejecting the way of the slave, the Negro freedman eagerly embraced the civilization of his white contemporaries. In 1877, a Carolinian observed that wealthy Negroes emulated the social behavior of the whites: "paying homage to the ladies, preventing the females from working, sending the children to school, living in fine houses, employing servants, supporting a good table, and keeping carriages and horses."[17] Nevertheless, whites were persistently skeptical of the depth of the Negro's acculturation.

> They have advanced rapidly in ideas, but t'is the views of others which they with their great power of imitation have adopted as their own. As for instance the sacredness of the mar-

13. Robert Somers, *The Southern States since the War, 1870–1871* (New York, 1871), p. 39.

14. Higginson, *Black Regiment,* p. 260.

15. *New York Times,* July 4, 1874, p. 5; Iza D. Hardy, *Between Two Oceans; or Sketches of American Travel* (London, 1884), p. 300.

16. MS Diary, entry for November 13, 1875.

17. A South Carolinian [Belton O'Neall Townsend], "South Carolina Society," *The Atlantic Monthly,* XXXIX (June, 1877), 676.

riage relation. Something unheard of before in negro morals, so far from it, that the owner would have to affix some penalty to the infringement of that relation. Now what more common than to hear 'I must go with my wife,' not because they have investigated the matter and seen the right of the thing, but such is the view of the white and the view suits present circumstances, as is shown in those who went with the Yankee and left their miss behind them. They take the white man['s] notions as they copy his manners, not for what they are but for the impression that's made by them on the world.[18]

It soon became evident, however, that the Negro's acceptance of the white man's culture was more than ape-like imitation.

At the end of the war, the Negro community in South Carolina consisted of some 400,000 individuals. To the whites the Negro mass seemed monolithic and somehow menacing, a black incubus bound together by some mystical tie which they could not fathom. This feeling existed in spite of the Southerner's claim that he understood the Negro better than the Northerner did, and, indeed, better than the Negro understood himself. The prevalence of this feeling was indicated by the frequent use of the term "the Negro" in the generic sense by the whites, as if one switched from a mental image of certain faces to one composite face, everywhere uniform. Many whites, who certainly knew individual Negroes by face, name, and personality, were manifesting the same spirit when they doggedly claimed that all Negroes looked alike to them. This was a persistent myth, reflecting that when a white saw a Negro, he was conditioned to see only black and to react in a distinct, fixed pattern which made little or no allowance for individual differences.

To a significant degree, the impressions of the whites were valid. The Negro was, indeed, inscrutable. ". . . he will know more of your character in three days than you will of his in three months," declared Beverly Nash. "It has been his business all his life to find out the ways of the white man—to watch him, what he means."[19] Further, homogeneous as the ante-bellum Southern white community was compared with that of the North, it was a gathering of strangers compared with the Negro community. Color, as the common mark of the oppressed caste, bound Negroes together with a firmness which the whites had never

18. Grace B. Elmore MS Diary, entry for March 4, 1865.
19. *New York Times*, August 9, 1867, p. 2.

experienced. Moreover, slavery operated aggressively to make Negroes seem and behave alike. Where there were variations in color, as in the mulatto population, or in status, as in the free Negro population, differences were reduced to negligible proportions by the fiat of the whites. Apparent sameness bred unity, and this tendency persisted through Reconstruction. "They are banded together with more than Masonic sympathy," wrote a Northern observer in 1866, "aiding and assisting each other when in trouble, and freely dividing the last morsel of food with travelers of their own color. Any piece of news obtained by them affecting their own race, is transmitted with telegraphic celerity throughout the whole county, and when a planter finds that his employees are exercised over something unknown to him, he is certain that his neighbors are similarly troubled."[20]

Negroes were bound together by race and the common experience of slavery, but individuals among them were also united in formal, institutional connections much as were their white contemporaries.

Many Negroes emerged from slavery with orthodox family associations already well defined. For instance, in July, 1865, on a cotton plantation in Kershaw District, 121 of the 133 Negro residents belonged to 35 families. Of these families 32 were headed by a husband and wife, 2 by women alone, and 1 by a man alone. In ages, sizes, and proportions between male and female these families were, apparently, entirely like those of the whites in the same time and place. On this particular plantation, all the younger children seem to have enjoyed secure family arrangements. Of the 43 children too young to be rated as quarter hands, 33 had both mothers and fathers, 7 had only a mother, and 3 belonged to a wifeless father.[21]

Nevertheless, among the legacies which slavery left the freedmen were remnants of shattered domestic arrangements. It was the adjustment of these which excited the pity and, more often, the humor of publicists, whose writings, in turn, led to faulty interpretations of

20. *Ibid.*, May 31, 1866, p. 5.

21. MS Contract, July 6, 1865, with annotations through December 23, 1865, A. H. Boykin Papers. Documents relating to labor arrangements in 1865 and 1866 on the three MacFarland plantations in Chesterfield District, on the H. L. Pinckney plantation in Sumter District, and on the Henry W. De Saussure plantation near Charleston indicated that the pattern of family relationships on the Boykin plantation were not rare. See: MS Contract, January 1, 1866, Allan MacFarland Papers; H. L. Pinckney MS Plantation Book, entry for January 5, 1865, and following; MS List, December [?], 1865, H. W. and W. G. De Saussure Papers.

familial patterns among Negroes before and after emancipation. Contemporary accounts are replete with instances in which husbands and wives, long parted by the vicissitudes of slavery, sought reunion in freedom. In the fall of 1865, a correspondent of *The Nation* heard of a case in which a man who had been sold to the West thirty years before returned to Columbia in search of his wife.[22] Frequently, one or both parties had taken another mate after separation, but settlements were quickly and often easily made. De Forest recorded the return of Caesar to Greenville to reclaim his wife after a fifteen-year absence in Alabama, only to find her married to a much older man. The Bureau officer then arranged a reunion in which the old man continued to live in the household, sharing in the couple's domesticity much as a venerated grandfather.[23] Within a few years after the war, however, the popular mind expected marital associations among ex-slaves to have been completed. Robert Washington, who had escaped North before the war, returned to Charleston in 1870 to claim his wife Lucretia and their child. Unfortunately for Washington, Lucretia had taken another husband. Magistrate T. J. Mackey, hearing the case, refused to allow Washington's claim, saying that he should have had interest enough to return long before.[24]

However arrived at, actual adjustments in marital relations among Negroes were soon legalized. Some Negro couples had been formally married in slavery and many of these performed the ceremony again in freedom. Many other permanent unions were solemnized only after emancipation. For instance, at the first meeting held in the church at St. Helena village after Emancipation Day, 1863, a Northern missionary married four couples who had been living together without clerical sanction. One groom was sixty-five years old.[25] Northern missionaries, teachers, and military and governmental officers consistently impressed upon the Negroes the necessity of formal ceremonies in perfecting marital unions. Southern whites were more peremptory. At its first postwar session, in the fall of 1865, the legislature disposed of the matter by giving blanket legal sanction to all unions of slaves recognized by both parties. Those having multiple arrangements were allowed until April 1, 1866, to choose one permanent mate. Thereafter, all marriages were to be properly contracted. Nevertheless, in the courts, common law

22. *The Nation*, I, No. 11 (September 14, 1865), 330.
23. Croushore and Potter, *A Union Officer*, p. 56.
24. *Daily Republican* (Charleston), February 19, 1870.
25. *Free South* (Beaufort), January 17, 1863.

marriages would be recognized.[26] In 1872, a Republican legislature again sanctioned informal unions persisting from the slave period and declared the children of such unions legitimate.[27]

Within the Negro family, the roles of individual members tended to be precisely what the social mores of the white community demanded of its own. These roles were defined to the Negro not only by the examples of the native whites, but by the preachments of his Northern friends as well. Thus, Union General Ormsby Mitchel, in October, 1862, admonished the Negroes in their church on Hilton Head to place their family responsibilities above all others. The husbands, he declared, must work at their jobs and provide a living; wives must keep their houses neat and clean and care for the children. To the general, this was a key element in the "Port Royal Experiment."[28]

Husbands and fathers, wives and mothers, parents, sons, and daughters learned their roles early and played them well. Like their white counterparts, Negro men revealed a distinct inclination to dominate their families and put an abrupt end to the matriarchy which had, perhaps, previously prevailed. In the economic sphere, Negro males asserted their dominance soon after emancipation. For instance, on Montrose, a plantation in Chesterfield District, in January, 1866, Ned affixed his wife Victoria's mark to the contract; and their son, Zack, made his own mark only "with Ned's consent." On the same occasion, Frank Tom made his own mark and those of Neil and Giles, his son and his wife.[29] Northern teachers in the Sea Islands noted a general trend toward masculine ascendency in the household. After gaining the vote, husbands were especially prone to show their superior importance by leaving the women in the fields while they attended political "conventions."[30] The most striking change among Negro wives wrought by emancipation was their partial withdrawal from the fields and greater concentration upon the management of the home. A notable change also occurred in relationships between parents and children. A visitor to the Sea Islands in 1865 reported that mothers spent more time than formerly with their children, and that both parents showed greater affection for their

26. *Statutes at Large,* XII, 270.
27. *Ibid.,* XIII, 162–63.
28. *New South* (Port Royal), October 17, 1862.
29. MS Contract, January 1, 1866, Allan MacFarland Papers.
30. Botume, *First Days Among the Contrabands,* p. 273; Holland, *Letters and Diary of Laura M. Towne,* pp. 183–84.

progeny.[31] Contrary to a common belief that Negro parents were generally cruel to their children, a Bureau officer in Greenville asserted that love of children was "one of the most marked characteristics of the race," though parents were prone to be strict disciplinarians.[32] Cynthia, who had served as a maid while a slave and who subsequently lived in Chester with her husband, her daughter Harriet, and her son Billy, described the manner and spirit in which discipline was administered in her family. Chided by her late mistress that she was not able to make Billy obey, Cynthia replied: "*Yes ma'am* I can. I makes Harriet hold him and turn up his frock and if I don't make these old bones (holding out her hand) work on him, he'll tell you." She paused a moment and added, "For you know Miss Grace, de Bibble says, use the switch and don't spile de chile."[33]

Like their white contemporaries, individual Negroes did not always play their family roles as society dictated. There were blatant cases of wife and child beating, of bigamy, illegitimacy, infanticide, and orphanage through desertion. Laura Towne, living on St. Helena, operated an early day welfare bureau which successfully deprived more than one brutal father of the privilege of abusing his offspring.[34] One Bureau officer, admitting that his office looked upon the seamy side of life, believed that bigamy was common among Negroes and that illegitimacy, though less prevalent than in slavery, was "disastrously abundant."[35] Nevertheless, in spite of individual transgressions, the average Negro family enjoyed remarkable success in its attempt to emulate the familial pattern of the whites.

A highly significant indication of burgeoning individual and family pride among Negroes during Reconstruction was their adoption of surnames. In slavery most Negroes were known only by given names and sometimes, to avoid confusion, by some identifying adjective. Thus, on Limerick, a rice plantation on the lower Cooper River, only one slave, Lewis Cockfield, boasted a family name. Many were identified beyond their given names by reference to a husband or wife. The two Binah's on Limerick were known as "Nat's Binah" and "Ben's Binah." Occasionally, the possessive was reversed. Nat sometimes became "Binah's

31. W. C. Gannett, "The Freedmen at Port Royal," *North American Review,* 101 (July, 1865), 6–7.
32. Croushore and Potter, *A Union Officer,* pp. 114–15.
33. Grace B. Elmore MS Diary, entry for November 30, 1866.
34. Holland, *Letters and Diary of Laura M. Towne,* pp. 213, 219–20.
35. Croushore and Potter, *A Union Officer,* p. 102.

Nat," or another husband was known as "Caty's Daniel." Often, Negroes were identified by a reference to some physical characteristic. On Limerick, a house servant, Martha, was known as "yellow Martha." Children were frequently differentiated by reference to their mother— as "Susey's Charles," or "yellow Martha's Henry."[36]

In freedom, Negroes hastened to adopt surnames. Lengthy casualty lists of Negro regiments recruited in South Carolina indicate that all soldiers had given and family names, and a few, like George E. Washington, had three.[37] In July, 1865, nine out of thirty-five families and four out of twelve single Negroes residing on a Boykin plantation in Kershaw were identified by family names. By the end of the year, three more families and one individual had adopted surnames.[38]

To that hackneyed Shakespearean query "What's in a name?" the freedman doubtless would have had an interesting answer. Implicit in his behavior in this relation was the rejection of his identity as a slave. Although Biblical names continued to be given as first names, the farcical, high-sounding, classical appellations of the slave period—such as Caesar, Primus, Scipio, and Bacchus—withered away before a host of Anglo-Saxon-sounding names—William, Charles, and George. Frequently, the names chosen traveled through several versions, reflecting the freedman's rather unsophisticated yearning for respectability. For instance, between June, 1866, and January, 1868, on a Sumter District plantation freedman Eddy became first Eddy Williams and then Edgar Williams.[39] Sometimes, the name seems to have been changed to fit the natural dignity of the man. During slavery and throughout the war, the captain of the *Planter* was known as Robert Small, the last name probably alluding to his physical height. When he sat in the Constitutional Convention in 1868, however, he was officially enrolled as Robert Smalls, a nominal change which nevertheless better comported with his stature in the eyes of his constituents.[40] The names of Negro women often changed in the same fashion. On the H. L. Pinckney plantation in Sumter District, slave Margaret became the wife of Captain and was subsequently known as Captain's Margaret. In Reconstruction years she was iden-

36. W. J. Ball MS Plantation Books, various entries.
37. *Palmetto Herald* (Port Royal), December 8, 15, 1864.
38. MS Contract, July 6, 1865, with notations through December 23, 1865, A. H. Boykin Papers.
39. H. L. Pinckney MS Plantation Book, various entries.
40. *Free South* (Beaufort), December 12, 1863; *New South* (Port Royal), September 6, 1862; Pearson, *Letters from Port Royal,* pp. 46, 268.

tified, simply, as Captain Margaret, a uniquely appropriate title since she was a strong and effective laborer, pacing the others in the field.[41]

Frequently, individual Negroes adopted the surnames of their former masters or of a respected white neighbor. Thus, there was an abundance of new Pinckneys, Middletons, Hayneses, Hamptons, and Pickenses in Reconstruction South Carolina. To some extent this was simply a matter of convenience and an obvious choice in view of the Negro's proclivity to identify closely with his plantation group. Nevertheless, it also indicates the existence of a certain degree of respect between freedmen and some ex-masters, an indication strengthened by the striking absence or dearth of the names of some large slaveholders (such as Aiken and Calhoun) among Negroes in this period. Some freedmen appropriated nationalistic names such as Washington, Lincoln, and Grant, but these were relatively few. Many Negroes chose names that described their work, surroundings, appearance, or personality. For example, on the H. L. Pinckney plantation in Sumter District in June, 1865, one Negro was known as Sam Tailor (the spelling had become Taylor by the following year); and another became Washington Sumptor, probably after the town or district of Sumter which was often spelled Sumptor.[42] On John Berkeley Grimball's Grove plantation in Colleton District, several families took the name Payas, probably in imitation of a respected lowcountry family. However, the spelling soon changed to Pious, perhaps in recognition of the religious aspirations of the family.[43] Many names were taken, or given, for no apparent reason other than the pleasure of the author. There were numerous Kings, Princes, and Dukes; Generals, Colonels, Majors, and Captains; and an occasional Senator, Governor, or Judge. Greens, Browns, and Whites abounded, but only a single Black, a resident of Beaufort, distinguished himself sufficiently to have his name recorded for posterity. Even he was known as "Jimmy of the Battery" as well as "Jimmy Black," and it is not clear that he acknowledged his more colorful name. A Northern teacher asked her students why his "title" was Black. "Oh, him look so," they chirped. "Him one very black man."[44]

Even at the time of emancipation, among Negroes the demands of kinship above the immediate family level were deep and wide. The

41. H. L. Pinckney MS Plantation Book, various entries.

42. *Ibid.*, entries for June 15, 1866; February 1, 1867.

43. Scattered references to the Pious clan are contained in the John Berkeley Grimball Papers (Duke).

44. Botume, *First Days Among the Contrabands*, p. 49.

freedman not only recognized the claims of sons, daughters, and wives but he also valued his ties with cousins, uncles, and aunts, with ancestors back through the generations, and with his children's children ad infinitum. This clannishness among Negroes, if it changed at all, grew richer in Reconstruction when they were relatively free to express their attitudes by actions. The feeling is evident on plantations where the nucleus of a clan remained year after year.[45] That the clan relationship was also frequently maintained in local migratory movements, is evident in the lists of settlers located on state lands by the Land Commission.[46]

There were also liaisons among clans, consolidated by long associations on a given plantation and intermarriage. A Northern teacher on the Sea Islands during the war noted a strong affinity among the Negro refugees for "massa's niggers," meaning those from their home plantation.[47] Apparently, much the same feeling bound the free Negro families of Camden together. There, the Boykins, Conways, Johnsons, and Scanlons (who had an Irish immigrant father) enjoyed a close and cordial intimacy before, during, and after Reconstruction.[48]

In addition to racial and familial bonds, individual Negroes were tied to one another by a host of organizations of greater or lesser, formality. In the early postwar years, the contract system itself tended to unite Negroes in the pursuit of their material interests. More important and lasting were the many mutual homestead, planting, insurance, burial, and savings and loan associations, organizations of tradesmen, and joint business enterprises which joined large numbers of Negroes together to achieve specific economic objectives. Religious and educational institutions and the myriad social activities emanating from them added further cohesiveness to the Negro community. Social clubs such as the Colored Freemasons carried on charitable enterprises, volunteer fire companies were practical as well as social and ornamental, numerous temperance societies were formed by the Negro leadership in

45. For instance, five of the eleven laborers who contracted to work on the A. H. Boykin plantation in Kershaw County in 1875 were Boldens belonging to two or three separate households. MS Contract, February 1, 1875, A. H. Boykin Papers.

46. About one-fourth of the commission's land in Abbeville County was occupied by seven families of Williamses and six of Moragues. See the reports of the land commissioner contained in *Reports and Resolutions,* 1870–1871 through 1883.

47. Botume, *First Days Among the Contrabands,* p. 103.

48. Bonds Conway Correspondence, various MSS.

the cities and the more populous towns. Thus, A. J. Ransier and others in 1869 secured a state charter for the Amateur Literary and Fraternal Association of Charleston, and another group formed the Columbia Educational Society.[49]

The one club to which practically the entire Negro population belonged was the Republican party. For the very ardent members, participation in meetings, caucuses, and conventions was possible. For the mildly devoted, Union Leagues and the militia provided outlets for enthusiasm. For the masses, there were parades, barbecues, picnics, and speeches. In the latter demonstrations, particularly those celebrating Emancipation Day and the Fourth of July, virtually the entire Negro community was involved, either as participants or spectators.

Monolithic as the Negro community appeared to native whites, there were divisive forces within it. Mulattoes were disdainful of blacks, and blacks resented the pretensions of mulattoes. Negroes who had been free before the war were liable to be scornful of those more recently freed, and ex-slaves were distrustful of the free Negroes. Servants scorned field hands, and the less prosperous envied the well-to-do. Urbanites were contemptuous of rustics and were repaid in the same coin. In addition, there were rivalries among religious denominations—particularly between the Northern and African Methodists, and among the various social clubs. Native Negro politicians often revealed a resentment of Northern-born Negro politicos. Finally, some Negro politicians and voters, occasionally, cooperated with Conservatives, and a few actually became Democrats.

Color variations within the Negro community were less important than native whites liked to think. Furthermore, they were infinitely less significant than the distinction between pure Caucasians and persons having Negro blood in any proportion at all. Generically classified as mulattoes, members of the mixed group were categorized by contemporary whites with exaggerated, almost agonizing precision. In the special meaning of the term, mulattoes were the issue of unions between pure Negroes and pure whites. White quadroons were the children of mulattoes and pure whites. White octoroons were the offspring of quadroons and pure whites. By the Constitution of 1895, the children of white octoroons and pure whites were allowed to marry white persons, and were, thus, legally white. Actually, however, any person having any known proportion of Negro blood, be it ever so slight, was not acceptable

49. *House Journal* (1868–1869), pp. 228, 255.

in white society. As one Northern-born Negro leader explained: ". . . they call everybody a negro that is as black as the ace of spades or as white as snow, if they think he is a negro or know that he has negro blood in his veins."[50] On the other side, the color code described the children of pure Negroes and mulattoes of various mixtures as black quadroons and black octoroons. Unions of mulattoes of various shades, of course, produced an infinite variety of mixtures.

Before 1890, census reports are not highly reliable concerning the mulatto population. In the aggregate, however, they do present a rough outline of the development of this class. In 1850, the first year in which mulattoes were counted, some 17,000 were found in South Carolina. This number represented about 4 per cent of the total Negro population. In 1860, when a more careful enumeration was made, the number rose to twenty-eight thousand, or about 7 per cent of the total. In 1870, when field agents were ordered to list as mulattoes all "quadroons, octoroons, and all persons having any perceptible trace of African blood," the number was recorded as slightly less than twenty-eight thousand.[51] Apparently, the mulatto population was heavily concentrated in the cities. On the Sea Islands during the war, a Northern official noted that in three Beaufort schools mustering 224 scholars he saw 43 mulatto children. On the plantations, he visited some schools with no mulatto children in attendance, others with two or three and none with more than six.[52]

Contemporary white observers probably exaggerated the extent of color distinctions within the Negro community. Prideful of race themselves, they were doubtless flattered by the deference which Negroes sometimes paid to whiteness among their own people. Conservative politicians, hopeful that mulattoes might be separated from the main phalanx of Negro Republicanism, were particularly articulate on this point. Yet, Northern observers appear to have been most sensitive to the distinction, and it was they who did most to publicize its existence. In Greenville, a Bureau officer reported a "deep and increasing jealousy between the blacks and the mulattoes," attitudes which were being institutionalized by the formation of "distinct cliques of society" and separate churches.[53] In Charleston, in the summer of 1872, a Northern cor-

50. *South Carolina in 1876*, I, 234.

51. *Negro Population*, pp. 207, 209, 218–21.

52. Pierce, *Atlantic Monthly*, XII, 303. See also: N. S. Shaler, "An Ex-Southerner in South Carolina," *Atlantic Monthly*, XXVI, 57; *The Nation*, XV, No. 372 (August 15, 1872), 105.

53. Croushore and Potter, *A Union Officer*, p. 124.

respondent observed that mulattoes held themselves aloof from those of pure Negro stock, and that the latter were jealous of them. "At the present moment," he reported, "on the walk outside my window, a couple of ebony damsels and a mulatto boy are belaboring one another in terms more vigorous than select as to each other's claims to 'respectability' on the ground of color."[54] Two years later in the same city, another Northern visitor thought that such recriminations were common. "Dat whitewashed nigger am just like a mule," he represented the black fieldhand as saying of the cream-colored city dandy. "He ain't got no country and no ancestor."[55]

Within the Negro community, mixed blood was frequently accepted as a warrant for increased social acceptability. Yet, color alone did not account for the mulatto's prestige. Large proportions of the wealthy, educated, and leadership classes were mulattoes. For instance, in 1869, a visitor to Howard School in Columbia observed that among some 600 students, who were probably closely representative of these elements, only 200 were of purely Negro ancestry, while 85 were black quadroons, 135 were mulattoes, and 185 were white quadroons, several of the latter being so white as to make it "very difficult to say that they are not white."[56] Doubtless, the typically high social status that individual mulattoes enjoyed added to the respect they were accorded as a group within the Negro community.

As individuals, mulattoes tended to regard with esteem their kinship with the whites. Surprisingly few of this class appear to have been the issue of backstairs and midnight romances. On the contrary, they seem usually to have been the fruit of more stable liaisons. Mulattoes, themselves, were frequently and rather proudly aware of precisely where and by whom white blood had been infused into the family tree. Moreover, the white community at large seemed to possess the same information, even though it was highly circumspect in expressing its knowledge. Thomas E. Miller, a late Reconstruction politician in the Beaufort area and a mulatto, was once saved from a severe beating and possible death by the intercession of a prominent white man. In the emotional heat generated by imminent violence, as Miller subsequently testified, his ally declared, "Miller, I knew your parents, both white and black from the days of boyhood," words which seem to carry much of the passion of a family friend.[57]

54. *The Nation*, XV, No. 372 (August 15, 1872), 106.
55. *New York Times*, July 4, 1874, p. 5.
56. *Ibid.*, July 4, 1869, p. 3.
57. *Recent Election in South Carolina*, Part 3, 170.

Proud as they often were of their white connections, mulattoes seldom discountenanced the black. Indeed, as individuals, mulattoes could not deny their Negro ancestry without denying a large portion of themselves. Robert Smalls or Francis Cardozo, for instance, might well have valued the legacies of their Jewish fathers, but this would hardly have led them to renounce their Negro mothers. What was true of the individual was true of the group as a whole. Theoretically, mulattoes were as much a part of the white race as the black, as much akin to the white as to the Negro community. In actual practice, they were rejected by their white relations. Yet, mulattoes still had a choice between forming a third "mulatto community," or identifying themselves with the society of the Negro. Soon after emancipation, quite deliberately, they chose the latter alternative. In July, 1865, a Northern visitor in Charleston found color distinctions within the Negro community pronounced. Visiting Columbia, he found few signs of such sentiments, and, returning to Charleston in September, he reported that "the old jealousy between blacks and mulattoes is disappearing."[58] Further, the census figures suggest that intermarriage between pure Negroes and mulattoes proceeded on a scale which belies the existence of any widespread pressure against it. Between 1870 and 1890, the proportion of mulattoes in the Negro community rose from about 7 to 10 per cent, and during the next two decades continued to rise to 16 per cent.[59]

Closely related to the division of the Negro community into pure Negroes and mulattoes was the distinction that Negroes made between those who had been free before the war (the "bona-fide free" as they termed themselves) and those who had been "sot free." Numbering about ten thousand in 1860, the former were about 70 per cent mulatto. They centered in Charleston, where many had long been prosperous, well educated, and respected. As early as 1790, sixty-one of the 320 free Negro families in South Carolina held slaves of their own and, during the war, many were reported as being ardent rebels.[60] Soon after the war, observers noted a cleavage between the free and the freed. "Late arrivals from the city say the really respectable class of free negroes, whom we used to employ as tailors, boot makers, mantua makers,

58. *The Nation*, I, No. 4 (July 27, 1865), 106; I, No. 6 (August 10, 1865), 73; I, No. 11 (September 14, 1865), 332.

59. *Negro Population*, pp. 218–20.

60. *Ibid.*, pp. 56–57; *The Nation*, I, No. 11 (September 14, 1865), 332.

etc., wont associate at all with the 'parvenue free'—but have the Orphan House Chapel (the O. H. itself being now for juvenile colored orphans) as a place of worship, Mr. Joseph Seabrook preaching," a Camden diarist wrote at the end of May, 1865. "They are exceedingly respectful to the Charleston gentlemen they meet," she prated, "taking their hats off and expressing their pleasure in seeing them again, but regret that it is under such circumstances, enquiring about others, etc."[61] Writing in 1925, Carter G. Woodson, a Negro and an eminent historian of his race, asserted that some of Charleston's "old issue free" had confided to him that they still practiced this form of discrimination.[62] Such a feeling, however, was not universal. Francis Cardozo, who was both a mulatto and "old-issue free," personified the statement of a Northern reporter in September, 1865, that "these wealthy slaveholding mulatto families of Charleston are fully identified in interest with the mass of the colored people, and are becoming leaders among them...."[63] Moreover, this form of discrimination grew increasingly less evident as individuals of the "sot free" class acquired wealth, education, and political and social influence.

Thus, there were both cohesive and divisive forces operating within the Negro community. In the balance, however, it is evident that the influences tending to unite the Negro community were far more influential than those which worked to divide it. Compared to that of the whites, the Negro community was indeed monolithic in its unity.

The social problems the Negro community faced during Reconstruction presented the same variety and complexity as did those confronting the whites. Like his white contemporaries, the Negro had to deal with problems of ill health, the care of orphans and indigents, crime, and antisocial behavior. Both during and after the period, these difficulties were exaggerated within his community by the peculiar problem of general poverty which the Negro encountered.

A major and vitally important difference existed in the numerical growth rate of the two races. Between 1860 and 1870, the number of Negroes in South Carolina remained practically static. A rapid increase in the Negro population followed during the two succeeding decades,

61. Emma E. Holmes MS Diary, entry for "End of May," 1865.
62. Carter G. Woodson, *Free Negro Heads of Families in the United States in 1830* (Washington: Association for the Study of Negro Life and History, 1925), p. lvii.
63. *The Nation*, I, No. 11 (September 14, 1865), 332.

and the population of the state became roughly 60 per cent Negro. By 1900, however, the rate of increase among Negroes had markedly declined, and in the early years of the twentieth century numerical superiority passed to the whites.[64]

A host of reasons could be advanced to explain the failure of the Negro population to expand during the early postwar years. A large part of the explanation lies in the decline of health and the increase in mortality among certain groups of Negroes. Even in slavery, medical care for Negroes (despite frequent exceptions and the arguments of proslavery apologists) had always been less extensive than for whites, and mortality rates among Negroes had been considerably higher than among their white neighbors. The colonel of the First South found that his men were usually less healthy than whites, and a member of an army medical board which examined men enlisted in the six South Carolina regiments found that they were three or four inches shorter than the free Negroes of the North. The latter stated that Southern-born Negro soldiers could expect to be "old men" by their forty-fifth birthdays.[65]

The dislocations of the war and emancipation resulted in a decline in sanitation and medical care among freedmen in many places. During the war, missionaries working on the Sea Islands found that sanitary regulations previously imposed by slaveholders had broken down, and their best efforts were insufficient to restore standards.[66] Epidemics, especially smallpox, were recurrent and devastating. "The children," wrote Miss Towne in January, 1865, "are all emaciated to the last degree, and have such violent coughs and dysenteries that few survive."[67] As emancipation spread through the state, the health of Negroes was often neglected. "The Freedmen are not sick these days," a Chester planter wrote facetiously in 1866. "The Dr. has not been sent for this year. A remarkable thing for this plantation, that is A Happy change wrought by Emancipation."[68]

The results of neglect were often disastrous. Debilitated by malnutrition and exposure, large numbers of Negro transients succumbed to diseases. In the year following the close of the war, a Northern teacher working on Edisto witnessed in one Negro family the death of both

64. *Negro Population,* pp. 44, 51.
65. Higginson, *Black Regiment,* p. 263; *New York Times,* April 2, 1866, p. 1.
66. Pearson, *Letters from Port Royal,* p. 15.
67. Holland, *Letters and Diary of Laura M. Towne,* pp. 153–54.
68. R. N. Hemphill to W. R. Hemphill, August 11, 1866, Hemphill Papers.

parents and the youngest four of seven children.[69] In the lowcountry, during the winter of 1865-1866, a smallpox epidemic was particularly deadly. On Edisto, the schools were forced to close. When they re-opened in February, one of the teachers asked a child if there were any smallpox patients remaining on her plantation. "No," the child answered, "the last one died Saturday."[70] Mortality during these winter months was so high that many whites confidently predicted the early demise of the Negro race. "The black thieves are rapidly dying out with smallpox and other loathsome diseases," declared one Charleston-ian in February.[71] Although never again so lethal, epidemics were recurrent and usually visited the Negro community with particular severity. "A great deal of sickness, & a great many deaths especiale [sic] among the Col. people & children," reported a Chester planter in the summer of 1873. "I am told there was 16 deaths within 5 miles of Blackstocks in a month."[72]

The common impression that mortality among Negroes was high was true of transients in general and in Charleston in particular, and it was from these sources that writers drew their conclusions. Highly reliable mortality figures for Charleston indicated that the death rate among Negroes there increased by about one-seventh between 1860 and 1870, whereas it decreased by about the same amount among whites. In the latter year, deaths among Negroes, in proportion to their respective total numbers, occurred roughly twice as frequently as among whites. In each of the six years, 1866 through 1871, about half of the Negroes who died were children. In 1866, smallpox accounted for about one-fifth of the Negro deaths in the city and decreased to nil thereafter, probably in response to a vaccination campaign. Negroes retained a comparative immunity to yellow fever, only twenty-three succumbing in 1871 to an epidemic which killed 189 whites. Venereal diseases also took their toll; but the most dangerous new killer was consumption, which claimed the lives of 75 Negroes in 1866, and 135 in 1871.[73]

69. Mary Ames, *From a New England Woman's Diary in Dixie in 1865* (Springfield, 1906), pp. 14–95.

70. *Ibid.*, pp. 112–13.

71. John Bachman to E. Elliott, February 1, 1866, Elliott–Gonzales Papers.

72. R. N. Hemphill to W. R. Hemphill, July 6, 1873, Hemphill Papers.

73. Shaler, *Atlantic Monthly*, XXVI, pp. 57–58; *The Nation*, XV, No. 372 (August 15, 1872), 105–6; *New York Times*, April 21, 1869, p. 2; Robert Somers, *The Southern States since the War, 1870–1871* (New York, 1871), pp. 52–54. Each of these sources relied upon the statistics published by the health authorities of Charleston.

Yet, it was not true that the mortality rate among freedmen was high everywhere. Scattered evidence suggests that Negroes who remained on their home plantations or who migrated only locally commanded roughly the same measure of medical attention which they had received as slaves and that the death rate among this class was about the same or, at the worst, only slightly higher than during the ante-bellum period.

Freedmen often deserted their late masters, yet, interestingly, they seldom abandoned their slave-period physician. Many labor contracts required the employer to advance medical care as "heretofore." Under these circumstances, the nature of medical assistance received by laborers remained substantially unchanged after emancipation.[74] The exorbitant fees charged, however, by physicians under this provision, perhaps explained why the laborers on the Peter B. Bacot plantation, near Mar's Bluff in Darlington District, adopted a novel but surprisingly common system of medical insurance. In 1867, they contracted to pay the physician four dollars for each of the thirty-two adults and fifty cents for each of the thirty children on the plantation in return for medical assistance as needed throughout the year.[75]

While the lowcountry was the most unhealthy portion of the state, missionaries, the military, and the Bureau were also most active there in pushing forward a program of public health. Particularly in Charleston, public medicine reached a high level of organization through the cooperation of the Freedmen's Bureau, which provided supplies, and the city, which furnished doctors, nurses, and buildings.[76] The good work continued after the Bureau retired. A British visitor to the city in November, 1870, found the public health program efficient and its hospital "an establishment of great extent, marked by scrupulous cleanliness and order, and devoted equally to white and colored subjects."[77]

A perusal of manuscript correspondence, labor contracts, plantation journals, and diaries indicates that mortality among Negroes in the interior was not significantly higher than it had been in the slave

74. For instances, *see:* MS Account submitted by Peter B. Bacot to Edward Porcher, 1866, Peter B. Bacot Collection; MS Physician's Journals, James R. Sparkman Books.

75. MS Contract, 1867, Peter B. Bacot Collection. *See also:* MS Contract, January 1, 1867, Allan MacFarland Papers.

76. *New York Times,* May 20, 1866, p. 1.

77. Somers, *The Southern States since the War,* pp. 53–54.

period.[78] As economic prosperity returned in the early 1870's, interest in Negro mortality among whites declined markedly. The state census of 1875 indicated a substantial increase in the Negro population, a trend which was confirmed by biennial censuses of the school population. The general enumeration of 1880 made it evident that, far from dying away, Negroes were living longer and births were exceeding both deaths and emigrations, suggesting that the Negro in freedom had learned to care for his health.

In the months which followed the war, many Negro children were deprived of mothers or fathers or both through death or desertion.[79] A large number of orphans were cared for by relatives or simply adopted informally by sympathetic adults. A few went into orphanages operated first by the Bureau and subsequently by the state. Apparently, most orphans were apprenticed out by the authorities. Because the apprentice might be trained in farm labor or domestic service where instruction was minimal and labor was hard, as well as in the trades, the practice was sometimes abused. However, conscientious officials frequently used the device as a very practical and fair solution to the problem of caring for parentless children. For instance, William Stone, a Bureau agent, in March, 1867, formally apprenticed to R. H. McKie, a planter residing near Hamburg, five Negro children between the ages of five and thirteen. However, he admonished the planter to have the children "taught the rudiments of an English education" and directed that he "should pay to each at the end of his apprenticeship a sum of money equal to four or five dollars per annum for each year that he serves."[80]

The very old, like the very young, were sometimes orphaned by emancipation and the war. Many of these were, in a sense, "adopted"

78. Between July and December, 1865, three out of the 133 Negroes residing on a Kershaw District plantation died; during the same interval, none of fifty-two laborers on a Christ Church plantation died. This compares favorably with the mortality rate of Negroes in Charleston in 1860 when one out of every 28.5 Negroes died. MS Contract, July 6, 1865, with notations through December 23, 1865, A. H. Boykin Papers; MS List with notations, December —, 1865, H. W. and W. G. De Saussure Papers.

79. Ames, *From a New England Woman's Diary in 1865*, p. 111; Croushore and Potter, *A Union Officer*, pp. 45–46, 54.

80. R. H. McKie to "Bureau Agent," March 1, 1867; endorsement of William Stone, March 7, 1867, R. H. McKie Papers. For other instances, *see:* R. I. Gage to "Patterson," January 14, 1866, James M. Gage Papers; MS Contract, January 17, 1866, John Fox Papers.

by relatives or friends. Some of the less fortunate were housed in local poor houses or "county farms" where conditions were often subhuman.

The Negro community also had its full share of the physically and mentally deformed. A Bureau survey of "unfortunates" in the state in March, 1867, indicated that among the four hundred thousand Negroes there were many blind, deaf and dumb, imbecilic or idiotic, insane, club-footed, malformed, and maimed persons.[81] A large number of the afflicted were without guardians, and they, along with the orphaned, were thrown for their support upon the not-too-generous assistance of the Bureau or the not-too-abundant charity of the communities in which they lived. In time, some achieved happier circumstances. The city of Charleston soon provided comparatively well for its unfortunates. The insane, for example, were cared for in a special ward in the City Hospital.[82] After the Radicals gained political ascendency, some of the more influential among the afflicted gained admittance to the state's insane asylum or the orphanage in Columbia. Most, however, were forced to pursue a miserable existence on the county farms.

The Negro community, too, had its criminal element. The traditional idea that the crimes of Negroes were largely confined to petty transgressions upon the property of others does not hold true after the first two or three years of freedom. Indeed, the Negro criminal, granting that his opportunities were not always equal to those of the whites, was fully as versatile as his white counterpart. His crimes included the full range of offences against property, persons, and society. They indicated among their perpetrators qualities of stealth and cleverness, audacity and cunning, militant bumptiousness, murderous temperament, ignorance, stupidity, and amorality.

A common jest of the slave period asserted that the Negro saw no harm in "putting massa's chicken into mass'a nigger." Whether the slave actually subscribed to this philosophy or not, many freedmen faced with starvation in the hard times of the early postwar years did steal food.[83] "Our fruit is beginning to ripen and is a large crop," ran a common complaint, "but the freedmen are very bad about robing [sic] orchards, and in fact they are bad about robing any place . . ."[84] As prosperity returned, there was a noticeable decline in such com-

81. *Report of the Secretary of War* (1867–1868), Part 1, p. 637.
82. Somers, *The Southern States since the War*, p. 54.
83. *New York Times*, August 9, 1867, p. 2.
84. "Mother" to Nickels J. Holmes, July 7, 1868, Nickels J. Holmes Papers.

ments, but in 1875 and 1876, as poor crops and low prices raised the spectre of hunger, thefts again became common. "The negroes are starving and stealing everything," lamented one Batesburg planter in the winter of 1875.[85]

Food was not the exclusive object of theft. In 1867, the mistress of a plantation near Adams Run declared that "You dare not leave out any article of clothing on the fence for one night for by the next morning it will be gone. . . ."[86] A persistent problem was the pilferage of un-ginned cotton, either from plantation storehouses or directly from the fields. Gathering conclusive evidence against a cotton thief was almost impossible since the larcenist could invade an unwatched field on a moonless night, pick two or three dollars' worth of the staple in a few hours, and mix it with his own harvest when he returned home. Detection was even more difficult in cases where the thief was a share-cropper stealing from his own crop before the division was made. Even an honest merchant obviously could not discern stolen cotton from that legitimately possessed, and not a few country storekeepers were much more interested in the offering price than the past history of their purchases. Once connections were established, other items joined cotton in the traffic. "Stealing and the traffic in Stolen Property," wrote a Bishopville planter in October, 1868, "which has become uni-versal among the negroes and encouraged by many White persons who are directly or indirectly engaged in the business is the greatest evil against which we have to contend. The enclosed proceedings of the Citizens of this Community Conveys an inadequate idea of its enor-mity."[87]

Occasionally, Negro robbers revealed great cunning and startling audacity. A white man floating a shipment of cotton downriver to Charleston in November, 1865, was called away from his post by a reported illness in his family. "I hired a guard of negroes," he explained to the owner, "and the next morning two bales of cotton were gone." Needless to say, so also were the guards.[88] Actually, piracy was not at all unique in the state, but train robbers were. In October, 1867, a party of Negro bandits tore up a section of the South Carolina Rail-road in Richland District, derailed a train, and looted the cars. On a highway in the same area two months later, eight Negroes stole at

85. T. S. Fox to John Fox, February 25, 1875, John Fox Papers.
86. Anonymous letter, September 10, 1867, Hemphill Papers.
87. J. S. Dennis to J. Y. Harris, October 7, 1868, J. Y. Harris Papers.
88. J. T. Davis to D. W. Jordan, November 15, 1865, D. W. Jordan Papers.

gun point a wagon, six mules, and two bales of cotton. Soon afterward, five Negroes entered a country store in Darlington District, posing as would-be customers. They soon produced guns, robbed the store, shot the owner, a neighbor, and the neighbor's wife, and fired on another neighbor who attempted to stop them.[89]

Negroes were also capable of executing frauds quite as grandiose as any produced by the white community. If the charges against R. H. Cain in regard to his real estate operations in the vicinity of Charleston were true, he ranks very high on the all-state list of confidence men. Yet, most of the frauds perpetrated by Negroes were picayune. For instance, in 1870, Harriet Washington, a Negro residing in Charleston, accused Alexander Hamilton, also a Negro, of selling her a defective love potion for twenty-five dollars and a gold cross. Arraigned before a trial justice, Hamilton argued that the root was supposed to work and complained that Harriet had failed to pay the money promised. Very astutely the trial justice nullified the contract and restored to the original owners both the gold cross and the impotent potion.[90]

Negroes, too, were guilty of crimes against society. Prostitution apparently flourished openly among some elements of the Negro community in Charleston. For instance, a Republican paper in the city in 1870 reported the arrest of three Negro women: "Ann Heyward, Eliza Aiken and Hannah Jenkins were arrested last night about half-past eleven o'clock, in a house of bad repute on Elliott street, while engaged in a free fight, during which they made use of violent and horrible language. They were all sent to the work house for one month each."[91] That bigamy existed among Negroes and was not considered acceptable was suggested by another note in the same paper to the effect that "Daniel Green was arrested this morning . . . for having two wives."[92]

The tradition that Negroes committed crimes against property rather than against persons was perhaps true in the first years of freedom. As Reconstruction progressed, however, the balance seems to have shifted increasingly to crimes against persons. In January, 1870, one reporter recorded four murders and three murderous assaults within a month. All eleven of those arrested as assailants were Negroes.[93] Violent crimes of a less serious nature were commonplace

89. *New York Times,* October 14, p. 5; December 27, p. 1, 1867; January 20, p. 2, 1868.

90. *Daily Republican* (Charleston), March 27, June 2, 1870.

91. *Ibid.,* April 13, 1870.

92. *Ibid.,* June 1, 1870.

93. *New York Times,* January 25, 1870, p. 2.

in the Charleston area. Highly typical was a case in which Mina Dennett and Nancy Manigault were hauled before a trial justice "charged with assaulting a woman with bricks and a piece of iron, painfully wounding her."[94]

The indications are that the Negro community did not wink at the crimes of its members any more than the white community condoned the transgressions of individual whites. Noting that theft had steadily diminished during his fifteen-months' tenure as a Bureau officer in Greenville, John De Forest thought that "Freedom had developed a sense of self-respect which made the prison more terrible than was the whip or the paddle."[95] In April, 1877, at the very end of the Radical regime, a visitor noted that there were over four hundred Negroes and only thirty whites in the state penitentiary. One could draw many conclusions disparaging to the Negro race from these facts, yet it is certain that the majority of Negro prisoners had been placed there by juries which were predominantly Negro and by judges, prosecutors, and officers of the law who depended on Negro votes for their support.[96]

94. *Daily Republican* (Charleston), May 14, 1870.
95. Croushore and Potter, *A Union Officer*, p. 103.
96. *New York Tribune*, April 6, 1877, p. 5.

XII...NATURAL, CIVIL, AND POLITICAL RIGHTS

As the war drew to a close, the victors turned from
fighting to consider the question of just how free
the freedman was to be. Few Northerners were willing to accord the
Negro perfect equality with the white man. Yet there was general
agreement that Negroes minimally should have the same "natural
rights" that Negroes in the North had enjoyed before the emancipation. As the intentions of Southern whites on racial issues became clear,
however, the North was convinced that these minimal rights could not
be preserved unless the Negro was admitted to full participation in the
courts. Moreover, although the extension of voting rights to Negroes
was the result of a complex combination of circumstances, one of the
arguments advanced in its favor was that the rights and privileges
previously granted to the freedmen would not be secure unless re-enforced by the ballot. In South Carolina, at least, this was a valid assumption.

Life, liberty, and property—those triple pillars of the Lockean social
world described well the degree of freedom that the North was willing
to concede the Negro on the day of his emancipation. It meant that
he was to be protected from bodily harm at the hands of other persons.
He was to enjoy the rights, privileges, and immunities detailed in the
national and state constitutions as bills of rights. But, most of all,

Negro freedom signified economic liberty: that the Negro was free to terminate disadvantageous connections, to seek the most profitable employment, to acquire property, to be secure in its possession, and to dispose of it as he pleased.

As in many areas of federal activity in South Carolina, the method by which the government sought to protect the freedmen in the exercise of their natural rights had its genesis in the Sea Islands during the war. Characteristically, the approach was judicial rather than administrative. On the plantations superintendents had early performed an informal magisterial function, and by late 1864 plantation commissions, each consisting of several Northern residents, had been established as courts to try the more serious cases.[1] Simultaneously, provost courts operated in areas under the military. When the occupation was completed, the military commander simply expanded this system of provost courts throughout the state and ordered all cases involving freedmen brought before them. These courts implicitly recognized the natural rights of the freedman, and the Bureau commonly worked through the courts in its attempt to make the fact conform to the theory.[2]

Sensing the imperative necessity of regaining legal jurisdiction over the Negro, native white leaders strove mightily to construct a system that would please both the North and their constituents. The Constitutional Convention of 1865 offered as a solution the establishment of a special court in each district (county) with "jurisdiction of all civil causes wherein one or both of the parties are persons of color and of all criminal cases wherein the accused is a person of color . . ."[3] These district courts would enforce a code exclusively applicable to Negroes. Ironically, the whites expected this to be successful. "I have no doubt Genl Gilmore will suspend his Provost Courts as soon as your Code is adopted," wrote Governor Perry to A. L. Burt in mid-October, 1865, as the latter was completing the draft of the Black Code.[4]

The apparent intention of the whites to deny Negroes natural rights through the Code led the military commander, General Daniel Sickles, to suspend the enforcement of the Code and the operation of the district courts until full assurance was received that all the courts would apply

1. Elizabeth W. Pearson (ed.), *Letters from Port Royal, 1862–1868* (Boston, 1906), pp. 86–87, 286–87.

2. Oliver Otis Howard, *Autobiography of Oliver Otis Howard* (New York, 1908), II, 255.

3. *Journal of the Convention of the People of South Carolina, held in Columbia, South Carolina, September, 1865* (Columbia, 1865), p. 148.

4. B. F. Perry to A. L. Burt, October 15, 1865, B. F. Perry Papers (Duke).

all the laws impartially as to color.[5] Under the skillful and earnest
prodding of Governor Orr, a special session of the legislature in September, 1866, yielded with only minor reservations to Sickles' requirements.[6]
Though not specifically applied to Negroes, many parts of the Code
(such as the vagrancy laws) were left intact and actually operated primarily against Negroes. Thus, the district courts, retaining jurisdiction
over the least important cases, became pre-eminently the tribunal for the
Negro. "The principle business claiming the attention of the court,"
wrote one reporter, after observing the district court of Anderson in
session in January, 1867, "seemed to consist in indictments against freed-
people for larceny, malicious trespass & c." Nevertheless, the informant
noted, the court commanded "dignity."[7] Both district courts and the
higher tribunals of the state generally evinced a laudable fairness in
dealing with Negroes. And occasionally, in their desire to be perfectly
fair, these passed beyond true justice and exhibited exceptional leniency
to individual Negro offenders. Such partiality was excused by the
Negroes' "disadvantages in the war of ignorance and social inferiority."[8]

Closely related to the issue of equal justice for the Negro in the
courts was his admission to the witness box. In the fall of 1865, the same
legislature which passed the Black Code authorized the acceptance of
the testimony of Negro witnesses in all cases to which a Negro was a
party.[9] Several months later, Sickles insisted upon the full admission of
Negroes into the courts as witnesses in all judicial proceedings, including
hearings before grand juries, magistrates, and coroners.[10] The legislature
complied, and when the civil courts resumed operations in October, 1866,
the testimony of Negroes was admitted without extraordinary restrictions. At first, native whites were horrified by the spectacle of Negroes
on the witness stand. Nevertheless, within months white jurors were
giving a large measure of credence to Negro testimony. In October,
1867, Johnson Hagood, as the foreman of a jury in Barnwell District,
delivered a verdict of not guilty after a Negro woman accused of stealing had, without corroborative testimony, sworn to her own innocence.[11]

5. *New York Times,* July 8, 1866, p. 8.
6. *Ibid.,* September 6, 1866, p. 8.
7. *Appeal* (Anderson), January 16, 1867.
8. *New York Times,* November 9, 1866, p. 1; John H. Croushore and David
M. Potter (eds.), *John William De Forest, A Union Officer in the Reconstruction*
(New Haven, 1948), pp. 1–14.
9. *Statutes at Large,* XIII, 263.
10. *New York Times,* July 8, 1866, p. 8.
11. *Sentinel* (Barnwell), October 27, 1866.

Still, the justice granted to freedmen by the courts and the credibility accorded to Negro witnesses was never entirely free from racial considerations. In April, 1867, Sickles considered the bias in Edgefield and Barnwell districts so great that he suspended the civil courts and, for a time, re-established the provost courts.[12] Negro leaders applauded and pressed for the admission of Negroes to the jury box as the only solution. "It's no use to give the black man the right to testify, unless you give him the right to sit on juries," argued a Negro leader in Richland District. "I've seen the working of it. A colored man testifies, and the jury goes strictly against it, saying the nigger is ignorant, and is this, that and the other; though I heard Judge Dawkins say in Court, here, last March, that he had never, in forty years, seen a better witness than a colored man that had been up testifying."[13] In September, 1867, the military cut through to an obvious solution. It ordered that every person registered as a taxpayer or voter was qualified as a juror.[14] Since practically every eligible Negro in South Carolina had been so registered by the military itself, the gate of the jury box was thus thrown open to every adult male Negro. Compliance with the order in the federal courts was rapid. However, the military found it necessary to remove State Judge A. P. Aldrich from the bench because of his refusal to execute the order, and the order itself had to be reiterated and amplified early in 1868.[15]

The rise of the Radicals to political dominance obviated the necessity of forcing native white officers to bow to federal imperatives. Indeed, the Radicals in power within the state revolutionized the judicial system of South Carolina in every way. The legal code was rewritten and procedure modified to conform rather closely to the model system then used in New York State. District courts, having become symbols of separate justice for Negroes, were abolished; jurisdictions altered; and the system was streamlined to function through local trial justices, multi-county circuit courts, and a supreme court. The most striking innovation was, of course, the opening of all judicial offices to Negroes. "The sensation is peculiar in this town of Beaufort," wrote a Northern resident in 1869, "to see a Court in session, where former slaves sit side by side with their old owners on the jury, where white men are tried by a mixed

12. *New York Times*, April 21, 1867, p. 1.
13. *Ibid.*, August 9, 1867, p. 2.
14. *Report of the Secretary of War* (1867), p. 306.
15. *New York Times*, October 17, p. 1; 26, p. 1, 1867; February 3, 1868, p. 1.

jury, where colored lawyers plead, and where white and colored officers maintain order."[16]

The highest judicial office ever given to a Negro in South Carolina went to Jonathan Jasper Wright who was elected to a seat on the bench of the supreme court by the first Radical legislature. Wright was born in Lancaster, Pennsylvania, attended college in New York, and returned to Montrose, Pennsylvania, to read law. After two years, he was admitted to the bar, the first Negro in Pennsylvania to be accorded that honor. After the war, Wright came to South Carolina as a legal adviser in the Freedmen's Bureau.[17] He was very active in the Constitutional Convention of 1868 and in the state senate before his elevation to the bench. Introduced to Wright by his brother robe, Judge Willard, the Reverend John Cornish found him a "full blooded negro."[18] One reporter pronounced the thirty-three-year-old lawyer "intelligent, fluent and facile."[19] However, Wright never distinguished himself on the bench and, in 1877, was ousted by the Redeemers.

It was certainly within the power of Negro members in the legislature to pack the benches of South Carolina with men of their own race. Yet, they exhibited a remarkable respect for the necessity of filling judicial offices with men of ability and integrity. To the supreme court, along with Wright, they elected Franklin J. Moses, Sr., an elderly native white lawyer whom the whites conceded to be fully capable of filling the office, and A. J. Willard, a New York lawyer of lengthy and creditable legal experience. To head the eight circuit courts of the state, they elected two very capable Northern lawyers and six native whites who had long been respected members of the South Carolina Bar.[20] Of these latter six, five might well have been elected by the preceding all-white legislature. The two jurists who sat on the benches of the federal district courts in the state throughout Reconstruction could be described in the same way.

Occasionally, the names of Negroes were offered for judicial posts, but in December, 1875, William J. Whipper, of Beaufort, a Negro, was elected to the bench of the Charleston Circuit Court by Radical legislators aroused against conservative tendencies within the Republican party. Whipper was born in Michigan and had served as a clerk in the office

16. *Ibid.,* June 14, 1869, p. 5.

17. Newspaper clipping, n.p., n.d., Morris Wright Cuney Scrapbook.

18. J. H. Cornish MS Diary, entry for April 14, 1870.

19. *New York Times,* July 27, 1868, p. 1.

20. *House Journal* (Special Session, 1868), pp. 274–84; *ibid.* (Regular Session, 1868–1869), p. 87.

of a Detroit lawyer. He came to South Carolina with the army and remained to practice law in the provost courts. He was not known as an excellent lawyer in the technical sense, but reputedly he did possess a high degree of practical intelligence and was a very effective pleader in the criminal courts. Like Wright, he was early active in the organization of the Republican party in the state and a leader in the Constitutional Convention. Outgoing, articulate, and flamboyant, Whipper was a perennial favorite of his race in the legislature. Apparently, he acquired money easily, and he certainly spent it extravagantly. On one occasion he hired a steamer to transport his Charleston friends to a celebration in Beaufort. He was known throughout the state as a horse fancier, and it was to Whipper that Speaker Moses lost the infamous $1,000 horse race that historians so often use to illustrate Reconstruction excesses. Impulsive as he was, even Whipper's friends considered him ridiculously radical in his advocacy of female suffrage, the abolition of corporal and capital punishment (being "conscientiously opposed to hanging"), and other humanitarian reforms of the day. It was true, perhaps, that not all of Whipper's money was honestly earned, and his election to the ermine occasioned a great outcry among both native whites, who pronounced him one of "these most rascally of rascally radicals," and the more conservative elements of the Republican party. Yet, though he was not the essence of integrity, Whipper was surely not the scoundrel which history has made him. Strangely, before his election to the bench, his press among the conservatives was rather favorable compared with that of many other Republican leaders. It was only after his election to a judgeship, which coincided with the resurgence of the straightout Democracy in South Carolina, that great vilification was heaped upon him. Whatever the truth of the matter, Whipper's enemies prevented him from assuming his robes.[21]

Radical Governors Scott and Moses, who retained the privilege of appointing local trial justices, were hardly as scrupulous in preserving judicial dignity as was the legislature. Virtually every community in the state had its trial justice, an officer who exercised final jurisdiction in very minor cases and disposed of others pending the sitting of the circuit courts. Although Scott did appoint a large number of very capable white Democrats to these posts, he also, apparently for purely politi-

21. H. E. Young to R. H. Gourdin, December 17, 1875, R. H. Gourdin Papers; *Intelligencer* (Anderson), September 30, 1868; *Daily Republican* (Charleston), January 20, 1870; *House Journal* (Special Session, 1868), p. 326; *ibid.* (Regular Session, 1868–1869), p. 240.

cal purposes, commissioned scores of Negroes whose qualifications for the office were less than adequate. One of these was June S. Mobley. In 1869, Mobley, who was also a member of the legislature from Union County, revealed his limited literary abilities in the following letter to another magistrate: "Der Set Mr Astues I thack you Ort to have thes parttys to garer be fore you trow thes peopl out the house I see thes to have A contack from the lady and if this is true you cant put theme out the house."[22] While the ignorance of Republican magistrates sometimes excited the ire and the amusement of the whites, many of these Negro officers revealed an earnest willingness to learn their duties well. "The appointee is Rev. James Hemphill, some Republican, Colored Brother, now of the fifteenth amendment, formerly of the peculiar institution of old Billy Hemphill Esq.," wrote the white James Hemphill from Chester in 1870 after one of his namesakes was made a trial justice. He observed, however, that the new official was in the courthouse that day "getting books, and some pints from David," the clerk of court and the son of the writer.[23] During his two-year tenure (1872–1874), scalawag Governor F. J. Moses "appointed negroes of the lowest class" as trial justices, the only qualification being that each man was, to use Moses's phrase, "a good political nigger." One such was Sam Dickinson of Charleston whom the whites found to be "a loud-mouthed, ignorant fellow," insolent to the whites and domineering over those of his race unfortunate enough to appear before his bar. In June, 1874, a Northern reporter, visiting the dingy room which served as Dickinson's office and courtroom, saw a sample of the justice meted out by the Negro magistrate. The accused was a young Negro man charged with assault and battery. "Young man, yer is charged with assaulten and battery, which are one of the most wust crimes which come before this yer court for interroration," lectured the judge. "Sar, yer has violated the law and struck a man, and outraged this court," he continued. "I fines yer $10, and if you don't pay quick I'll make it four more for contempt."[24] Racial bias probably made whites hypercritical, but, doubtless, justice did suffer under the Moses appointees. During the Chamberlain administration which followed, many of the least capable and most corrupt trial justices were relieved by better men of both races.

The offices of jury commissioners, clerks of court, reading clerks, bailiffs, and constables also came to be filled in some instances by

22. *New York Times,* February 12, 1869, p. 2.
23. James Hemphill to W. R. Hemphill, May 14, 1870, Hemphill Papers.
24. *New York Times,* July 3, 1874, p. 2.

Negroes exhibiting the same variances in capacity and integrity. One of the most important and lasting innovations of the period, however, was the admission to the bar of Negro lawyers. The latter supplied a service sorely needed by the Negro in defending and expanding his new freedom as he, himself, interpreted it. In addition, it opened an important avenue of professional advancement to individual Negroes. Finally, like so many of their white contemporaries, Negro lawyers found the simultaneous pursuit of law and politics not only practicable but profitable.

A few Negro lawyers of considerable native ability had been trained abroad and in Northern schools. These were worthy rivals of their native white colleagues, who, as a group, enjoyed a high reputation for professional capacity. Robert Brown Elliott, Boston born and reared, was educated at High Holborn Academy in London and at Eton, from which he was graduated in 1859 at the age of seventeen. Afterward, he returned to the United States and studied for two years in the Massachusetts School of Law. In 1863, he enlisted in one of the Negro regiments and served in South Carolina until the end of the war when he returned to Boston to complete his legal training. Nine months later, he was again in South Carolina as the editor of *The Leader,* a newspaper published in Charleston by Northerners. Elliott, too, was an early organizer of the Republican party in South Carolina, went to the Constitutional Convention, and passed into the legislature in 1868. In September, 1868, along with Wright and Whipper, he was one of the first three Negroes admitted to the bar in South Carolina. Of pure Negro blood himself, he soon found a mulatto bride among the prosperous free Negroes of Charleston. Elliott was very effective as a lawyer, politician, and parliamentarian. One conservative native white reporter pronounced him "the ablest negro in South Carolina." In the first Radical legislature, he served as a member from Edgefield. In 1870 and 1872 he was elected to Congress and on the floor of the House he delivered a very learned and impressive speech in support of the Civil Rights Bill. In 1874, he again entered the state legislature to become the speaker of the house. While there was much evidence that Elliott was guilty of accepting money from the spoilsmen, he was strangely immune from the post-Redemption prosecutions of the Democrats. Elliott remained a strong and vigorous Radical in the crisis of 1876–1877, but in the latter year he accepted a treasury post in New Orleans and practiced law there until he died in 1884.[25]

25. James Grant Wilson and John Fiske (eds.), *Appletons' Cyclopaedia of*

One of the most important innovations of the Radicals was the opening of the jury box to Negroes. In the state courts, the legislature ordered that juries, both grand and petit, be composed of Negroes and whites in the same racial proportion as that of the voting population of the county in which they sat.[26] Although juries in the federal courts were supposedly chosen without regard to race, the results were very much the same. A Northern lady residing in Charleston in 1871, after a social call by the federal district judge, reported his statement "that in all the lower Counties the Jurors are now mostly colored men, because there are so many of them."[27] Illiteracy, ignorance, and poverty did not necessarily result in the corruption of all jury panels; yet where such conditions existed spoilers were sometimes present to take advantage of them. Politicians appointed by the governor to offices as jury commissioners were obviously able to stack juries as they chose and sometimes did so. For instance, the jury list from which men were selected to sit in judgment of the alleged Ku Kluxers brought before the United States District Court in Charleston in the spring of 1872 was generally believed to have been packed so as to preclude any chance of acquittal.[28] Illiteracy was a particularly critical problem among members of grand juries whose duties included general supervision over the financial affairs of local officials. In the spring of 1874, the apparently honest and reform-minded state solicitor of the Charleston circuit persuaded the court to order the grand jury to investigate the books of the notoriously corrupt county commissioners. ". . . but as the foreman and most of the jury were ignorant negroes who could not read, the Solicitor was instructed to go with them and point out any irregularities he could detect."[29]

During and after 1874, major reforms in the jury systems were effected. In that year, federal juries were much improved in efficiency and effectiveness by a reorganization under regulations which required that

American Biography (New York, 1888), II, 331; _New York Times,_ April 3, 1869, p. 7; October 18, 1870, p. 5; July 26, p. 5; November 25, p. 4, 1874; December 13, 1876, p. 1; _Intelligencer_ (Anderson), September 30, 1868; _Congressional Biography_ (1950), p. 517; _Congressional Record_, II, Part 1, 43rd Cong., 1st Sess., 407-10; George Brown Tindall, _South Carolina Negroes, 1877-1900_ (Columbia, 1952), p. 43.

26. _Intelligencer_ (Anderson), April 15, 1869.
27. M. C. M. Taylor to J. Wilbur, January 23, 1871, Jeremiah Wilbur Papers.
28. "G. I. C." to W. P. Miles, April 4, 1872, W. P. Miles Papers.
29. _New York Times_, June 14, 1874, p. 1.

jurors be able to read and write.[30] An attempt in the Constitutional Convention of 1868 to require jurors in the state courts to be able "to read and write legibly" ultimately failed.[31] However, as reform agitation within Republican ranks became increasingly intense in 1874, a general disposition among the leadership to overhaul the system became apparent.[32] Once in power, reform Governor D. H. Chamberlain achieved this object without altering the law simply by appointing as jury commissioners honest and capable men of both races and parties. Soon after taking office, he was able to report to a friend that even in Richland County (Columbia) the courts had good, dependable juries.[33]

Corruption and incapacity did mar the judiciary of South Carolina during the first six years of Republican ascendency, but it does not appear to have assumed the magnitude that the whites charged then and subsequently. Doubtless some courts were biased in favor of Republicans and Negroes; but the participation of Negroes in the judiciary of South Carolina during Reconstruction produced no Scottsboro case in which the defendants were white rather than black, and no Negro, either on or off the bench, was ever heard to declare that the white man had no rights that the Negro was bound to respect.

"The emancipation never can be anything, in short, but a bitter failure," wrote an anonymous New Yorker to the *Times* in the summer of 1865, "unless some equal right of suffrage is given to the emancipated race; for without this safeguard they are and must be totally defenceless."[34] While public opinion in the North was rapidly tacking to favor the extension of the vote to the Negro in the South, refugee Negroes along the coast of South Carolina had already begun to savor the flavor of political activity. As early as 1862, an autonomous Negro village was established on Port Royal Island as another of the many island "experiments."[35] Another test in political self-determination by the freedmen

30. *Ibid.*, August 18, p. 3; October 10, p. 1, 1874.

31. *Convention Proceedings* (1868), pp. 86–87; *New York Times,* February 3, 1868, p. 5.

32. *New York Times,* August 18, p. 3; July 21, p. 5, 1874.

33. MS Commission as Jury Commissioner of Chesterfield County, issued to G. E. Spencer by Secretary of State H. E. Hayne, January 4, 1876, George W. Spencer Papers; D. H. Chamberlain to F. W. Dawson, June 24, 1875, F. W. Dawson Papers.

34. *New York Times,* July 18, 1865, p. 4.

35. The village was named Mitchelville in honor of the commanding general, Ormsby M. Mitchel. *New South* (Port Royal), October 4, 18, 25, November 1, 1862.

was envisioned by Sherman's resettlement order which prescribed that
under the general supervision of the military "the sole and exclusive
management of affairs will be left to the freed people themselves . . ."[36]
In the "virtual" sense, the Negro population of the coastal area was well
represented in Washington during and immediately after the war by
their friends in the government. More directly, their views were voiced
by such informal agents as Rufus Saxton and Mansfield French. Finally,
impromptu organizations among the freedmen, spontaneous in greater
or lesser degree, were effective in influencing the actions of federal
authorities. The Negro population of Charleston was particularly
vociferous, making its desires known in Columbia and Washington
through the resolves of numerous mass meetings. For instance, an assembly in the fall of 1865 protested vigorously against the passage of the
Black Code and appealed to Congress for redress, supplying the Radicals
in that body with highly potent ammunition for the coming attack.

Agitation for the vote among South Carolina's freedmen actually
lagged somewhat behind that of the Radicals in Washington, although
the most active element among the Negro population along the coast
obviously desired that their race be granted the franchise at the close of
the war. The delay was partly caused by the fact that Northern Republicans generally led the Negroes to believe that the event was then
politically impossible. Chief Justice Chase, himself, speaking to a
throng of Negroes in Zion Church in Charleston in April, 1865, assured
the cheering crowd that suffrage would come to them "sometimes;
perhaps very soon; perhaps a good while hence."[37]

However, as Congress turned toward Negro enfranchisement, the
Negro leadership in South Carolina moved quickly to press their obvious advantage. William Beverly Nash, as a delegate from the state
to the National Freedmen's Convention in Washington early in 1867,
strove vigorously to have the convention endorse Negro suffrage without
educational or property qualifications. Asked if his people, once enfranchised, would vote for their former masters, he replied that they
would vote for "loyal and patriotic men, whoever they might be." When
practical suffrage came shortly thereafter in the form of the first Reconstruction Act, the response of the Negroes was enthusiastic. Sitting
in the gallery of the House of Representatives when that body over-

36. *Official Records,* Ser. 1, XLVII, Part ii, 60–62.
37. Whitelaw Reid, *After the War; A Southern Tour, May 1, 1865, to May 1,
1866* (London, 1866), p. 585. See also: *Daily Republican* (Charleston), April
20, 29, 1870.

rode Johnson's veto, Nash felt "that the clock of civilization had been put forward a hundred years."[38]

The Reconstruction Acts gave adult male Negroes in South Carolina the opportunity to vote for or against a convention to re-organize the government of the state. At the same time, they were allowed to vote for delegates to that convention should the decision on the first question be in the affirmative. Actually, the problem of just who should vote in subsequent elections was to be decided by the convention itself. A surprisingly large number of delegates to the convention in South Carolina were conservative on the matter. After extensive discussion concerning linking suffrage to the payment of a poll tax for the support of schools, the appropriate committee reported a provision which granted universal manhood suffrage until 1875, after which each potential elector coming of age "shall be able to read and write . . ." William J. McKinlay, a well-to-do member of the free Negro society of Charleston and a teacher, argued for the literacy qualification, saying that "in order to have wise men at the head of our government, it is necessary that the people should be educated and have a full sense of the importance of the ballot." Most delegates disagreed. A. J. Ransier, a native Negro delegate from Charleston, asserted that the vote "is our chief means for self-defense"; and Robert C. De Large, of the same background, looked "upon suffrage as the inherent right of man." Richard H. Cain spoke for many when he denied the necessity of perfect sophistication among the electorate. "He may not understand a great deal of the knowledge that is derived from books; he may not be generally familiar with the ways of the world," declared the African Methodist missionary, "but he can, nevertheless, judge between right and wrong, and to this extent he has as much ability to cast his vote and declare his opinion as any other man, no matter what may be his situation in life."[39] The result was a constitutional provision calling for universal male suffrage.

The Fifteenth Amendment, coming before the South Carolina legislature in March, 1869, was speedily adopted. Many Negro leaders regarded the final ratification of the document a year later as the ulti-

38. *New York Times*, March 23, p. 2; April 15, p. 5, 1867. Home again twelve days later, Nash led a meeting of Richland County Negroes which resolved thanks that Providence had "seen fit to cause this great nation to release them from the disadvantages and deprivations that they labored under as a people, and to acknowledge their manhood, and return to those great principles of the Declaration of Independence, which declares all men to be equal . . ." *New York Times*, March 21, 1867, p. 1.

39. *Convention Proceedings* (1868), pp. 352, 713, 723, 725–32, 832–35.

mate triumph. Joseph H. Rainey, soon to serve four terms in Congress
upon the suffrage of his racial brothers, declared at a Fourth of July rally
in Georgetown in 1870 that distinctions of color had been "to a great
extent destroyed by the adoption of the Fifteenth Amendment to our
National Constitution—the keystone to the arch of our political structure . . ."[40]

Claiming the vote for themselves, many Negro leaders were also
willing to accord the same privilege to others. During the convention,
and later in the legislature, some Negro leaders evinced a readiness to
have the restrictions Congress placed on their white opponents removed.[41] Frequently, to the horror and always to the amusement of
native whites, many leading Negro politicians also endorsed female
suffrage. W. J. Whipper, arguing in the convention that it was wrong
"to deprive these intelligent beings of the privileges which we enjoy,"
unsuccessfully moved to have the new constitution extend the suffrage to
all adults.[42] Early in its first regular session, Louisa Rollin, prominent in
the free Negro society of Charleston, and one of four sisters born of
a French father and a Negro mother, appeared on the floor of the House
of Representatives in Columbia to make a speech urging sexless suffrage.[43] Two years later, another meeting in the capital promoted female
suffrage. Lottie Rollin, Louisa's sister, directed proceedings in which
Whipper and scalawags F. J. Moses, Jr., and Thomas Jefferson Mackey
rendered highly favorable speeches.[44] Of course, the movement did not
achieve any significant progress during this period, but, as we shall see,
the role of Negro women in Radical politics was far from negligible.

Having won the vote, it remained to be seen what use the Negro
would make of this privilege. While they pondered the question of
Negro suffrage in the first months following the war, whites, North and
South, wondered whether the Negro as a voter would follow his late
master and present employer or join the ranks of the Republicans. Even
the friends of the Negro in the South subsequently interpreted the well-
nigh universal adherence of the Negro to Radicalism as the logical result

40. *New York Times,* March 12, 1869, p. 5; *Daily Republican* (Charleston),
April 15, July 8, 1870.
41. *Convention Proceedings* (1868), pp. 877–80 and following. For precon-
vention sentiment in the same vein, see: *New York Times,* April 15, p. 5;
August 9, p. 2, 1867; February 3, 1868, p. 5.
42. *Convention Proceedings* (1868), p. 838.
43. *New York Times,* April 3, 1869, p. 7.
44. *Daily Republican* (Charleston), January 20, 1871.

of the failure of the native white conservatives to seize the initiative in winning the support of their ex-slaves in the days immediately following the passage of the first Reconstruction Act.[45] On the other hand, conservatives blamed the alliance of Radicals and Negroes on the misrepresentations of native white sentiments which were made by unscrupulous emissaries sent into the state by Northern Radicals.[46]

In retrospect, it is apparent that Negroes could only have become Republicans, regardless of the exertions which conservative native whites might have made. It was clear to the Negro leadership and, presumably, to the mass of Negroes in South Carolina that the men who had consistently acted in the interest of their race, who had pressed the war as one of emancipation as well as union, who had urged the arming of Negroes, who had insisted upon the recognition of the Negro's natural, civil, and finally his political equality, were the same men who dominated the Radical Republican element in Congress. It was no less clear that the native whites who had held them in slavery and resisted emancipation, who had sought to restrict their liberties by the Black Code and to minimize their participation in the courts, and who, by the rejection of the Fourteenth Amendment, attempted to deprive them of full civil and political equality were the same men who allied themselves with the Northern Democracy in opposition to the Negroes' friends in Congress. Furthermore, it was a patent truth to most Negroes that only a portion of the Southern white leadership recognized their new freedoms, had done so only at the point of a bayonet, and persistently minimized these freedoms. Between the two sides the Negro had no real choice; for him, freedom and Radicalism were one and inseparable.

The cement which joined the Negroes of South Carolina with the Congressional Radicals in a durable alliance was historical, but it was also anticipatory of future advantages. Concisely, Negroes supported the national program of the Radicals in return for a recognition of the principle of equal rights for their race. Particularly in the coastal area, many Negroes, having fought for their freedom and the Union, felt that they were partners in (rather than wards of) the party which supported these ideals. Further, Negroes everywhere—without being less grateful for past services—carefully measured their loyalty to Radicalism

45. For instance, see D. H. Chamberlain's comments in an interview with a Northern correspondent, *New York Times*, June 22, 1874, p. 1.

46. Robert Somers, *The Southern States since the War, 1870–1871* (New York, 1871), pp. 50–51. See also A. G. Magrath's estimate of the situation, *New York Times*, June 21, 1874, p. 1.

in terms of future benefits. They were aware, as the Reverend Henry Turner told a Columbia audience in April, 1867, that the North had not fought the war entirely for the freedom of their race and that the government's support of their rights was not entirely altruistic. Many Negroes, doubtless, saw wisdom in Turner's advice to befriend the government only while it befriended them, to affiliate with any party that would give them the right to ride on the same cars and to vote at the same polls with the whites. "He would have all to have and exercise the right to vote, to be voted for, to go to Congress, to the penitentiary, to hell, or to heaven, just as they pleased!"[47]

In the national sense, Radical Republicanism was the party for the Negro, but in South Carolina it soon became pre-eminently the party of and by the Negro. Negroes early realized that their votes gave them a controlling interest in the party within the state and that this power could be used to achieve the goals which they most fervently sought. Thus, Radical Republicanism in South Carolina became all that national Radicalism was and more. In its first statewide meeting in Columbia in July, 1867, the Republican party of South Carolina resolved to support not only the Northern Radicals and equal rights for the Negro, but also to insist upon a broad program of reform addressed to the specific interests of the Negro. Opposed only by a scattering of native whites within their ranks, the Republican convention adopted a platform calling for a system of free, public education; internal improvements; "the division and sale of unoccupied lands among the poorer classes"; the revision and re-organization of the judicial system; and public support for "the poor and destitute, those aged and infirm people, houseless and homeless, and past labor, who have none to care for them."[48] The manner in which Negro voters sought to achieve these goals and the large measure of success which they realized suggests that the great mass of Negro electors possessed a degree of political sagacity comparable to that of their white contemporaries.

In exercising his suffrage, the Negro evinced several, rather distinct patterns of behavior.

Tradition describes the Negro elector in Reconstruction South Carolina as ignorant of the meaning of his vote, as the dupe of unscrupulous Northern emissaries and unprincipled Southern "poor whites." It is said that the Negro voter was incited against the whites, leagued against

47. *New York Times,* May 5, 1867, p. 1.
48. *Ibid.,* July 31, 1867, p. 1.

them in secret meetings which appealed solely to the Negro's alleged proclivity for ceremony and elaborate garb. By bribes of flattery, food, liquor, and money, the Negro was marched to the polls where he cast a ballot dictated in detail by his political masters who thereupon discarded him until the next election. There is a grain of truth in this description. During the first months after receiving the franchise, some Negroes obviously did not fully understand the implications of their new power and the procedures by which they would exercise it. During the registration period in the summer of 1867, a mulatto registrar working in a rural precinct near Charleston found some Negroes who thought that enrollment would lead to a grant of land and, he reported, it was "a common thing to find them slyly bespeaking from the Registrars the selection of a good tract." Some of these argued over whether mules were to be given with the lands. "For what's de use of bein' sot free widout lands," they reasoned. "And what's de use of de lands widout mules?" they continued with impeccable logic.[49] One Southerner subsequently claimed that during the election Negroes came to the polls at Adams Run with halters to lead off the mules they expected to receive, and a lowcountry Bureau officer reported that some Negroes cast their ballots into the post office, or any hole they could find, while others took them home.[50]

Such tales seem to have been designed to amuse rather than inform. Certainly, they were not indicative of the intelligence manifested by the Negro electorate at large. A Northern reporter wrote from Charleston in April, 1867, that awareness of the general meaning of their new rights had spread among the Negroes throughout the state "with marvellous rapidity." "Regarding the precise character and value of their new privileges," he added, "of course, those in the interior have, as yet, rather vague impressions; but everywhere their interest in political affairs and their curiosity concerning their changed social status is now fairly awakened, and it is safe to predict that they will not be slow to learn their own importance as an element in the body politic, and to make their weight felt in local and national elections."[51] During the first election in which Negroes participated, the Bureau officer in Greenville, in pointed contrast to his lowcountry contemporary, found that "the freedmen voted quietly and went immediately home without even a

49. *Ibid.*, September 19, 1867, p. 1.
50. Myrta Lockett Avary, *Dixie after the War* (New York, 1906), p. 346; Croushore and Potter, *A Union Officer*, pp. 126–27.
51. *New York Times*, April 3, 1867, p. 1.

hurrah of triumph." Further, he asserted, the most stupid among them understood that by voting Republican he was acting "again de Rebs," and "for de freedom."[52] Finally, such abnormal political ignorance as did exist among Negroes was soon erased by experience. A Northern resident on St. Helena noted that in the first election the Negroes "came on in armed bands, as if expecting to fight to maintain their rights. . . ." By November, 1868, however, the Negroes were better informed and during the elections held that month "perfect order was maintained from beginning to end without the slightest difficulty."[53]

Far from falling into political slavery, the Negro voter could be fully as capricious under the hand of the professional party manager as his white counterpart. Observing a caucus of Republicans in Beaufort township, a Northern resident noted that the pre-arranged slate of candidates for township officers was discarded, and the Negroes "nominated their men without regard to party dictation," filling some of the lesser offices such as road surveyors and constables with Negroes "who give measureable satisfaction in performing their duties."[54] Republican politicians could be reasonably confident that Negroes would vote Republican, but they were most uncertain which Republicans they would vote for.

In the first few years after they had won the vote, Negro Republicans were prone to promote their campaigns by parades, barbecues, rallies, meetings, and caucuses. Frequently, these affairs drew upon the most remote plantations for participants. For instance, on August 8, 1868, "Mike & wife, Primus & wife, Scipio & Briny" each lost a day of labor on H. L. Pinckney's Sumter County plantation by attending a "Radical meeting at Stateburg."[55] Whites were often irritated by such events because they led the Negro to desert his labor; but, more importantly, they were frightened into the conclusion that the Radicals were pied pipers who thus used frivolity to make political slaves of their employees.

Loud as he may have been during the campaign, the Negro at the polls was sober and purposeful in recording his vote. On election day, 1870, a native white lawyer in Bennettsville noted: "few whites out— negroes come in early—vote & go home. No excitement—have all things their own way."[56] At twelve noon on the same date across the state in Aiken, Reverend Cornish made a similar entry in his diary. "The voting

52. Croushore and Potter, *A Union Officer,* pp. 126–27.
53. *New York Times,* December 30, 1868, p. 2.
54. *Ibid.,* June 14, 1869, p. 5.
55. H. L. Pinckney MS Plantation Book, entry for August 8, 1868.
56. Joshua Hilary Hudson MS Diary, entry for October 19, 1870.

is mostly over," he wrote, "Large numbers of men—black & white in the streets—all very quiet & orderly—no hustling nor crowding at the polls—"[57]

A strikingly large proportion of the Negro electorate actually exercised its suffrage. In the convention elections in November, 1867, nearly 69,000 of a possible 81,000 Negroes, roughly 85 per cent, participated. If the records are accurate, not a single Negro voted against the convention.[58] In the spring of 1868, about 67,000 of a possible 84,000 Negroes went to the polls to ratify the new constitution and to return Republicans to all major offices. At the same time, less than 60 per cent of the 50,000 registered white voters bothered to cast any ballot at all, and only 54 per cent of the total white electorate voted against the constitution and for Democrats. "The controlling party is the black man's party, in the main identical with the Radical Party," glumly and accurately concluded one Southern Democrat.[59] Registration rolls and election returns reported by Republican state officials in subsequent canvasses are not totally reliable; nevertheless, it is apparent that throughout Reconstruction the overwhelming majority of adult, male Negroes exercised their suffrage in the Republican direction at every opportunity.[60]

The mass of Negroes not only voted Republican themselves, but insisted that every member of their race do so. On the eve of the election of 1878, the Negro foreman of a Santee River rice plantation told his employer that all hands would vote Republican and so would he. He would do so to retain the loyalty of the workers. All of the workers would do so because every Negro who had voted Democratic in the previous election had been punished by having a cow killed, his rice stolen, his house bombarded, or had suffered other damage.[61] Negro women were very active in insuring the Republicanism of their men.

57. J. H. Cornish MS Diary, entry for October 19, 1870. See also: *ibid.,* entry for November 3, 1874; William Mauldin MS Diary, entry for October 19, 1870.

58. *Report of the Secretary of War* (1868), p. 521; *Appletons' Annual Cyclopaedia,* 1867, p. 705.

59. *Report of the Secretary of War* (1868), pp. 521–22; *New York Times,* May 7, 1868, p. 5.

60. For example, even in the strongly Democratic county of Spartanburg, roughly 80 per cent of the potential Negro electorate voted Republican in every election, a proportion which was ostensibly unaffected by intensive Ku Klux activities in 1870–1871 and by the pressures exerted by the Red Shirts in 1876. *A History of Spartanburg County,* pp. 145–46; *Appletons' Annual Cyclopaedia,* 1869, p. 637.

61. Avary, *Dixie after the War,* pp. 346–47.

"The women are the head & fount of the opposition," complained the wife of the Democratic leader in Union County. "Some going to the polls to see that the men voted right, threatening them with assassination if they did not vote as they wished—& when things went for us some were seen passing by the Yankee camp weeping."[62] During the campaign which preceded this election, the Sumter Guard became violently ill after drinking coffee served by a Negro woman. Questioned sharply, the Negro woman confessed that she had liberally laced the refreshments with croton oil, thereby seriously impairing the martial dignity of that brave company.[63]

The Negro voter persisted in his determination to cast a Republican ballot in spite of all obstacles. The real obstacles, of course, came from the conservative native whites who made prodigious efforts either to convert the Negro or to keep him away from the polls. "All kind of contrivances to keep the negroes from the Pol[l]s are contemplated by those who employ them," wrote a Charlestonian in November, 1868.[64] The use of economic coercion, violence, and the threat of violence have been discussed. In addition, white employers frequently resorted to outright bribery. "I feel almost sure that three out of four of my freedmen will not vote," declared John F. Calhoun, an Abbeville planter. "It will *cost me* something, but their voting might cost me more."[65]

Even in 1876, when the Democrats claimed victory in the statewide canvass, Negro voters continued to hew closely to the Republican line. After the election, Thomas G. Clemson (who, through his wife, the daughter of John C. Calhoun, had inherited Fort Hill, Calhoun's country seat in Oconee County) reported to a friend that "all I could do on Fort Hill was to gain *two* who did not vote and I have done better than many around." After working like Trojans, with only slight effect, many of his neighbors were firing their employees for voting Republican and sending them "to their Radical friends." Yet, the Negroes were not without resort. "My neighbor Lewis has had a barn and other buildings burnt the night of election, because he dismissed at Seneca (the voting precinct) all of his tenants, all having voted the Radical Ticket."[66]

Militant demonstrations by the whites put the Negro electorate to the severest tests. On the same date that Oconee Negroes were casting

62. E. B. Munro to her mother, November 9, 1876, J. B. Grimball Papers.

63. Elizabeth Munro to Emily Elliott, October 2, 1876, Elliott–Gonzales Papers.

64. William Heyward to James Gregorie, November 8, 1868, Gregorie–Elliott Papers.

65. John F. Calhoun to A. L. Burt, April 15, 1868, J. C. Calhoun Papers.

66. T. G. Clemson to A. L. Burt, November 10, 1876, T. G. Clemson Papers.

Republican ballots in defiance of their white employers, Democratic leaders in Edgefield County were executing a most daring plan to keep the Negroes entirely away from the polls. As soon as the box in the village of Edgefield was opened, the one Democratic manager, over the protests of his two Negro colleagues, simply carried the ballot box from its customary position on the portico of the courthouse into an interior room. During the previous night, armed whites had filled the courthouse. The whites voted and remained, allowing their friends to enter and leave, conspicuously displaying their pistols, and packing themselves so closely in the corridors and on the steps that no man could pass without their approval. According to the Negro managers, this formidable barrier was further reinforced since "several hundred horsemen were crowded around the C. H. steps in such a manner that colored men could not approach the CH." The violent mood of the whites was made evident by raucous shouting and a brandishing of arms. The Negro managers deposed that "not more than 35 or 40 Colard [*sic*] men voted at this box during the entire day, and that most of these voted late in the evening when they were accompanied to the Box by a U. S. Marshall." The managers named 257 Negroes who were qualified to vote but did not. Under the circumstances, it is indeed amazing that some two score Negroes had the temerity to cast their ballots.[67]

If political intelligence is measured by success in getting the friends of one's interests into office and in establishing an effective program to promote those interests, then the Negro's political capacity during Reconstruction was on a par with that of his white contemporary.

Indeed, in the matter of winning offices the Negro community was probably more successful than most other interest groups in the nation. During 1868, on the state level, they and their white allies won all eight of the principal administrative offices and elected the legislative delegations from twenty-five of the thirty-one counties. These successes gave them power to choose two United States senators and all the judicial officers of the state, and also gave them varying degrees of control over county and municipal offices. In the federal election of 1868, Republicans clearly won three out of the four Congressional seats to be filled and returned the Grant-Colfax electors. During 1869, as their reward, they gained a host of federal offices—postmasterships, customs

67. MS Deposition by Woly J. Williams and Abram Landrum, November 9, 1876, South Carolina Reconstruction Papers.

and internal revenue positions, marshalships, and judicial posts. In addition, they won by election a host of county and municipal offices.

Of course, Republicans (and, presumably, the mass of Negro voters) were eager to claim for their party all the offices which majority rule gave them, but they also exhibited a striking determination to use their numerical superiority to move beyond this toward the almost total exclusion of the minority from power. This all-or-nothing bent on the part of the Republicans lent a special flavor of bitterness to politics in South Carolina during Reconstruction. Native whites had long held that representation in a republic should be based at least partly upon wealth. Once in power, Republicans not only placed representation firmly in the hands of the numerical majority, but were frankly hostile to wealth in the hands of their political enemies. Furthermore, Republicans were unwilling to concede the considerable fraction of white voters any measure of representation above that which they gained by having indisputable majorities in a few counties. In 1870, for instance, when white voters constituted about two-fifths of the total electorate, conservative native whites took less than one-sixth of the legislative seats.[68] Conservative native whites and even some leading carpetbaggers suggested that electing the legislature by cumulative voting would be more equitable. This would have given the white minority seats in the lower house in proportion to their total voting strength. However, the Republican legislature refused even to consider such a plan.[69] Many Negro leaders supported amnesty for ex-Confederates, but when Congress was considering a general amnesty in 1871 the South Carolina House of Representatives passed a resolution requesting the state's representatives and directing its senators "to vote against all such laws . . ."[70]

Maneuvering for more power, Republicans often resorted to devices which were blatantly unjust. In the white counties, many local offices would normally have remained under the control of the whites. Yet, the Republican leadership deliberately increased the powers of the central

68. John Schreiner Reynolds, *Reconstruction in South Carolina, 1865–1877* (Columbia, 1905), pp. 154–55. In 1868, about two-fifths (54,000 of 138,000) of the voters in the state were white. In 1875, roughly three-eighths (74,000 of 185,000) were white. *Report of the Secretary of War* (1868), p. 522; *Appletons' Annual Cyclopaedia,* 1875, p. 706.

69. *New York Times,* May 12, p. 1; 14, p. 1, 1871; February 16, p. 4, 1874; James S. Pike, *The Prostrate State: South Carolina under Negro Government* (New York, 1874), pp. 23, 54–55.

70. *New York Times,* January 12, 1871, p. 1. See also: *ibid.,* February 22, 1872, p. 1.

(state) government in order to give Republican governors and legislators extensive control over such county officers as tax assessors, treasurers, and sheriffs.[71] The decision of the legislature to allow the governor to appoint trial justices rather than having them chosen by popular election as the Constitution of 1868 provided is an obvious example of how the Republican party used centralism to perfect its control over local offices. Less obvious, but infinitely more important, was the fact that the budget of each county had to be approved by the legislature, and legislative courtesy did not always apply. Republicans were also adept in gerrymandering. White voters formed two-fifths to three-eighths of the electorate. Yet, by stretching each Congressional district to include heavily Negro counties, the Republicans succeeded in claiming each of the four or five (after 1870) seats in every election. The same device was applied to expand town boundaries to include Negro suburbs and thus pass their governments into Republican hands.[72] Frequently, conservative white candidates claiming victory were simply unseated by Republican majorities in the legislature or in Congress on the pretext that the conservatives had gained votes by illegal means.[73]

Where all else failed, Republicans sometimes resorted to outright fraud. An open invitation to deceit was the Republican legislature's election law which allowed the governor to appoint three managers for each polling place and a board of three commissioners for each county to oversee the managers. Managers were allowed to keep the ballot boxes for three days after the election and the county commissioners to retain them five days longer before making a final count and reporting the returns to Columbia. In many cases, Republican managers and commissioners obviously and grossly exaggerated the vote polled by their party. For example, in 1870, returns submitted by Republican managers in Laurens, Newberry, and Chester counties indicated that their party had increased its voting strength in each place by about 50 per cent in two years. Presumably, these gains represented new Negro voters. If they had been legitimately achieved, the adult male Negro population in each county must have increased from 20 per cent to 30 per cent within the two years, an event which the census figures belie.[74] Often the fraud was perpetrated boldly. In 1870, Joseph Crews, the notorious scalawag leader of Laurens County, as the chairman of the board of

71. *Daily Republican* (Charleston), August 13, 1870.
72. *New York Times*, January 25, 1870, p. 2.
73. *Ibid.*, July 12, p. 5; 14, p. 5, 1868; November 21, p. 1, 1870.
74. *Report of the Secretary of War* (1868), pp. 521, 522; *Appletons' Annual Cyclopaedia*, 1869, p. 637; *Reports and Resolutions* (1870–1871), p. 518.

commissioners of elections tallied the results and destroyed the ballots while fleeing from bands of rioting whites. He reported 3,021 votes for himself for a seat in the legislature. Eight other Republican candidates for local offices were elected by a vote of 3,020, and another by 3,019. Even among Negro voters such unanimity was unlikely and, indeed, did not occur in any other place or even in Laurens subsequently.[75]

Beginning in the election of 1874, when eight counties were conceded entirely to the "reform" coalition and partial representation was accorded reformers in six counties, Republicans in power turned against the use of fraud in elections and showed an inclination to yield to the opposition a reasonable share of offices. Nevertheless, until the very end of their dominance in the spring of 1877, Republicans were determined to make the most of the powers they did possess. Working through the Republican party, Negroes secured, at least in legislative form, the inauguration of a program which they believed would advance their special interests. They broadened the range of possibilities for economic advancement, enlarged opportunities for acquiring an education, promoted an expansion of the public services of the state to win more security for the unfortunates of their race, and, finally, they won, if only on paper, recognition of their "public equality."

By far the most striking facet of the political behavior of Negroes in South Carolina during Reconstruction was their tendency to dissociate themselves from white persons. This was abundantly apparent in the racial constitution of the two parties, but it was also evident within the Republican party itself.

To some extent, the segregation of Negroes and whites into Republican and Democratic factions was the result of the prejudices each entertained toward the other. Yet the gap was not impassable. For their part, Negroes, at least ostensibly, earnestly entreated white voters to join their party. The price of admission was simply the acceptance of the "Union Republican platform."[76] On the eve of the ratification of the Constitution of 1868, R. C. De Large begged his white neighbors to join him on this ground. "I ask—nay, I plead—" he cried, one imagines with arms outstretched, "that you, the whites, come forward and bridge over the breach, which should not exist."[77]

75. *Reports and Resolutions* (1870–1871), p. 499.
76. *New York Times*, May 25, 1867, p. 1. See also: *ibid.*, March 23, p. 2; April 15, p. 5; 21, p. 1, 1867.
77. *Ibid.*, March 27, 1867, p. 8. See also: *ibid.*, April 9, 1868, p. 1.

Some native whites did accept De Large's offer. Acceptance was greatest in the three areas where Unionism had been strongest before and during the war—the city of Charleston, Lexington County, and the mountain districts. Outside these strongholds, the white Republican electorate consisted primarily of officeholders, their immediate families, and persons whose economic interests were directly involved with Negroes and the Republican party. The number of native whites who voted Republican probably fluctuated between three and four thousand, though groups of white voters entered and left the party at various times.[78] Apparently, many native whites voted Republican not because they really approved of political collaboration with Negroes or hoped to achieve office, but because they found appealing a program that endorsed an expansion of educational, economic, and political opportunity. Some few of these were strangely persistent in their loyalty to Republicanism. For instance, during the campaign of 1876, when every power of the white community at large was turned toward Redemption, about one hundred white Republicans attended a meeting at Oconee courthouse at which Richard T. Greener, a Negro and a member of the faculty of the University of South Carolina, spoke.[79] However, the great mass of white voters refused to accept political partnership with Negroes; and many of these even denied Negro Republicanism the dignity of formal opposition.

On the other hand, the Democratic (or Conservative, or Reform) party was spectacularly unsuccessful in winning Negro votes in spite of herculean efforts spent in that cause. Many of the ante-bellum leaders in South Carolina politics simply abdicated after the war; some of these rather gracefully retired after the failure of their great experiment, others were passed over without their consent, and a few withdrew out of revulsion against the "levelling" tendencies of the immediate postwar months. The men who emerged as dominant had generally belonged to

78. For instance, at least 574 whites in Lexington District supported the convention movement in the fall of 1867. However, some 500 of these refused to vote for the constitution and voted with the conservative Reform party in the election of 1870. *Report of the Secretary of War* (1868), pp. 521, 522; *Reports and Resolutions* (1870–1871), p. 518.

Registration and election figures compiled by the army in 1867 and 1868 indicate that at least 1,300 native whites voted Republican in those years. In 1868, Republican spokesmen claimed 5,000 native whites had joined their party, a figure which was probably too generous. *Report of the Secretary of War* (1868), pp. 521, 522; *New York Times,* May 2, 1868, p. 11.

79. *Weekly Republican* (Charleston), October 25, 1876.

upcountry, national Democratic, and co-operationist factions in the prewar years. Benjamin F. Perry and James L. Orr were typical of this
class. Separate, but closely associated with these leaders, were men who
had been of the "aristocracy" before the war and had risen in politics
only after gaining high rank and reputation in the Confederate military
—men such as Wade Hampton, Joseph Kershaw, Matthew C. Butler,
and James Conner. The postwar leadership was sometimes assisted by
those who had marched somewhere near the head of the aristocratic
political column in the prewar period—men like A. P. Aldrich (who even
opposed acceptance of the Thirteenth Amendment) and A. L. Burt
(who lent his Abbeville home for Jefferson Davis's last cabinet meeting).
These men led the native whites into a firm alliance with President
Johnson and a tentative, suspicious, and shallow union with the Northern Democracy.

During the summer following the war, when they were certain that
the ruthless heel of the conqueror was upon their necks, the active leadership came amazingly close to making a bid for a Negro following. The
offer would have consisted of an extension of the franchise to Negroes
on the basis of literacy and property qualifications, so restricted to suit
both a lingering aristocratic spirit and the upcountry's fear that lowcountry Negroes might become the political pawns of their late masters.
"We might probably even have procured what was then called
'impartial suffrage,'" wrote a member of the Constitutional Convention
of 1865 six years afterward. However, Johnson had "held up before us
the hope of a 'white man's government,' and this led us to set aside
negro suffrage."[80] There was much hindsight in this statement, but
there was also much truth. Indeed, as Johnson struggled with the
Radicals through the critical year of 1866, South Carolina's leaders
understood from their alert and energetic "commissioner" in Washington, William Henry Trescot, that readmission without Negro suffrage
was very possible.[81] When Johnson began to lose ground to the Radicals, the state's leaders maintained a remarkable flexibility as they
maneuvered to effect a prospective exchange of a qualified Negro suffrage for reunion. In December, 1866, they allowed the Fourteenth
Amendment to be rejected in the state legislature by, as Trescot aptly

80. C. C. Memminger to Carl Schurz, April 26, 1871, in Fredric Bancroft
(ed.), *Carl Schurz: Speeches, Correspondence and Political Papers*, II (New York,
1913), 256.
81. W. H. Trescot to J. L. Conner, May 7, 1866, W. H. Trescot Papers (Duke).

phrased it, "our old colleagues of the South."[82] They expected an impasse to follow in which they would be able to strike the bargain. Ironically, while Beverly Nash was in Washington in the winter of 1867 pressing for universal male suffrage, Governor Orr was also there, lobbying for the compromise settlement which he hoped would hold his faction together and in power in South Carolina.

Defeat in the war had cast traditional politics in South Carolina adrift. The Reconstruction Act of March 2, 1867, was the rock upon which it crashed. The white leadership now grew thinner still. Many, including Ben Perry, simply refused to participate in political affairs which they deemed unconstitutional and trusted that the Supreme Court would soon disallow. Belatedly, Orr and Hampton made a brief and spirited attempt to woo Negro voters into their camp. By mid-summer, however, shattered by the coolness of the Negro electorate and dismayed by what they considered the freedmen's ingratitude, the white leadership gave up the struggle.

Organizing as Democrats, native white leaders again tried to win Negro votes in the spring of 1868 when the new constitution was to be submitted to the people and, if adopted, state and local officers elected. In several areas, they succeeded in organizing clubs of Negro Democrats. In Columbia, for instance, a Democratic Association of Colored Citizens was formed in mid-April with about forty charter members. By mid-June, it reputedly mustered one hundred Negroes on its roll.[83] Again, the efforts of the whites went unrewarded. Citing the local press in several counties, an upcountry editor lamented after the April elections that the Democrats of Newberry and Fairfield counties had each won only about one hundred Negro votes, though Greenville apparently counted none, and the Edgefield *Advertiser* complained that fewer Negroes voted Democratic there than anywhere.[84] Outside of Charleston, where the Democrats made up a purse of $631 for a Negro named Riley who voted Democratic despite the threats of his Radical neighbors, apparently little effort was made by the Democrats in the lowcountry to win the Negro vote.[85]

Emerging as the most prominent leader among the Democrats after their losses in the spring of 1868, Hampton struggled to get his cam-

82. W. H. Trescot to W. D. Simpson, December 22, 1866, W. H. Trescot Papers.
83. *New York Times,* April 26, p. 10; May 7, p. 5; June 15, p. 5, 1868.
84. *Intelligencer* (Anderson), May 6, 1868.
85. *Ibid.,* November 25, 1868.

paign in motion for the national elections in November. However, early Radical victories in the North and West vitiated the effort before it was well underway. By October 9, a month before the election, most native whites would have agreed with the Spartanburg farmer who thought "that the Radicals are going to elect their candidate for the Presidency."[86] With this failure, the first series of attempts by the Democracy to win a Negro following came to an end.

The failure was not, as many Republicans subsequently alleged, because the Democrats had not tried to win Negro votes. Essentially, it was unsuccessful because the party of the white man presented no program which addressed itself to the special interests of the Negro. Indeed, it even attempted, with painfully apparent ineptitude, to eschew recognition of the Negro's right to vote. Possibly, a few Negroes became Democrats because they deprecated the racial antagonisms that Negro Republicanism engendered. Certainly, some succumbed to personal persuasion and coercion. Ultimately, however, the appeal of the Democrat to the Negro was negative or meaningless, resting heavily upon the ballyhoo and barbecue which the white, in his own naiveté, was certain would play effectively upon the "childish nature" of the Negroes. For instance, on the Fourth of July, 1868, the Democratic Negroes of Aiken celebrated with "dancing under the trees——" In the same place, a month later, a Democratic rally featured speeches by Wade Hampton and M. C. Butler. "There was a stand also," the Reverend Cornish noted, "for the 'Coloured Auxiliary Democratic Club' & two negroes spoke."[87] In Anderson, a special—and separate—meeting was held for the Negroes in which they were addressed by the Democratic candidate for Congress. Afterward, a song composed for the occasion was sung:

> To set carpet-baggers a-walking,
> And scalawags close in their rear,
> We must all keep continually talking,
> And vote for our Seymour and Blair.

In the evening, a "candlelight meeting" was held for the instruction of the Negroes in the proper exercise of their suffrage. However, the Democratic county chairman was depressed to note that it was only poorly attended.[88] In sum, the only concession made to the Negro voter

86. *Ibid.*, August 19, 1868; David Golightly Harris MS Farm Journal, entry for October 9, 1868.

87. J. H. Cornish MS Diary, entries for July 4, August 4, 1868.

88. *Intelligencer* (Anderson), September 2, 1868.

by the Democracy was permission to vote the all-white leadership of that party into office.

The inability of the Democratic party to raise a respectable leadership among their Negro converts was indicative of the hollowness of their appeal. For instance, in Barnwell, they pressed forward Richard Gayle, an elderly Negro who had been brought from Virginia as a slave. He had earned the respect of the whites by laboring long and arduously to buy himself and his family out of bondage. Tragically, some members of his family died immediately after he had purchased their freedom, and he managed to buy the rest only shortly before they would have been liberated anyway. Gayle, in speeches unreservedly endorsed by the Democrats, advised his Negro neighbors that the whites were their true friends. Moreover, opposition to the white man was useless. The whites were certain to win any struggle, Gayle thought, because they had conquered the Indians and the forest, had built cities, telegraphs, railroads, and steamboats.[89] The paucity of leadership among Negro Democrats was so great that Orr developed a two-man team of Negro orators which he apparently sent upon demand from Columbia into critical areas.[90] The vein of leadership was only slightly richer in Columbia where Pleasants Good, "an old family servant of the Gregg family," headed the Negro Democratic club; but even in the capital city the practical results of Negro Democracy were negligible.[91]

After the fiasco of 1868 and until 1876, most native whites virtually surrendered the state to Republicanism. A few Democratic leaders— among them James L. Orr—accepted office at the hands of the Republicans and soon passed into that party. Most whites simply withdrew from active politics, concentrated upon improving their economic situation, and gave up hope of regaining political power. Those who did remain active fell into the strategy of "fusion." That is, they allied themselves with conservative elements splintered from the Republican plank. Thereby, they hoped to siphon off enough Negro votes to regain control. In 1870, they combined with a carpetbag judge of questionable reputation to campaign as the Union Reform party. In 1872, they supported a "reform" bolt within the Republican party led by Orr. In 1874, they endorsed a supposedly reforming group which nominated

89. *Sentinel* (Barnwell), November 7, 1868.
90. J. H. Gooch to J. L. Orr, May 6, 1867, Freedmen File.
91. *New York Times*, April 26, 1868, p. 10.

a respectable scalawag for governor and Martin R. Delany (a Negro) for lieutenant-governor.

Basically, fusion failed. In 1870, when they enjoyed a true partnership with conservative Republicans, their candidates were overwhelmingly defeated. In 1872 and 1874, when they enjoyed a more respectable numerical showing, they were actually only "fellow-traveling" with rebel Republicans who hardly deigned to recognize their support. In 1874, nevertheless, in some counties in which the white electorate was or approached the majority, the fusionists won qualified successes and were much encouraged. "The great battle for Constitutional liberty is not now," declared one, "it will be fought two years hence."[92] Such optimism was hardly warranted. In the winter and spring of 1876, fusion faltered as the mass of native whites returned to the political posture they had assumed in 1868. By the summer of 1876, the last of the fusionists had capitulated unreservedly to a straight out, all-white Democracy which would accept the Negro's vote (as long as he had one) but not his dictation.

Fundamentally, fusion did not succeed because it misrepresented not only the basic attitudes of the great mass of white voters, but the deep-seated feelings of the fusionist leadership itself. By allying himself with the Negro voter and officeholder, the fusionist was, in practice, recognizing the Negro as his political equal, a concession very few whites were willing to make either in theory or practice. In every election in which the fusionists participated, possibly more eligible white voters stayed home than went to the polls.[93] Furthermore, the fusionist leadership was aware of its duplicity. Francis Warrington Dawson, the English émigré journalist who probably introduced the idea into the state for the first time during the municipal elections in Charleston in the summer of 1868 and who was largely responsible for its inauguration in the statewide campaign of 1870, candidly recognized it as an attempt to "overturn our negro governments and re-establish white supremacy."[94] A. P. Aldrich was purely Machievellian about

92. A. P. Aldrich to J. C. Chesnut, November 5, 1874, Williams–Chesnut–Manning Papers.

93. "They are acting the part of out Heroding Herod," wrote one white Democrat who expected to stay home on election day in 1870. J. M. Dennis to J. Y. Harris, April 16, 1870, J. Y. Harris Papers.

94. F. W. Dawson to his father, July 30, 1868, F. W. Dawson Papers; F. W. Dawson to R. R. Hemphill, June 28, 1876, Hemphill Papers. In the letter to Hemphill, Dawson claimed that he "alone" was responsible for starting the fusion movement in South Carolina.

fusion. "It may be called the New Departure, or any other name," he explained after the defeat of 1870, "but what we want is to get the State, we can't get it under the name of Democracy, for the nigger has been taught to hate that as he does cold & we must spread our nets to get in all the disaffected of the Republican Party, white & black, & they are not a few."[95] Interestingly, honorable men among the fusionists felt that self-respect had been damaged by their actions in 1870. Several days after the election, Joseph B. Kershaw outlined a new approach to fusion which would effect a partial repair. ". . . hence forth while we reiterate our acquiescence in the political status of the negro in the language and spirit of the Platform of the Reform Party, and while we shall most gladly welcome the co-operation of any and all who may come to our aid in restoring good government to our bleeding and prostrate State, upon the same liberal platform and principles, yet *they* must seek *us* for that end, since they *will* have it so and we as a people shall pursue that course of conduct 'most likely to effect our safety and happiness.' "[96] This tact may have salved Southern consciences, but conservative Republicans remained reluctant to embrace the erstwhile Democracy for fear of receiving the kiss of political death.

Quite obviously, Negro voters recognized that in adopting fusion the whites were being untrue to themselves. Republican editors were fond of indicating what was apparent to all, that the fusionists recognized Negro suffrage only after "the bayonet compelled it." ". . . before the war you wouldn't let me join your party," a Republican journalist reported one Negro as saying to the whites in 1870, "and now I don't choose to."[97] Of course, much of this was editorial rubbish; the great mass of Negro voters hardly bothered to verbalize their feelings. Actually, Negroes went to fusionist meetings, rallies, and speakings, ate their barbecues and picnics, listened attentively to their candidates, and, on occasion, even promised them their votes. Nevertheless, on election day, they appeared early at the polls and quietly cast their ballots for the opposition. "I have been very busy for the past two months," complained the Democrat-become-fusionist clerk-of-court of Chester County after the election of 1870, "not only in my office, but

95. A. P. Aldrich to A. L. Burt (probably late spring or early summer), 1871, A. L. Burt Papers.

96. J. B. Kershaw to F. W. Dawson, November 6, 1870, F. W. Dawson Papers.

97. *Daily Republican* (Charleston), April 27, 1870; June 2, 1870. See also: *New York Times,* September 8, 1868, p. 1; *Daily Republican* (Charleston), May 11, June 10, 1870.

electioneering among the infernal negroes, and after all my trouble, and all the humiliation which I had to undergo, and the concessions made I am defeated by over thirteen Hundred Majority." The crestfallen candidate had made it his special business to pay his "respects to the 'colored friends'" on his uncle's plantation "and got the promise of several votes, but I understand that they all marched to the Polls by sunrise and voted the full Radical ticket."[98]

In 1874, F. L. Cardozo attempted to explain to a Northern correspondent why the Negro voter rejected the fusionist bid. The colored men, he said, had no confidence in the professions of whites. They did not believe that the whites deliberately sought to deceive them, but that the Democrats, if returned to power, would assume to be the judges of the rights of the Negroes and would remand them to a condition of subjection and dependence tantamount to slavery. The Negroes did not believe that those who had considered slavery a divine institution and fought a long and bloody war to defend it could have changed so soon. They felt that the whites would go to any lengths to control their labor and that they were more interested in exaggerating the corruption in the government than they were in reform because they hoped to excuse their use of intimidation by its existence. The Negroes, Cardozo maintained, were distressed by corruption and the antagonism of the whites, but they would not act to establish "concord and harmony, if concord and harmony meant the sacrifice of their political and civil rights."[99]

Cardozo may have spoken as a politician, but the response of the Negro electorate at the polls attested to the accuracy of his analysis before, during, and (as the events of 1876 were to prove) after the fusionist phase had passed.

Negro voters rejected the leadership of the white Democracy largely on grounds of principle; but within the Republican party there was an increasingly prevalent tendency among both Negro leaders and voters to dissociate themselves from their white colleagues. Often the withdrawal was caused in part by the conservatism of some white Republicans, and more often it was accelerated by the ambitions of individual Negro leaders to occupy offices held by their white partisans. But,

98. David Hemphill to R. R. Hemphill, October 27, 1870, Hemphill Papers. See also: J. H. Hemphill to W. R. Hemphill, November 13, 1874, Hemphill Papers; *The Nation*, XV, No. 367 (July 11, 1872), 23; Avary, *Dixie after the War*, pp. 245-46.

99. *New York Times*, June 22, 1874, p. 1.

most importantly, it bore unmistakably the mark of the racial prejudices which the Negro community held against the whites.

The proclivity of Negro voters to elevate members of their own race
to positions of public and party trust was early evident. In the Convention of the Republican party which was held in Columbia in July,
1867, no less than 64 of the 80 delegates were Negroes. After a strenuous contest in which the cry of race was frequently heard, the convention chose as its president R. H. Gleaves, a Pennsylvania mulatto
who had come to Beaufort after the war to enter business with Robert
Smalls. Two native-born Negroes and a scalawag were elected vice-
presidents and four Negroes designated secretaries.[100] Of the 124
delegates elected to the Constitutional Convention of 1868, at least 71
and probably 74 were Negroes. In the state and local elections of that
year, Negroes were victorious candidates for many lesser offices. For
instance, 71 of the 124 places in the house of representatives and 11 of
the 31 senatorial seats were filled by Negroes. On the other hand,
higher offices were pre-empted by white Republicans. Only one Negro,
F. L. Cardozo, who stood for secretary of state, appeared on the state-
wide ticket consisting of eight men.[101]

To some extent, the absence of Negro officers in high places during
this early period was the result of the conservative advice of their own
leaders. In the summer of 1867, Delany urged Negroes to "be satisfied
to take things like other men in their natural course and time, preparing themselves in every particular for local municipal positions, and
they may expect to attain to some others in time."[102] Cardozo opposed
a move to offer a Negro candidate for lieutenant-governor in 1868
and even refused the nomination himself, arguing that "to have yielded
to it would simply have been a surrender to the enemy by going
beyond the limits of true victory."[103]

Nevertheless, a large element of the Negro leadership (particularly
among those who were Northern born) pressed for a larger share of the
offices for Negroes. J. J. Wright, in the July, 1867, convention of the
party, noted the "commanding position that we now occupy in the
South, in conjunction with the Republican element of the North," and
demanded "a representation in the councils of the nation commensurate
thereto"—namely, the vice-presidency.[104] In the fall, a Northern cor-

100. *Ibid.*, July 31, 1867, p. 1.
101. *Ibid.*, March 13, p. 5; July 12, p. 5; December 14, p. 2, 1868.
102. *Ibid.*, August 21, 1867, p. 4.
103. *Ibid.*, May 1, 1868, p. 11.
104. *Ibid.*, July 31, 1867, p. 1.

respondent observed an increasingly determined aggressiveness among the Northern-born Negro leadership and a willingness among them to use their color to gain "an advantage over their white rivals."[105] Taking the leadership for his race on the floor of the house of representatives in Columbia in the following summer, W. J. Whipper pressed for the election of R. B. Elliott to the speakership on purely racial grounds. Losing this campaign to a scalawag, he then demanded a judgeship for his race, a demand which was satisfied some eighteen months later by the election of Wright to the state Supreme Court.[106]

During the winter of 1870, the Negro leadership suddenly became markedly more assertive, perhaps encouraged by a stirring of the Negro masses after the ratification of the Fifteenth Amendment. One manifestation was an attack upon the separation of the races in public places. Another was an insistence upon a larger share of important offices for Negroes. The first assault was launched against Charles P. Leslie, the Van Buren style Democrat from upstate New York who had so badly "bungled" his job as land commissioner. Not only was Leslie incapable and corrupt, but he had also excited the racial animosity of his Negro colleagues by referring to them by such sobriquets as "daddy Cain" and "The Reverend Burt District Randolph."[107] Significantly, the ouster was effected by Cardozo and a purely Negro faction in the legislature, and the cabal demanded that a Negro be chosen to fill the office.

During the spring, the movement for more offices for Negroes gained headway rapidly. At a Republican rally at Christ Church in May, Abram Smith oratorically claimed the lieutenant governorship for his race, but was generously willing to allow Christopher Columbus Bowen, a scalawag, to retain his seat in Congress "provided no colored man desired the place."[108] In Charleston, A. J. Ransier attacked the conservative Republican senator, F. A. Sawyer, for his failure to appoint more Negroes to federal posts, and R. H. Cain called for a division of the state's four congressional seats between the races.[109] Even Martin Delany had become suddenly ambitious. Arguing that "black men must have black leaders," he asked for "a colored Lieutenant Governor, and two colored men in the House of Representatives and

105. *Ibid.,* November 25, 1867, p. 8.
106. *Ibid.,* July 7, p. 5; July 12, p. 5; July 27, p. 1, 1868.
107. *Ibid.,* July 20, 1868, p. 8; *Intelligencer* (Anderson), September 23, 1868.
108. *Daily Republican* (Charleston), May 16, 1870.
109. *Ibid.,* June 24, July 28, 1870.

one in the Senate, and our quota of State and county offices."[110] R. C. De Large, maneuvering to win Bowen's place in Congress, came very near to political apostasy. For three successive nights in Charleston in June, he held meetings in which he denounced Bowen and the "white ring" in Columbia (exempting only Scott) and urged the Negroes to form a party of their own. "If the white men in the party think that the Republican party was made for them," he warned, "they are badly mistaken." The Negro should no longer yield to the white Republican leadership. "When a colored man is capable of filling an office, I say give it to him; and I shall fight this over the entire State." If the party objected, then the party was dispensable. "I hold that my race has always been Republican from necessity," he darkly menaced.[111] By August, a correspondent of the *Nation* thought that "negro senators and representatives may be looked for regularly, and that the colored man has definitely decided that he will no longer 'take a back seat!' "[112]

Rather mysteriously, the movement lost momentum as summer waned. Even De Large declared publicly that he had not really meant to advocate the desertion of the party. Nevertheless, in terms of important offices gained, the Negro leadership profited greatly by the maneuver. Ransier became the lieutenant-governor. Cardozo retained his position as secretary of state. B. F. Whittemore, a carpetbagger, withdrew from the congressional race in the northeastern quarter of the state in favor of a native-born Negro, Joseph H. Rainey. S. L. Hoge, another carpetbagger, did the same in his district for a Northern Negro, R. B. Elliott. Bowen, in the Charleston area, allied himself with Sawyer and other conservative Republicans but ultimately lost his place to the ever-ambitious De Large. Ransier also became the chairman of the state-wide Republican executive committee, upon which he was assisted by Cardozo, Beverly Nash, and a scalawag who was reputedly married to a Negro woman.[113] The Negro majority in the legislature increased to 86 out of a total of 156 places as 11 Negro senators and 75 Negro representatives took their seats. The new legislature evinced an inclination to cap these triumphs with the election of Cardozo to the United States Senate. Finally, however, the Negro majority yielded to the claims of the incumbent, Thomas Jefferson Robertson, a wealthy, respectable native white who covered his natural conserva-

110. *Ibid.,* June 24, July 5, 1870.
111. *Ibid.,* June 24, 1870.
112. *The Nation,* XI, No. 267 (August 11, 1870), 82.
113. *New York Times,* August 1, 1870, p. 2.

tism with a good show of Republicanism.[114] After the election, the
Charleston *Daily Republican,* formerly the party organ for the state,
was driven to the wall by the withdrawal of the state's official patronage,
by its own claim, for its endorsement of Bowen and its general opposition to the ambitions of the Negro leadership.[115]

Both the continuing desire of the Negroes to win more of the important offices and their success in accomplishing that end were apparent in the years which followed. White Republicans were irritated
and alarmed by the flooding tide of black officeholders. "The negro is
bound to have office," Governor Scott observed ruefully. "When they
smell blood they are in for it."[116] In 1872, a delegate to the South Carolina Colored Men's Convention demanded a cabinet post for his race;[117]
and, in the elections of that year, Negroes gained four of the eight state-
wide elective offices, increased their majority in the legislature from
86 to 106 of the 156 places, and won both the speakership of the house
and the presidency *pro tempora* of the senate. In addition, they took
four out of the state's five Congressional seats. Two years later, this
current was apparently still running high among Negro voters. A
Northern reporter visiting the state in the summer of 1874 thought that
the Negroes were "becoming tired of the political servitude" and were
"already talking of assuming, themselves, the management of the political machinery of the State."[118] The trend was partly reversed by
election results as white Republicans took three of the Congressional
places and white fusionists and bolters gained more than a score of
legislative seats. However, Negroes retained other political salients
and moved forward to win sixteen Senate seats—one-half of the total.
In 1876, the slate of candidates advanced by the Radicals reflected very
nearly the same racial complexion exhibited by Republican incumbents.

The first object of attack by those Negroes who sought more offices
for their race were the ignorant and, typically, more disreputable scalawags. In areas where the Negro leadership was strong, this element
disappeared from Republican ranks after the first few years. On the
other hand, those native white Republicans who were well educated
and able and who had been considered respectable by the native white
community—such as the Melton, Mackey, and Moses clans—enjoyed
a durable popularity among both Negro voters and leaders.

114. *Ibid.,* December 8, 1870, p. 1.
115. *Ibid.,* September 13, 1871, p. 4.
116. *Ibid.,* April 25, 1871, p. 5.
117. *Ibid.,* March 31, 1872, p. 1.
118. *Ibid.,* June 21, 1874, p. 1.

Strangely, the heavy losers in the Negro's drive for office were carpetbaggers. A preference among Negroes for the scalawag over the carpetbagger, other things being equal, was early manifested. "We would rather have white people that have lived among us than strangers," Nash had said in the summer of 1867, while making the point that his race did not want high offices for themselves. "The colored people have grown suspicious of strangers," he explained. "They know that good men don't come South—they have business at home, and from what we have seen those that come are adventurers with both hands open, like birds of prey."[119] The most spectacular display of this bias was the decision of the overwhelming majority of Negro voters in 1872 to place in the governor's chair Franklin J. Moses, Jr., a scalawag whose good reputation had already been impugned, in preference to carpetbagger Reuben Tomlinson, the scrupulously honest and highly capable reform candidate of the bolters who had done so much for Negro education in the state. Chafed by the prospect of certain defeat, B. F. Whittemore, a carpetbagger himself and one of the bolters, demanded irritably of his nominal leader, James L. Orr: "Do you think an honest Northern man will triumph over a dishonest Southern man when you remember the hatred entertained toward the carpetbaggers?"[120] By 1876, no white Republican politician could expect long to survive who was not willing to grant Negroes access to all offices. In 1875, an upcountry Republican editor found it a matter of no surprise that some white men, presumably including himself, were willing to see Negroes in office from the "highest to the lowest."[121]

A striking feature of political life in the post-Reconstruction period was the preciseness with which opposing parties and races exchanged places and performances. Just as Negro Republicans had done previously, white Democrats during and after 1877, were determined, as one Northern correspondent observed, "to run the opposition into the ground completely . . ." In the house of representatives, the white Democratic majority, "amidst derision," forced Negro members to

119. *Ibid.*, August 9, 1867, p. 2.

120. B. F. Whittemore to J. L. Orr, September 9, 1872, Orr–Patterson Papers. In the following year, the Negroes of Charleston chose a scalawag over a carpetbagger for mayor of the city. "He is identified with the City & his nomination indicated the disposition of the negro to separate from the carpet bagger," asserted Redeemer James Conner to a friend. "The current sets that way at present, and it is a hopeful sign." James Conner to W. P. Miles, September 17, 1873, W. P. Miles Papers.

121. *Republican* (Greenville), August 10, 1875.

"crawl" and make "abject apology" before being allowed to take their seats. Similarly, whole delegations of Republicans were arbitrarily and summarily excluded from the places they claimed.[122] Precisely as Democratic officers had been driven into the few solidly white counties during and after 1868, now Negro Republican officeholding was pressed into a few lowcountry counties in which the Negro population possessed an overwhelming numerical superiority. By 1892, only two counties, in which the Negro population was some 85 per cent of the total, continued to send Negroes to the legislature. A decade later, even these were lost.[123]

By intimidation and outright fraud and by increasingly stringent election laws, the white made the Negro's exercise of his suffrage steadily more difficult. Negro voters answered these pressures much as the whites had responded to the political dominance of the Negro during Reconstruction. A few became Democrats, and some of these did so because they genuinely endorsed the Redeemer program of reform and retrenchment. Thus, some Negroes practiced their own brand of scalawagism. Others accepted the Democratic programs without changing their party and, hence, became fusionists. However, the average Negro voter was apparently afflicted by a severe and crippling case of defeatism. "This election was quiet—we had fifty to their one —but they beat us," wrote Jake Adams to a friend after the elections of 1878.[124] Like native whites during Reconstruction, Negro voters responded by withdrawing entirely from political participation. In 1878, the Republicans failed even to offer a gubernatorial candidate, and Hampton ran 50,000 votes ahead of his own lieutenant-governor, a margin which perhaps measured the Negro turnout.[125] "There is certainly a great change in the negro population, & it is refreshing to be rid of the political scoundrels that have been such pests to our peace & general security," wrote an old citizen of Georgetown in 1879, feeling the pulse of the people. He concluded, "I think their political aspirations are nearly if not entirely at an end."[126]

122. *The Nation*, XXIV, No. 621 (May 24, 1877), 305–6.
123. Tindall, *South Carolina Negroes*, pp. 309–10.
124. Mary Boykin Chesnut MS Diary, entry for November 12, 1878.
125. *Appletons' Annual Cyclopaedia*, 1878, III, 771.
126. T. P. Bailey to R. H. McKie, March 22, 1879, R. H. McKie Papers.

XIII...THE POLITICOS

The alliance of Negroes with the Republican party was a logical outgrowth of the pursuit by individuals of their own interests. Yet, some allowance must be made for the leadership that focused and organized the political energy of the Negro masses. The men who supplied this leadership and the manner in which they pursued their objectives are the subjects of this chapter.

The traditional story that Radical Republicans in the North dispatched paid organizers to South Carolina to encourage Negroes to claim their political rights and join the Republican party only after they plotted to pass the first Reconstruction Act is a patent exaggeration. Actually, Republican organization in South Carolina began during the war. As if by deliberate selection, the great majority of Northern civilians and the higher officers of the military who came to the Sea Islands before the surrender were of the Republican persuasion. In 1864, Republicans on the islands were well enough organized to send a delegation to the national convention of the party and in the following year to elect the Radical editor of the Beaufort *Free South*, James G. Thompson, to the otherwise all-Democratic state constitutional convention which met at Johnson's call. Many of these Sea Island Republicans were abolitionists who, after emancipation, passed on to Radicalism. Before 1867, however, most of them were much more avid in pursuing their professions than in organizing potential Negro voters as Republicans.

The tradition also asserts that governmental employees, military officials, and, particularly, the agents of the Bureau were hand-picked
Republican emissaries. Assuming that subsequent political prominence
would mark most such people, this, too, is clearly untrue. Indeed, with
the exception of the educational department of the Bureau, less than a
dozen Republican leaders emerged from the hundreds thus employed.
Albert Gallatin Mackey, Daniel T. Corbin, and Charles P. Leslie were
the only federal officials who took leading parts in organizing Republicanism in South Carolina. Mackey, a native Charlestonian and a persistent Unionist, received the choicest post in the state—that of collector of
the port of Charleston. Mackey became the very able presiding officer of
the convention that drafted the Constitution of 1868. Corbin, a Ver-
monter who had been a captain of Negro troops during the war, became
the federal district attorney after the war. Corbin acted as a legal
adviser to the Constitutional Convention of 1868, was a perennial senator
from Charleston, and remained an active Republican leader in the state
long after Redemption. Leslie came to the state as a collector of internal
revenue. By the spring of 1867, however, when he emerged an active
Republican, he had already left the service of the treasury department
and was eminently unsuccessful as a planter in Barnwell District.

The military was even less political. From early 1866 into the summer
of 1867, the commanding general was Daniel Sickles, a close personal
friend of Orr. Sickles's relief, E. R. S. Canby, evinced a mild Republicanism which even the native whites found inoffensive.[1] Only two
officers in the entire command became active Republicans. One of these,
a Colonel Moore who commanded the Sixth Infantry, was relieved after
appearing at several political meetings in the Columbia area. The other,
A. J. Willard, pursued a peculiar political career. A New York lawyer
who came South as the lieutenant-colonel of a Negro regiment, he
remained to become a legal adviser to the commanding general. In
1867, he was given the duty of registering voters in the two Carolinas.
There is no indication that he was an active Republican until after
he was seated on the supreme court bench by the first Republican legislature.

Outside of its educational division, the Bureau was hardly more
political. Saxton had never been able to make an abolitionist stronghold
out of his various commands. His successor in the Bureau, Scott, became
the first Republican governor and laid the Bureau open to the obvious
charge. Yet, the Bureau under Scott was as often accused of anti-

1. *New York Times,* September 4, 1866, p. 1; November 25, 1867, p. 8.

Republicanism as otherwise. Indeed, his staff seemed to tend away from Republicanism and certainly from Radicalism. "They are often more pro-slavery than the rebels themselves," scandalized Laura Towne, "and only care to make the blacks work . . ."[2] Leaving aside its educators and Scott, only three Bureau agents were active Republican organizers. R. C. De Large and Martin Delany held minor offices in the Bureau, and J. J. Wright was Scott's legal adviser.[3]

It is true that before the passage of the first Reconstruction Act South Carolina Negroes were not organized by and as Republicans in any significant degree. They were, however, organized *for* Republicanism. They were associated in such a way that when they were enfranchised, the establishment of the party amounted to little more than formalizing a pattern which already existed. The elements most responsible for this pre-conditioning of the Negro voter-to-be were the Bureau schools, the Northern churches, and the native Negro leadership. Moreover, these three sources supplied a ready-made core of chiefs to South Carolina Republicanism.

Many early Republican leaders found their first postwar employment in the educational division of the Bureau. Reuben Tomlinson, a Pennsylvania Quaker who had been among the first experimenters to come to the Sea Islands during the war, was for nearly three years the Bureau's superintendent of education in South Carolina. In the summer of 1868, he took a seat in the first Republican legislature. Two of Tomlinson's assistant superintendents, Whittemore and Randolph, were front rank leaders in the organization of the state's Republicans. Whittemore was particularly influential in the northeastern quarter of the state, represented Darlington in the Constitutional Convention of 1868, and became the first Republican congressman elected in that area. Randolph was active in the vicinity of Orangeburg and was that county's first Republican state senator. A number of Northern-born Negro soldiers also became Bureau teachers and passed into the Republican leadership.

2. Rupert S. Holland (ed.), *Letters and Diary of Laura M. Towne, 1862–1884, Written from the Sea Islands of South Carolina* (Cambridge, 1912), pp. 157, 171.

3. For De Large's Bureau role, see Martin L. Abbott, "The Freedmen's Bureau in South Carolina, 1865–1872" (Unpublished Ph.D. dissertation, Emory University, 1954), *passim*. For Delany's Bureau history, see Frank A. Rollin, *Life and Public Services of Martin R. Delany, Sub-Assistant Commissioner, Bureau Relief of Refugees, Freedmen, and of Abandoned Lands, and Late Major 104th U. S. Colored Troops* (2nd ed.; Boston, 1883), *passim*. For Wright's background, see the *Charleston Mercury*, February 24, 1868.

London S. Langley and Stephen A. Swails were two who belonged to this class.[4]

In addition, the Bureau recruited as teachers a host of Charleston Negroes (many of whom had been free before the war) and sent them into the hinterland. There they did yeoman work, not only as educators, but in imparting a sense of political awareness to the parents of their scholars. Many of them returned to Charleston as delegates to the Constitutional Convention of 1868. Examples of such cases are numerous and worth close attention because they indicate one means by which Republicanism spread among the Negro population before they actually obtained the vote. These examples also reveal much of the character of what might be called the second echelon of Republican leadership in the state. Henry L. Shrewsbury, twenty-one years old in 1868, a mulatto offspring of the free Negro population of Charleston and well educated, was sent to Cheraw as a Bureau teacher soon after the war. In 1868, he returned to Charleston as Chesterfield's Negro delegate to the Constitutional Convention. Henry E. Hayne, who had also been free before the war and became a sergeant in the First South, was sent to Marion as a Bureau teacher and returned to Charleston in 1868 as the leader of the three-man Negro delegation from that district.[5] William J. McKinlay and T. K. Sasportas went to Orangeburg from Charleston as Bureau teachers. Both were scions of free Negro families which were prominent in the trades. Sasportas was the son of a butcher who had himself owned slaves before the war. Sasportas was educated in Philadelphia, remained there during the war, and was said to be intelligent and very well informed.[6] The work of Randolph, Sasportas, and McKinlay goes far toward explaining the large Negro vote cast for the convention in Orangeburg District in the fall of 1867 and the subsequent development of Orangeburg as the stronghold of Republicanism, Northern Methodism, and Negro education. All three of these educators returned to Charleston in 1868 as delegates to the convention. What these men did in Orangeburg was duplicated by James N. and Charles D. Hayne in Barnwell District. Offspring of the free Negro society of Charleston, the brothers probably came to Barnwell as Bureau teachers and, along with Northern Methodist minister Abram

4. *Charleston Mercury,* February 24, 1868; Luis F. Emilio, *History of the Fifty-Fourth Regiment of Massachusetts Volunteer Infantry, 1863–1865* (Boston, 1894), p. 336.

5. *Charleston Mercury,* February 24, 1868.

6. *Ibid.;* Laura Josephine Webster, *The Operation of the Freedmen's Bureau in South Carolina* (Northampton, 1916), p. 159.

Middleton, formed the core of Republican leadership in that district. James Hayne was apparently the leader of the trio which combined with ex-slave Julius Mayer to represent Barnwell in the Convention of 1868. Interestingly, in the convention, Sasportas voted with Randolph on every recorded vote, and the Negro delegates from Barnwell paralleled Randolph's vote six out of seven times.[7]

Frequently, the Bureau licensed local Negroes to teach in their native communities. At least two of these attended the Constitutional Convention of 1868. Calvin Stubbs, who had been a slave in Marlboro District, became a Bureau teacher and represented the district in the convention. With Stubbs came George Jackson, an elderly Negro who had bought his freedom. In the three recorded votes in which he participated Jackson cast his lot with Stubbs.[8] W. Nelson Joiner, a Negro who had gained his freedom in Tennessee before the war and settled in Abbeville, was also a schoolmaster before coming to the convention.[9]

Technically all these teachers were employed by private parties, the function of the Bureau being simply to supply the physical materials necessary. Actually, however, as superintendent of education, Tomlinson had a large degree of control over recruiting, assigning, and overseeing the performance of teachers in schools supported by the Bureau.

Also prominent in early Republican organization in South Carolina and in the Constitutional Convention of 1868 were two Negroes who came to the state as the direct agents of the American Missionary Association for the purpose of establishing schools and, hence, were closely associated with the Bureau. These were F. L. Cardozo, who was the principal of the largest Negro school in the state, and J. J. Wright who passed into full Bureau service soon after entering the state.[10]

Of the seventy-four Negroes who attended the Constitutional Convention of 1868, certainly eleven and probably thirteen (if the Hayne brothers were included) came by way of their involvement in Negro schools. Even though Tomlinson did not himself attend the convention, he followed the same path into the Republican legislature. It could hardly be denied that this phase of the Bureau's program in South Carolina was politically vital.

7. *Charleston Mercury*, February 24, 1868; *Convention Proceedings*, 1868, *passim*. For numerous references to the Haynes brothers, see Martha Schofield MS Diary.

8. *Charleston Mercury*, February 24, 1868; *Convention Proceedings*, 1868, *passim*.

9. *Charleston Mercury*, February 24, 1868.

10. *Daily News* (Charleston), March 9, 1868; *Charleston Mercury*, May 17, 1867; February 24, 1868.

Probably as significant in conditioning the Negro population for Republicanism were the labors of religious missionaries from the North. The real meaning of their work was that they taught and practiced a religion which did not discriminate against the freedman because of his race. The official ambivalence of the churches toward political activism has been discussed. Many leading ministers did manage to avoid direct political participation. Many others, however, devoted themselves wholeheartedly to promoting the interests of the Republican party.

Northern Methodists were especially prominent politically. French, Whittemore, and Randolph might well be considered politicians rather than ministers, but when formal Republican organization began in the spring of 1867 they moved easily and familiarly among the Northern Methodist congregations of the state. It is no coincidence that the very areas in which Northern Methodism was strongest—Camden, Greenville, Kingstree, Orangeburg, Summerville, Florence, Maysville, Sumter, Darlington, Aiken, Barnwell, and Charleston—were also areas in which Republican organization proceeded comparatively rapidly and successfully.[11] Some indication of how this was done was noted by Reverend Cornish early in May, 1867. When his Charleston-bound downtrain stopped at Branchville, a station of the South Carolina Railroad, he saw "the notorious parson French" debark from the uptrain along with Senator "Willson" of Massachusetts. Cornish watched the two men stroll around the station while waiting to resume their journey. "Hear they are on their way to Aiken to enlighten the people," he observed cynically, "especially the negroes."[12] Obviously, Northern Methodist churches provided a ready meeting ground for a communion not so holy between Republican organizers and prospective Negro voters.

At least five of the 124 members of the Constitutional Convention of 1868 were Northern Methodist ministers. At least one delegate—Barney Burton, a forty-year-old ex-slave who had moved to Chester after the war—and perhaps several others were among the 102 local preachers in the conference.[13]

Aside from Bishop Payne nearly every leading minister in the African Methodist Church was also a practicing politician. R. H. Cain was the most successful in both careers, but there were others who were hardly less active than he. William E. Johnston of Sumter was a

11. Compare statistics contained in *Northern Methodist Minutes*, 1868, p. 11, with those in the *Report of the Secretary of War*, 1868, p. 522.

12. J. H. Cornish MS Diary, entry for May 7, 1867.

13. *Northern Methodist Minutes*, 1868, p. 12; *Convention Proceedings*, 1868, pp. 6–7; *Mercury* (Charleston), February 24, 1868.

delegate to the Constitutional Convention of 1868 and later the senator from that county. Richard M. Valentine was an early organizer for the African Church in Abbeville and, although not a delegate to the convention, he sat as a representative in the first Republican legislature. It is virtually a fact that the African Methodists moved their 30,000 members into the Republican party as a solid phalanx.

Individual ministers in other churches were also active politicians. Altogether at least thirteen of the seventy-four Negro delegates who sat in the convention of 1868 were professional or lay ministers.[14]

By 1867 in South Carolina, a numerous resident leadership had already evolved among Negro laymen to make the work of Republican organization easy. The coastal Negro population who had won their freedom before the end of the war supplied a disproportionately large number of top-level leaders for their race. Many of these came directly out of the Union Army to assume prominent places in their communities. At least nine members of the Constitutional Convention of 1868 had been soldiers in the Negro regiments. Three of these had been in South Carolina regiments and became active Republican organizers in the interior districts—H. E. Hayne in Marion, Prince R. Rivers in Edgefield, and Richard Humbird in Darlington. Six were Northerners who had joined the Massachusetts regiments and remained in the coastal area after the war. The careers of Elliott, Whipper, Swails, and Langeley have been described. George H. Lee, 25 years of age at the time of the convention of 1868, had been a sergeant in the Fifty-fourth Massachusetts and left the army to become a planter.[15] W. H. W. Gray had also been a sergeant in the Fifty-fourth and was widely known in the islands after the war as an organizer of Negro Masonic Lodges, in themselves prefabricated Republican clubs.[16]

Many native Negro leaders emerged in the early postwar years by dint of their participation in arranging meetings, parades, and celebrations. R. C. De Large was one of these, ubiquitously the secretary of assemblages of freedmen in Charleston. Two others were Joseph H. Rainey and Alonzo J. Ransier, both of whom had been free before the war. Rainey was born in Georgetown in 1832 and was trained as a barber by his father. For a time, he worked at his trade in the Mills House in Charleston. During the war, he served as a steward aboard a

14. Derived by checking the list of delegates against numerous other sources.

15. Emilio, *History of the Fifty-Fourth Regiment*, p. 352; *Mercury* (Charleston), February 24, 1868.

16. Emilio, *History of the Fifty-Fourth Regiment*, pp. 129, 350.

blockade runner and then on the fortifications around Charleston before he fled to the West Indies. Returning to Charleston after the war, he became a leader in the Negro community. Afterward, again taking up residence in Georgetown, he became a delegate to the Constitutional Convention. He then went into the state senate and, after 1870, served four terms in Congress.[17] A. J. Ransier, thirty-four years old in 1868, had been a shipping clerk in Charleston before the war and afterward became a leader in the Negro community of the city. In 1865, he was an eminent figure in The Friends of Equal Rights Convention which was held in Charleston and presented a petition from that body to Congress. He was later a delegate to the Constitutional Convention, a congressman, and lieutenant-governor.[18]

Soon after the war, many wide-awake Negro leaders from the coast plunged into the interior as Bureau teachers, employees of the benevolent societies, and religious missionaries. Others, like Charlestonians Charles Jones and John Bonum, apparently went later for the specific purpose of mustering Republican voters. Jones worked in Lancaster and returned to Charleston as a delegate to the convention of 1868. Bonum, once the slave of a hatter and after the war the operator of a small store in Charleston, became a delegate from Edgefield.[19]

Negroes in the interior were not without their natural leaders and some of these appeared in the Constitutional Convention of 1868. W. Beverly Nash, a middle-aged, ex-hotel waiter who had once belonged to William C. Preston, gained national attention in 1866 by his criticism of the Bureau's activities in the middle districts. By 1868, Nash was unquestionably the chief spokesman for the Negro electorate of Richland, a position which he maintained over all rivals throughout Reconstruction.[20] Even in the most remote districts, Negro communities pressed forward a home-grown leadership. Some, like Wilson Cooke of Greenville, an ex-slave, literate, half-white, and a tanner by trade, retained their political prominence throughout the period.[21] Others, like Thomas Willliamson of Abbeville District, who had been free and well-to-do (reputedly owning slaves) before the war, came to

17. *Congressional Biography* (1950), p. 1440; Allan Johnson and Dumas Malone (eds.), *Dictionary of American Biography* (New York, 1928–1958), XV, 224–25; *Mercury* (Charleston), February 24, 1868; *New York Times,* October 18, 1870, p. 5.

18. *Congressional Biography* (1950), p. 1719; *Mercury* (Charleston), February 24, 1868.

19. *Mercury* (Charleston), February 24, 1868.

20. *Ibid.; New York Times,* August 9, 1876, p. 2.

21. *Mercury* (Charleston), February 24, 1868.

the convention, but soon lost their influence to more aggressive political entrepreneurs.[22]

Utilizing the ready-made organization and leadership provided by Bureau schools, churches, and the native Negro community, Republicans in South Carolina rapidly marshaled their powers. Almost simultaneously, in mid-March, organizing meetings were held in Columbia and Charleston.[23] Early in May, Republicans from as far away as Greenville met in Charleston for the purpose of establishing the party on a state-wide basis.[24] The Charleston meeting was decidedly not representative, but it did call for a Columbia convention in July and formed a committee to accelerate formal organization in areas not represented. Within a few weeks, this committee established Republicanism throughout the coastal counties and in Orangeburg, Kershaw, and Sumter Districts. The Columbia convention drew a hundred delegates from nineteen districts and formally launched the Union Republican party in the state.[25] Shortly after the Columbia meeting, party organization was perfected in every district. "They are organizing over the State, having lectures among them to disseminate the views of the party," wrote an elderly Chester Democrat. "One meeting has been held here, and there is to be a second one tomorrow when I suppose speeches will be made."[26] When the referendum on the calling of a constitutional convention was held in November, Republicans were able to present a slate of candidates in each district and to muster some 69,000 votes to secure their election.[27]

Obviously, Republican organization in South Carolina was largely homespun rather than imported as tradition maintains. However, Northern emissaries were not entirely lacking. In March, 1867, heretofore strange Negro ministers from Washington appeared in Charleston and Columbia.[28] In May, Senator Wilson (escorted by Parson French), was circulating through the state, and "Pig Iron" Kelley was expected to follow soon. A white woman residing in Abbeville in August saw

22. *Ibid.*
23. *New York Times,* March 21, p. 1; 23, p. 1; 27, p. 8, 1867; *The Nation,* IV, No. 89 (March 14, 1867), 203.
24. *New York Times,* May 25, p. 1, 1867; Lizzie Perry to A. L. Burt, May 11, 1867, B. F. Perry Papers (Duke).
25. *New York Times,* July 29, 1867, p. 1.
26. J. C. Hemphill to W. R. Hemphill, August 2, 1867, Hemphill Papers.
27. *Report of the Secretary of War* (1868–1869), p. 521.
28. *New York Times,* March 21, p. 1; March 23, p. 1; May 5, p. 1, 1867.

some of the lesser lights in the field. "With Rev. Nick Williams's & Armstrong's lecturing our semi-chimpangee brethren at our very doors," she wailed, "God only knows what will come, & I have decided to hide my head."[29] A few of the lesser Northern politicos remained to participate in the constitutional convention. William N. Viney, for instance, was an Ohio-born Negro who came to the state as a paid political organizer and went to the convention as a delegate from Colleton District.[30] Even after the organization was completed Northern Republican agents continued to visit the state. In April, 1868, Congressman J. M. Ashley of Ohio spoke in Columbia, and in the following September, John Mercer Langston, a Northern Negro who gained a wide reputation as a Republican organizer in the South, came into the state disguised as a Bureau school inspector and, as one upcountry editor saw it, he "spouted for the darkies . . ."[31]

In 1867 and 1868, Union or Loyal Leagues were an important part of Republican activity in the state. Possibly, Leagues had existed in South Carolina in 1865 and 1866, but it was only after the passage of the first Reconstruction Act that the organizational device was widely used. Leagues were used to indoctrinate Negroes with Republicanism, but they were also schools to instruct Negroes in their civic responsibilities. It was perhaps no accident that the first president of the League in South Carolina was Gilbert Pillsbury, a long-time abolitionist who had first headed the military's school system in the Charleston area. Negroes must have found the Leagues entertaining. Visiting his low-country plantation near Adams Run in December, 1867, the Reverend Cornish found that "Sam—the then negro boy that waited on me when I lived at the Hermitage on Edisto Island— . . . is now president of the Loyal Leage [sic] & a very influential character among the Negroes —is Sam Small——"[32] Leagues were not always harmless, however. Sometimes they assumed a militant front. Early in January, 1868, the mistress of Social Hall, also near Adams Run, noted that the Negroes in the vicinity were well organized. "The men have weekly meetings for the purposes of drill—fife, fine dinners, uniforms, drum, flags & c.

29. Louisa McCord to A. T. Smythe, August 27, 1867, A. T. Smythe Letters. This Armstrong was probably William J. Armstrong, notorious to Southern whites as a political agitator among Negroes. George R. Bentley, *A History of the Freedmen's Bureau* (Philadelphia, 1955), p. 189.

30. *Mercury* (Charleston), February 24, 1868.

31. *Intelligencer* (Anderson), September 30, 1868; Bentley, *Freedmen's Bureau*, pp. 188–89.

32. Diary, entry for December 3, 1867.

Prince Wright acting Brig. Gen., Ned Ladson (R. knows him) Colonel!"[33] As described above, in the mountain district of Oconee, the threat passed into open violence when members of a League killed a white boy in the course of a riot and proceeded to seize control of the community. Occasionally the whites retaliated. A year after the Oconee riot, Elias Kennedy, a Negro minister living in adjacent Anderson County and well known as a League organizer, was killed while on a League mission in a neighboring Georgia town.[34] Leagues were numerous in South Carolina, but outside of the cities they were not durable. After the heated campaigns of 1867 and 1868, the great mass of Negro voters apparently faded out of the organization. The subsequent character of the League in South Carolina was accurately reflected in the politics of their president, F. L. Cardozo, one of the most conservative Negro politicians in the state.

Far more permanent and effective than the League was the regular party organization, which had developed in the traditional pattern. The grass roots were represented by individual Republicans who met either in township or, frequently, in county conventions to nominate candidates for local offices and to choose delegates to conventions representing larger districts—counties, congressional districts, or the state and nation. Each convention chose its permanent executive committee which, with its chairman, was responsible for carrying on the party's business until relieved by the next convention. At the peak of the pyramid was the state executive committee. After 1870, control of this committee by Negroes gave them important power in the heart and core of Republican politics in South Carolina.

The character of professional Republican politicians in South Carolina during Reconstruction has often been debated. The Redeemers, who wrote most of the history of the period, damned them all. The scalawags were poor whites without character, education, or position. The carpetbaggers—except those with money—were bootless ex-officers of the Union Army and unprincipled adventurers in search of political plunder. And Negro politicians were either Northern-sprung zealots in various stages of mental derangement or ignorant and deluded freedmen who moved directly from the cotton fields into office without

33. H. R. G. (Harriett Gonzales) to "Emmie," January 8, 1868, Elliott–Gonzales Papers.
34. *Intelligencer* (Anderson), September 2, 1868.

so much as a change of clothes. Even a cursory survey of these groups reveals the inaccuracy of such a description.

Actually, scalawags represented—in economic status, education, and, to a large extent, social standing—every phase of Carolina society. The single quality found in the backgrounds of most native white Republican leaders was a spirit of Unionism distinctly deeper than that of their neighbors. Even here, however, scalawags as a group were still in some degree representative of the community, mustering a few first-line fire-eaters in their ranks. Franklin J. Moses, Jr., for instance, had been the secretary of the secession governor and had personally hauled the United States flag down from over Fort Sumter in 1861. Some scalawags were poor. Solomon George Washington Dill of Charleston and Kershaw, by his own report, had always been a poor man and identified himself with the interest of the poor. Others were rich. Thomas Jefferson Robertson, a United States senator throughout the period, was reputedly one of the wealthiest men in the state after the war. Precisely as South Carolina exhibited a high degree of illiteracy in its white population, so too were there ill-educated scalawags. Dill of Kershaw, Allan of Greenville, Owen and Crews of Laurens, and many others apparently possessed only common school educations. On the other hand, many scalawag leaders were at least as erudite as their conservative opponents. Dr. Albert Gallatin Mackey graduated first in his class in Charleston's Medical School, and a Northern correspondent, visiting him in the book-lined study in his Charleston home, found him highly learned. Further, Mackey was nationally known as a writer on the subject of Masonry, having been for many years the Grand Master of the Order in South Carolina. The Junior Moses, T. J. Robertson, C. D. and S. W. Melton were graduates of South Carolina College and personally intimate with classmates from the state's leading families. J. L. Orr completed his education in the University of Virginia, and J. F. G. Mittag of Lancaster was an artist of some reputation who had studied under S. F. B. Morse. Doubtless some native whites became Republicans out of expediency, but it is also certain that many adopted the party out of principle. John R. Cochran and John Scott Murray of Anderson and Simeon Corley of Lexington, for instance, were Republican leaders whose principles were above reproach even by the opposition. Although none of the self-styled aristocracy became open Republicans, a fair proportion of the scalawag leadership had been accepted in the elite social circle of their own communities before becoming Republicans, and in most cases, apparent-

ly they did not immediately lose social prestige by crossing the political divide. Practically the whole team of scalawag judges—Orr, Green,
Vernon, Moses, Sr., Bond, and Bryan—along with the Melton and
Robertson clans and the mountain district leadership could be described
so. Indeed, very generally anti-scalawag snobbery was much more a
post-Redemption myth than a Reconstruction reality.[35]

Carpetbaggers exhibited the same degree of variety. John J. ("Honest
John") Patterson, a Pennsylvanian, railroad manipulator, and protégé of
Thomas A. Scott, was a wealthy man before he came to the state in
1869 to interest himself in the Blue Ridge and Greenville and Colum-
bia Railroads. J. P. M. Epping had made himself famous as well as
rich by introducing the state to soda water in bottles. Reuben Holmes
and J. D. Bell, Beaufort's two white delegates to the Constitutional
Convention of 1868, were both Northern businessmen who had come
South for economic reasons. Others, like D. H. Chamberlain, D. T.
Corbin, and Frank Arnim were young, former officers of the Union
Army. Admittedly they were on the make. Nevertheless, they had
begun to seek their fortunes in the South long before the spring of
1867, and, as a group, they were certainly not bootless adventurers when
they entered Republican politics in South Carolina. And, far from ex-
ploiting the natives, Reuben Tomlinson and Justus K. Jillson contributed substantial sums of their own money to further education in
South Carolina. The average carpetbagger was rather better educated
than his Southern counterpart of the same age and economic back-

35. Scalawags, of course, always ran the risk of social ostracism. For instance,
Orr, in August of 1867, expressed his reluctance to cross political lines for this
reason. See: New York Times, August 11, 1867, p. 3. Still, whether or not the
white community invoked social sanctions against carpetbaggers and scalawags
depended very much on what kind of Republicans they were. Far from condemning the best class of scalawags, like Orr, for becoming Republicans, many
native whites praised them for attempting to save their state by elevating the
character of the dominant party. For a sampling of the favorable reaction of conservatives to the scalawag judges, see: Intelligencer (Anderson), December 2, 1868;
January 28, February 4, 1869. Furthermore, in the pursuit of fusion politics, many
conservative whites so blurred the party line that they were, themselves, barely
distinguishable from the more conservative Republicans. A distinct change began
during the campaign of 1876, when Straightouts deliberately used the threat of
ostracism as a tactic in the strategy of defeating the Republicans by hacking their
leadership into inaction. "Many have joined the party to their eternal disgrace,"
thundered one white-liner at a political gathering in May, 1876, "and they will
never recover from it. No sir; nor their children, nor their children's children.
[Cheers.]" Recent Election in South Carolina, Part 2, 40; see also p. 41.

ground. Chamberlain, who was a graduate of Harvard and had been among the top four scholars in his Yale law class, was a man of high literary attainments. Others, like F. A. Sawyer, were well trained and experienced teachers and educational administrators. Indeed, one seeks in vain among the leading carpetbaggers for one who was ill-educated, and many of those least educated in the formal sense were, like Timothy Hurley, intelligent men of wide experience. Few political carpetbaggers were received socially by the aristocracy, but they obviously remained fully acceptable in their home communities in the North. Chamberlain, for instance, constantly drew moral strength from his New England friends, particularly from the legal community in New Haven. In 1875, he was accorded the honor of addressing Yale Law School's commencement audience. Returning North in 1877, Chamberlain became a prominent New York lawyer and a leading member of the American Bar Association. Even "Honest John" Patterson, the most notorious of bribers, returned to Pennsylvania after Redemption to win praise for his continuing success as a railroad chieftain.

The Redeemers' estimate of Northern Negroes in the South was nearly correct—they were zealots. Some, like R. H. Gleaves, came to further their material fortunes by business pursuits. Others, like Whipper and the lawyer class in general, probably saw a chance for personal profit in representing the claims of the newly emancipated. But, most of them came (or, having left the army, remained) primarily as religious, educational, and cultural missionaries, hoping to accomplish an elevation of their racial brothers which was not possible in the restricted and less populous Negro communities in the North. Just as the Massachusetts Negro regiments drew off the cream of young manhood from the Northern Negro population during the war, Reconstruction attracted the cream in peace.[36]

The one thing that most native Negro leaders were not was fresh from the cotton fields. Of the seventy-four Negroes who sat in the Constitutional Convention of 1868, fourteen were Northerners. Of the

36. Carter G. Woodson theorized that the draining of leadership away from the North into the Reconstruction South debilitated Northern Negro communities for two generations, accounting for the marked lack of aggressiveness which prevailed among Northern Negroes until the twentieth century. Carter G. Woodson, *A Century of Negro Migration* (Washington, 1918), pp. 123–24. Apparently, South Carolina, being the one state in which Negroes were politically as well as numerically ascendent, was like a magnet to ambitious young Negroes. Scattered sources suggest that there was a considerable influx into the state of an educated class of Negroes and that the ingression continued well into the 1870's.

fifty-nine Negroes who had been born or settled in South Carolina before the war, at least eighteen and probably twenty-one had been free. A dozen of these were Charlestonians. Nearly all had been tradesmen. Roughly two-thirds of this group continued to pursue their trades after the war and at least until the time of the convention. The remainder took service as Bureau teachers. T. K. Sasportas, Henry Shrewsbury, and others had risen to the educational level of the high school graduate in the North. Most possessed the equivalent of a common school education, while several were, apparently, barely literate. F. L. Cardozo, of course, having attended the University of Glasgow and the London School of Theology, was as well educated as any man in the state.

Thirty-eight of the delegates were clearly former slaves. The occupations of twelve of these are not known, but not one was described as an agricultural worker. Twenty-six were trades-, professional, or business men. Eight of the twenty-six were ministers (some being tradesmen as well), four were carpenters, two blacksmiths, two shoemakers, two had been coachmen and the remaining eight included a businessman, a businessman and steamer captain (Smalls), a tanner, a barber, a teacher, a waiter, a servant, and a carriage maker. Most of those who were tradesmen had pursued the same occupation as slaves. For instance, John Chesnut, the barber, was the son of a Camden barber whose father had been freed by the first General James Chesnut. John was born of a slave mother and, hence, was a slave but had been allowed to learn his trade in his father's shop. The degree of education possessed by these freedmen was not high. However, nearly all appeared to be literate in some degree, and a few were amazingly well read. Nash, for example, could quote Shakespeare with apparent ease and obviously read the leading Northern papers. During the war, Robert Smalls had been taught intensively by two professional educators while he was stationed for a year and a half in the Philadelphia Naval Yard. It is true that conservatives had considerable grounds for complaint against the ignorance of their late-slaves become legislators, but their charges of stupidity changed with the political climate. Early in 1866, the Camden press lauded John Chesnut and Harmon Jones as "two intelligent freedmen" for their speeches to the Negroes denying that the government was to give them lands and urging them to return to work.[37] After 1867, when John Chesnut went into Republican poli-

37. Thomas J. Kirkland and Robert M. Kennedy, *Historic Camden* (Part 2, Columbia, 1926), p. 198, quoting the *Camden Journal,* January 6, 1866.

tics, became a delegate to the convention which drafted a new constitution, and served thereafter in the Republican legislature, words strong
enough to describe Chesnut's lack of talent were not available.[38]

In view of the high degree of natural ability extant among leading
Republicans of both races, it is hardly surprising that the higher offices
were filled with men who were quite capable of executing their responsibilities.

In the executive area, the abilities of such white office holders as
Dr. Ensor as the director of the insane asylum and H. L. Pardee as
superintendent of the penitentiary, and such Negro office holders as
F. L. Cardozo and H. E. Hayne withstood the closest criticism. Although he was frequently overridden by a less careful legislature,
Cardozo as treasurer of the state from 1872 until the summer of 1876
(after which his office was virtually nullified by a boycott of white taxpayers) revealed the highest capacities. Even the conservative editor
of the Chester *Reporter*, after a visit to the Capitol in December, 1869,
conceded that Cardozo, then secretary of state, was "courteous and
accommodating," and the "most respectable and honest of all the State
officials." Observing the house in action the same journalist found
Henry Hayne, "a little yellow fellow," able in arguing for the sale
of state lands in plots of fifty acres or less with provision made for the
addition of a mule.[39] The records themselves, particularly those of the
land office and of the state census of 1875, indicate that Hayne as secretary of state from 1872 until the Redemption executed his duties well.

Even political opponents generally recognized the capacity of leading
Republican legislators. South Carolina's Negro congressmen—Elliott,
Rainey, Ransier, De Large, Cain, and Smalls—were usually conceded
to be able enough for their posts. Though Democrats in the House
scoffed, Elliott's speech to Congress on the Ku Klux was widely cele-
brated.[40] Capable Negro solons also appeared in the Constitutional
Convention of 1868 and in the Republican legislatures which followed.
Ransier, Gleaves, and Swails as presiding officers in the Senate and

38. Much information concerning the background of the delegates to the Constitutional Convention of 1868 was contained in the February 24, 1868, issue of
the Charleston *Mercury*. However, the above discussion was based on charts constructed by the author outlining the biographies of leading carpetbaggers, scalawags,
and Northern and Southern Negroes. The information was gathered from numerous sources during the course of research.

39. *Reporter* (Chester), December 9, 1869.

40. *New York Tribune,* April 3, 1871, p. 1.

Samuel J. Lee and, again, Elliott as speakers of the house were remarkably effective managers in view of their sudden elevation to their posts.[41] There were others, like Whipper, who were virtually professional legislators and became excellent parliamentarians.

It was inevitable that combinations of intelligence, education, experience, and natural ability were in short supply among Republicans in South Carolina. After all, there were comparatively few Negroes in South Carolina who could claim to possess a high level of education or significant experience in government. In the legislature, and in local offices in many areas, there was obviously a lack of competence among Republican leaders. This absence was usually indentified with the presence of the Negro officeholder.

Yet, what one saw in the legislature was obviously determined by what one was conditioned to see. A liberal English observer noted that on the floor of the Senate Negro members were decorous and dignified.[42] In January, 1869, Martha Schofield visited the new Capitol. In the senate chamber, she was the special guest of her friend, the presiding officer, D. T. Corbin, "and it was with strange feelings I sat in that body where all men were equal before the law, where those whose race had been oppressed for two centuries, were now making laws for the oppressors. . . . The colored members appear as much at ease and at home as the others," she pointedly observed. Crossing the broad entrance hall to the house chamber, the Quaker schoolmistress was delighted to see that "colored, and white, democrats and republicans were sandwiched in a way that would disturb the dead bones of many of Carolines proud sons." She heard Tomlinson speak for a bill to abolish capital punishment and De Large's answer. "London [probably London S. Langley] came to us and we had a nice chat," she continued, "also Henry Parris & Mr. Wells from Beaufort—or St. Helena." Having served in the islands during the war period, she saw "a good many acquaintances among the colored ones." "Who could have prophesied this 10 years since," she marveled.[43] The more astute visitors, however skeptical they may have been of the results, invariably saw something vital in the proceedings of Republican and Negro legislatures in the state. "It is not all sham, nor all burlesque,"

41. Edward King, visiting the Capitol in the fall of 1873, found the presiding officers of both houses (Negroes) very able. Edward King, *The Great South* (Hartford, 1875), p. 460.

42. *Ibid.*, p. 461.

43. Diary, entry for January 22, 1869.

wrote James Pike after his celebrated visit in the winter of 1873. "They
have a genuine interest and a genuine earnestness in the business of
the assembly which we are bound to recognize and respect unless we
would be accounted shallow critics."[44]

Conservative native whites were distressed by what they saw even
before they entered the legislative chambers.

A Baptist minister in November, 1870, reported:

> The entrance halls both upstairs and down was thronged with
> negroes, who were keeping up a sort of saturnalia, haw-hawing,
> buying and selling peanuts, candy and gumgers, 2 or 3 walking
> arm in arm with noisy demonstrations, one party wrestling,
> another tugging at each other's coattails in play, somewhat
> after the manner of the game of 'last tag'. . . . an uproar was
> kept up, which ascended through the building into the open
> door of the Legislative halls, and did not facilitate hearing
> what was going on there.

Going on was a debate over the action to be taken in answer to the
Laurens riot and other "Ku Klux" activities. The clerical gentleman
continued:

> I heard a pretty incendiary speech from W. J. Whipper, the
> head negro member, in regard to alleged outrages in Laurens
> and threats in Edgefield against the Radical members; then
> a pitiful narration of his "suffrinks" from Jo Crews, who had
> like to have been killed several times over, and a zealous tirade
> from a nameless darkey who wanted to know if anybody had
> been punished yet of it—if they had killed any of the rioters,
> or tried to kill them. . . . It is a dark looking set, set off, how-
> ever, with a wonderful new carpet and 5 huge chandeliers—as
> gorgeous as Cuffee usually delights in—when somebody else
> pays for it.[45]

The proceedings of the House particularly offended whites. In
August, 1868, an upcountry editor was shocked to find seven "dusky

44. James S. Pike, *The Prostrate State: South Carolina Under Negro Government* (New York, 1874), p. 20. Pike's words must be weighed in the balance
established by the high scholarship of Robert F. Durden's *James Shepherd Pike:
Republicanism and the American Negro. 1850-1882* (Durham, 1957). Evaluated on
this scale, Pike's statement becomes highly complimentary to the legislature.

45. Basil Manly, Jr., to Charles Manly, November 28, 1870, Basil Manly, Jr.,
Letters and Letterbook.

belles" seated on the platform with Speaker Moses.[46] A year later, another observer noted that members frequently defied the chair, conversed with debaters on the floor, and, on one occasion, T. K. Sasportas answered an argument from Representative De Large with his fist.[47] A Northern visitor in 1874 was amazed by the lack of respect accorded to some members by others. As an instance, he noted that Representative Holmes of Colleton called on the speaker for the yeas and nays on a measure, but the speaker refused to recognize him until the vote had been announced. Holmes then rose to a question of privilege and was overruled. He persisted and other members began to cough. Holmes tried to talk over the noise. The coughing grew louder. Finally, E. W. M. Mackey suggested that someone call a doctor and the house roared in amusement, while the exasperated Holmes collapsed in his chair.[48]

Capacity and incompetence frequently traveled side by side in the legislature, but incapacity was often glaringly in evidence among office-holders of the lower echelons. "Our letters are often lost now," wrote a resident of Camden to her son, "Adamson is travelling Agent to distribute the letters and Boswell and Frank Carter, Ned's son, are Postmaster[s] here." The cause, of course, was apparent: "In Columbia and elsewhere, they have negroes in the Post office, and I have no doubt our letters go astray."[49] County and city officers elicited similar complaints. Much distressed, the grand jury of Williamsburg County, in the spring of 1871, charged that the county commissioners permitted the county's prisoners to roam the streets of Kingstree after the jail burned in 1867, kept no records worthy of the name, and had allowed the roads and bridges of the county (some of which had not been worked upon in two years) to become almost impassable. Further, they feared that the county poor farm was "calculated to do more harm to the County than good."[50]

The great problem of the Republican regime in South Carolina, however, was not so much a lack of capacity among its leaders as it was an absence of a sense of responsibility to the whole society, white as well as black. In the idealistic days of the Constitutional Convention

46. *Intelligencer* (Anderson), August 19, 1868.
47. *New York Times*, April 3, 1869, p. 7.
48. *Ibid.*, March 11, 1874, p. 10.
49. Mrs. E. W. Bonney to her son, November 29, 1869, E. W. Bonney Papers.
50. William Willis Boddie, *History of Williamsburg County, South Carolina, 1705 until 1923* (Columbia, 1923), pp. 441–44.

of 1868, Republicans often reflected verbally upon the fact that their work was for the benefit of all. Yet, within two months after the close of the convention, election results showed that, willingly or not, the Republican party in South Carolina was the party of the Negro and for the Negro. Within a short time, it also became a party by the Negro. This was a line which the whites themselves had helped to draw. There emerged among Republican leaders a new concept that their first loyalty was due, not to their total constituency, but to that particular Republican and Negro element which had put them into office. This attitude was evident in the inclination of Republicans to drive Democrats and native whites of the conservative persuasion completely out of the government. It was also evident in a certain superciliousness which developed among members of the party in power toward the opposition. In this atmosphere, the protests of the white minority became proper subjects for Republican disdain and, indeed, ridicule. "Please read where I have marked, and judge the class of men which composed the late Taxpayer's convention of South Carolina," Negro Congressman Rainey jeered quietly in a confidential communique to President Grant's secretary early in 1874.[51] Three years earlier, while the first taxpayers' convention was in session, A. O. Jones, the mulatto clerk of the house, suggested to his partner in a corruption-laden ring of public printers that their Republican Printing Company enter a bid for the printing of "Ye Taxpayers." "R. P. C.," he jested, "That's as effective on the State Treasury as the other terrible triad is on Radical office holders—eh?"[52] If the opposition had no political rights, they also had no economic rights. Attacks on the property by heavy taxation and then by the theft of those tax moneys was perhaps within the limits of this new morality.

Among Republican politicos in Reconstruction South Carolina, there is no correlation between intelligence, education, wealth, experience, and competence on the one hand and, on the other, integrity. The thieves included men who claimed all or most of these qualities, as well as men who could claim none. The relationship which did exist was the logical one: among those who did steal, the most successful thieves invariably combined high intelligence and large administrative talents with generous endowments of education, wealth, and experience. Petty frauds were numerous and widespread, but the truly magnificent peculations were conceived and executed by a relatively few men,

51. J. H. Rainey to General O. E. Babcock, February 24, 1874, J. H. Rainey Papers.

52. A. O. Jones to Josephus Woodruff, May 5, 1871, Hemphill Papers.

usually residing in Columbia or Charleston. However, these larger schemes frequently required the purchase of the co-operation of scores of state officers and legislators, and thus corruption was spread.

The first and always the most gigantic steals consisted simply of issuing state bonds in excess of the amounts authorized by the legislature. In the summer of 1868, the legislature sanctioned the issue of one million dollars worth of bonds to pay the interest on the state debt and to re-establish its credit. The financial board, consisting of Governor Scott and the other leading officers in the state government, was authorized to market the bonds through a financial agent, H. H. Kimpton, in New York. The authorized issue was promptly made. Probably under Kimpton's management, another million was clandestinely added.[53] Since Scott had to sign each bond and Treasurer N. G. Parker had to issue them and honor payments of interest, it is certain that they were implicated in the plot, but the involvement of other members of the board is not clear. When the legislature directed the issue of another million dollars in bonds in 1869, the fraud was repeated.[54] After passing and repealing an act to re-finance the debt through London sources, the legislature repudiated about half of the state's twelve-million-dollar debt and converted the remainder into a single loan guaranteed by about six million dollars worth of "Conversion Bonds." But again the actual issue almost doubled the amount authorized.[55] By flagrantly misrepresenting the state's finances and by buying and selling his own issues, Kimpton kept the bond bubble afloat. To its authors, a part of the appeal of the bond scheme was that it needed the co-operation of the inner few only and did not require the wide-scale bribery of state officials. Indeed, the fewer to profit the better. Moreover, the ring only served its own interest when it encouraged efforts at financial reform and re-establishing the state's credit, because these displays tended to drive up the market price and to prepare the way for further illicit issues.[56]

As in the first bond fraud, the extent to which state officers were involved in the bond ring is hazy. Scott, and Moses, his successor as governor, Parker as treasurer, and J. L. Neagle as comptroller general were clearly in collusion with Kimpton. Cardozo, first as secretary of

53. John Schreiner Reynolds, *Reconstruction in South Carolina, 1865–1877* (Columbia, 1905), pp. 115, 463.
54. *Ibid.*, pp. 463–64.
55. *Ibid.*
56. *The Fraud Report*, pp. 1685, 1586. The *Fraud Report* is contained in *Reports and Resolutions* (1877–1878).

state and after 1872 as treasurer, and Chamberlain, as attorney general
until 1872, may have suspected something of the truth but obviously did
not profit by the bond ring's activities. Even before 1870, however, the
concept of the bond ring was expanded to include the purchasers as
well as the purveyors of fraudulent issues. Speculators for the most
part, those holding the bonds became as interested as the inner ring
in maintaining the value of their paper by displays of financial responsibility in South Carolina. Before the Taxpayers' Convention of
1871, for instance, a group of native white financiers in Columbia and
Charleston combined with a group of New York speculators to hire
M. C. Butler and M. W. Gary (subsequently two leading Redeemers)
to influence the convention to declare the debt valid. Gathered for
the purpose of condemning financial corruption by Republican officers,
the convention ironically ended by giving the regime a clean bill of
fiscal health. Though Butler and Gary obviously had a large part
in arranging this result, the speculators reneged on their bargain.[57]
Nevertheless, the bond ring continued to operate, and, indeed, during
Hampton's gubernatorial tenure was eminently successful.

The influence of the spoilers in spreading corruption was much
more effective in the activities of the "Railroad Ring." This fraud
began with Governor Scott's seemingly genuine interest in the completion of the Blue Ridge Railroad, but in the end it certainly included
the early members of the bond ring and a number of others. The
key idea, a common one in the state since the 1830's, was to link Charleston with the west through Chattanooga and thus tap the southern-
going trade of the great northwest. Before the war, the Blue Ridge
Railroad had begun to build toward this goal by running its rails from
a junction with the Greenville and Columbia at Belton to Walhalla
in the northwestern tip of the state. There it stopped, however, and the
very expensive labor of tunneling through the mountains remained
to be done. In 1868, Scott and others persuaded the legislature to
guarantee loans to the Blue Ridge amounting to four million dollars.
There was nothing illicit or even unusual in this movement to encourage internal improvements. However, the scheme soon grew larger.

57. Documents tending to support the authenticity of the charge against Butler
and Gary are contained in both the M. W. Gary Papers and the F. W. Dawson
Papers. Dawson himself may have become involved in the plans of the bond ring
to transfer its business to London. See: F. W. Dawson to C. P. Leslie, August 1,
1871; C. P. Leslie to F. W. Dawson, August 1, 1871; F. W. Dawson to H. H.
Kimpton, August 1, 1871; H. H. Kimpton to F. W. Dawson, September 13, 1871;
F. W. Dawson Papers.

Twelve state officers combined to buy the Blue Ridge, including a large share owned by the state itself. Then the plan was expanded to include the purchase of the Greenville and Columbia and its spurs, also partly owned by the state. If the Blue Ridge could be completed, the ring would then have control of the shortest all-weather route from the northwest to the Atlantic.

Here John J. Patterson, an associate of Thomas A. Scott and a veteran railroad manager and financier, entered the ring, probably as its technical manager. Assisted by native whites James L. Orr and General B. H. Harrison (the past president of the Blue Ridge) and by Redeemer M. W. Gary, the ring bought shares from private parties.[58] At this point, the operations of the ring were clearly legal. In 1870, however, certain officers of the state who were also shareholders in the ring arranged to sell the state's interest in both railroads to the ring at greatly devalued prices. Early in 1872, Patterson attempted to push through the legislature a bill which would have the state issue four million dollars in tax-guaranteed scrip to the Blue Ridge Railroad as a direct loan in lieu of its previous guarantee of the bonds of the road in that amount. The manner in which Patterson, acting as the bribe-broker, pushed this affair in the legislature is a good case study in corruption.

On February 22, 1872, Patterson had his legislative henchman, Prince Rivers, lately the first sergeant of the First South and chairman of the House Military Affairs Committee, arrange a caucus in his committee room. If South Carolina ever had a monarchy, Thomas Wentworth Higginson had once said, Rivers would be its king. Patterson spoke in behalf of the measure at the caucus. Then, he or one of his emissaries approached each likely supporter individually. For instance, he had Governor Scott himself attempt to enlist the support of H. H. Hunter, a Negro member from Charleston and a minister. Hunter refused to commit himself to the governor, and when he left Scott's Capitol office he was met by Patterson. As they strolled down Main Street, Patterson informed Hunter that he, Patterson, had told the governor that Hunter was "a good little fellow and that he wanted to make some money as well as the rest of them." Hunter conceded that money was one of "those necessary evils which we all had to have."

58. Orr was busily engaged in this operation in the spring of 1870. See: W. W. Marshall to "Charlie" [Smith?], April 12, 1870, J. W. W. Marshall Papers. See also MS Contract, written by Gary, signed by Patterson, August 5, 1871; T. S. Sterns to M. W. Gary, February 28, 1874, M. W. Gary Papers.

Urged to vote with the ring, Hunter replied that he had been doing so all along. When the vote was taken Hunter continued to go along and got $500 for his loyalty.[59] When the bill came up on the floor of the house, Patterson, with startling audacity, was actually in the chamber, having stationed himself behind one of the curtains which closed off the alcoves at each window. There, he sent for and "button-holed" each member worthy of his attention. In one case, he even paid a member to vote for the bill after it had passed. W. C. Glover, a Negro member from Charleston and a laborer by profession, was absent when the bill passed its third reading by a safe majority. Brought to Patterson by a friend who chided him for being too negligent of his own interests, Patterson instructed Glover to go to the clerk and have his vote recorded and promised that he would be paid. As his sobriquet implied, Glover was paid and "Honest John" Patterson's reputation remained intact: if he promised a bribe, he would pay it.[60] In the senate, Nash led a group of Negro senators in opposing Patterson's bill. Nash refused an offer of $25,000 to support the measure, but his group finally compromised upon the issuing of $1,800,000 in scrip to the Blue Ridge Railroad as a direct loan. When the measure passed the senate, Patterson watched the proceedings while comfortably seated on a couch in the rear of the chamber.

In spite of the opposition of the Nash group, there was a payoff in the senate, and Nash and his friends participated. After the act was passed, this group gathered by arrangement in Leslie's railroad committee room. The clerk of the senate entered and placed a large square package on the table in front of Leslie. Nash left, but the clerk later saw the committee's doorkeeper, a deaf-mute well known in the Capitol as "Dummy," emerge from the room "just after the distribution, making most expressive signs, indicating filling of pockets, & c." Later, Leslie passed Nash a brick-sized package containing $5,000 in the very scrip that the legislature had loaned the Blue Ridge Railroad.[61]

The payoff for house members was in the best cloak-and-dagger tradition. Everidge Cain, a Negro member and a farmer, voted for the bill, he said, because some of his Democratic friends (including General Harrison) had urged him to do so and a Patterson man had promised to pay him for it. Several days after the bill became an act, Cain received a note instructing him to call at a Richardson Street address.

59. *Fraud Report*, pp. 1631–32.
60. *Ibid.*, p. 1638.
61. *Ibid.*, pp. 1649, 1652, 1659.

Arriving there at dusk, he found a doorkeeper who silently directed him upstairs where another man opened the door for him to enter a darkened room. There, a man, with his face averted, handed him an envelope and pointed toward another door. Beyond, still another man stood at the head of an outside stairway. "Go on down," whispered the sentinel, "you're all right." Opening the envelope later, Cain found $200 in scrip. The man who had spoken to him he believed to be his Democratic friend, General Harrison.[62]

There were a number of other major "jobs" pushed through the legislature. During the first Scott administration, a group of native white conservative Charleston businessmen combined with several carpetbag politicians to gain, over Scott's veto, a fabulously lucrative monopoly of the mining of phosphates (for fertilizer) from the river beds of the state. Agent for the job was Timothy Hurly, a Boston-born Republican who reportedly came to Columbia carrying a carpetbag containing $40,000 which he used, partly through scalawag Speaker Moses, to win the desired legislation.[63]

The most effective jobber, however, was always Patterson. It appears that the Pennsylvania financier enjoyed legislative bribery as a game. In the fall of 1871, he and his henchman, H. C. Worthington, one-time Nevada congressman, Union general, and minister to Brazil, volunteered to defend Governor Scott from a threatened impeachment. They used $50,000 of the state's money provided by Scott. On the morning before the vote initiating proceedings was taken, Patterson arranged the usual caucus through Rivers, who "was always looked to as a leader of certain members, about fifteen or twenty." As host, Rivers served drinks, "viands," and cigars. Patterson and Worthington attended and spoke against the impeachment. Afterward, only Patterson and Rivers were in the room. "So when Patterson saw me in the room," Rivers later testified, "he just said: 'You go and vote against the impeachment and I'll give you $200;' and I said: 'All right.'"[64] By the same methods, and at the cost of $40,000, Patterson bought himself a seat in the United States Senate and promptly had Worthington appointed collector of the port of Charleston where both doubtless soon earned several times that amount by soliciting bribes from merchants. In the fall of 1873, Senator

62. *Ibid.*, p. 1631.
63. *Ibid.*, p. 1677. Democratic members were charged with accepting bribes in this instance, but the charge seems more political than real. *Daily Republican* (Charleston), March 26, 1870.
64. *Fraud Report,* pp. 1612–14, 1614–33, *passim.*

Patterson again lent his special legislative talents to a friend, Hardy
Solomon, and succeeded in getting legislation passed to pay the obligations of the state to that merchant and banker.[65]

There were other patterns of corruption in the legislature. Presiding officers in both houses and their clerks conspired to issue fraudulent
pay certificates and to honor claims for legislative expenses which were
without justification.[66] Between 1870 and 1874, a steady source of
bribe money was the Republican Printing Company, an organization
administered and ostensibly owned by the clerks of the two houses,
A. C. Jones, a Negro, and Josephus Woodruff, a Charleston and Columbia journalist become scalawag. Through bribery, the clerks patched
together enough support to secure the contract for state printing, but
actually they were constantly pressed for funds by some legislators as
if the company were co-operatively owned by the members and Woodruff and Jones merely the managers.[67] Virtually every election by the
legislature elicited a rash of bribery; but there were also other forms of
graft. The sumptuous furnishings of Columbia committee rooms somehow seemed to find their way into the homes of members and of attachées
in all parts of the state. A committee clerk from Aiken later testified
that Speaker Samuel J. Lee, a Negro also from Aiken, during one
session furnished rooms for himself and his wife over a Columbia
restaurant as a "Committee Room." Later the clerk saw the same
"marble-top table, settees, cushioned chairs, sideboards, &c" in the parlor
of Lee's Aiken home. John Williams, the sergeant-at-arms for the
house, furnished rooms for himself and Prince Rivers in the same way.
Williams, too, carried furniture to his Hamburg residence and transferred other pieces so that "a house of ill fame kept by a colored woman
named Anna Wells was also furnished."[68]

Corruption at the local level was less spectacular, but it was prevalent

65. *Ibid.*, pp. 1548–62, *passim.*
66. *Ibid.*, p. 1486.
67. In the elections of 1874, for instance, Woodruff claimed that R. E. Elliott
insisted upon the company's giving him $500 for his campaign to win first a seat
in the house and then the speakership; Joseph Woodruff MS Diary, entries for
October 4, 5, 1874. This diary, upon which so much of the Redeemer's indictment
of the Republican regime rests, may not be fully accurate. Amendments in
pagination and the use of terms which apparently became current only after
Reconstruction suggest that an earlier draft may have been altered. Certainly,
Woodruff was actively trying to retain his clerkship of the Senate under the
Redeemers and was, for a time, successful. See Woodruff correspondence in the
W. D. Simpson Papers.
68. *Fraud Report*, p. 1213.

enough. In many places, e.g., Beaufort, Negro officers maintained high standards of integrity, but all too often Negroes and whites were knaves together. The grand jury of Williamsburg, looking over the books—such as they were—of the clerk of the county commissioners in the spring of 1874, found that "upon many occasions when money was received, it was forthwith divided out between the members of the board and the clerk." Further, the commissioners had drawn pay for more than the maximum number of days allowed per year; the Negro school commissioner could not account for his funds; and the county treasurer paid only such claims as he chose to honor.[69] By June, 1874, no less than twenty-four county commissioners, three county treasurers, two sheriffs, and one school commissioner had been presented by grand juries, indicted, or convicted.[70] During Moses's gubernatorial term, punishment was neither swift nor certain for the guilty. The three county commissioners of Barnwell (two Negroes and a white man), interviewed by a Northern correspondent as they were en route to prison in June, 1874, announced that Moses would pardon them within fifteen days, an occurrence which the sentencing judge had pessimistically predicted.[71] After 1874, when reform was in the air and public peculation had become precarious, thievery seemed almost entirely halted. Even then, however, official thieves were more liable to take to their heels than to prison. "Burrel, (a son of Big Sam), was County Commissioner and is under indictment for malfeasance in office, and it is said, has gone to parts unknown," exulted a Chester resident in November, 1874, citing a typical case.[72]

Cities, too, frequently fell victim to the spoilers. Columbia, which underwent an expansion of its boundaries to give the Republicans absolute control and Negro officers from mayor to policeman, suffered an increase in its debt from some $426,000 in 1872 to $620,000 in 1874, and to $677,000 in 1875.[73] Meanwhile, Charleston's debt swelled prodigiously beyond the two-million-dollar mark.

The average Negro officeholder realized very little profit by resorting to rascality. Those who became wealthy by thievery were few, and all

69. Boddie, *History of Williamsburg County*, pp. 441–43, quoting the presentment of the grand jury.

70. *New York Times*, June 15, 1874, p. 1; *The Nation*, XVIII, No. 468 (June 18, 1874), 389.

71. *The Nation*, XVIII, No. 466 (June 4, 1874), 355–56.

72. James Hemphill to W. R. Hemphill, November 13, 1874, Hemphill Papers.

73. *New York Times*, June 8, 1875, p. 1.

the most successful were white—Scott, Parker, Kimpton, Patterson, and, perhaps, Neagle and Woodruff. These were the men who conceived, organized, and directed steals on a state-wide basis. Key figures who abetted them in their predatory operations, either as officers of the government or as lobbyists, also received substantial sums—Moses, Hurley, Leslie, Worthington, Whittemore, Elliott, Samuel J. Lee, and Swails—amounting over the entire period from scores of thousands to several hundred thousand dollars each. The average Negro legislator and officeholder, however, found that the wages of sin were pitifully small. There were only four occasions when large sums of money were passed out as bribes; other divisions were made of the printing money, and occasionally some office seeker was willing to buy votes. Senators were usually paid from $500 to $5,000 for their support on such occasions. Members of the House received much less. For voting for the Solomon claims, James Young, a Negro member from Laurens, received only $30, R. S. Tarlton of Colleton got $50, Charles H. Simons got $13 in cash and a box of provisions from Solomon's store, and Joseph J. Grant got only provisions. J. T. Gilmore, a Negro member from Richland and a farmer, was more astute. He collected a total of $250 from men working for the Solomon claims and promptly traded the money for four cows. Rivers got $500 for setting up a caucus to support the claims and for his vote in its favor.[74]

The real profits of the corruptionists, large and small, were often much less than quoted. For instance, the bond ring sold its issues to doubtful investors at much less than par value (usually at about sixty cents on the dollar). As more bonds flooded the market and criticism of the government rose, good issues and bad dropped to fractions of their face value. One issue eventually fell to 1 per cent of its nominal value. Blue Ridge Railroad scrip, used to pay the largest bribe bill contracted during the Reconstruction Period, circulated at less than its face value. Legislative pay certificates, whether or not legitimately obtained, were usually sold at a considerable discount by impecunious members to businessmen like Hardy Solomon. Such circumstances existed because the treasury was itself perennially empty and those having claims against it had to await the pleasure or indulgence of the treasurer. While Parker held that position, large sums of tax money were sent North to Kimpton to keep the bond bubble inflated by interest payments on both good and bad issues. Local obligations were very liable to be neglected. After 1872, each claimant had to face the suspicious

74. *Fraud Report,* pp. 1548–62, *passim.*

Cardozo, who soon became the bane of every corruptionist's existence by his miserly management of the treasury. The officers of the Republican Printing Company, to which a generous legislature appropriated $385,000 for the state fiscal year 1873–1874, had the greatest difficulty during the summer of 1874 in squeezing $250 to $300 out of the treasurer every Saturday to meet their minimum operating expenses.[75] Lecturers in history are fond of titillating their classes with the story of how the Negro legislature voted Speaker Moses a gratuity of $1,000 for his services as presiding officer after his having lost that amount to Whipper in a horse race. Yet, Moses probably thought the gesture something less than generous since pay certificates, if the holder were fortunate enough to find any buyer, seldom sold at more than three-fourths of face value. Moreover, Moses probably considered it an ordinary reward for the extra duty demanded by his office, a burden which many legislatures, North and South, customarily eased by voting special compensation.

There *was* plush living in Columbia during Reconstruction. The senators maintained a bar in one of their cloak rooms in the Capitol and fine food, smooth whiskey, and the best Havana cigars were copiously available. The legislative halls, the offices in the Capitol, and the committee rooms located in privately owned buildings (many were in Parker's Hall, often spelled "Haul" by contemporaries) were lavishly furnished. Yet the bar, which was allegedly supported by the senators from their private resources, was closed to other officers except by invitation, and the enjoyment of the accommodations afforded by other rooms were usually limited to those who used them officially.

The average Negro representative came to Columbia on his own money. He roomed and took his meals—usually on credit—in an ordinary boarding house with a dozen or so other legislators, clerks, and legislative attachées. Many could not afford appropriate clothing. Hardy Solomon found one member on the street so ill clad that he took him to his store and fitted him into a suit without requiring a vote in return. Occasionally some affluent Republican might offer the favorite "oyster supper" at a local dining room, or a caucus be held in which refreshments were served; but these were rare events. Such high living as was done by the legislators was done in the barrooms and, typically, on credit. "John A. Chesnut and W. J. Whipper, members of the House of Representatives from Kershaw and Beaufort," a Columbia barkeep known as "Uncle" advertised in a local paper as the session of 1869

75. Woodruff Diary, various entries for July, August, and September, 1874.

closed, "will please call on the undersigned and settle their bills at once."[76]

Far from a jubilee, attending a session of the legislature was for many Negro members a prolonged torture. Occasionally, political excitement ran high, as during the Ku Klux troubles and recurrently during elections. But the typical legislator followed a dull, drab, daily routine. During the mornings, he attended committee meetings or caucuses, stood on the streets or about the Capitol grounds, or remained in his boarding house. Beginning at noon, he attended a three- or four-hour legislative session, most of which were uneventful and, indeed, unimportant. In the late afternoons, he repeated the morning's performances, had his communal dinner at his boarding house, and retired. Throughout the session, he was plagued by a lack of money and by a worrying uncertainty whether he would be able to collect his pay at all, regardless of how much he voted himself, and whether he would realize from his nominal salary enough cash to meet his debts in Columbia and his obligations at home, familial and otherwise. Retrospectively, the life of the Reconstruction Negro legislator was rather monkish when compared to the annual excursions to the capital of his ante-bellum counterpart.

There are many partial explanations why Republican politicos in South Carolina stole. If prevalence of delinquency is acceptable as evidence in mitigation of crime, one has only to point northward to "Grantism" and Boss Tweed, and afterward, in South Carolina itself, to the continued success of the bond ring and the phosphate monopolists during the Redeemer period. To some extent, there was a very general loosening of moral restrictions in the state after the war. Even as the Radicals moved into Columbia during the summer of 1868, an elderly native white farmer in Spartanburg District despondently complained of "dishonesty from once honest men" without racial or political distinctions.[77] Simple greed is an obvious reason for theft, and no doubt this existed in a large measure among corruptionists in South Carolina. Further, opportunity had much to do with it. Men who might have remained honest in other circumstances found the easy temptation offered by a Patterson or a Hurley irresistible, and their yielding made it more likely that other, more sturdy, souls would also succumb. It is possible to construct a grand rationalization for the corruption-

76. *New York Times*, April 3, 1869, p. 7.
77. Edward Lipscomb to Smith Lipscomb, June 5, 1868, Smith Lipscomb Papers.

ists. Since the whites themselves essentially had withdrawn from political participation, most Republicans felt relieved from the necessity
of representing their interests in the legislature and in the government
at large. The attack on the property interests of the whites was a
deliberately contrived part of the Radical program; it would promote
a redistribution of landed wealth and the public welfare program which
their constituency wanted. From there, a quick moral slip might bring
one to rationalize that anything that drove the cost of government up
would promote the Republican program, the focus of one's primary
loyalty. Thievery might thus become service to the party. Though no
Republican ever publicized this rationale, many came very near to publicly espousing something close to it. "I believe in Mr. Cain's doctrine,"
cried A. J. Ransier to a lowcountry audience in 1870, " 'Get all the
money you can, but vote right!' "[78] Public morality for the Republican
(and Negro) politico was thus defined by party (and racial) loyalty,
and not by the ethical standards which they themselves had first established and which conservative whites, at least ostensibly, continued to
serve.

A large number of legislators practiced precisely what Mr. Cain
preached: they took bribes, but only after having voted "right." S. E.
Gaillard, a Negro senator from Charleston after 1871, refused a $5,000
bribe to support Patterson's Blue Ridge scrip and other bills in 1872
but finally came to support a compromise measure. After the compromise
was effected, he joined with other Negro senators who had promised
their votes for specific amounts but were having trouble collecting.
"I got in with this crowd," Gaillard later testified, "because I had
supported the Financial Settlement Bill after it had been amended."[79]
He later refused an offer of $500 to support Solomon's claim, voted
against it, but the ever-generous Solomon deposited $500 in his bank
account anyway.[80] Many other members testified that they had voted
for the claim because it was "just," "honest," "right," and that the bribe
was a "present" given in appreciation of their having voted right.[81]

Virtually every bribe-taker felt the necessity of excusing his conduct,
however specious his explanation may have been. Prince Rivers asserted that his followers began to accept bribes only after they had
held office for a couple of years and that they did so then only because

78. *Daily Republican* (Charleston), June 24, 1870.
79. *Fraud Report,* pp. 1649–50.
80. *Ibid.,* p. 1562.
81. *Ibid.,* pp. 1548–62.

they learned that the lowcountry members were taking all that was offered. Moses later stated that almost every member took fraudulent pay certificates believing that each dollar collected was so much retained in the state rather than drained off through Kimpton to New York by the bond ring.[82] Nash offered the same excuse to explain why he took $5,000 in Blue Ridge scrip after having successfully led a fight to give Patterson less than half of what he wanted. "I was supporting these Bills because I thought," he swore, "after hearing the arguments of these men, that it was right, and I merely took the money because I thought I might as well have it and invest it here as for them to carry it off out of the State." In the fall of 1877, he still had the scrip in his possession, obviously being very certain that it remained in South Carolina.[83] A few members described their motive as simple economic necessity. After having voted for Corbin for United States senator in the fall of 1876, L. J. Keith, a Negro representative from Darlington, admitted: "I would have voted for any other candidate under the same circumstances. I was pretty hard up and I did not care who the candidate was if I got $200."[84]

If, as Chamberlain alleged in the summer of 1874, the mass of Negro voters thought that public peculation was no less wrong than private thievery, the question arises of how the thieves remained in office year after year. The circumstances suggest a series of obvious answers. First, the period of blatant corruption was actually quite short, beginning when the railroad and printing schemes got out of hand in 1870 and ending as reform pressures became increasingly strong in the spring and summer of 1874. Further, the full extent of corruption became known only after Redemption, if then. Very few Republican officials admitted to any robbery before 1877, and even the conservative native whites, in the Taxpayers' Convention of 1871, certified the soundness of Republican fiscal administration.

Rumors there were of fraud, and probably many Negro voters realized something of the state of affairs, but Republican politicos sagaciously chose to accentuate the positive aspects of their activities and to call the roll of the offenses of the whites. With a fair degree of honesty, Republican campaigners could point with pride to a legislative program dedicated fully to the Negro's economic, educational, and political interests, and the paper pattern had at least some fraction of

82. *Ibid.*, p. 1486.
83. *Ibid.*, p. 1652.
84. *Ibid.*, p. 963 *et seq.*

reality in every county. The Republicans had given the Negroes, A. J. Ransier declared before a Negro audience at Christ Church in the spring of 1870, a constitution, a homestead law, "abolished the old patrol laws, whereby the poor colored man was hunted and whipped to death," and had secured for him his wife and children.[85] Just as Republicans in the North waved the bloody shirt, those of the South waved the "black shirt," and, even more potently, rattled the chains of slavery. "We have played together, you say," read a transparency draped across a Charleston street during the campaign of 1870, "but were we ever whipped together."[86] During the same campaign, Ransier viewed with alarm the attempts of the whites to bring in immigrant labor to supplant that of the Negro and concluded elliptically, "Shall I mention the 'negro code?'"[87] Later, in a Charleston address, Rainey dwelt with typical Republican fondness upon the willingness of the whites to concede to the Negroes what they had already won for themselves and pointed to the irony of men "who used to take so much pleasure in lacerating our backs in the past" now wooing the Negroes for their votes.[88]

The violence of the Ku Klux period, though never repeated in the same form, provided a fresh weapon for Republican orators in the state and was applied by them most ingeniously. The semisecrecy of the Grange, which justifiably alarmed the Republicans, was used to identify it as "a trick of the Ku Klux Democracy."[89] "I understand Whitemore [sic] is telling the negroes that these granges and Temperance Societies, that are formed all over the Country are nothing more than Ku Clux Societyes," complained an outraged Granger from Darlington in the summer of 1874.[90] After 1874, the Republican and Negro electorate moved out to secure its own style of reform, but, before that time, the Negro voter had only two choices. Either he could vote for a bolting faction supported by the conservative whites, or he could adhere to the regular nominees. There was really no choice. As Ransier put the question to a Charleston audience in June, 1870: "Would you not prefer their [the last legislature's] legislation to the old state of things, though not perfect?" "Yes! Yes!" cried the crowd.[91]

85. *Daily Republican* (Charleston), May 16, 1870.
86. *Ibid.,* May 4, 1870.
87. *Ibid.,* May 16, 1870.
88. *Ibid.,* April 29, 1870.
89. *A History of Spartanburg County,* p. 168.
90. W. A. Law to his wife, August 29, 1874, W. A. Law Papers.
91. *Daily Republican* (Charleston), June 24, 1870.

Politics for the Republican professional during most of the Reconstruction period was not so much how to beat a white Democrat as it was how to beat some rival Republican first out of the regular nomination and then, if he bolted, as he usually did, how to beat him at the polls. Thus, after 1868 and before 1876, many political contests in South Carolina were merely fights between Republican factions standing on the same program and principles, the real issue being personal. Comfortably entrenched behind a "natural" majority of 30,000 Negro votes and with the Democracy in retirement, Republicans could indulge in such political luxury. However, the result was the proliferation of personal machines, scores of factions led by chieftains who always demanded and often won a rather uncritical loyalty from their political cadre.

The first, and perhaps always the most potent, machine was built by Scott who used his gubernatorial powers during his first term to construct a gigantic organization which won him a second term in 1870. Using his appointive powers he placed his friends in positions as county treasurers, jury commissioners, election officials, and trial justices. He organized scores of thousands of militia "throughout the State."[92] He buttressed the militia with a 500-man police force (staffed in part by importations from his home town, Napoleon, Ohio) which operated as his political secret service. He won the support of local politicos who were themselves the heads of lesser machines—Rivers, Elliott, Whittemore, Swails, Nash, Smalls, Crews, De Large, Rainey, Cain, and others. He added to these the endorsement of various institutions—the persisting Union Leagues, the Grand Army of the Republic, and the various churches. In return he offered, besides patronage and gubernatorial support in local elections, a large share of public offices for Negroes. The result was a resounding victory over his Republican opponent, R. B. Carpenter, who had accepted the kiss of political death from the white conservatives. The only serious opposition to Scott's dominance came from C. C. Bowen, Charleston's scalawag congressman who had used his office to construct for himself a large personal machine. However, Bowen was crushed by the Scott engine, lost his congressional seat to De Large, and never again won high office.

By 1872, Scott had passed under a cloud, and the mantle of leadership was snatched away by Moses whose primary strength lay in an often publicly demonstrated devotion to the interest of the Negro and a private dedication to the interest of himself. The campaign, while

92. *Fraud Report*, p. 1601.

ostensibly between bolting reformers and regular reformers, was actually between combinations of personal machines. Once in office, Moses employed all of the devices that Scott had used to build a personal following and added the practice of pardoning criminals whom he considered "good political niggers."[93] The campaign of 1874 assumed much the same form as that of 1872, but the heads of both tickets probably really intended to reform the state's government. The factions aligned behind each candidate, however, might as easily have fallen on the opposite side.

Such politics produced strange electoral bedfellows. In 1872, the campaign of scrupulously honest Reuben Tomlinson was prominently supported by B. F. Whittemore, the carpetbagger who had admitted taking money for a West Point cadetship. In 1874, Chamberlain's campaign manager was Dr. Ensor. Chamberlain was supposedly an original corruptionist, and Ensor was the carpetbagger who managed the state asylum for the insane so excellently. On the other hand, the bolting reformer Judge Green, a scalawag, had as his campaign manager T. C. Dunn, who was soon to buy the post of comptroller general for himself, and as his prime stump speaker, R. H. Cain, who had been indicted for fraud and libel.

The success of the Redeemers in casting odium upon all Republicans for the admittedly widespread corruption that marked their regime has obscured the admirable integrity of such leaders as R. Tomlinson, J. K. Jillson, J. L. Orr, D. H. Chamberlain, L. C. Carpenter, J. G. Thompson, F. A. Sawyer, A. J. Willard, J. M. Morris, Lemuel Boozer, Simeon Corley, J. H. Rainey, A. J. Ransier, and Cardozo and the sincerity of others who had perhaps been involved in corruption but sought to participate in reform. Also obscured is the fact that reform was largely achieved by these men under the banner of Republicanism well before Redemption occurred.

As early as the first session of the Republican legislature in 1868, a native white Republican from Lexington resigned "in disgust for the rottenness" of the Radicals and two Negro members from Marlboro, Thoroughgoods Stubbs and Richard Grant, elected as Republicans, an-

93. The loyalty of the Moses following was often astounding. One young Negro went to prison rather than testify against Moses. O. R. Levy, a Negro legislator from Charleston whom Moses had made a trial justice, voted for the scrip bill merely because Moses asked him to and refused to accept the offered bribe. "I did not sell my vote," he proudly declared, "and did not want the scrip, and never took it." *Fraud Report*, p. 1641.

nounced their intention of voting with the Democrats. Shortly afterward, Stubbs resigned his seat.[94] As corruption spread, some of the
party's leaders became visibly distressed. The first reaction took the
form of private protest and withdrawal. For instance, Cardozo, sus-
pecting the thefts of Leslie and others through land commission purchases, withdrew from the Commission's advisory board and refused
to act with it until the office was placed under his own supervision.
Chamberlain, too, on the advisory board by dint of his position as
attorney-general and responsible for the legality of titles to land purchases, was disturbed by what he saw. In the spring of 1870, apparently
discovering the fraud involved in the Schley purchases, he threatened
to bring its principal perpetrator, Treasurer Parker, to trial. Parker
engaged a New York lawyer, D. M. Porter, to assist him. Porter's
counterattack was indeed awing. He hastened to make the title to the
Schley tracts good, and then he turned to menace Chamberlain. "I
am satisfied you have too much discretion to do what you say or intimate," he wrote. "In other words," he explained with painful candor,
"Mr. Cardozo is the only State official who would not be carried down
and made odious to every honest man."[95] Whether Chamberlain yielded
to this threat or not is unclear, but he did not bring the case to a jury
and no hint of the matter appeared in the press. During this same period,
Chamberlain held a twelfth share in the railroad scheme—as did Tomlinson and several other apparently honest men—a share which he had
purchased for $10,000. He later rued his participation. "That I hoped
to make money—dreamed of thousands—there is no doubt," he wrote
to a political confidant in 1875, "but I never knew of or consented to
any transaction even in this connection, which involved any injury to
the State as I then understood it." Patterson's activities, however, soon
opened his eyes to the fact that something more than foolishness was
underway. "We went on until owing to the treachery of our copartners
and the unwarrantable proposition pushed in the Legislature in behalf
of the concern, led Mr. Tomlinson and me to insist that we should be
relieved of our share in the concern. From that time I had no pecuniary
interest in it in any way."[96] In 1872, apparently unwilling either to
continue in association with or to expose his erstwhile colleagues,
Chamberlain retired from active politics and pursued the practice of

94. *Intelligencer* (Anderson), September 9, 16, 1868.
95. D. M. Porter to N. G. Parker, June 6, 1870; D. M. Porter to D. H. Chamberlain (a copy in Porter's hand), June 6, 1870; D. M. Porter to N. G. Parker, June
9, 1870, Samuel Dibble Papers.
96. D. H. Chamberlain to F. W. Dawson, June 9, 1875, F. W. Dawson Papers.

law in Columbia in partnership with the very respectable scalawag, S. W. Melton.

During the campaign of 1872, reform was in the air. Though it is by no means clear, James L. Orr had supposedly been commissioned by Grant to clean up South Carolina. When the regular convention nominated the notorious Moses for governor by a vote greater than the combined vote of his three honest rivals, Orr bolted and secured the nomination of Tomlinson on a reform ticket. J. Scott Murray of Anderson and John T. Green of Sumter, two men whom a Redeemer historian pronounced "above reproach," joined Tomlinson's ballot. Some prominent Negro politicos of dubious integrity, e.g., Samuel Lee and S. A. Swails, also joined the bolting reformers, but most of the Negro leadership who were influential throughout the state and inclined to favor reform, namely, Cardozo, H. E. Hayne, Rainey, and Ransier, chose to work within the regular organization. Cardozo and Hayne actually took places on the ballot with Moses.[97] Replacing Parker as treasurer after the election, Cardozo exposed an attempt by Moses to steal some $25,000 immediately after his inauguration and almost succeeded in his attempt to have Moses tried for the crime. Moses used his executive powers to avoid prosecution, however, and continued his thefts.

By the spring of 1874, virtually every Republican leader in the state was talking reform, and a strong minority was moving energetically to achieve it. In February, Elliott, whose own reputation was not unsullied, spoke in Columbia, denounced Moses and corruption, blamed the Negro majority for the circumstances, and predicted the unseating of the party if reform were not achieved.[98] In May, Judge T. J. Mackey, who had supported Moses in 1872, spoke in much the same vein.[99] Taking their cue from the Northern press, the party journals in South Carolina took up the cry. "The Republicans of this State must see to it that in the coming election every county shall elect none but honest and competent men, without stain or reproach on their private or public reputation," warned L. Cass Carpenter of the Columbia *Union Herald*, "or we shall be driven out of the house of our friends as a leprosy and a curse."[100] Official Washington soon made the warning explicit. In the summer, T. J. Mackey returned from an interview with Grant in

97. Reynolds, *Reconstruction in South Carolina*, pp. 224–26.
98. *New York Times*, February 21, 1874, p. 6.
99. *The Nation*, XVIII, No. 465 (May 28, 1874), 341.
100. Quoted in the *New York Times*, June 3, 1874, p. 4. See also June 1, 1874, p. 4.

which the latter had said that he would hold all Republicans in the state responsible unless they "reformed at the ballot-box." With wonted grandiloquence, Mackey continued: "And while the President speaks calmly of all the great battles in which he participated, yet when I talked to him of South Carolina, his apparently pulseless lips quiver, his veins and his eyes enlarge, and he says, 'You must stop the robbery!' " Mackey felt that he had received a "field order" for reform which had to be executed, cost what it might.[101] Congressmen Rainey, Ransier, and Cain all returned to the state with the same message from Capitol Hill, and added the warning that failure to reform might result in the levying of certain restrictions upon the suffrage.[102] As chairman of the Republican state executive committee, Elliott issued an address demanding reform and urged that the duty rested "peculiarly" upon the shoulders of the Negro electorate.[103] "Without a great change," E. W. M. Mackey commented presciently "in less than two years from now the Republican Party in this State will be dead. If we want to save it we must at once commence a fight against the band of thieves in our midst."[104]

At this point, Chamberlain re-entered active politics and easily won the nomination for governor. A bolting group offered Green and secured the endorsement of the conservatives.[105] Both candidates campaigned vigorously on identical platforms of reform and retrenchment. In many counties, Republican reformers now turned against their more corrupt partisans and fought them with an effectiveness—indeed, a vehemence—which the conservatives could not have matched. In the Republican county convention in Chester in October, Jim White, a Negro, interrupted the machinelike proceedings to attack the county boss, the Reverend Dublin Walker, also a Negro. White charged

101. *The Nation*, IXX, No. 477 (August 27, 1874), 129.
102. *Ibid.; New York Times*, August 19, 1874, p. 3.
103. *New York Times*, July 26, 1874, p. 5.
104. *Ibid.*, July 10, 1874, p. 3.
105. In August and September, Grant apparently flirted with the idea of supporting Joseph B. Kershaw for governor, the leading candidate of the conservatives. However, in the last hours before the Republican convention sat, a conservative emissary telegraphed the final decision from Grant's summer retreat at Long Branch: "Grant is thoroughly committed to Chamberlain. I can accomplish nothing." The telegram was quoted by F. W. Dawson in a letter to his wife, September 8, 1874, F. W. Dawson Papers. Dawson also attempted to defeat Chamberlain's nomination by bribing members of the Republican convention, but, as he complained to his wife, "They beat me out by using more money than I had." F. W. Dawson to his wife, October 13, 1874, F. W. Dawson Papers.

Walker with inefficiency and corruption, acidly pointing to the irony of
a supposed minister of the Gospel thus disrupting the operation of that
"staff-wheel of life," the public schools. During the ensuing wrangle,
Judge Thomas Jefferson Mackey entered the hall, cast aside his judicial
dignity and took a rough oratorical cudgel to Walker and his cronies.
Pointing to South Carolina's national reputation as the "Prostrate State,"
he promised that the nine indictments then pending against county
officials "can and shall be tried." Reform on the local level, he urged,
could be achieved by electing one or two large property holders as
county commissioners. Challenged by John Lee, a local officeholder, to
explain himself, Mackey, who had tasted physical combat while fili-
bustering in Nicaragua with William Walker twenty years before,
minced no words. "I am determined," he cried, "to break up the band
of thieves to which you belong." Shortly afterward, the meeting ended
in a riot in which the judge and his cane acquitted themselves well.[106]

After the election, it became obvious that Chamberlain's reformism
was more than campaign deep. Immediately, he began to press vigorously for an excellently conceived program of economy which he
presented in detail to the legislature. When that body passed a measure
which exceeded his recommendations, he stiffly vetoed the bill. Reluctantly and belatedly the legislature complied. Chamberlain also won
from the legislature a more equitable and efficient system for the levy,
collection, and expenditure of taxes. Finally, he sought and, to a large
extent, achieved improvement in the administration of the laws, particularly those relating to the schools, and this led him to remove a large
number of Republican placemen and appoint in their stead honest and
capable men of both races and parties.

As Chamberlain's intention became obvious, many conservative
native whites who had strenuously opposed his election moved rapidly
to his support. By the summer of 1875, even A. P. Aldrich, a leader of
truly reactionary tendencies, was urging the future lieutenant governor of
the Redeemer regime, William D. Simpson, to support Chamberlain in
his fight with "the Radical Ring."[107] Particularly sympathetic to Chamberlain's reform efforts were the top echelon financiers and businessmen
of Charleston. Their political cat's-paw was Francis Warrington Dawson, the editor and half-owner of the *News and Courier*, by 1874 the
leading newspaper in the state. By bitter experience, the business elite

106. *Reporter* (Chester), October 15, 1874; Mary Conner Moffett (ed.), *Letters
of General James Conner, C. S. A.* (Columbia, 1950), p. 10.
107. A. P. Aldrich to W. D. Simpson, June 30, 1875, W. D. Simpson Papers.

had found that political corruption was bad for their profession (a lesson which Customs Collector Worthington doubtlessly reiterated daily); but they had also found, in 1868 and 1870, that political violence was infinitely worse. What they needed was reform by orderly, legalistic processes, and Chamberlain showed himself to be much more able at this task than any native white conservative (Democrat) then in view. Within a month after Chamberlain's inauguration, Dawson "called on the Governor . . . and had a long and very pleasant talk with him."[108]

On his side, Chamberlain welcomed the support of the business community and channeled it to promote his reform program. "You can do much, and I write privately to ask you to do all in your power to keep down appropriations to the limits of our income," he told Dawson in February, 1875. "Members should be moved to feel that they will be watched and their names paraded and remembered if they fail of their duty in this respect," he continued. "My sole object is to give good government to S. C. and I believe that is yours too."[109] Chamberlain got precisely what he wanted from Charleston, and he repaid them in kind. By early spring, the alliance was smoothly functioning. "Let me serve you," the governor wrote, "in any way that is right and proper—which is all of course which you would ask—Cela ira sans dire."[110] The depth of the alliance between the Chamberlain reformers and the Charleston business elite has been neglected by historians, probably because both parties chose to keep it that way. "You know," Chamberlain once cautioned Dawson, "we must not be *too good* friends."[111]

Chamberlain bought success in reform at the cost of sacrificing a measure of unity within his party. First among his critics were not his nominal opponents, the conservatives, but those of his own party whose espousal of reform had been for campaign purposes only. "The truth is there were very few men in my party last fall who *meant* reform," Chamberlain informed Dawson "doubly" confidentially in February, 1875. "They sang that song because it was demanded, not because they loved it," he continued. "My inaugural chilled them, my

108. F. W. Dawson to his wife, November 22, 1874, F. W. Dawson Papers. Ironically, in August, Dawson had told his wife that Chamberlain differed from Moses much as a "footpad" differed from a forger. F. W. Dawson to his wife, August 2, 1874, F. W. Dawson Papers.

109. D. H. Chamberlain to F. W. Dawson, February 7, 1875, F. W. Dawson Papers.

110. *Ibid.,* May 7, 1875.

111. *Ibid.,* June 24, 1875.

special message enraged them, —and nothing keeps them from attacking me . . . openly . . . except the power of my office and the support which the conservatives and Country at large give to me in all my efforts at reform." Among the friends of reform, Chamberlain found Cardozo steadfast. "Cardozo was one of the few men who *meant* to improve the condition of the State, who felt that party success and good personal character, all demanded a thorough change of course," he asserted, and concluded that Cardozo "has consistently held to that view and is today the wisest and truest adviser I have, —the man who will stand longest by me and all who determined to stop stealing."[112] Also prominent on the side of aggressive reform were James G. Thompson, editor of the Columbia *Union Herald* and wartime editor of the *Free South* in Beaufort; Thomas Jefferson Robertson, the wealthy scalawag United States senator; and Judge T. J. Mackey. In December, 1874, Mackey virtually promised the solicitorship of his circuit to a Democrat because there was no Republican available who was capable of molding the office into an instrument of reform.[113] At the same time, true to his pre-election promise, "playing prosecutor, Judge, and every other department," he kept up "a constant war and stress" upon "all these fellows who were once his intimate associates and friends, but now, like Goldwaites dog,—'The dog to gain his private ends went mad and bit the man,'" reported an observer in Chester. "The darkies here," the commentator added, "are deadly enemies to him now, and will get him out of the way if they can, provided he doesn't get on their side again."[114]

The opposition to reform advanced no clear leadership. The legislature evinced a certain reluctance to reduce its own salary and, perhaps in resentment of Chamberlain's lashing as much as for other reasons, attempted unsuccessfully to impeach Cardozo and arrest editor James G. Thompson for contempt. However, in the spring of 1875, as Chamberlain intensified his attacks on the corruptionists, the opposition stiffened. Chamberlain energetically pressed the prosecution of ex-Treasurer N. G. Parker who retaliated, as he had in 1871, with a threat to expose Chamberlain's own supposed misdeeds. In this case, he threatened to tell all about Chamberlain's involvement with the railroad ring. Chamberlain, now prepared to speak with the candor which he should have shown four years previously, authorized Dawson to publish

112. *Ibid.*, February 18, 1875.
113. J. F. Hart to W. H. Brawley, December 14, 1874, N. A. Hunt Papers.
114. J. H. Hemphill to W. R. Hemphill, April 12, 1876, Hemphill Papers.

a defiant reply. "My evils have heretofore come from the friendship
of bad men," the governor asserted. "Perhaps I shall fare better if I
now have their hatred. At any rate I'm ready to try it." In the vanguard
of his enemies Chamberlain thought, no doubt accurately, that he saw
the adroit fist of Senator John J. Patterson "and those men who hate
me now because my words last fall have not been proved *lies*." In his
mind Chamberlain visualized Patterson, along with Scott, "old R. R.,"
in Washington "pouring his venom on me, 'Squat like a toad' at the
ear of the President and spitting his venomous filth on me at every
chance." They hated him, he felt, "for being more decent than they."[115]

Not all of the opposition to Chamberlain came from men who were
dishonest or opposed to reform. Some Republicans, very astutely, saw
the danger in being too friendly with the conservatives. In June, 1875,
A. P. Aldrich noted that Judges R. B. Carpenter and S. W. Melton were
afraid that Chamberlain was coming dangerously close to giving the
conservatives the very weapons which could be used to "kill him off
with his own party and prevent him from carrying out his policy of
reform."[116] In December, the legislature rebelled briefly against the
executive whip by electing Moses and Whipper to judgeships which one
year previously they had filled by dazzling majorities with native white
lawyers of the highest ability and integrity. Then, as Chamberlain—
probably at the insistence of the Charleston merchants and certainly
with the support of Senator Robertson and Federal District Court
Judge Bond—moved out against the stronghold of corruption which
H. C. Worthington, Patterson's henchman, had erected as the collector
of the port of Charleston, the opposition to Chamberlain crystallized
and came openly into the field under the marshalship of Patterson. By
early April, the senator was actively at work in the state. "Patterson
is here openly fighting me, and with him are Dunn, Carpenter, (L. C.
& *R. B.*), Hardy Solomon, but not Sam. Melton," flashed Chamberlain
from the battle front.[117]

Chamberlain felt that he had won the approval of reform Republicans
in the North.[118] However, in South Carolina he found himself between

115. D. H. Chamberlain to F. W. Dawson, May 11, 1875, F. W. Dawson Papers.
116. A. P. Aldrich to W. D. Simpson, June 30, 1875, W. D. Simpson Papers
(Duke).
117. D. H. Chamberlain to F. W. Dawson, December 27, 1875; January 3,
March 13, April 7, 1876, F. W. Dawson Papers.
118. D. H. Chamberlain to Charles Nordhoff, February 3, 1876, D. H. Chamberlain Papers; D. H. Chamberlain to Samuel Bowles, March 30, 1875, Samuel Bowles
Papers.

two fires. The "Straightout" Democracy was on the rise. To counter Straightout criticisms of the Chamberlain regime, which the fusionists wanted to support for re-election in 1876, the fusionists in general and the Charlestonians in particular urged Chamberlain to make more appointments favorable to the conservatives. On the other hand, every such appointment frightened his Republican friends, particularly the Negro electorate, added fuel to the fire which Patterson had started, and diminished his chances of winning the Republican nomination. Such tensions worked a visible strain on Chamberlain. He became chronically ill and highly irritable. In May, the fusionists protested the appointment of a Radical to an office in Marion. "To urge me to try to get the nomination of my party and then to denounce me for taking only a small step in that direction and one which does no harm to them is idle," he exploded in exasperation to Dawson.[119] Meanwhile, Patterson was rapidly organizing a coalition designed to unseat Chamberlain (and presumably reform) and pledge the state to O. P. Morton for president. Chamberlain's group favored either Blaine or Bristow. In mid-April, a fevered convention of the Republican party met in Columbia. The ever-ready battler, Judge T. J. Mackey precipitated a fight on the floor of the convention in which pistols were drawn and women went screaming from the galleries. In the early hours of the following morning, seemingly by sheer force of oratory, but actually with the assistance of hard, persuasive work by Cardozo and others, Chamberlain swung the heavily Negro membership of the convention away from Patterson and to himself. Quite clearly, the politicos of Republicanism (and, presumably, the Negro electorate) in South Carolina had decided to continue in the path of reform under Chamberlain.[120]

External forces prevented Chamberlain and his friends from perfecting their program. Most important among these was the resurgence of the Straightout Democracy. Feeling themselves oppressed by what they still interpreted as "confiscatory taxes," increasingly pained by the declining price of cotton and the rising costs of agricultural production, finding credit scarce and costly, and sparked by the success of the native whites in Mississippi in overthrowing their Negro majority, the mass of native whites in the state concluded between the fall of 1875 and the

119. D. H. Chamberlain to F. W. Dawson, May 22, 1876, F. W. Dawson Papers. For partial appraisal by Chamberlain of the delicacy of his position vis à vis the Negro voter, see D. H. Chamberlain to Samuel Bowles, February 2, 1876, Samuel Bowles Collection.

120. *New York Times*, April 12, 1876, p. 1.

summer of 1876 that the "natural ruling element" could and should regain political control of South Carolina. Particularly in the middle and
upper counties was this sentiment strong. In essence, it was a return to
the stand which Democrats had assumed in 1867 and 1868. The Negro
would be invited to vote the Democratic ticket; here and there Negro
leaders might be accorded local offices; but, ultimately, the Negro would
be expected to follow in the path laid out by his white superiors, and
such offices as he obtained would be given in evidence of his mentor's
generosity and not as the Negro's due. At their very best, the Straightout Democrats gave the Negro paternal politics as they had given him
paternal slavery. At their worst, they gave him promises which they
never expected to honor.

If fusion had been an aberration, then the return to Straightoutism
was a return by the native whites to their true selves. Quite obviously,
the thousands of white voters who had previously refused to participate
in fusion politics entered enthusiastically into a campaign launched on
this basis. To carry their banner, it is hardly surprising that the Straightouts turned to the man who had remained ever true—Wade Hampton.
The general's champions argue that somehow he was more willing than
any of his followers to give the Negro political justice. Yet, Hampton
actually offered Negroes only the privilege of voting for himself and
his followers, and he was in perfect harmony with those native whites
who steadfastly refused to recognize the Negro's political equality by
joining with him in any political partnership. As Hampton wrote to
his close friend, Armisted Burt, soon after the inauguration of Congressional Reconstruction, he was "willing to concede partial suffrage
to the negro; suffrage limited by educational qualifications & this test
should be applied irrespectively to the whites also, but I can not bring
myself to the recognition of universal suffrage as a fixed fact, one to the
support of which we will pledge ourselves." Well before 1871, Hampton
saw the Straightout approach as the only path consistent with honor.
It would give the whites a strong minority in the House, he thought,
and by sheer quality of candidates it might give them a majority in the
Senate. "If we could accomplish this result it would in my opinion be
far preferable to any affiliation with Radical elements white or black."
Fusion, he feared, might "commit ourselves to a policy which will fix
on the state negro rule & negro equality." "It would be better for the
State to be remanded to military government," he argued, "rather than
that [policy be pursued] which places the negro permanently in power."
Even though he had little faith in the Northern Democracy before

1876—if, indeed, he had much then—Hampton also felt that "no permanent relief can come to us of the South save by the general overthrow of Radicalism in a national election."[121] Hampton was absent from the state during the canvasses of 1870, 1872, and 1874. During this period, like so many Straightouts, he turned his attention to the reparation of his economic fortunes. Even had he been in the state, however, as he told Burt, he could not have reconciled himself to playing the fusionist game. When South Carolina found Hampton in 1876, it was as if she had re-found herself. Indeed, she had. Hampton was, above all, the creature of the society that had reared him. He was the personification of its ideal, carrying in his human form the inflexible rectitude, the sober courage which all South Carolinians idolized but few possessed. He could no more be untrue to the values of that culture than those values would allow him to be untrue to himself. In turning to Hampton in 1876, white Carolinians were listening again to their consciences. Whatever else Straightoutism may not have been, at its best in the Hampton tradition it *was* honest.

During a May, 1876, convention of conservatives, the fusionists still had enough strength to defeat a Straightout attempt to nominate an all-white, Democratic ticket. However, when the conservatives met again in August, the membership was altered, and a Charleston delegate was surprised to find that "the idea of refraining from opposition to Chamberlain was scarcely entertained out of Charleston. . . . The people of the State are so sick at heart of the failure of every attempt

121. Wade Hampton to A. L. Burt, n.d., Wade Hampton Papers (Duke). This letter is undated; however, internal references indicate that it was certainly written after the passage of the first Reconstruction Act, and probably written on the approach of the elections in the spring of 1868. Regardless of the date of this particular letter, Hampton consistently held to this view. As early as August of 1867, he had written to a Charleston comrade: "I am willing to give the negro all his rights, but I cannot deny all to the whites at the same time. I can never agree to universal suffrage though I would consent to 'impartial suffrage.'" Wade Hampton to James Conner, August 1, 1867, James Conner Papers. Precisely the same views are expressed by Hampton in another letter to Burt commenting on the election of 1870. Wade Hampton to A. L. Burt, January 2, 1871, Wade Hampton Papers (Duke).

Too, Hampton was always dubious of the efficacy of the assistance of the Northern Democracy. In May of 1868, he wrote: "It will not do for us to trust to the Dem. party for deliverance for putting out of the question the doubt of their success in the Presdt. election, there remains a recollection of their Punic faith—as shown of old." Wade Hampton to James Conner, May 24, 1868, James Conner Papers.

they have hitherto made, and so disgusted with the Republicans with whom they were forced to make alliance that they revolted against any coalition." The immediate cause of the change, he thought, was Chamberlain's letters to Grant and Patterson's speeches protesting the Hamburg riot. These, he believed, "gave universal offense and disgust." Furthermore, the *News and Courier* "by its injudicious championship of him excited suspicion and disgust and alienated very many good men who would otherwise have supported him." The Charlestonians had surrendered at last. James Conner, Confederate brigidier, grandson of an Irish immigrant, son of one of Charleston's leading financiers, sang the swan song of fusionism in one last plea on the eve of Hampton's nomination by acclamation. "If there had been a ballot many would have voted against H. but it would have only done harm to oppose him ineffectually," reported a confidant of Conner. Thus, the fusionists gave up their "certain and lasting" program for "the greatest thing unity."[122] Once again, the issue became Democrat versus Republican; or to put it more precisely, white versus black, contrasting colors upon a common background of reform.

Stressing Hampton's promises to the Negroes of "free men, free schools and free ballots," Democrats in many areas actively wooed Negro voters. The white Richland Democratic Club in Columbia brought Negro members into the Club and held weekly meetings to convert others. During the meeting of October 5, a Negro Democrat named Robinson made a speech indicative of the character of the converts. Robinson declared that he had been campaigning with Hampton and "that he believed Gen Hampton could not tell a lie; that Gen Hampton had told him that he would give his people good teachers both male and female, and that he would Keep the School House open more than four months in the year; that Gen Hampton will be and that he shall be our next Governor."[123] Democratic Clubs were frequently very careful to protect their Negro members from forceful reconversion. The Richland Club retained a lawyer to press the prosecution of a Negro Republican for assaulting another Negro for expressing Democratic sentiments and to free a Negro Democrat who had been arrested in Columbia and spirited off to prison in Lexington for a debt of five dollars.[124] Similarly, the Black Oak Democratic Campaign Club in Berkeley County organized a military company

122. Richardson Miles to W. P. Miles, August 24, 1876, W. P. Miles Papers.
123. Minutes of the Richland Democratic Club, September 5, 1876.
124. *Ibid.*, August 31, September 7, 1876.

"to protect all members of this Club (without regard to race color or previous condition) in the due exercise of their political rights."[125]

Actually, few Negroes joined the campaign on the Democratic side. In October, a carpetbag correspondent of the *Times* believed that not 2,000 Negroes in the entire state would vote Democratic freely, and 1500 to 1800 of these were in the nine counties where the white population possessed a decided majority.[126] Occasionally, Democrats inadvertently referred to the paucity of their Negro following. The Black Oak Democracy, for example, pessimistically resolved to protect "the few colored democrats who have & will join our party," while the chairman of the October 5 meeting of the Richland club lamented: "I do regret that our colored friends are not here in larger numbers."[127]

James Davis, a Negro tradesman of Columbia, probably spoke the minds of thousands of his race when he explained extemporaneously to the Richland Democratic Club why he could not support their ticket. He had been an "Independent" (a reform) Republican, he said, "but as you have seen fit to frame a ticket discarding my race I must stand aloof." He had attended the postwar meeting in which Hampton had offered biracial suffrage with literacy and property qualifications and he was "ready to concede that when we asked for unqualified suffrage it was a matter you could not readily grant." His basic objection to joining the Democrats, however, was that he did not believe Hampton could persuade his supporters to carry out his pledges to the Negroes. He assessed the situation with startling perception:

> I have come to the conclusion that you have made up your minds that this is the white mans land and must forever remain so. If you come to my people and say to them we will give you what belongs to you we will grasp your hand and help you drive out the carpetbagger. Colored men that are South Carolinians love South Carolina as well as you do. If this government is to continue the same as has been in the past I feel it that we will suffer. You have money and have lands and if Hampton is elected you can readily obtain amounts from the North, but what have we? Whilst I know that if the men that you have nominated had their way, none of our rights would be endangered, yet what guarantee have I that their

125. MS Constitution and notes, Black Oak Democratic Campaign Club, n.d.
126. *New York Times,* October 21, 1876, p. 8.
127. MS Constitution and notes, Black Oak Democratic Campaign Club, n.d.; MS Minutes, Richland Democratic Club, October 5, 1876.

opinion will be regarded? . . . . I will agree with you that I
and many like myself are not competent to run this government,
but you must not draw a line and exclude all of my race.

Davis scoffed at the character of Negro Democrats. "You may sift all
that have come over to you and you will find that you will have to bull
pen them to obtain their votes," he warned. "We want a good government; give us a fair showing and we are with you for reform and
Victory!" What he was asking for, of course, was a place for Negroes on
the statewide and Richland tickets and this was something local whites
had already decided would never be given again.[128]

Democratic campaign managers actually expected few Negroes to
join them. In the upcountry districts, very little effort was made to
recruit Negroes for the party, but a tremendous effort was made to keep
them away from the polls. In the lowcountry, emphases were reversed
but converts were never numerous. The exception was Charleston where
several minor Negro office holders came out for Hampton.

Democratic managers expected few conversions among the Negroes,
but they were determined to make the most of what they did get.
Mississippi in 1875 provided the plan. "The negro was not with us,"
wrote a Mississippi Redeemer to an inquiring Carolinian in January,
1876, "did not vote with us, and still has an idea that he did not, but
he had no one on the spot to show him how the thing was done, but he
sees that it was done, hurras for the winning side, and, now, it is a hard
matter to find a negro *who did not vote the people's ticket*. All that is
necessary is to obtain the result, no matter how, and Mister Nigger ac-
cepts it as satisfactory, and claims that he helped to work out the
problem."[129] Looking toward the day when they would claim that the
Negro was with them, Democrats were very careful to give the Negroes
who did join them conspicuous positions in meetings, parades, and
other gatherings, and everywhere to exaggerate their numbers. During
the Hampton Day celebration in Laurens, for instance, "the campaign
managers were solicitous" about their Negro friends and "gave them
front seats at the stand."[130] In Spartanburg, the Negro Democratic Club
rode in the Hampton Day parade and two Negroes were made vice
presidents of the county organization.[131] Similarly, in a redshirt parade

128. MS Minutes, Richland Democratic Club, October 5, 1876.
129. S. W. Ferguson to T. G. Barker, January 7, 1876, M. W. Gary Papers.
130. William Watts Ball, *The State That Forgot: South Carolina's Surrender to Democracy* (Indianapolis, 1932), p. 161.
131. *A History of Spartanburg County*, pp. 163-64.

in Edgefield in October a carpetbag reporter counted nine Negroes among the 1600 horsemen, although the Democratic press claimed 200. In Sumter, 13 Negroes were seen among 1200 mounted whites, although the Democrats claimed 300. The same reporter knew of only seven Negro Democrats in Columbia where he lived; in Barnwell, he could not find a hundred; and only one Negro attended the Democratic convention in Beaufort County.[132] On September 28, A. C. Haskell, Hampton's campaign manager, told Negroes at the weekly meeting of the Richland Club that 7,000 Negroes would vote Democratic.[133] After the election, he raised his estimate to 9,000.

There are no authoritative statistics on the subject, but scattered references indicate that the great mass of Negroes remained loyal to Republicanism through election day. The son of the Democratic county chairman in Laurens conceded that only "A few score, possibly more than a hundred negroes in Laurens voted for Hampton . . ."[134] "The day of the election was quiet," a young woman reported from Lexington, "there were about ten negroes voted our Ticket at the precinct where our neighborhood voted at." If the conversion rate was not greater in other precincts in Lexington County, then certainly less than a hundred Negroes voted Democratic in that district. Interestingly, for the few defectors from Republicanism retribution was soon forthcoming. "A colored Democrat was severely beaten and had his house burnt by a colored rad, near my Uncle A. H. Wolfe," the young lady added.[135] With the exception of Charleston, it is improbable that more than a hundred Negroes voted Democratic in each county in the state. Further, it is almost certain that had not several thousand Negroes been kept from the polls by sheer physical force, the natural Negro majority of more than 20,000 votes would have decisively defeated Hampton. As it was, the Republicans threw out the vote of Laurens and Edgefield to count Chamberlain in by a majority of 3,000, while the Democrats eventually won a count which gave Hampton a majority of only slightly over 1,000.[136]

After the Redemption, Democrats, as the Mississippian had advised, usually claimed that the Negroes themselves had voted Hampton into office. Occasionally, however, they found it convenient to discard the fiction that the Negro was with Hampton in 1876. Samuel L. Bennett,

132. *New York Times,* October 21, p. 8; 29, p. 1, 1876.
133. MS Minutes, Richland Democratic Club, September 28, 1876.
134. Ball, *The State That Forgot,* p. 163.
135. Lizzie Geiger to "Leaphart," November 13, 1876, John Fox Papers.
136. *Appletons' Annual Cyclopaedia,* 1876, I, 724, 727.

a Negro and once Republican auditor of Charleston County, supported Hampton in 1876 and averred that 400 Negro votes were given to Hampton by the county. When he sought to get Negroes onto the local Democratic ticket in 1878, however, he thought he saw a conspiracy to exclude his race from such honors. The editor of the *News and Courier,* having undergone a profound metamorphosis since Reconstruction days, replied that there was no such plot. Unwittingly previewing events to come, he declared that what a party did within the party was its own business, that Bennett's estimate that 400 Negroes in the county had voted for Hampton was "excessive," and that opposition to the whites by Negroes could only turn the victors against them.[137]

Republican politicos did not yield easily. Their ranks were reinforced by such newcomers as Bruce Williams, the new senator from Georgetown, and T. E. Miller, a freshman member from Beaufort, both of whom were well educated and of impeccable reputations. After the election, Republicans held the senate by a clear majority of three. In the house, protected by the military, they organized under E. W. M. Mackey. The Democratic members of the House withdrew, organized separately, and proceeded to swear in their candidates. For an anxious four months, the "dual government" continued.

The position of the Republicans was gradually undermined. Of primary importance was the refusal of the great mass of taxpayers to support the Republican regime, instead paying a portion of their taxes— at Hampton's request—to his officers. Without positive federal intervention, this alone would have caused the fall of the Chamberlain government. Early in April, both Hampton and Chamberlain went to Washington and conferred with President Hayes. Shortly after they returned, the federal garrison was withdrawn, and every major department passed into the control of the Democracy.

Redeemer propaganda would lead one to think that, to a man, carpetbag leaders of both races forthwith fled the state, pursued by whites quivering with indignation and bent on bringing them to swift, uncompromising account for the peculations which, again to a man, they had been guilty of perpetrating. Native Negroes, who had been the victims of their own inferiority, were forgiven by the indulgent, protective whites and returned to their ante-bellum loyalty. Repentant scalawags were either unscrupulous poor whites who passed from sordid power

137. Clippings and letter, S. L. Bennett to W. H. Wallace, December 5, 1877, March 15, 1878, Wallace–Gage Papers.

into ignominious oblivion or respectable whites who had made an honest mistake. These latter were allowed to recant and return to their Democratic allegiance.

In actual fact, a large proportion of the carpetbaggers remained and continued to work as they had before. Willard on the state Supreme Court and D. T. Corbin, R. B. Elliott, J. P. M. Epping, and R. H. Cain in various federal offices remained active Republicans for many years after redemption. For many reasons others did go North and West. The native Negro element not only continued to be overwhelmingly loyal to Republicanism but also supplied an increasingly influential portion of the local leadership. Some of these men, Robert Smalls, for instance, had been active from the beginning. Others, like Thomas E. Miller and George W. Murray, were young men of excellent character who came into politics only as the Reconstruction regime was passing away. A few, such as Cardozo and H. E. Hayne, left the state, but in Cardozo's case it was to take a high post under Hayes in the Treasury Department. A few others, like Beverly Nash, lent a grain of truth to the tradition by making humble apologies to the whites and retiring from politics. True to the Redeemer myth, the scalawag element very nearly evaporated. E. W. M. Mackey, C. C. Bowen, and L. E. Northrup, second- and third-rank politicians during Reconstruction, remained active in the lowcountry but were never powerful. Subsequently, other native whites became Republicans, perhaps for the purpose of winning patronage, although at the turn of the century this group was still insignificant. But most scalawags simply disappeared from public life. Those like T. J. Mackey and T. J. Robertson who were allowed to come back into the conservative fold soon found themselves laboring under informal but inflexible political disabilities.

Republican politicos of both races in post-Reconstruction South Carolina sustained themselves largely by doling out federal offices.[138] Still, behind the politicos was a party that had been hardened and, to some extent, purified by its adversities. Recognizing the Hampton pledges as a Trojan Horse, hard-core Republicans now fought Democrats for principle as vigorously as they had previously fought each other for petty personal advantage. That they were reduced to virtual political impotence by the turn of the century was not because they had refused to fight.

138. See James W. Patton's close and conclusive study of post-Reconstruction Republican leadership in South Carolina. James Welch Patton, "The Republican Party in South Carolina, 1876–1895," in *Essays in Southern History,* ed. by Fletcher Melvin Green (Chapel Hill, 1949), pp. 91–111.

In a large measure, Democrats were so completely successful because they were able to convince themselves and the mass of Americans that every Republican in the state was either incompetent or corrupt or both. They had begun the campaign in the early 1870's, and they had happily measured its effect among reform-minded men of both parties in the North. By 1876, it was the keynote of their cause and one which deliberately ignored the faithfulness with which reform Republicans had adhered to Chamberlain's promises in 1874, the endorsement of his administration by a large number of white conservatives, his crushing of the Patterson corruptionists in the convention of 1876, and his pledge to continue his reform program along lines which the white Democracy itself advocated. After Redemption, the campaign continued. Using the power of official office, Democrats proceeded publicly to smear charges of corruption across the face of Republicanism in the state, unqualifiedly damning every Republican officeholder and every man— excluding themselves, of course—who had ever voted for a Republican candidate. The strategy was to establish guilt by accusation. The method has since become familiar. A legislative committee was chosen to investigate the frauds of the previous regime. Supposedly, the committee was bipartisan. Actually, the Republicans on the committee were hand picked by the Democratic managers and were themselves in the process of changing their political clothes. The committee investigated only four or five selected cases, usually having the same seventy-five witnesses testify again and again to the same sordid instances. At the same time, the committee carefully refrained from inquiring into the current status of the bond and phosphate rings in which some Democrats were then very much involved. When the committee finished, it published the testimony in a 1700-page report, then the longest single publication in the state's official library. Among those testifying were men who had been at the very heart of corruption—Parker, Moses, Scott, and Josephus Woodruff. Ironically, these were given clemency. On the other hand, only a few Republican leaders were actually brought to trial, the most influential—Chamberlain, Cardozo, and Smalls— being arraigned with those who were confessedly most corrupt. The effect was to condemn the good with the bad, and all at once.

That such was the deliberate intention of the Redeemers was made clear in a letter written in the summer of 1877 by James Conner, the attorney-general under Hampton, to W. D. Simpson, the lieutenant-governor. "Briefly & all this in confidence," he wrote in relation to those Republicans who had fled, "I think our course is to get the Inditments & not issue requisitions [for extradition], but publish in Shape of a Report, the testimony the Committee has taken: an immense deal of it, & the most captivating parts are historical & would not stand test as legal evidence, but the moral evidence would be crushing." "The press would revel in it," he continued with prophetic accuracy, "& we would politically guillotine every man of them." The effect was precisely as Conner predicted. The press did revel in it. *Every man* was, in the eyes of the whites, politically executed. Northerners used it as a license to desert the Negro, and few historians have since failed to use eight-dollar spittoons, one-dollar cigars, and a bar in the Capitol to lighten their prose and delight their students. "If we bring them back—can we convict?" asked the attorney-general, "& a mistrial is equivalent to a defeat & re-habilitates every man of them. The one course is certain & safe. The other doubtful, as Juries are doubtful, & the only gain in the latter, if sucessful, is the putting their bodies in the Penitentiary." Perpetual political banishment, not legal justice was what was desired. Conner's plan would yield just that. "It will be needless for them to say that the evidence of Moses *et al* is false," he argued. "The reply is conclusive. If you believe it false, why dont you stand yr trial & face the charge & prove the falsehood. Refusal to meet it is confession of guilt." Conner conceded that the investigating committee would oppose his plan, but, he asserted, "If we had listened to Committees or public [opinion?] Hampton would never have gone to Washington." For those Republicans who remained within the state, the Charlestonian offered a different policy. "I ought to say that I do not include in this any man in power," he explained. "I would go, viciously, for Patterson, Wright & any of the Congressmen [Rainey, Cain, and Smalls], as any man in place." "Think it over," the attorney-general insisted, "& let me have your views, of course in confidence, for these are matters that should be confidential until the policy is determined on, & when you do write—write large & round. Do as I say & not as I do."[139]

Conner carried out his program with great effectiveness. Scores of indictments were obtained against Republicans who had left the state, and the most notorious—Parker, who had already been convicted in 1875 by a Republican jury, judge, and prosecutor—was again convicted, thus implying that all the others could be convicted as easily if they dared to return. However, such strategy wore thin on Cardozo, who chose to stand trial on the nine indictments brought against him. The prosecution countered adroitly by choosing to try Cardozo on only one

139. James Conner to W. D. Simpson, August 24, 1877, W. D. Simpson Papers.

count—that of cashing in his capacity as treasurer certain coupons on
state bonds which had been fraudulently obtained by the holders but
which were identical with legitimate coupons of their type. Ironically,
the same charge had been brought against Cardozo by angry corruptionists within his party during the legislative session of 1874–1875. Interestingly, although Cardozo was convicted of conspiracy, four other state
officers indicted with him on this count were never brought to trial.
Three of these had turned state's evidence and confessed to the fraud.[140]
Conner also went "viciously" after L. C. Carpenter and Robert Smalls,
two Republicans claiming to have been elected to Congress in 1876. He
secured the conviction of the former on a very doubtful charge of forgery
and the latter on a case of bribery. Thus, only four Republicans were
convicted of frauds by the Redeemers before a jury.

Redeemers barked much more than they bit, but once in power they
hastened to salve the very wounds they had induced. Cardozo, for
instance, was soon pardoned and the eight remaining indictments against
him dismissed. In the spring of 1879, a very general settlement, largely
engineered by F. W. Dawson, was made providing that Republicans in
the federal courts would drop charges against Democrats for interfering
in the election of 1876 in exchange for the dismissal of charges against
Republicans pending in the Democratic state courts.[141]

Had the Redeemers been truly outraged by Republican thefts, they
would doubtlessly have gone "viciously" after all of the corruptionists at
home and abroad, punished each to the fullest possible extent, and
produced an impressive group of new inmates in the state penitentiary.
After all, the question of guilt, the determination of the degree of trans-
gression, and the measure of punishment deserved in each case were
decisions which properly belonged to judges and juries, not to state
officers in their capacities as party leaders. That they failed to perform
their duties in this respect, leaves the Redeemers open to charges of
public duplicity, personal dishonesty, and political opportunism.

During their first dozen years of freedom in South Carolina, Negroes
realized a progressive expansion of the meaning of their new liberty.
From slaves and quasi-slaves they burgeoned into soldiers, farmers,

140. James R. Leland, *A Voice from South Carolina* (Charleston, 1879), pp.
226–29.

141. Numerous documents relating to these negotiations between April 17 and
April 22, 1879, are in the F. W. Dawson Papers.

lawyers, businessmen, and investors; elders and bishops; college students and teachers; jurors, voters, and politicians; family men, Masons, and, even, criminals. In a large measure, this growth was made possible by an outside political power which, early in the period, expanded the basis of that power to include the Negroes themselves. Yet, an irony of the post-Reconstruction history of the Negro is that the very political freedom under which other liberties were early nurtured could not sustain itself in a period in which those liberties continued to grow. Negro losses in the political realm were largely the result of the effectiveness of the Redeemer campaign in vilifying Republicanism in South Carolina. The extravagant charges levied in the report of the Fraud Committee (attested to by scores of witnesses who were confessed participants) seemed ample by its very volume and redundancy to cover the whole body of Republicanism with layers of slime. The numerous indictments against absent Republicans and the apparent ease with which convictions were obtained where the state chose to prosecute was proof enough of the guilt of all. It is hardly surprising that many native white contemporaries convinced themselves and the following generation that Republicanism meant "corruption," and that Negro Republicanism meant "corruption compounded." In time, Northerners accepted the Southern argument as it applied to the South and found in it a certain measure of relief from a sense of guilt for their apostasy. The results were unique; the men who had lost the war in South Carolina had won the peace. Not many vanquished can claim such a victory.

BIBLIOGRAPHY

I. Primary Sources

A. MANUSCRIPTS

Bennett College Library, Greensboro, N. C.
  Norris Wright Cuney Papers.

Duke University Library, Durham, N. C.
  Benjamin Allston Papers.
  John Daniel Bivens Account Books and Papers.
  Thaddeus S. Boinest Papers.
  Edward Earle Bomar Papers.
  Eli Whitney Bonney Papers.
  Armisted L. Burt Papers.
  John C. Calhoun Papers.
  Ellison Capers Papers.
  Daniel H. Chamberlain Papers.
  Rachel Susan Cheeves Papers.
  Thomas Green Clemson Papers.
  Ann Pamela Cunningham Papers.
  Francis Warrington Dawson Papers.
  Henry William and Wilmot Gibbes De Saussure Papers.
  Samuel Dibble Papers.
  Thomas Rhett Smith Elliott Papers.
  John Fox Papers.

Robert H. Gourdin Papers.
John Berkeley Grimball Papers.
Wade Hampton Papers.
John Y. Harris Papers.
W. R., J. C., and R. R. Hemphill Papers.
William Hill Papers. (Photostats.)
John W. Holland Papers.
Nickels J. Holmes Papers.
N. A. Hunt Papers.
Daniel W. Jordan Papers.
William A. Law Papers.
Allan MacFarland Papers.
Louis Manigault Papers.
Joseph Warren Waldo Marshall Papers.
R. H. McKie Papers.
Jacob Rhett Motte and Mary Motte Papers.
James L. Orr Papers.
Lalla Pelot Papers.
Benjamin Franklin Perry Papers.
Francis Wilkinson Pickens Papers.
Henry L. Pinckney Plantation Book.
Octavius Theodore Porcher Papers.
Robert A. Pringle Papers.
Joseph H. Rainey Papers.
(Merged with South Carolina Reconstruction Papers.)
William W. Renwick Papers.
James Burchell Richardson Papers.
Daniel Edgar Sickles Papers.
William Dunlap Simpson Papers.
South Carolina Militia Papers.
South Carolina Reconstruction Papers.
George W. Spencer Papers.
Augustin Louis Taveau Papers.
William H. Trescot Papers.
Jeremiah Wilbur Papers.
Benjamin S. Williams Papers.
Josephus Woodruff Diary. (Photostats.)

Southern Historical Collection, University of North Carolina, Chapel Hill, N. C.

Peter B. Bacot Collection.
Peter B. Bacot Papers and Diary.

John and Keating S. Ball Plantation Journal.
William J. Ball Plantation Books. (Microfilm.)
Alexander Hamilton Boykin Papers.
Mary Boykin Chesnut Diary.
John Hamilton Cornish Diary.
Richard Dozier Papers.
Elliott–Gonzales Papers.
Habersham Elliott Papers.
Grace B. Elmore Diary.
James M. Gage Papers.
David Gavin Diary.
Gregorie–Elliott Papers.
John Berkeley Grimball Papers.
John Berkeley Grimball Diary.
Meta Grimball Diary.
David Golightly Harris Farm Journal. (Microfilm.)
Heyward–Ferguson Papers. (Microfilm.)
James B. Heyward Plantation Book.
Emma E. Holmes Diary. (Microfilm.)
Wilmot S. Holmes Collection.
Charles Howard Family, Domestic History. (Typescript.)
Edward Lipscomb Papers.
Basil Manly, Jr., Letters and Letterbook.
William L. Mauldin Diaries.
N. R. Middleton Papers.
William Porcher Miles Papers and Books.
Thomas J. Myers Papers. (Typescript.)
N. A. Nicholson Papers.
Orr–Patterson Papers and Books.
Benjamin F. Perry Papers. (Microfilm.)
Pickens–Dugas Papers.
Martha Schofield Diary. (Typescript.)
John McKee Sharpe Papers.
William D. Simpson Papers.
Sparkman Family Papers.
James R. Sparkman Books.
George Coffin Taylor Collection.
Sally Elmore Taylor Memoir.
Daniel Augustus Tompkins Papers.
Trenholm Papers.
William Henry Trescot Letters.
Wallace–Gage Papers.
James Wilson White Papers.

South Carolina Department of Archives, Columbia, S. C.

> Freedmen File.
> Trial Justice File.

South Carolina Historical Society, Charleston, S. C.

> James Conner Papers.
> Augustine Thomas Smythe Letters.
> List of Emigrants for Liberia, November 17, 1867.

South Caroliniana Library, University of South Carolina, Columbia, S. C.

> Black Oak Democratic Campaign Club, Constitution and Notes.
> Bonds Conway Correspondence.
> D. T. Crosby Papers.
> Edward Crosland Papers.
> [—. —.] Deas Papers.
> Martin W. Gary Papers.
> Louisa Gervais Papers.
> John Berkeley Grimball Papers.
> Reuben S. Holmes Papers.
> Joshua H. Hudson Diary.
> J. J. McIver Papers.
> F. W. McMaster Papers.
> J. A. Mitchell Papers.
> Noisette Family Papers.
> Richland Democratic Club Minutes.
> J. Y. Simons Papers.
> Edward L. Stoeber Papers.
> Williams–Chesnut–Manning Papers.
> George Wise Papers.

Yale University Library

> Samuel Bowles Collection.
> W. D. Whitney Papers.

B. OFFICIAL RECORDS AND DOCUMENTS

1. Publications of the United States Government

Biographical Directory of the American Congress, 1774–1949. Washington: Government Printing Office, 1950.

Bureau of the Census. *Negro Population in the United States, 1790–1915.* Washington: Government Printing Office, 1918.

————. *Religious Bodies, 1906, 1916.* Washington: Government Printing Office.

Census, 1860, 1870, 1880, 1890. Washington: Government Printing Office.

Congressional Record, 1873-1877. Washington: Government Printing Office.

Hemphill, James Calvin. *Climate, Soil, and Agricultural Capabilities of South Carolina and Georgia.* Department of Agriculture, Special Report No. 47. Washington: Government Printing Office, 1882.

The Journal of the Joint Committee on Reconstruction at the First Session of the Thirty-Ninth Congress. Washington: Government Printing Office, 1866.

The Ku-Klux Conspiracy. Testimony Taken by the Joint Select Committee to Inquire into the Condition of Affairs in the Late Insurrectionary States. Vols. III, IV, V. Washington: Government Printing Office, 1872.

Mayo, Amory Dwight. "The Final Establishment of the American Common School System in North Carolina, South Carolina, and Georgia, 1863-1900," *Report of the Commissioner of Education for the Year Ending June 30, 1904.* Washington: Government Printing Office, 1905.

Recent Election in South Carolina. Testimony Taken by the Select Committee on the Recent Election in South Carolina. House Miscellaneous Document No. 31, 44th Congress, 2nd Session. Washington: Government Printing Office, 1877.

"Report on Cotton Production in South Carolina," House Miscellaneous Document No. 42, Part 6, 47th Congress, 2nd Session. Washington: Government Printing Office, 1883.

Report of the Secretary of War, 1867. House Executive Document No. 1, Part 1, 40th Congress, 2nd Session. Washington: Government Printing Office, 1868.

Report of the Secretary of War, 1868. House Executive Document No. 1, Part 1, 40th Congress, 3rd Session. Washington: Government Printing Office, 1869.

R. N. Scott, *et al.* (eds.). *War of the Rebellion: a Compilation of the Official Records of the Union and Confederate Armies.* 130 vols. Washington: Government Printing Office, 1880–1891.

South Carolina in 1876. Testimony as to the Denial of the Elective Franchise in South Carolina at the Election of 1875 and 1876. Senate Miscellaneous Document No. 48, 44th Congress, 2nd Session. 3 vols. Washington: Government Printing Office, 1877.

Use of the Army in Certain of the Southern States. House Executive Document No. 30, 44th Congress, 2nd Session. Washington: Government Printing Office, 1877.

Young, Edward. "Labor in Europe and America," House Executive Document No. 21, 44th Congress, 1st Session. Washington: Government Printing Office, 1876.

2. Publications of the South Carolina State Government

Hammond, Harry. *South Carolina Resources and Population, Institutions and Industries.* State Board of Agriculture. Charleston: Walker, Evans & Cogswell, 1883.

Journal of the Convention of the People of South Carolina, held in Columbia, South Carolina, September, 1865. Columbia: Julian A. Selby, 1865.

Journal of the House of Representatives of the General Assembly of the State of South Carolina, 1868–1877.

Journal of the Senate of the General Assembly of the State of South Carolina, 1868–1877.

Proceedings of the Constitutional Convention of South Carolina held at Charleston, South Carolina, beginning January 14th and ending March 17th, 1868. Charleston: Denny & Perry, 1868.

Reports and Resolutions of the General Assembly of the State of South Carolina, Passed at the Annual Session of 1865. Columbia: Julian A. Selby, 1866.

Reports and Resolutions of the General Assembly of the State of South Carolina, 1866–1894.

Revised Statutes of the State of South Carolina. Columbia: Republican Printing Company, 1873.

Statutes at Large of South Carolina, 1861–1877.

C. NEWSPAPERS AND PERIODICALS

African Methodist Episcopal Church Review, Vol. III.
Anderson *Appeal*, 1867.
Anderson *Intelligencer*, 1865–1877.
The Atlantic Monthly, 1861–1877.
Barnwell *Sentinel*, 1866.
Beaufort *Free South*, 1863–1864.
Bennettsville *Journal*, 1869.
Charleston *Courier*, 1865–1873.
Charleston *Daily Republican*, 1869–1871, 1872.
Charleston *Mercury*, 1865–1868.
Charleston *News*, 1865–1873.
Charleston *News and Courier*, 1873–1877.
Charleston *Southern Patriot*, 1832.
Charleston *Weekly Republican*, 1876.
Chester *Reporter*, 1867, 1874.
Columbia *Daily Union*, 1873–1876.
Columbia *Union Herald*, 1876.
Conway *Horry News*, 1869.

Greenville *Republican*, 1875.
Greenville *Southern Enterprise*, 1869.
Harper's Monthly Magazine, 1861–1877.
Methodist Review, 1865–1896.
The Nation, 1865–1877.
New York Herald, 1865–1877.
New York Times, 1861–1877.
New York Tribune, 1865–1877.
North American Review, 1861–1877.
Port Royal *New South*, 1862–1864.
Port Royal *Palmetto Herald*, 1864.
The Rural Carolinian, 1869–1876.

D. ARTICLES, MEMOIRS, TRAVEL ACCOUNTS, REPORTS, AND MISCELLANEOUS WRITINGS

Ames, Mary. *From a New England Woman's Diary in Dixie in 1865*.
Springfield, Massachusetts: The Plimpton Press, 1906.
Appletons' Annual Cyclopaedia, 1865–1878.
Bancroft, Frederic (ed.). *Speeches, Correspondence, and Political Papers of
Carl Schurz*. New York: G. P. Putnam's Sons, 1913.
Botume, Elizabeth Hyde. *First Days Among the Contrabands*. Boston: Lee
and Shepard, 1893.
Cauthen, Charles E. (ed.). *Family Letters of the Three Wade Hamptons,
1782–1901*. Columbia: University of South Carolina Press, 1953.
Croushore, James H., and Potter, David M. (eds.). *John William De Forest,
A Union Officer in the Reconstruction*. New Haven: Yale University
Press, 1948.
De Forest, John William. *The Bloody Chasm*. New York: D. Appleton and
Company, 1881.
De Leon, Edwin. "The New South," *Harper's Monthly Magazine*, XLVIII
(January, 1874), 270–80.
Fox, Henry J. "The Negro," *Methodist Review*, January, 1875, pp. 79–97.
———. "Our Work in the South," *Methodist Review*, January, 1874, pp. 29–
45.
Gannett, W. C. "The Freedmen at Port Royal," *North American Review*,
CI (July, 1865), 1–28.
Hardy, Iza D. *Between Two Oceans; or Sketches of American Travel*.
London: Chapman and Hall, 1884.
Helper, Hinton Rowan. *Negroes in Negroland, the Negroes in America and
Negroes Generally; Also the Several Races of White Men Considered as
the Involuntary and Predestined Supplanters of the Black Races*. New
York: G. W. Carleton & Company, 1868.

————. *Nojoque; a Question for a Continent.* New York: G. W. Carleton & Company, 1867.

Higginson, Thomas Wentworth. *Army Life in a Black Regiment.* Boston: Lee and Shepard, 1890.

Holland, Rupert S. (ed.). *Letters and Diary of Laura M. Towne, 1862–1884, Written from the Sea Islands of South Carolina.* Cambridge: The Riverside Press, 1912.

Howard, Oliver Otis. *Autobiography of Oliver Otis Howard.* Vol. II. New York: The Baker & Taylor Company, 1908.

King, Edward. *The Great South.* Hartford: J. Wells Champney, 1875.

Lawrence, William H. *The Centenary Souvenir, Containing a History of the Centenary Church, Charleston, and an Account of the Life and Labors of Reverend R. V. Lawrence, Father of the Pastor of the Centenary Church.* Philadelphia: Collins Printing House, 1885.

Leland, John A. *A Voice from South Carolina.* Charleston: Walker, Evans & Cogswell, 1879.

Matlack, L. C. "The Methodist Episcopal Church in the Southern States," *Methodist Review,* January, 1872, pp. 103–26.

Minutes of the A. M. E. Church, 1876.

Minutes of the Annual Conference of the Methodist Episcopal Church, 1865–1891.

Minutes of the Annual Conference of the Methodist Episcopal Church, South, 1860–1877.

Minutes of the Sixth Session of the South Carolina Annual Conference of the Methodist Episcopal Church, held at Claflin University, Orangeburg, South Carolina, December 22, 1870. Charleston: Republican Book and Job Office, 1871.

Minutes of the Eighty-Third Session of the South Carolina Annual Conference of the Methodist Episcopal Church, South. Charleston: publisher not given, 1871.

Minutes of the Eighty-Fourth Session of the South Carolina Annual Conference of the Methodist Episcopal Church, South. Charleston: publisher not given, 1872.

Payne, Daniel Alexander. *Recollections of Seventy Years* (Compiled and arranged by Sarah Pierce Scarborough; edited by Reverend C. S. Smith). Nashville: African Methodist Episcopal Sunday School Union, 1888.

Pearne, Thomas H. "The Freedmen," *Methodist Review,* July, 1877, pp. 462–81.

Pearson, Elizabeth Ware (ed.). *Letters from Port Royal, 1862–1868.* Boston: W. B. Clarke Company, 1906.

Pierce, Edward L. "The Freedmen of Port Royal," *The Atlantic Monthly,* XII (September, 1863), 291–315.

Pike, James S. *The Prostrate State: South Carolina under Negro Government.* New York: D. Appleton and Company, 1874.

Proceedings of the Colored People's Convention of the State of South Carolina, held in Zion Church, Charleston, November, 1865. Together with the Declaration of Rights and Wrongs, an Address to the People, a Petition to the Legislature, and a Memorial to Congress. Charleston, 1865.

Proceedings of the Tax-Payers' Convention of South Carolina, held at Columbia, beginning May 9th, and ending May 12, 1871. Charleston: E. Perry, 1871.

Reid, Whitelaw. *After the War; A Southern Tour, May 1, 1865, to May 1, 1866.* London: Sampson, 1866.

Rollin, Frank A. *Life and Public Services of Martin R. Delany, Sub-Assistant Commissioner, Bureau Relief of Refugees, Freedmen, and of Abandoned Lands, and Late Major 104th U. S. Colored Troops.* 2nd ed. Boston: Lee and Shepard, 1883.

Shaler, N. S. "An Ex-Southerner in South Carolina," *The Atlantic Monthly,* XXVI (July, 1870), 53–61.

Somers, Robert. *The Southern States since the War, 1870–1871.* New York: Macmillan and Company, 1871.

South Carolina Baptist Convention Minutes, 1866.

South Carolina State Gazetteer and Business Directory. Charleston: R. A. Smith, 1880.

A South Carolinian [Belton O'Neall Townsend]. "South Carolina Society," *The Atlantic Monthly,* XXXIX (June, 1877), 670–84.

Trowbridge, J[ohn] T[ownshend]. *The South, a tour of its Battle Fields and Ruined Cities, a journey through the desolated States, and talks with the people, etc.* Hartford: L. Stebbins, 1866.

Martin, Isabella D., and Avary, Myrta Lockett (eds.). *A Diary from Dixie, as written by Mary Boykin Chesnut.* New York: D. Appleton and Company, 1905.

Moffett, Mary Conner. *Letters of General James Conner.* Columbia: R. L. Bryan Company, 1950.

Williams, Ben Ames (ed.). *A Diary from Dixie by Mary Boykin Chesnut.* Cambridge: Houghton Mifflin Company, 1949.

II. Secondary Sources

Abbot, Martin L. "The Freedmen's Bureau in South Carolina, 1865-1872," Unpublished Ph.D. dissertation, Department of History, Emory University, 1954.

Albert, A. E. P. "The Church in the South," *Methodist Review,* March–April, 1892, pp. 229–40.

Allen, Walter. *Governor Chamberlain's Administration in South Carolina: A Chapter of Reconstruction in the Southern States*. New York: Putnam, 1888.

Anderson, R. Earle. *Liberia, America's African Friend*. Chapel Hill: University of North Carolina Press, 1952.

Avary, Myrta Lockett. *Dixie after the War*. New York: Doubleday, Page & Company, 1906.

Ball, William Watts. *The State That Forgot: South Carolina's Surrender to Democracy*. Indianapolis: The Bobbs-Merrill Company, 1932.

Bentley, George R. *A History of the Freedmen's Bureau*. Philadelphia: University of Pennsylvania Press, 1955.

Boddie, William Willis. *History of Williamsburg County, South Carolina 1705 until 1923*. Columbia: The State Company, 1923.

Chapman, Harry Aubrey. "The Historical Development of the Grange in South Carolina," Unpublished Master's thesis, Department of History, Furman University, 1952.

Cornish, Dudley Taylor. *The Sable Arm: Negro Troops in the Union Army, 1861–1865*. New York: Longmans, Green and Company, 1956.

Durden, Robert Franklin. *James Shepherd Pike: Republicanism and the American Negro, 1850–1882*. Durham: Duke University Press, 1957.

Emilio, Luis F. *History of the Fifty-Fourth Regiment of Massachusetts Volunteer Infantry, 1863–1865*. Boston: The Boston Book Company, 1894.

Farish, Hunter Dickinson. *The Circuit Rider Dismounts; a Social History of Southern Methodism, 1865–1900*. Richmond: The Dietz Press, 1938.

Gould, John M. *History of the 1st-10th-29th Maine Regiment*. Portland: S. Berry, 1871.

Historical Records Survey Program, Division of Professional and Service Projects, Works Projects Administration. *Inventory of the Church Archives of Michigan, AMEC, Michigan Conference*. Detroit: MHR Survey Project, September, 1940.

A History of Spartanburg County. Compiled by the Spartanburg Unit of the Writer's Program of the Works Projects Administration in the State of South Carolina. N.p.: Band & White, 1940.

Hood, James Walker. *One Hundred Years of the African Methodist Episcopal Zion Church; or the Centennial of African Methodism*. New York: Zion Book Concern, 1895.

Hyde, A. B. *The Story of Methodism*. Greenfield, Massachusetts: Willey & Company, 1887.

Jackson, Luther Porter. "The Educational Efforts of the Freedmen's Aid Societies in South Carolina, 1862-1872," *Journal of Negro History*, VIII (January, 1923), 1–40.

Johnson, Allen, and Malone, Dumas (eds.). *Dictionary of American Biography*. New York: C. Scribner's Sons, 1928–1958.

Jones, Frank Dudley, and Mills, W. H. (eds.). *History of the Presbyterian Church in South Carolina Since 1850*. Columbia: R. L. Bryan, 1926.

Kirkland, Thomas J., and Kennedy, Robert M. *Historic Camden*. Part Two, Columbia: The State Company, 1926.

Knight, Edgar Wallace. *The Influence of Reconstruction on Education in the South*. New York: Teachers College, Columbia University, 1913. (Teachers College, Columbia University Contributions to Education, No. 60.)

Korn, Bertram Wallace. *Jews and Negro Slavery in the Old South, 1789–1865*. Elkins Park, Pennsylvania: Reform Congregation Keneseth Israel, 1961. Printed by Maurice Jacobs, Philadelphia, Pennsylvania.

May, John Amasa, and Faunt, Joan Reynolds. *South Carolina Secedes*. Columbia: University of South Carolina Press, Columbia, 1960.

Morrow, Ralph Ernest. *Northern Methodism and Reconstruction*. East Lansing: Michigan State University Press, 1956.

Nicholson, Alfred William. *Brief Sketch of the Life and Labors of Rev. Alexander Bettis; also an Account of the Founding and Development of the Bettis Academy*. Trenton, South Carolina: The Author, 1913.

Patton, James Welch. "The Republican Party in South Carolina, 1876–1895," *Essays in Southern History*, ed. Fletcher Melvin Green. Chapel Hill: The University of North Carolina Press, 1949.

Pegues, Albert Weitherspoon. *Our Baptist Ministers and Schools*. Springfield, Massachusetts: Willey and Company, 1892.

Quarles, Benjamin. *The Negro in the Civil War*. Boston: Little, Brown, 1953.

Reynolds, John Schreiner. *Reconstruction in South Carolina, 1865–1877*. Columbia: The State, 1905.

Simkins, Francis B., and Woody, Robert Hilliard. *South Carolina During Reconstruction*. Chapel Hill: University of North Carolina Press, 1932.

Sinclair, William A. *The Aftermath of Slavery: A Study of the Condition and Environment of the American Negro*. Boston: Small, Maynard and Company, 1905.

Taylor, Alrutheus Ambush. *The Negro in South Carolina During the Reconstruction*. Washington: Association for the Study of Negro Life and History, 1924.

Tindall, George Brown. *South Carolina Negroes, 1877–1900*. Columbia: University of South Carolina Press, 1952.

Webster, Laura Josephine. *The Operation of the Freedmen's Bureau in South Carolina*. Smith College Studies in History, Vol. I. Northampton, Massachusetts: Department of History of Smith College, 1916.

Williams, George Washington. *History of the Negro Race in America from 1619 to 1880*. New York: Putnam, 1883.

———. *A History of the Negro Troops in the War of the Rebellion, 1861–1865.* New York: Harper & Brothers, 1888.

Wilson, James Grant, and Fiske, John (eds.). *Appletons' Cyclopaedia of American Biography.* New York: D. Appleton and Company, 1888. 6 vols., 1887–1889.

Wilson, Joseph T. *The Black Phalanx: A History of the Negro Soldiers of the United States in the Wars of 1775–1812, 1861–65.* Hartford: American Publishing Company, 1891.

Woodson, Carter Godwin. *A Century of Negro Migration.* Washington: Association for the Study of Negro Life and History, 1918.

———. *Free Negro Heads of Families in the United States in 1830.* Washington: Association for the Study of Negro Life and History, 1925.

INDEX